ADVENTURERS

ADVENTURERS

The Improbable Rise
of the
East India Company,
1550–1650

David Howarth

YALE UNIVERSITY PRESS
NEW HAVEN AND LONDON

Published with assistance from the foundation established in memory of Oliver Baty
Cunningham of the Class of 1917, Yale College.

All reasonable efforts have been made to provide accurate sources for all images that appear
in this book. Any discrepancies or omissions will be rectified in future editions.

For information about this and other Yale University Press publications, please contact:
U.S. Office: sales.press@yale.edu   yalebooks.com
Europe Office: sales@yaleup.co.uk   yalebooks.co.uk

Set in Adobe Garamond Pro by IDSUK (DataConnection) Ltd
Printed in Great Britain by TJ Books, Padstow, Cornwall

Library of Congress Control Number: 2022946489

ISBN 978-0-300-25072-5

A catalogue record for this book is available from the British Library.

10 9 8 7 6 5 4 3 2 1

To Saskia, Grace and Thomas, with love, and gratitude for not mutinying

CONTENTS

ILLUSTRATIONS AND MAPS

PLATES

1. *Sir Robert Sherley* by Matthaus Greuter (Greuther), or by Diego de Astor, 1609. © National Portrait Gallery, NPG D33608.
2. The tomb of Sir Thomas Smythe in St John the Baptist church, Sutton-at-Hone. By permission of Revd Emma Young.
3. *Sir Thomas Roe* by Michiel Janszoon van Miereveldt, 1640. © National Portrait Gallery, NPG 1354.
4. *Sir Thomas Roe at the Court of Ajmir* by William Rothenstein, 1927. Artepics / Alamy Stock Photo.
5. *Ships Trading in the East* by Hendrick Cornelisz Vroom, 1614. National Maritime Museum, Greenwich, London, Palmer Collection. Acquired with the assistance of H.M. Treasury, the Caird Fund, the Art Fund, the Pilgrim Trust and the Society for Nautical Research Macpherson Fund.
6. An East India Company share certificate. By permission of Chetham's Library.
7. Itakura Katsushige. The History Collection / Alamy Stock Photo.
8. *Jahāngīr Preferring a Sufi Sheikh to Kings* by Bichitr, *c.* 1615–18. Alamy Stock Photo.
9. *Naqd 'Ali Beg, Envoy from Persia* by Richard Greenbury, 1626. © British Library Board. All Rights Reserved / Bridgeman Images.
10. The Bell Carpet, *c.* 1630. By permission of the Girdlers' Company.
11. Jan Pieterszoon Coen by Ferdinand Leenhoff, 1887. © xHollandsex-Hoogtex / xxANPx x414083060x.
12. *Dutch Vessels in Harbour* by Wenceslaus Hollar, 1647. By permission of Christopher Mendez.

MAPS

PREFACE

This is a book I have wanted to write for fifty years. It is about the romance of making money and the thrill of commercial history. As a research student in Florence in the early 1970s, I looked at documents about works of art exported from Tuscany to the court of Charles I. Allocated a desk in the crepuscular Archivio di Stato, at a time when that institution found itself between the Arno and the *Birth of Venus*, not even Botticelli could have lifted the sense of doom. Months passed, as did mood – from gloom to joy.

Eventually, unable to find what I was looking for, I took myself off to the basement, where, after rummaging among closely packed files, I chanced upon something special, a letter where, stitched down the right-hand margin, were samples of all the silks that London had summoned from Florence in an attempt to get Van Dyck's sitters to dress a little better. Just short of four hundred years old, so lambent were the corals, so subtle the laurels, these postage-stamp beauties could hardly have been exposed to light for more than seconds in those 350 years since someone had taken quill to paper and a needle to margin. Moving down the Arno, from Florence to Livorno, such bales of silk became parcels of profit that, shipped aboard some Levant Company vessel, were bound for the Thames and the workshops of Whitehall Palace.

Forty years later, and the scene changes to Euston Road in the rain. Here, in the British Library's India Office Records, are to be found the papers of the East India Company, all 8 miles of them. Here too is history in all its rustling, tumbling abundance; so huge a challenge to master as surely demands that Dante's exhortation *'Lasciate ogne speranza, voi ch'intrate'* ('All who enter here despair!') be tooled in gold above the issue desk. But just as in the Uffizi, so at the British Library, the possibilities appeared boundless. For these papers tell a tale unparalleled in any other early modern English archive.

PREFACE

As with all the best stories, a study of the improbable rise of the East India Company throws up a hundred questions to answer. I do not pretend to have mastered the British Library archive – no one can do that when those unmatched archivists who were trained by the Victorian Public Record Office threw in the quill at so impossible a task. And who can blame them? In transcribing merely the ten years when a Company factory existed in Japan, that is to say from 1613 to 1623, the British Library has found itself obliged in modern times to run to two fat volumes of 1,500 pages. As for the 'other', the record of those from whom the Company was buying, I have relied on some of the small portion of primary sources in Asia that have been published to date.

In what follows, there are many hostages to fortune between the Red and the Yellow Seas, many questions begging for answers. But that is the inevitable consequence of so much about the East India Company that is of interest to every intellectual discipline. From its first days, the East India Company was much more than a commercial organisation. It was part of the culture of the realm. Once established, the Company became the investment of choice for the flower of commercial, cultural and political life in an island fast gaining continental reach and global significance. If I have suggested that there remains the most formidable of challenges in acquiring a mastery of so voluminous an archive, what is within our grasp is a description of those stormy petrels, the Company's fleets, as they ventured out over troubled waters.

Any number of literary tropes, from Captain Hook to Captain Haddock, have made it too easy to assume that the servants of the Company were splashed in brine and pickled in rum. It is a travesty of the truth. 'General' Sir Henry Middleton, for which read 'Admiral' in today's parlance, kept the most splendid of tables. Here was to be found the best of Tudor silver winking against the verdure hangings of Brussels. Within what was known as the 'great cabin', Company captains would entertain guests dressed in such splendour as to have made the costume galleries of the Victoria and Albert Museum look like a charity shop. But beyond show there was performance, and beyond cupidity, creativity. Middleton was a very fine musician who loved the well-tempered viol, whilst many of the merchants he carried, carried home more than was to be found in a ship's log. Take the merchant Augustine Spalding, who first appears in the records in 1607 as the Company's interpreter in Bantam.

Spalding not only tried to sell heavy West Country cloth in the middle of a monsoon – an epic challenge in itself – but hardly less painfully set about constructing a Malay dictionary for the use of mariners that he had translated out of a Dutch version taken from a primer in Latin.[1] Far off the coast of Senegal, too, and on the Company's Fourth Voyage, the ships put on the first performance on water of Shakespeare's *Hamlet*. In the months that separated the west coast of Africa from the north coast of Java they took to a parley of instruments, believing that music soothed the soul of the most mutinous of crewmen.

For all the cultural richness encountered on these earliest voyages, no visual trace remains. Such a lack of material is in marked contrast with what is to be found in the Rijksmuseum in Amsterdam.[2] Here the heroics of the Dutch East India Company (the Vereenigde Oostindische Compagnie, or VOC) are recorded in abundance. Part of the difference is because at that time the visual arts were much more sophisticated in Holland than in England. But in the grander sphere of nation-building and national rivalries, not until the East India Company annexed Bengal in 1757 did the English think ambitiously of territorial conquest. By contrast, however, and from its very foundation in 1602, the Vereenigde Oostindische Compagnie's impulse was to manufacture national identity via the creation of colonies in the Far East. In early East India Company history, however, appeals to past glory or future greatness are as hard to find as the horn of a unicorn.

What follows, then, is an account of the rise of England's most powerful overseas commercial organisation, as it came to be defined in the perennial rivalry with the Dutch. This is less a tale of two nations than two companies whose activities had profound effects on the creation of respective empires in England and Holland in the early modern world: the one commercial, the other colonial.

ACKNOWLEDGEMENTS

I would like to thank my wife Saskia for her patience during the years it has taken me to write this book, but also for her formidable skills in tracking down rare and out of print books during the gestation of a project that has taken far longer than she ever bargained for. In addition, my children, Grace and Thomas, have managed to put up with my absence in mind if not in person.

I owe much to many at Yale University Press: Heather McCallum carried me through failures of nerve, Julian Loose conducted me out of mazes, providing strategic creative input to bring new angles to bear upon our story, and Rachael Lonsdale wafted me across the finishing line with what to me seemed effortless ease but must have been enormous focus on all and every detail of a complex manuscript. Frazer Martin rendered the business of illustrations as much fun as a night at the pictures – sweets included. Felicity Maunder and Elizabeth Stone made rough places plain, whilst Lucy Buchan, who dropped not a stitch in making a seamless garment out of the proofs, Stuart Weir, Marika Lysandrou, Katie Urquhart and Stephanie Lee clarified important aspects of production and publicity.

Having lost my way in the vexatious business of trying to find a publisher, I found it thanks to timely advice from both Zoë Pagnamenta and Jenny Uglow who deposited me at the front door of Yale University Press in Bedford Square, London.

Marigold Atkey, best of listeners, was able to provide reassurance and direction at a critical moment too. Margot Magee Sackett read the whole manuscript, an act of great kindness which has saved me from many errors of both fact and judgement. Frances Stadlen and Roger Ellis have, too, advised on significant parts of the manuscript. For the shrewd comments of all three I am especially grateful.

ACKNOWLEDGEMENTS

In addition, I thank Fergus Hall most warmly for essential financial support. This made a vital difference in the early stages of research.

Ideas for the book were facilitated by invitations to speak at two conferences. I was asked by Dr Christina Anderson to deliver the keynote address at *Early Modern Merchants as Collectors* (Ashmolean Museum, Oxford) in June 2012. This provided vital stimulus. I would also like to thank Dr Toby Osborne for an invitation to deliver a paper at a conference on international diplomatic culture at Durham University held in connection with his Arts and Humanities Research Council project 'Translating cultures: Diplomacy between the early modern and modern worlds'.

The staff of the London Library are a rare and endangered species, for the survival of which so many scribblers are deeply grateful. I cannot thank Rosalie Davidson and her colleagues enough for their support, efficiency and courtesy, most especially during a time of illness. Besides unparalleled input from that quarter, I spent many hours working in Chetham's Library, Manchester, where Fergus Wilde did so much to facilitate my research. In addition, I owe hardly less gratitude to the staff of the John Rylands Library, also in Manchester.

Finally, the following have offered support at various stages of this project: Philippa Atkey, Cees Bakker, Stephen Bann, David Bartie and the Haberdashers' Company, Mervyn Bassett, Heather Beattie, Alex Bremner, Viccy Coltman, Helen and Ron Cox, Ingrid Cox-Lockhart, Suzanne Foster, Simon Franses and Franses and Co., Alison Games, Marc van de Griendt, Bill Hamilton, Anna Howard and the Girdlers' Company, George Lockhart, Arthur MacGregor, Peter McCullough, Christopher Mendez, Stethanis Petracopoulos, Frances Pollard, Neil Rennie, Thomas Reilly, René Weis, Carolyn Wilkinson, Stephen de Winton and Emma Young.

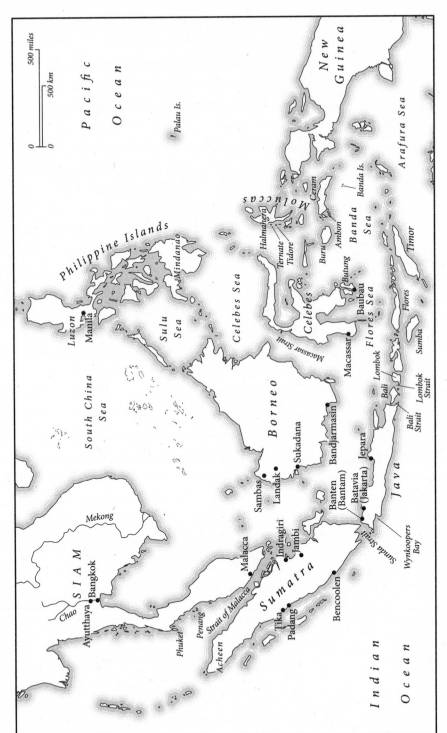

1. The East Indian Archipelago.

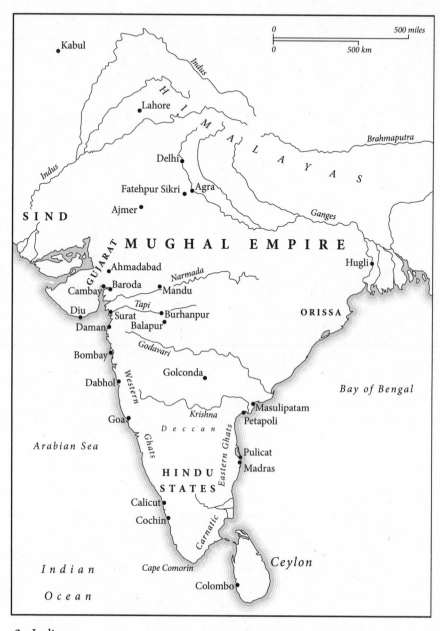

2. India.

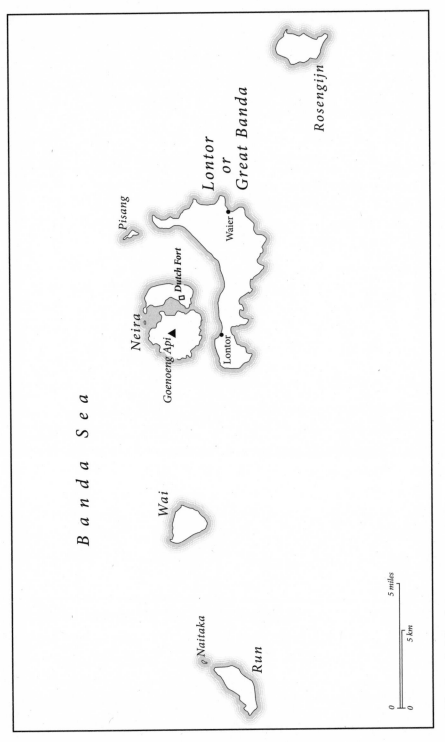

Banda Sea

Naitaka

Run

Wai

Pisang

Neira

Goenoeng Api ▲

□ *Dutch Fort*

Lontor •

Waier •

Lontor
or
Great Banda

Rosengijn

0 ——— 5 miles
0 ——— 5 km

3. The Banda Islands.

INTRODUCTION

Our story properly begins in a room in Westminster on the last day of 1600 with the formal launching of the East India Company, or EIC, under the sonorous title of 'Governor and Company of Merchants of London Trading into the East-Indies'. But that halcyon moment had been preceded by a number of discussions, the most important of which had been held on 24 September 1599, when 101 business interests had assembled, and the result of which was the issuing of the nascent Company's first royal charter.[1]

Not all the congregants are identifiable, though some of the biggest names in the City lurked in the shadows of a long September day. Here we find men of both reputation and scandal.

Take Sir William Cockayne (d. 1626), who would be responsible for the biggest financial scam of the entire seventeenth century when in 1614 he convinced James I that English wool should be dyed at home, not as hitherto finished in Holland, before onward transmission to the markets of Europe. Cockayne's argument was that monies would be repatriated; privately, he calculated that he might also fleece the Merchant Adventurers Company which controlled the management of what was England's principal export. It proved a disaster, and by 1617 the Adventurers had regained control just as Cockayne gained his evil reputation as the most grasping of the money-men.[2]

Or Sir Baptist Hicks (d. 1629), who, beginning a mercer, ended a viscount. Before reinventing himself as a great Gloucestershire landowner, Hicks had been notably grasping and much criticised for grinding his customers in his shop at the White Bear in Cheapside. Besides manipulating the money markets, Hicks had also massaged the Crown with large cash loans. Sir Baptist's career perfectly illustrated how the princes of the City could become the potentates of the realm.[3]

The meeting's convenor was the roistering earl of Cumberland (d. 1605). Most noble among sailors, most colourful of these movers, Cumberland thrust himself forward with as much gusto as any figurehead upon a ship. Later damned as 'a great but un-amiable man', and one whose career 'admirably illustrates the difference ... between fame and virtue',[4] Cumberland was ideally suited to get things launched. He had had 'a good war'. Celebrated for commanding the *Elizabeth Bonaventure* at the Armada in 1588, party to the famous capture of the *Mãe de Deus* in 1592, lauded for leading a raid on Puerto Rico, his lordship had done well by England. Cumberland had courage, charisma and a title. With such assets, indeed, he now managed to get the shareholders to fall into line like so many children on a Tudor monument.

Soon enough, these men – and the very first investors were all men, though it would not be long before women took their place in the story – came to be referred to as 'Adventurers'. Such a name points not to exciting events at sea – though goodness knows, many a shareholder would long for the outfit to be altogether more 'adventurous' than any governor was ever going to allow – but rather the venturing of capital. The East India Company's roots ran deep in the loam of English commerce.

By no means all who crowded into these inaugural meetings were interested just in money. The Sandys and the Ferrars stood for rectitude more than rials, religion more than receipts. As an MP, Sir Edwin Sandys would be the furious, highly charged leader of all those who despised the Stuarts and just about everything else to do with the country from whence the new dynasty had hailed. By contrast, Nicholas Ferrar was to be converted from rising to his feet at Adventurers' meetings to falling on his knees in prayer after establishing the sequestered hamlet of Little Gidding, his little community of penitents chanting amidst the bullrushes, which T.S. Eliot would immortalise in one of the great poems of the twentieth century.

It is hardly an exaggeration to say that in late-sixteenth-century England the few thousand who ran the country were either drawn to, worked for or envied the new overseas companies of which the East India was the latest and would become the most successful. Anyone who paid around £200 in subscription qualified as an Adventurer, and so by rights would be admitted to the General Court. At the meetings of all these shareholders or Adventurers, factors' letters from foreign stations would be read out. Behind the arras however, muttered the twenty-four-strong Court of Committees. It ran things on a quotidian basis, taking all the important decisions, of which the most crucial was to make sure that it was given every means to emasculate the General Court. The Court of Committees could always be relied upon to work hard at concealing what it felt the General Court should never know. Though the Adventurers were well aware of this, with the exception of a disaffected minority who could never be reconciled to a culture of the nod and the wink, the generality knew better still that the gains to be made in throwing savings into the Company meant it was best to overlook the Court's wilful exclusion.

By 1610, only a decade since the Company had first opened for business, traffic wardens employed to keep things moving in the gridlocked streets of the City found coaches backing right up Eastcheap. Every manner of royal and royal officeholder was determined to become an Adventurer. Who do we find pressing for entry? Here were Sir Francis Bacon and Thomas Hobbes, among the greatest thinkers of the age. Here too was to be found the entire judiciary. As for the servants of the royal household, Adventurers ran from cook to chaplain, via the Chancellor of the Exchequer and the Royal Librarian. This is not to say that all these men from high places had much or any influence on how matters were actually conducted. The East India Company's first governor, Sir Thomas Smythe (d. 1625), was obliged not only to manage a raft of competing interests but also to thrust off those who thought themselves entitled to influence. How Smythe set about trying to maintain the integrity of the Company, with determination if not always success, is clear from the way he managed to repel a peremptory demand of the Lord Treasurer, who the Court minutes record:

'useth much persuasion to the Company to accept of the employment' of Sir Edward Michelborne, on the voyage, as a principal commander; resolved not to employ any gentleman in any place of charge or command in the voyage; Mr Garway requested to move the Lord Treasurer 'to give them leave to sort their business with men of their own quality, and not to expect that they should make any further motion of this matter to the generality lest the suspicion of the employment of gentlemen being taken hold upon, do drive a great number of the adventures to withdraw their contributions'.[5]

3

It was not only the constant business of keeping sweet those who might become sour that represented a major challenge. Retaining the contributions of stakeholders who had ventured upon the Company's first journeys was paramount, whilst encouraging others to chance their money too required all the skill and experience Smythe had accumulated over many years as a successful governor and counsellor of earlier trading companies. Amongst these, the most notable with which Smythe had had dealings were the Muscovy and Levant Companies. Cartels in their own right, these two would provide critical experience to the nascent East India Company. Indeed, such avuncular advice was to prove essential not only to the launch but also to the very survival of this new venture.

There was always strenuous debate as to how to get to those places where European wares might be offloaded at profit. Was it to be the Cape or the cap – round the Cape of Good Hope or over the ice cap of the North Pole? The support of the Muscovy Company was essential for those who championed the possibility of either a north-east or a north-west passage over the Arctic to China, and who were prepared to embark on a highly strenuous journey. From the vastly experienced Levant Company, which had already been bringing luxuries from the Middle East to Europe for some twenty years, the Company learned that the way to survive was to import in order to re-export. What came up the Channel had to go out through the 'Pillars of Hercules' – which was how Gibraltar was then described – and from there to Italy, Greece and Turkey. But despite it being doubtful whether the Company could have survived had it not been able to borrow invaluable experience from the Levant, relations were often strained.

As for supplying the ships that might take English goods as far as Japan, this process exposed the thoroughly ad hoc nature of the business. Whilst everyone scrambled to load the three ships that would set out for the East at the end of February, there was every manner of thing posted from Stepney to Surat and Poplar to Penang. Not all was from England either. Whilst there would be a good stock of tin from Bodmin and kerseys from Woodbridge, there was also coral from Marseilles and 'elephants' teeth' (tusks) from Senegal, with which to make many an ivory throne. As for the Company's ships, returning after upwards of three years cruising Eastern waters, these would be loaded with indigo from Ajmer, silver from Japan, silks from Persia, cinnamon from Ceylon, cottons from Coromandel and, as ballast, upwards of 80 tons of stone for every ship. This might then be donated to make walkways in the City.

Victualling the fleets was a massive logistical challenge. To begin with there was the issue of finding ships of sufficient size and seaworthiness. Less than one week before the departure in April 1601 of the first historic 'Voyage', as the annual departure to the Far East was known, it was suddenly discovered that the *Great Susan* was so grossly overladen it would be lucky if she made Greenwich before sinking. What was to be done? Sir James Lancaster, Armada veteran and Company 'General', scurried off to Gravesend to find a seaworthy vessel. No time to haggle, whipping out his purse, Lancaster offered a quick £300 to buy the *Gift*. At 120 tons she could just about be counted to get to the Azores, ploughing along behind her three sisters carrying what the main ships of the voyage could not. The receipt for her acquisition is minuted as late as 18 February, when the voyage should already have left.[6]

What is surprising about the launch of the East India Company is how little was planned and how less was prepared. Looking at the Company in these first chaotic years suggests just how wrong it is to think there was something inevitable about its so-called rise as a systematic monolith that was somehow predestined to govern India. Indeed, all too often these early voyages only just got away in time to allow for a successful round trip. But as we shall soon discover, what successes they could be!

Here was an outfit that ought to have been as solid as a bulwark. When a good return was achieved, profits were staggering: if the swabber aboard the good ship *Peppercorn* was crafty enough to steal just one bag of spice, he might expect to gain a 2,000 per cent profit. But whilst returns were good for a number of years, by the onset of economic depression in 1618, what should have been a copper bottom became a rotten hull. Late arrivals, glutted markets, private gain and a house divided between the Court of Committees and the General Court of Adventurers brought the whole show to the very verge of bankruptcy. But for all the difficulties, profits *did* accrue and capital *was* accumulated. So, although painfully and laboriously, the Company was able to conquer recession to become both secure and profitable.

There is a strong case for thinking that the first of all these voyages was the most chaotic. Six months before departure the Company owned not a single ship; none had been built and none were on order. To tackle the problem, a subcommittee set off to the docks of Deptford, Erith and Gravesend. Overlooking the merits of the *Mayflower*, which instead of harvesting pepper in Malaya came to sow Protestantism in Massachusetts, the subcommittee lighted upon the *Malice Scourge*. This was a vessel of 600 tons owned by the earl of Cumberland. Grudgingly, and only after a great deal of wrangling, a price of £3,700 was agreed. But that was far from fair. Waiting until the money was in the mattress, Cumberland told the Company how they would be well advised to buy a water pump in case the *Scourge* decided to follow what men had feared the *Great Susan* was going to do, and sink to the bottom of the Thames. As for the overburdened *Susan* herself, she belonged to Sir Paul Bayning, who was another of those 101 first investors. The deal with Bayning was that if the *Susan* made it home, he would buy her back at half price, never mind her condition. Such obvious conflicts of interest would stay with the Company throughout its entire history.

Nevertheless, if in 1600 no one was ready, the Company found itself part of a world ready enough for bold enterprise. Overseas associations, of which the East India was to be one of the last, benefited from what had been the institution of new administrative structures following the accession of Henry VII in 1485. Eschewing ecclesiastical strictures about usury, the Tudor revolution in finance had seen the ruthless pursuit of other men's wealth. This it had done with strategies that were interim solutions to old problems, dilemmas that exercised the mind of administrators from one Cromwell to another: from Thomas in the 1530s, creating his new order of wealth, to Oliver in the 1650s, granting his new charter to the East India Company.

How can a large organisation generate profit and sustain solvency? These were acute questions faced by those who ruled England; until, that is, the finances of the Crown were ordered upon something of a regular basis after the 'Glorious Revolution' of 1688. Exactly a century before then, Lord Burghley, chief minister to Elizabeth I, had been doing much to create the optimum conditions that would allow the overseas companies to emerge. It is no exaggeration to say that Burghley changed the face of society. He was foremost in creating such a culture of adventurism as was well suited to the high-risk business of sailing eastward. No less important was the vastly enhanced sense of nationhood following the 'great deliverance' of the Armada in 1588. Such an accretion of new commercial skills, so manifest a celebration of 'Englishness', created the necessary confidence in this high-risk enterprise. Accordingly, the Company was able to attract vastly experienced men who had benefited from old lives at sea and new thinking about money, revenue-raising and company formation.

English court and English commerce were more creatively entwined than in any other polity in Europe. Essential to the effectiveness, influence and survival of the Company would be its close and conflicted relationship with the executive. Elizabeth I bore down upon the Company. For instance, she sent a letter from her Privy Council bemoaning 'Her Majesty's mislike of the slackness of the Company' during their first voyage, 'propounding unto them the example of the Dutch who do prosecute their voyages with a more honourable resolution'.[7] Such an unambiguous rebuke was wholly different from James I's vacillation whenever he was to have dealings with this new outfit.

The Stuart Crown not only insisted on being involved in Company business but it also conducted its own in such a way as to seriously undermine the bargaining position of the Company with European rivals. Largely because of the way in which James I viewed the Company, Governor Smythe became enmeshed in things that had as much to do with foreign relations as overseas commerce. A constant fight between England and Holland, conducted now in London and then at The Hague, was just part of a larger battle between the City and the Crown that would include much more than just commerce and taxation. The barbed relationship with the Dutch and the sulphurous dealings between James I and Governor Smythe that Dutch intransigence did so much to provoke serve to show how from first bright morning the Company was a 'piece of state'. The EIC belonged to the globe of politics as much as it did to the sphere of commerce.

Many of those who attended those famous first meetings wanted to do more than simply sell pepper in Pudding Lane, buy estates in Kent or help themselves to large parts of America. They wished to benefit the 'commonwealth', something that had nothing to do with colonies. America appeared to be suitable in this respect, but only the seriously insane ever thought of laying down settlements upon the banks of the Tapti. The Tudor 'commonweale' meant social cohesion and the health of the body politic, and most definitely not the subjugation of others. But if very few were interested in settlements, the Company was always in constant tension about the pursuit of wealth and the morality of profit.

Critics deprecated how the Company took irreplaceable specie out of the commonwealth, constantly denouncing what they saw as a fatal weakening of the realm. Governor Smythe's critics kept on telling him how once money had left the realm it was not only gone but gone forever! Starting as it sustained a national debate about wealth creation – moving from bullionism to monetarism – the EIC and its troubles, the profits it made, the distrust it provoked, all this and more, made it gather as it grew the best thinking about the wealth of the English nation. Thomas Mun (d. 1641) headed up the Company's departments of Human Resources and PR – an inspired choice, and a member of the Court of Committees whose spate of publications prevented the Company from dying of exposure beneath a hail of denunciation. So persuasive was Mun's rejection of bullionism that he is regarded as the most acute British thinker about money until Adam Smith established his pre-eminence with *The Wealth of Nations* (1776).

Questions about how economics worked, how to get rich and, still more important, how to stay that way leached into the broadest possible social questions. Because the Company attracted the Forbes list of Tudor England, it could never avoid public scrutiny. But soon enough, within the span of its first few years, a process began that might suggest how it would become a 'fourth estate', always in an uneasy relationship with the Crown, which would strive to bend the Company to its will; a Parliament that resented its growing wealth; and a Church that deplored its usurious ways. Throughout these early tumultuous years, the Company bore a striking resemblance to one of its own ships trying to get to China over Russia. Searching for a passage through its difficulties, it found itself pressed from all sides, timbers groaning, orlops creaking and mizzens cracking; everything looked doomed. And yet the Almighty read the Company motto 'Deo ducente nil nocet' ('With God leading, no harm arises') and heartily approved of what he saw. Often enough, Smythe had absolutely no idea where he was going. How, then, could those twenty-four godly men comprising the Court of Committees have survived had they not believed that the hand of God was upon the wheel?

INTRODUCTION

This story begins with a survey of European transoceanic trade that had been developed by Portugal, Spain and Holland before the East India Company opened for business. Such a survey exposes the nature of the challenge that the Company faced in getting on terms – especially with Portugal, which enjoyed a head start of more than a century.

Although during the two decades after that first formal inaugural meeting at Westminster in 1600 there was every chance that this extraordinary enterprise might sink at any moment, somehow that did not happen. What helped was how the Company was buoyed by its enhanced sense of what it meant to be 'English'. Chapter 2 is therefore a survey of the Tudor process of nation-building. This is of great importance to our understanding of how it was that men were willing to put themselves forward for what would otherwise have been incomprehensible risks. Chapter 3 explores the Tudor 'City' to consider the resources Smythe was able to fall back on from his power base within the livery companies. The social and economic profile of Tudor London provided the Company not only with impediments to overcome but also with opportunities to exploit. The Company was a London organisation; Bristol, the nation's second port, played very little part. Here there is an exploration of how the crooked mile worked for the benefit of Smythe and his Adventurers.

Chapter 4 bristles with all the hustle and bustle of Smythe House, the Company headquarters and home of its governor. Here all was pandemonium prior to the moment a new voyage launched and the Company's ships set their course for the East. So follows the biography of the *Peppercorn*, one of the seventy-odd ships that would do the round trip during Smythe's governorship. By looking at how *Peppercorn* was prepared, who sailed her, where she went and what she carried, we are transported back to life upon a seventeenth-century wave.

Adventurers then turns to the first thirty years of the Company's life and its forays into the Spice Islands, India, the Middle East, Persia and Japan. It is a story of frustration, retreat and improvisation. Not only the Spice Islands but also the fabled riches of 'Cathay' had long been the goal of Tudor entrepreneurs. Yet the failure to find entrées to China, and the neglect in funding trading posts across the broadest reaches of the Indian Ocean, condemned the enterprise at a time when the Dutch were so conspicuously providing for their own outlets. Another costly mistake was Smythe's pushing for a Japanese 'front'. This he did because he thought it would provide the means with which he could scale the great trade wall of China. Instead he was mired in ten years of disappointing returns. What to do about the Dutch, and in particular the Dutch East India Company (the Vereenigde Oostindische Compagnie, or VOC), represented the most important failure of Smythe's governorship. In those early years it seemed as though by not finding a modus vivendi that might allow both nations to trade in peace, a terminal wound must be inflicted upon London. Digging into the detail of those negotiations speaks to the brittle, weak and confused nature of the Company. The Dutch triumph in the Moluccas, the most valuable islands upon the face of the planet – the very places that the Company had been called into being to grab in the first place – forced London into a wholesale rethinking of what could be achieved. All the while, India was emerging as the focus of attention.

Why the subcontinent proved so successful was in no small part down to the endeavours of Sir Thomas Roe, the Company's ambassador in India. Here and at last, there was substantive sustainable profit. And so it came about that a reluctant acceptance of playing a junior part to the Dutch in seas east of Bengal, a willingness to be bullied by those so conspicuously more successful than itself, would set up the abiding success story of the EIC. Had the Dutch not got the Spice Islands, the English would not have got India.

The overwhelming impression made by focusing on these early years is how survival was a surprise. The perilously low and slow trajectory of the Company must challenge those who think that from the first there were a subjugation of peoples and a march to riches. Such assumptions would be characterised by the sword of Robert Clive ('Clive of India') and the rule of Warren Hastings, but ways which brooked no compromise, methods as merciless in execution as they were sometimes disastrous in consequence, these were absent from the collective thought of the Company until very late in the seventeenth century. *Adventurers* is therefore both a counter and a caveat to those who would argue that the quarter-millennium during which the Company traded was one long uninterrupted progression in which the *spoils* of conquest and the dividend of commerce trumpeted superiority over subjected peoples.

INTRODUCTION

Whatever later writers thought about a 'British' involvement in India –
from Malthusian economists, Benthamite reformers and Clapham evangeli-
cals to Thackeray and twentieth-century supporters or detractors of the British
in India – in 1620 twenty-odd Englishmen in India had been interested
neither in people nor in politics. For them, it had been all about saffron not
slaves, *rials* not religion, cinnamon not conquest. All this was of course unlike
America, where a first British presence was motivated not merely by greed for
riches but by a need to subjugate. In places where the parties to a deal traded
in mutual prejudice but sudden liking and admiration too, in Agra as in
Isfahan, in Aceh and Edo, the Company was more despised than despising.
Here were to be found factories where the East India Company was wholly
insignificant, places where the Company was more sinned upon than sinning;
where, indeed, the EIC was to the powerful economies of the East no more
than lichen upon a trunk. In 1620 the East India Company had just, but only
just, become a growth. It would be generations before it was also to become a
parasite.

1

THE SMOKY AYER OF SPANISH GREATNES

Our first foray is global in its geography. What follows has to do with the trans-oceanic accomplishments of Spain, Holland and, especially, the astounding achievement of the Portuguese who had given birth to the marvellous leviathans of the deep known to the world as 'carracks'. First venturing into the Atlantic and then conquering Asia, such triumphs of the naval architect had an astounding effect on the mindset of the Tudor merchant, who would become the Stuart Adventurer.[1]

The English had felt the closest ties with Portugal since the Aliança Luso-Inglesa had been ratified by the Treaty of Windsor in 1386. As the sealing wax dried on that parchment so came to be solidified the oldest political treaty the world has ever known. Two centuries on from the alliance's signing, those men in white ruffs fiddling their way through the arcades of Gresham's Exchange – the future directors of the East India Company – could not but have felt that Portugal was far over any financial horizon they might compass. Such had been the head start of the Lusitanians in cornering the world's most lucrative consumables: that holy trinity of maize, clove and nutmeg. All this had come about because of the fillip given to trade with the accession in 1460 of Henry the Navigator, prince of the house of Aviz and son of Philippa of Lancaster. Under Henry's enlightened patronage, the smallest of European nations henceforth came to harbour the largest of ambitions.

From the taking of Ceuta in Morocco in the same year the English won the battle of Agincourt (1415), the Portuguese colonial regime went on to enjoy a hegemony in Eastern waters which was to last 150 years. The beginning of the end came with the snatching of the Portuguese crown by Philip II in 1580 from under the noses of several rivals. Privately a man of conservative, narrow and austere habits, Philip's assiduous patronage of those who would divine the secrets of the new world had succeeded in provoking not merely the avarice but also the curiosity of the old. His accession dealt a blow not only to Portugal's independence but also to its élan, and suggested to European commentators that now, indeed, the Spanish would become as dominant upon the seven oceans as their conquistadors had for so long been in the Americas.

But the pundits were wrong. None could have foreseen the bursting upon the scene of an unconquerable unknown nation: the United Provinces, or Holland. As we shall see, the fight to the death between Spain and its erstwhile dependencies in the Low Countries eventually yielded the commercial laurels to that North Sea nation. Within one generation only, Amsterdam was to eclipse Lisbon, emasculate Madrid and humiliate London by turns.

From the arrival of the Portuguese upon the mainland of North Africa in 1415, a sense of manifest destiny seemed to light the way. Captain and pilot, viceroy and bishop, all subscribed to the belief that nothing could prevent investment in Macao and intercourse at Peking when the arms of Portugal and the merchants of Lisbon were carrying all before them. And none had more belief in the infinite than the Portuguese explorer Pedro Nunes (d. 1573) who, in his *Tratado em defensam da Carta de marear* (*Treatise in Defence of the Sea Chart*, 1537), considered the nature of that *perpetuam mobile* which was the country of his birth:

> There is no doubt that the navigations of this kingdom [Portugal] from one hundred years to this part are the greatest, most marvelous, of higher and more discreet conjectures than those of any other people in the world. The Portuguese dared to take on the great sea and ocean. They entered it without any fear. They discovered new islands, new lands, new seas, new peoples, and what is more, new heavens and new stars.[2]

Of all the wonders of a Portuguese 'vasty deep' none was so monstrous as the *nao*. Known as the carrack by the English, the *nao* towered over all other European vessels. As an instrument of aggression and means of transport, the only thing that could have been compared with it was the junks with which Grand Eunuch Cheng Ho had made his stately progress through the southern seas between 1405 and 1433. The exceptional displacement of the carrack was best appreciated at water level. These were ships the size of cathedrals, sterns of carved exuberance, windows fretted like the honeycomb, escutcheons hanging like so many lanterns at a festival, with such splendours of the deck giving way to hobbit-sized burrows beneath. At less than 4 feet, these cabins could not afford the grandee even the privilege of standing up.

The New Christian Pedro Nunes,[3] one of those Portuguese mathematicians and navigators responsible for getting the 'great ships' to Goa and home again, dedicates much of his *Tratado* to grappling with trying to solve the perennial problem of taking a longitude bearing. But Nunes's numerous publications were not merely confined to the rudder and the rope house but were destined to have a place in the study of the humanist and the historian. The author was himself ambitious for future generations to understand the pre-eminence of the Portuguese in world exploration; in short, this was the age in which navigation and nationalism were twins as the practitioners of this fine art of measurement sought to steer the state to greatness. To the extent that his compatriots agreed with Nunes, they marvelled at how such triumphs of knowledge and conquest had been achieved by the smallest country in Europe, just as they marvelled how carracks also carried men and, in the case of Portugal itself, women to China and back.

With not just one but three castles between raft and stern, one carrack alone might weigh more than the entire flotilla the East India Company sent out east every spring. Take the *Mãe de Deus*. A *nao* captured by the English privateer Sir John Burgh (d. 1594) with his *Roebuck*, the *Mãe* had been built in 1589. It weighed a staggering 1,600 tons because it had no fewer than seven decks and a crew of 600. Depending on the weather, manoeuvring this into Lisbon would have required the very best of pilots. As it lay deep in the water, great care would be needed crossing the bar in case the *Mãe* came to be shaken into a thousand spars. Sometimes there were spectacular wrecks within sight of home after voyages lasting thousands of miles. For example, of the homeward-bound carracks dispatched from Goa in 1592, only the *São Cristóvão* got through: two were lost through natural disaster, the *Bom Jesus* ran aground and the *São Bernardo* disappeared without trace. But then the percentage of 'acts of God' was deemed acceptable given the enormous profit engendered by the safe return of just one vessel.

During most of the sixteenth century total Portuguese losses by shipwreck on the outward voyage were just short of 10 per cent and on the return

15 per cent. However, once decline started, losses went beyond the tipping point: 20 per cent during the period 1590–1630. This was far higher than the equivalent for either the English or the Dutch. As has been remarked, 'Portugal developed one of the richest shipwreck literatures in any European language.'[4] Indeed, and it comes as no surprise to discover how it was that the Portuguese published the most famous anthology in all of maritime history – all about drowning; it comes with the lachrymose title *História trágico-marítima*.[5]

For those who had the misfortune to travel in a carrack there was some reassurance in the fact that they were enormously strong. If properly handled, they could outlast the working life of most seamen: one of 1,200 tons plied between Lisbon and Goa for a full twenty-six years before being reduced to a hulk in 1582. It had been built not in Lisbon but in Goa, where, following the creation of the most important of all Portuguese *ultramarino* (overseas) cities, a number of local families became vastly wealthy dynasties of ship-wrights. As for the *Santa Catarina do Monte Sinai* of 800 tons (built in Kochi, India, *c.* 1512), such was the wonder of that particular world that the famous painter Joachim Patinir (d. 1524) took its portrait. In Kochi, where the *Santa Catarina* had been built, there was a pool of vast experience. Overheads were pleasingly low because materials lay about in prodigal abundance: pyramids of wood, pools of tar, fields of hemp and battalions of labour exploited in such numbers that less care was taken of the unskilled than devoted to the skilled business of laying a keel.

But as with the carrack, so with its owners. The Portuguese turned out to be much less powerful than their rivals thought. When the English East India Company came to be founded in 1599–1600, many Adventurers thought that the Portuguese would never be caught, let alone conquered. As was to become apparent, though, the real challenge was to find that self-belief necessary to take the fight to the enemy. The man who enabled these Adventurers to do just that was Richard Hakluyt (*c.* 1552–1616).[6]

Hakluyt is the greatest of England's naval historians. Cleric not sailor, Hakluyt always made sure to confine his own experience of adventuring to crossing the Channel only. Notwithstanding, from peering out of his oriel at Westminster Abbey, Hakluyt somehow contrived to compass the whole span of the oceans' drift. Writing over a million and a half words about sailors,

15

Hakluyt became a figure of national importance in promoting nationhood. In brief, he dedicated his whole life to making his compatriots believe that it was within the power of England to gain pre-eminence over the glassy medium. Thanks to Hakluyt's aggressively nationalistic views, the last of the Tudors but the first of our Adventurers were vastly encouraged to take to the sea. That was all well and good, or so Elizabeth and her ministers thought when they were being constantly lobbied by Hakluyt to do more to encourage an 'English' marine, but there was a problem: Lisbon lay between London and Lahore. The Portuguese had what appeared to be well-established colonies and, with the viceroyalty of Goa, one of the great cities of the world. But what the English saw coming into Europe by way of the fabulous riches of the Far East, they not only liked but also determined to have for and by themselves.

The early history of European contact with Asia had begun after Vasco da Gama made his first landing in India when he touched at Calicut in 1498. A hundred years later and there was luxury right across Europe: silk and spices, carpets and porcelain coming in by the shipload. This was not just a golden era for learning but for shopping too: no banker's wife wanted to miss out on a visit to Lisbon, then Europe's most exciting city, even if few of them could have afforded the rarest porcelain that was to be spotted in six boutiques dedicated to ceramics alone to be found along the Rua Nova dos Mercadores. Just how fabulous all this was is suggested by the report of the French ambassador who, unobserved, observed 'Philip of the Indies' at a palace window in Lisbon 'watching with great pleasure' through the length of a long autumn day as his treasures emerged from the cavernous holds of ocean-going merchantmen.[7] For a hundred years before the foundation of the East India Company, Iberia had nurtured a transcontinental network that was dedicated to the creation of such wealth as had not been experienced since the most rapacious days of Tiberius Caesar.

Portuguese intrusion within the Indian Ocean, indeed its pre-eminence as the sole importer of Eastern luxuries, had been maintained because of critical differences in shipyard production between West and East: if Europe nailed, Asia sewed. The hull of a Portuguese *nao* was bound with nails, which enabled it to absorb massive ballistic discharge at a time when, by contrast, the hulls of Asian vessels, secured only with raffia, meant that a fusillade could blow them away like leaves before the wind. This was of considerable advantage to the Portuguese, who therefore had no trouble in selling the Indian trader security from Portugal's own violence when Europeans operated protection rackets not city by city but on a positively oceanic scale.[8] In the sixteenth century the Portuguese also enjoyed advantages through the deployment of their nimble caravelles. Swallows dipping their wings, these lightsome carriers complemented the famous 'great ship of Amacon', a *nao* of such prodigious size that Japanese 'Master of Lacquer' Kanō Naizen (d. 1616) made this leviathan the hero of a strip cartoon in the form of a multifaceted screen, the best examples of which are to be seen in either Lisbon or Tokyo.[9]

The *nao*, accompanied by the lighter caravelle, should have been able to return with prodigious cargo and handsome profit; or at least that is what the merchants of Venice feared when it became known that the Portuguese had rounded the Cape of Good Hope for the first time. For example, that merchant of gloom Girolamo Priuli, whose image still haunts the walls and ceilings of the Doge's Palace, recorded what was being said on the Rialto: 'to-day, with this new voyage by the king of Portugal, all the spices which came by way of Cairo will be controlled in Portugal, because of the caravels which will go to India, to Calicut, and other places to take them . . . And truly the Venetian merchants are in a bad way, believing that the voyages should make them very poor.'[10] However, by the 1560s Venice was importing more pepper than she had been able to handle. As for the Portuguese, 'imports declined despite a large increase in demand in Europe during the century'.[11] This was because the Estado da Índia – the bureaucracy placed within metropolitan Portugal and charged with managing its overseas possessions – from the first permitted the most gross inefficiencies. Never able to take full advantage of a hard way to new wealth, the Portuguese had suffered the lamentable consequence that 'not even 10% of cloves coming out of the Moluccas [the Maluku Islands or, as they were called in 1600 in England, the Spice Islands] found its way in Portuguese ships round the Cape'.[12] Nevertheless, to those English Adventurers who possessed a sense of history, what had once been little more than the kingdom of the cork and the sardine now appeared to have become something vastly powerful.

What Henry the Navigator mapped, Afonso de Albuquerque (d. 1515) subjugated. This furious but charismatic soldier, joining a genius for administration to a mastery of the battlefield, earned for himself the sonorous epithet 'Captain-General of the Seas'. Fancifully compared with Tamburlaine, Albuquerque gave full sail to such ambitions as recognised no limits, his deeds provoking the commanding epitaph after his death 'Y quien mas hiziere passe a delante' ('he who does more, let him walk in front').[13] Between 1503 and his demise in 1515, Albuquerque captured Socotra and Hormuz (1507), Goa (1510) and Malacca (1511). As governor of India, he sent his subordinates to discover Sumatra and Siam (1511) and the Moluccas (1512). But beyond that, when making the king of Portugal the first European monarch to reach China, this same colossus sent his countrymen to Timor and Papua New Guinea; perhaps as far as *terra australis* itself: who knows?

But all this was not enough for such a man. Albuquerque went on to declare his intention of subjugating the Mamluks by diverting the Nile. But how was it done? This, Albuquerque was at a loss to explain, when armed with a thousand Portuguese and four hundred Malabaris, he issued them with garden spades only. Rather than diverting the river, Albuquerque resolved instead to steal the body of the Prophet. With the cadaver secured and the 'Moor' thereby held ransom, it was thought by Albuquerque (if by no one else) that the infidel would be obliged to give up Jerusalem. Beyond that, Albuquerque, thinking that the enemies of Christ would also be forced to evacuate the Holy Land, thought too of how his master Manuel I of Portugal would be rendered triumphant in a place where England's Richard Cœur de Lion had been trounced.

But then it was just such madness that made the king of Portugal begin to entertain the enemies of this demented man. Dismissal, when it came, was a surprise to Albuquerque, which was hardly surprising for one who had always commanded but rarely obeyed. Returning to Goa in 1515, Albuquerque was startled to discover how a sovereign hitherto gratified was gracious no longer. Manuel dismissed his lieutenant from such an accumulation of offices as had made the most extraordinary soldier in Portuguese history sovereign of the southern seas. As for Albuquerque himself, forced to consider his melancholy eclipse, he expostulated: 'Grave must be my sins before the King, for I am in ill favor with the King for love of the men, and with the men for love of the King.'

Things were never the same after Albuquerque died and the glory days of Portugal began to fade. During close on the two centuries after the death of

Manuel I (d. 1521), viceroys of Goa lasted no more than an average of two years in post. Yet a deep commitment had been made to colonisation, a process of engagement that, whilst exhausting the Portuguese, enlightened the English to the manifest folly of putting down settlements of any sort. As for the Company's Adventurers, those on the directing board who were known as the Court of Committees, they would think it better to adopt a light touch in trading with indigenous peoples, a feeling induced by what they had discovered about the baneful experience of the Portuguese. It would not be long after its foundation that, at the beginning of the seventeenth century, the Company began to discover a more successful network of trade than the Portuguese could ever have hoped to match.

Still more serious than the bad business of muddling conquest and coin had been Albuquerque's failure to take Aden. Here was the finest of deep water ports, so placed as to allow for the arrest of unwanted traffic entering the Red Sea. Aden was the port of resort to Cairo from Calicut, Coromandel and Canton, control of which was necessary for anyone aspiring to dominate the western Indian Ocean. But where Albuquerque failed, there came the armies of the 'Grand Sophy'; as with the Ottoman conquest of Aden, the crescent prevailed over the cross, and the imam discountenanced the missionary. When the 'Moor' first invested Aden in 1538, the dividend yielded was an accommodation by the maritime nations of the West to a disagreeable truth. Henceforth, dominance of the Indian Ocean was to be contested between a resurgent Islam and an intransigent Europe. When Aden fell, it fell to the West to concede not only the revival of Turkish arms but also the resurgence of Ottoman globalism.

Yet it must be doubted that if Albuquerque had only managed to take Aden, then a monopoly of trade would have been guaranteed. Quite simply, there were too many powerful economies steering more profitable courses than the Portuguese. The existence of highly sophisticated indigenous markets from the Horn of Africa to the Gulf of Hormuz meant that the smallest country in Europe was not to enjoy the largest hegemony in Asia for more than an interval. Neither Portugal, Spain, Holland nor England – the four European nations that invested most in Asian trade – would ever be more than tesserae within a mosaic of buoyant, burgeoning economies in a vast region where the fabled Spice Islands alone describe an area larger than the continental United States. European nations were drawn to the East by a growing awareness that there existed beyond Alexandria wealthy economies with whom it might be opportune to do business. During the brief period when fabulous profits were to be enjoyed through European exploit and exploitation, these were relished in the West because its traders relied upon indigenous and not Western banking facilities. It was an English observer who recognised the dependence of West upon East when he began to think of the challenge that Asia represented compared with the Americas. 'These people,' the East India Company's agent in Madras was to observe in 1650, 'are not like ye naked, unlearnt Americans but a most subtle and pollitique nation.'[14]

Fatal to the single-minded focus necessary to the maintenance of so vast an enterprise was that peculiarly Portuguese disaster of maintaining the Catholic faith. Such allegiance, such fatal ambition, was often distracting and always debilitating. Churches were put up, missions established, massacres punished, missals distributed at vast cost and doubtful value. And all of this across unaccountable uncountable miles. Just how fatal was subscription to the *Reconquista* is best suggested by the ways in which the Lusitanian episcopate made massive demands upon the secular arm. It had all begun with the taking of Ceuta, when the Portuguese had heralded a soldiery that had raped and ravaged its way across North Africa with the collusion, the blessing and the remission of a militant if ineffective Church. Whereas, to put it too simply, a 'Portingale' had a sword in one hand and a crucifix in the other, for the Estado da Índia, Portuguese Catholicism was like beri-beri: sapping, paralysing and recurrent. It weakened the system, as it infected what might otherwise have been clear-sighted decisions about where profit lay. As has been remarked, 'This commitment cost vast sums of money . . . [extracting] from the population men of military age and women with large dowries; few complained of this.'[15]

The powerful presence of the Church militant within the great bastion of Goa created a house divided. Viceroys of Goa, and there were far too many of them, resented the Jesuits whilst relying upon them to regulate a society divided equally in its devotion to the Virgin and to Venus. It was St Francis Xavier, whose death casket still stands upon the marble of Bom Jesus in Goa Velha, who himself had once stood against the fly-blown regime that in India had assailed him upon every side. This particular St Francis, worldly and transcendent, cynic and saint all at once, found himself moved to remark upon the sexual and fiscal laxity rolling about Goa in its salad days of apparent prosperity: 'all go the way of *rapio, rapis* (I steal, you steal). And I am astonished how those who come from there find so many moods, tenses and particles for this poor word *rapio, rapis!*'[16] Such comment was delivered just as another, answerable to João III and not Jesus, signed off the annual audit with his despairing flourish: 'This is what Goa in 1545 yielded last year, apart from what was stolen by officials.'[17]

Yet for all the drain upon resources which the 'Faith' represented, the Goanese establishment could not do without the 'Society' at a time when the brotherhood was proving so adept at diplomacy. The most adroit of these was Jerónimo de Ezpeleta y Goñi (d. 1617), St Francis Xavier's great-nephew, and Navarrese superior of a mission sent to the Mughal court in 1595.[18] This may be the same Jerónimo depicted in a miniature now in the Chester Beatty Library in Dublin.[19] He comes apparelled in all the colours of Coromandel: tea-cosy black hat set off by turmeric robes and midnight-blue cloak. Hirsute and barefoot, looking more like a Sufi than a saint, Jerónimo travelled to Lahore, where its courts of alabaster made the wood and plaster of Lisbon look like a pie-house. Although no Westerner could have picked up on all the tensions in the Mughal court, Jerónimo observed how 'Some who were supreme yesterday, are no one today. Some fell due to their own faults, others by way of rumours, and others because they believed that the world with all its tricks, could not beat them.'[20]

Despite the skills that Jerónimo and his tribe could deploy, the Jesuits were too often regarded by the secular arm as a pestilence in the body politic. Many a viceroy was as maddened by the swirl of a cassock as a horse by the sting of a fly. The problem of ecclesiastical influence in the affairs of Portugal, both *ultramarino* and metropolitan, developed into a canker which served only to erode timbers in the ship of state. Within the supine and somnolent deliberations of a decayed Estado da Índia, orthodoxy came to trump initiative in the affairs of a nation so loyally but disastrously devoted to the strictures of the Holy See.

All this may be demonstrated by noting a very Lusitanian habit of 'christening' a ship. In Portugal carracks were named after the Holy Family and the Passion, but never the things of this world. Take the *Cinco Chagas de*

Cristo (*The Five Wounds of Christ*), which was to be sunk by the English sea-rover Nicholas Downton (d. 1615). In marked contrast to all this, we must look in vain for salvation among the Adventurers of the East India Company, the *Ascension* being the one ship in the entire fleet whose prow might be thought to have pointed upwards. Different choices reflected different priorities: *Malice Scourge, Dreadnought, Trade's Increase, Peppercorn* and *Clove*: these were the names that the English preferred. Think, too, just how aggressive these are compared with all those suffering Portuguese saints. The 'Portingale' was propelled by the Holy Spirit, not by the trade winds. No wonder not a single Company ship was ever to be stung by a Portuguese man of war. Such distinction may seem small, yet perhaps not.

Technology, or rather a lack of it, had a bearing on how the Iberians began to stall from the mid-sixteenth century onwards. Neither Portugal nor Spain evolved state-of-the-art shipyards, maintained research or standardised production in an era as competitive for shipbuilding as artificial intelligence today. Such failure to invest in order to advance damaged Spain as much as Portugal. This was remarked upon by Duarte Gomes Solis (d. 1632), a New Christian who had had a remarkable career that culminated in his becoming special adviser to the conde-duque de Olivares (d. 1645), chief minister to Philip IV (d. 1665).[21] Born in Lisbon in 1561, Solis had run the pepper market in Goa before running onto a reef and being captured by African tribesmen. With experience as various as it must have been terrifying, this man of many seas was well qualified to discourse upon the eddies and currents of competitive Europe:

> The nation that has made the greatest progress in this art is Holland, which makes its ships very strong, elegant in design, and very light. They secure many advantages in giving a very broad floor, for in this way the ship is not deep in the water, and it is easily careened [cleaned], and is light. In Spain everyone used to build ships each after his own fashion according to the measures desired by the ship master. Ships were made short by the keel, and for this reason they pitched heavily; the floor was narrow and the depth great, so that they shipped much water, and in entering or leaving ports with bars affording little water, they were lost, to the damage of their masters and the merchants who loaded cargo in them.[22]

Both Iberian nations came to believe in colonisation, as would the Dutch, though with these particular Protestants, this was to be for *raisons d'état*, not faith. Sir Thomas Roe (d. 1644), the Company's first ambassador to India, scrutinising the Portuguese Empire with a mixture of professional concern and studied contempt, was never convinced by what he had to observe: 'It is the beggering of the Portugall, notwithstanding his many rich residences and territoryes, that hee keepes souldiers that spendes it; yet his garrisons are meane. He neuer Profited by the Indyes, since hee defended them.'[23] But if Roe was unmoved by what he had long dismissed, it was Solis who deplored his countrymen's devotion to national pride: how, for the Portuguese, metal always meant armour, not money: 'It was the advice of our first conquerors, that the more fortresses we had, the weaker we should be, and that to make ourselves masters of India, it would be more safe to bring large fleets there in order to enrich ourselves by trade. But the Portuguese thought more highly of soldiering than of knowing something about trade and such other matters, which with industry might have brought them riches.'[24]

Perhaps, though, Solis was being rather too harsh. Things were by no means over for either Portugal or Spain when the East India Company Adventurers first formed up. Although by 1600 both the Dutch and the English had entered the scene, the Portuguese could still shoot up like a cork upon the water. The first decade of the seventeenth century proved to be the busiest in the whole history of the *carriera*. At that moment, 77,000 tons left Portugal in seventy-one departures.

Indeed, it was of this interval that a historian writes: 'From 1570–1610 the Portuguese enterprise shows a far greater predilection for territorial adventurism than in any other earlier period.'[25] It might be added that such a late flourish may have been provoked more by national humiliation than any necessary reforms in the practice of book-keeping. The painful truth for those who sat in Lisbon whilst trying to run Goa was how Portugal had been suborned at the altar of Spain's ambition, forced into the most painful of marriages when Philip II had annexed the Portuguese Crown to that of Spain in 1580.

The Portuguese Empire was vast in extent but weak in reserves. From its earliest days, the hold that Portugal sustained upon its overstretched dominions was dependent upon economies richer, bureaucracies more efficient and regimes more powerful than itself. This meant that control was always nominal, often peripheral. How could it have been otherwise? Brazil and Goa had their own viceroys, but that made little difference to effective control of either of these principal Portuguese 'possessions'. The regent of the first could do little more than poke his baton into the sugar cane only to retrieve it, whilst those who made their private fortunes in Goa never knew whether they might not be pushed into the sea before what they had stolen from the Estado could be stowed safely aboard the returning *nao*. As for India, with the passage of time this came to be seen as a liability that, if only it could be dropped, might open a more fruitful path to the riches of South America. As matters stood, if there was ever much vision in Lisbon there was always myopia in Goa, as upon that occasion when the viceroy Francisco de Mello e Castro kicked an assistant down the stairs for having been impertinent enough to suggest that reform might not be such a bad thing after all. De Mello's words encapsulated the problems that by 1650 had sapped the initiative of the Estado: 'Senhor so-and-so, you can go and say whatever you like in Portugal, for when the punishment comes hence, either Portuguese India will no longer exist or else we will no longer be around, for we are very old and this place is a long way off from Portugal.'[26] Chancing upon anecdotal evidence of so vivid a nature as this, the student of history may be taken less by the glory that is Goa than by the indolence that was the Estado. As a moment's reflection will suggest, though, not all was hopeless; far from it.

The old assumption that because Spain and Portugal were Catholic and corrupt they were no match for the vigorous rationalists of Protestant Europe has long been exposed for the Manichaean dichotomy it always was.[27] However, even during the lifespan of the current generation of economic historians, the view that the Estado da Índia had somehow been doomed from the first was promoted by a Danish historian. Niels Steensgaard's examination of the impact of European commerce in Asia has been enormously influential. In what settled in status to become the primary study, Steensgaard simply wrote off the Portuguese like a bad national debt. He described the bureaucracy of the Estado as having to 'be regarded as one of the purest examples in history of constitutionally determined corruption'.[28] Nice phrase, but it won't do to dismiss a culture with what at the time was the rattle of a typewriter. By contrast, a more nuanced view came to be expressed by a reviewer of the book in which Steensgaard argued his case. That critic had some telling things to say about the overemphasis historians had traditionally placed on the revolution effected by the opening up of the Cape route to European ships. The reviewer suggested too much significance had been placed upon the dependence of Portugal in going round Africa when all the time they were going through Basra to Aleppo:

> in the long term the skill, initiative, and shipping resources of the Portuguese merchants stimulated all the varied routes of the overland trade. Even the key monopolized commodity, pepper, was shipped overland in large quantities by Portuguese middlemen who could not afford to give obedience to the restrictive edicts of their own king. Before 1590 the Cape route, exclusively in the hands of the Portuguese, rarely supplied as much as 70 percent of the pepper consumed in Europe, and sometimes supplied as little as one-half. Spices other than pepper, and all the many other commodities in the overland trade, were scarcely affected by the Cape route.[29]

But if Goa was on the slide at a time when the Company was on the up, in 1600 matters looked anything but secure for Englishmen contemplating a challenge to these pioneers of Far Eastern trade. What happened with that marriage between Spain and Portugal in 1580 seemed almost as threatening to the Privy Council as what was to transpire with the Armada in 1588. In 1580 Philip II had simply helped himself to Portugal when he had grabbed the vacant throne. What did this mean for English trade prospects? Fortunately, much less than might have been the case if Spain had not also found itself with a major rebellion from within its most prosperous territories. This had begun in 1566, and it would only end in triumph for the Dutch when Spain was obliged to cede independence to the United Provinces in 1648. But if that eighty-year civil war was to represent an enormous blow to Spain, it was a relief to the Adventurers. Had it not been for the distraction of that war, Holland would have wiped the East India Company quite off the map.

In order to understand the seeming potency of the Iberian menace, something that involved England in a twenty-year war with Spain (1585–1604), it is necessary to go back to the end of the fifteenth century. Alexander VI, most corrupt of Renaissance pontiffs in what was always a hotly contested field, had come up with the bright idea that the world should be divided between Spain, which was the country of his birth, and Portugal, where many of his best friends resided. Such a parting of waters, initiated with Alexander's bull *Inter Caetera* (1493), had then in turn been 'confirmed' by the Treaty of Tordesillas (1494). By this, Spain had been 'granted' everything west of a meridian 'drawn north to south 370 leagues west of the Cape Verde Islands', whilst for its part, Portugal had been prevailed upon to looked resolutely eastwards.[30] And yet despite such apparent accord, it was difficult to pick up in London the tensions that had existed between these Iberian kingdoms right through the sixteenth century. For example, upon visiting the royal map house of Lisbon, after that outrageous annexation of 1580, fondly thinking that each state was in accord with the terms of Tordesillas, Philip II had met with a most disagreeable discovery. Upon unrolling the maps, massive discrepancies at once became apparent between the *cartas* of Spain and the *mapas* of Portugal. Thus alerted, this man, one of the greatest regal patrons of the sciences, doubled his efforts to improve the accuracy of charts and the science of navigators.

As Philip determined that his cosmographers must gain a more accurate view of a Spanish world, it would have seemed entirely accurate to have thought that Spain was the richest nation upon the face of any globe, however imprecise the markings upon such a sphere may have turned out to be. Hoarding Colombian emeralds in its treasuries, papering its sacristies in gold, Spain had cushioned itself from the menace of tumultuous wealth. However, as the annual treasure fleet continued to paint Europe silver, so Spain began to drown in its own riches. Trouble had come by the 1570s when Spain had first ceded the transportation of its precious metals to the Dutch. Had Spain but controlled all this itself, the kingdom might have invigorated its own economy. Disastrous failure to exercise all that silver, by creating an industrial base and a service infrastructure, meant that circulation became sclerotic. And so it was that by neglecting to dismantle its pyramids of silver, Spain failed to put its own peoples to the loom. So far from doing that, by a disastrous irony it served merely to give the Dutch such incentives to the creation of their own wealth as would come to fund their first titanic struggle against the mother country – the 'Revolt of the Netherlands' that broke out in 1566 – which would only find resolution when peace was brokered at the Peace of Westphalia and the Treaty of Munster (1648).

In grasping the carrying trade from Iberia in the 1570s, the northern regions of the Low Countries, most prosperous and progressive of all Spain's dependencies, rejected control from Madrid. Beyond that, the United Provinces, as this grouping called itself, went on to run the most successful haulage business in Europe. This it was able to do by carrying Peruvian silver for the bourse, Patna cotton for the matron, Persian rugs for the cardinal and Pomeranian corn for Spaniards themselves when at the beginning of the seventeenth century there arose widespread cereal failure in Valencia and Aragon. Where Spain counted the cost, the Dutch capitalised on the profits. From the 1570s onwards, the 'Hollander' became the chief rival in European waters to what had been his erstwhile ruler. With profits accruing, the Dutch earned sufficient reserves of specie to build an infrastructure that encouraged the most virtuous of commercial circles. As the stone was cast upon the water, as new keels slipped into the Ijssel, new wealth expanded to the very circumference of Europe. During these critical years Spain stalled and Holland stole. Observing all of this, if too late, Philip II issued a *pronunciamento*. Published in 1592, this edict proved disastrous for the kingdom and deleterious for the empire. Instead of promoting a healthier Spanish economy, as would have been the consequence of opening Iberian ports to whoever could freight at the lowest price, all that Philip's policy succeeded in doing was to put up such trade barriers as created a siege economy within the Peninsula.

Such a disastrous policy proved to be the liberating moment for the Dutch. Turned away from the ports of Iberia they struck out into an ocean of wealth. Confidence in Holland had been checked by that disastrous edict of 1592; but only for a pulse. Defiance broke out, optimism leapt up, and though crisis loomed, it was but a squall giving way to sunshine upon tropical waters. Spanish *reales* continued to jingle in a Dutch pocket because here was a people of the waters long used to sinking their *reales* in a silver sea, adopting as they adapted Spanish coin to float home industry upon distant enterprise. In the face of relentless belligerence, huge numbers in Holland flocked to invest in their gilded merchantmen riding upon the Zuider Zee before those great ships beating round Texel set a course for the Spice Islands.

Such transoceanic voyages served as the means to escape the financial chaos that always threatened that nascent republic, following furious attempts by Spain to strangle a new nation at its birth. But instead, soon enough indeed, buoyant interest rates came to prevail in the bourse of Holland. As from 1600, the Seven Provinces found themselves able to adjust to any restrictive practices that hereafter their enemy might try to impose.

Beyond issues of comparative economies, there were to be critical differences between the fleets of Spain, England and Holland. These help to explain why the northern nations were able to overtake the Mediterranean powers of Spain, France and Italy. For example, the English commercial fleet was to prosper because England 'was able and willing, to extract a much larger share of the "national product" than the French or Spanish state'.[31] Such capacity on the part of the English was a prime illustration of that maxim 'he who taxes best sails furthest'. But it was the Dutch, now emerging as the pre-eminent maritime power of the early modern world, who were also evolving the most efficient system of revenue extraction in Europe. In turn this encouraged a flexible marine that enabled the VOC to create one type of vessel for breaking the ice floe but quite another for breasting the coral reef. Compare all this with the system in Spain, if system it could be called. Here the terms of unification through dynastic marriage in the case of the Aragonese Crown (1479), conquest of Navarre (1511) and the takeover of Portugal (1580) stipulated clearly that existing fiscal and representative systems would not be changed by the senior partner Castile; in other words, traditional 'liberties' (*fueros*) would not be touched. Thus by the late seventeenth century the formerly 'international' borders still functioned in the same way as they had done since these separate kingdoms had been incorporated into a greater Spain. From first to last, from Ferdinand and Isabella to Napoleon Bonaparte, export and import duties charged – and spent – were the province of independent Castilian, Navarrese and Aragonese treasuries. But still there were internal customs functioning on the boundaries between the old kingdom of Castile on the one hand and Galicia, Cantabria and Asturias on the other.[32] A national inability to raise taxes goes far, therefore, in explaining why the Spanish commercial empire came to be overmastered by the Dutch.

Here is an irony. Philip II had moved his capital from Valladolid to Madrid (1561) in order to be at the centre of things, only for it to be discovered that although Madrid might lie at the centre, it stood in the middle of nowhere. How different from London! Madrid was a tent of bureaucrats and a camp of grandees; the River Manzanares a latrine running through a town where the only discernible industry was effort expended in trying to obtain a sinecure, or finding a place in the sun alongside an inbred king. In contrast to all this, Tudor London dominated the economy of England. Astride one of the great commercial rivers of Europe, London also commanded the tributaries of the Severn, Humber and Tyne, none so distant that when coal and rope were required they could be summoned with all dispatch. The dominance of London made for simplicity as it encouraged expedition. By contrast, the direction of a Spanish home-waters fleet, as the whole thrust of its *ultramar* affairs, was divided between the Basque, the Galician and the Andalusian ports; termini accessed from that lonely capital only by journeys of hundreds of miles over desperate roads made for romance, though hardly, it may be thought, rationalisation.[33] And so it was that although Iberian barns might have looked well built and better stocked, once they were given a good kick the rusted hinges flew off.

From the first, the more percipient Adventurers of the English East India Company saw this for themselves. Richard Hakluyt, for example, made it his business to try to persuade these investors that they had nothing to fear from either the Portuguese *nao* or the Spanish carrack. As for Sir Thomas Roe, he had observed Spain at uncomfortably close quarters when in 1611, and paddling up the Amazon, he had been detailed by James I's chief minister Lord Salisbury to note the strengths and weaknesses of Spanish settlements. Roe formed a view he would see no reason to modify in a diplomatic career that was to take him from Agra to Stockholm via Constantinople: Spain was all show and no go. Englishmen would therefore do well to blow away 'the smoky ayer of Spanish greatnes', as Roe put it when writing a few years later from the palace of an Indian emperor to the Lambeth palace of an arch- bishop of Canterbury. Roe understood that empires are all about perception, which too often, in Roe's opinion at least, had taken the form of unwar- ranted despair in the face of Spanish might or trepidation under the stern of a Portuguese *nao*. But Roe was to have none of it. When he was to get out to India in 1615, he made it his principal business to face down the pretensions of the Portuguese viceroys.

By the time England came to blows with Portugal in India, from 1608, it was in fact the Dutch and not the English East India Company that had become principal beneficiary of Iberian atrophy; though Holland might never have taken that lead but for what had been a diaspora of wealth out of Antwerp that had followed Philip's attempts to reassert control over the Netherlands. Richer than the kingdom of Naples, more populous than the duchy of Milan, both Spanish possessions at this time, the Netherlands was the very barn and wellhead of Iberia. In the north were the fish, from the east came the grain, whilst out of the fat lands to the south, the ancient kingdom of Burgundy, the identity of the Spanish Habsburgs had issued. Philip II's father, Charles of Ghent, had so identified with the Netherlands that when he had first arrived in Spain in September 1517 as Charles I, co-ruler with his mother Joanna of Trastámara, he had spoken not one word of Castilian. So beholden had Charles been to his Burgundian heritage that he had supplemented Spanish revenues from the prodigal abundance of northern dependencies. Out of Franche-Comté tumbled the products of Rhine and Rhone; out of the North Sea and the Mediterranean had issued the fruits of oceans in all their prodigal abundance.

By 1550 Antwerp had succeeded Lisbon as Europe's 'city of culture'. Through its legendary printing resources it supplied missals for the pious and *naturalia* for the curious. A mart of exchange and an exchange of nations, Antwerp also attracted Europe's best painters. These pursued a truly cosmopolitan clientele, including England's foremost exchange dealer, Sir Thomas Gresham, who, living in Antwerp in 1563, had sat for Antonio Mor, the unblinking portraitist of the king of Spain himself.[34] The greatest gift that Antwerp gave Europe, however, was the abundance of printing presses that the city sustained; of these, the most creative was presided over by Christophe Plantin. He was the founder of the celebrated partnership of Plantin-Moretus, which by the middle of the sixteenth century had overtaken the Venetian house of Aldus Manutius in the business of creating Europe's bestsellers. The Plantin-Moretus was an enterprise that in time would include the most cultivated man in Europe on its payroll: Sir Peter-Paul Rubens (d. 1640). Plantin the type designer and Rubens the graphic designer were both citizens of what was still a very Spanish Europe as they were both passionate patriots of Spain's richest dependency, the fabulously wealthy duchy of Flanders. For his part,

Christophe was deeply embedded in a Spanish-directed culture marked by his close friendship with Abraham Ortelius, cartographer-royal to Philip II. As for Rubens, in a career which in its productivity surpassed even the output of that other Spaniard, Picasso, he was to receive his most important commissions from the Habsburgs of Madrid.

But if for a felicitous pulse Flanders looked to achieve what Florence had created, her citizenry made a tragic, fatal error. Entertaining heresy, retribution followed when one weekend in 1576 eight thousand men, women and children were put to the sword; not an ethnic but a sacred 'cleansing', this attempted resolution of the difficulties for Philip II came to be known as the 'Spanish Fury'.[35] Those who survived, unwilling to risk disembowelment a second time, decamped instead to the plashy sluices of Friesland where, safe from the long end of a Spanish pike, they afforded learning, crafts and loyalty to a newly invented United Provinces.

The sixteenth century witnessed the rise of Iberia to what appeared to be a position of unassailable dominance everywhere south of the Azores. However, this was more apparent than real. Portugal had over-extended herself, not only in the brevity with which she achieved her victories, but also in the extent of her conquests. Albuquerque's path of rapine had created the very conditions that would overwhelm the resources of a mother country, which then had a population the equivalent of Glasgow today (1,689,000). Besides the little matter of ruling over Brazil, so vast had been the extent of Albuquerque's Eastern 'triumphs', so impossible were the geographies of his annexations, that what the *gran capetan* had served up came to prove to be the most impossible of legacies. So it was that atrophy had set in after a brief interval of febrile and muscular exertion. Soon enough, the sheer enormity of what Portugal had done smothered initiative in her overseas dependencies. The alacrity with which the 'Captain-General of the Seas' had pushed his enemies over a cliff had served to disarm those whose task it was to consider the longer-term consequences of what had been assumed must only be a gradual investment in Asia. Hobbled by domestic prejudices that would render future viceroys ill-equipped for such pragmatism as might have yielded the very profits that the home country desired, the administrations of Goa and Macau came to be disabled by a toxic mix of religious bigotry and misplaced chivalry. The Estado, proving unable to get on equal terms with the powerful, contingent and indigenous economies of both India and the Far East, found itself knocking at the side door, not entering the main gate.

As for the incumbents of the palace themselves, passing through the vice-regality with an alacrity that served only to militate against settled policy or momentum of effort, in the pulse available to each in turn, these all too numerous incumbents devoted themselves on the one hand to futile endeavours in support of *limpeza de sangue* (purity of blood), whilst on the other bending themselves to the onerous business of self-interest and familial aggrandisement. Most if not all viceroys were devoted to the paramount task of taking home so many diamonds as ensured dependents at home would be rendered rich until eternity. With regard to the metropolitan throne itself, after Portugal regained its independence from Spain in 1640 kings began to declare, within the theatre of diplomacy if hardly from a public platform, how they would rather have sold India to profit from Brazil, than be required, as unhappily was the case, to continue in that dispiriting business of sustaining the hapless and the helpless settlers of the subcontinent.[36]

But what of Holland? Although it seemed to have far more in common with England than with its erstwhile overlord Spain, as the two North Sea nations became the fastest-growing European economies in Asia, so profound differences between them began to emerge; difficulties that meant that without intermission either armed neutrality or open conflict came to define Anglo-Dutch relations between the death of Elizabeth (1603) and the deposition of James II (1688). As for Holland's thrust eastwards, this was a projection of the new and a rejection of the old: pursuit of nationhood and denial of subservience. The sudden aggressive appearance of the Dutch in the East Indies was as much a matter of definition as of defiance. The grabbing by the Dutch of lucrative trading posts once Iberian was not only the expression of a nation coming of age, but also the essential aid to enrichment. Imagining financial ruin through the exigencies of civil war, wrongly as it turned out, the Hollander strained to consolidate his freedoms until the moment when Spain ratified what had been the implication of the Twelve Years' Truce (1609), when with the Peace of Westphalia and the Treaty of Munster (1648) it granted the independence of its once contumacious provinces.

Hakluyt, most incontinent of English historians, suggested that any continent was there for the taking if only compatriots would once start believing in themselves. For those persuaded by such partisan nationalism, Hakluyt's achievement had been to prepare 'the cheafest captains at sea, the greatest merchants, and the best mariners of our nation' to prosecute what he saw as England's calling. In Hakluyt's second and definitive edition of the *Principall Navigations* (1598), that is to say the precise moment when the first Adventurers were founding the East India Company, the author issued less a call to arms than a summons to sail:

> the first carak that ever was taken comming foorth of the East Indies; which the Portugals tooke for an evil signe, because the ship bare the Kings owne name . . . the taking of this carak wrought two extraordinary effects in England: first, that it taught others that caracks were no such bugs but that they might be taken . . . and secondly, in acquainting the English nation more generally with the particularities of the exceeding riches and wealth of the East Indies; whereby themselves and their neighbours of Holland have bene incouraged (being men as skilfull in navigation and of no lesse courage then the Portugals) to share with them in the East Indies, where their strength is nothing so great as heretofore hath bene supposed.[37]

2

✂✁

NORTH SEA NATIONS

On 17 November 1558 Queen Mary breathed her last in St James's Palace. One month later, Anthony Jenkinson (d. 1611), who had gone down to the Caspian Sea to sell English 'kerseys', felt his end was nigh too. Anthony had been working for the Muscovy Company, given its first charter by Mary herself a mere three years earlier. There, however, the connection ends: Mary died in a palace; Anthony foresaw his demise in the grass. His luck had run out that December morning when he had spotted not 200 yards off his caravanserai thirty-seven heavily armed 'rovers', presaging, in his own reckoning, slow torture and an agonising death. But then a miracle occurred, a seemingly divine intervention to save his life that had been denied to the most Catholic of sovereigns.

The miracle was made of metal, and it was hot after what had proved to be the hottest of days. It was a four wheel-lock pistol, which Anthony had, but the raiders didn't.[1] Those guns made all the difference. Ferocious fighting erupted between Anthony's group of merchants and the nomad raiders which seems to have lasted several hours. As battle drew to a close a truce was eventually agreed, though both parties expected to be at it again the next day. As evening came on so Anthony's spirits sank when he saw how the bandits had positioned themselves between himself and the river. These rovers knew full well that the men from Muscovy had fought all day without water. Shrugging his shoulders, Anthony could only regroup on a hillock behind, putting bales between himself and the arrows, driving camels into the stockade and, after setting the watch, settling under a camel-hair rug to await what he was certain was going to be his last dawn. As it turned out, however, although there was indeed a reckoning, it was not the one that Anthony was expecting. When the sun came up the bandits came forward. They were now

34

suggesting that if they were given enough bounty they would leave. Mightily relieved, 'that night [the survivors] came to the river Oxus, where we refreshed our selves, having been 3 days without water and drink, and tarried there all the next day, making merry with our slain horses and camels'.[2]

Thus spared, Anthony rode into Bokhara five days later. Despite the delay that had been caused by this fight with the tartars, he was just in time for the merchant fair. This was a huge annual gathering that brought merchandise to the city from no fewer than three continents. Undoing sacks, what Anthony now discovered therein was to prove his own undoing:

> The Indians do bring fine whites, which the Tartars do all roll about their heads, & all other kinds of whites, which serve for apparel made of cotton wool and crasko, but gold, silver, precious stones, and spices they bring none. I inquired and perceived that all such trade passeth to the Ocean sea, and the veins where all such things are gotten are in the subjection of the Portingals. The Indians carry from Boghar [Bukhara] again wrought silks, red hides, slaves, and horses, with such like, but of kersies and other cloth, they make little accompt. I offered to barter with merchants of those countries, which came from the furthest parts of India, even from the country of Bengala, & the river Ganges, to give them kersies for their commodities, but they would not barter for such commodity as cloth.[3]

England's economy had been overly dependent on wool long before Anthony thought he could dump it on Uzbekistan. Indeed, wool would be a commercial dependency in England still in the ascendant at the end of the seventeenth century, when the country's traditional export of cloth remained the largest entry in its port books.[4]

If over-dependence on one commodity might be considered a disadvantage at the dawn of the eighteenth century, having so modest a fleet as the English possessed in the sixteenth was even worse. It militated against large-scale diversification in either imports or exports. English marine tonnage was the smallest amongst the seafaring nations of Europe. In 1570 Spain and Portugal had upwards of 300,000 tons, the Netherlands 232,000 tons, the Holy Roman Empire 110,000 tons, France 80,000 tons and England a paltry 58,000 tons.

Evidently, then, England was at a disadvantage when it came to the size of its fleet. Nevertheless, as the tribulations of Anthony Jenkinson suggested, what England possessed in abundance were people willing to chance everything to open up new trade routes. Fearless men backed by City moguls, ruthless and rich alike, sallied forth to make England sail.

From the accession of Henry VII onwards, pressure groups would focus on trying to find shorter routes to the Spice Islands round the North Pole than had been available at the start of the golden age of Portuguese voyaging. During that long doleful *durée*, hopes, ships and money were to be sunk beneath a grey forlorn Atlantic in an unremitting series of tragic outcomes, relieved by only the occasional acts of astonishing if frustrated heroism. For example, William Baffin (d. 1622) was to graduate from life as a pilot at a whaling station on Spitsbergen to piloting Captain Edward Bylot's *Discovery* (1615) into a more northern latitude than would be unsurpassed until Franklin's celebrated expedition of 1852.[5] The earlier endeavour had been sponsored by what called itself 'The Company of Merchants of London, Discoverers of the North-West Passage': established in 1612, this had been presided over from its inception by Sir Thomas Smythe (d. 1625), who was, of course, the first governor of the East India Company.

What Baffin did came to be memorialised in Baffin Island, nominally yielded to the English, almost 197,000 square miles constituting the world's largest and, at the time, most useless land mass. As it was, Elizabethan adventure capitalists had invested in ships from which there would be no return. Desolate islands sewn with the windy sea grass but not the pepper, bluffs patrolled by the ferocious bear but not the ruminant camel, empty lands in emptier seas, these were but poor substitutes for the cottons of Coromandel and the emeralds of Colombia. The regime in England had long endeavoured to do something to encourage wealth, but islands and sounds so suddenly 'English' were but small compensation for the loss of life and the expenditure of savings. Here was a primitive nation goaded into trying to find the fabled shortcut to China coming to realise just how far behind it was.

If such lands were unprofitable, that in no way dampened ardour. Blinded by avarice and perpetual snow, explorers had been instructed to find a shorter route to reduce time and expense in getting at 'Cathay'. Thus it was that in pursuit of a perilous but fruitless goal, expeditions had been fitted out and launched, waved off indeed, with a princely hand. The most celebrated had been a fleet consisting of three ships (the largest of 160 tons only) under the command of Sir Hugh Willoughby as captain-general and Richard Chancellor as pilot-general. This had departed from Ratcliff on the Thames in May 1553. Making the bravest of shows when festooned in flag and streamer, and with its mariners 'all apparelled in watchet or skie-coloured cloth', the little fleet had paused off Greenwich to salute Edward VI.[6] It may be wondered whether, had the boy-king been well enough to attend to such a compliment, he might have asked himself if vessels appearing hardly more robust than paper boats in the royal fountain could ever return. Such doubts were well placed. What braved the oceans came to grief amidst the shrouds of the Bering Sea.

But although a search for the 'Passage' proved of no obvious benefit, it was far from wasted experience. Nudging the bottle-green icebergs of northern waters proved something of a nursery of endeavour and an exercise in courage. The attempt to avoid hitting any of the 36,563 islands that lie in wait for the unwary traveller about the Canadian Arctic gave William Baffin just the self-belief that the East India Company's orders to site a battery in the Persian Gulf required of him, as it also gave a whole school of navigators good grounding against grinding into the reefs of the Maldives. Although Martin Frobisher, most intrepid of the Arctic men, seems to have spent more time looking for hair of mermaid and horn of unicorn than investors might have felt was wholly justified, what he found and chroniclers burnished was patriotism and duty in the face of impossible odds. These qualities would prove no less valuable to the Adventurers of the East India Company than were to be the cannon and the astrolabe. That desolate lid of the earth that turns its circle from Karelia to Murmansk, via Yellowknife and the Great Bear Lake, represented many things for future adventures of the English East India Company. Above all, perhaps, what the frozen round of Arctic endeavour provided was a training ground for that 'virtue' which the Tudors were the first to feel and the Victorians the last to believe.

This supposed 'virtue' was what some have seen as a peculiarly English delight in being the loser. It was something Elizabeth I played up to and Shakespeare played with: the first in the 'Armada Speech' when she roused waiting troops at Tilbury, and the second when Henry V tells his own crew to brace up and get on with it the night before the battle of Agincourt. What seems to have been a peculiarly British need to be defeated, however, came to be given definitive expression by Sir Henry Newbolt (d. 1938) with his notorious exhortation to duty, the *Vitaï Lampada* (1892). In what is less than an epic, the poet is positively heartened by the fact that 'the sand of the desert is sodden red ... the gatling's jammed and the colonel dead'. Regrettable though such a state of affairs might have been, that sort of thing had always allowed the chaps to 'play up and play the game'. What Newbolt had celebrated at the twilight of the British Empire in 1892, the old Etonian George Best had discovered in the Arctic in 1580.

Best sailed those icy waters as something of a journalist. His self-appointed task was to contrive myths of English prowess in northern wastes that would provide fingerposts to the future; pointing his avid readership, safely tucked up in London, to silver fish and white fur – all wrapped up in breathless tales of 'dering-do's and 'dering-don'ts'. Having no difficulty in rowing over the flotsam of wrecked hopes, the emptiness of English achievements becomes, for George, boundless field for boldest of claims:

> In the economy of exploration where high costs and innumerable dangers were to be offset by the similarly infinite number of profits – which Best painted in the opening inventory of his *Discourse* – the uncertain accomplishments of Frobisher's voyages led the chronicler to turn to a different kind of profit. It actually forged the pride it professed, offering both the state and the community the necessary conditions to develop a sense of nationhood: the battle against the odds was turned into a national cause of epic dimension, and the narrative sought to project an image of the Englishmen as mythic heroes.[7]

One who would surely have met with the warmest approbation from the Homeric Newbolt was that same Anthony Jenkinson whose heroics in the grass were described earlier. Jenkinson was one of the earliest converts to the pleasures of grappling against hopeless odds, and so he must have been mortified in 1611 to find himself dying in a four-poster looking over sheep cropping his Northamptonshire meadows. Before so serene an exit, however, he had had an audience with Suleiman the Magnificent, most magnificent of Turkish sultans, before then travelling on to become the intimate of Ivan the

Terrible. In Moscow Jenkinson had found resolution sufficient to drink with a tsar whose appetite for indulgence was surpassed only by his delight in instruments of torture, of which Jenkinson was fortunate enough to dodge the sharp end.

Once back in England, Jenkinson had been summoned to debate the putative existence of a north-east passage with Sir Humphrey Gilbert. But thereafter he petitioned the queen so that he might find a way to 'the famous region of Cathaye and infynyte ilondes neare thereunto, all wiche are replenished with infynyt treazures, as golde, sylver, precious stones, bawmes, spices, drogges and gumes'.[8] Though Jenkinson never could find that 'famous region', his odyssey from Archangel to Moscow, down the Volga to Ovid's Scythia, induced him to go public with his much-creased 'plots'. These he donated to his friend Abraham Ortelius, who went on to use them for 'Russia' in his atlas entitled *Theatrum Orbis Terrarum* (1570, and dedicated to Philip II). Though that new way to China was never to be found, in failing, Jenkinson succeeded in gaining a reputation as the bravest of the brave. His tenacity impressed Elizabeth I as his intrepidity inspired her apologists, less for the promise of riches than for the promotion of knowledge. Although Tudor explorers had only sea water and pebbles to show for all their efforts, they certainly helped to create an 'English' school of history, writers bold enough to imagine the country changing from an island to an empire; men who proved themselves to be as much the adventurer as those investors who would later purchase shares in the East India Company.

The first of these promoters of England at sea was the magus Dr John Dee. Dee had a mass of credulous disciples, whilst for his own part he passionately believed in the importance of overseas trade. He wrote his influential book *General and Rare Memorials pertayning to the Perfect Arte of Navigation* (1577) in support of an expanded navy. England had always been a maritime empire, and now was the time to reclaim that birthright. As if to make the point, he commissioned a frontispiece to go with the *Navigation*. Here Elizabeth I is enthroned upon a deck, looking less like a captain than a conductor warming up an orchestra.

It has been claimed that Dee coined that infamous term 'the British Empire'. He didn't, although we can be certain he would surely like to have done so. He used it often – so often, indeed, as made the phrase familiar at a time when others were also beginning to conceive of history in quite new terms. Although Sir Thomas More's *History of King Richard III* (composed *c*. 1513–18) represented a serious attempt to record facts to an extent that had not been essayed before, the book was more a 'life' than a 'times' – less concerned with the wellsprings of societal change than the Elizabethans, who would largely reject the temptation to extrapolate morals out of history.

Foremost among those whose canvases would be larger than More's were William Camden and Sir Robert Cotton. Whereas history had been little more than a moralist's tale about the ways of God before these two got going, Camden and Cotton concerned themselves with *real* events, albeit conceived as a picture set within a deep frame of providentialism. Hitherto 'chroniclers', for we hesitate to use the term 'historians', had embroidered a life of *virtú*, if they hadn't made the whole thing up in the first place. From now on, the past came to be reconstructed by allowing what had gone before to speak through the exposition of events, the transcription of documents and the broadcast of testimony. Where the earlier men had been fabulists putting words into the mouths of 'heroes', as if the narration of history was no more than speech bubbles in a cartoon, Camden and Cotton began to offer their readership history with a small 'h' but capital potential. All this was in marked contrast to mellifluous Latinists who had invented set pieces that approximated as closely to truth as *Macbeth* to Scottish history – embellishments in the form of 'orations' set forth to justify and inspire, admonish or sanctify.

We turn first to William Camden as being first to publish. His *Britannia* (1586) established him as foremost among the British historians: as the first to find roots of history *within* history and not among the contrivances of myth or the periods of rhetoric. But if Camden's sense of history was comparatively realistic, it was also a species of polemic informed with deep patriotism, his writings guided by a determination not merely to tell of the past, but to encourage a place for England in a grander scheme of things. For Camden, 'Britannia' was not so much an island as part of a greater whole, to which she naturally gravitated. The point here is that Camden was central to encouraging compatriots to be proud of where they had come from, though his scholarship was hardly less critical in making Englishmen think of where they wished to go. As the title of his great work implies, Camden was taken with the continuities of Rome in a work that proffers as much sociology as antiquarianism: trade, commerce, food production, new industries and the growth of urbanism appear for the first time in a history that is itself a first; translated from Latin into English in 1611, and about the English for the English. If *Britannia* had to do with old times, it was a tract for its own; something of lasting value for the descendants of those to whose Roman colonial heritage Camden had so painstakingly dedicated himself.

Proclaiming the greatness of 'Great Britain', and so unshackling Englishmen from constricting insularity, all this created a growing sense that England could yet defeat Portugal, as it also nurtured one of the fondest of national myths.[9] This was that the salty sea dogs of Devon spent their time capturing Spanish treasure. Nothing could have been further from the truth, however.[10] Occasions when big prizes were taken were rare. But of these, unquestionably the most sensational was the capture of the *Mãe de Deus* at the battle of Flores in 1592. Constructed in Lisbon just three years before, the seven-deck, 1,600-ton *Mãe* carried 900 tons of luxury only. Between the ribs of a heaving diaphragm and within the cavernous bowels of a great ship came to be discovered nothing that was needed but all that was indulgent: tapestries to delight the eye and spices to beguile the tongue, cochineal to adorn the artist's palette and emerald to sparkle among the silver gossamers of a Tudor dress.[11] The discovery had Hakluyt crowing about 'God's great favour towards our nation, who by putting this purchase into our hands hath manifestly discovered those secret trades & Indian riches, which hitherto lay strangely hidden, and cunningly concealed from us'.[12] Such a triumph succeeded in arousing the cupidity of a whole generation when the treasure was valued at more than the entire annual revenue of the Exchequer. Never has such a prize been captured as Sir Walter Ralegh (d. 1618) brought into Plymouth he 'returned to London . . . with booty estimated to have been worth £600,000, possibly earning for his investors a staggering 4,700% profit. The Queen received in the region of £300,000.'[13]

All this was no doubt excellent copy for government propagandists, but in truth it was a complete sideshow. The damage inflicted on the coastal fleets of Spain during the war with England between 1585 and 1604 made a far greater impact on the Iberian economy than the occasional theft of a carrack. Of course all the small stuff went on in the Western Approaches, the Bay of Biscay and the English Channel. Hugely profitable to the rogues of Plymouth, the decimation of Spain's coastal traders was also no less useful to lobbyists working for such a trade war with Iberia as could be exported to the Spice Islands.

Among the most vociferous of the lobbyists wanting to take the battle to the Spice Islands was William Sanderson (d. 1638), a wealthy entrepreneur who was so smitten with England's daring deeds that he named his sons after his heroes of the Tudor seas: Ralegh, Cavendish and Drake. Sanderson was just the sort of City figure who would make others look beyond the confines of Leadenhall Street to consider the riches of the East. Like many others, he had thrown money at the proposed 'short route' to China, rightly described as 'the most alluring geographical concept of the late sixteenth century'.[14] In such a pursuit, Sanderson not only supported Ralegh but also John Davis, the most experienced pilot in England. When Davis was making repeated attempts to break out into the Pacific, Sanderson lent him his *Moonshine* to sail away 'alone and without further comfort'.[15] Davis was never to find his way to riches, but his backer went on lending boats and a purse of £1,000 for the construction of the first English celestial and terrestrial globes. Our tireless Hakluyt wrote of 'the comming out of a very large and most exact terrestriall globe, collected and reformed according to the newest, secretest, and latest discoveries, both Spanish, Portugall and English, composed by Mr. Emmerie Molineux of Lambeth, a rare Gentleman in his profession, being therein for divers yeeres, greatly supported by the purse and liberalite of the worshipfull marchant M. William Sanderson'.[16] Sanderson's commitment to maritime 'R&D' made him central to the Elizabethan sea.

But Sanderson's high profile did not protect him. Made umpire for the dangerous game of dividing up the *Mãe de Deus* swag, he appears unfortunately to have laboured under the misapprehension that because Sir Walter Ralegh was a hero he must be honest. Named 'Marchaunt for Sir Walter Ralegh and for the captains, masters, gentlemen, and mariners in the voyages',[17] Sanderson's job was to see to the distribution of the prize money which came to be extracted from the capture of the *Mãe*. First the subject of envy then the object of contempt, Sanderson's inability to control a chaos of greed and storm of avarice caused immediate loss of his reputation and the subsequent ruin of his estate.

Riches on the *Mãe*'s scale provoked mayhem. Everyone was after the spices, porcelain, carpets and pearls, whilst rubies bounced along the jetty like golf balls across a green when a posse of London jewellers descended upon Dartmouth to snatch what they could and stuff it into their hose, hoping no one was looking. As confusion mounted, Elizabeth I's treasurer Burghley heard how much had 'disappeared into the pockets, caps and other orifices of men whose custom was to enrich the taverns and bawdy houses, of south-west England for months to come'.[18] When order was at last restored, prizes worth £500,000 had been reduced to £140,000. For all the stress endured, Sanderson had himself been able to savour his own exciting discoveries. For deep within the secret recesses of the *Mãe*, he had chanced upon a Latin account of China printed at Macao in 1590, 'inclosed in a case of sweete cedar wood and lapped almost an hundredfold in fine Calicut cloth, as though it had beene some incomparable jewell'. (A must for Hakluyt and sure enough, it bobs to the surface in the second edition of his *Navigations*.)[19] As a result of all the excitement these treasures caused, men began to say, if the Spanish can sweep all this up, why not us too?

English cartographers began to fathom the mysteries of the sea by getting the measure of a famous Dutch and Delft school of navigation. One of those who had to thank the Dutch for making the seas if not the English safer was the Welshman Martin Llewellyn (d. 1634). Llewellyn was a cartographer whose work suggests that English research at desk and on deck was quite as good as anything undertaken by the Dutch when that nation was regarded as pre-eminent in this field. Llewellyn's *Atlas of the East* consists of sixteen portolan sea charts.[20] At 25 by 36 inches, these are about four times the size of the average Portuguese effort, and four times as useful.[21] Llewellyn had probably been 'super-cargo' on the first Dutch voyage to the East Indies (1595–7), commanded by Cornelis de Houtman (d. 1599). What Llewellyn achieved out there, however, could not have been done without an apprenticeship under the Dutch cartographers who already had their studios established in the Dutch settlements.

On Java in the summer of 1596 the Dutch had run into the Portuguese cartographer Pedro de Tayda, 'a famous Pilot who had frequented all the coasts and Islands of the East Indies and made Maps of them all, which he promis'd to shew the Dutch. This gave them great Hopes of discovering more of that Country, than he had discover'd before.'[22] No sooner had he given away his secrets than the authorities, taking a dim view of any academic willing to share his researches, promptly arranged for Tayda to be murdered. Though Llewellyn had had no contact with Tayda, what he had learned viva voce out in the Indies had been supplemented with important printed material then coming out of the United Provinces, 'the *Nieuwe caerte op Java geteeckent* compiled by G.M.A. [i.e. Willem] Lodewijcksz, engraved by Baptista à Doetechum and published at Amsterdam by Cornelis Claesz probably in 1598' being perhaps the most distinguished of these publications.[23] From such hybridisation Llewellyn had gone on to create 'The earliest known sea atlas expressly designed for navigation in the East by a chart-maker of any nationality'.[24] But there is a problem. Llewellyn's *Sea Atlas* remained hidden in the deepest recesses of an Oxford library until its redis-covery in 1975. No matter. It is likely that there would have been manuscript copies in the satchel of every captain employed by the Company Adventurers.[25]

But of other English chart-makers, the most notable was Gabriel Tatton who moved between London and Amsterdam as easily as a bookseller between Bodley's Library and St Paul's Churchyard, where the best of London's book trade was to be found. It seems Tatton was no less beholden to Dutch colleagues than Llewellyn had been. The charts that this *celebrum hydrogeographico* created had evolved from further collaboration with Dutch pilots working out of Bantam and Batavia. Tatton's work had been informed by what Hessel Gerritsz (d. 1632) was doing when that famous cartographer, snug and dry behind his desk in Amsterdam, was awash with notes supplied by the VOC.[26] Chart-making was important but dangerous work. Baffin of Baffin Island was better at making a map than sighting a gun because he was to be shot dead by a sniper when trying to calibrate weaponry during the Company's attack on Hormuz in 1622. Or take John Speed, scion of a dynasty famous for churning out maps that once adorned every boarding house in the land. After spying for England, Speed died too, though in the Red Sea not the Persian Gulf. But what of Tatton? His demise was neither useful nor heroic. Aboard the good ship *Elizabeth*, somewhere off Java, he 'being drunk, fell over board, and was drowned'.[27]

But if mapmakers were in debt to the 'Hollander', their masters would have died rather than acknowledge Dutch superiority in this vital field. Startling indeed was the dislike that the dominant classes felt for 'the great bog of *Europe* . . . and the buttok of the world, full of veins and blood, but no bones in't' as one critic of Holland described the country.[28] Distrust, dislike, a sense of inferiority: all this and more is suggested by looking at the prejudices of Sir George Downing (d. 1684). Taken on as special adviser on Dutch affairs and ambassador to The Hague, Downing was most remarkable for his intense dislike of the 'Hollander'. Asking himself why the Dutch did better than the English, he had discovered much the same problem that Philip II had encountered sixty years earlier: Spain first and England afterwards, both had failed to learn from a Dutch genius for good preparation and better logistics. No other people had such self-belief as did the Dutch; not surprising, therefore, that it would be they who invented the national anthem.[29]

Although the English laboured under a sense of inferiority when presented with so many apparent Dutch triumphs, in no sphere had the Hollander proved more adept than in that of espionage. The most effective exponent of such penumbral arts was Jan Huyghen van Linschoten (d. 1611) who, in accomplishing what may well have been the greatest theft in the history of commerce, helped to transform power relations across a hemisphere. Catholic at a time when the Low Countries was becoming Protestant, hiding devotion to new politics under old pieties, Linschoten migrated to Portugal where he became secretary to João Vicente da Fonseca, newly appointed cardinal-archbishop of Goa.

After Fonseca and Linschoten had travelled out to Goa in 1583, it has been suggested that the archbishop encouraged Linschoten to begin a compendium of rutters[30] which, taken with other information to be found in the Portuguese records, was being gathered for future transmission to Philip II himself.[31] Since it now appears that Linschoten's master had from the first encouraged him to search the maritime records, he cannot stand accused of spying *tout court*.[32] But Linschoten was always artfully manipulative in exploiting any opportunity to benefit his compatriots at the expense of those who paid his expenses.

Whatever the truth, Linschoten was quick to insinuate himself into the confidence of a master who was now disarmed by so plausible a *dévot*. Having won the esteem of the archbishop, Linschoten now set about acquiring such a trove of classified information as would prove vastly more valuable than any chest of diamonds stolen from the grandest carrack. Entrusted with the keys of both the archiepiscopal and the viceregal archives, such was the *embarrass de richesses* Linschoten was to find therein that his challenges became legion: how to transcribe, how to transmit it all? Despite such logistical difficulties, Linschoten triumphed. In running off with those reams it can be said that no theft of classified material of comparable significance would occur until Klaus Fuchs began sending the secrets of the Manhattan Project to the Russians in 1941.

But how had Linschoten been able to get away with so grand a larceny? Just as he was wondering what to do with his contraband, none other than Philip II himself had provided him with the exit strategy needed. Philip had summoned Fonseca back to Spain for audits spiritual and commercial, but then Fonseca himself leaving Linschoten behind as his major-domo of the archiepiscopal palace afforded his amanuensis just that latitude required to tidy up his papers, pack his bags and leave. Making his way to the Azores, Linschoten spent days in the sun pumping visiting sailors for such knowledge as they had about their own voyages, information duly squirrelled away for future use. In the Azores, too, Linschoten succeeded in replacing the income he had foregone when departing Goa by salvaging some of the ships that, once the property of the Estado, had been sent to the bottom by the English. Having thus reinvented himself several times, Linschoten now began to have the fondest thoughts of home, looking forward to fame and wealth as the fruits of guile and duplicity. Rich as a scrap merchant, Linschoten would become richer still as the pensionary of a grateful nation. He reached Enkhuizen upon 3 September 1592, and national congratulation thereafter.

Safely back in Holland, the thief became a bestselling author. After several years of rumination and comparative study, Linschoten was able to give the watery world his *Itinerario* (1595–6).[33] This was widely popular outside the United Provinces and nowhere more so than in the offices of the East India Company. At the mere opening of a folio, the Company accrued such local knowledge of the East Indies as must otherwise have taken a generation to amass by other means. A sense of just how important Linschoten's *Itinerario* was to the EIC's founders is suggested by the survival in the Company archives of a long memorandum by Fulke Greville (d. 1628), Treasurer of the Navy during the period when the EIC had been founded, to Robert Cecil (or 'Salisbury' as he is better known), chief minister to the Crown, who had always followed his father Lord Burghley in the assiduity with which he tended to the commercial prospects of England's trade. Written on 10 March 1600, the memorandum reflects the importance in which the leading English maritime enterprises held Linschoten's publications. Greville writes: 'respecting the places to which the English might trade in the East Indies. Names of such kings as are absolute in the East, and either have war or traffic with the King of Spain . . . Has made these collections out of Osorius, Eden's Decade, and specially out of the voyages of John Huighen.'[34] Indeed, the part of Linschoten's published researches that really absorbed the Court of Committees was his book entitled *Itinerario: Voyage ofte schipvaert van Jan Huygen van Linschotenn naer oost ofte Portugals Indien, 1579–1592*, which came to be rendered into English as *Iohn Huighen van Linschoten his Discours of Voyages into ye Easte & West Indies* (ed. J. Wolfe, 1598). The book appeared against a background of tension between the Dutch and the English, some of it quite possibly provoked in Amsterdam when Linschoten's co-authors got wind that an English translation was in the offing.

Perhaps the most important of those who had assisted Linschoten with what was a multi-authored volume was Petrus Plancius (d. 1622). Mathematician, radical Calvinist preacher, spymaster and teacher at the Amsterdam nautical academy, Plancius may have heard about the imminent English translation being edited by John Wolfe; a 'threat' affecting his own thinking about the need to protect Dutch commercial secrets in a world becoming increasingly defensive, where competition for trade routes was intensifying with every passing month. From the first, Portuguese carracks had had orders that rutters should be destroyed in the event of a ship being taken,[35] not unlike U-boat commanders in a quite other battle of the Atlantic whose first priority would be the destruction of radio code books when surfacing after a depth-charge attack. As the Portuguese had realised, by the 1590s the Dutch had become major players; the Estado da Índia needed to do all it could to guard its secrets. But then of course the Dutch found themselves in exactly the same predicament as had the Portuguese, though in the case of Amsterdam it was London it had to fear. And so it was that in the face of an imminent English translation of what were the most sensitive parts of Linschoten's *Itinerario*, Plancius commanded that all scientific data for the fleet of Jacob van Neck (d. 1638) was to be compiled in books and delivered to him alone upon the fleet's return. The crewmen responsible for gathering data were forbidden from keeping their own copies and had to sign an oath of secrecy.[36] But alas for the Dutch it was too late; the English sail had unfurled. Thus we read in General John Saris's *Journal* how, when pocking about among the islands of Japan, he thanked God for Jan Linschoten who was keeping him out of trouble: 'We steered alongst Southwest to bring the point of the shoale called Pulo Citi a starne; then wee sounded about two Glasses after, and had fifteene fathome. Note that wee found Ian Huijghen Van Linschotens booke very true, for thereby we directed our selues from our setting forth from Firando.'[37] Yet for all the help that Linschoten had vouchsafed the Adventurers, the damage done by his reaching into the *armario* was irreparable; though it must be added that by the time Linschoten gave the world all those secrets, Portugal was fast being overhauled as it was. Nevertheless, this most nerveless of Dutchmen had been able to sabotage an empire that, but for his studied disloyalty, like the Third Reich might have lasted a thousand years.[38]

Although Linschoten's *Itinerario* was primarily a grand theft from Portugal, and of the sixty-seven rutters contained within it, no less than sixty-three are of clear Portuguese origin, the text looked beyond the resources of Lusitania alone. Quotidian experience was also garnered from Linschoten's friends and contemporaries to make the book an all-round compendium, useful for every specialist aboard any ocean-going ship. For example, Nuno da Silva, pilot for Drake's circumnavigation of the world in 1579, and thus the man who made possible an 'English' performance across the theatre of the world, is the hero of chapter 54. In this we find a technically accurate account of the crossing of the world's most dangerous seas: the running of the Magellan Straits. Then there was Linschoten's old sailing mate who looms through the mist. This was Dirck Gerritsz Pomp (d. 1608), who donated so much of his first-hand experience as had made it possible for Linschoten to write knowingly about the sea route from Nagasaki to Canton and all the riches of China. So it was that among a hundred directions from a thousand thefts, Linschoten suggests how, for example, the Malay Archipelago was a vulnerable run. He therefore recommends his not-so-gentle readers that they would do well to consider gliding with all stealth from Sumatra via the Straits of Sunda, thereby avoiding Portuguese men of war awaiting those who, more greedy than guarded, were bent upon the shorter if more dangerous route to those far off but glittering riches.

Cornelis de Houtman, a compatriot of Linschoten and the one who had probably taken Llewellyn to Java as 'super cargo', had himself sailed to Portugal in 1592 on what turned out to be his own epic voyage of discovery organised from the Amsterdam-end by Petrus Plancius, that fiery collaborator of Linschoten's *Itinerario*. With Houtman and his brother, who had come along too, it had been a case of voyaging through the map houses of Lisbon rather than rummaging amongst the archives of Goa. This was because the Houtman brothers, brothers in crime, having failed to acquire any rutters, had fallen back instead upon acquiring above-the-counter maps from the Portuguese cartographer Bartolomeu de Lasso. Bent upon the same endeavours, and recognising themselves as two of a kind, Linschoten and Cornelis de Houtman joined forces to found the Compagnie van Verre (1594) or 'the long-distance company' which came to be absorbed into the VOC in 1602. Before then, however, the two men had sent their *Amsterdam, Hollandia, Mauritius* and *Duyfken* to the Far East in 1595.

Although that particular voyage was to prove a commercial disaster, it certainly afforded the Dutch a critical head start as it gave the English a big fright. As we know, by 1599 discussion had begun in London about setting up the EIC. As for Linschoten, of him it has been well said how he 'had shewn the way, and had opened up illimitable possibilities of future commerce; and this was enough to inflame the enthusiasm of his fellow countrymen'.[39] So with his *Itinerario*, this too had 'illimitable' success: translated into English, German and Latin out of Frankfurt, its diaspora concluded with an appearance in French (1610), though we must look in vain for a Portuguese or a Spanish translation. Linschoten changed everything. Adaptability, pragmatism, the rejection of convention, a strict separation of the sacred from the sail, breakthroughs in technology, better logistics and support systems, industrial espionage: all this and more accounts for why the new got the better of the old and why the Dutch became world leaders in voyages of oceanic magnitude.

Meanwhile, what of the English? While all this was going on in Amsterdam, in London such Adventurers as could muster themselves by 1600 had only managed to set out four second-hand boats bought at a knock-down price because no one else wanted them. And this they had done solely because the Establishment regarded it as an outrage that the Dutch were getting a head start in the business of transoceanic trade. Although the English moaned like wind in the rigging about their rivals, had they but reflected just a little, they must have been less astonished to see their erstwhile protégés transformed from sorting washed herring to selling washed silk when these Dutchmen had dominated the European carrying trade for as long as anyone could remember.

However, for all the élan with which the Dutch left for Bantam, once through the Straits of Sumatra it proved difficult for them to offload European goods. Challenging questions thus arose: how was the imbalance to be paid for? Would export of silver from Holland serve to damage the home economy? The problem was this. In the United Provinces there were more goods imported than exported. And so the Heeren XVII, or 'Seventeen Men', who governed the VOC responded by investing heavily in short routes across Asia. It was thought that brisker voyages would allow for the steady accumulation in Holland of silver out of Japan. By such means was compensation found for the increasing difficulties everyone in Europe was now experiencing with a shortage of silver from Peru, whence the precious metal had been imported into Europe since the mines of Potosí had been discovered by the Spanish in 1546. Japanese silver, coming on line during the first decade of the seventeenth century, represented a significant compensation for the massive haemorrhaging of Western specie, as easing the pressure on European mints, an existing shortage of coins in Europe came to be made up by turning Eastern metal into Western money. This way, too, came relief for the beleaguered merchant who could ignore, if he could never silence, those who saw the outflow of precious metal as no less of a crime than the practice of usury that Clement V had condemned in 1311. If the trick was to be seen bringing specie back, so the profit was to do business within the Far East. Soon enough, sooner than with England, Holland made herself a very rich country. This she achieved through efficient trading practices and ruthless exploration of colonies, both floated upon an efficient system of public finance underpinned by a well-managed national debt. From the first, this had involved massive public investment in Holland in return for secure and regular payments of interest.

The joys of the earth were transported by the Dutch, who had the most versatile fleet in Europe, its efficiency and accessibility greatly aided by the appearance of the *fluyt*. Invented at Hoorn in 1595, this combined ingenious pulleys that allowed for less manpower, whilst its building costs undercut competitors and shallow draught permitted inland riverine journeys. What helped the Dutch fleet enormously was plentiful and proximate supply of wood from the Baltic. This was in sharp contrast to the difficulties the English encountered. They were forced to import much of their timber from Russia and four-fifths of their canvas from Brittany. The English were superior to the Dutch in gunnery, however, and their ships tended to last longer.

For the majority of sailors, standards of hygiene were almost non-existent, a disregard that in part accounted for high mortality rates in both the EIC and VOC. The Dutch were frankly astonished by the fastidiousness with which the indigenous they encountered conducted their bodily functions, remarking at Guinea that 'They are curious to keep their bodies clean, and often wash and score them . . . they cannot abide that a man should Fart before them, esteeming it to be a great shame and contempt done unto them.'[40]

But soon, marked political as well as economic differences between the English and the Dutch became clear enough. There were closer links between politics and trade in Holland because of closer identity between governors and governed. In Amsterdam the direction of commerce was better attuned to the demands of new enterprises than was the case in London. In Holland start-up companies paid 3–4 per cent interest on loans, whereas the English government demanded 10 per cent. This was a prohibitively high rate that induced major problems for private borrowers. In London James I was much less concerned to protect the mercantile interest than to exploit it. By contrast, Prince Maurits, Stadtholder of the United Provinces, saw the state and the VOC as indissoluble. In the earliest days of the East India Company, James encouraged the notable privateer Sir Edward Michelborne to attack with powder the very traders the Company was peaceably targeting in the Indian Ocean.[41] This was in flagrant contravention of the monopoly that James himself had just granted the Company, terms of which had specifically excluded rivals such as Michelborne from the Company's sphere of interest. No matter: James got his rials and Michelborne his knighthood, one of many who were to be ennobled at a time when disregard for the laws of the sea seems never to have been an impediment to respectability on land. But then if 'Sir Edward' represented a present threat, the Crown committed its own acts of interloping. Short of cash, it would sweep upon the City to carry off a forced loan here or impose a fine there. Predictably enough, such interventions served only to create bad relations between the Crown and the City. By contrast, there was relative harmony between the executive and the commercial arm in the United Provinces.

Technology was more advanced in Dutch boatyards, where docks were so appointed as made it easier to put the right vessel in the right waters. No one understood this better than Jean-Baptiste Colbert (d. 1683), who before he was to finance Louis XIV's wars against William of Orange had inspected the shipyards of Amsterdam as an impecunious student touring Europe on a rial a day. In Holland Colbert had engaged in a little industrial espionage. Creeping about Dutch yards, he had made careful account of the wizardry of cranks and saws, wind-driven lifting-gear and ingenious sluices. Had he made a comparative study of the broader ways of Amsterdam and London, however, he would have noticed profound differences that distinguished the VOC from the EIC. English merchants kept their distance from government but the Dutch did not. In contrast to the EIC, which from the first would be admonished not to engage in acts of war with rivals, as an extension of the state the VOC was positively charged with extirpating Portugal and Spain in the Far East.

The situation could not have been more different in London. The English were deeply suspicious of Whitehall at a time when the East India Company viewed the aristocracy as unfit for the direction of its affairs, however valuable they might prove for investment purposes as Adventurers. In Holland, though, government and commerce became indistinguishable in a country where all classes were deeply engaged with the VOC, if only as small-time investors in a state within a state. While there were pockets of resistance to synergy in Holland, the contrast between London and Amsterdam was pronounced. Many from the City would come to side with Parliament when Civil War broke out because of the damage caused by the Crown's disastrous handling of City companies, initiatives marked by insensitivities unusual even by the standards of the Stuarts, policies that have been described as 'shot through by ambivalence and inconsistency'.[42]

It was rare for separate and conflicting interests not to be rapidly resolved within the United Provinces. In England, by contrast, the regime would sell a monopoly to one cartel only to sell the same to another business interest. This was something that the Crown was obliged to do if it was to remain afloat in the face of a recalcitrant Parliament, for whom the iniquity of taxes was an article of faith at a time when the executive was trying to rid itself of scrutiny by the House of Commons. In contrast to such break-ins upon the EIC by the English Crown, the Stadtholder had a very different perception as to the place of trade within a nation where interests overlapped more seamlessly. If Maurice of Nassau respected the aspirations of the VOC, Charles I would come to spurn those of the EIC.

Although major differences between the EIC and the VOC would always be apparent, their structures moved towards one another. With the renewal of the East India charter in 1609, the captains of the EIC were furnished with authority to pursue self-defence, jurisdiction and retribution, initiatives hitherto licensed by the Crown alone. This resulted in two approaches, the first conducted by the Crown in Europe, the second by the Company in Asia. Secretaries of State pursued a quite different tack towards the Dutch as *Europeans*, compared with how the EIC regarded them as *Asians*. Such a contrast meant that when crises arose with Holland, decisions were conflicted and action vitiated. In Holland the interests of the nation were also the interests of the VOC.

Two distinctions characterised the EIC: reluctance to use violence, and vigilance to avoid land commitments. With such a credo the Court of Committees was encouraged to view the aristocracy with suspicion at a juncture when so many titled men were drawn to the idea of colonisation. But if the Committees kept Whitehall at oar's length, things were different in Holland. Here there was an identity of interest between overseas expansion and a state in which a man may well have been a Heren XVII precisely because he had been a 'regent' of a province. But there was no such hybridisation among the worthies of the EIC. If there had been, Sir Thomas Smythe would have been a privy councillor, not merely an assiduous if largely mute attender of Parliament in his capacity as MP for a string of English ports.

In contrast to Holland, expansion in England happened with no appeal whatever to national glory. In England policy towards overseas commitments came to be shaped by the commercial well-being of the Company, not the status of the nation. Of all the overseas trading enterprises of Europe, the English version was distinct. It endeavoured to operate independently of existing political institutions. From the moment that Smythe chaired his first gathering of all the Adventurers, something that was called the General Court (as distinct from the Court of Committees, or the 'board' in modern parlance), Smythe took care to exclude non-City groupings, and he did his best to dampen any suggestion that the Company get involved in colonisation. The ambivalence of the Company towards the Establishment was demonstrated when Smythe refused membership to James I. Since no king could be an Adventurer, because he could never be on terms of equality with his subjects, it followed that if the king was to have been admitted, the Company must have become the property of the Crown.[43] The Court of Committees was determined to maintain its independence. In contrast, over the sea and not so far away, the Heren XVII refused to make their accounts public because their business had become affairs of the state, and so henceforth everything needed to be secret.

In Chapter 1 it was suggested how the contrast between what the Portuguese and the English chose to call their ships was redolent of important distinctions. So too with the respective flags or 'ancients' of the English and Dutch East India Companies, which displayed different values as well as colours. In London, the motto spoke of an Almighty who could be relied upon to issue a competitive dividend, provided the Adventurers made a good investment in piety: 'Deus Indicat Deo Ducente Nil Nocet' (With God leading, no harm arises).[44] Such a worthy if jejune sentiment could hardly be in starker contrast to the thoroughly aggressive intent proclaimed upon the flag of the VOC. With the Dutch, two furious lions hold a shield upon which a third, with slavering tongue and penis erect, holds a blade in one paw and fasces in the other. 'Red in tooth and claw', these fearsome beasts support an imperative to imperialism, admitting of neither argument nor dissent and the more awesome for its brevity: 'Je Maintiendrai' ('I will maintain'). That was precisely what the VOC was about to do. It would be a battle the EIC had neither the will nor the resources to win.

3

MERCHANTS OF LIGHT

It is not our conquest, but our commerce; it is not our swords but our sails that first spread the English name . . . over and about the world; it is the traffic of their merchants, and the boundless desires of that nation to eternize the English honor and name, that have induced them to sail, and seek into all the corners of the earth.

Lewes Roberts, *Treasure of Traffic*, 1641[1]

'Merchants of light' is a phrase taken from the writings of Sir Francis Bacon: not only the greatest philosopher of the age – for some indeed *the* greatest of English philosophers – but the foremost English apologist for the importance of international trade in international relations. The tag comes from Bacon's description of the enlightened merchants of Bensalem, capital of Bacon's mythical New Atlantis in his allegory of that name which was published in 1627. It is these 'men of business' who bring not only money but also enlightenment to the corruptions of an Old World.[2]

One who Bacon might have described as just such a 'merchant of light' was Lewes Roberts (d. 1641), with whose argument in favour of trade for the well-being of any 'commonwealthe' we begin. His career was typical of some who, having made good in the City, went on to make better writing about means of wealth creation. In a series of important books Roberts encapsulated as he epitomised many of the debates about the nature of money and its social impact, centring on the place of international companies upon a national stage. Alongside other writings on economics, for instance the miscellaneous contributions of de Malynes, Mun, Keridge and Roe, Roberts generated such a debate about how wealth creation impacted 'common-wealthes' as would not be rivalled in British thinking until the appearance of Adam Smith's *Wealth of Nations* in 1776. And so this chapter charts not only the steady progress of wealth creation by the East India Company but also the social challenges it confronted during its improbable painful birth.

For his part, Roberts was convinced that national greatness came out of commerce. But then he was no less taken with the social utility of the merchant class of which he himself was an adornment with his gracious civility, social ease and sensible thinking. Roberts's writings, epitome of progressive thought on the ways to further commerce and promote social cohesion, infer if they do not always proclaim the need for national conscious-ness and confidence as necessary preconditions for the 'rise' of a body such as the East India Company. That said, there were enormous challenges in early Stuart London, the mortar to the pestle of the EIC. And these problems, so Roberts believed, the Court of Committees needed to come to terms with if the launch of their business was to be a success. It is, then, to late Tudor London, that engine house of the East India Company, that we travel to see how the cogs and wheels began to rotate.

Lewes Roberts had been a Levant Company merchant. Founded in London in 1592 out of an amalgamation of the Turkey and the Venice companies, the 'Levant' was essential to the birth of the East India Company. Indeed, it is inconceivable that the EIC could have survived without absorbing so many directors of the Levant into its own executive board. If Roberts generated good sales for the Levant Company, his *Treasure of Traffic* sold hardly less well; the good sense of its contents might have merited a jacket endorsement from Bacon himself, such was the congruity of the two authors' sentiments as to the nature of wealth creation.

Treasure of Traffic represents Roberts's valedictory reflections upon a life which had been busy and various.[3] The son of a merchant of Beaumaris, Lewes had been destined for the university when crisis in the family business demanded he be thrust instead from the study of 'arts' to the study of 'marts'. But if change had been unexpected, disappointment was short-lived when the ledger proved more exciting than the lecture. No one can have had more fun failing to get to the university of his choice than Lewes Roberts: Newfoundland and Malaga, Algiers and Tunis were all savoured before he came to rejoice in a long interlude in Europe (1619–24), visiting Rome and Byzantium before settling to live in Delft, where he was admitted into the

Merchant Adventurers; though Vermeer had not yet been born, the place was already one of the glories of a Golden Age.

Having circled Europe, Roberts's life continued to have a certain geometry about it. In his later London days his career came to be marked along the diameter which stretches from St Martin's Ludgate Hill to St Olave's Hart Street, churches that still mark the extremities of the City of London. But if Lewes's travels contracted, his mind expanded. By now the Roberts and the Harvey families had long been intimate. Lewes himself had been apprenticed in 1612 to Thomas Harvey, the brother of William, who would go on to tell the world how blood got about in his *De Mortu Cordis* (1628). As for Roberts, he too was a serious thinker, albeit about circulation of currency and not the substance of life. His most important work was his *Merchants Mappe of Commerce* (1638). This has commendatory verses attached, which were composed by Izaak Walton, of *Compleat Angler* (1653) fame. Such accolades as Roberts's *Mappe* attracted were in part a favour from a friend, but assuredly it had been earned. If Walton recognised the distinction of that book, it rapidly found its place as one of the key English publications on trade prior to the age of the Enlightenment. In this work, as also in his other publications, Roberts has no doubt that the merchant's realm extended far beyond a mere counting house; as a recent analyst of the *Mappe* comments, 'through merchandising and learning the skills of the merchant overseas, individuals could "perform the greatest employments that are incident to the service of a state or kingdom" – "those that have had their education thus . . . have proved not only good commonwealth's men, but also excellent statesmen" '.[4]

Lewes Roberts's career began when the East India Adventurers started to assemble and their company to operate. As his opportunities expanded, so did those of the Company. This was in part because of the eloquence with which he would go on to argue for the critical importance of a healthy export market. Roberts had always seen this as essential for the generation of domestic wealth. It was a brave thing to do when the more conventional economic thinkers like Gerard de Malynes (d. 1641) were hostile to exports. In contrast to Roberts such Jeremiahs felt that the export of specie alongside goods fatally weakened the sinews of the nation. They believed that once money left the realm it sank beneath the waves. For Roberts, however, sending money abroad was merely a profitable casting of bread upon the waters.

This broad debate about what exports were, a discourse in which Roberts played so distinguished a part, was held within the wider social context of a powerful growth of nationalism that had long been gathering momentum but which had received a particular fillip after the transition from the Tudors to the Stuarts. What greatly enhanced a sense of self-worth and optimism with the arrival of James I in London in 1603 was how this new and foreign regime was able to promise a blessed continuity of succession that biology had denied the Tudors. And yet although the last years of Elizabeth had been embattled, the empowerment of England had marched on. 'Elizabethan globalism'[5] came to be promoted, of which the most notable aspect was the monarch's non-Christian alliances. Elizabeth had cultivated the interest of the Ottoman, something first achieved through the medium of the Venetian and Turkish merchants who as we have seen had amalgamated as the Levant Company in 1592. The prime movers in all this were Edward Osborne and Richard Staper in London with William Harborne as the Company's ambassador in Constantinople. Here it has been aptly remarked, 'William Harborne had achieved the exclusive favour and privileged access he sought for the English in Istanbul, forged out of a common enemy in the Holy Roman Empire and a closely related common abhorrence of idols and idolatry, an identification between Protestantism and Islam that both sides worked to sustain over the years'.[6] What had long gone on in the bazaar of Constantinople now proved something of a dress rehearsal for when the East India Company found itself having to deal with the Muslim powers of the Indonesian archipelago.

Momentum for looking East had owed much to the famous legend of Gloriana, as Elizabeth came to be referred to with the passing of the years. Gloriana was a myth which had it that this virgin queen had held out against wicked Catholics heaven-bent upon destroying the nation. But if the Armada of 1588 had been something of a crisis, and England's plight had certainly provoked some sympathy among her onlookers, neither cash nor arms had come out of Europe. As for Elizabeth herself, with the immediate challenge over, she had become rather more interested in Pashas than in Protestants. Time and money had been put into life beyond the Golden Horn. Accordingly, the Levant Company had been able to scoop such a cornucopia of wealth as would prove compulsive to some who, casting eyes as envious as they were avaricious upon the carpets of Persia and the rubies of India, would constitute the Praetorian Guard of that perilous cartel the East India Company.

In the decade before the EIC came into being, soldiers of commerce tracing the silver cords of the Tigris savoured the markets of Falujah as they sounded the defences of Ormuz. Covering vast distances, the entrepreneur of greed sensed in so many ways the Eastern promise of Western engagement. Within the crescents describing those arcs between the Hellespont and the Pyramids, the Indus and the 'Mountains of the Moon', the Levant Company bequeathed the experience as it ignited the ambition of those who, having savoured new markets as old as the pharaohs, were now willing to go to the ends of the earth in pursuit of wealth no Englishman had experienced before.

It is all too easy to back-end the great Tudor century of enterprise when in fact long before Elizabeth had succeeded in 1558 England had seen expansion in productivity and output of variety, small-scale production, skilled workers arriving from persecutions in Europe, new industries, new ways of making things and more. No less critical had been mindset – a revolution in attitudes to 'otherness' that had allowed an insular nation to become abundant in trade and exuberant in confidence. England's population had been rising, prosperity had become more widespread and innovation was being encouraged at every turn, not least by the masterful Lord Burghley (d. 1598), Lord Treasurer of England.

Burghley's papers demonstrate a vastly expanded concern with promoting public greatness through national wealth. His memoranda positively burst out of their bindings with suggestions for introducing foreign trades: inventions for increasing yield; anti-fraud devices; countless interesting if not mad ideas.[7] But Burghley was no passive listener. He took pains to access advice when, for example, a foreign business might be thinking of relocating from Rouen to Rochester or Haarlem to Harwich. During the thirty years when Burghley dominated Elizabethan life, he sent out trusted agents such as Alexander King and William Herle. They travelled the length and breadth of England to enquire as to the state of a thousand businesses: woad growing; the salt industry; and the frayed state of the rope makers whose business was essential to the maintenance of an English fleet. But then Messrs King and Herle were not simply bent upon a little industrial espionage; they acted as

consultants. They provided critical links between free enterprise and government, just two out of an army sent out to truffle for talent by a master who
was thirsty for opinion and tireless with statistics. On one occasion Burghley
is to be found consulting the experts about whether a fall-off in imports
would damage royal finances by reducing taxes. He received the reply that
the growth in bays, says, frisadoes, owlterfines and other textiles 'much
hindered Her Majesty's customs inwards', though there was also gain, as 'it
is not only beneficial to Her Majesty in customs outwards, but also profitable to our Commonwealth, for it cannot be that such number of these
commodities can be wrought in this realm by strangers only, but that they
must set many of the poor people of this realm on work'.[8]

Bold patronage and cautious husbandry, twin supporters to his badge of
office, helped Burghley encourage Tudor savings to grow into Jacobean dividends. But then not all the credit can be assigned to this giant among
Elizabethan statesman. Lord Leicester (d. 1588), the queen's favourite, and
Sir Francis Walsingham (d. 1590), head of what was a Tudor stab at an MI5,
both anticipated Lewes Roberts in understanding how the wealth of the
nation lay not in her conquests but her commerce. A felicitous combination
of congruence and momentum within the counsels of the Privy Council
would mean that as from 1600 the East India Company Adventurers found
themselves enjoying the calm waters and prosperous voyage of early Jacobean
prosperity. Such indeed were the indecent profits to be made from the very
earliest voyages of the Company that the merchants running it shuddered to
remember their childhoods and the parsimony of the nation during the
bleak mid-winter mid-century interlude of darkness which was the reign of
Edward VI (1547–53). That had been a period of acute economic crisis, but
what now? Those who had had the good sense to pile into the East India
Company, as they had poured into the founders' meeting, would be gratified
soon enough to find themselves happy recipients of disbursements consequent upon 400 per cent gross profits.

What had long made things different in England from the continent was
how ministers mixed with merchants, in a well-oiled system of viscosity that
served to discourage friction. When the commercial elite merged new money
with old blood, meetings about property deals or the coupling of children
took place. Such melding would have been unthinkable in France or even

Italy, where the elites of Lyon and Lucca had by now stepped out of the trade fair and into the palazzo. An absence of snobbery about the grime of commerce characterised key Elizabethans such as Sir Francis Walsingham, who kept easy company with moneylenders as well as spies. From the City, Walsingham received such douceurs as made him a fast if expectant friend of the livery companies.

But all this is to look at the top end of things. Far beyond the City of London, England, had developed into 'a consumer society that embraced not only the nobility and the gentry and the substantial English yeomen, but humble peasants, labourers, and servants as well'.[9] Such inclusiveness had come about following the 'conspicuous redistribution of wealth' that had resulted from a flooding of the land market after the Dissolution of the Monasteries (1538). That was when covetousness had become 'consumer choice'. By the reign of Elizabeth life had become more pleasurable with every passing year.

For example, one fine morning in 1599 Henry Buttes, Master of Corpus Christi College, Cambridge, could have been spotted stalking down what is now King's Parade with a manuscript under his gown. He was heading off to his printer; not with a learned exegesis on Ezekiel's 'Valley of Bones', but his own instructions as to how to make gravy out of a quite different sort of bone: the *Dyets Dry Dinner*. If the recipes in the book were reliable, the title was certainly not. One look inside and we find our Master Chef salivating over his prune of Damascus. This, he professes, is a positively divine *bonne bouche*. As for Egyptian and Judean dates, assuredly these were better than Italian; though alas never ripe as, regrettably enough, was also the case with the Spanish varieties. These tended to be sour.

But the good life that Buttes extolled, his neighbour deplored. As a Fellow of Queens' College, Cambridge, Sir Thomas Smith had lived not 500 yards from where Buttes had his rooms. Smith was a distinguished grammarian, public servant and ambassador by turns who whispered into an assortment of royal ears in his capacity first as adviser to Edward VI and then to Elizabeth.[10] But holding the Regius Chair of Public Law, Smith perched in an eerie from which he would swoop down to pick over what he saw as the rotten carcass of public morals. Smith's *De Republica Anglorum: the Maner of Gouernement or Policie of the Realme of England* (composed in 1562–5, circulated in manuscript thereafter, and published in 1583) was an influential text in which the author gives vent to outrage when, upon walking up Cornhill under the shadow of Old St Paul's, he had made the mistake of glancing into a shop window: 'I have seen within these twenty years, when there were not of these haberdashers that sell French or Milan caps, glasses, daggers, swords, girdles, and such things not a dozen in all London. And now, from the Tower to Westminster along, every street is full of them.'[11]

This relish for luxuries that Buttes enjoyed and Smith deplored had to be serviced. Nothing Buttes enjoyed needed an East Indiaman to bring it to a Cambridge high table. Yet who could have predicted what other delights people might now be induced to enjoy from just those markets that the East India Company was about to sample? New sensations from afar would arrive soon enough, if only the carrying trade could be properly organised. A widespread delight in luxuries is to be found in what is a positive soufflé of culinary literature that rose in Tudor England, with books suggesting a new value put upon the perishable.

The sort of frenzy for food promoted by, among others, the well-connected Countess of Kent was fed by a range of specialised kitchen shops fitted out with as many instruments as could be discovered in a surgeon's chest. Lady Kent's *The Daily Exercise for Ladies and Gentlemen* (1621) recommends fritters to garnish meats and salads, though if Goody Housewife wants to do them well, she simply must get hold of those special moulds exclusively supplied by Thomas Dewe of St Dunstan's churchyard. Purses were bulging as a broad spectrum of society spent on luxuries.

Joy at this world and confidence in the next would never be more exuberantly expressed than by that incomparable topographer of London John Stow (d. 1605). Compiler of the *Survey of London* (1598), Stowe is remembered today in St Andrew's Undershaft, where behind his desk and so visible from waist up only, the assiduous recorder composes his paean to what even then was one of the great cities of Europe. The author could personally recall the reign of Henry VIII, telling his famous story against naughty Thomas Cromwell (d. 1540) whom Stowe roundly condemns as one of the worst of Tudor developers. Sixty years after Cromwell had died, what that autocrat had done was still being resented by Stow's family. Cromwell had shoved John's father out of his own garden by thrusting a building on rollers through their dividing fence: 'ere my father heard thereof. No warning was given him, nor other answere, when hee spoke to the surveyors of that worke, but that their mayster, Sir Thomas, commanded them so to doe; no man durst go to argue the matter . . .'[12]

Stow was the Pevsner of the saddle bag, if hardly the glove compartment. He was wildly successful, giving Londoners what they wanted when tourists were turning the wheel of the *Golden Hind* as its famous captain Drake had once turned the world. After paying the vessel a state visit, Elizabeth I had made it the prime original of English Heritage, ordaining that it should be maintained in perpetuity and open to the public. And so it was designated a national monument.[13]

But for all the hundred parishes that Stow describes, he is never parochial. In the 1633 edition of the *Survey* there is just the one architectural illustration. It is a tomb not of an alderman, as might have been expected, but rather of a Persian.[14] Dying in 1626, this particular follower of the Prophet is honoured not once but twice. The first tribute is a twiggy woodcut illustrating this man's monument that had once been found in St Botolph-without-Bishopsgate. Here the curious reader can discern an epitaph in Arabic which is banded about a box of alabaster.[15] But then on he comes again in an oration describing the ceremonies performed at the graveside. Once there had been mutterings at the number of foreigners taking jobs, but what had been Tudor tirade had now become Stuart tolerance.

For all that, Stow is contradictory in important ways which have a bearing on the East India Company and the indivisible, intimate relationship it had with Londoners who provided the vast majority of its employees. The *Survey* may be full of London pride but there are also passages here, as there were passages in the capital indeed, where life was not only 'nasty, brutish and short' but dark and diseased. There is mention of places with names such as Gropecunt Alley and Cock Hill, presumably where only the foolhardy would enter. A sense of how parts of the early modern City were rabid and rank is suggested by glancing down Katherine Wheel Alley off Thames Street. Once there had been nine salubrious tenements here, but by 1584 these had fallen on evil days as those nine had come to be divided into forty-three. Such subdivision had made for enormous local anger, causing parishioners to complain that what had been a decent enough place to live in had now become:

so streighted, as that two persons canne hardly passe those by the other whereby the Aire is greatelie pestered, which maye breede daunger in the tyme of Infeccion. The poore tenementes beinge highlie rented, receave many Inmates and other base and poore people of badd condicions to the great trouble and annoiuance of the honest neighbours that inhabit there and the whole warde who have made very earnest and importune suite for reformacion of the said ally by plucking down such unnecessary buildinges.[16]

All this might suggest that London's birth rate was rocketing when in fact it was in decline. What caused such dangerous overcrowding was therefore the influx of 'strangers' (those who came from overseas) and 'foreigners', Englishmen who had drifted into the capital. Inflation frightened Justices of the Peace and the parish beadles who were ordered to control an underclass of the angry, whose difficulties might condemn many to sleep in a room with twenty others. Problems were not just about somewhere to rest, however. Some of those who wanted to work could not. Although it is suggested that 'thousands of merchants were admitted to companies without incident between 1550–1650', such a comment must refer only to the relatively stable relationships between the twelve great livery companies and their nascent workforce.[17] Beyond the deference displayed towards the master and his wardens in the Great Hall of the Drapers' Company, life could be very different for those much less fortunate and yet who aspired to the acquisition of life skills. For example, 'Following a riot which began on June 29 1595 by apprentices marching on Tower Hill, five were hung drawn and quartered as an example to encourage the others to stop misbehaving,'[18] whilst the next year the same suffered the privation of being ordered to be kept locked up in their masters' houses during the hottest summer months with plague in full swing, that is to say between the beginning of August and Michaelmas (29 September).[19] The statistics suggest that more than half of London's apprentices failed to complete their training,[20] whilst so vulnerable was the class to abuse that there were numerous cases of apprentices 'being corrected with horrifying severity'.[21]

London was facing huge social problems that were subject to a chaos of improvisation because of the manifest inadequacies of an ad hoc Poor Law.

Although the livery companies had a commendable record of charitable works that was as moving as it was remarkable, private enterprise was no substitute for state provision, of which there was woefully little. Furthermore, the causes of vagrancy and unemployment was a subject which provoked the deepest divisions. It seems that few, if any, grasped how it was possible to look for work but not find it. In any event, if the mayor was usually beneficent, too often his minister was baleful in condemning the regiment of the unfortunates. One cleric, distinctly over-excited by the poor, looked upon vagrancy as a sin: 'the very filth and vermin of the common wealth . . . the very Sodomites of the land, children of Belial, without God, without minister: dissolute, disobedient, and reprobate to every good work'.[22]

A comparison of the sources of poor relief in London during the respective periods 1570–3 and 1594–7 demonstrates that legacies and benevolences to the three great London hospitals of Christ's, St Thomas's and Bart's rose from £372 to £858 per annum, a jump of 57 per cent. However, if price index and population increase be applied to these figures, real-terms relief actually shows a drop from 0.0818 to 0.0742 per capita expressed in terms of £ p.a.[23] The black holes into which so many fell may therefore have induced the idle apprentice to consider whether there was anything to choose between prison on a charge of seditious assembly or three years spent between the wooden walls of a ship; that is to say, the time it would take a Company ship such as the *Peppercorn* to sail to Japan and back. Endemic violence, widespread rack-renting and disabling accidents being constants, was it not therefore preferable to risk the rigging than beg upon the stumps at London Bridge; better to be hanged from the yardarm of an East Indiaman than live upon the doubtful dependence of uncertain charity?

But what had the sufferings of an indigent cooper in Hanging Sword Alley have to do with an East Indian sailor like Owen Bodman? Both were brutalised, one on land and the other at sea. Getting drunk and setting fire to the VOC's *Black Lion* out in Bantam, Bodman came to be viewed by his fellow delinquents hanging from a spar and as straight as any sword. For their part, Bodman's accomplices waited to be given ten stripes on the back at every ship in the fleet. The truth was that for the Bodmans of that nasty world, the abject squalor of urban destitution made the furious life of a sailor more attractive than festering amidst the stews of London; though all who signed up for a Voyage knew that of any twelve sitting down at a mess table aboard the *Peppercorn*, four would be pitched into the sea in the course of the journey.

Although employment aboard *Peppercorn* was hell on sea, the Company could always rely on recruiting full crews. Every voyage came to roll upon a sea of cheap labour as it ground upon a shoal of extreme violence, brought with the men from London alongside the single chest they were permitted by the Company to stow aboard. Such indeed was the savagery displayed before the mast by those who had groped their way out of the caverns and taverns of Limehouse and Blackwall that keeping discipline at sea was as much of a challenge as keeping cargo dry. The parish beadles of London could have provided valuable advice as to how they sustained a community of souls; no wonder we find such relentless insistence by governor and captain alike upon the supposed 'discipline' of daily prayers and morning psalms. Although standards of living were indeed rising spectacularly for some living in London, life was mixed for most, any number of success stories being challenged by those who in failing to find employment hoped to be able to fall 'down from Graves-end into *Tilbury* Hope and set sayl for *East-India*'.[24]

Broader economic trends, though, were moving in the direction of an upward curve. There was a growing market among London's rich and the country's prosperous for the sort of goods that the East India Company would import. If Elizabeth I had ever been inclined to award a Tudor rose for enterprise, Burghley's hometown of Stamford, Lincolnshire, must have been on any shortlist. Once a market for hay, the place had reinvented itself after the revolt of the Netherlands in 1566. The burghers of Stamford, having seen the immigrants, had spotted their chance. Forthwith, they had issued their fulsome welcome to weavers of bays, says, stammet, fustians, carpets, fringes, linsey-wolseys, tapestry, silks, velvet and linen, to hatters, rope makers, cofferers, craftsmen in metal who were able to make knives and locks, besides workers with steel and copper. But soon enough the town had come to be outbid by faraway Maidstone, which was nicely placed for direct access to the Dutch ports being on the River Medway. This Kentish town now succeeded in upping the stakes. Here the worthies had invited in purveyors of bays, says, mocka-does, grograyn chamletts, russells, stammer, frisadoes, Flanders woollen cloth, patterned linen diapers, damask, plain linen, sackcloth, ticks for feather beds, arras and tapestry, Spanish leather, Flanders pots, paving tiles, bricks, brasiers, makers of white and brown paper, corselets, headpieces and all kinds of guns and armour: enough, surely, to have set up fifty workshops for all those rowdy Dutch boys clattering into town. But Stamford and Maidstone were acting under coercion and not in concert. Behind such demands was the directing hand of Burghley, as ever encouraging enterprise.

England accumulated as it accommodated: new peoples, new skills, new materials, new laws. These were wholesale changes discernible from Whitehaven to Penzance and from Dover to Newcastle. Foreigners brought into the country their different ways, different skills, lifestyle, foods and religious confessions, opening minds to the attraction of change, opening mines for the extraction of material. Each and every process demanded risk and relocation. But more generous definitions as to who was 'English' made for the most productive of paradoxes. As scattering of trade and sowing of difference arose, a sense of what it meant to 'belong' began to coalesce. Such spread of enterprise, specialisation of markets, appeal and accessibility of luxury goods helps us to understand why the Company appeared when there was such a rush of enterprise and rash of expansion: lace-making in Manchester; band-string making in Blandford; knives in Sheffield; sail-making in Ipswich; fustians in Lancashire; liquorice in Worksop; hops at Farnham; saffron at Saffron Walden; tobacco in Winchcombe; stuffs, silks, satins and velvets at Norwich, Canterbury, Colchester, Spitalfields and the London suburbs; thread-making at Maidstone; madder at Swindon; serges at Exeter; tulips once from Amsterdam but now in Mildenhall. Not all were new industries, however, as Saffron Walden implies (charter granted *c.* 1300), but most had been revitalised with construction or re-equipment for a homespun economy. Hunger to establish what was new, a desire to expand what was established, could not have created increased demand but for a broad customer base. The silks and satins, ruffs and riches that had always been worn by the aristocracy were now desired by the Lewes Roberts and their wives in what was rapidly becoming a well-stuffed world.

Although detailed statistics have not surfaced as to the breadth of the base of the pyramid, the East India Company could not have survived the lean years following the onset of economic depression in 1618 had there not been a greatly expanded consumer market by 1600. Although there can be no doubt that the creation of the Company was overwhelmingly a 'London' achievement, all of the great cities of England were becoming larger, richer and more populous. Middling houses were now more social and less defensive as new ways of promoting social intercourse were adopted which reshaped floor plans to allow for conspicuous consumption and dazzling display. As for the walls of both country and town houses, every major city had painters catering to the demand of what were now passingly sophisticated provincials. So too in London, for the benefit of those up from the country with the onset of the 'season', there were as many books on etiquette as comedies of manners to be truffled out of the bookshops of Old St Paul's Churchyard.

But what of the seemingly dimmest recesses of rural England? Take Kirkby Lonsdale, the modest centre of Westmorland, one of the most economically backward counties of England. Yet when taking a stroll before turning in, the commercial traveller wandering up the High Street was as astonished at what he could see as he was startled by what he could find in the window of Backhouse and Sons. Here was a draper with only two grandees within 30 miles, yet with a range of trumperies fit for such a bonfire of the vanities as must have gratified the godliest of ministers. James Backhouse, the proud prosperous proprietor, would open his boxes to regale 'Madam' with London, Spanish and Scottish silk; white, green, black and Coventry thread; Norwich and Scottish lace; girdles and fringes; daringly, too, a seductive range of enticing garters, Oxford gloves and much else from under the counter. The 'Mrs Smiths' of that world indulged themselves because wages in England doubled between 1580 and 1620, from 4d a day to 8d, and not just in Kirkby Lonsdale. Life was thawing. Those with spare cash now had their chance. Living further south, for example in Winchcombe in Gloucestershire, it was possible to copy your neighbour by growing tobacco. If that did not appeal, then just a short walk into town and any surplus might be lent to the general store at rising interest rates. Although the proportion of value assigned to luxuries from the Far East was tiny at this stage, there was a growing appetite for the higher life.

Alongside tobacco growers, grander figures worked hard in the challenging business of indulging themselves. Of these, Sir Henry Sidney (d. 1586) of Penshurst was an interesting case. Despite best efforts, a great career eluded him. Sir Henry would never be able to penetrate the inner sanctum of government; he was forced instead to settle for the consolations, if such they could have been called, of the Presidency of the Marches of Wales and the Lord Deputyship of Ireland. As for this last, it always yielded but one of two results, or if the benighted incumbent happened to be particularly unlucky then both: disgrace to person and the beggary of his rolling acres.

Lingering in Ludlow but longing for London, Sidney would make sure to visit his tailor when in town. There, this grandee readied himself to impress the provincials. Sir Henry would buy bone lace of gold and silver costing 6s 8d, or, if feeling really good about himself, 7s the yard. He would invest in the latest fashion – hoping to be noticed at court. But buying for position was complicated: it required much careful thought about going in for the finest gradations of quality, marked off with a farthing here or a penny there. Sidney dispatched his steward to Lancashire from Ludlow on two separate occasions; riding north to buy linen at either 7½d, 8d or the finest at 8½d for half a yard. But what was wrong with Welsh linen? Why make a round trip of 284 miles for a pair of sheets? But Sidney was no more fastidious than those much less grand. When the Hatchers of Careby wanted a new bull, they only had to tell their steward to go the 7 miles into Stamford. But no, the beast had to be led by the nose all the way from Derbyshire. As for Hatcher horses, these needed to be sourced in Northamptonshire. What was important was the demand the Sidneys and the Hatchers of Tudor England created for goods, networks, markets and differential means of supply. Now all this indulgence, in good time, would encourage the East India Company to come knocking upon the doors of Europe's dealers and England's milliners.[25]

To consider the late Tudor economy is to open a hive upon a thousand cells, workers moving among the humming octagons of workshop, lathe, garden shed, garret, loom, oven, furnace and forge. As for the customers, every one of these small outlets was sought out by prospective buyer or passing pedlar; buyers knew what they wanted, where to get it, when, how and where to sell it. It is no wonder then that the East India Company was going to make massive profits from importing 150 different grades of Indian textiles; no wonder that African chocolate, Arabian coffee and China tea would socialise English literature through the institution of the coffee house. Long before all that, however, new produce for the kitchen was complemented by new products from the still room, now an outlier of the manor house where rose water was distilled with a dozen other perfumes – some derived from the new plants from the East that were brought together in a popular compendium, John Hester's *True and Perfect Order to Distill Oyles out of all Manner of Spices, Seeds, Rootes and Gummes* (1575).

If the English were ready for luxury, this was never at the expense of social exclusion. It has been suggested that one reason many of the great merchant princes of the City were so disposed to give to the poor was because those who came to be buried in ermine had been born in sackcloth; many of these men were the first-generation success story of their family.[26] Still less would the winnings of the East India Company be scooped by the aristocracy and gentry alone. Adventurers consisted of all sorts of men, and a few women too. Although a high proportion of the Establishment was to invest in the Company, grandees never gained that leverage some desired. The first governor of the Company, Sir Thomas Smythe, made it clear that earls need not apply for vacancies on the executive. For the titled, colonisation rather than commerce was always the first priority, whilst for those who had an intelligent interest in trade there was no entitlement to meddle. In drumming up support for colonisation, 'imperialism by public subscription' as it has been nicely described, the aristocracy was motivated by 'elementary patriotism mixed with the more complex desire to strike the right figure in the great world'.[27] Whilst many with a handle played indispensable roles in raising capital for the settlements of Virginia and the Somers Islands, only the earls of Cumberland and Southampton would have more than walk-on parts in the drama of the East India Company.

Although the momentum of growth and the expression of extravagance would be checked periodically, as during the big dip in the economy from 1618 to 1622, some twenty years afterwards one observer could remark on how 'the lowest member, the feet of the body politic are the day labourers who by their large wages given them, and the cheapness of all necessaries, enjoy better dwellings, diet and apparel in England, than husbandmen do in many other countries'.[28] Or take the contemptuous words of the Grand Jury of Worcestershire, this august body thought it was becoming difficult to distinguish between master and servants, 'except the servant wears better clothes'.[29] As patterns of investment suggest, putting money into the Company was not just about pennies but whether pockets were going to remain wool or become silk. It was not just about business but the business of status. Here was a nation recently divided by hostile confessions but now united through the adroitness with which Elizabeth I had refused to prosecute those whose faith she may not have understood but of whose loyalty she was certain. In what is taken to have been a letter drafted by a young Sir Francis Bacon, she is famously supposed to have declared, 'I would not open windows into men's souls'.[30] In thus backing off where her sister had borne on, Elizabeth had poured a balm of toleration upon the inflammation of bigotry. Yet if this most consummate of erastians had kept the window closed as to the precise nature of the deity, another was thrust open to the chance of commerce. Like her greatest minister Lord Burghley, Elizabeth I saw how in encouraging international relations she could make England a figure in the world, through the channel offered to selfhood by the rise of these first overseas companies.

This was a process which, beginning with the foundation of the Muscovy in 1555, and promoted by the establishment of the Levant in 1592, came to be realised with the creation of the East India Company in 1600. The rise of the Muscovy had been something of a fairy tale on ice. Navigating the White Sea and sledging the tundra, London merchants had long made English goods attractive to Muscovites. Indeed, so successful had the Muscovy Company become by the 1580s – that moment when these forerunners of the East India Company now began to think of a passage to India – that what had long been a print in northern snows was followed by those desirous of extending trade with Russia far to the south-east. However, in failing to take the subcontinent from the Caucasus, the successors to these Muscovy men turned to the sea-route to India via the Cape.

Sir Thomas Smythe had burnished his credentials for appointment to the governorship of the East India Company by virtue of his tenure as ruler of the Muscovy. Such had been his success, so gratifying the kudos he had garnered from his time in 'Mosco', that when he came to make his will, and recalled how he had prosecuted a great trade through castles of ice, he would remember 'the manifolde mouthes of [the] Volga' before the generous waters of the Indus.[31]

Failure to penetrate India from Afghanistan, fatigue in pursuing a path to 'Cathay' over the North Pole, such dual frustrations must have frozen endeavour but for the early success of the Levant Company. Cotton wool from Smyrna, currants from Candia, carpets from Anatolia, tumbling in all their prodigal abundance upon the quayside of Blackwall, kindled a determination to shift the compass from the Cape of Desolation to the Cape of Good Hope – from 'Greenland's icy mountains' to 'India's coral strand'.[32] Without the remarkable achievements of the 'Mystery and Company of Merchant Adventurers for the Discovery of Regions, Dominions, Islands, and Places unknown', as the Muscovy Company first described itself, without the Levant freighting its rum and spices, cottons and woollens, currants and kerseys, indigo, galt, camlet, tin, pewter, maroquin and soda ash, tulips and pottery, the Adventurers of the East India Company could not have become a force with which to be reckoned at the Royal Exchange.

With the rise of the East India Company, much has been made of the centrality of textiles. Yet paper was as important as fabric to the emergence of the Company: writers as well as shipwrights floated English fleets on Asian seas. Critical to the identity of the Company was the strenuous debate that took place between the covers of books. Some of these economists who wrote about the effect of the Company on national wealth were in the pay of the EIC, and so wrote in defence of their employer. Here the argument was all about the business of trading when some among the less intelligent Adventurers thought that the means favoured to prosecute just that actually represented a threat to the nation. The issues centred on a controversy provoked by the conservative thinking of Gerard de Malynes and the progressive theories of Thomas Mun.[33] This last, in his *A Discourse of Trade, from England unto the East-Indies answering to diuerse objections which are vsually made against the same, by T.M.* (1621), seems to have anticipated Lewes Roberts in defending the Company with a demand that it be allowed to take out progressive amounts of currency to open up trade on as many fronts as possible.

As these strenuous arguments suggested, the need to supply the Company's factories with liquidity proved a major public relations challenge. A balance of payments deficit was the steady state in the early years of the Company when it was as hard to find things to appeal to Indian buyers as it was to sell to them in bulk. Lead and tin, fewer textiles, a little quicksilver, coral and 'elephants' teeth' (tusks), a smattering of trinkets – this was the best that could be done.

Since more silver was exported than could be generated by sales out East, so to the hostility of the Portuguese and the competition of the Dutch came to be added the sniping of an enemy within.

Those of a conservative way of thinking deplored a system of exchange whereby England's coin was cashed.[34] Observing precious Spanish rials – the only truly international currency of the day – disappearing into the strong-room of the Company's ships, pessimists began to think that the process would render anaemic what had once been a puissant nation. In the face of such mounting criticism, the Court of Committees came to feel it had to push back on all this negative talk and damaging publicity.

Mustering support, mastering argument, sometime merchant and present-day mercantilist Thomas Mun was the Company's man for the moment. There were some richer than Mun but none so well endowed as regarded an under-standing of how cash flows. A key figure on the Court of Committees, Mun believed that money must travel if trade is to return. He was quite certain that the Company needed to export as much coin as the markets demanded, since with its dispersal would arise the requisite inflow of wealth. Profit was to be generated not with English exports to India, however, but rather with sales of imports, either to the home market or re-exports of what had been Asian sent into Europe and still further afield. Beyond this, though, Mun lobbied hard for a creative commercial partnership with the Levant Company. Thereby, Far Eastern goods could be pushed through the Pillars of Hercules and into Arabia Felix. What was bought in Benares had to be repacked in Bermondsey before being sold in Baghdad, if the Company was to generate the sort of returns demanded by its Adventurers.

The prominent economist Gerard de Malynes, who was the sparring partner of Thomas Mun, was the implacable opponent of allowing money not only to find its level but also its location, a state of affairs that for his part Mun felt wholly unthreatening.[35] The trouble with Malynes was how he remained wedded to what was not merely an old but a medieval school of economic theory. Malynes held fast to two maxims: there had to be an unchanging supply of specie and in order for such to be confined within the fortress which should be England, it could never be allowed out of the country. Instead, merchants needed to rely either on credit facilities or bills of exchange. But here was the dilemma. If Englishmen wanted Indian textiles but Indians did not want English goods, what was required was coin. How then could this imbalance be resolved? By creating free markets. Indigo from Rajasthan would be paid for by carrying goods for others and souls for the *hajjd*.

It was for this reason that the so-called coastal trade – whether from port to port in Asia or in Europe – was so critical to the growth of the East India Company. On the face of it, profit from bringing goods from Asia to Europe could be astronomical for the Adventurers. However, because of the time it took for the Court of Committees to pay out Adventurers' dividends, gross percentage profit needed to be divided by the number of years that had elapsed between investment and dividend. Accordingly, the Company always required the greatest possible geographical spread of activity. This was achieved by becoming a carrier for other regimes. Thus it was that the transport of Muslims to Mecca became an important subsidy for the regular transport of goods, either around the Cape of Good Hope and so home, or by harbour-hopping when engaged on this so-called coastal trading – a process which often entailed something little more enterprising than moving from one Eastern entrepôt to the next and often within sight of land. But in truth, matters were not as dire as Malynes liked to suggest. Silver was exported but it was imported too, albeit with a Japanese not a Peruvian provenance. After the Company had opened its factory on Hirado in 1613, so the London Mint regularly received an influx of Japanese silver. With this it was able to replenish its dwindling supplies of Spanish metal. If that migration eased an acute shortage of coin, it also saved the Company. Without such circulation, there would have been no servicing of interest payments; nor, for that matter, dividends for the Adventurers.

From the moment the Company got to India in 1608, it started to borrow heavily on the Indian money market. In other words, the cash needed was raised in India for Indian markets, as it was also serviced by profits generated in the subcontinent. These loans were necessary because of the insurmountable delay in getting rials to India in an age of sail. Had it not been for Japanese silver coming on stream, James I would have been quite unable to resist public opinion stridently clamouring for an end to the East India Company, that wicked and unpatriotic institution as so many took it to be. Those who looked so darkly upon the affairs of the Company argued that such was the threat that the Company posed to the integrity of the nation that the entire East India fleet should be confiscated at once. Yet for all that, Mun remained the ever-confident apologist: 'For let no man doubt, but that money doth attend Merchandize, for money is the prize of wares, and wares are the proper vse of money; so that their Coherence is vnseparable.'[36]

This was in marked contrast to the argument of Thomas Keridge who as 'President' of Surat lorded it over the Company's principal trading entrepôt in India. If anything, Keridge was even more liberal than Mun because he was always arguing for multilateral exchanges right across the globe. As for Mun, he believed how in times of conflict the diminution of trade generates wealth by other means: victualling, loans, interest, fees, contracts – all these things being demands created by states of and states at war. Mun was putting forward such arguments when Turkey and Persia had been fighting each other for as long as anyone could remember.[37] What Mun had to say has been endorsed by subsequent scholarship: 'the huge scale of the specie trade between Turkey, Persia and India . . . such movements between sworn enemies were part of the properly functioning international commercial system'.[38] Mun was first in England to understand how currencies obey changes in the strength of economies, not of armies.[39] But Mun was also first to defend the Company when after a singularly profitable first decade it was to fall upon evil days.

For this reason alone, Mun has an honoured place among later luminaries who served the Company: Malthus, Ricardo and Mill were all to become employees. Even Adam Smith, alone rejected by the Company, was to contribute his own understanding of its affairs within the pages of his incomparable *The Wealth of Nations*. But whatever Smith would say about things that had worked and others which had not, Mun had anticipated the Scotsman in perceiving how money-making is part of what we now call the 'economy'.[40] What Mun knew, and in thinking thus he was himself new, was how commerce can never defer to social obligation. Through all the bad times the Company was to experience, Mun held to his conviction that only if the economy was appropriately exercised would its health lead to the wealth of this particular nation.

No one appreciated Mun's support for the Company more than Governor Smythe. But then Mun's reputation was by no means confined to the dark alley of Philpot Lane. He was the only member of the Court of Committees who was respected by Parliament. Drafted onto both the Committee on the Decay of Trade and the Standing Commission on Trade, Mun was thought of as a public rather than a partisan figure. It was for this reason that Smythe would champion Mun as a future Company ambassador to India. Rising to address the Court of Committees, Smythe would suggest how:

> their affairs in the Indies lye a bleeding, and that partly by the dishonesty of some factors, partly by the weakness of others that are overmatched with those that govern there for the Dutch, the Company's stock hath been strangely consumed and lost to the general hurt of the adventurers and the utter undoing of some of them; that Mr Munnes might discern the hand of God beckoning him to undertake this great work of certifying the factories and restoring the trade.

Somehow though Mun seems to have failed to spot that omniscient hand. He refused and Smythe reacted. At first Mun was 'pressed with an unanimous consent of the whole court', promised unlimited powers, told that if he would go, not only would he be afforded passage on the best ship, but he would also be allowed to take 'such equipage as he himself shall hold fitting'. Notwithstanding all that, Mun would not be moved.[41] More concessions followed. Once out there he 'might *ex re nata*, begin and reform as he pleased'. But it was no good. Mun claimed 'he hath matter for his charity to work upon at home, and doth cast his eye upon his family with as much and perhaps more tenderness than another'.[42] Refusal did not mean withdrawal of regard, however, still less release from the onerous role of being both public relations officer and chief apologist. With these responsibilities, Mun then became tasked with exposing the bad faith of the Dutch over a treaty of 1621 which had been supposed to have put an end to the venomous rivalry between the two companies. That particular exercise in pushing back against the Dutch having been finished, however, Mun would then come to be asked to start a paper war after news of the Massacre of Amboyna reached London in the spring of 1624.

What had happened was this: the Dutch commander on Amboyna had tortured and killed ten Company factors, claiming they were plotting to seize the island. Once news reached Europe of this incident, Mun directed 'the number of books to be printed and compounding with the press' as the Company strove to pin the guilt squarely on the VOC:

The Court having been specially called to hear Munns' answer to the chief objections made against the Company's trade, that gentleman offered his 'collections' to be read; but first it was thought necessary to examine the state of the business between the English and the Dutch, to prepare it for the Lords when they should meet, as they were to be urged to do speedily. Meanwhile the 'commissioners of the treaty' were to be called together that afternoon, Mr Deputy [Maurice Abbott] and Sir Thomas Roe having promised to attend. Ellam and [Robert] Bacon were ordered to be present then. Munns proceeded to read his 'collections' and these were approved as being set down with great judgement and good words; but he was desired to soften some passages in which he had 'bitterly lashed' the Company's opponents as the Court had no wish to exasperate the latter. In the main his work was applauded. Alderman Halliday, however, thought that Munns was too sanguine about the attitude of the Dutch, his own opinion being that, unless they proved in the future more faithful to their engagements, no profitable trade by this conjunction was to be expected. He believed that whereas before the Treaty the Dutch had endeavored to expel the English from the Indies by force, so since that agreement they had been trying by underhand methods to discourage and drive them out of the trade, in order to monopolize it themselves.[43]

It is hard to exaggerate the significance of Thomas Mun in the affairs of the Company. At the end of what had been a resoundingly successful first decade, in coming under heavy fire thereafter, the Company seemed well-nigh overwhelmed by its critics. By 1620 it stood condemned for its inability to sustain early promise, hated for monopolies, dismissed for conservatism and despised for lack of direction. Yet here was Mun in stout defence of what so many saw as the indefensible.[44] Beyond quotidian crises, however, a supportive Tudor culture had created the ideal environment in which all these overseas cartels could thrive, provided directors held a collective nerve. It is then to the Tudor mindset we now turn to understand the rise of the City of London to its position as the fourth estate in the realm of England by 1600.

4

ENLARGING THE BOUNDS OF
HUMAN EMPIRE

Treatises and treaties, pill boxes, paper, books: whatever was formed from pulp was as important to the genesis of the Company as the canvas from which its sails were made. Letters, share certificates, memoranda, inventories, ships' sermons and ships' log books, Acts of Parliament, statutes of the realm – all these helped the merchants of London start to believe what up to that point had appeared to be the impossible: the opportunity to penetrate to the Spice Islands and beyond. Advances in medicine, controversies about the Church, the evolution of law, definitions of 'commonwealthes' and 'corporations', even the thoughts of philosophers, began to create what it meant to be 'English' in Tudor England. The rise of cultural nationalism that all this paper represented was a catalyst for the expansion of commerce.

None of these things would have scored had it not been for important advances in medicine and the understanding of disease which spread like a bacillus out of Europe. Of those English practitioners who espoused the new medicine none was as fearless as Dr William Clowes (d. 1604). He was a thoroughly bad-tempered man whose colleagues crossed him at their peril. Clowes was always angry, often at what he saw as the scandalous state of medical practice in London. In the 1586 edition of his learned study of the 'French pox' or syphilis, entitled *A short and profitable treatise touching the cure of the disease called Morbus Gallicus, by unction* (1st edition, 1579), Clowes scorns the mountebanks, those passing themselves off as doctors:

> painters, some glaziers, some tailors, some weavers, some joiners, some cutlers, some cooks, some bakers, and some chandlers . . . it is too apparent to see how tinkers, toothdrawers, pedlars, ostlers, carters, porters, horse-gelders, horse-leeches, idiots, apple-squires, broomsmen, bawds, witches,

conjurers sooth-sayers and sow gelders, rogues, rat-catchers, renegades, and proctors of spittle-houses, with such other like rotten and stinking weeds . . . in town and country . . . abuse both physic and chirurgery.[1]

Once all that was off his chest, Clowes went on to do exactly what in this same book he had said he would accomplish. He raised the standing of medicine in England until it became a viable proposition to send a three-ship voyage to the East Indies and back without everyone dying in the process. However, Clowes's achievement owed more to the close reading which medical practitioners were to give his second publication, *A Proved Practice for All Young Surgeons*, published in 1588, than to such nostrums as they had been able to extract from his *Morbus Gallicus*. As its title suggests, its aim 'was practical guidance for the young practitioner based on what was known, by experience, to be successful, and it included a series of case studies with methods of treatment as well as various compounds and preparations, some of them his own which he generously shared with the reader and some inherited from his master, Keble'.[2]

Clowes was lobbyist and reformer. Proud of his open-mindedness, he once declared how, 'if I find anything that may be to the good of patients, and better increase my knowledge and skill in the art of surgery, be it either in Galen or Paracelsus; yea Turk, Jew or any other infidel: I will not refuse it, but be thankful to God for the same'.[3] Successful in bypassing the Royal College of Physicians, who for as long as anyone could remember had been more interested in privileging than in promoting practice, Clowes's own publications, as also his own proselytising, now ensured that 'From England there emerged some of the finest vernacular medical works in Europe . . . William Gilbert, William Harvey and their followers gained for the English in the field of the medical sciences a reputation for versatility, originality and distinction.'[4]

Serving as both military and naval surgeon, Clowes acquired invaluable experience of gunshot trauma. This would prove of great value to the Company when Clowes passed on his knowledge to the first generation of East India Company surgeons. Part of Clowes's value to the Company was how he had always been abreast of the latest thinking in Europe on trauma surgery. The most important publication for his own work as a naval surgeon had been the collected works of Ambroise Paré (d. 1590). Paré had worked with the French armies at a time when the art of amputation was being promoted. Presumably much to the relief of his soldiers, Paré had stopped pouring boiling oil into wounds. That said though, others then had to brace themselves instead for Clowes to start hacking into healthy rather than gangrenous tissue in order to try to prevent their infections from spreading.[5]

Clowes, who ended his days as senior surgeon at Bart's, had the revolutionary idea that his patients benefited from fresh air, at a time when the 'chymistes' of London were also promoting a quite new approach, this one relating to the practice of drug-taking. There began to appear a whole range of books that had been inspired by a famous alchemist from Basel, Philippus Aureolus Theophrastus Bombastus von Hohenheim, known to his friends as Paracelsus (d. 1541). The impact of Paracelsus has been neatly summarised thus: '[he] replaced the herbal remedies of Galenic medicine with chemical remedies. He saw these, and indeed all essences, as containing an internal alchemist's arcana or ferment that had the power of separating the assimilable from waste. This reasoning was applied in detail to the processes of digestion and excretion, as well as fermentation.'[6]

Clowes became 'a leading proponent of chemical therapy', uniting with a group who 'not only advocated chemical therapy but also projected themselves as allies of the Paracelsian'.[7] But what impact did all this have on the progress of English medicine – and indeed the East India Company? The discoveries associated with the efficacy of mineral distillations, something that had always been central to the teaching of Paracelsus, would be of the utmost value to the surgeons of the Company. Suddenly a vast new field for cures had been opened up. Now mineral and plant extracts could be relied upon to be effective when fresh specimens had been unable to survive the rigours of transport from India to England.

But what is the connection between the fulminations of Dr Clowes and medicine as it was practised not in the field but at sea, not at Bart's but in Bantam? Without Clowes there would not have been the famous Dr Woodall (d. 1643).

Though something of a scoundrel, John Woodall, with a surgery at Wood Street, in the financial district of the City, was London's most expensive doctor. He went on to establish the post of surgeon-general in the East

India Company. Placing in every vessel his vast trunk of instruments – things of surgery and torture alike – the 'Surgeon's Chest' looked like, and was viewed as, an Ark of the Covenant, worshipped by the people of the sea as their means to salvation. Doubtless its contents killed as many as they cured, but without the saws and unguents, the bandages and the braces, the whole crew must have gone down. If many owed much to wealthy Woodall, he owed most to cantankerous Clowes whose painful extractions of wisdom out of books and elixirs out of crucibles meant that for the first time it was practical to consider voyages to the Yellow Sea and back.

Important changes were clearly afoot within the medical professions which would prove quite as critical to the capacity of the East India Company to put in the miles as would advances in an understanding of aerodynamics to long-distance flying in the twentieth century. But such a story of progress was by no means confined to the chemist's laboratory and the dissector's table. Every intellectual endeavour of Tudor England was in ferment.

A gathering of cerebral enquiry in the medical field had been complemented by a much broader revolution in society which had strengthened the capacity of government at both national and local level. This had been the necessary precursor to that economic growth which we have described in Chapter 2. The momentous changes that Henry VIII had presided over during the 1530s, changes to which Burghley would later give added momentum, had allowed for both the raising of capital and its allocation to these new overseas trading companies. Such a process of centralisation and premium on efficiency in the administration of national wealth, although it would be squandered under the Stuarts, was as essential as it was enabling for the precursors of the EIC. What took place has been called 'the Tudor revolution in government', the title of Sir Geoffrey Elton's celebrated book published in the early 1950s. Although much of the impact of what Elton argued came to be blunted upon the shields of hostile reviewers, the book succeeded in transforming approaches to an understanding of Renaissance England. It posited Elton's belief that the 'revolution' which Henry VIII had realised had not been initiated by the king but enabled by far-reaching bureaucratic reforms set in place by Thomas Cromwell after he had succeeded Cardinal Wolsey as chief minister to the Crown. Cromwell's quill was mightier than Henry's sword.

Elton then turned from cause to consequence, from suggesting how change had come about to considering its impact upon the 'commonweale'. This Tudor 'revolution' had enabled the crown to centralise power with the result that it gathered to itself such prestige as Henry VII must have envied. Had it not been for Cromwell's transformation of the means of control, the collection of data and the dissemination of command, the administrative achievements of Lord Burghley would never have been possible. Burghley was the constant gardener who in tilling the soil to nurture the seed took his tools out of Cromwell's shed.

How effective, indeed how 'real', was this famous revolution has been the subject of argument for the seventy years since Elton gave the world his theories. But what cannot be in doubt is how, menacing and mendacious by turns, Cromwell generated a vast amount of paper. But then so had the printing presses of London since William Caxton had started to set type back in 1476. What issued from the City of London's publishing houses some sixty years after Caxton, however, was no less germane to the eventual launch of the Company than any number of statutes which Cromwell had drafted in his study at Austin Friars.[8]

Important Tudor texts devoted either to what today might broadly be thought of as politics or sociology – canonical books such as Sir Thomas More's *Utopia* (1516) and Sir Thomas Elyot's *The Boke Named the Gouvernor* (1531) – provoked interest as they influenced the thinking of the Tudor merchant who looked to learn the means of control and the methods of business involved in running a complex organisation. As More, Elyot and, later, Sir Thomas Smythe (of *A Discourse of the Common Weal of this Realm of England* fame) considered what an ideal society might be like, what they applied to the macrocosm of England would be applied by Smythe through a species of reductionism to the microcosm of his enterprise. As the national mind had been on the march, so the social studies that Tudor students of political science presented to the world came to have a fecund bearing upon the culture of the East India Company and its competitors. Although an accretion in thinking and imagination, argument and illustration had been gradual, it was a necessary and sufficient prelude to the foundation of the EIC. A notable corpus of works about society, its ills and its aspirations, things which have descended to us as canonical texts, helped Governor

Smythe to envision ways in which he might yet manage that hazardous business of survival amidst the chaos of improvisation, the underfunding of capital and the fusillade of enemies that would characterise the early years of the East India Company.

Not least among the thinking which was to make Smythe himself think was the acerbic religious controversy that raged through much of the sixteenth century and provided – or generated – a crucible for the expansion of mental horizons; boundaries that needed to be stretched if the East India Company was to stretch itself to the boundless wastes of China and Korea. The hot controversies that had for so long engulfed the churches in England appealed to Smythe who, taking himself to be a godly sinner, extracted from theological furies cool reasoning as to how to organise communities. Though no presbyter himself, Smythe of Low Church inclinations was the patron of St Dionysis Backchurch, a house of worship not 300 yards from his own front door.

In the process of getting rid of the Middle Ages and getting rid, too, of the Roman Church as that had been expressed in glass and stone, indulgences and taxes, Cromwell had given Henry VIII big ideas about how he might become the giant upon a European stage that he had always wanted to be. One of the most intoxicating of the lies which lay at the heart of Henry VIII's *Act in Restraint of Appeals* (1533) was his claim that he was an emperor and not just a king. In the preamble Henry declares: 'Where by divers sundry old authentic histories and chronicles, it is manifestly declared and expressed that this realm of England is an Empire, and so hath been accepted in the world'. Not a word of this was true, but that was not the point. Such inflammatory rhetoric was a flare upon the high road to nationalism as it was also the means to make the governing class feel good about itself. What Henry's claims encouraged was a sense of national pride and individual worth which was liberating for those who set up the East India Company, and in doing so released the rope from the capstan of English commerce.

Whilst Henry's daughter Elizabeth I came to feel harboured about by a fleet of enemies, all intent upon bringing her down and bringing Rome in, she never forgot that quixotic vision of her tyrannical father: the idea that England should step forward to play its part in world affairs. So too for the first generation of the East India Company's Court of Committees – its earliest directors – either born like Smythe in the reign of Queen Mary (d. 1558) or early in the first years of Elizabeth's tenure, the impetus to nationalism and the impulse to expand was something they took in with their mother's milk. Nevertheless, it could not have become so well advanced by 1600 but for the struggles which centred around the religious establishment of Elizabethan England and Elizabeth at its heart.

For a time, however, such a capacity to nurture ambitions as wild as they were unsettling went underground during the interval between the death of Henry VIII in 1547 and the accession of Elizabeth I in 1558. Chimeras of greatness, scrolled upon proclamation and trumpeted by herald, declarations vainly promised but prodigally pursued by Henry VIII, all of this descended into impotence, fanaticism and depression during the reigns of Edward VI and Queen Mary. The year before Henry VIII had acceded to the throne in 1508, the Retail Price Index had stood at 100. By the accession of his son Edward VI in 1547, things had started to look bad. A run of appalling harvests between 1549 and 1551, an attempt to exterminate the Scots, renewed hostilities with France, all contrived to send that same Index to 248 in 1546 and 285 in 1551. By the time Elizabeth I had ascended the throne in 1558, matters looked frail indeed. But although the first years of the new reign were hedged about with every sort of threat, beneath the surface strength was mustering. Since the accession of the Tudors in 1485, England had been forging new and stronger identities than had prevailed under the Plantagenets. During the forty-five-year reign of Elizabeth I, England gathered strength, its economy expanded and its enemies drew back.

Despite the hazard of Elizabeth's reign, something she artfully and archly played for all it was worth to bind her courtiers closer to her person, challenges had been legion throughout a century which saw England reshaped as never before. The real menace to England's growth, because it was a menace to the country's stability, had been and would remain the issue of religion.

In 1529 England had possessed the full armoury of European Catholicism, monasteries included. But then Henry had removed the Pope and the consistory courts, while he had rendered monasteries such 'bare ruin'd choirs' as were best left to the poets. Henry had been succeeded by Edward VI who, having repudiated his father's home-grown Catholicism, imposed a sour and acerbic Protestantism upon England. The austerity of that grey and cheerless regime lasting only five years, and with Mary coming in, Cardinal Pole came out. The prelate enflamed the queen's febrile devotions, and Catholicism was reignited by setting fire to such English bishops as refused to drop the fustian of Geneva for the brocade of Rome. After so much turmoil, bitter quarrels about the relationship between Church and state erupted at Elizabeth's accession in 1558. What followed was the so-called 'Elizabethan Settlement' referred to above. It was a fudge whereby Anglicanism was retained but some of the old ritual returned. Supposed to please all but satisfying few, the business of selling what was sold as a 'compromise' gave Henry VIII's title 'Defender of the Faith' a quite new meaning for this, his defenceless daughter. Finding herself charged with keeping the peace, Elizabeth looked to a veritable army of apologists to sustain a balance between the treachery of the seminarian and the disaffection of the presbyter. None was more eloquent in defence of that 'Settlement' than Richard Hooker, sometime Master of the Temple and all-time master of prose.

Hooker's *Of the Laws of Ecclesiastical Polity* (1593) is the most mediated of all defences mounted to protect the Anglican Settlement from the assaults of its enemies. Hooker casts the Settlement as at one and the same time national Church, political creation, corporate body and community of souls. Although the author has nothing whatever to say about the formation of overseas trading cartels, and here it must be remembered that when Hooker first published the foundation of the East India Company was still almost a decade away, still, much of what Hooker writes about social obligation in his consideration of 'church in society' would be of the greatest interest to Smythe, not least because he was the biggest employer in London and also charged with keeping a dozen little commonwealths, too often at sea in every sense, afloat.

It may be thought that Smythe found Hooker's *Polity* compelling as the cleric writes with such limpid exposition about the proper ordering of both the macro and the micro when each in its own degree is pushed and pulled by different priorities and prejudices. In Hooker's compendious volumes, the churchman ostensibly offers his nostrums for those interested in the dynamic between a national Church and the society within which it is incorporated. However, what Hooker also has to say as the supreme apologist for the *via media* of Anglicanism could have been applied to quite other contexts.

What in no small part makes Hooker so attractive an advocate of compromise is his deep concern with how communities order affairs so as to ensure that differences are not only respected but resolved. This most irenic of churchmen has rightly been held up as offering an early prospectus of a rational way to define society and its needs: 'If there is any single point that must be chosen as the beginning of the English Enlightenment, as the first glimmering of its dawn, then that would have to be the publication in 1593 of the first four books of Richard Hooker's *Of the Lawes of Ecclesiasticall Politie*.'[9] Beyond that it could surely be suggested that what Hooker pleads Bacon would soon enough advocate in publications promoting the marriage of mental and natural philosophy.

What Hooker had to say about Church governance leached into a still broader analysis of the nature of authority. Governance of parish or convocation of bishops, charity commissioners, governors of schools, directors of multinationals, all these and more had difficulties in common; and all had much to learn from Hooker's acute sociological analysis. The value that Hooker places on the expression of orthodoxy and obedience, as these things were manifested in the ceremonies and buildings, the hierarchies and the organisation of the Anglican Church, was something that may have been of compelling interest to Smythe. In those days the parish and the pinnace were not so very different.

Such a parallel – that is, between an Elizabethan ship of state and Smythe's ships of India – is worth pursuing when attempting to imagine how Smythe set about creating the future shape of the East India Company. It would be nice to be able to alight on Smythe's own church of St Dionysis, rebuilt to designs of Sir Christopher Wren after the medieval structure had been burned in the Great Fire of 1666; but it was demolished in 1878, and sadly neither crocket nor quoin survives. With the average size of a late Tudor inner City parish such as St Dionysis being eighty households, the congregation would have closely complemented the number of adult males that sailed out on that first three-ship Voyage on 20 April 1601. Managing congregation or crew demanded much the same delegation and many of the same skills. Both parishioner and purser had a multitude of tasks all to do with care and discipline, reportage and accountability, which if properly discharged, would allow for the proper functioning of these separate nuclei. For someone like

Smythe it may be argued that there were suggestive parallels between the presbytery of his church and the governance of his ship, especially to one such as himself who worshipped God and gold with equal fervour. A church and a ship were paternalistic microcosms which 'fostered a social dynamic remarkable similar at times to that found in a tightly knit workshop ruled by a domineering master'.[10]

Workshop or worship? If the domineering Smythe may never have owned a workshop, he had always worshipped in tiny communities which demanded much more from their well-to-do members than merely removing their hats upon coming through the door. Anyone who lived prosperously in a large house in Seething Lane, as Samuel Pepys would do and many navy men had done, was required to do something about seething London. As a recent authoritative account of the London poor makes abundantly clear, the parish, its ministers, patrons, beadles and wardens together constituted an employment exchange, a benefits office, a medical dispensary, a police force and just about everything else you can think of which social services are supposed to provide for the citizen of the twenty-first century. And all of these services needed to be supplied on an East India Company ship, along with the bread and wine.

As for Smythe and such paternalistic care as he was required to show in both dockyard and ship, his family and the Juddes, from whence his mother had descended, had been famous for family charities still going today; largesse which in Tudor times, if not in ours, was dispensed through the hundred tiny parishes which made up that glittering mosaic of capital worship. As for the governor himself, it would seem that he had had a long apprentice in easing if hardly solving the ills of small communities; fieldwork which was invaluable experience when it came to ordering the wretched lives of those thrown into the prison which was an East Indiaman setting out upon its travels.

As a monopolistic corporation like the Anglican Church, the East India Company not only had to think about its nature but also had to be alert in defence of its privileges. There had never been so urgent a need to consider the nature of corporations as there was in the closing years of Elizabeth's reign. The Anglican Church had had to invent a past to suggest how the break with Rome had been no more than a return to Anglicanism's roots before Catholicism had corrupted the purity of worship. So too the East India Company was required to think about a future with its pluralities and hierarchies, not unlike the steeple of authority which with the Anglican Settlement (1559–63) had passed into law when Smythe was a boy.

The massive changes in Church governance witnessed during the mid-Tudor decades needed new courts to promote respectability in spiritual matters. But then so too enhanced legal structures arose because of the closer identity of Crown and Church following the break with Rome. Enhanced powers of the monarchy in the realm of domestic disputes had multiplied exponentially as a consequence of a massive redistribution of wealth following the immolation of the monastic orders; a presence in the body politic that had been second only to the Crown in the extent of its assets. A recently empowered Crown, fattened upon the marrow of the monasteries, had then initiated land sales of such complexity as demanded the creation of new courts and the scaling-up of old. As for trade and commerce, now that the ambition was to get halfway round the world, the logistics involved were on a quite different scale than in the past. In pursuit of providing a legal frame-work for new enterprises, entrepreneurs looked into how other social groups promoted their sectional interests. An Erastian Crown, a national Church, statute versus precedence, Parliament and monarchy together changing the face of the nation: never was there such public debate about the nature of corporations and the meaning of 'commonweale'.

The vast changes in how society had come to be ordered had a profound effect on the thinking of managers as to how to manage. But what about 'Law' with a capital 'L'? Further stimulus to understanding what corporations meant and how they worked, whether these were of body or mind, was provided by 'the most significant statement of English common law on corporations in the early modern period and one that still receives mention in today's law journals'.[11] This was the case of *Rex v Sutton* or what is also known as *Sutton's Hospital* (1612). The issue at hand revolved around the supposed disposition of the City merchant Sir Thomas Sutton when his intention of incorporating a charitable foundation became the object of embattled litigation.

There was not much to choose between the brilliance of the counsels representing the opposing parties in the case. Legal historians have often taken Sir Edward Coke (d. 1634), acting for the defence, to have been the prime exemplar of what Sir Francis Bacon would suggest in 1625 judges should always be: not just lions, but lions under the throne.[12] Such an accolade came to rest upon Coke for his apparent fearless defence of Common Law. What is certain is that Coke had the highest public profile of those who sat upon the Jacobean judicial bench, though in truth, his attitude had rather less to do with defending 'Everyman' than in promoting himself; in the words of a recent commentator, for Coke 'the role of the common law was a moveable feast, from which he supped differently depending on which position he held'.[13]

As for the plaintiff in the Sutton case he had a quite different champion, albeit one who thrust himself into the public eye in quite different ways to the publicity-seeking Coke. This was no less than Sir Francis Bacon himself (d. 1626), who at this stage of his marvellously varied career was Attorney General. Here Bacon was representing Simon Baxter, who as a cousin of Sir Thomas Sutton had put himself forward in claiming to be the old man's rightful heir.[14] Bacon argued that although Parliament had approved the foundation of Sutton's hospital, and it could not be disputed that a grant of incorporation had been issued, it was open to challenge in the courts because the drafting had been neither finished nor approved before Sutton had died. Sutton's intentions could not be validated as the precise terms of what had been proposed could not now be retrieved. Bacon therefore asked that Sutton's will be set aside. Besides the fact that Sutton's intentions were not clear, the text of the will did not specify either title or place for Sutton's foundation, features that, Bacon argued, were essential in any legitimate act of incorporation.

Coke denied this, while being in agreement with Bacon as to the immaterial and artificial nature of corporations, though the whole spinning-top of legal nicety then began to turn on 'whether this immaterial and artificial person can nevertheless be real and how it could be so'. As the proceedings wore on Bacon cited Sir Thomas More's *Utopia* 'to construe the corporation as a purely imaginary body politic, since it lacks any concrete foundation while Coke argues that this same immaterial and artificial person corresponds to a substantial, actually existing thing, possessed of property, an endowment, and a distinguished board of governors'.[15] This was a group of which Coke happened to be one himself. That aside, the point is this: the light that the *Sutton's Hospital* case shed upon the nature of trusts was of great interest to the City and to men such as Sir Thomas Smythe. The case had come to court soon after the EIC had had its constitution ratified by the issue of a new charter (1609). But in due course that would require yet another licence, something that would need to be lobbied for in the face of ever-mounting pressures, from the King for gratuities and from Parliament for reform.

If the law had acted as a catalyst for thinking about how to create societies that would promote change or pursue profit, the new initiatives also found reflections in the popular literature of the day. The excitement of change and the challenge of travel, the romance of the sea and the riches of East and West alike eddied their way into the Elizabethan mind. 'Thus we find the whole of Elizabethan literature strewn with gold and silver,' wrote Virginia Woolf, 'with talk of Guiana's rarities, and references to that America – "O my America! my new-found-land" – which was not merely a land on the map, but symbolized the unknown territories of the soul. So, over the water, the imagination of Montaigne brooded in fascination upon savages, cannibals, society, and government.'[16] None of course expressed those 'unknown territories of the soul' more poetically than Shakespeare (d. 1616) who was lodging in Silver Street and living amid men on the make and on the move. Such was his understanding of the patois of sailing, so sure his mastery of maritime technology, that it has even been suggested in a book deemed respectable enough to have been published by a university press that the bard was a sailor.[17] As for the inspiration of his plays, there are allusions to seafaring from first to last: from *Henry VI* (1591) to *Henry VIII* (1613).

The first production of *Henry VIII* in 1613 had resulted in the burning down of the Globe when a live cannon had been fired onstage by boys from the special effects department. And just at this very moment there was something astir on the north bank of the Thames too. Sir Thomas Smythe, no less, was readying himself to put his own match to powder with the launch of the First Joint Stock (1613), shortly to be fired at those investors who ran off with their money just as soon as the ship's pilot ran into Blackwall. With this Joint Stock, however, everyone was going to have to keep their money in longer and the Company was going to be able to build up capital assets.

Walking from the smouldering ruins of the Globe at Southwark to the Curtain at Finsbury Fields, no Adventurer could have helped but notice the logo of the Company stamped from Saffron Hill to Cinnamon Street: *impresa* set over mansion and sealed upon letter, scribed upon gate and stamped across wood – a proud badge announcing not just the departure of a flotilla but the arrival of a nation. The EIC came into existence in 1600 because England had come into its own. The country believed in itself, confident that it was not merely the equal of but superior to all European rivals.

If today most people can recite a few lines of our national playwright (though doubtless not from *Henry VIII*), they may be surprised to know how familiar they are with the writings of that other 'William', William Tyndale (d. 1536). It is often thought that Shakespeare said it all. In fact, it was Tyndale: 'salt of the earth', 'fat of the land', 'flesh pots', 'milk and honey', 'let my people go' and that ornithological curiosity 'bald as a coot', among many other aperçus. These had all been minted by Tyndale the master coiner whose currency has been rubbed to cliché through its overfamiliarity. But Tyndale did more than merely give the language its quotidian phrases. He was the first to dare to suggest how 'Everyman' should gain access to his own Bible rather than have it 'licensed' through the agency of a parish priest. As Tyndale became ever more snared in controversy, he was questioned as to what he believed; a challenge to which the great chronicler of the English martyrs, John Foxe, has him respond: 'If God spare my life, ere many years I will cause a boy that driveth the plough shall know more of the scripture than thou doest!'[18] It was because Tyndale had himself contrived to elide religion and nationalism (albeit as a modified form of Catholicism, not an Anglican Church) that on these first East India Voyages the boy who ploughed the waves sang the psalms in his proud vernacular.

Setting about translating the Bible in order to let his own people go, Tyndale had gone on to create 'the most important book in the English language'.[19] And so it was that Tyndale contributed mightily to a burgeoning sense of national identity. With slow maturation and the accretion of other 'national' texts, those who formed corporations found that courage which was a prerequisite for the strenuous business of sending English ships to Asia ports. Tyndale had doggedly set himself to his translation, sustained by his recollection that if St Jerome had dared to turn the Greek Bible into the Vulgate, 'Why may we not also?' Such questions, such pride, as much nationalistic as they were spiritual, Tyndale's resounding phrase 'Why may we not also?', resonated with the merchants of the City as they came to pose a different if more secular question: Why may we not challenge Spain?

One of those who would be inspired by Tyndale was that same Sir Edward Coke encountered as counsel in the Sutton Case. Coke's admiration for Tyndale's contribution to 'Englishness' was expressed through his own defence of the 'rudeness' of its language: 'Our English language is as copious and significant, and as able to express anything in as few and as apt words, as any other native language . . . And (to speak what we think) we would derive from the Conqueror as little as we could.'[20] Such plain rejection of the supposed superiority of French culture in favour of promoting robust 'English' is what this is all about. But then Coke went further. Through the genius of English legal practice, England had arranged its disputes so as not to need recourse to foreigners, nasty or otherwise. For Coke, Norman or French law had never been as efficacious as the flexible evolution of English Common Law; an inheritance which with characteristic conceit Coke declares he had been brought into this world to project, to progress and to defend. For Coke, the source of justice was popular law and custom, not the arbitrary fiat of a tyrannous monarchy who for centuries had been imposing the 'Norman Yoke', or the 'Norman Conquest' as it is known today – the imposition of Norman and Angevin culture upon Anglo-Saxons who had previously flourished in a milieu of ancient 'English' liberty. Writing in the first days of the EIC, Coke was placing law at the service of nation-building, just as others were encouraging Englishmen to be more expansive and ambitious. Tyndale, Shakespeare and Coke all contributed to the gathering of a wave.

It was Sir Francis Bacon, however, who in his vast corpus of publications wholly recast assumptions regarding the purpose of 'Natural Philosophy' – what we call the physical sciences – and inaugurated a very English revolution in thinking about the world and phenomenology. This would in turn cut a path to the foundation of the Royal Society in 1660. Bacon's fifty-eight *Essayes or Counsels Civil and Moral* (3rd edition, 1625) is all the non-specialist now knows of one whose intellectual curiosity was unsurpassed in a century that included Boyle, Newton and Locke. Bacon was proud of these essays, dedicating them to the duke of Buckingham with the comment 'of all my other works, [these] have been most Currant: For that, as it seems, they come home, to Mens Businesse and Bosomes'. But whilst the essays are still read, most of Bacon's oeuvre was accessible only to those who understand Latin, with the notable exception of his extended allegory *The New Atlantis* (1626).

If Bacon's corpus is now neglected, prior to the disappearance of Latin as the lingua franca of Europe, no great mind had been unaware of the distinction of those once influential works. D'Alembert, oracle of the *encyclopédistes*, called Bacon 'the greatest, most universal, the most eloquent of philosophers', uniting with Diderot in adopting the Baconian system of classification as being the most exact enumeration possible.[21] Bacon became dedicatee of Kant's *Kritik der reinen Vernunft* (1781) before Darwin took Bacon's *opera omnia* with him as a pillow when he left for Patagonia aboard the *Beagle* (1831). Thomas Babington Macaulay (d. 1859) suggests in his biography of Bacon the most important reason for the universal admiration of him among the thinkers: the exceptional achievement of Bacon in liberating the English mind. 'The knowledge in which Bacon excelled all men,' he writes, 'was a knowledge of the mutual relations of all the departments of knowledge.'[22]

Bacon was important for the new commerce because of his declaration that 'I have taken all knowledge to be my province.' No English thinker had previously had such boundless curiosity; none would ever match Bacon's capacity to see all branches of knowledge as nurturing a society prosperous in wealth and settled in spirit. A thirst for knowledge, openness to experience, adaptation and pragmatism, these Bacon marked up for others to pursue in England's quest for foreign trade. In order to express what he meant Macaulay compares the philosopher's achievements to the difference between a globe and an atlas:

> His knowledge differed from that of other men, as a terrestrial globe differs from an atlas which contains a different country on every leaf. The towns and roads of England . . . are better laid down in the atlas than in the globe . . . We may go to the Atlas to learn the bearings and distances

93

of York and Bristol . . . But it is useless if we want to know the bearings and distances of France and Martinique, or of England and Canada. On the globe we shall not find all the market towns in our own neighbour-hood; but we shall learn from it the comparative extent and the relative position of all the kingdoms of the earth.[23]

Macaulay may have likened Bacon's effect to a more rounded system of thought, that is to say the globe and not the map. But what Macaulay might have added was how, like Shakespeare, Bacon could be inspired by the sea. It has been suggested that Bacon's *New Atlantis*, fitting snugly between More's *Utopia* and Swift's *Gulliver's Travels* as it does, was inspired by the philosopher's awareness of the epic story of William Adams (d. 1620), the famous English pilot who brought the Dutch to Japan for the first time.

Bacon deeply affected the culture of early modern England; of that there is no doubt. This said, there is nothing to suggest that anything he wrote had any *direct* effect on the foundational thinking of Smythe and his fellow directors. There is not a shred of evidence that he was ever recruited as a consultant, and he is only found amongst the papers in that unexceptional capacity as an Adventurer at a time when everybody in London life had become an investor in the East India Company. As for Smythe, assuredly he was no intellectual, and there is no evidence that he was ever in touch with Bacon to ask for help in promoting the arts of navigation and invention, astronomy and physic, language and diplomacy, all of which were in urgent demand if the captains of the Company were to be sufficiently armed for the challenges ahead. Bacon's works and Company profit were never in a relationship of cause and effect. And yet Bacon's inductive method was of great influence upon the savants whom Smythe recruited for the challenges of sailing ships over the edge of what was then the known world. Bacon and Smythe both reflected the zeitgeist. The Company could not have survived without a marriage between mind and matter, between what Bacon argued and Smythe applied. There was something in Bacon's claims about the nature of experimentation and the revelation of natural law, assumed by him to be a combination of human ingenuity and divine illumination, that resonated powerfully in the counting house; there was a natural affinity between Bacon's attitude to knowledge and Smythe's pursuit of wealth. Both replaced the idea of a fixed, exhaustible stock with the concept of uninterrupted flow. It must also be said that Smythe shared Bacon's ineradicable optimism, though his belief in progress took a rather different form. For Smythe, there could be limitless expansion of commerce, regardless of those economists such as Malynes who deplored the Company's export of money. In the great debate about what money is, precisely, something provoked by the appearance of these overseas companies as from 1550, Bacon was on the side of Mun in famously declaring that 'money is like muck, not good except it be spread'.[24]

What caused the launch of the Company to happen when it did were things of this world and the next, of the mixed and mundane: critical texts which had to do with how society should best be ordained; slow maturation of a thousand changes in forge and workshop; transformations wrought by shipwright or cartographer; skills honed, battles won, enterprise promoted. The encouragement of an 'R&D' culture, nurtured by Burghley and supported by Walsingham, gave technical advantages over Spain and Portugal; just as the same offered new delights to the consumer. Though numerous Tudor navigators had become entombed in boundless ice-floes, those who had been fortunate to make it home had discovered something other than black rocks in grey seas. Heroes constructed from basalt not flesh, these desperados had been as important to the arrival of the Company as for its survival.

Essential too was a sense of nationhood that induced abundant self-belief. From the mid-sixteenth century, a powerful awareness of what it meant and what it might mean to be English had matured in the writings of theologians, philosophers and playwrights alike: residue of so much thought, so much imagination, so much industry. History is as much about men as it is about movements: the inspiration of Drake, the writings of Dee, the prophecies of Bacon; these countless efforts, painful and creative by turns, gave birth to the surgeon's chest, the sextant and the dividend. By 1600 all these and more had come together to create the necessary mass for combustion. We turn now to a consideration of how the Company operated under the most unusual man in the history of English business. He was that force of nature known to his admirers as 'Neptune' Smythe.

5

RAISING THE MONEY

We begin not in the stews of London from where so many Company sailors were recruited, but rural Kent. This vast county, so various in its topographies, became for the East India Company what far-off Devon had been for the sea dogs of the Armada. Kent was the Company's heart of oak. It was the best of recruiting grounds, this particular bend of the river producing that legendary English pilot William Adams. Among putrid estuaries and leaden waters, within blousy garrisons and tarred yards, ships came in before standing out for the Downs, deals were rigged and contraband shuffled through marshes quite as sinister as terrifies Pip in *Great Expectations*. In places rank with rushes and malarious odours, the thief would come in the night to excavate well-gotten gains which he had taken out of an East Indiaman anchored at Gravesend and waiting to get into Blackwall. With such contraband one who may have been a private trader but who was certainly a public thief readied himself to sell silk from Tabriz to the ostlers of Tonbridge.

Here in Kent, too, was the royal dockyard at Chatham on the River Medway, up which in June 1667 would come the Dutch to destroy an English fleet with all the ruthlessness the Japanese would deploy at Pearl Harbor in December 1941. But before its grand humiliation at the hands of the Hollander, Chatham was a proud naval base, long connected, though at long distance, to Sandwich, where Smythe would insert spies between his sacks of spice to tell him who exactly was stealing what out of warehouses operated by his company. Kent was a source for victualling; out of Chatham, too, the Company could borrow a mast as you might borrow a car. Among the flats and dunes of a promiscuous coast thrusting up against the Dutch were to be found experimental firing ranges where new weaponry destined for Company fleets would be tested. Further inland and across the Weald was a forest to stoke a forge. Here Burghley had encouraged German engineers to make such balls and ballistics as had made splinter out of splendour at the Armada.

For those in the East India Company wishing to move from the counting house to the country house, Kent was every estate agent's dream. Here was the liveliest market in England for those wishing to plant respectability and a nectarine. One such was Lionel Cranfield (d. 1645) who as governor of the Eastland Company directing trade in the Baltic was close to Smythe, and to Smythe he sold his father-in-law's manor house at Sutton-at-Hone. All that now remains of this once splendid affair is a flint retaining wall dividing the churchyard from the ground upon which the mansion once rested. As for its church of St John the Baptist, rebuilt by Smythe in 1615, the village has since moved down the hill, so that for most of his days St John is left preaching in an English wilderness, with as companions only rooks wheeling about a flinty tower, frowning upon waving corn below.

Not all is disappointment, though. Against an aisle lies the tomb of Smythe himself. Despite its solid alabaster, there is something strangely provisional about the whole ensemble: it is so shoved against a Perpendicular window as to block one of its three lights. Smythe's relationship with his children was almost as unsatisfactory as this final placement: that is clear enough from the contrast between what is to be found here and the monument to Smythe's father, Sir Thomas Smythe the Elder. This is at St Nicholas's church, Ashford, also in Kent, and some 40 miles down the Dover road.

Whereas the hands of Thomas the Younger are held in prayer hoping for eternity, Sir Thomas the Elder is caught reading a book, inattentively waiting for the years to pass before discovering his fate. Smythe the Elder is accompanied by his wife, beneath whom are a brood of offspring lined up to look like so many ducklings heading for the village pond. In contrast to such conviviality in Ashford, Smythe the Younger rests alone at Sutton. But then Sir Thomas the Younger was the most private of men in the most public of offices: his letters are confined entirely to business, and very dull they are too, much like his effigy. Doubtless the second-rate sculptor who did all this could do no better, but the outcome is curiously appropriate. No one could look into the soul of Sir Thomas Smythe: the man playing for everything gave nothing away.

But if Smythe lies alone in death, from birth he had been the favourite out of many. Second of his twelve siblings, Thomas was regarded as the best hope for a dynasty rich in wealth and connection. Product of a mid-Tudor union between the Juddes and the Smythes, the marriage of Thomas's parents had been the outcome of a strategic alliance between those prodigiously powerful livery companies the Skinners and the Haberdashers. Thomas's maternal grandfather, Sir Andrew Judde (d. 1558), had been prominent in the wool trade at Calais. In addition, he had profited from currency exchange in Europe, gold dust from Guinea, furs at Moscow and oil from everywhere. Having more contacts than contracts, the Crown owed Judde far more than just the huge financial debts for which he held sureties no doubt well locked away in his desk. Lord Mayor of London Judde had suppressed the Wyatt rebellion and so saved the reign of Queen Mary; but then he had made it his business to have friends not just in high places but in others too. During his tenure as mayor of Calais, he had entertained an unusual guest: the king of Spain. And as for Lady Judde she could claim an illustrious descent from the Chichele brothers, one an archbishop of Canterbury, the other founder of All Souls College, Oxford.

Fascinated by the romance of Russia, intrigued by the darkness of Africa, Sir Andrew taught his grandson Sir Thomas Smythe the Younger how commerce should be rightly leavened by civility and its profit tempered by charity. Always sensible of God's abundance to his own abundant family, Judde had been charitable to a fault: treasurer of London hospitals, he was the founder of both Tonbridge and Judde schools. Generous to the indigent and mindful of the scholar, Sir Andrew's epitaph demanded not just tablets but walls. Judde's son-in-law, known as 'Customer' Smythe (d. 1591) and the man buried in Ashford, has a splendid portrait at Queens' College, Cambridge, where appropriately enough, given how close a man the Customer was, his face is buried in a marmalade beard. Though qualified to follow his father-in-law to the Skinners' Company, the Customer became Farmer of Her Majesty's Inward Customs for the Port of London in return for an annual fee that came to weigh less each passing year as profits from this emolument began to soar. Bold and corrupt, the Customer wasted no time in making the leading politicians of the age his 'pensioners'. For example, the royal favourite, Robert Dudley, earl of Leicester, remarked in his will upon his own 'great love' for Smythe. But then the Customer was relieved to discover that when Lord Burghley asked him how to raise taxes, he was careful never to enquire as to how Smythe had done so well for himself.

But if the Customer found it possible to take a stake in his friends, rather less easy was that ticklish question that exercised the mind of many a Tudor mogul: how to make the best marital investment. In the Customer's case, the answer was to join the Smythes with the Juddes. Such a base secured, this arriviste son of a Wiltshire yeoman now began to change his bread into stones by building Corsham Court (1575–82) in his native county. Hardly had that great mansion been finished, however, than Smythe the Elder decided to move nearer the merchants of the Staple who possessed an enviable monopoly on wool exports. Such sheep Smythe made sure to fleece every time they came up the Thames, returning from their wool fairs in Brabant. In order to be closer to the pulse of commercial life, the Customer now moved from Corsham to Ostenhanger, in Kent. Ostenhanger, he was gratified to discover, had once belonged to King Canute. So it was that its new owner was able to conceal his modest beginnings beneath a veneer of respectability. In the spirit of such self-advancement, the Customer next commissioned so splendid a group of family portraits as has provoked the verdict that 'No comparable contemporary group of English paintings, of such extent and quality . . . has survived.'[1] It would seem, then, that both sides of the family, the Juddes and the Smythes, knew well enough just how to come out top in the ruthless world of London commerce.

As for Sir Thomas Smythe the Younger, his first experience of responsibility was running the Muscovy Company. This would prove the best possible apprenticeship for heading up the EIC. However, no sooner had he been elected to the top position in the newly founded East India than in turn he found himself overwhelmed in the most serious crisis of his life. A mere six months after he had been elected one of the two sheriffs of London in November 1600, Smythe became implicated in the Essex rebellion. In February 1601 the earl of Essex moved on the City of London and, disastrously for Sir Thomas, stopped bang outside Smythe's back door, to try to gain the support of the sheriff himself. What exactly happened is not clear and can never be known. However, after the rebellion had been put down, Essex and his supporters together with some suspected of being sympathetic to him were questioned. Much of the testimony certainly looked bad for Smythe; the earl of Rutland, for instance, admitted 'That the Earl of Essex said, he was sure of Sheriff Smith'.[2] However, it was then the turn of Essex himself:

I went to Sheriff *Smith's* House, and after my coming thither, I sent the Sheriff and Mr. Alderman *Wats* to my Lord Mayor, desiring him to come to us; if he would not, to send four of his Aldermen to see if we demeaned our selves Loyally, with Intent to put our selves into their Hands to use us as they would, or to put us into any Prison; yet in regard of our private Enemies, and the Fear of their Treachery, we desired them to shut their Gates; and this was the end for which we went into the City.[3]

Although none of this could be made into charges, Smythe came to be fined a staggering £40,000. This was one of the biggest fines ever to have been raised by an unscrupulous government upon the shifting sands of mere surmise. On 2 March Smythe was imprisoned in the Tower, there to remain at 'her Majesty's pleasure'.[4]

Still inside at Christmas 1601, Smythe wrote to Elizabeth's first minister Salisbury, pleading that 'the innocence of his cause will move her Majesty's heart',[5] and praying that his recipient would graciously intercede for his liberation. Nothing happened. Nevertheless, that letter may have cleared a path. When Smythe came to be released, he would adopt a tone of deference towards Salisbury he was to afford none other. And well he might. Secreted within the folds of Salisbury's papers is a sinister little aide-memoire that, if Smythe had only known about it, would have made him realise just how close to the blade he had in fact been. Headed 'Memorial' and dated 'Before 17 February 1600–1', that is to say just a week after Essex's attempt on London, it is a list of those who needed further interrogation. Heading this prompt are the words 'Remember Michelborn's words to Smyth.'[6] Whatever that might have meant, such talk as it was believed the privateer Sir Edward Michelborne and Thomas Smythe may have exchanged could have been just one of those things that had put Smythe in gaol.[7]

Running the Muscovy was a big challenge when shipping lanes were so often closed. But if Smythe had a difficult time getting through to Archangel, Russians came in large numbers to London. Smythe had been a notably successful fixer when a delegation had arrived in 1600. This had been led by Grigori Mikulin,[8] who whilst in London decided to have his portrait painted. It has the singular distinction of being 'the earliest image of a Russian person made from life that has survived until our time'.[9] Looking at the portrait, it comes as no surprise to discover that Mikulin had been the minder of Ivan Ivanovich, son of Ivan the Terrible. Thirty years later and here he was now striding into the English . . . court, accompanied by sixteen retainers who seem to have provoked astonishment and mirth in equal measure:

> [there] went before him two and two together . . . great fat men, espe-
> cially he himself, a man of tall stature, fat with a great face and a black
> beard cut round; of a swarfy colour his face, and his gait very majestical.
> His attire was nothing differing from the rest of his company . . . but in
> richness and garnishing thereof. He had on a gown of gold down to the
> small of his leg . . . a great fur cap upon his head, and underneath that a
> cap . . . embroidered very richly with great pearls . . . His buskins were of
> red leather with high heels.[10]

The visit proved a huge success: enough alcohol consumed to have launched a ship, enough shouting to break the windows of the livery halls where carousers were entertained. Smythe had picked up the tab and the Russians had picked up private education, taking such a shine to it that they promptly sent their children to Winchester and Eton, Oxford and Cambridge.

One thing led to another. After Smythe had been released from the Tower, he was appointed ambassador to Russia in June 1604, where he was to present his credentials to Tsar Boris Godunov.[11] Before setting off for Moscow that July, however, Smythe had been inducted into the royal presence at Greenwich Palace. Asked how long he would be away, he had replied: 'full xv. moneths, by reason of the winters cruelty, whose Frosts were so extream, that the seas were not at those times Nauigable', to which the king responded, 'It seemes then that Sir Thomas goes from the Sun'. This was the cue for a hovering attendant to make an interjection for which the king had been angling: '[Smythe] must needes go from the Sunne departing from his resplendant Majesty'. At once this most feline of monarchs, to whom no flattery could be too gross, began to purr before 'giuing sir *Thomas* his hand to kisse and bestowinge the like grace vpon all the Gentlem. that were for the voyage'.[12]

Although the embassy was to achieve less than had been hoped, it was of value for rehabilitating Smythe – a return to grace that came to be noted in the published narrative:

but as if our Ambas. were againe in the *Tovver of London*, as he is in the ship: now tost, then becaulmed: in feare and hope within one moment, wher sometime God *Neptune* like a Prince, will haue his subiects know his force, and feele his rigor . . . but as God brought him out with much honor and praise, onely by the benefit of patience, clothed in Innocency, so shall I by the help of God, deliuer our selues safely at our Port and han[v]en.[13]

Though direct accounts of Smythe's first audience with Godunov have not survived, Moscow set much store by his arrival.[14] As for Smythe himself, he suggested how seriously his hosts took him when he told his minder Salisbury how he had been met 'with diverse messengers, who bought orders for my easy passage and supplies for my journey'. As he made his way from Archangel, he went on to report: 'At my coming near the Mosco diverse dukes and noblemen and at least 5000 men on horseback were sent to bring me into the city, who conducted me to my lodging, the fairest house in all the Musco.'[15] Upon arrival, protocol demanded a dignified interval before the emperor deigned to receive his visitors. Eight days passed before Smythe 'was sent for to the Emperor's presence, who sat in great state in a throne of gold with his imperial crown on his head, his sceptre in his hand and many other ornaments of state'.[16] Despite the formality that Smythe had been strictly enjoined he should maintain, a man could have much fun in Moscow.

Carousing apart, there was the serious business of having to counter the Dutch who were now infringing an English monopoly of trade between Russia and Europe. Could that special privilege be retrieved and the Dutch pushed back across the Neva? To please the tsar and annoy the Dutch, a state-of-the-art coach in kit form was put together before presentation to Godunov. Thrilled to be driving around Moscow all wrapped up in fur, the emperor at once warmed to his visitors.[17]

What did this bode for the Muscovy Company? Smythe was only able to obtain freedom from taxation and permission to trade within old Russia, not within the south-eastern perimeter where it had been hoped lucrative cross-border deals with Persia could have been hammered out. As critical of the ignorance of Russian officials as he was contemptuous of their negotiating skills, Smythe was just preparing for home when news came through that Godunov had died. This brought scant benefit when Godunov's successor, Feodor II, had only just enough time to float new concessions before being strangled.

The embassy to Moscow had drawn Smythe close to the Salisbury orbit, and so it was to Salisbury Smythe first wrote when 'being returned out of Russia, I could not omit the first opportunity [of] my service as the best acknowledgement I can make for your favours; and to entreat your directions concerning my coming to the Court to attend the King, with an account of my service or a conclusion of this employment'.[18] What Smythe had achieved in 'Mosco' was sufficient to get him re-elected as governor of the East India Company in 1607. As we have seen, Smythe had been first elected to the top job when the EIC had been founded in 1600, but had then been forced to resign at the time of the Essex rebellion the next year. Now back in charge in 1607, this was an appointment that would last fourteen more years. From election day onwards there was much to do.

Underfunding of the Company was a serious problem. The first voyages had shown that investment could not be sustained when Adventurers took their money away after a single voyage, meaning that everything had had to start again whenever a new voyage needed to be mustered. Joint-stock financing was now required because the Court of Committees had come to think it better to issue dividends at those times that were best for Company profitability than be required to disgorge at the demand of the Adventurers. As it was, the prevailing system encouraged unpredictability as it discouraged growth. Furthermore, such a process, ordered by Adventurers, not the Court of Committees, militated against forward planning. A Company failure to build up reserves demanded too much attendance on the money-lenders of Cheapside, now offering rates way in excess of what could be obtained on the Amsterdam money market.[19]

Buttonholing one director here, dining another there, Smythe garnered sufficient support to have it agreed that single-voyage investment be replaced by medium-term joint-stock financing. Here Smythe was merely following what had long been the practice in the Muscovy Company. Although such a move was decisive to the financial viability of the EIC, it was certainly not a reform that Smythe had thought up for himself. Furthermore, it would not be until Cromwell was to put things on a quite new footing for the Company in 1657, with his granting of a new charter, that permanent joint-stock funding came in. Nevertheless, such a change as Smythe negotiated in 1613 meant that henceforth the Court of Committees could make decisions with a capital sum disposable over several years and not as hitherto, when all depended on what could be scraped together year on year. This new system had other advantages. It meant wresting control from the General Court or, in other words, the full congregation of the Adventurers. From when this new system was adopted in 1613, control and deployment were more strongly in the hands of the twenty-four members of the Court of Committees. Henceforth, it would not only be possible to conceal the dire state of finances from the Adventurers, but also put increasing focus on strategies of investment rather than the ducking and weaving required of Thomas Mun in hoodwinking the ordinary members of the Company. However, discounting short-termism in this way meant that interest owed to Adventurers might not be returned for seven years, even when the amount of capital any one of them might be willing to release could be as much as £14,000. London was awash with money, and that would save the Company from disaster.

Important changes that Smythe pushed through allowed the Company to manage the savage recession that would start in 1618. Prior to this, the adoption of joint-stock financing had the gratifying effect of clustering power into the hands of the Court of Committees, and from 1613 it was able to take a much tighter grip. But if that solved some problems, it exacerbated others. From the first, the more paranoid had sustained marked hostility towards the Court. Rightly enough, Adventurers always felt that vital information was being withheld. Their only redress was to go to the press, and this in turn generated much damaging publicity about what the Company's critics regarded as malfeasance.

Of these published assaults the most damaging was a pamphlet written by Robert Kayll. Printed by Nicholas Okes and issued in London in 1615, *The trades increase* was a defence of the home fishing industry and an attack on the East India Company. Too many resources were being directed at the East Indies, so Kayll claimed, where profits were nugatory and effort damaging. Instead of all that, so Kayll argued, London should be doing much more to protect the English fishing and whaling industries from incursions by the Dutch who were giving the men of Hull a hard time whilst disputing the rights of English whalers at Spitsbergen. According to the arguments that

Kayll deployed, protection for the fishing industry was more patriotic than sailing to the East Indies. It put food in the mouths of the poor instead of silk on the backs of the rich.

The title that Kayll had chosen referred to the loss on its maiden voyage of the most expensive ship the Company had ever built. Also named the *Trade's Increase*, this stricken vessel had subsequently come to stand as a symbol for what the country suffered in suffering the Company. As for Smythe, he took the whole thing very personally. Incandescent about Kayll's claims, he had the offending article sent over to Abbot who in his capacity as archbishop had the unenviable job of scanning publications for the presence of either treason or heresy. Abbot thought 'it should rather be suffered to die than be suppressed, which would cause many men to seek after it the more earnestly, but promising a warrant to that effect if the Governor desired it'.[20] That the suppression of the pamphlet may not have been the best way was clearly Abbot's thinking; but most Adventurers thought its author should be punished, 'and thereby discover the dislike the State hath to such pamphlets that shall tax what the State hath approved'.[21]

At this point Sir Francis Bacon was brought in for a second opinion in his capacity as Attorney General. By temperament one for much order and no argument when it came to protecting the status quo, Bacon thought it 'very near to treason and all the rest very dangerous'.[22] But why was this pamphlet so contentious? Because Kayll said the only way to change things was to stand society on its head. By this time the entire Establishment had a stake in the East India Company, and so it followed that a wholesale attack on how things were run at the Company was more than a critique of big business. This was a root-and-branch attack on the governing class as a whole, as a passage from the pamphlet itself serves to suggest:

The East India men, not able to furnish those places they resort to, keepe out other from comming amongst them, and to looke into those parts they know not, and would giue out of their largenesse and riches, entertainment to all the Marchants in the Land. Besides, how tedious and costly they, and all other Companies, make it to their own Associates, when as out of orders, and cause of their vpholding their Trade, men can neither dispose of their owne as they would, nor haue the benefite vnder a long time.[23]

105

As for Kayll, nothing is known about him beyond the fact that he recanted his views under pressure, confessing the errors of his ways and the impertinence of his views. Wholly untraceable otherwise, he is to be found neither in the Company's records nor on the high street. Smythe himself managed to push back, convincing the economist and his fellow ambassador to Russia Sir Dudley Digges (d. 1639) to publish a riposte. Entitled *The defence of trade* (1615), Digges protested not so much at Kayll himself, but at any imputation that Digges's own arguments were not backed up by the statistics. In his postscript, Digges assures fellow Adventurers that what he writes he researches:

> Reader, It may please you then to know that the substance of this which you have read, was taken out of Customes-bookes, out of the East-India Companies bookes, out of Grocers, Warehouse-keepers, Marchants bookes and conference with men of best experience. As for errors of pen or presse, you will either not mark them or can mend them; all I aske for my paines. And so I leave you to commend (if you list) piperi et scombris that Trades Increase to packe up fish and this Defence of Trade to wrappe up spice: a couple of Inke-wasting toies [toils] indeed, that if my heartie wishes could haue wrought it, should haue seene noother light then the fire. So farre from the ambition of your acquaintance was D.D.[24]

Books could be dangerous things in those days. But this was not always the case: Smythe and fellow members of the Court of Committees were often gracious in allowing their admirers to dedicate offerings to themselves. Though not a bookish man himself, Smythe never doubted the power of print, as it was refracted to fallen men through the word of the Lord himself. For instance, he took a special interest in a certain 'Doctor Wood' whose book 'for the comfort of navigators and such as shall travaile by sea' Wood dedicated to the Company, with Smythe commending it as a 'very good work'.[25] Its title is worth citing in full since it gives a sense in which Smythe and his godly brethren felt that a voyage was not only a quest for spices, but a spiritual renewal: *The trve honour of navigation and navigators; or, Holy Meditations for sea-men. Written vpon our Sauiour Christ his voyage by sea . . . whereunto are added certaine formes of prayers for sea trauellers, suited to the former meditations, vpon the seuerall occasions that fall at sea* (1618). This pious offering Wood dedicated not only to Smythe but also to 'all the rest of the Honorable and worthie aduenturers of the same Societie'.

Elaborate, pompous even, such a dedication supports the view that these merchant princes took seriously the business of looking after the spiritual welfare of the whole company. No less satisfactory than Wood's godly animadversions on the hazards of life at sea was how Wood's own printer, Felix Kingston, keen on becoming an Adventurer himself, had offered the Company 1,000 copies 'of the said book for his freedom'. As for the author, he netted 20 *jacobus* for his pains, not only for producing the book in the first place, but also for taking himself off to Blackford where, climbing aboard ships 'waiting to fall down to Gravesend this week', and so from there out to the Downs and on to India, the good doctor shouted into the wind about the ways of God to mariners.[26] The printer, Felix Kingston, had his offer accepted and so he became an Adventurer, 'By service or otherwise' as the column against his name states. But what other names surrounded his? Under this year of '1618' alone, and Kingston was accepted on 9 January, there is such a galaxy of talent as suggests that the Company had become the dominant commercial force in England less than twenty years since its foundation. In this same year, and coming in as new Adventurers, were the prince of Wales and his solicitor; Sir Julius Caesar, Chancellor of the Exchequer; Sir Francis Bacon, Attorney General; Sir Edwin Sandys, great parliamentary man and greater opponent of Smythe as treasurer of the Virginia Company, a position he had held since its foundation in 1607; the philosopher Thomas Hobbes, whose witness to the fight between Smythe and Sandys over control of the Virginia Company had been quite enough to make Hobbes himself begin to think that life was indeed 'nasty, brutish and short'. Beyond these were William Trumbull, English agent to the archducal court in Brussels; Dr Theophilus Field, the king's chaplain; Bodley's librarian; and Lionel Cranfield, now earl of Middlesex, who some years before had enabled Smythe to become embedded as a significant landowner and Kent notable when he had sold him the fat lands of Sutton-at-Hone.

For Smythe himself, suppressing bad publicity was one thing, disappointing suitors another. He was afraid of no one, courtier or king. Repeatedly refusing James I's request to join the Company, Smythe also rebuffed the earl of Northampton (d. 1614), who was not only a minister in the highest favour with the king, but also someone who had been instrumental in

Smythe's rehabilitation after the Essex rebellion. It became intimated that Northampton, too, wished Smythe to encourage one of Northampton's creatures, a Captain Harris, only for Northampton to receive Smythe's masterly retort: 'the Company expect a man qualified for such a place to be partly a navigator, partly a merchant, with knowledge to lade a ship, and partly a man of fashion and good respect'. Now this was too much even for the best of CVs, and everyone knew it. But then what was Northampton to do? Captain Harris would eventually be employed, but only in Smythe's good time. The point is this: recruitment to the Company was largely on merit, not contacts. This vital distinction Smythe flagged up with a note on file that reads thus: 'this answer was hoped to be a good means to urge against him or any others of his rank or condition who may be pressed upon them'.[27]

So what did Smythe make of St Stephen's Hall, when as an MP and chief spokesman in Parliament for the City he went there to defend what many regarded as the indefensible?[28] Although Smythe would represent no fewer than four constituencies, and so was in the Commons over many years, he was regarded as a good committee man but no orator.[29] Assiduous over the detail, Smythe was dogged, too, in facing down James I when the two confronted one another in the Presence Chamber. They had endless rows about money, but in largely resisting his sovereign's demands for a gift here or a loan there Smythe rendered his Company a capital service. Before recession set in as from 1618, the Company had been alluringly profitable. Just how much money was being made was reported by London's leading newsmonger: 'The goode return of our East Indian ships hath put such life in that trade, that our marchants mean to go roundly to worke, and in lesse then a fortnight have underwritten for fowre hundred thousand pounds to be employed in that voyage in fowre yeares by equall portions; by which means yf they and the Hollanders can agree, they are like enough to ingrosse the whole trade of those partes.'[30] But the king, though he could see the critical importance of solvency and even the reform of royal finances, was temperamentally disqualified from encouraging the conditions that made such a happy outcome possible.[31] Indeed, by July 1615 Crown debt stood at £700,000, which prompted the Secretary of State Sir Ralph Winwood to declare 'the confusion and dissolucion of the monarchy yf there be not a p[re]sent remedye'.[32] And so it was that the king's men resorted to mounting smash-and-grab raids that it fell to Smythe to foil. The Lord Treasurer might be ushered into the boardroom of Smythe House, where so many early meetings were held. There he would advise the Court of Committees how it might be in their best interests if they could see their way to a donation now or, if they preferred, a loan on ruinous terms later. Smythe performed stoutly in fending off such attempts to steal the money, though he paid a price for that.

When the Crown found itself unable to squeeze the City, it turned to other stratagems. Of these, privateering was the most notable. Privateers formed syndicates that might rig out a small flotilla to challenge the Company in the waters around the Middle East and India. Such things were never a direct threat to Company voyages, if only because privateers could not take on the Company's much more heavily armed ships. Instead they fell upon the defenceless Indian merchants who were customers and partners of the Company. When complaints were duly made to the authorities by these understandably aggrieved Indians, blame inevitably fell on the Company – and the consequent sanctions were burdensome.

First cousin to the privateer was the pirate. Travelling around coastal waters could mean the unwelcome appearance of any number of Captain Hooks. The problem had become especially acute when the pirate Henry Salkeld declared himself king of Lundy, from whence he would sally forth to rob merchantmen bound for Newfoundland out of Bristol. But once Salkeld had been thrown overboard by his friend and fellow pirate Peter Easton, the island became both an Islamic republic and a nest of Barbary pirates. Violence and disruption spreading thereafter, the Crown struggled to suppress these desperadoes from appearing in home waters. Bristol could offer little to help, though its plea of poverty was hardly consistent with a port that had played so important a role in maritime exploration. As one party after another fell away, James became furious, rounding on Smythe to tell him that the City was holding back over the king's bill for policing. This came to the tidy sum of £7,554 15s. Smythe could only assure an irate James that he had done his best: 'The Merchant Adventurers owe £1000 but beg that £700 may be taken in gunpowder, bought by them for service to the state. The Muscovy Company owe £1000 but allege poverty. The Turkish and Spanish Companies owe nearly £6,000. The French Company owe £1,100 but excuse themselves on account of the troubles in France. The Trinity House plead that the Council remitted them £1000 and have paid the remainder.'[33]

If there were pirates at sea there was mutiny in the docks. These centred on the Company's operations at Blackwall in the early summer of 1619. The unrest was watched carefully by the City because the Company was the biggest employer in London and who knew where it would stop? Two to three hundred carpenters of the King's Yard, together with others from the Company's own premises at Deptford, violently took hold of the apprentices and marched them out of the yards 'with a drum stick before them'.[34] However, during the disruption Smythe was notable for listening to the men's grievances. What may be thought of as his paternalism, which it seems he deployed with good effect on this occasion, became something the Court of Committees was to sustain even when the business started to be far less profitable: 'The EIC stuck doggedly to upholding the interests of its labor force long after the business case had ceased.'[35] Notwithstanding good labour relations, the financial pressures induced by the 1618 depression, something that may have provoked the crisis in the summer of 1619, may also have been the catalyst for *The Lawes or Standing Orders of the East India Company* (1621). This was basically the Company rule book, and fascinating it is too for anyone wanting to know how things worked, or at least were supposed to work.

The *Lawes* runs to 82 pages and 335 clauses. No clause is muddled, no problem disregarded, with clarity at a premium and precision foregrounded: all this and more in a book in which no one from the Court of Committees to a caulker could be in any doubt as to when they were transgressing regulations. Henceforth, none was to be trusted because all were required to be their brother's keeper. It was one thing to encourage the master to welch on the gunner, but every paper was now going to require two signatures, with every law bound with the twist and twine of regulation. Everything puts a premium on efficiency and avoidance of duplication. For example, the Master of Timber and Plank is instructed to see 'the said Timber, Plank, and Boards, [be] lodged in the most convenient places of the Yard near their use, laying the straight Timber, Beam timber, Floor timber, Phittocks, Squire knees, Racking knees, and the several sorts of Planks by themselves, to avoid the great labour and charge, which hath bin heretofore in the often removings of the said Materials in the occasions of their use, when they were mingled all together'.[36]

The challenge was to ensure supplies arrived in one piece and in the correct quantity. The gathering of wood from Ireland, canvas from Normandy, iron from Spain, cordage from the Baltic suggests how logistics were as complicated in Deptford as at a car plant in Cowley today. An attempt was made to stop planks dropping off a barge by branding each piece with 'a number near the Mark, or at both ends of every piece of Timber, Plank, boards, and the like'. As for the larger issue of design, shipwrights 'bring in convenient time unto the said *Court of Committees* his Plots and Models compleat, of all the new Ships which are intended to be by him builded for the Company'.[37]

The *Lawes* stipulated how quarter-masters and boatswains be 'daily present in the Ships hold . . . and that the boatswain, gunner, cook, steward, carpenter, and other officers, do attend in the ships, to receive and take charge of their several stores for the voyage, and to give a true account . . . unto the Purser'.[38] Most dangerous to profits, though, was the haemorrhage that occurred at unpacking; a time when the 'Committees for Discharge of the Companies Ships' needed to be warned about preparing 'strong and good padlocks (of their own choosing) with which they shall lock the Hold carefully, when they retire to Dinner, and when they give over the work at night, always commanding the Porters and others to be searched, when they come out of the Hold, to prevent such deceit, as they might use by secret conveyance of wares, in their breeches, or otherwise'.[39] Further caution was urged when full discharge was granted, officers of these 'lawes' being required to 'diligently . . . search, that nothing do remain between the ceilings, or in any other place of secret conveyance';[40] though they did make the concession that every man be allowed a small chest in which he was free to pack goods not included on the list of prohibition.

What needed most scrutiny, however, was the account books. These were required to be kept 'diligently' and in a place 'fit for purpose', so all could inspect them. As for those judged incompetent, bad accountants were condemned along with the 'common drunkard', 'notorious gamester', 'whoremaster' and 'wronger' by 'private trade'. Anyone demonstrating neither remorse nor reformation was to be shipped back 'so the Company may proceed against them, according to the quality of their offence'.[41]

By the time that Smythe had got on top of Blackwall, he was beginning to tire with running the Company. From now on things started to slip as his grip began to slide. Long years of complacency running the Virginia Company had provoked its nemesis. Smythe had been in charge since the foundation of Virginia in 1607, but in 1618 his downfall had come about as a result of the machinations of the dashing earl of Warwick and co-conspirators. They had prompted disgruntled shareholders into believing that all the time Smythe had been running Virginia he had been asset-stripping: he was accused of channelling funds into marketing and away from the sort of investment, it was argued, the returns from which might have been more to the advantage of settlers. That said, these same critics were prepared to concede that such immediate gains as might have been forthcoming had their approach been adopted were likely to have been nugatory. Nevertheless, Smythe was removed and someone else was put in his place. It was a rare humiliation, but one that was to be followed by mutterings about how he was handling the East India Company.

Despite all the troubles of Virginia, Smythe still continued to have his triumphs. In the spring of 1618 he was to raise a loan that opened up the possibility of much-expanded trade relations with Russia. With this he was able to congratulate himself on having pulled off a deal no one else could have orchestrated. As governor of both the Muscovy and the East India Companies, he had contrived a float of what was reported to have been £10,000 to Tsar Michael (d. 1645), who needed money for reconstruction after Poland had occupied Moscow and threatened the future of the Romanovs.[42] The loan was especially attractive to Smythe's colleagues in both Companies because thereby 'they hope to ingrosse that trade of cordage as of many other reall commodities, besides the hope of a trade into Persia that way'.[43] At the end of January 1618 it was reported how the East India Company had set out a fleet of nine ships of 'great burthen' and was now showing itself 'stronger than ever'. If now a viable trade between Moscow and India via the Caspian could be built, then that in itself would be the most tremendous fillip to the Company.

Something that represented the killing off of what had been in some senses both an external and an internal threat was a settlement with the Scots which occurred around this same time. A patent had been granted to Sir James Cunningham with rights which not only represented a Scottish rival to an English East India Company but something more than that.[44] The worrying thing for Smythe was that Cunningham was not going to be confined to

Scotland. The patent expressly stated how Cunningham would be allowed 'to set fourth schippis or veschelllis out of anie poirt harbry or hevin within or belonging to any of his majestes kingdoms'.[45] Such a threat had, however, been welcomed by James I for the leverage it might represent when the Crown wished not only to extract money from the EIC but to persuade them to lend it to a third party. But then it came to be reported to Sir Dudley Carleton, who was at the time English ambassador to the United Provinces, how:

> Our East Indian fleet is setting out and some of them gon down to Gravesend. They go stronger and more then ever heretofore, beeing nine goode ships and of great burden, three or fowre of them new built . . . The King hath geven a patent to one Sir James Cunningham a Scottish knight to raise an East Indian companie there, whereof he and his heyres are to be Governors, and none to be admitted but by his and theyre approbation. They have libertie to trade into the East and West Indies, Turkie, Muscovie, Greenland or to any other place alredy discovered or to be discovered: they may furnish themselves of shipping, mariners, vitayle or anything els they need in any port of England, where all officers are to assist them, as likewise they may vent theyre commodities here, and that which in the reading yt seemed to me most strange that not only Scots, but English or any other stranger may be admitted into this societie, and yt must be called and accounted the Scottish Companie, with a number of other large privileges, which do directly infringe former graunts, and crosse the whole course of our trafficke. But the best is they do only yet make a noise and shew, and seek all over for partners and adventurers which come slowly in, and as I heare wold faine compound and sell theyre rights and interest to the East Indian Companie.[46]

What was reported was performed and the Scots were indeed bought off. The encouragement James had given his compatriot had been a way of putting pressure on Smythe and the Court of Committees. Certain it is that to have allowed matters to have got thus far when the attorney general could have told James the Cunningham licence was entirely contrary to the terms of the East India English Company charter was wholly characteristic of how James I could never stick either to the law or a bargain.

Conceivably James had too, encouraged the whole project in order to manoeuvre Smythe into coordinating the work of the East India and Muscovy companies in making that critical loan to Russia. Subsequently James then removed the threat of a 'Scottish' company once rials became roubles. In other words, the Scottish idea had been a means to threaten Smythe over the Russian loan whilst the cancellation of the Scottish patent was Smythe's 'reward' for putting through on an aspect of James's foreign policy. Although the Scottish idea had been short-lived, Adventurers had been rightly concerned about how the threat of a patent patently threatened their interests.

No sooner was the Russian situation settled than Smythe began negotiations with the Dutch to see whether a better trade deal could be managed, after numerous previous attempts had served merely to create rancorous discord. On 19 April 1619 it was reported that there had been a great feast 'to your States and other Commissioners here at Merchant Taylors' Hall for a farewell; the artillery have also given them a great supper, with a warlike dance or mask of twelve men in complete armour'.[47]

All this was followed by congratulations to the king for the part that people were expected to believe James himself had played in bringing the two parties together: 'The King has dissolved the difficulties of the East India business, and by his own wisdom and authority brought them to an accord.'[48] Such delusions were entirely characteristic: here was one who alone regarded himself as the broker of peace in Europe. Soon enough, however, widespread anger greeted the realisation that Amsterdam had done much better than London. This caused short-term damage to the morale of the Company, but permanent eclipse for Smythe. A sense of despair at how the Company had been sold down the Thames by the king was palpable:

> but say what they can, things are passed as the other wold have yt, which makes the world suspect that they [the Dutch] have found great frends and made much use of theyre wicked mammon. Our men shall never have like meanes and advantage to bring them to reason as they had now, both in regard that we are sought to combine either with the Portugale, French and Dane, as also and that specially, that our marchants were generally animated and thoroughly resolved to set up theyre whole rest

upon yt, which was never so great nor perhaps will easilie be again, now the opportunitie is lost and the heat cooled.[49]

Smythe's critics grew bolder, though enemies could do nothing whilst he had the support of the king. Furthermore, was it now really time to change the pilot when the Company had not yet emerged from the pitch and toss of a major economic recession? 'The East India Company with some difficulty have chosen Sir Thomas Smythe their Governor this year. The King sent them word it was not fit to remove him, now that he had taken so great pains in the treaty, and that the Articles had been ratified under his hand as Governor.'[50] Pains or not, there had been a maritime disaster over which Smythe had presided and from which his reputation never really recovered. Not since Henry VIII had watched the *Mary Rose* sink in front of his eyes in 1545 had there been anything like this.

What happened took place in the Thames, not Portsmouth harbour, as with the *Mary Rose*. The merchantman *Anne Royal*, with a burden of 900 tons, was coming up the river from India when she sank with a cargo worth £16,000. The tragedy occurred at Gravesend, appropriate it may be thought, given the loss of life resulting. It was the worst public relations challenge Smythe had faced in what was now becoming a decidedly over-long career with the Company. The 'disaster', as the Minutes described this sinking, provoked a massive salvage operation. No fewer than a thousand men were deployed at £100 a day to fish things up. It was hopeless. After fruitless weeks it came to be suggested they simply cut 'her in pieces' and save what they could by 'morsels'. As a result of such a massive embarrassment, 'factions and jars among themselves, have much impaired the reputation of the Company'.[51] In a real sense Smythe went down with the *Anne Royal*.

And yet he was the great survivor too: he had been thrown in the Tower before he had been thrown out of the Virginia Company, but here he was still. And what was more, he certainly wasn't going to give up yet. That said, his popularity was haemorrhaging. At the elections for the upcoming year of 1620–1, indeed, he was only able to continue because it was made known that James would take it in ill part should he be removed. And so it was that the king could only squeeze not ease Smythe into the chair by leaning on the electors. Things had not been looking good when a courier came into the meeting with an express stating with studied euphemism, if rare tact, how His Majesty did not 'wish' the Company to 'alter their officers and committees'.

What was clearly a tricky meeting was reported on by Lord Egerton after he returned home. He began by mentioning how someone had threatened them all with a ballot box. Dismissing this as some 'kind of lottery', he was then mightily relieved to be able to report how that extremely bad idea had been circumvented by Lords Southampton and Digby, together with Sir Thomas Edmondes, commissioner with the Dutch, Lord Sandys and Dudley Digges who had of course done his own part in seeing off the wild democrats when he had attempted to rebut that scandalous pamphlet which Robert Kyall had had the sauce to publish. Such a mustering of some of the biggest guns on deck worked. For the moment at least no more was to be heard of such a thing as a 'ballot'. Moving on, Egerton related how matters then progressed. The king 'delighted not in change of his ancient Officers':

he was now an old king and loved not to have new faces repair unto him (insinuating after a sort his Mates asserted[tion] unto Sir Tho. Smyth) and besides, that there were now new deputies and commissioners either come or coming out for the States to make a final commission about their traffick into those partes, which with commissioners and business their old Officers are best acquainted and most expert, and therefore his matie without prejudice to their free election thought they should do well to continue them for this one year. This speech was seconded by Sir Thomas Edmondes and Sir Dudley Digges a very [word indecipherable] and well-spoken gentleman. This request (as it were) of his Majesty seemed very reasonable (as I thought in the ears of the most reasonable and greatest number of the Assembly which was great so that when it came to hands it was carried clear). By which Sir Thomas Smythe for this year: and for the next year Alderman Hallyday is chosen.[52]

Such manoeuvrings clearly did the trick; if only for the last time. Royal intervention would not have worked thereafter, and it would not be tried again. In July 1621 the old clam would be duly winkled off the hull, as Chamberlain was to report to Carleton, who as the English ambassador at The Hague had the closest interest in what was happening in London: 'Sir Thomas Smythe was at last removed from his warme' seat of beeing so long governor of the East India companie.'[53] It would seem that he went not a moment too soon. Four months later and it was being reported how a man might 'guess the state they are in and how sound at heart (for all our fair shows) when neither lord mayor, aldermen, farmers, no, nor whole companies, as the East Indian, Muscovy, and others, are able to hold out and pay their debts'.[54]

Although Smythe formally retired in July 1621, he never left the Company. A consultant thereafter, he calmed things down when disgruntled Adventurers started to make their usual fuss about how the Court of Committees had cheated them. Now working at arm's length, Smythe began spending more time promoting the charities his maternal grandfather, Sir Andrew Judde, had founded all over London and Kent. Remembering family and friends in his will, Smythe ordained that there should be a tripartite division of his immense wealth: one part for his wife, another for his son Sir John, 'in regard that neither before nor since his marriage he hath not been advanced by me', and the third divided into a score of *remembrancia* – so much money given to friends to buy 'memorial rings' as might have caused a hike in the London metals market.[55]

Smythe remembered the great companies, though it was the Muscovy not the East India that was treated most generously, not only 'because they have testified their love to me many years' but also because it had been his first great business success. It received £500. As for the EIC, Sir Maurice Abbot, Smythe's deputy since 1614, received £5 and Smythe's treasurer £3. The twenty-four Committees received 40s apiece, with the proviso they hurry off to have yet more rings made. Virginia and Bermuda came by £100 each to build a church in each colony. The four ancient hospitals fared thus: St Bartholomew's £40, and Bridewell, Christ's Hospital and St Thomas's £20 each. Sir Thomas Roe, Company ambassador to India, and John Woodall, surgeon-general of the same, are the only others mentioned by name: 'I give to my assured good friend Sir Thomas Roe to make him a ring to wear for my sake the sum of ten pounds', whilst Woodall got the same but no testimonial. Looking to his end, Smythe declared how 'I would have my funeral without pomp or vain glory'.

Smythe was swept off by the plague in early September 1625. It had killed thousands as it had postponed the coronation through fear of contagion. Unlike fellow mogul Sir William Cockayne, himself to be remembered at Old St Paul's in a sermon composed by John Donne no less, Smythe's obsequies went unpublished if not unmarked.[56] His orbit was recalled, not in anthem or sermon, but in the silent stone of St John's church. Here is to be found Smythe's epitaph: unlike Donne's great sermon about Smythe's friend Cockayne, this alas is notable only for the jaunting allegro of cursive script and bathos of jejune sentiment. If the lines are weak, at the least they evoke that wise warning of the Caroline poet who admonishes those tempted to go out with a flourish to remember how:

> Poets that lasting marble seek
> Must carve in Latin or in Greek[57]

But if there was no swelling anthem by Bull, no periods out of Donne, there is a lively if hardly profound tribute to a life now stilled, a cosmology of ambition and a fable of achievement:

> To the glorie of God and to the pious memorie of the Honble. Sir Thomas Smith, Kt, late Governor of ye East Indian, Moscovia, French and Sommer iland companies; Treasurer for the Virginian plantation Prime Undertaker (in the year 1612) for that noble designe, the discoverie of the north-west passage; Principal commissioner for the London Expedition against ye Pirates and for a voiage to ye ryver Senega upon ye coast of Africa; one of ye cheefe commissioners for ye Nauie Roial, and sometyme ambassador from ye Matie. of Gr. Brit. to ye Emperour and Grand Duke of Russia and Muscovia etc. Who having judiciously conscionably and with admirable facility managed many difficult and weighty affairs to ye honour and profit of this nation, rested from his labour the 4th day of Septem. 1625, and his soul returning to him that gave it, his body was here laid up in ye hope of a blessed resurrection

> From those large Kingdomes where the sun doth rise,
> From that rich newe founde world that westward lies,
> From Volga to the flood of Amazons,
> From under both the Poles, on all the Zones,

From all the famous, ryvers, landes and seas,
Betwixt this place and our Antipodes,
He gott intelligence, what might be found,
to give contentment through the massie Round,
But finding earthly things did rather tire
His longing soul, the[a]n answer her desire,
To this obscured village he withdrew,
From hence his heavenlie voyage did persue
Here summed up all, and when his gale of breath
Had left becalmed in the port of Death
The soul's frail bark (and safelie landed her
Wher Faith his factor and his harbinger
Made place before) he did no doubte obtaine
That wealth which here on earth we seek in vaine

More elegant than persuasive, here lies the body of one who did not tire of discovering earthly things, a governor who never gave up bringing fruits to 'Britain's bourse' by virtue of his 'many difficult and weighty affairs'. The final word on Smythe can do no better than recall Samuel Johnson's remark of how 'in lapidary inscriptions a man is not upon oath'.[58] So now it is time to leave a country churchyard for a confined alley in the heart of the City, where in narrow Philpot Lane, Smythe worked to make the possibilities of English commerce unconfined. It is therefore to observe exactly how on a daily basis 'our honourable Smith ... at whose forge and anvil have been hammer'd so many irons for Neptune' spent his days at the office that we now turn.[59]

6

RUNNING THE OFFICE

The foundation of the East India Company was met with neither fanfare nor flourish. Not a stone survives of the house where first meetings began. It belonged to Smythe, and though no visual record survives it would have been very similar to Pindar House. This was constructed in 1599–1600 within the parish of Bishopsgate Without, on the site of what is now Liverpool Street station. A creation of wood and plaster, it once belonged to the great Turkey merchant Sir Paul Pindar. Today part of the house's façade totters precariously upon the disdainful marble of the Victoria and Albert Museum.

To make a pilgrimage to the site of Smythe House, emerge from Monument tube station, turn left and there it is – or would be if there was anything left to see. Such romance as may once have been found in a place with the less than romantic name of Philpot Lane is, however, now confined only to the most discreet of ceramic tiles. These bear the arms of the East India Company. Here too is what has been described somewhat preciously as 'London's tiniest sculpture': it is of two mice fighting over a hunk of cheese, just the sort of thing Smythe's mariners did on those early voyages. But the visitor to Philpot Lane must look in vain for a plaque telling where Sir Thomas was once domiciled. What is known, though, is how in 1600 the Lane was clustered with spires like candles on a birthday cake. Today, by contrast, it terminates in Starbucks and Vodafone. Smythe would surely have approved: the multinationals of our time provide caffeine and a WiFi signal, whereas in his day they offered pepper at home and contact across the world.

Smythe was appointed first governor of the Company on 31 December 1600. Although there would appear to have been some competition for the post, no one could match his business record. As was noted in Chapter 5, Smythe had managed the Muscovy Company very well; thus it was thought that his good work in hosting Russians might pay dividends when it came to Indians. If it proved difficult to get to Asia by sea, hope was held out that the subcontinent might yet be reached via the Caspian and the passes of the Hindu Kush. That had always been Smythe's patch.

But Smythe's knowledge of the wastes of Central Asia was by no means his only attractive quality. What trumped his familiarity with the tsar of Russia was how he had also cosied up to the sultan of Turkey. At the likelihood of trade relations opening with Persia, once the East India Company got going, it was thought that the secure position Smythe had established in the Levant Company by 1600 could prove essential. The Levant factories at Aleppo, Constantinople and Smyrna could surely become way stations for the caravanserais setting out for Isfahan, Kabul and beyond. Such thinking proved absolutely right. No one in 1600 knew what would happen when the EIC began to trade in India. However, if sales turned out to be only meagre to start with, then the influence Smythe could bring to bear in the Levant might allow the Middle East to subsidise the subcontinent until India could stand upon her own resources. The synergy between the Levant (est. 1592) and the East India (est. 1599–1600) companies was decisive for the success of both. As the leading historian of English commerce and British revolution has put it:

> The East India Company was founded in 1599, and was dominated by the Levant Company merchants, who saw the project as essential to maintaining an important segment of their old trade . . . Levant Company merchants composed more than one-third of those present at the first meeting of the new company in September 1599, and seven of the original fifteen directors elected at that meeting were Levant Company merchants. The first governor of the East India Company was the Levant Company governor Sir Thomas Smythe, and seven of the twenty-four directors (known as 'committees') chosen under the original charter of 31 December 1600 were also Levant Company directors. In addition, Levant Company members provided between one-fourth and one-third of the total fund, invested in the first, third and fourth joint stocks.[1]

Smythe was the most exceptional of businessmen, for his tireless energy and contacts as well as the shrewdness of his decisions. He was the boardroom chairman par excellence. In one important sense, however, there is nothing to show for it all. Although references to portraits abound, the only certain likeness now available is a dismal little engraving which has as much conviction as the King of Diamonds; though that of course might have been just what Smythe considered himself to have been. Frustratingly enough, once there were likenesses aplenty, things of sufficient quality to have impressed Emperor Jahāngīr (Mughal emperor of India 1605–27) who, looking upon himself as the world's leading connoisseur, was mighty pleased to hang a portrait of Sir Thomas because 'he esteemed [it] so well for the worksmanship'.[2] But if portraits of Smythe have gone, so have his letters; at least those of a confessional sort.[3] We are left instead with a *deus ex machina*: someone who seems today more machine than man. Did his papers go up in the Great Fire, which started 200 yards from his own front door? If so, that hardly explains his absence from the correspondence of others. Perhaps the weightier Smythe became the more invisible he grew as preferring to pluck the sleeve than grasp the quill. Yet in pursuit of the private life of so private a man, it can be established that he was a collector of the choicest rarities, living and dead. Though no inventory survives of his various properties in London or Kent, it is known that he possessed an Inuit kayak and a relative of Pocahontas. Whilst the last died of tuberculosis, the kayak remained suspended above the Court of Committees, mordant reminder of the vicissitudes of fortune in a sea of troubles.[4]

From the first, Smythe had much to do. The earliest meetings of the Company were divided between various livery company halls and Smythe's place in Philpot Lane. Although moving about when holding general meetings of shareholders was common enough with chartered companies, for example, the Levant was never to have somewhere it could call its own; such 'make-do' was very different from the commodious arrangements that prevailed from the first across the water and with the Dutch.[5] The Heren XVII had built themselves an Oost-Indisch Huis in Amsterdam, and mighty impressive it still is. Brindled like streaky bacon, the 'Huis' is as solid as a meat loaf and has been attributed to Hendrick de Keyser I (d. 1621), pre-eminent architect of the United Provinces. Finished in 1606, the Huis now houses one of Holland's most distinguished universities. But of the various places in the City where the first East India Company meetings were held, unquestionably the one most favoured was Crosby Place in Bishopsgate. This is described as having been 'one of the tallest, grandest houses in the older part of town, and with one of the largest walled gardens – it was at Crosby Place that Richard III had lodged in 1483 as he plotted to usurp the throne'.[6]

What mattered still more than where to hold annual elections were the perennial problems with storage. With the EIC, the lodging of bales and the security of spices was always to be an exercise in improvised chaos. Leadenhall Street had some offices and committee rooms, together with warehouses leased by the Company. Some personnel were accommodated within the Staplers' Company, though clerks were inconvenienced by those living in flats above and others leasing rooms as workshops. In August 1614 'Munden the Painter', coming into one of these warehouses, startled employees by grandly announcing how he had his eye on 'one or two' of the Company's spaces as being fittest 'for making and painting of the pageants'.[7] Having arrived on the lord mayor's behalf, he now demanded every facility for the important business of staging the lord mayor's annual show. This was all rather awkward, until someone suggested Munden take himself off to the Staplers' chapel, which seemed to double as a theatre. What belonged to the Company in Leadenhall Street was a hybrid of flats, offices, chapels, cafés and studios.

But somehow business was conducted and profits accrued. Lord mayors no less would compete against the candle for Japanese lacquer and Lahore carpets, Indian miniatures and Ming vases.[8] These auctions, sometimes conducted in Leadenhall Street, also took place at Smythe House. For example, the Company's ship *Consent*, reckoned worn out by going to Indonesia and back too often, was auctioned off in Smythe's Great Hall. Weighing in at a little over 100 tons, there it was knocked down for £195, 'furniture' thrown in.[9]

Leadenhall Street was one of London's most crowded thoroughfares, and it made no sense at all to have the place brought to a standstill by carters coming up from Blackwall loaded with the goods of a returned fleet. There were complaints by the Adventurers about how the precious things in which they had invested were lying about in heaps, and they also wondered whether properties stacked right across London should be given up in favour of a single purpose-built headquarters – everything contained under several roofs but crucially on one site. Storage facilities existed at Lord Compton's, though there was better space still at the Countess of Warwick's. As for Smythe, he was asked to pull rank at the Haberdashers whilst also leaning on the Skinners, in both cases so that they would provide space in the cellars under their halls. If, however, things became tricky with livery companies such as these, there was always Gresham's Royal Exchange where units were readily available to rent.[10] One way and another much time was wasted, with Company surveyors sent off to find a medium-term solution to logistics. For example, one such got excited by the earl of Craven's town house, described by those keen to take it as: 'a large building with Spacious Rooms, very commodious for such a purpose, having a large Hall and Court Yard for the reception of people having business here, to attend on the Company, on Court Days. There is also a little Garden with Warehouse at the back part towards Lime Street to bring the goods into the Warehouse.'[11]

Smythe may have owned the title deeds, but he was never master in his own house when the unwary found themselves somewhere that must have seemed to the biblically minded like the Tower of Babel and Noah's Ark rolled into one. Here was a resort for nations and a nest for animals. Sailors from five continents jostled the alderman who, picking his way through them, was all the time intent upon dodging the deserving widow there to beg for charity after her husband had 'drowned in service'. The smell, the noise, the crowd can only be imagined, with a dozen languages ululating against the shriek of a parrot and the laughter of monkeys. Despite the chaos, however, many Adventurers wished Sir Thomas might remain governor *in perpetuam*, if only the God Lord might allow such an outcome. Yet others were not pleased at all, feeling that 'Neptune' Smythe had far too many nets in the water to allow the steady attention that disgruntled investors felt the Company merited. This lot, and fortunately for Smythe they were never more than a minority, wished him gone, and what is more they often said so. Yet what Smythe's supporters liked was the calmness, the fearlessness and the independence their governor maintained in the face of those who were forever bearing down upon the Company.

Agendas at biweekly meetings of the Court of Committees were as varied as they were exhausting. Among a thousand questions, some appeared much harder to solve than others. How to identify those 'painful and laborious men' who might be relied upon to become godly chaplains was just one of the problems, and this was something Smythe spent infinite pains addressing. Who to choose was ticklish enough, especially when some candidates were deemed too young. Take Wilson of 'Brazenose Col. Oxford', of whom the appointments board felt 'especial exceptions were against his youth, and that he is too much in the fashion, whereas a man of a grave countenances is rather to be required, because it will be unsavoury to have a young man reprove ancient men, especially of such vices as may reign in themselves'.[12] Youth may have been an impediment but deceit was a snare. It was devilishly difficult to know if an applicant would provide a good example or, once exposed to the carnal lusts of the East, be found to be swimming in 'filthy lusts'.

The Reverend Mr Sturdivant was called upon to deliver a trial sermon before the Court of Committees. Upon this august occasion Smythe chose direction from the Beatitudes, wherein it is declared that 'Blessed be the poor in spirit'.[13] Was such a choice intended to encourage such fellow directors as may have been swollen with pride not to count on an inheritance in the next world? Whatever the truth, Sturdivant passed his exam. Once in India, however, it came to be reported how he had 'a straggling humour, [and] can frame himself to all company, as he finds men affected, and delighteth in tobacco and wine'.[14] Packed up with the indigo, Sturdivant was bundled off, never to be heard of again. Too often Smythe had a hard time persuading his factors to take all this seriously. The business of religious observance was a frail, tentative affair, which explains why the Company made only the most perfunctory attempts to convert the indigenous. What mattered far more than conversions to the men of Leadenhall Street was that their chaplains should never, but never, let the side down. At all costs they were not to bring Christianity into disrepute.

To Smythe, moral was more important than physical health. There is not one reference in his letters to health, hygiene or diet. For him it was soul not life that mattered, his abiding concern being to provide an answer to the psalmist's rhetoric: 'Wherewithal shall a young man cleanse his way?' And so it was he ordered ships' libraries be stocked with 'books of divinity for the soul, and history to instruct the mind'. Among these was Foxe's *Book of Martyrs*, which in vivid admonitory detail recounts the agonies of the blessed who had been martyred for their faith during the reign of Queen Mary. Not content with all this, Smythe became so vexed by the conduct of his factors that he set about admonishing all to be 'the more respective and shun all sin and evil behaviour, that the heathen may take no advantage to blaspheme our religion by the abuses and ungodly behaviour of our men'.[15] This went down very badly indeed. Here were employees obliged to live half the year like rabbits in a burrow to escape the heat and the other half drowning in a monsoon as impenetrable as chain mail. And in the places where these wretches lived, there were only the whore and the bottle to ease their pain.

Who were these factors for whose morals Smythe cared so much? Most going East discounted the enormous risks that such an odyssey must involve. After all, they mused, the lure of untold wealth was still more gigantic than the fear of an early death. A minority, though, signed on less for lucre than liberation, hoping to escape a restrictive economic system in England to reinvent themselves in India. Notwithstanding such chancers and their chances, those to whom these jobs went were well connected, well educated and well off; though rarely well balanced, it has to be said. Often brilliant linguists, ever fearless and always charged with energy, these men were not only endowed with libraries but were possessed of that amulet against despondency which was 'curiositie'. Intellectual ambition, something often met with in these first factors of the Company, was, it has been suggested, what makes the seventeenth century still more important for how we live now than the Renaissance itself.[16]

Take Richard Wickham from Bristol who was to sign up for the Company in 1607.[17] One of the ablest of the factors at the Company's house in Japan, Wickham was to die of the 'bloody flux' (dysentery) at Bantam in 1618. His post-mortem inventory is a remarkable document, including an astonishing £5,000–6,000 in cash, not counting the 933 rials that were lying around his study and bedroom.[18] As the accountants sniffed about, they identified one who had prospered mightily and, so it began to seem, at the expense of the Company. Of table silver, there were nine great basins, ewers, tankards, a great cup; one 'silver boat' and a small silver civet box – quite enough to furnish the grandest Indonesian table. But Wickham's first love was clothes, and upon these he spent freely: ash-coloured lace; a doublet with gold lace; an orange-coloured doublet with hose of satin trimmed by black lace; a black stripped satin suit; black satin suit cut upon yellow taffeta; and a striking white satin doublet. Also found were purple stockings trimmed with gold lace, together with a pair of scarlet hose trimmed with gold as could have been intended for a portrait when, home at last, Richard Wickham, the first of the nabobs, could begin that good life he had been planning after so many years spent defrauding the Company.

Wickham's possessions were divided West and East. Fifty-nine chests of books were sold at auction in Bantam in aid of Bristol Grammar School, though in rather more demand was a wardrobe of kimonos of different weights according to the season: green damask and one of 'changeable taffeta', a white damask creation lined with red taffeta and others besides. There was a gilt mirror to ensure the chapeau was at just the right angle, rugs, both white and yellow, a China quilt embroidered with silk and gold, another of damask carnation, two Japanese beds and two Macao-ware writing desks; these last were decorated with animals or plants in dusted gold on midnight black or Chinese red.[19] Wickham had always been mesmerised by the weaponry with which the Japanese cut a figure and often a belly: here a saddle, and there lances, a bow and arrow, a coat of mail. There were rubies and agates, pearls and diamonds, rough cut as well as 'sparks'. As the resolute mariner he had always been, Wickham possessed a fine collection of nautical instruments: astrolabe and Jacob's staff, five pairs of compasses, a semicircle and an equinoctial dial; surprisingly, though, there were no sea charts. Perhaps these had all got soaked on the *Sea Adventure*. This was a Chinese junk that the Company had bought and Wickham had commanded. Acquired to ply between Japan and Vietnam, but being something of a fish basket, it had made those whose job it was to stop her sinking think she spent more time under than on the water.

If we wish to get a surer sense of the sort of person Smythe chose to run things, it is as well to turn to one of the wealthiest of those who made up Bristol's caste – also a long-standing friend of Richard Wickham. This was John Whitson (d. 1629). John Aubrey, Whitson's godson and author of the celebrated *Brief Lives*, tells us how his godfather had acquired such a house in St Nicholas Street as Aubrey reckoned contained 'the stateliest dining room in the city'.[20] Seemingly built out of oranges, this had been erected with the wealth its proprietor had made trading with Spain. Within that banqueting chamber Whitson entertained lavishly, until, with spiritual indigestion drawing on, our immensely rich man was at last induced to meditate upon the vanities of this life. This he did by composing a valediction with the decidedly cheerless title *The Aged Christian's Final Farewell*. Here the some-time mayor of Bristol and MP for the same invites us to commiserate over the difficulties anyone must find with a soul weighed down by investments of £10,000.

Yet at the eleventh hour what Whitson had clearly enjoyed for the previous ten he now discounted as the 'idols of earthly minds'. Wealth, material splendour and charitable foundations: these were what characterised the lives of those who made it good out of overseas companies such as the EIC. Just as Sir Thomas Smythe's forebears, the Juddes had provided for half a dozen schools, so Whitson now did the same, though not, it must be said, on such a heroic scale. He left the residue of his vast estate for the foundation of the Red Maid's Hospital (est. 1634), not an institution for the reformation of prostitutes as might be supposed, but a charity dedicated to qualifying girls for what was then the lucrative Bristol marriage market.[21]

As for those 'idols of earthly minds' to which John Whitson refers, there were plenty of these to be truffled out of St Nicholas Street.[22] In the Great Hall hung a large map, though what it represented is not specified. If it were something of a cartographic biography, it must have been a vision of the world as it was understood in 1630. Whitson's web was France, Spain, the Mediterranean and America. In 1603 he had been a backer of the future East India captain Martin Pring who had made a celebrated excursion into Vermont, Maine and New Hampshire, accompanied by two ferocious mastiffs and groceries supplied by 'Kimono' Wickham – who before he was to disappear to Japan had been a retailer in Bristol.[23] Whitson's map complemented the 'two great pictures', three small pictures and two stags' heads that hung alongside it. But none matched the value of a pair of kinderkins described as 'of powdered sugar weighing nearer one hundred a quarter and twenty one pound'. In the Little Parlour was a 'drawing table', sideboard and two leather-backed chairs, whilst in the Upper Hall, conceivably a gallery above a screens passage, was a 'bone cabinet'. This was no ossuary but a *scrittoria* probably all the way from Goa. A table carpet, nine small pictures and books, 'some Latin, some English and one Spanish', finish the tally – enough to suggest that global merchants were men of real standing and passing sophistication.

This is certainly what Johan Albrecht de Mandelslo (d. 1644) thought, if he doesn't exactly spell it out. The first foreigner to take a look at a Company factory, Mandelslo was a guest of the East India Company who stayed at Surat in the 1630s. An impressionable twenty-four-year-old from Mecklenburg, Mandelslo had decided to head East, but finding himself marooned after missing the monsoon, threw himself upon the generosity of the principal English factory in Gujurat. Although no elevation survives of the entrepôt in Surat, at least from this earliest period in its existence, what Mandelslo describes suggests a cross between an Oxbridge college, a hotel and a warehouse.[24] At Surat Mandelslo was at once made welcome by its 'President', William Methwold (d. 1653), who certainly spoke Dutch and would surely have known some German. In any event Methwold was a firm believer that all Christians 'were obliged to assist one another', and so he made Mandelslo warmly welcome. Palepuntz was served to the assembled company before dinner: this toddy derived its name from a Bombay corruption of the English 'bowl of punch'. Consisting of aqua vitae, rose water, lemon juice and sugar, what Mandelslo has to say about it is the first known reference to the invention of that indispensable aid to civilised living, the cocktail.[25] After the aperitif, the factors proceeded into the great hall, where what followed may have been something of a challenge. Despite the heat, Methwold liked to keep 'a great Table of about fifteen or sixteen dishes of meat, besides the dessert'.[26] Afterwards, they all took the 'cool of the sea air' in an open gallery atop the roof. Here tea was on tap and *khan* (coffee) in the pot.

Divine service happened at six in the morning and eight at night, and no fewer than three times on a Sunday, a regimen as strenuous as was to be found in any Oxbridge chapel at that time. After Friday prayers a toast was drunk by three merchants to their absent wives, a touching gesture on the day that they had bidden their farewells. The 'fair garden without the City' was taken in after Sunday sermon. Here all had fun putting a fiver on seeing who was best at archery. Games over, there were fruit and preserves before everyone dunked themselves in a water tank, upon the lip of which perched 'some Dutch Gentlewomen who were there to serve and entertained us with much civility', though 'civility' did not extend to those extra services then being provided by Indian 'dancers' in the lesser English factories. From all that Mandelslo had to say, it was eminently civilised, though hardly conducted with such indulgence as would be enjoyed by Warren Hastings in eighteenth-century Bengal.

So much for the sort of animal the factor turned out to be. If back home, however, Smythe spent too much time trying to prepare morals for export, here he was alert to the need for a good R&D department. In this he proved notably successful. Smythe succeeded in recruiting the best mathematicians to ease, if they could never solve, the vexatious problem of longitude. This centred on the difficulty of knowing the angular distance on its meridian of any place on the earth's surface north or south of the equator. The failure to master the single greatest challenge to safe sailing caused Smythe to contribute towards the stipend of Edward Wright (d. 1615).

Wright may have been unsurpassed at plotting a course, but he was rather less conscientious with the accurate trajectory of his own life. Autobiographical passages are filleted into the life of his patron, that extraordinary man George Clifford, earl of Cumberland. Described as 'the rudest Earll by reason of his northerly bringen up', such a disadvantage was more than compensated for by his being one of 'great personal beauty, splendid in dress and of romantic valour', all of which is true in Cumberland's portrait in miniature by Hilliard. The best that was to be said by his contemporaries about this roistering man is what is to be found in Wright's important contribution to safer sailing: his celebrated *Certaine Errors in Navigation* (1599). As a mathematician, Wright certainly owed much to the patronage of Cumberland, something he readily acknowledges in the *Epistle Dedicatorie* that fronts the Preface to his *Certaine Errors*. Here Wright pays fulsome tribute to one whose own life was to prove something of a gyroscope. This Wright does by informing his reader of how it was through Cumberland's largesse that his work had first been promoted: 'Right Honourable, and my very good Lord, being first induced, by occasion of your Lordship's imployment of me at sea, to apply my Mathematicall studies to the vse of Nauigation I thought, these first fruits of those my sea-labours, could not bee more justly due to any, then to your self: as by whose beneficiall hand, they haue been chiefly cherished, to growe.'[27] His other claims, as having nothing to do with mathematics and navigation, need to be read with some scepticism.

What is certain, though, is that Wright was a Fellow of Caius College, Cambridge (resigned 1595). There he had passed his days in circumnavigating the courts until, with the onset of a sabbatical, he was looked for in vain within its chained library, having, he tells us himself, thrown off his own chains to reinvent himself as 'Captain Carelesse' – taking off in 1589 with Cumberland in order to harry the Spanish main. Such fellowship in arms had come about from their shared delight in mathematics that the two had discovered as students. If maths can hardly be thought a qualification for shooting a Spaniard, their time at sea now proved the highest of adventures. Soon enough, however, they parted, amicably enough – Cumberland to try to sink massive debts in the sea during what would turn out to be his woefully unsuccessful career as a privateer, whilst Wright, returning to Cambridge, came to experience the difference between guns on the high seas and gossip on a high table.

Abandoning cannon for calculation, Wright reverted to teaching, though after the resignation of his Caius fellowship in 1595 his students were no longer undergraduates but captains, who found squeezing into a lecture room rather more taxing than sailing across a bar. If these lessons were tough for them, they were liberating for Wright. As for Wright's most celebrated book, his *Certaine Errors*, this made Mercator's work much more accessible to those who were navigators not mathematicians, for example, over the crucial business of how to establish an accurate straight-line course. A side effect of what Wright did in taking the work of Pedro Nunes and Mercator into the practical sphere was how all of this led to corrections to charts, compasses and cross-staffs.[28]

Having returned to land and respectability, matters were set in readiness for Wright to enjoy a distinguished public career following his appointment as mathematics tutor and librarian to the prince of Wales. All was frustrated, however, by the death of the prince himself in November 1612 at the early age of eighteen. After this check to what might have given Wright something of the authority with Charles that Dee had enjoyed with Elizabeth, this new prince had to be prevailed upon to ask the Company to lend Wright money against the future sales of his books. These arrangements became void after Wright's own death in November 1615. That unexpected event represented a real blow to the progress of applied mathematics, projective geometry, hydrography and engineering. At the time of his death, Wright had published books on armillary spheres and sundials, whilst the learned were looking for much more from that creative pen.

Wright's lasting, alluring epitaph was his famous exercise in cartography that is the world map known as the Molyneux-Wright. In directing the

Company towards the object of its lust, this has been described as 'a diagram of corporate desire stretching itself across the body of the earth'.[29] Based on Mercator, Wright's creation appeared in the second and much-expanded edition of Hakluyt's *Navigations* (1598). It is an astoundingly beautiful object, or so Shakespeare seemed to think since it provided him with copy for *Twelfth Night* (III.ii): 'He does smile his face into more lines than is in the new map, with the augmentation of the Indies'.[30] Wright's further contribution to knowing where you are was his *A Description of the Admirable Table of Logarithmes* (1616), which is his translation of John Napier's *Mirifici logarithmorum canonis descriptio* (1614). Beyond those who liked to rattle 'Napier's Bones', as the work of the man who invented logarithms was colloquially known, Wright's public place in a larger history of mathematics was his fond belief that the discipline should be of practical value and not merely of abstract delight. At the forefront of his research was his *Admirable Table*, tribute to a life admirably passed.

Now known only to historians of science, Wright was one of many outstanding minds attached to the Company through the assiduity of Smythe. When in March 1614 Captain Nicholas Downton of the Company sent in a testimonial pointing up the value of Wright's researches, such was Smythe's own debt that he concurred readily enough with the minute that was to represent the Company's obituary to what had been a man of many instruments: 'Mr Wright, the mathematician, who has gathered great knowledge in the Universities, and effected many worthy works in rectifying errors formerly smothered.'[31] From Wright's first association with the Company, Smythe and Sir John Wolstenholme (d. 1639), the Farmer of the Customs, had been paying Wright a stipend of £50 per annum for him to give lectures to Company employees, the costs of which these two had been dividing between them.

Smythe's patronage of Wright is a testament to the governor's capacity for talent-spotting, something Smythe was then to repeat with England's celebrated tribe of cartographers, the Speed family. The maps of its most famous son John were then appearing in the *Theatre of the Empire of Great Britaine* (1606), and later in that Speed bestseller, the *Historie of Great Britaine* (1611–12). But it is William not John Speed who is of most interest to us here, though surprisingly enough, given his importance to British cartography,

132

William has no entry in the *Dictionary of National Biography*. But if William is obscure now he was obscured too in the early seventeenth century, Smythe using him first as a fly upon the wall to report on things happening in London and then as a spy upon the water, when he went to sea under cover as the official 'Keeper of Record': William was expected to tell Smythe what his captains were cooking up. In this connection there is an incomplete transcription by William of a lost journal for the *Hector*. This report is described as 'made [1608] by Wm Speede by the appointment of Sir Thos. Smythe, governor of the East India Company'.[32] During its gestation William was aboard the *Hector* off the coast of Yemen, on which the factor Lawrence Femell asked his 'general': 'I pray you to lay out for 6 pretty maps of the road for Mahomet Aga, if there be no better aboard the ships; Wm. Speed hath small maps.'[33] William died soon afterwards; though not before he had garnered valuable cartographic research that came to be assimilated into the family's later publication, entitled *Prospect of the most Famovs Parts of the World* (1627).

There was never a quiet moment for Smythe who, though a man of strong faith, was not a Puritan with a capital 'P'. He relished the prospect of many a feast promised by the beneficiaries of his largesse. Southampton was close to him, if only because their two lives had entwined in dangerous ways. Southampton had followed Smythe into the Tower at the time of the Essex rebellion, and had been still luckier to have got out with his head still on – if only because he really had been up to his neck in treason. But then, celebrating with the likes of Southampton could never be done without a vote, not even it seems the smallest of gatherings. However, once these were approved and the stoves were lit, there was always excess of merriment.

But the diurnal round of feasts could be interrupted by the most shaming of revelations. One day in January 1615 what should turn up but a fardel of erotica, specimens of that Japanese genius for *osokusu-no-e*, or, as we might loosely translate that phrase, 'peep-shows in a roll'.[34] The arrival of these things caused 'great speeches to be made' at the Royal Exchange, with Smythe biting his nails lest it be thought such 'wicked spectacles' were generally encouraged by the Company. He therefore resolved that they should be put into the fire, 'where they continued till they were burnt and turned into smoke'.[35] As for naughty Captain Saris (d. 1643), he who had brought in this corruption in the first place, fortunately he was as interested in cartography as in coitus. By also presenting the Company with the earliest known map of China, he was able to save his job, if hardly his reputation.[36] Nothing if not enterprising, the good captain remained long in service, dying during the Civil War at his cottage in Fulham.

Exposure of a different kind was experienced by Captain William Keeling (d. 1620) who, having commanded the *Third Voyage* (1607), was made 'general' for the 1615 departure.[37] In addition to a multitude of other burdens, Keeling had been detailed on this second of his two voyages to take Sir Thomas Roe to India as the Company's first ambassador. For this Keeling placed his flag in the *Dragon*, whilst the *Lyon*, *Peppercorn* and *Expedition* fell into line behind. But there were problems. Keeling was yoked with Captain Christopher Newport who, having travelled to America many times, had been confident that he, not Keeling, would become the figurehead for the prow. But to his chagrin, Newport found himself captain of the *Lyon* only. Although the ship was brand new and as bright as a carousel, this was poor compensation for the fastest man on water – one, indeed, whose legendary feats caused grateful passengers to name a Rhode Island town Newport News.

Keeling's problems were compounded by Roe himself. Suddenly it was discovered that Roe was itching to get behind the wheel himself. Having taken the *Lyon's Clawe* in search of the 'Large and Bewtiful Empire of Guiana' when Roe had pushed that boat up the Amazon in 1611, he could not see why he too might not have a go at running down the Channel. Keeling had absolutely no intention of sharing his command, though, and in dismissing the request caused Roe to confess: 'It goes against my stomach [that am very moderate] to be denied a candle, or a draught of beer of a steward, without asking the Captain's leave; whom yet, I must say, used me well: but loved that I should know his authority, and then denied me nothing.'[38] Although all this made for tensions, Keeling grew fond of Roe, and also his wife, to whom he was to present a small keepsake as his calling card – 'You will be pleased to consider of how little ceremony I am' – yet wishing to acknowledge 'the many affectionate favours received [from your husband] . . . in our joint passage to East India', adding how she would find him 'more willing to perform your commands than ceremonious men usually are'.[39]

That little keepsake arose because of the shared grief that the two wives had experienced on the departure of their husbands for India. As Keeling had prepared to leave, travel arrangements had still to be sorted. He had wished to take his wife, who was pregnant, though he knew full well there was a ban on women travelling. As Keeling was considered of excellent character, what many on the Court of Committees thought an entirely reasonable not to say touching request came to be defended on the grounds that it be 'very fitting for the quiet of his mind and the good of his soul, and as a curse befalleth those that keep man and wife asunder'.[40] In the end, however, Keeling's petition was refused. Notwithstanding all that, arrangements for her to travel with him went on apace; but what Keeling could not have known was how, suspecting this captain was up to no good, Smythe had inserted a spy among the sacks at the Company depot in Sandwich, where the outward bound voyage was due to stop. Unhappily for Keeling, this man had overheard him suggesting to his wife she make feint to return to London, whilst all the time doing what she could 'underhand with a midwife to go with her to the Indies'.

For this clear case of disobedience, Keeling received something of a broadside from Smythe who disliked the evidence of defiance as much as he feared the prospect of childbirth aboard. Severely reprimanded, Keeling wrote an open letter noting an 'extremely unkind letter from Sir Thomas Smythe, never obliviable'.[41] What was to be done? The fleet was ready but its 'general' was not! There was nothing for it but to turn to the Committees as the court of final appeal. Thanking Smythe for trying to resolve the issue, the Court of Committees continued to think a wife in the hold better than a whore in the wheelhouse. In the end Smythe prevailed, and Keeling was brusquely informed that 'if he return his wife to London, they will hold their former opinions firm, but if she accompany him they will hold him unworthy their service'.[42]

The unhappy business ended with Roe telling Keeling to be a man and not a husband. This did the trick.[43] Not long afterwards Keeling was able to record the most romantic of entries in his journal: 'This day we lost sight of the Lizard and began our course for the Cape of Good Hope.' But whilst Keeling was sailing down the coast of Africa, Smythe remained office-bound, continuing the business of reading logs and letters, and, when able to creep out of his own front door, tracking what was afoot at court and Commons, dock and warehouse, all vital work if he was to discharge his office effectively.

One of the most important official engagements over which he was required to preside would be the launch of ships like the *Trade's Increase*. This was the mightiest vessel the Company would build until building came to be given up in favour of leasing. The *Increase* had been scheduled to hit the water on 30 December 1609, an event that was graced by the attendance of not only the king, but also the queen and the prince of Wales. All began well enough, and for none more so than Smythe, who found the burden of office lightened with the royal bounty of a 'great chain of gold' and a medal 'put about his neck by the King's own hands'.[44] No sooner was that part of the ceremony done, however, than stillness descended. The *Increase* refused to budge and tension rose palpably. Perhaps either the slipway had buckled under the weight of a far heavier hull than had ever before been accommodated, with the result that the ship could not get over the 'hill', or insufficient animal fat had been applied to grease the rails. Whatever the truth, with minutes passing a waiting king found himself waiting in vain. Famously impatient and much given to making scenes, James flounced off, leaving a stricken governor clutching a gold chain with which he would gladly have pulled that wretched ship into the water. Yet the day had not been a total disaster: Smythe had been able to persuade Prince Henry to give his name to yet another expedition to discover a north-west passage, though a further two years were to elapse before anything happened. This was because of the tragedy that overtook Henry Hudson (d. 1611), after whom Hudson's Bay is named.

One of the most intrepid explorers of the Tudor age, Hudson was a depressive who was killed as much by the force of his own nature as by nature itself. With his last and fatal voyage, on 22 June 1611, a sizeable minority raised a mutiny aboard the *Discovery*. Resolving to bear their captain's moods no longer, they overpowered him, his son and six others, and, setting them adrift, left them to one of two fates: either to be frozen to death or eaten alive. As for the mutineers, they survived a later ambush by Inuit, only to stagger ashore in Galway. Carted over the water, the mutineers then stood trial in London. There they were acquitted, on the reasonable grounds that since there were no witnesses there could be no guilt. Once the trial was over, Smythe approached the ringleader Robert Bylot to ask him if he needed a job. Smythe's thinking was this. Given that Bylot was one of the

Company's best pilots, who was he to be overly officious about what might have happened so far away?

If Smythe favoured recruitment over righteousness, he could never dodge the 'deserving poor'. Perhaps the most affecting was Hudson's own son Richard, upon whom the Company looked kindly 'in regard his father perished in the service of the commonwealth'. But how to attend to Richard's needs, alongside those of so many others? Appeals came up with monotonous regularity: issues about money to be borrowed at 8 per cent, Smythe's daily appearance in the Commons 'to answer any imputations that may be cast upon the Company', Baltic cordage and Normandy canvas, relocation of storehouses from Deptford to Blackwall, admission of new members, stores for the ships and a thousand other vexations.

As if all this wasn't enough, Smythe, who by now was a very big fish in the Pool of London, was called upon by the City authorities to do his bit in driving down the crime rate. Accordingly, he arranged for twenty jailbirds to be sprung from Newgate. These were then mustered on the quayside at Blackford where, much to Sir Thomas Roe's alarm, they came to be packed aboard the same ship that was taking him to India. Dumped on Robben Island, this menacing crew did not survive for long. Their ringleader, Captain Cross, once a Beefeater but often a murderer, came to a terrifying end slipping beneath the waves while fending off circling whales.[45] Meanwhile, and back home, when not helping to empty London's jails, Smythe was busy running a parole board. Approached by Bridget Grey, who had come to see him on behalf of her grandson John Throckmorton, described as a 'prisoner in Newgate', she told Smythe why she had asked to see him. Apparently John had helped steal a 6s hat, and now here she was begging Smythe to have him 'conveyed beyond seas' so that he 'may escape an infamous death'. Why not? thought the governor. After all, Throckmorton's accomplice, Robert Whisson, 'old thief' and chief culprit, had been hanged, and so, provided Mrs Grey's appeal to the Council was upheld, there was no harm in giving the lad a fresh chance among the lions of South Africa.[46]

The worst of it for Smythe was not whether to let a man swing or no but those relentless hard-luck stories of all the widows with whom he was required to deal. It became too much, and so it was decided that Mr Offley 'was to underwrite the petitions of mariners' wives for part of their husbands' wages, the governor being so troubled with their clamours and petitions as that he cannot have that freedom in his house which is needful for the preservation of his health'.[47] Immediate relief afforded, Smythe was freed up for the more productive task of considering short ways to new wealth and long lists of possible patrons, among whom was Prince Henry, whose father put his name to the Bletsoe Proclamation. This was all about that old quest for new ways to China: 'In regard, it is an enterprise tending to so worthy an end, and which now at last after many proofs hath obtained so happy and likely a beginning, we have thought of some extraordinary means to grace and honour the same', and therefore constitute 'our dear son immediately under ourselves (whose protection is universal) supreme protector of the discovery and the company'. Although this sort of thing had been going on before anyone alive had been born, the venture attracted an astonishing number of important supporters: Nottingham, who as Lord Howard of Effingham had been the hero of the Armada; Sir Francis Bacon, who was of course committed to opening up trade all across the globe; the archbishop of Canterbury; the Earl Marshal; the Lord Privy Seal – all of whom had to be kept sweet by the Company; plus any number of 'the lesser sort'. With no authority so to do, the Bletsoe Proclamation announced free trade between the Cape of Desolation on 'Groynland' to the 'lands of America . . . unto the very territories of Tartaria, China, Japan and Coray, and to all other coasts, countries, or islands, either known or unknown, discovered or undiscovered, lying upon or in the sea of Suz'. Thomas Button, captain of the *Resolution*, John Ingram, master of the *Discovery*, and 'all the mariners and companies of those ships who set to sea in April 1612, for the discovery of the said passage, and to their executors' were granted customs from December 1615 until December 1617, half to the use of Captain Button, the rest for the benefit of the crew. It comes as no surprise to discover that 'Sir Thomas Smythe is appointed first governor'.[48]

For the majority of the time that Smythe was in charge, these were years of plenty, returns on investment being so phenomenal that what had started as a business became a business of state. As profits exceeded those of any of the other overseas companies, the whole Establishment piled in. With both the king and the prince of Wales clamouring to become Adventurers, the Company became the Fourth Estate. It could not be allowed to fail because the fractured structure of royal finances looked to the City for its salvation. So in an important sense the East India Company was nationalised, as English society moved ever closer to grasping a fully developed sense of nationhood.

When first and fat years were succeeded by lean, and European-wide depression set in, such troubles began as it was doubted whether Smythe could continue to manage things. The one area in which he had not shone for the Company was in Parliament. Although he had sat for a number of important maritime constituencies, the Company port of Sandwich included, he had contributed very little to debates. No doubt he had played a part in shaping economic policy through membership of some key financial committees; though that is very hard to assess since the minutes do not survive and he was almost entirely mute in the chamber itself. Since a massive assault on the Company was gathering strength, not in just one but both Houses of Parliament, it was as well Smythe was out of it all by the early 1620s.

No less fortunate, however, was how he came to be replaced by Sir Maurice Abbot from the spring of 1624. Even by Jacobean standards the 1624 Parliament stands out for the ferocity of its conflicts, and Smythe would have been wholly unsuited to fending off assault. Instead, that great showman Sir Maurice would rise from where Smythe had roosted to fight with great effect a battle in which the very survival of the Company hung: not upon the outcome of balanced debate but according to how many of its critics, many an Adventurer among them, had felt themselves excluded from entering the winners' enclosure. This was that famous occasion when the king's favourite, Buckingham, arrested the entire East India fleet amidst a chorus of its enemies calling for the dismemberment of the very institution itself. Before the great events of that famous parliament come to be described, we turn to see how the Company got the fleet into such a state of readiness that it presented an alluring target to a bankrupt Crown. What follows is the biography of *Peppercorn* which though broken up in 1623, less than a year before the dramatic events of the 1624 Parliament, had been just the sort of ship that Buckingham now had his eye on.

7

A VOYAGE EXCEEDINGLY TROUBLESOME

It is 20 February 1610. Though it is still dark, the nightwatchmen have opened the great gate of Blackwall Dock. There is no time to wait for sunrise to load the boats, though everyone agrees that the less stowage done with open flame moving about within the fecund wombs of wooden hulls the better. Here stand *Trade's Increase*, *Peppercorn* and *Darling*, the three ships which will make up the Company's Sixth Voyage. Here too standing in their stoles and stamping in their boots are those of the Court of Committees who have been delegated to work in groups to get the ships away. As they wait to enter the offices to check the inventories and the balance sheets, outside can be heard the shore porters shuffling in the dark like a heard of animals: moving carcass to quayside and crate to wagon for that moment when it is safe to penetrate that tight enclosure of wealth which was the interior of an East India ship.

The challenge of getting out to the Far East was not just acknowledged on that raw February morning by those unfortunate enough to have been roused from their beds at Amen Corner in the City to tumble along for their day's work in the docks, but still more publicly and twice-weekly at the twenty-four-strong Court of Committees, which met every Tuesday and Thursday (plague permitting). This executive board was all too conscious as to the immanence of hazard, and so forever inclined to issue the most minute instruction as to how the general and officers of each and every Voyage were to conduct themselves. These directors, merchant sailors first and possibly merchant tailors after that, tough as any ship's rope, had visited every port known to Tudor man. With no comfort but much advice, Committees tasked the general of the Sixth Voyage – the vastly experienced if volcanically choleric Sir Henry Middleton – with responsibilities they well knew could

140

become insupportable, as it would indeed prove to be the case with this fatal journey.

The theme of this chapter is, then, the less than poetic subject of 'packing': the business of getting the boats ready for the East India Company's annual voyage round the Cape. It was the first theme of Committees, for whom preparation was all; stowage was the foremost priority for a voyage when the utmost care had to be taken to minimise the dangers of the ocean. The Company's annual voyage would always try to get away between the start of February and the beginning of April, in order to take advantage of the monsoon cycle and favourable winds off Africa: leave London any later, and homeward-bound ships would be rendered motionless for six months at least. Yet the Company was never as obsessed with getting away as the Portuguese had always been: they held it to be an article of faith that 'The last day of February is time enough, but the first day of March is late.'[1] Such anxious interrogation of the calendar mattered less in England, since a galleon was faster than a carrack and lost time could be made up. But for all that preparation to be completed well before the blossom blew in Greenwich Park depended on years of trial and error when Tudor seamen had begun to acquire the first painful, rudimentary experience of putting, but then keeping, to sea.

Sir John Hawkins (d. 1595), for example, had won many encounters with Iberian ships. Notwithstanding Hawkins was never to win the more protracted 'battle of the rats'. On one voyage, for example, he was thoroughly dismayed to be told that 20 per cent of the food had been eaten by his 'noddies' (sailors) but the rest by *Rattus norvegicus*.[2] These were brown rats, and although they ate the comestibles, such a shortage could hardly have accounted for the massive price rise that threatened the profits of the privateer. Food costs went up sevenfold between 1500 and 1650. But even on those rare occasions when there was enough to eat, sufficiency created a plenitude of problems. Things went off and men stopped eating.

One of the few to consider the dangers of cooking at sea was Sir Hugh Plat (d. 1609). A man who was interested in everything, Sir Hugh had created a bestseller with his *The jewell house of arte and nature, conteining divers rare and profitable inventions, together with sundry new experimentes in the art of Husbandry, Distillation, and Moulding, faithfully and familiarly set downe, according to the Authors owne experience* (1594). When not recommending 'a cement for mending glasses; and how to know what cards your opponent is holding', this high priest of household management was having the greatest difficulty in getting Sir John Hawkins himself, together with famous Francis Drake, to talk food. Eventually, however, the three did get together, and the two found themselves disarmed upon hearing such good sense after all. For that notable meeting there was just the one item on the agenda, and it was macaroni.

Plat regaled the nation's best heroes with the merits of 'a cheap, fresh and lasting victuall, called by the name of Macaroni amongst the Italians'. What was said round that table came to be well digested. Macaroni could be stored, and although the rats would be sure to have a go, what they left would not go off. Such was Plat's persuasiveness that macaroni migrated from agenda to menu. It came to be served on Hawkins's last voyage, and but for his death in 1595, future management of food at sea might have been transformed. Although a late convert to pasta, Sir John had always taken the health of his crews very seriously, if hardly that of the thousands of slaves he had shipped from Guinea to the Caribbean. Indeed, so solicitous was Hawkins over questions of diet that he has been described as the 'single greatest innovator in [England with] regard to shipboard cleanliness and shipboard health'.[3] Macaroni not muskets made the Empire, or, as George Orwell put it, 'I think it could be plausibly argued that changes of diet are more important than changes of dynasty or even of religion.'[4]

What Orwell had to say of a later age can be applied fruitfully enough to what went on before men had even begun to think of such a thing as that British Empire Orwell despised.[5] A scarcity of food was disastrous but then it must be said too that its very presence was never less than a threat. Food and its safety was the single most important thing about the survival of the East India Company, not just in the period under discussion but always. Mastering the challenge of food in the hold was as important as the presence of gunpowder upon the deck, not only to the business of getting there but of not getting ill.

When Smythe groaned and ground a way to Archangel, he had not needed to invent the freezer, as Sir Francis Bacon would attempt, only to die a hero's death in the process.[6] Supplies could not rot on Smythe's watch when his own watch froze in his pocket, whilst those who traded in the Mediterranean, for example, were rarely more than two days' sailing from land and thus from food. How different the predicament of others like Middleton charged to take ships to the Spice Islands! The stretches of water which had to be traversed, often many hundreds of miles from landfall, were an enormous challenge not merely to health but survival itself. Given the vulnerability of the vessel and what in those days was still only a rudimentary knowledge of navigation it was like attempting to fly from London to New York in a biplane. But then the currents and the calms were something quite else. Often enough a man heading for the west coast of Africa found himself on the east coast of America, a quandary which all too often provoked scenes straight out of *The Rime of the Ancient Mariner*, a poem full of desperations and despairs about being becalmed upon plates of steel under a burning sun and without a 'drop to drink'. Such enormous distances challenged even the best of pilots, though surely the worst must have been the benighted Portingale who, swearing he had delivered his crew upon the coast of Coromandel, confessed soon enough that he had landed them in Angola and not India after all.[7]

For some reason Englishmen found the business of getting out to the East Indies an awful lot harder than their Dutch competitors. At this time, the VOC was able to mast and muster much larger flotillas than the standard issue of three English boats; small boys standing expectant upon the sands of Texel would be rewarded with the sight of ten great East Indiamen issuing out of Amsterdam to hammer the English upon the farthest boundaries of the Eastern seas. By contrast, the East India Company's outward-bound flotillas consisted of three vessels, with a luggage carrier tagging along behind: this would be burned in the Azores to stop it falling into the hands of the Portuguese. Very few of the big ships were lost through error, though too many were worn out well before their time. Some were tall and some were heavy. As for the grandest of these great vessels, a sense of which may be obtained from looking at the etching of a Dutch East Indiaman which the artist drew probably in the 1630s, these represented kinetic art of a high order when throughout the seventeenth century the East India Company was the patron saint of woodcarvers.

One of the earlier ships to be commissioned for the East India Company was the *Peppercorn* (1609–23). She had been built in the same dock and at the same time as the mighty *Trade's Increase*, pride of the Company fleet. There the similarities end: the *Increase* was proud, the *Peppercorn* humble; the *Increase* lost when *Peppercorn* lived. Although the *Increase* was getting on for three times the size, it sank on its maiden voyage. By contrast, *Peppercorn* sailed 100,000 miles or more.

As with all Company vessels, there were countless things to be done before the departure of the *Peppercorn*. Loading the ship was long in planning, albeit short in packing; it was a frantic time when everything had to be stowed within a period of roughly four months. The vastly complicated process started in October. This was what came to be called at the time 'victualling', or the proper preparation of supplies. Readying the *Peppercorn* was more demanding than whatever might be necessary for preparing its return under a tropical sun. When coming home there were fewer stops, and fewer crew because so many died going East. Getting *Peppercorn* sailworthy required prodigious feats of organisation from scores of suppliers, though many of the food-handlers were themselves a hazard to health at a time when food hygiene had yet to be invented.

But then there were other threats to the physical well-being of employees besides the obvious dangers of consuming rotten food. Some of the trades associated with trying to keep food edible, if they were not positively carcinogenic, were nonetheless lethal for those exposed to them. In 1633 John Woodall, who for many years had been Surgeon-General of the East India Company, was asked to look into the lamentable condition of the saltpetre workers. A noxious mixture of potassium nitrate (75 per cent), sulphur and charcoal, such a brew had a savage irony attached to its preparation: though used to preserve meat, it killed those preparing it. Woodall's report makes pitiable reading. There is the distressed condition of those whom Woodall had examined, but also a sense that such 'remedies' as he suggested would be wholly ineffective:

> the sickness of their saltpetre refiners is occasioned by their coming fasting in a morning to the work, and therefore he propounded that the Court would allow them some hot caudles to eat before they fell to their work to keep out the steam and smoke, which otherwise will get into their stomachs and in short time kill them, their bodies being already

sunk and much impaired. The Court ordered him to prepare such break-
fasts as he shall conceive to be good to recover their healths and prevent
their sickness for a month or two . . .[8]

Wider problems, however, and having to do with the spring preparation for
the departure of the fleet, began in the Company kitchens. These were just
one great big laboratory for germ warfare, created by butchers exporting
death through a thousand cuts: shin and brisket, chuck and blade, transformed into slimy protein marinated in saltwater. In the early spring when
Blackwall was all abustle, what had been wholesome became noisome quickly
enough. But in winter too, a mountain of suppurating flesh was stacked in
overheated, airless buildings. The horror of what lay in wait for the men of
the *Peppercorn* was highlighted in the Minutes of the Court of Committees
for 26 February 1619, when the assembled dignitaries were obliged to listen
to Smythe reciting 'Complaints from India of tainted beef; the fault of the
butchers knocking down so many oxen together and letting them lie in their
blood until it be settled, without cutting their throats whilst alive, whereby
they would strive and strain the blood out of their bodies, and for want
thereof their flesh cannot take salt'.[9]

A multitude of regulations having to do with storage, preparation and
consumption suggests that various subcommittees charged with getting the
ships away had only the most rudimentary understanding of what a balanced
diet might mean. But then no amount of print could have compensated for
faulty preparation, still less for comestibles that should have carried a 'sail by
date' in the boldest of type. For example, James Demaistres of Pudding Lane
sold the Company 60 tons of mouldy beer. The scandal came before the
Court of Committees on 20 December 1619, when it was resolved that
formal complaint be made to the Lords of the Council, though it was noted
how with this particular crook 'all his wealth and life cannot satisfy'.[10]

With any voyage, there were 'manifests' or estimates of overheads. These
were inscribed under the heading 'A View to the Charge'. Such guesstimates
were largely correct, despite being forecasts. They included the cost of 'dead'
stock that was carried forward to the next voyage; in one case this was valued
at a prodigious £3,000. There were also significant bills for capital sums
associated with the building of the *Peppercorn* and monies added to running

expenditure for repairs, refurbishment or alterations. One big boat cost £2,400 16s, with subsequent unspecified charges an additional £4,770 and beyond that further outlay on crew of £2,895. Thus the 'setting forth' in that case, totalled £10,849 16s. A middle-sized vessel came in at the much lesser figure of £6,464 overall, whilst a pinnace might cost only £2,600 to get ready: a daunting total of £22,913 16s 0d nonetheless.

Shipbuilding was prodigiously expensive, though the costs could vary wildly. This depended on the size of the ship and which yards had been used, at a time when tenders could be let out to builders as far afield as Ipswich and even Ireland. In July 1609 estimates of £50,000 came in for the building of the *Trade's Increase* and the *Peppercorn*.[11] From this it becomes apparent that the biggest boats only took six months from commission to completion. That order of July 1609 was followed in January 1610 by an outlay of £50,000 for supplying everything needed for the Sixth Voyage. This consisted of the *Trade's Increase*, *Peppercorn* and *Darling*. The *Increase* was by far the most expensive boat the Company had built to date. But these large sums also suggest that *Peppercorn*, too, was designed to a high specification. Perishable or just plain valuable things demanded expensive outlay for specialist equipment and protective materials. Such devices were ordered to prevent rotting in what had long proved the most adverse and varied environmental conditions possible. One type of boat, provided it had been built with the appropriate materials, sufficed well enough for the cold waters of the northern hemisphere; but the same specification hardly met the exigencies of the southern oceans, where the fleets ploughed ever further into humidity that hung between the fetid decks like so many wet blankets. No wonder that many English boats failed to last the time that might have been expected had they not been required to reconcile two wholly different metrologies.

An army of craftsmen was needed to get *Peppercorn* ship-shape. These were skilled artisans able to command the highest wages in both London's artisanal and manual sectors. As for the crew, separate 'imprest' for their wages came in at £784, modest enough for a muster of three hundred men, as, for instance, came to form up for the Sixth Voyage. But then that was not a true figure. Accountants laid aside a top-up of £10,000 for wages; this to be allowed for the impossible outcome that everyone would get back alive. Unscrupulous rather than creative, such accounting saved at least £3,000 when 30 per cent of any complement would never be seen again. There was no provision for death-in-service pensions for dependants. Although there was a quite well-developed industry in ship insurance, personnel were excluded from any policies.

As for mariners themselves, they could take out money with them, though they were well advised not to do so because the whole lot might be stolen by the man in the next hammock. There was little opportunity to spend, except on what Smythe deplored as wicked vices. On the other hand, there was a good chance a man could embezzle a fair amount. Afraid of private trading and fearful of overloading ships with contraband, the Court of Committees declared for the maiden voyage of *Peppercorn* that 'No officer or sailor in any of the Company's ships to have more than one chest of a certain size'.[12]

Run-up to *Peppercorn*'s maiden voyage in 1610 was frantic. One man was delegated to go to the 'cordage house' to see if he could get hold of some serviceable second-hand rope for tying *Peppercorn* to moorings in foreign ports. Another went off to the Customs House, where he was pleased to discover officials minded to remit the tax on French wheat that had just been brought up river for *Peppercorn*. Meanwhile, Jeffry Hamlet truffled about the *Dragon*, trying to take whatever might be useful. Frayed old Andrew Roper was told he was too decrepit to be taken on as a factor, though there was much interest in George Cockayne as one of the factors who was to travel out on *Peppercorn*. It helped that George was a relation of Sir William Cockayne, who would run for the governorship in 1624 when Sir Maurice Abbot was to be elected. Despite such connections, however, George wholly justified his selection: he would prove utterly dauntless in the face of Dutch fury, though it was his very courage that would do for him. It was reported in July 1620 how he had been 'long since most inhumanely murdered by Chinese'; though in the margin of that letter is the laconic annotation 'about May 1619'.[13]

Rather less satisfactory was Hugh Greete, a diamond merchant who had been directed to go out on the *Peppercorn*. Although Greete was recruited as one of London's leading hard-stone brokers, Smythe could see through him and he would be accused of stealing a whole pyramid of sparklers. Notwithstanding, Greete was to have the last laugh. At his death in 1619 he left his very considerable fortune to the Company for the building of alms-houses in Poplar High Street. Smythe objected strongly on the grounds that the money was not his to give in the first place but rightfully belonged to the Company: all of it had been stolen by Greete during his long and successful career as a private trader when he had wrapped himself in the Company's flag. Much to Smythe's chagrin, however, the Hugh Greete Almshouses opened in 1628, only to close in 1866 – thus outliving the very Company itself. Fortunately for Smythe, he died before being obliged to witness the triumph of his enemy.

The costs for what was designated by the Court of Committees as the Sixth Voyage (1610), *Peppercorn*'s maiden voyage, have regrettably not survived. So to get a sense of the magnitude of expenses that must have been involved, we are obliged to turn instead to those costs that had been incurred with the Third Voyage (1607), for which happily a full set of accounts do exist.[14] However there was an important distinction between the relative costs of the Third and the Sixth Voyages. The Third consisted of only two ships because a pinnace which accompanied the outward leg had been burned in the Azores. By contrast, the Sixth consisted of three major vessels. Thus it would seem to be prudent to factor in a putative extra 25 per cent to the costs of the Sixth to account for three, not two, vessels and the enormous size of the *Trade's Increase*.

For the Third Voyage of 1607 to 'Bantam and the Moloccos', there was 'the some of the whole chardge outwarde' that had been incurred in preparing the *Dragon*, *Hector* and their accompanying pinnace of 120 'tunns', the whole serviced by 280 men. Getting these away was anticipated to cost a formidable £28,915 12s 8d. As for their return, that was reckoned at the much lesser sum of £17,100 0s 0d, in part because the pinnace was broken up in the Azores and, for the return leg, there was a smaller complement of crew because of death at sea. Such a reduction was not disabling, though, since imports were less bulky: indigo was a lot easier to handle than iron. All thrown in, and the throw included an extra £10,000 for wages, the bill for 'setting forth', returning, unloading and discharging, something spread over three years, came to a remarkable £56,015 12s 8d. Once these estimates had been presented, there was an exercise in cost-pruning to be undertaken. Somehow accountants managed to shave £6,015 12s 8d off the estimates:

'the wch Computatōn being reuiewed is reduced from £56015 12s 8d to aboute £40000-0s-0d'. An audible sigh of relief went round the room, but even so the sums were simply enormous.[15]

Assuming things were much the same three years later, for *Peppercorn* and the other two, once 25 per cent is added £50,000 at a conservative estimate must have been found. It was a massive investment, enough to keep 250 skilled artisans employed for close on a decade. More times than not, there was little problem raising this kind of money as there were any number of Adventurers willing to queue twice round Old St Paul's to put savings into such a vastly capital-intensive endeavour.

But why did it cost quite so much to put three ships into the sea? The heaviest outlay was the men's wages, then there was the cost of the actual merchandise. Most of this consisted of cloth, England's staple export. Though many of the bolts had the most alluring of names, that cannot have appealed very much to a Japanese trader, and in any event these things proved difficult to shift anywhere east of Persia.[16] But there was other merchandise too, and judging from what *Dragon* and *Hector* had carried out three years before, *Peppercorn* and *Increase* might have stowed something in the order of 150 tons of lead, 150 of iron and 5 of tin. When, however, it is stated that the 'somma totalis of all the mr.chandise' only came to a total of £6,001 it can be seen that this represented going on towards 15 per cent of the gross sums involved. That was not much at all. Indeed, it reinforces the argument that the two great costs were the men and their food.

What then were the amounts of food stowed aboard until this could be supplemented by foraging, barter or purchase? Dried and salted beef amounted to 11 tons, pickled beef 21 tons and pork in brine 30. There was also dried stockfish at 35 hundredweight, codfish or *backalew* (from the Spanish *bacallao*) at 208 hundredweight, with lynge weighing in at 7 hundredweight. A prodigious 63 tons of bread might seem to have been less of a challenge than storing putrid meat between decks where it was hard to breathe. But bread had its own risks too: it was prone to attack by weevils and had to be kept in a lead-lined safe. This was not only useless as a method of storage but a major health hazard in its own right. Captain Downton, commanding *Peppercorn* on her maiden voyage, confessed how 'the best we can [do] for safety of our bread and corn [is] by [setting aside] a tight room to contain it, in regard of the innumerable sort of Cacara, a most devouring worm with which this ship doth abound to our great disturbance'.[17] However, problems with bread began before the first loaf was taken aboard: there was enormous pressure to bake enough to supply an outgoing fleet. In January 1614 the Company's baker, pressed to increase production, claimed 'he has not above 80,000 [loaves] ready' whilst try as he might he was only able to make '18,000 bread in a week'.[18]

With those loaves on the water, it is astonishing any weevil could make headway when, with the passing of the months, the bread must have been as hard as pumice. As for Downton of the *Peppercorn*, he was much better at fending off the 'Portingale' than in wrestling with weevils: *sitophilus granarius* did for the wheat, *oryzae* simply loved the rice, whilst that most prodigious spoiler of all, the formidable little beast known as the *zeamaias*, couldn't get enough of the maize. In the warm waters of the Yellow Sea it became a case of worm within, worm without. But of all these minute enemies, it was the sea-borne clam, *Teredinibacter urnerae*, that had the greatest firepower. It would turn *Peppercorn* into sponge if the ship was not regularly careened.

So much for eating: whether that was conducted by the men or their pests. As for drink, there were no fewer than 110.5 tons of 'sider'. This needed to be carefully sampled to ensure that it would not wring the belly 'extraordinarily'. 'Ship's Beer' at 60 tons and 'Strong Beer' at 20.5 both brewed 'by Mr Campion by order of the Court'. Then, for the better sort, ninety pipes of wine (each pipe being 126 gallons) were supplied through Messrs Humble and Harrison, vintners by appointment to the Company. Some was best Bordeaux, because it was thought important guests needed if not to be incapacitated then to be disarmed before they would surrender their trade.

Ships fell to bits, sailors fell overboard, crews fell into disease. That said, the standard of medical care was more advanced than on land. Without all that lobbying by William Clowes, the Company would have failed entirely. Lemon water was carried because Smythe had been influenced by the rebarbative Clowes, who had long recognised the value of anti-scorbutics. But there was a more general concern with vitamins. One flotilla was supplied with 15 tons of white wine because the medics thought that it was a sovereign remedy to 'refresh the men and scour their maws, and open and cool as well as lemon water'.[19]

But how was food prepared without a galley? Cooking was done at a free-standing stove placed behind the stoutest mast available. This was a waiting hazard at a time when many chefs passed their days more drunk than sober. Richard Hancock, the cook aboard the *Peppercorn*, was no exception, and Captain Downton confided feelings of relief and anguish at the man's disastrous if final escapades: 'The 25th day. I pray God to withhold all deserved plagues from us. At noon our ship came afire by the cook his negligence, o'erguzzled with drink, digged a hole through the brick back of the furnace and gave the fire passage to the ship's side, which led to much trouble besides spoil to our ship.'[20] To the relief of all, there was to be no repeat. Two days later and here is Downton again; reporting how 'At noon Richard Hancock our cook died.' Clearly there had been one binge too many.

Whatever Hancock had been preparing, there were firkins of butter, either 'sweet' or rape oil for frying and any amount of nutmeg, ginger, powdered sugar, pepper: all things piquant and powerful. In cupboards were 'raisins of the sun'. *Peppercorn* served as both silo and sack: meal 179.5 hundredweight, beans 196 bushels, peas 392 bushels, oatmeal 263 bushels and steel wheat 263 hundredweight, 'steel' referring to French wheat, which being harder than the English was supposed to last longer. However, by far the most important thing aboard was water: 780 tons taken on one voyage alone. As for this most precious of commodities, just as *Peppercorn* was leaving Blackwall heading out to sea, two Frenchmen had sidled up to Smythe, offering to sell him their secret formula for keeping water fresh on long voyages. Water was not an option, though soap was. For men who could be bothered to wash, there was the comforting presence of a hundredweight of the suddy stuff, those more fastidious than others praying they might make port before it all ran out. Without it, there was nothing with which to clean up after squatting in the 'heads'. Privies were far from private, being located in rows either side of the bowsprit. They were equipped with slatted sides to allow the sea water to cleanse them.

For the arduous process of victualling, the grocer had to wrestle with the cordwainer charged with stowing vast quantities of canvas for replacement sails, together with all the heavy instruments required for their cutting and sewing. Anchors sourced from Lübeck were the business of chandlers William Greenwell (deputy-governor 1604–15) and William Harrison (treasurer 1613–20), both thrice bound as high officials, major Adventurers and main suppliers. But there was more to be taken abroad than Greenwell, Harrison and Co. could supply: boatswain, gunner, steward and a dozen specialists needed to do their bit. It suggests those great big East Indian beasts must have been superbly designed, but drawings have not survived to tell us more about these prodigies of engineering in wood. *Peppercorn* was filled with 80 tons of ballast as bedrock. Packers worked for weeks to create the most adventurous of playgrounds for rats on their own maiden voyage. Documents detail any number of times that sails were torn, but there was never a tectonic shift in cargo.

Finesse and experience of a rare order were required of the highly skilled shore porters – men whose knowledge of how the multilayered sandwich should be prepared could make a huge difference to profits. In this important sphere of activity, what has been observed of the VOC can be applied equally to the *Peppercorn*: loading a ship with a cargo of various products was not an easy task. The difference in light and heavy goods in requirement to the balance of a ship had to be taken into account. The necessity to store products in such a way as to ensure that their quality was preserved, and that they did not contaminate each other, during the trip back home – such as highly aromatic goods polluting other cargo – was equally important.[21]

That said, however, nothing had quite so much care lavished upon it as the 'Surgeon's Chest', which doubled as a repository for surgical instruments and an apothecary's store. Once the lid was opened, here were to be discovered teeth for sawing, knives for slicing, spatulas for insertion, pliers for excision and all the unguents the generous Orient could supply in prodigal abundance. Under the supervision of the Company's first 'surgeon-general', Dr John Woodall, whom we met in Chapter 4, the chests were assembled so that their contents were well pigeon-holed. There would be nothing wanting for Robert Comely, who was the first of the many surgeons who would serve aboard the *Peppercorn*. But alas, Comely was to be defeated by the dark arts of poisoning. Returning in the summer of 1613, he was visited in his surgery by Abraham Lawes, one of the signatories on the orders dispatching the Sixth Voyage and who was now complaining of stomach cramps. What followed had all the drama of an *Anatomy Lesson* by Rembrandt: 'The 12th [June 1613]

Mr Lawes' disease came on so fast that he began to droop . . . July 2nd Mr Lawes conceives he is poisoned for that his stomach falls away, and he hath often inclination to vomit, for he saith he was so at Venice when he was formerly poisoned . . . The 27th [July] This day Mr Lawes died and is opened by the surgeon who took good note of his inward parts which was set down by the surgeon and divers witnesses to that note.' As for Lawes, there was nothing for it but to tip him over the side and sweep ever onwards.[22]

All dreaded 'this great and terrible instrument' that was known tactlessly enough as the 'dismembering saw'. With this, the surgeons were warned to employ three strong men to hold patients down when it came to the actual flourish. The victim himself was urged to 'prepare his soule as a ready sacrifice to the Lord by earnest praiers'.[23] But if Woodall and his weaponry were feared at sea, the man himself was feted in London. He remained at post whenever the plague swept in and the *beaux-monde* swept out. Here was a man who, extraordinarily enough, was to catch the plague not once but twice; experiences that, always alert to the main chance, Woodall put to excellent use in his learned disquisition upon what he himself would describe with some relish as 'that most fearful and contagious disease'. Woodall's first-hand account of what the plague could do, and how it felt, is, however, only part of a book that every London surgeon needed, *The Surgeon's Mate* (1617). In no time at all it established itself as the indispensable text for the hard-pressed surgeon working the author's 'bone nibbler' in a hurricane.

Woodall was the outstanding practitioner of early Stuart England, though he was never gifted with either the prescience of Clowes or the originality of Harvey. Ambitious and avaricious, Woodall owed more than he could say to the Company. The nature of Company practice and the demography of its employees provided perfect case histories for his further edification. Cadavers that today the mortuary might expect to receive from a motorbike accident, Woodall discovered in the remains of ships' boys. Such lads falling between gunwale and quayside, taking huge risks at great heights, at once fell under the knife of the most formidable of anatomists. Extemporising from such experience, Woodall's nostrums would achieve their most elegant expression in the 1639 folio edition of *The Mate*. The full title pronounces our man 'Surgeon General' whilst unintentionally revealing its author's bottomless conceit:

A Treatise Discovering faithfully and plainely the due contents of the Surgion's Chest the uses of the instruments, the vertues and operations of the Medicines, the cures of the most frequent diseases at Seas Namely Wounds, Apostumes, Vclers, Fistulas, Fractures, Dislocations, with the true manner of Amputation, the cure of the Scurvie, the Fluxes of the belly, of the Collica and Iliaca Passio, Tenasmus, and exitus Ani, the Callenture; WITH A BRIEF EXPLANATION of Sal, Sulphur and Mercury; with certaine characters and tearmes of Arte

Published chiefly for the benefit of young Sea-Surgeons, imployed in the East-India Companies affaires

By John Woodall Mr in Chirurgery

Upon an architectural frontispiece stands the head of Woodall, wearing a ruff of such extravagance as must have made even a turkey jealous, whilst himself ensconced between Hippocrates and Galen, the legendary founders of the Greek and Arabic branches of the high art of medicine. The two have been wheeled on to pay their respects to the great man, just as the reader is invited to look upon Woodall as the world's greatest physician.

Woodall was an instrument maker too, his most successful device coming to be called Woodall's Trephine. With this, the Company would make holes in the heads of its sailors for 300 years or more. Besides prospecting skulls, there was nothing Woodall was not prepared to have a stab at: surgeon, doctor, dentist, druggist and shrink all rolled into one. But if Woodall enjoyed high status, he practised low cunning: instead of procuring fresh lint for bandages, he did a little bandage laundering on the side by offering old as new. The racket unravelled, though. On 9 November 1642 he was asked 'whether he did not new Boyle the salves again and so make the Company pay for them twice'. What a suggestion – of course not! However, when London's wealthiest doctor asked if the Court of Committees 'would be pleased towards the repair of his languishing necessities and his better support now in his declining and dying days to bestow somewhat upon him', the executive 'did by erection of hands deny to bestow anything upon him'.[24] Such denials came after years when so many had claimed how he had been up to no good with the Company. Though Woodall could hardly indulge in the besetting sin of 'private trade', he could and he did devise as many methods of making money out of overcharging as there were instructions for cures within his famous surgeons' chests.

As for the basics of sailing, these were sometimes sourced from Europe or even beyond. For example, Russian hemp was hung out to dry on the tenterhooks of Goodman's Fields. Iron from the Hanseatic ports, canvas from Rennes, sailors from Amsterdam, cheese from Edam – much better than those awful rocks from Cheshire formerly stowed aboard. There were 90 pounds of paper carefully placed in watertight chests. Quality paper needed importing since the first English mill had only started in 1588, and there was nothing local of sufficient calibre. For his watercolours, Inigo Jones always sourced from Geneva; his costume designs needed to be laid upon things as smooth as ivory. Best quality was hardly less important to Smythe, however, when in these earliest days paper might lead to pepper.

Reception of a document in the East was markedly different from how it came to be docketed in the West. Fingered, sniffed, stroked, caressed, kissed, placed upon the head, letters would be laid aside for perusal later. Such epistles were not only gifts but also transmissions of power from recipient to receptor. As the person proffering the document needed to be presentable in his own person, and care was always taken that anyone acting as a representative of the Company smelled good before kneeling, so the material qualities of the letter were every bit as important in the East as whatever information it might contain. Nothing found in the safe of the *Peppercorn* could be more valuable than the golden letters of James I, which have been described as 'technologies of power that constituted the sinews of the Company's long-distance connections in the early years'. These were often left blank at the head so that names could be filled in on the spot, according to which authority was being targeted.[25] However, too much can be made of cultural differences. Company employees were themselves freighted with elaborate expectations as to the efficacy and the significance of what was scribal.[26] For example, when Captain Best received a long-awaited *firman* (or royal decree) that allowed the Company a degree of trade, 'he stood in doubt wether yt was the firma or no, for that yt was brought in no statt nor fashion, nott beseaming the letter of so great a kinge as the Magolle was'.[27]

Much was taken out for security rather than sale. For example, canvas suits were used to protect against pepper dust; these were supplied without pockets to discourage theft. Then there were what were described ominously as 'waste clothes for the close fights'. Such things came in handy for wiping blood off the slippery deck after a 'good bang' with the enemy. Gunpowder was precious but volatile; once wetted it was wasted. When friends came in from the sea, captains ashore fired their guns until *Peppercorn* rattled like a cage of lyre birds. Though no vessel was lost, one commander certainly was; paddling ashore to attend the funeral of his mate, soon enough his own funeral needed to be prepared. The chief gunner was primed to fire the customary salute, but failing to notice that his charge was live and so touching his match-hole, this unhappy man succeeded in blowing his commander sky-high. That unfortunate episode resulted in the Court of Committees issuing a command which forbade 'shooting at drinking of healths, and at the captains going on shore or otherwise'.[28] No one paid any attention.

So much for food, medicines and rather a lot of blood, but what about presents? *Peppercorn*'s safe was stuffed with luxuries, not merely artful but state of the art. Take the beautiful 'emerald-cased watch', alarm and calendar appended, which is part of the legendary 'Cheapside Hoard'. Described as 'one of the most remarkable jewels in the world', this astounding little thing was dug out of a cellar in 1912. It is reckoned to have been made by Gaultier Ferlite of Geneva between 1610 and 1620. One of many clever tricks about it is that its maker has transposed the twelve and the six o'clock, which meant that 'the wearer could tell the time with a quick downward glance': it was 'not until the twentieth century with the introduction of the type of watch commonly worn by nurses that this idea was re-introduced'.[29] Although there is no evidence that this jewelled octagon ever came near *Peppercorn*, similar beauties certainly did.

Smythe spent much money on high-end luxuries. Puritan by confession and close by habit, he disapproved of such vanities and resented paying for them. Still, it had to be done, so *Peppercorn* had her full complement of 'artificers' to attend to such treasures as the famous one that emerged from a cellar in the City exactly 300 years after it had been made. As for *Peppercorn*, London's finest artificers were stowed aboard simply to make sure that everything was kept ticking along nicely. Whilst it was hoped that the likes of the Ferlite watch would be acceptable, never mind what may have been intended as to its fate, what of the beginnings of such an astounding object? Its genesis stands as an epitome of the sources and resources upon which Smythe could now call. When Ferlite was bending over his lathes in Geneva and Smythe was turning his wheels in London, contacts were being activated across thousands of miles. These connected the unskilled and the skilled. Stones dug out of shale in Colombia and acquired in Amsterdam, assembled in Geneva but paid for in London became so many emerald panels that, thinner than the leaves of a maple (measuring a mere 3.8 by 2.3 millimetres), by the alchemy of a craftsman came to be made into an octagon of time upon which would depend not just the hours of the day but the years of trade.

The export of jewels, as attractive to steal as to own, meant that the strongroom of the *Peppercorn* looked like a delicious still life by Willem Kalf (d. 1693). In total, £50 was spent on buying up silver plate and £13 6s 8d on 'sweet meats and banquetting stuff, for banquet and entertainment of such strangers and others, as shall come aboard the ship for the honour of our nation and the credit of the Company'.[30] Just how sweet that 'meat' might have tasted after years at sea nobody seems to have enquired. On no account were the compasses, sextants and sea charts to be given away; so valuable that they too were kept secure. Last to note as first to signal departure were the chests of 'ancients'. These were flags made from silk and metal, which always had to be as splendid 'as shall be thought fit'. Silhouetted against the taft rail, the 'ancient' of St George was complemented by the Company's arms, fearsome lions in treacle gold. Beneath the mane flickered the scales of a merman in azurite blue, allusion to the sparkling waters over which the *Peppercorn* conducted its endless merry-go-round. Above the fearsome pair floated the Company crest: armillary sphere bound with zodiac and lodged between two split pennons. Here was appended 'Deus indicate, Deo ducente nil nocet' or, as might be said in English, 'Don't worry! God [i.e. Sir Thomas Smythe] will lead us to the land of profit.'

Before setting a course for Africa, the critical thing was to settle the complement of crew and passengers. Once the captain had been commissioned, the next thing was to find the right pilot for the right ship. Here no effort should be spared, if only to maximise the chances of getting home safely. Matthew Mollineux, not the globe-maker but a relative, was chosen to go alongside *Peppercorn* as master of the *Increase*. Everyone thought Mollineux the best who could be had, and so he was awarded the prodigiously generous salary of £10 a month: 'for that, besides his skill in the Indies, at Bantam and at the Moluccas, he hath been at Surat, where none of our people formerly have been'. Mollineux was not just well travelled but well tested. While everyone had been busy victualling the *Peppercorn*, he had been rewarded 'for his extraordinary pains in bringing home the *Dragon*, very much distressed, and without the help of any mate'.[31]

Between interviewing officers for key appointments, the Court of Committees was hard pressed to identify the prodigious sums that have been itemised here and which were needed to pay for all this. By now it was far too late to postpone the voyage. Smythe was nettled in having to reveal that only £50,000 had been promised when costs would amount to £80,000, including unlooked-for sums that had to be found before the ships left the dockside. What made matters worse was that 10 per cent had been set down by people other than Adventurers. This was not good since Smythe always liked to keep the Company as tight a ship as possible. Nevertheless, recruitment had to go on, even if it was not clear how salaries were to be paid. Henry Boothby, 'skilled in calicoes' and speaking Spanish, who threw in £100 from his own account, was commissioned for seven years. By mid-January, though, the *Peppercorn* was awash with petitioners wishing to be taken on: people with experience of merchandise, foreign countries or the sea. But others had no qualifications whatsoever. These might be sons of judges or minions of court, virtuosi keen on foreign travel or young men looking for a free ride. Often just out of university, this lot thought that talk of Ahmedabad would carry more kudos than tales of Rome. But if there were parasites, there were others who, though unable to pull ropes, could pull strings. Among such were the rarest linguists in all England. No graduates these, at a time when neither Oxford nor Cambridge offered degrees in Ashanti or Classical Malay; they were autodidacts who had chanced upon their natural gifts. Such a cauldron of talent had unlooked-for benefits. It ensured that if the food was bad the conversation would be better.

Take George Strachan (d. 1634). Born in Kincardineshire when Scotland was if not the Wild West then a still wilder North, Strachan mastered Arabic and Persian, possibly Turkish and Hebrew too. Much respected in the halls of learning, he corresponded with Maffeo Barberini, the future Urban VIII and most pontifical of all the Baroque popes. Born a Calvinist but caressed by a cardinal, Strachan determined to burnish his credentials within the republic of civility, and elected to become personal physician to the Emir Feyyad, an Arab potentate whose demesne described lands between Syria and the Euphrates. But then Strachan made a huge mistake: he took a job with the Company. Enduring two years but unable to stand it another minute, he melted into the desert, never to be seen again.

Aboard were assayers of gold, and others who could judge between ballast and ruby. One was called 'Milward, a jeweller, well skilled in rough and cut diamonds and the author of certain rules to judge of their worth, [and] thought very fitting for employment at Bantam'.[32] At first this careful man did well enough, though as with many others out East, he soon became unbalanced. Company factor at Tecoe, Milward got it badly wrong. When the *Rose* left port she carried his letters of complaint against the local governor. The recipient of such missives who was the king of Aceh, siding with Milward and never one to do things by halves, cut off the testicles of the miscreant; whereupon the 'capon', as the Tecoe governor was now referred to somewhat insensitively by the Company's factors, having lost his manhood, thought it only fair that Milward should lose his life. Accordingly, the plaintiff died of poisoning not long afterwards.

In addition to experienced artisans and skilled craftsmen were the young. *Peppercorn* was expected to find room for the likes of a Japanese page-boy to Captain David Middleton and an 'Indian youth' brought home by Captain Best and taught English by the Reverend Mr Copland so he 'may be sent home to convert some of his own nation'.[33] Of a still more exotic nature was a 'young man' dispatched by the virtuoso Sir Walter Cope 'to go for parrots, monkeys, and marmosets for Lord Salisbury'.[34] Another of note was 'The youth, an apothecary, skilful in distillation and commended by my Lord Carew'. For Roe in India, Carew was his most loyal correspondent, and with contacts such as this, no one was going to deny the boy his passage thence. Once on board he turned out to be something of a chemist in the making, coming to feel 10-feet tall when told that he was now to become the 'surgeon's mate's mate'.

Then there were the 'on-board entertainments' that all needed to be carefully planned: playbooks brought aboard and viols stowed away to prevent mutiny when becalmed. Although there certainly would have been entertainments organised by Captain Downton for the maiden voyage, *Peppercorn* could not claim the credit for having hosted the first performance of Shakespeare on water; that honour went to the *Red Dragon* with *Richard II* and *Hamlet*. As for music, hymns were constantly sung, so too madrigals. Psalms were chanted every morning and prayers offered morning and night.[35] The Company was an important patron of music. It made sure to seek out the best instruments, as when the Company organist was asked to try out a virginals made for two. This had a pin that 'pulled out by [one] man, will make both to go, which is [a] delightful sight for the jacks to skip up and down in such manner as they will'.[36] This beauty cost £15. That was a lot, but then such things were luxuries when not art: there was one knocking around London that had been painted by Rubens. As the boats rode on a satin sea in a velvet night, there was lots of water music but fireworks too, someone having remembered to bring along leather buckets to stop a ship from behaving like a Catherine wheel.

With the Sixth Voyage assembled, all that remained was for the officers to form up for a public recitation of their 'instructions'. On this occasion, 'General' Sir Henry Middleton, the flag officer, was gratified to read why command had come his way: 'Of an espetiall trust and confidence we haue of the Integrity, wisdome and resolucon of or loueinge freind Sir Henry Middleton Knight, So doe appointe and authorize him General to goe in the *Trades increase* and to Comand all or said Ships and the men in them, haveinge pcured him sufficient authority from or Souereigne Lord the kings matie.'[37] It was added, with truth if hardly tact, how it would be a 'long and tedious voyage . . . exceedingly troublesome and costly'. In addition, it was ordained that 'prayers be said eury morneinge and eveninge in every Shipp and the whole Company to be called therevnto wth diligent Eyes'.[38] Thus it was hoped there would be:

> Noe blasphemeinge of God, Swearinge, Thefte, Drunkennes or otherlyke disorders be vsed but that the same may be severelie ponished, and that noe diceinge or other vnlawfull games be admitted for that most comonlie the same is the begyninge of quarrellinge and many tymes the occasion of murthers[;] a iust provokacon of God's wrath and vengeance (from wch the Lord deliur us all) therefore yt shall be needful that such orders be sett vp and published in eury Shipp.[39]

But if the Court of Committees thought prayer important, its members were more fervent about record-keeping, though the impossible standards expected showed wholesale disregard for the reality of life on the ocean wave. It was demanded that 'Continual and true Journals' be maintained every day; with duplicates from no fewer than six people on each ship. But then the Court went further. It stipulated whole-fleet meetings be called once or twice a week, 'to the end yf any haue forgotten what an other hath observed, the same may be added, soe as a pfect discourse may be sett downe'.[40] How anyone thought this could happen beggars belief when a voyage could so easily be scattered, with one ship in Africa, a second off South America and a third going round and round Ascension Island. There was always something provisional about arrangements once past the Needles. For instance, in January 1609 it was reported to Dudley Carleton, then staying at Eton, who was then serving as English ambassador, how 'The least of our East Indian ships, called the pinnace, arrived at Dartmouth with 100 tons of cloves, without seeing or hearing any thing of her consorts since they parted from the coast of England.'[41]

Organisation of trade, accountability of employees, quality control, buying policy, money exchange and an awful lot more besides was required in the face of the enormous complexity of Far Eastern markets. But then this had always been the nature of world trade. Hangchow, a thirteenth-century Chinese trader, had had an astonishing array of different rice: 'There are numerous varieties of rice, such as early rice, late rice, new-milled rice, winter-husked rice, first quality white rice, medium quality white rice, . . . ordinary yellow rice, short-stalked rice, pink rice, yellow rice, and old rice.'[42] No surprise to learn, then, that four centuries later there was still more to master. If Hangchow saw a world of riches in a grain of rice, Company factors required their stock books to run from 'A' for aniseed to 'Z' for za'atar. It was an enormous challenge, one well illustrated by a report from Fujian in 1616. This suggested how things in China had become still more minutely calibrated since those far-off days of Hangchow in the thirteenth century: 'In both China and Japan, farmers experimented with different types of rice – quicker ripening (even if lower in yield); resistant to salt (for use near the sea); resistant to cold – until over one hundred and fifty varieties were in use in Fujian alone, over two-thirds of them found in only one location.'[43] And so it was with *Peppercorn*. The colours it carried in kersey, or what would now be called worsted, always magical are now mysterious: Venice red, Popinjay green, French greens and Grass greens, Violet and 'Murryes', 'Grain', 'Azar' Blue, ten different 'Yallowes' and a Flame colour. Last but least attractive, there was something they called 'Horseflesh'.[44]

Given the vast complexity of markets, not to mention currencies, final briefing in town acknowledged that discretion must prevail.[45] As Middleton stood listening at the end of the long table in Smythe's Great Hall, he was relieved to hear that he would not be censored when using such initiatives as occasion might demand. Nevertheless, the accumulated experience of the Court of Committees, every member of which had travelled to the most outlandish places, would prove invaluable. Clause twenty-one suggests how best to manage the run between Banda, the Moluccas and Bantam. On that route 300 tons of nutmeg might be purchased, though that is not insisted upon. What is made clear, however, is that if it was to be nutmeg, then it must be free from dust and 'rumps . . . [because if not] the same will not be worthy the freight and charges'. Twenty tons of mace was also required, 'the largest and brightest that may be gotten but none that is dark coloured red maces, which are called femenyn maces and here little worth'. Finally it was proposed that if Middleton should find it convenient to go to the 'Maluccos' [the Spice Islands] whilst nutmeg and maces 'are providing' at Bantam, there he was 'to seek for Clou[v]es, and haveing gotten to your content therein, to retourne to Banda, there to take in the mace and nutmegs and then to return to Bantam, where having settled the business . . . then in God's name with all due speed to return for England'.

On what would prove a sadly prophetic April Fool's Day, at last Middleton drew off, setting his prow for India. So much for all these hopes that were every bit as assorted as the coral and the kersey, the cider and the cheese that had been packed between the ballast and the deck. But what now of those highs and lows experienced as these three ships headed down to the Azores, up into the Persian Gulf, to finally anchor on the coast of Indonesia? What actually happened, as opposed to what the Court of Committees had prayed might have come to pass?

· 8 ·

ー゛゛゛〜

OCEANS OF WEALTH

Nicholas Downton had enjoyed a reputation as a very able seaman long before he had been appointed captain of the *Peppercorn* under Sir Henry Middleton for the Sixth Voyage of 1610. Downton had won notoriety for having sunk the Portuguese carrack *Cinco Chagas de Cristo* as far back as 1592, a feat of arms or annihilation, depending on which side you might have been (Chapter 1). Albeit a feat of pyrotechnics, Downton's victory had been entirely pyrrhic. By the time he had given the order to cease firing and the smoke had cleared, the boat sank, and with it all but thirteen of the Portuguese crew.

By contrast to such earlier successes, the Sixth Voyage, under General Middleton, was to cost Downton much and his many friends more. Of those who had subscribed to Middleton's 'Orders' of January 1610, many were to disappear either 'into the wide sepulchre of the ocean sea' or into its margins of sand: Middleton of wounds and heartache; Gyles Thornton, master of the *Trade's Increase*, of causes unknown; and Abraham Lawes, master of the *Peppercorn*, as a stiff upon a surgeon's table. As for the cape merchant designate, Lawrence Femell, he would find himself splashing about in the Red Sea surf with Turkish janis-saries intent on severing head from body. By a stroke of great good fortune, however, he survived in one piece, only to die in India shortly thereafter.

The *Increase*, *Peppercorn*, *Darling* and the lighter *Samuel* of 40 tons set off in March 1610.[1] There was also a pinnace in kit form stowed aboard the 1,298-ton *Increase*, something to be assembled when tidal estuary or oozing river demanded a shallow draught. The squadron made first landfall at the Cape Verde islands. But things were not well even as early as this: *Increase* needed repairs to a worn-out mast that had only been fitted six months before. This was the first time that everyone sensed the *Increase* had been rushed in its building; ominously enough, all of that was now beginning to show. Taking advantage of the delay, however, officers came aboard for one of those 'councils of the sea' the Court of Committees had demanded of Middleton.

With *Increase* bound up, *Samuel* was broken up to make sure that the Portuguese could not add it to their naval inventory. That done, and the fleet staying in approximate formation, all came safely to Table Bay. There they found a mighty fleet of thirteen Dutchmen lying at anchor. Arrival at the Cape also meant news via letters wrapped in oiled vellum stuffed under stones. So it was that Middleton had to make do with the news that his brother David had been alive in 1609. But a more permanent marker was the graffiti scored upon boulders scattered over the veldt – interesting if laconic entries. Nothing survives from this Sixth Voyage, though doubtless there would have been incisions similar to the one that reads: 'Hereunder lie letters from the commander Dirk van der Lee and vice-commander P Crook with the ships Nassau, Frederik Hendrik, Nimegen, Wessel and the galliots. Arrived here 9 April 1632 from Batavia and departed 15th ditto.'[2] Although these were meant primarily for compatriots, they were a challenge to the enemy. Dirk van der Lee might have been responding to what an Englishman had written on the other side of that very stone: 'Richard Arnutt Co. Of London arrived July 4 an[no] 1621 dep[arted] xxi.'

As crews poked about and the ships remained at anchor so that stores could be replenished, Downton wandered into what seemed the Garden of Eden itself, 'At this time was there spring, both trees and all hearbes blowing over the earth . . . It much repenteth me that yt I came unprovided of all sortes of garden seeds, wch might be helpfull or necessarye for reliefe of Christians coming here for refreshments. Also planting acorns might in time be useful, as they grow here more quickly than in our cold country.'[3] Glad to sniff the plants, he was less pleased with quite other odours:

> These people are the filthiest for the usage of there bodyes that ever I have heard of, for besides the naturall uncleanes (as by sweat or otherwise) whereto all people are subject; wch the most by washing cleare themselves of, contrarywise these people doth augment by annointing there bodyes with a filthy substance, wch I suppose to be the juice of hearbes . . . also another most strange and filthy wearing . . . as the guts of cattle about there neckes, wch makes them smell like a butcher's slaughter-house"

have heard of: for besides other uncleanness which most people clear off by washing, this people, on the contrary, augment their natural filth, anointing their bodies, with a nasty substance which I suppose to be the juice of herbs . . . !ey wear also a most filthy and abominable thing about their necks, being the nasty guts of their slaughtered cattle, making them smell more offensively than butcher's shambles.[4]

Relieved to get aboard again, Downton took *Peppercorn* to join the others in a five-gun salute to the Dutch before they sailed up the coast and into danger:

> We left St Augustine bay on the 9th September, leaving the *Union* still there. The 29th, the wind being E.S.E. and the current, as I judged, setting S.W. we were entangled with a lee-shore, which we called the Carribas, being several small islands with sundry ledges of rocks among them, only to be discovered by the breaking of the waves upon them . . . we spent six days before we could get disengaged from among them, the wind . . . still forcing us to leewards, though using every effort by towing and otherwise to get off. The great danger arose from the strength of the current, and the want of any place where we could anchor; as, although we had ground near the rocks, it was very deep and foul. There are several of these islands, mostly full of trees. Every night after dark, we could see fires on shore made by the natives, but we had no inclination to go ashore to speak with them. When it pleased God that we got clear of this danger, we found the current to our amazement carry us to the northwards.[5]

Drowned, eaten or saved? All depended upon the skill of the pilot. Pulling off, the flotilla came safely to Socotra, an island 250 miles off the southern coast of Arabia, unrivalled for tamarind and aloes of the finest quality. The tamarind was thought an 'extraordinary good fruit against the scurvy', whilst the Socotrine aloe (*Aloe Perryi*) was held in special esteem as being effective against burns, bad breath and a host of skin complaints. The most famous of all Portuguese herbalists, García de Orta (d. 1568), had had much to say about the medical benefits of Socotrine aloes. In a famous apologia, his *Colóquios dos simples e drogas da Índia* (1563), he claims that Socotra aloes are four times more efficacious than others.

At Socotra, Nestorian Christianity had once been in the ascendant. The place had then been captured by Tristão da Cunha and the duke of Albuquerque back in 1507. Thereafter it had been abandoned following the wreck of the *San Antonio* on its shores in 1511. In the century before Downton and *Peppercorn* arrived, however, the island had reverted to an isolation so profound that even today a third of its flora and fauna are not to be found elsewhere. But Downton had not come all this way merely to spot the Socotra starling. Rather, he was sizing up chances of breaking into the Arabian market. Carrying a medley of gifts and arriving beneath an 'orange tawny tent' set against an azurite sky, he found the sultan awaiting him 'attended by the principal of his people, being Arabs, and a guard of small shot'. At once Downton proffered a 'fair gilt cup of ten ounces weight, sword-blade and three yards of *stammel* [red] broad-cloth'.[6] Information duly solicited by such douceurs, it was decided that *Increase* and *Darling* should sail into the Red Sea whilst Downton took *Peppercorn* into Aden in order to seek such business as might be on offer. But hardly had Downton arrived there than he found himself outwitted by its Turkish governor. Trouble began when the men landed:

> Being informed by my boatswain that he was much in want of small cordage for many purposes, and that he wished he and others might go ashore to lay some on the strand by the town wall, I sent to ask permission from the governor, with assurance of their safety. This was immediately granted with the utmost readiness and complacency, desiring that they might use the most convenient place for their purpose, and offering the use of a house in which to secure their things during the night. Yet after all these fair promises, every man who went ashore was seized, stript of their money and every thing they had, and put in irons. My pinnace was lost, all the ropes taken away, together with the implements for laying it over again. Thus there were now prisoners, two merchants, the purser, a man to wait upon them, a prating apothecary, my surgeon, master-caulker, boatswain, one of his mates, two quarter-masters, the cooper, carpenter, gunner's mate, cockswain, and five of his crew, in all twenty persons.[7]

Meanwhile *Increase* and *Darling* ran into still more serious difficulties. Anchored off Mocha, the crewmen were warmly received and so took advantage of a comfortable house provided by the harbour authorities. There 'General' Sir Thomas Middleton was sunning himself when, hearing noises round the back, he was pole-axed by a glancing blow. This would have killed him had he been walking. The whole thing had been a trap to confiscate the ships. Eventually he came round, but with such severe ache in his hands he thought they had been severed. What was to follow was hardly relief. Middleton was thrust into a cupboard where he was left 'all that day in a dirty dog kennel under a stair . . . my company to keep me awake were grief of heart and a multitude of rats'.[8] Finding himself chained by the neck to one of his crew, he was asked how he had dared approach Mecca, when the place was forbidden to the unbeliever; he replied that there had been no suggestion they were unwelcome when they had first arrived in Yemeni waters. So far from that, indeed, Middleton told his tormentor how he had been encouraged to offload goods by the promise of doing a brisk trade to the satisfaction of all parties. At this point the governor sent his prisoners up to the capital San'aa. This was 250 miles across a desert, the most daunting of terrains that required prisoners to walk upon molten steel by day, only to find themselves shrouded in spiky frost by night. Notwithstanding, all were heartened by the escape of the master of the *Darling*:

> That same evening, though the Turks guarded our men very narrowly, Mr Pemberton slipt aside among the bushes, and made for the sea-side, where he chanced upon a canoe with a paddle, in which he put off, committing himself to the danger of the sea, rather than trust to the mercy of the Turks. Through the fatigue of his long journey, he was forced to give over rowing by the morning; but it pleased God that the canoe was noticed from the Trades-increase, and picked up by her pinnace, which brought Mr Pemberton on board, hardly able to speak through faintness.[9]

When the party eventually staggered into Sana'a, somehow with no one dying, the Pasha afforded scant reassurance: 'Is not my word sufficient to overturn a city? If Regib [the Pasha of Mocha] wrong you, I will pull his skin over his ears, and give you his head. Is he not my slave?'[10] Less interested in the head than his liberty, Middleton pushed back sufficiently as to obtain promise of freedom for all. But release was not just thanks to stout bearing.

Things might have ended quite differently had it not been for the large Indian business community that feared that if it did not intervene, the Company would have made matchsticks out of their masts. Thus it came to pass that the Indians made a decisive intervention that helped to resolve the deadlock. As the party returned, Middleton was sufficiently alert to notice that 'Here grow poppies of which they make opium', though after lighting up himself, he was forced to conclude 'but it is not good'. Meanwhile, all were wondering what had become of Pemberton. They did not have long to wait before hearing decidedly encouraging news, when Pemberton wrote:

> To satisfy your worship of my arrival and safety after I gave you the slip . . . I came down to the sea side about 7 or 8 miles to the southwards of the ships, where going by the sea side I found a canoe, but never an oar, but God so provided me that wading along with her to windward, found two gengathoes and with them an oar with a pole, which pole I put out like a bowsprit, and with my garter made it fast, and thereon hung my shirt, and with the oar, though with much ado, and great pain, steered her but could not guide her so as I would, but came the 23rd of December on the off side of the Increase, and so far that had it not been for one poor fellow, under God, I might have been in danger of perishing, this being about 9 of the clock in the morning, but bless be God, I arrived, all spent with labour and want of drink, having drunk all my own water that nature could afford me, for the which blessing, with many other, God make me thankful.[11]

Now Middleton began to think of his own escape, encouraged by a bevy of letters that advised how this might best be done. Pemberton wrote from aboard the *Increase* safely behind English guns: 'I stand in doubt your Worship was not pleased of my rash advice, in advising to disguise yourself', before turning to the Old Testament as solace for both: 'I rest, desiring that God, who delivered the prophet David from the hands of wicked Saul many times, and Daniel from the jaws of the lions, even that God I desire to deliver you out of the claws of those bloodthirsty lions, and grant you with speed your former liberty.'[12] With questions and advice flying hither and thither, Middleton started to wonder whether disguise might not be the best thing after all. This Pemberton now approved:

Right Worshipful, Yours of the 9th received, your intent I like well of. I make no question but God, who is your guide, will effect it. I think in disguising yourself in apparel, and to have your hair cut from your face, and besmutting yourself, and with a burden, then there will be no doubt, but if you think to effect it otherwise, in the name of God, I make no question being once in the boat, that then it is out of fear in bringing you away, in despite of them all, for before they can make after you, you shall be almost aboard: I doubt not but God will so provide that it shall come to pass. I would have shaved myself and disguised myself to have effected this business, but doubted my pockeated face, with some kind of show [of recognition] with our men, make me know.[13]

Fretting at his impotence, Middleton now began to act the sailor on shore. This greatly annoyed Downton, who having cut himself loose from his own difficulties in Aden only now found himself ordered about as if by remote control. Accordingly he complained in the strongest terms at what he regarded as Middleton's meddling ways: 'Wherefore Sir, since you are in the tyrant's hands . . . I pray you, with patience, give ear and consider that while you were in your place I embraced you with honourable respect, and did no way disobey your command, but now you are separated from us, . . . I will no way obey you, but by the help of our great God, I propose so to command and dispose of these ships, as I shall think fittest.'[14] Meanwhile Middleton fell upon a ruse: incapacitating his guards with drink and stepping into the empty barrel, he was trundled down to the sea to spring upon the sand.[15] Blinking in the sun and looking about him, Middleton leapt into the nearest boat and proceeded to tack down the coast, picking up others who had been detailed to leave town two by two so as to avoid suspicion:

All things fell out well for my purpose. The *subasha* [pasha], who was our guardian, and left in town only to look after me, fell to hard drinking at a rack house. The boat being come, and my keepers all drunk, the subasha came home to our house about noon. I then sent away the carpenters, two and two only together to avoid suspicion, as if to walk, with orders to shift for themselves in the appointed boat. Mr Femell, and those others I was to take in to leeward of the town, I ordered likewise to walk by twos at the shore, and to wait my coming for them. Having given all these directions, I was put into my cask and safely carried to the boat, on which I gave immediate orders to bear up to leewards, where I took in Mr Fowler and ten more of our people. Mr Femell and others, being too late of coming out of town, were taken before they could get to the boat. Having got safe on board the Darling, we espied the boat with the carpenters coming towards us, in which four escaped, but a fifth was too long of coming to the boat, and attempting to swim on board, was drowned.[16]

So much for officers and crew, but what of the factors? Some had been left behind when Middleton had made it out to the *Trade's Increase*. Of these the unluckiest was unquestionably Lawrence Femmell, who was new to the East India Company. Stranded on shore when the Turkish assault had begun, and hoping to get away with Middleton, Femmell had rushed after the escaping party but disaster had struck. He missed Middleton's pinnace owing to the 'foolish dealing of that idiot and white-livered fellow the coxswain'. Struggling to get into deeper water but with the enemy now gaining, he then found himself with no choice but to turn and fight: 'My pistol, I thank God, was a means to save my life, for two soldiers assailing me I placed two bullets in one of them, who lieth by, as I hear. The second purposing to have cloven my head, I warded it with my pistol, the blow was so violent that his sword fell out of his hand into the sea, by this time there came a Turk who knew me and protected me from further harm.'[17] Returned for the time being to shore, he received a letter from Middleton in which the general asked his fretting subordinate: 'If you hear of the cornet or treble viol hereafter you may send for them, . . . for the concert is spoiled without them. The cornet was left standing in a corner of the house where John Cook died.'[18]

Whether Femmell found those instruments is not clear; though the 'harm' he had avoided from that scimitar of the janissary came in a different guise all too soon. Designated to run the factory at Surat, and eventually getting out to India, he died in Surat shortly after arriving. Before then, however, he had developed a taste for coffee when he was summoned to the great cabin aboard the *Increase*, there to listen to whatever could be pulled together to make up 'Middleton's Consort'. It seems that music was in much demand. For Middleton it soothed the wounded pride of failing in the Red

Sea, whilst for Femmell it allowed him to forget about falling into the same. But as for the presence of music at large, it was supposed that for the generality it did more important things still. Captains believed that a consort of viols quieted vile bodies ready to rise up in fury against their masters.

India was only marginally less threatening than the Yemen. The Portuguese made landing extremely hazardous. But with resistance and rest, Middleton returned to the Red Sea where he was determined to settle old scores. So it was that the Sixth Voyage came to anchor off Aden once again, two years to the day since leaving London. *Peppercorn* was left to blockade Aden, while *Increase* and *Darling* moved up to anchor off Bab-el-Mandeh. As the two nosed through the narrow waters, who should they find waiting for them but that captain of pornography John Saris who was now in charge of the Eighth Voyage. Promoted general of this Eighth Voyage, Saris had left London for Japan. Such an unlooked-for encounter vastly complicated things, serving to frustrate Middleton's intentions. But that was no bad thing, since if Middleton had succeeded in shooting up the bazaar, it would have destroyed any chance that the Eighth might have been able to do business upon its own account.

Middleton now made the extraordinarily tactless suggestion that once revenge had been enacted, the Sixth should get two-thirds and the Eighth one-third of any booty that might accrue. Treating such a suggestion with the disdain it deserved, Saris left Middleton little choice but to depart empty of reparation. But before the disgruntled general hauled off, there was time for an errand that Smythe had delegated to Saris. This involved paddling from the *Hector* to the *Increase* with a trunk of books Smythe was keen that 'Master Femmell' should have it, if only to set the right tone for his new appointment:

for the better comforte and recreation of such of our factors as are reci-deinge in the Indies, wee have sent the works of that worthie servant of Christe, Mr W'm Perkins,[19] to enstruct their mynds and feede their soules w'th thatt heavenlie foode of knowledge of the trueth of God's word, and the Booke of Martirs in twoe voleumes, as alsoe Mr Hakluit's Voyadgs to recreate their spiritts wth varietie of historie, w'ch bookes wee desier to have lefte w'th Mr Lawrence Femell our cheefe agent . . . that they should have espetiall care to sanctifie the Sabboth daye and to reade upon those devyne books for the instruccion and comforte of all those that shall be there remayninge.[20]

Could it be that Smythe had deliberately chosen Saris to stagger around in the blistering heat of the Yemen with Master Foxe's *Book of Martyrs*? If so he might have been punishing Saris because Smythe had heard how this lustful 'General' had left London with a life-size picture of a naked woman hanging in the officers' mess aboard his flagship. Perish the thought, but Smythe might have had a sense of humour.

Once returned to Surat, however, Middleton came again upon the enemy: 'A mile from us rode at anchor seven sail of Portuguese frigates or men of war, there being thirteen more of them within the river of Surat.'[21] At this point an envoy from the Portuguese felt sufficiently emboldened to ask Middleton if he possessed the trade pass that the man spuriously claimed Philip III always granted aliens wishing to trade in what the king of Spain regarded as his 'possessions'. A showdown became inevitable. All the while, the Portuguese were doing their best to sink the English at sea or ambush them in the sand. Although these depredations were fended off with no loss of life, it was resolved to turn the Sixth southward in search of more tractable markets. Heading for the Malay Peninsula and voyage set fair, suddenly disaster struck. This was due to poor piloting from Martin Mollineux, the man who had done so well in bringing the Company's *Dragon* home after its travails in the Bay of Biscay. On this occasion, however, Mollineux proved rather less adept; indeed, he contrived to drive the Company's most expensive boat onto the only two rocks between India and Indonesia:

About midnight of the 20th November we set sail in clear moonshine, having the wind at N.E. off shore. Notwithstanding every care and exertion to avoid the two known rocks three leagues from Tekoa, we got fast on a rock . . . God in his mercy gave us a smooth sea and no wind, so that the set or motion of the ship seemed quite easy; yet the water flowed in upon us so fast, that both chain-pumps with infinite labour could not in a long time command the water. With all possible expedition we got an anchor out astern, with two-thirds of a cable, which God so blessed, that before we could heave the cable taught at the capstan, the ship of her own accord was off into deep water . . . After consulting together on what was best to be done, we returned to Tekoa, there to endeavour to stop our leak, which we found to be in the fashioning pieces of the stern. Accordingly, about sunset of the 21st we came to anchor there in a place well-fitted for our purpose. The 22d, 23d, and 24th we laboured hard to land indigo, cinnamon, and other things, using every exertion to lighten the ship at the stern where the leak was, and were busily engaged till the 8th December in mending the leak and reloading our goods; which done, we set sail again from Tekoa, and arrived on the 20th at Pulo-panian.[22]

Increase was in desperate need of massive overhaul when she finally limped into Bantam. All seemed to be progressing well when fire broke out: this was so extensive the great ship had now to be abandoned altogether. Grievously disappointed, vexed beyond endurance, Middleton expired on 24 May 1613. It was a melancholy end for one who had been second only to James Lancaster in reputation. Meanwhile, himself weary of 'this our every way thwarted journey, where my contents are small, and my hope of profit less', Downton cut his losses, and in the same month that he buried Middleton, he took home 'this poor little ship' as he describes his *Peppercorn*.

Returning home, *Peppercorn* came into Table Bay without mishap. There Downton chanced upon Sir Robert Sherley, curse of the Company and confidant of the shah. By far and away the most devious operator in the early modern world of diplomacy, Sir Robert, who had awarded himself an English knighthood upon the strength of having received a papal gong, was going to finally break the patience even of his devoted secretary. Hearing his master's voice once too often, and so throwing off the dust of the desert, this unhappy man would be heard to wail as he went, how his erstwhile master had had one fixed principle only in life – arranging 'his conscience like a water-mill in keeping with the material to be ground'.[23] In 1613, however, honest Captain Downton had yet to fathom the full depths of Sherley's duplicity, and so with much joint experience of the Middle East between them and the hope of opening a textile trade between England and Persia, the two talked silk deep into the night.

Departing Cape Town, *Peppercorn* fell in with the *Hector* and *Thomas*, setting course for the Cape Verde islands. By September Downton was approaching Pembrokeshire when, offshore winds making it impossible to get into Milford Haven, he found himself obliged to berth in Waterford Bay with a crew of twenty-six, not the forty-six with which *Peppercorn* had left Bantam. Leaning over the side, Downton spotted his old mate Stephen Bonner, who had come over from Lyme Bay for a day's fishing. Bonner was horrified at the condition of *Peppercorn*, and so 'laying aside his own business, used the utmost diligence in doing the best he could for the ease and relief of our weak and sick people'.[24] Comforts material and spiritual were afforded by the bishop of Waterford, who 'very kindly came to visit me'. The bishop offered communion, but Downton declined, feeling himself 'unprepared' though 'at hearts' ease'. Having qualified for a fortnight's leave, those able to went ashore. No sooner had they put first foot on harbour step, however, than it threatened to be their last. The commander of the fort had hired a 'villainous fellow' whom Downton had thrown into jail to swear Downton was nothing but a pirate. So Downton went to Dungannon jail, from whence he came to be sprung by Walter, eleventh earl of Ormonde, the uncrowned king of Ireland.[25]

Free to turn rudder south-east, thanks to the gracious intervention of his lordship, Downton found Beachy Head looming through a clear dawn before reaching Dover Roads by eight o'clock on the night of 12 September. Anchoring against the battleship *Assurance*, he was arrested a second time: 'Mr Cocket her master came immediately aboard, and again arrested my ship till further orders from the lord high admiral.'[26] He was released soon enough, and *Peppercorn* groaned up the Thames into Blackwall. On 20 October 1613 'Mr Deputy' and several members of the Court of Committees came down to congratulate Downton upon his laborious return. And so at last he was able to surrender his 'charge' of three and a half years' keeping.

Exhausted officers and crew feasted, probably fiddled, and most likely did both. Invoices were altered and bills of lading doctored whilst for those who could not grasp accountancy there was much to seize anyway – silk stuffed into bags and emerald sewn into doublets. Security guards were to be found on every ship once docked but crews were well experienced in evading them. As for *Peppercorn*, it badly needed a rest. Salt-begrimed, worm-devoured, paint-peeled, it was sent off to deep dock for a well-deserved refit. There it remained a year before emerging, reinvented as a heavily armed merchantman.[27]

Peppercorn played no part in Downton's crushing defeat of the Portuguese at Swally Hole in January 1615. When, however, the ship eventually left dry dock at Blackwall, it was declared ready 'for any occasion': the 'occasion' selected was Japan no less. This was a journey *Peppercorn* had never attempted before. Contact was lost on the outward leg, but *Peppercorn* was eventually plotted returning in May 1617, signalling to the *Globe* far off the coast of Africa. Labouring in a swell, Captain Harris, who had succeeded Downton as commander of the *Peppercorn*, tried to close on the *Globe*, signalling to 'keep him company to the uttermost of his endeavours'. But if boats fell in, officers fell out. Suddenly the Portuguese *Salvado* bound for Lisbon, seeing the danger, chivalrously offered Harris assistance. This he gladly accepted, guaranteeing his unarmed Samaritan safe passage. But hardly had Harris made this gesture than it was confounded by Martyn of the *Globe* who, firing upon the *Salvado*, boarded it, tortured a crewman to reveal the valuables and encouraged his crew to rape the women. Harris was outraged and, confronting Martyn, such 'extraordinary foul language ensued' that those standing by feared that the two might actually kill each other. Eventually Harris backed down, though the encounter had made one witness suggest that the ranking of every 'prime servant' should be expressly named in commissions, otherwise there would be continual 'heart-burnings and discontents'.[28] Safely home, Martyn thought he had got away with it, but he was reckoning without the Dutch crewman Jacob Bowingson who, having witnessed the horror, denounced Martyn as a rapist, torturer and extortioner. At this point, Smythe quietly fixed things. Well experienced at helping men evade justice, he decided that Harris should be dismissed and Martyn retained. The choice was harsh, but then so was Smythe. From the first, he had been willing to disregard depravities when the calculus of advantage demanded that expediency should trump morality.

After that year-long refit, when *Peppercorn* had become as much warship as merchantman, it was now qualified to take station in the Straits of Molucca at the end of 1618. Here the plan was to join a large English squadron to confront the Dutch in such a battle as would finally decide who was to be King of the East. However, there were serious difficulties with all of this, the most pressing being the state of the English fleet. Of all the ships in bad repair, *Peppercorn* was in the worst shape because she had made such heavy weather of getting to the Far East. It had taken ten months to make Bantam, during which the master had been lost, seven men had drowned, seventeen were dead and there were but 'six men able to work'. Indeed, *Peppercorn* had barely been able to crawl across Bantam Roads and into dock. But there was a much larger problem, and this affected not just that jocund little boat but the entire English fleet being assembled to fight it out with the Dutch. The officer who identified this larger issue had long been in the fast stream: the Bristolian Martin Pring whose brace of mastiffs had proved so effective against Native Americans. Pring was number two in command of the squadron that now included *Peppercorn*. Here Pring had been struck by the grievous quality of the men under his command, so horrified that he became wholly dismissive:

> this irregular and almost incorrigible scum of rascals, whom the land hath ejected for their wicked lives and ungodly behaviour. Our misery is that we so often see the proverb fulfilled, which is if they be good for nothing send them to the East Indies. If it were to be wished that your worships would not lend so free and gentle ears unto the unreasonable requests of many who think they have made an East Indian voyage if they lose an ungracious and disobedient son or an unruly depending kinsman.[29]

But this was not all. Operations were severely compromised by simple men burdened with complexities they could not grasp. Here Pring was thinking of what he described as *semi nautae*; that was to say, people 'who cannot want entertainment if they know what point of the compass is opposite N.E.'[30] Once such undesirables were taken on, they went to sea with few clothes but many diseases, and if denied money 'their fingers are like live twigs, nothing being too hot or too heavy for them, that lies in their way; many honest men being robbed of the little money they had brought to sea by these wicked villains'.

Here Pring was choosing to ignore the biggest villain in the sea. The general under whom he served was just as ignorant as were those hopeless crewmen which Pring dismisses. This was the redoubtable Sir Thomas Dale who, soldier not sailor, and hardly knowing the difference between a prow and a poop, had been made commander of the biggest battle group that the

Company had ever assembled. The fault for all this lay firmly with Smythe who had pushed for Dale's appointment because when Smythe had had his back against the door of Virginia over accusations of malfeasance, Dale had charged in to help out.

In Virginia Dale had proved to be a notably cruel man. Sent to knock heads together, he had done that by hanging them in pairs with such gusto as had convinced Smythe that one who could correct a convict settlement might be relied upon to create a community of enterprise. Knowing just how badly things were going in the Far East, Smythe thought that in flogging his way through the fleet, Dale might yet serve to stiffen the mast.

But once Dale got out there things changed with the changing circumstances he encountered. In the Far East Dale adopted a different policy to the 'hang 'em high' approach which worked among the drunks of Virginia, but proved much less efficacious with the merchants of Bantam. Some, but only a few, seem to have applauded, but most deplored Dale's philosophy of management. This was to allow Company seamen to assault the indigenous population because he thought this would slake the lusts of the swabber and lead to better behaviour aboard the fleet. Dale regarded the Pribumi of Indonesia with as little respect as he had formerly accorded the Chickahominy of Virginia. In contrast to the contempt which Dale nursed for the Indigenous were attitudes held by others in the same station who utterly despised the egregious Sir Thomas Dale. One such was the merchant Augustine Spalding, who, taking time out of compiling an English–Malay dictionary, reported to the Court of Committees how he thinks 'worser thieves live not in Newgate than most of the men in this fleet; Sir Thomas Dale's favour in allowing them to pillage at pleasure has made them worse'.[31] Here there was something of an irony since Spalding himself was in the Company's crosshairs having been suspected of making off with a sack of their money. If trouble was still to come for Spalding, soon enough death was to overtake Dale – though even then not soon enough for many – as he was swept away with dysentery upon the coast of Coromandel.[32]

Despite the disappearance of the overall commander, senior officers remained intent on closing with the Dutch, and English decks were cleared for action. Thus it was that *Peppercorn*, along with eleven other East India Company ships, came to be primed to take on a much superior fleet of sixteen

Dutch battleships, with the result that a 'cruel bloody fight' seemed apparent. Any brave English spirits who were looking forward to the final reckoning with the Dutch, who for nearly twenty years had bested the English in the seas beyond Ceylon, must have been crestfallen when the whole thing was called off. Had it in fact taken place, the Company must surely have suffered its terminal defeat. This was partly because of the disparity in numbers but also due to the lamentable condition of the English ships. Nine of these, including *Peppercorn*, were 'pitifully distressed in their provisions and stores', whereas the Dutch were in better trim. But then, Captain Adams (Robert, not the famous pilot William), coming up in the *Bull* from the Cape in the nick of time, signalled that a truce had been brokered in Europe. And so by this means was prevented such an encounter as 'if they had met there had never been such a day amongst Christians'.[33] The respective commanders, now directed to join in amity in discharging fireworks not grapeshot, found much joy at so happy a union 'before any more Christian blood was spilt, and heathens to stand laughing at us, and make benefit of our dissensions'.[34]

With Captain Adams's intervention, the Company was granted a short reprieve from the unstoppable advance of the VOC. It was a moment to catch breath when this crisis-ridden year of 1619 had been so disastrous. There had been a serious haemorrhage of commanders and an unacceptable loss of shipping. Dale had died: though he was missed by none. But the death of the president of the Indies was quite another matter. This was John Jourdain, who had been taken out by a Dutch sniper when Jourdain had been parleying aboard the *Samson*. The Dutch had captured the *Dragon*, *Bear*, *Expedition*, *Rose*, *Samson*, *Hound* and *Star*, whilst all that the Company had got its hands was the *Zwart Leeuw* (Black Lion). That apparent success turned out to do more harm than good, however. At two in the morning on the very day when the *Black Lion* was to have been unloaded, sailors had broken through her orlop and broken open her rack. Next thing and one of those high-octane bottles, overturning next to a candle, caused the *Zwart Leeuw* to go up like a rocket. No mercy was shown to larcenists cum arsonists. A 'court' was at once convened aboard the *Moon*, where the ringleader Owen Bodman was arraigned together with his accomplices. For 'burning the Black Lion, breaking open the chests, mutiny, and breaking the master's head', Bodman was to be hanged from the yardarm until he be dead, whilst his accomplices were forced to look on, before themselves receiving 'ten stripes upon the bare back aboard each of the seven great ships of the fleet'. The end of the *Leeuw* was deeply to be regretted when there was precious little encouragement in trying to meet the Dutch gun for gun.[35]

Out of that peace now arose the so-called Fleet of Defence. Ostensibly formed against Portugal and Spain, in fact the true purpose of this conspiracy to murder was to immolate the Chinese junk trade to and from the Philippines. The alliance between the Dutch and the English companies lasted just the two seasons (1621–2), until the parties resolved to separate and 'each to bear their own charges' in pursuit of security and quest for trade.[36] As it transpired, *Peppercorn* played no part in the first campaign season. There was further delay in getting it into battle for season number two because three of the crew, together with three from the *Bull*, had run off with the help of a 'Japon of Nangasaq' (Nagasaki); but the six 'were so hotly pursued that they were over-taken and brought back again'. As to their punishments, these had had to wait until the Japanese governor of Hirado returned from Nagasaki; where he had gone 'to put to death many Japon Christians for harbouring of Papist pristes secretly'.[37]

All the while, *Peppercorn* and *Bull* were tied up until the authorities decided what to do with compatriots who had encouraged the six English crewmen to run off. If the ' "Japponers" were to be put to death . . . so then the ringleaders of our runaways must be executed as well as they': this was the matter-of-fact way in which Richard Cocks, the cape merchant of Japan, who would be one of the judges, anticipated what might happen. Eventually the English renegades were brought into 'the English howse at Firando in Japan'. In presiding over this second ad hoc 'court', Captain Adams went through the motions of urging his colleagues to be open-minded, though in suggesting that the six were 'raisors of mutiny in the highest degree', Adams was clearly working for the result. And so it was that Edward Harris, boat-swain, and Thomas Gilbert, crew of *Peppercorn*, and William Harris and Alexander Hix of *Globe* were sentenced to death, the sentence being carried out immediately when each of the miscreants was made to swing from their respective ship. That done, it was recorded how 'it hath pleased Captaine Robart Adames, w'th the free consent of his private councell, to reprive and for present to give them there lives, hopinge the example of justice executed uppon the other fowre will breede a terror and feare in the hartes of all others to comitt the lyke offence, w'ch God of his Mercy grant'.[38]

At last released after being lighted of crewmen, *Peppercorn* partnered the Dutch *Moyen* 'the better to surprise Chinese junks sailing to Manila'. On 20 April 1622, when stationed off Hartes Bay in the Philippines, *Peppercorn* ran out her guns when 'three Christian Chinese' had revealed that there were two China junks lying under the island of Luan. There was no sign of them, however, so it was resolved to land 400 men. But having heard the Europeans were coming, these Chinese merchants had gone to Manila, taking everything with them.

In a way, violence clearly achieved results: it has been computed that 'In 1621 the fleet had captured: five junks with goods and two frigates, one empty the other carrying fifty sacks of rice. In 1622 it took a frigate and a junk, both "richly laden", five other junks and a few small boats.'[39] In the second of the seasons, goods and silver to the value of 199,256 rials was snatched.[40] Adams, having himself contributed to the killing, was well qualified to write to the president of the Indies about a much broader Dutch investment in death, describing how the Hollanders were 'like so many develles or raveninge wolves sekinge after there prey w'ch abuses I have at full certified to the President at Jaccatra and therefore here omytt them'.[41] But whilst Adams was professing to Jakarta, Cocks was protesting to London. Writing as the cape merchant at the English base in Hirado, Cocks had this to say when addressing Smythe and his Court of Committees: Right Wor'll Ser and Sers, . . . the 29th June last our whole fleete of 9 shipps, English and Duch, arrived in saffetie from the Manillias, very few of the men being dead, and having taken and pillaged 5 junckes, the Duch using much crueltie in killing many Chinas after they hadd rendred themselves, and many more had kild yf the English had not prevented them.'[42] But was this collusion? Is it just coincidence that the two senior men in Japan should both be writing within seventy-two hours of one other? It seems likely that they were conspiring to put blue not red water between themselves and the VOC, using Company paper to wipe blood off English decks.

That this may have been happening is also suggested in quite another sort of letter, same scene same time, which implies that the Dutch were not the only killers. Joseph Cockram (d. 1626) had this to say about the behaviour of his own: 'The abuses of the Dutch this last year I am sory wee are [have]

not yet righted heare according to your desires, but in theis voyadges soe
many abuses and complaints on eytheir syde by wicked and unrulie people
that it is hard to judg betwine our two nacions wheare lyeth the greatest
fawlt, for on eytheir syde are knaves enough.'[43] In fairness to the Dutch, so
grievous were these reports that Batavia was visibly shaken and the whole
operation closed down. Whatever the degree of complicity, the Dutch were
famous for drowning. Wearing his hat as secretary to the Council of Flanders
and not as a painter, Rubens wrote to the French savant Palamède de Fabri,
Sieur de Valavez, about what had been happening much nearer home, in the
waters off the coast of Dunkirk:

> The Hollanders, with their usual severity, and notwithstanding all the
> courtesy imaginable shown by the Most Serene Infanta and the Marquis
> [Spinola] to their prisoners (as I myself have seen at Dunkirk), have
> thrown into the sea, tied in pairs, back to back, about seventy of our men
> who were serving on private ships under the royal standard. They have
> done this at different times, but there were thirty on one ship alone. I
> hope, and I believe it is true, that orders have been dispatched to these
> private vessels, though not yet to the royal ships, to take reprisals up to
> the same number of men.[44]

As for the English East India Company's relations with the Dutch, dealings
were made a whole lot worse by this misalliance. Out in the Far East there
was a permanent sense of resentment whenever a Dutchman came in sight.
Part of the reason for this was that the Dutch had nurtured what the English
had neglected: a proper infrastructure of maintenance. Logistics were too
complicated when London had never financed a proper repair department,
and still less had been willing to pay for deep water facilities in Japan. And
so it came about that the Company base in Japan was ordered to 'leave affe
our consortshipp of the Fleet of Defence w'th the Hollanders'.[45] As for
Peppercorn itself, she would be 'left off' too. By 9 February 1623 the boat was
at Jakarta and in a desperate state. Sadly, now there was nothing for it but to
join the *Globe*, *Fortune*, *Bear* and *Clove* at the breaker's yard.

Between them, this flotilla of five had discharged a prodigious span of
service. Yet somehow the Company had spent more energy firing guns than

gathering gains. The presence of so many warships dedicated to piracy and not trade ought to have alerted London to what was afoot. The Fleet of Defence had been welcomed in London as heralding a more positive attitude by the Dutch. Soon, however, Holland was to revert to its default position, which was to remove altogether the English from the East. It was a policy of unremitting aggression that resulted in the so-called Massacre of Amboyna, which would occur early in 1623 (see Chapter 15). At best, Amboyna was an 'incident' rather than a 'massacre', though that was precisely what the Company claimed to exploit public outrage. But to the extent that Amboyna was a massacre of national pride, it was to prove quite fatal to relations, not only between the two companies but also between the two nations. What mattered more to the 'Hollander', though, was that the VOC had won the 'Battle of the Spice Islands' with the expenditure of much less powder than they had once feared was going to be necessary.

Amboyna signalled the end of relations with the Dutch until William of Orange landed in Devon in 1688 on the anniversary of the Gunpowder Plot, that much earlier crisis for the Stuarts. As for the supposed Massacre with a capital 'M', that had coincided to the day with the death of the *Peppercorn*. Through stormy endeavour, expectation had always been that she and her sisters might yet deliver the Spice Islands to the Adventurers back home. But as death unfolded in Amboyna, *Peppercorn* was dismembered, the break-up symbolic of a much greater loss. Writing from aboard the *Elizabeth*, riding in Bantam Roads, Edward Lenmyes confessed to a miasma of despondency that was fast settling on him and his mates. He writes of 'how the Dutch flourish here, we being subjects unto them both in government and in tribute, which might have been ours when time was'.[46] All that now remained was to see if the Company might yet find its salvation. What Lenmyes could not have known was that some 5,000 miles away, India was well on its way to becoming the consolation prize for all that had been lost in a part of the world to which untold riches had summoned the Company back in 1600.

9

THE FLYING DUTCHMEN

Company relations with the VOC were conditioned by pride and prejudice. Although the two nations might have seemed natural allies, the English always expected gratitude for the help they had given the Dutch during their war of independence against Spain (1560–1640). As for the Dutch themselves, they greatly resented such a presumption.

Difficulties between the two powers had begun when the Dutch had been forced to become an English protectorate under the terms of the Treaty of Nonsuch (20 August 1585).[1] Although such dependence might have seemed gratifying to the English monarch, Elizabeth I had discovered her new-found protégés to be hardly less distasteful than the Spanish themselves. Yet although she despised the Dutch, she found herself obliged to associate with them, if only because of her horror at the thought that Philip II might launch the invasion of England out of Ostend. As for the Dutch themselves, their first treaty as an independent nation hardly supported claims to autonomy when, as a result of the Treaty of Nonsuch, Elizabeth had insisted on nominating Leicester as military and political head of what the rebels had declared to be the 'United Provinces' (Utrecht: 23 January 1579). A combination of the terms upon which Leicester was obliged to operate, his own failings and resentment at what had been imposed had contributed to creating enormous strains between the two countries. There was also the vexed question of the 'Cautionary Towns', prosperous little Dutch places given to Elizabeth as security against default on the massive loans that rebels had obtained from England. And so the seeds of conflict had been sown. Starting in the 1560s when war in Holland with Spain had also begun, difficulties between England and Holland would not be resolved until the 1690s, when a republican Dutchman became a king of England.

Anglo-Dutch relations were shot through with complexity. Although there were shared values there were divisive tensions too. Economic and social development at the same stage of growth made for armed competitiveness; a Protestant faith that was mutually supportive in confession proved divisive in profession. A similar lack of natural resources within a wet and windy climate where both countries hovered about the same latitude induced frictions, whilst both nations suffered from an insufficiency of commodities to sustain their exports. Although Dutch maritime technology was ahead of England's, their respective fleets had a parity of know-how, in part because they had been nurtured in the same home waters. This meant, however, that when armed conflict was to occur in the waters of the Far East, a failure to deliver the decisive blow by either party against the other served to encourage the next round of killing.

The English were rankled by the provocative thought that it had been the Dutch who had got to Asia first, their inferiority enshrined as an article of faith in the founding charter of the Company itself where it had been declared how Adventurers had been 'induced by the success of the voyage performed by the Dutch nation . . . they were stirred up with no less affection to advance the trade of their native country than the Dutch were to benefit their commonwealth'.[2] Although the two nations shared many ambitions, how they realised them was to be very different. For the EIC, patriotism did not mean annexation of territory, extermination of peoples, fabrication of forts and sowing of settlements, as was the case with the VOC. For the English, what was to be ambition in America after the foundation of the Virginia Company in 1607 would never be the vision in Asia. In England, no one cared a clove for colony when profits sat more heavily than patriotism in the scales of national self-interest. A letter written in Amsterdam on 8 August 1597 seemed to contain good news for those wishing to follow the Dutch into the rising sun. From what had now become Europe's financial capital, this informant, whoever he was, reported to the City of London how the Hollander had been in mighty disarray during a first foray to the Far East. The letter referred to the famous voyage of Cornelis de Houtman, whose assiduity in the map rooms of Lisbon was referred to in Chapter 2. Apparently Houtman had just returned with his pox-ridden crew, having presided over a humanitarian and commercial disaster: Houtman's celebrated if disastrous foray of 1595–7.

The unknown writer must have cut some figure in Amsterdam, since 'Touching the East India voyage' he had informed recipients how 'the captain and original attempter of the voyage' is lodged with him and that at their 'coming' he will impart 'so much as I shall learn'. This he promised to do by drawing out as many 'secrets as possible', adding how the Dutch adventurers had lost their nerve and, being 'now well cooled', would be glad of their money back: 'More than 60,000 royals of eight returned, not through want of will in the inhabitants to have traded, or for want of merchandise to have loaded twenty ships, but absolutely for want of government and through the jars of the commanders, everyone seeking sovereignty.' The Dutch fleet had been required to lie at Bantam for six months without 'trafficking, through their own disagreement'.[3]

Whereas the English East Company was and would always remain focused on the English capital, nothing could have been further from the case over the water. Those who took part in the deliberations of the VOC joined in something of a six-part motet. Though the headquarters of the VOC were in Amsterdam, the 'XVII" delegates who met there represented what was known as the 'six chambers'. These stood for the six Dutch ports with the wealth, ambition and know-how needed to undertake the complexities of adventuring thousands of miles from home: Amsterdam, Rotterdam, Middelburg, Enkhuizen, Hoorn and Delft. Nevertheless, it is surprising that the intra-urban rivalries which had scuppered Houtman had not sunk the federation of six before it got its ships out of harbour. Here the decisive input preventing the dissolution which might have been expected, was this very structure of the Heren Zeventien, or Heren XVII, which 'came into being to neutralise the power of Amsterdam'.[4] Such then was the prelude to the emergence of a fully integrated VOC (1602). In England, by contrast, the genesis of the Company was a wholly 'London event'. Though Bristol was to supply key personnel, and Shoreham, Ipswich, Dublin and Newcastle provide some boats, none of these outliers was a party to the negotiations that had created the EIC. But this different way of doing things cannot explain why the Dutch became dominant in the Far East. With colonies to run and people to exterminate, it may be thought that all the expense and effort these root and branch changes demanded must have been a formula for disaster. Nevertheless, the fact is that the Dutch triumphed, and so the question remains why.

Unlike the English, the Dutch had boundless self-belief, a bottomless purse and a baleful amount to lose if they were to fail in the great work of nation-building. For all their confidence, the United Provinces was a small and new nation fighting for survival against the most powerful force in Europe since Charlemagne's empire had stood astride the Rhine. This was why the VOC always enjoyed that forthright backing from the public purse which the EIC habitually lacked. In contrast with the consistent support the state afforded the VOC, the English Crown was keen to take revenue but deny resources, in ways quite unthinkable with the Stadtholder who, though a republican, was something of a king in the United Provinces. It has been pointed out that 'Up to 1625, Dutch warships were not built by the VOC but provided by the State as support for the role the VOC played in conflicts.'[5] Such subsidies were because Stadtholder Prince Maurits knew that the United Provinces and the VOC were indivisible.

By contrast, James I felt that if he could only crush the cartels he could corner the markets. When in 1624 he equivocated about forthright action over Amboyna, as London was demanding, the newsmonger John Chamberlain got the national mood well enough: 'The time hath ben, when so many English as have ben sent into those parts within these sixe or eight moneths wold have don somewhat, and made the world talke of them, but I know not how we that have ben estemed in that kind more then other nations do begin to grow lesse then the least, when the basest of people in matter of courage dare brave and trample upon us.'[6] But had such a thing happened to the United Provinces, hell on water would have been released. For that newly evolved homo sapiens who was the 'Dutchman', possession in the East was affirmation in the West. The capture of territories by the sailors of Hoorn, their settlement by the burghers of Haarlem, was a 'process' no less important to nation-building than the endless sieges that Stadtholder Prince Maurits spent his life conducting. Here there is an irony. The castles of Batavia and the warehouses of Ceram (Seram) were as sacred to the Dutch as were the missionary stations of Mexico City and the basilicas of Macau to the Iberians. Each was non-negotiable.

Although Smythe may not have known it, the Company was doomed from the very start over the business of getting on terms with its rival. The Dutch were bound to prevail. Time and again they deployed bigger fleets as they built more efficient shipyards. This was entirely right, given the enormously testing conditions that arose from voyages of vast distance and epic challenge. As from 1619, when the VOC headquarters was moved from Amboyna to New Batavia, there came about 'the effective deployment of specialised homeward-bounders . . . [they] had to be specially constructed; not available ready-made on the home market, they were designed to meet the specific needs of Far Eastern trade'.[7] But beyond that, the Dutch knew much better how one stretch of Eastern sea differed as radically from another as the *Hollandia* from the *Zwart Leeuw*. Boats and waters alike needed handling in very different ways. For example, Dutch mariners knew how the seas around Formosa (Taiwan) were 'a harde en swear vaerwater' (hard and heavy waters), whereas the ocean between Batavia and Siam was much easier. This meant that in discrete zones old stock could be risked. First in Bantam (Banten) and then in Batavia, the Dutch created an infrastructure sufficiently robust as to allow its yards to victual fleets commonly to be twice the size the English could muster. But if the East India Company was to lose out in the craze for maize, what prolonged its presence in the Far East was less the resolution of its commanders than the nature of geography. The Spice Islands consist of over a thousand outcrops, whilst the seas between the Indonesia archipelago and the Philippines are so studded with inlets it was always going to be hard for the Dutch to press the advantage. Such accidents of terrain allowed the EIC to hold out much longer than had the issue simply been put to the cannon.

In 1579 Drake had landed on the Moluccas, where he had contacted the king of Ternate. There the king had told him how he was most anxious to find an ally to deflect the Portuguese, and so had 'sent to our Generall with speciall message that hee should have what things he needed and would require, with peace and friendship, and morever that hee would yeeld himselfe and the right of his island to bee at the pleasure and commandement of so famous a prince as we served; in token whereof he sent to our Generall a signet'.[8] It would be upon that accord that a major defence of England's claim to the Spice Islands would rest. Lading cloves, Drake left around new year 1580, confident that England had now gained possession of a fabulous resource.

Meanwhile, back in England, Elizabeth I had been approached by the Spanish ambassador who, aghast at the damage that Drake had inflicted on Spanish colonies, had demanded the rogue be punished. But Elizabeth was having none of it, telling him that her commander would certainly be dealt with if it could be proved that he had done something wrong. After all, Elizabeth had never signed up to the Treaty of Tordesillas, and she was damned if she was going to allow Spain to have it all. But she also upheld the right of the English to trade or colonise where the Spanish had not already settled. Still less would she concede that Spain was to be permitted to prevent her subjects from going wherever they wished: 'The use of the sea and air is common to all; neither can any title to the ocean belong to any people or private man', as the queen told her startled petitioner.[9] This was a bold assertion which anticipated by some years Hugo Grotius's famous theory about 'international waters' which he would enunciate in his *Mare Liberum* (1609), less with the confident assertion of a crown than with all the cavilling of a jurist (see Chapter 14). Having shaken her ruff at the Spanish ambassador, to humiliate him further, Elizabeth made straight for Deptford where, climbing aboard the *Golden Hind*, she knighted Drake before opening his ship to the public.

What then followed had proved wholly disastrous. In 1582 Sir Edward Fenton had left Southampton for the Spice Islands.[10] Given that Fenton's brief was to follow up on Drake's first important contacts, it is hard to understand how such a man should have been charged with deep sea responsibilities at all. The Muscovy merchant Sir George Barne had helped prepare the voyage, but after a close encounter with Fenton had concluded that 'our generaul [is] but a foolish, flattering, fretting creeper'.[11] This notwithstanding, the *Galleon Leicester* of 400 tons, named after Fenton's patron, queen's favourite and disastrous ruler of Holland, Robert Dudley, earl of Leicester, sped down the Channel. The flagship was accompanied by the queen's own *Edward Bonaventure* of 250–300 tons and two barques of 50 and 40 tons apiece, called the *Elizabeth* and *Francis*, this last, however, running off somewhere near the Cape. Trouble began when the fleet was slow in getting down the coast of Africa. Anchoring at Sierra Leone on 6 August 1582, 'before we went from thence, upon a fair stone at the watering place, where all the ships water that come to that place, we graved or names, the year of the Lord, and the month wherein we departed, as we had seen Sr ffrans drake and Capt Candish that had been there before us had don'.[12] But for all the inspiration these two Elizabethan heroes might have furnished, it soon became clear that the flotilla was not going to make it round the Cape because the expedition had left England too late and winds were now against it.

Striking out for South America and anchoring in the River Plate instead, Fenton learned that a strong Spanish squadron was waiting for him at the Cape of Magellan, or that was what he was led to believe. In fact, he was now jumped upon in the river itself. Giving fight, he sunk one ship before deciding to go back to England because the enterprise had been overwhelmed by confused command and capricious direction. The journal of the expedition vividly suggests what it was like when everyone was either aggressive or mutinous: 'Then the General would have drawn his long knife and have stabbed Hawkyns, and intercepted of that, he took up his long staff and therewith was coming at Hawkyns, but the master . . . stayed his fury.'[13]

One expedition after another tried to make lasting contact with the Moluccas, where the overstretched Portuguese were no longer considered an insurmountable threat. In October 1589 Sir James Lancaster had been much involved in trying to create an English footfall: 'Great benefitte will redound to our countree, as well for the anoyinge of the Spaniards and Portingalls (now our enemyes) as also for the venting of our comodities (which, since the beginning of thes late troubles, ys muche decayed), but especially our trade of clotheinge; of which kinde of comodities, and others which our countree dothe yeald, no doubte but a lardge and ample vente wil be founde in those partes'.[14] Nothing much came of that, though, and so it was decided to victual three ships for the South Sea, the Philippines, and the coast of China. On 10 April 1591 the Armada veteran George Raymond, placing his flag in the *Penelope* and accompanied by the *Merchant Royal* and old-stager *Edward Bonaventure*, set off once again. But with a typhoon raging all about, the look-out on the *Bonaventure*, turning to look back at the flagship, now came to observe what made the most melancholy of entries in the journal: 'in the evening we saw a great sea break over our admiral, the *Penelope*, which struck out their light, and we never saw them anymore'.[15] Lancaster lost his mate and fourteen men who, landing on the Comoros, were taken to have been eaten. Nothing daunted, he made it to Sumatra by June 1592 after overwintering at Zanzibar. But little was achieved there, and so returning up the coast of Africa, and passing St Helena in April 1593, Lancaster headed over to the West Indies, where a mutiny left him stranded on Mona with just eighteen men. There they were obliged to wait until picked up by a Frenchman from Dieppe. For his part, Lancaster reached Rye in Sussex in May 1594. Like Drake, he had been away for three years but, unlike him, he had nothing to show for it, except it may be supposed to add his name to the gilded honours board of English failure.

Now the challenge was to reverse all these setbacks. Slowly the Company prodded its way into Borneo, which was reputed to be rich in gold washed out of rivers. The place was also possessed of the world's best antidote against a universal fear of the sixteenth-century English mind: the prospect of being poisoned. What, however, was seen as a sure means to frustrate such intentions was the fabulous 'bezoar stone', calcified food boluses retrieved from animal intestines. The marketing of bezoars was allowing the Company to make money from widespread credulity. People believed them to be a capital investment against poisons of every description, despite the best efforts of William Clowe's inspiration, that famous French surgeon Ambroise Paré. Paré had commandeered a cook from the royal kitchens who, sentenced to death, had elected to die by poison. With the victim's agreement, Paré had inserted the stone, and, standing well back, allowed room for the Crown poisoner to administer his potion. When the convict died in agony some seven hours later, Paré was thrilled because he had long thought bezoars to be bogus.

Besides such quackeries there were also eagle-wood, benzoin, camphor and many other substances, both perfumed and medicinal. Attempts to extend trading links up the coast were, however, frustrated by the hostile presence of the ferocious Dayaks who, much to the disappointment of the factors, turned out to be rather more interested in headhunting than trading. This provided something of a disincentive to the intrepid Sophony Cozuck (i.e. the Kazak) who had got himself the job of heading up the Borneo mission. A man of courage, Sophony had managed to see off a large hoard of those man-eaters with just two companions, something achieved through one decisive advantage: these three had gunpowder when the three hundred did not. Reluctant to risk having a hash made out of his head a second time,

Sophony now waited for the arrival of the *Darling* after retreating behind the stockade of Sukadana. Once aboard this ship he then left for Pattani. Thereafter the incompetence of factors, the intransigence of the Dutch and the hostility of locals spelt the end of Borneo. A sudden attack launched from Java resulted not only in heavy losses for both English and Dutch, but also in the abduction of the queen herself. After that, local tradesmen had run for the jungle. By February 1623 the English president at Jakarta had declared that the debts of the Sukadana factory were irrecoverable. So much for setbacks in Sumatra, Java and Borneo. But what was happening on the Spice Islands themselves? Matters might have gone better had the resolution of Captain Jourdain been backed by the resolve of the Company.

Jourdain had been wrecked aboard the *Ascension* on the coast of Gujurat in 1609. After getting to Agra, he had made his way up country where he had succeeded in joining Sir Henry Middleton, who was then returning to the Red Sea. Sufficiently impressed by Jourdain, Middleton sent him in the *Darling* to Amboyna, where he came to be confronted by the Dutch resident who told him he could not buy cloves. And worse was to come. Crops would never be shared when the Dutch held the very strongest sense of resentment. At this point the Dutch explained to Jourdain how they had been 'at an extreame charge in buildinge and mainetayneing castles to defend them against their enemyes'.[16] Furthermore, they had constructed forts to protect against the Iberians and indigenous alike, and the English had benefited – but not contributed. The problem was the English had always refused to 'go Dutch': refusing to ante-up on maintenance costs when, truth was, they had for long slept in peace under the shadow of a Dutch cannon. The whole issues of payment for protection had become something of an ulcer in the stomach of the VOC, an acidic resentment which the Dutch could always be replied upon to try to drain whenever delegations from the EIC and the VOC pursued the hopeless quest of arriving at a resolution of difficulties and an accommodation of difference.

Brushing such inequity aside, Jourdain told his adversary how Amboyna was 'free for all men'. Furthermore, the people had not agreed to become 'vassalls to the Hollanders'. As it was, the indigenous had wanted to trade with the English, but the Dutch had forced them to buy Coromandel fabrics at a fixed price, in exchange for pepper for amounts the Dutch set. Finding

Hitu chiefs afraid to trade, Jourdain had had no choice but to yield.[17] So he had left for Ceram (Seram Island), where he was told that here, too, the locals would have dealt with the English had it not been for the Dutch threat 'to build a castle, if they did trade with us, and they durst not to displease them without order from the Kinge of Turnatto'.[18] Provoked beyond endurance, Jourdain marched up to the gates of the Dutch factory to confront a young and very angry Jan Pieterszoon Coen who would prove the most successful governor-general in the history of the Dutch East Indies; though indeed, there had already been others queuing up to compete with him for the laurels of being the cruellest. Prior to Coen's arrival there had been all too many willing to adopt a policy of ethnic cleansing if that would help clean up on the clove harvest:

> The shift of the VOC policy makers towards violent action is best exemplified by the secret instructions for governor-general Pieter Both, written in May 1612 by Henrik Brouwer. He brutally advises to cut off the Bandanese trade to and from Java; to destroy part of the trees in Banda, their only source of income (a means of pressure considered much 'cheaper' than an attack on their strongholds); to build a fort on Lonthor; and to kill any Bandanese who dares to resist.[19]

It may be asked whether such men might not have been efficient commanders of *Einsatzgruppen* units in Russia in 1941. No such pitiless agenda is to be found among the papers of the East India Company, or at least until the Company became a ruler as well as a business.

Responding furiously to what were the all-too-familiar English arguments, Coen talked in the most 'chollericke manner' about how Jourdain had come out to interfere 'in the countries that were under their [Dutch] proteccion, as itt were in dispight of them'.[20] As the two stood shouting at one another, Coen then added that should Jourdain even attempt to buy any cloves without his consent 'it was soe much stolne from them, and therefore they would prevent itt, if by any meanes they might'. Getting nowhere in arguing that 'the countrye was as free for us as for them', Jourdain now fell upon the ruse of challenging Coen to summon the local chiefs so as to test the issue. Coen declining, Jourdain did it instead. Heads assembled and the chiefs, demanding the presence of the Dutch, told how they would willingly trade with the English but fear had prevented it.[21] But Jourdain's determination was not supported by the Company. Thus it would be the Dutch who prevailed in a place where the Company had once hoped to plant its flag.

Leaving Bantam in the summer of 1619, Jourdain proceeded with the *Sampson* and the *Hound* up the Malay Peninsula to visit the English factories at Jambi, Pattani and elsewhere. It was a fatal step when his ships were in bad repair, and knowing this, Coen fell upon him. After a furious if short engagement Jourdain surrendered, the terms of which were being discussed when Jourdain was mortally wounded by a shot from one of the Dutch vessels – accidentally according to the Dutch, intentionally thought the English. The passing of Jourdain was widely marked because he had been the most able of the Company presidents. However, for the Dutch his death was merely pawn taken by queen. His murder was certainly gratifying, but hardly more than an incident in what was a much longer game.

What had really done for Jourdain, though, was how the Dutch, and Coen especially, had identified the real enemy as not the Portuguese but the English. From his earliest encounter with Jourdain, Coen had sustained a coruscating contempt for the EIC. This was because he believed it only capable of taking spoils, never of supremacy in the Far East. Shrewd enough to see how the English did not have the capacity to turn servitude into triumph, Coen rightly believed that the EIC lacked the resources to make itself an equal and cooperative ally of the VOC. Indeed, he was to say as much when writing in January 1622:

> It was impossible to deal with the English. They would do as much damage to the Dutch interests as they could, and then claim that it was they who are the aggrieved party. The jealousy, the distrust and the envy that these people had was unlikely to be neutralised by any regulations, agreements or orders. The more apart the two stayed from each other, the greater were the chances of continued friendliness between the two.[22]

Coen was right. The Fleet of Defence would hold together for just fifteen months, proving richer as a source of conflict than as a means of mutual support. So stretched was the Company that during this disreputable interval the resources that could be allocated to the Fleet were so meagre that it proved quite unable to step up to the mast with obligations that floated in Europe were sunk in Asia. Through Dale's incompetence, Coen had been able to obliterate any hope that what lay east of Ceylon might yet be grasped by the Company. With the creation by Coen himself of massive defences to skirt Batavia, never again could the English expect to capture a *Zwarte Leeuw*. But if the Company was beaten on the Malay Peninsula, it was also besieged in the Spice Islands. On an outcrop called Pulau Run hunkered down a tiny knot of desperate Englishmen determined to hold out against hell, high water and a Dutchman.

Nathaniel Courthope had come late to the Company, and his baptism had been unfortunate. Allocated to the Sixth Voyage, he had accompanied Middleton across that terrible Yemeni desert, and despite the horrors they all endured he asked for more. Promoted to purser of the *Increase*, and gaining respect for doing that rarest of things, eschewing private gain, he got a reputation for himself as one who relished a station the nastier it became. Posted as factor on Succadana, when that godforsaken place had been abandoned by Sophony the Kazak, Courthope seems to have thoroughly enjoyed himself despite being surrounded by headhunters. Thus, once more making a success of a challenging outpost, and subsequently offered command of the *Swan* and the *Defence*, he was next detailed to sail with all speed for Pulau Run on the Bandas. This was a mission of exceptional danger but one that, true to form, Courthope welcomed. He reckoned it a break whilst appreciating at the same time that this new posting might give him the chance of altering the face of the Far East by outfacing the Dutch. What had given hope as it had spurred incentive was how only the year before Courthope had been appointed, the *Swan* and *Defence* had sailed in convoy to Pulau Run, in what the English thought a 'rescue' mission. The chiefs of Pulau Run and Wai had made a formal surrender of their islands to James I, in defiance of the offshore presence of a strong Dutch naval force.

Courthope landed with the irrepressible Sophony. With them were Thomas Davis, Richard Hunt and Thomas Spurway. Before Jourdain had been assassinated, he had instructed Courthope that should he find the inhabitants still desirous of becoming British subjects, they were to be induced 'to ratifie under thare hannds and seales the former surrender, yf lawfully made; yf not, then to make a new surrender of all or parte of such ilannds as are yet under thare owne commannds and att thare owne dispose, leavinge out thease whare the Flemings are possessed and have command'.[23] The island of Wai was to be left to one side; though if the surrender that Jourdain had claimed had been mooted was indeed found to be valid, then the same was to be communicated to those Dutch ships now standing off the islands. If the inhabitants wanted it, Courthope was to land guns and put up defences against the hated Dutch. Should this provoke the 'enemy' into offering violence 'to the countries of our soveraigne lord the Kinge, or to the shipes, goods, or persons of his subjects, you are, to the uttmoste of your power, even to the losse of lives and goods, to make good the same'.[24] Richard Hunt was to be installed on Pulau Run as chief factor.

Leaving Bantam at the end of October 1616, Courthope had taken two months to get out to where he now took up position. To begin with, matters looked most encouraging as he discovered that local chiefs wanted both Pulau Run and Wai to become British possessions. Besides, as they assured Courthope, they had not concluded any agreement with the Dutch. Judging all this should be forthwith confirmed, a ceremony of cessation was repeated: writings were 'drawn and confirmed by the principals of Polaroon and Polaway', who 'delivered us nutmeg-tree with the fruits thereon, in the earth, with other fruits and a living goat'.[25] The 'ancient' of St George was raised, guns landed, battery constructed; all of which provoked the Dutch, who regarded the whole performance as brazen theft of something that belonged to them.

On 3 January 1617 the Dutchman Cornelis Dedel sailed over from Neira with three heavily armed ships. When the inhabitants gathered on the beach, Dedel retreated in short order. A week later, and a Dutch pinnace was observed taking soundings off Nailaka. Since its seizure would allow the Dutch to dominate the road to Pulau Run, the English opened fire. Though smoke brought relief, subordination heralded disaster. John Davis, head-strong master of the *Swan*, insisting on taking his ship over to Lontor against the protest of his compatriots, was captured when turning for home on 2 February 1619. The *Swan* was then towed into Neira, whereupon the Dutch summoning local chiefs made them witnesses: 'much glorying in their victorie and showing the Bandaneses their exploit, in the great disgrace of the English what they could, saying that the King of England might not compare with their great King of Holland, and that one Holland ship would take ten of the English ships, and that St George is now turned child'.[26] The loss of the *Swan* was a massive blow, yet worse was to come. Courthope knew he had to preserve his last ship, because without the aptly named *Defence* there would be little chance of holding out until relief came. So it was at once resolved that stores and ammunition would be taken out of the boat, whilst the *Defence* herself came to be laid up under a new battery established on Nalaika. But then on the night of 19–20 March 1619, when drifting from her anchorage, the *Defence* floated out to sea. Some leaping into a lifeboat regained Run, whilst the rest ran her into Neira Road, where the ship was surrendered. This had been no accident, but the contrivance of those who had determined to escape a predicament that was becoming more unpleasant with every passing day.

Everything was now against Courthope, yet still he held out with his desperados. A few days later, and the governor-general of the Dutch East Indies arrived in person. A doctor of laws, cautious in command, studied in moderation, Governor Reael deplored the aggression of his compatriot as much as he lamented their coarseness. At once resolving to see if he could not come to terms with the heroic Courthope, Reael was determined to relieve his enemy of the predicament he now found himself in. If Courthope might yet be persuaded to yield, a surrender Reael devoutly hoped for, further bloodshed could be avoided and surely accord reached? Offered the restoration of captured men and his two ships, beguiled with the prospect of compensation, proffered assistance to depart, permitted to carry what spices he might yet be able to gather, such largesse made Courthope pause for careful consideration. Relaxing his grip on his sword, if only for the moment, eventually he came to give Reael his answer: how 'I could not [accept your terms], unlesse I should turne traitor unto my king and countrey, in giving up that right which I am able to hold, and also betray the countrey people, who had surrendered up their land to our Kings Majestie'.[27] Discharged of the burden of his feelings thereby, Courthope then sailed over to Pulau Run to talk things through with his council. Returning, he offered Reael his counter-proposal. The English would depart, provided Reael was willing to leave the question as to who owned what to be settled by negotiation either at Bantam or in Europe. Reael would also be required to give written under-taking that he would neither molest nor bully the islanders. These terms were refused, but Reael cautioned against making an immediate assault. There matters remained for the time being.

For fourteen months thereafter, Courthope held out against the most determined efforts to winkle him off the island. Conscious of the vital impor-tance of keeping the flag flying, he even managed to overcome the horror of witnessing his longed-for relief falling into the hands of the enemy. In March 1618 the *Solomon* and *Thomas* were captured in sight of the shore, whilst the following June a determined assault was repulsed by the Indigenous. Maddened by what they had heard of Dutch cruelty, and despite the obvious disadvantages, the inhabitants of these islands had won. They had seen off a force that was feared only marginally less than those terrible Japanese pirates who spared no one.

In August 1618 Courthope took the huge risk of sending out a small boat imploring help. Soon enough, that disappeared upon an empty ocean. But unknown to Courthope, towards the end of this same year Sir Thomas Dale dispatched his swiftest pinnace in the opposite direction. The purpose of this was to encourage Courthope to hold fast to await what was promised would be speedy assistance. However, the pinnace too was never seen again. A further year went by, but with Dale and Jourdain now dead so was any chance of succour. Thus passed the first ten months of 1620. Then, towards the end of that October, whilst returning from Lontor, Courthope was inter-cepted near Wai. Mortally wounded, he threw himself into the sea to avoid the indignity of dying in the hands of his enemies. And so ended the life of a man who had fought with desperate resolve and madder courage to hold an island measuring under 2 miles in length and just over half a mile in width, a resolution that had earned him huge admiration from his enemies. In the regrettable absence of his corpse, however, all that Courthope's foe could afford their inveterate implacable adversary was an epitaph and not a grave. This they performed with full military honours upon those waters that had closed over him.

The loss of Pulau Run, the most valuable real estate upon the face of the earth, was the end of a whole generation of what had been missed opportuni-ties. Drake had stopped there, though had he only stopped longer, in annexing these jewels he would have secured them for Englishmen before anyone had heard of such a thing as a 'Hollander'. Instead, the loss of Courthope some fifty years later meant the demise of the whole cause. By expelling the EIC from these islands, the Dutch extinguished any hope the English had that the Company might yet partition with them the greatest prize that the East could yield. Yet because of Pulau Run, the Company chanced upon India and England lighted upon a place called Manhattan. This was to come the way of the nation with the Treaty of Westminster (1674), which was one of those endless attempts to bury perennial animosity between the two countries.

Disaster in the Moluccas could not be taken in isolation, however. There was abject failure across the whole theatre of South-East Asia. There may never have been the money to sustain infrastructure, but an absence of rials was not the whole problem: for the English, motivation was in short supply and imagination often lacking. By contrast, the Dutch positively thirsted for the East. This was in order to neutralise economic warfare conducted by Spain. For so long now, the Spanish had not been able to reconcile themselves to the loss of their fattest provinces. The Hollander also craved a drum-roll presence to impress the West, to win a place at the council table and to join the great powers of France and Spain.

Yet of course securing Indonesia and the Moluccas was not enough to achieve this ambition. But what of China and, for that matter, the prospect of Burma, the rivers of Vietnam, the forests of Siam? The first East India Company employees in Siam were the two Dutchmen Lucas Antheuniszoon (d. 1640) and Pieter Willemszoon Floris (d. 1615).[28] They had bought into the EIC by contributing £1,500 towards the cost of the Seventh Voyage (1611), which had been readied under the watchful eye of Captain Anthony Hippon sailing in the *Globe*. All three set out for India, Antheuniszoon working out of Petapoli and Floris in Masulipatam. Leaving India and arriving at Bantam on 26 April 1612, the *Globe* departed in June for Pattani where Floris set out one stall, whilst Antheuniszoon went on to Siam to begin business at Ayutthaya, then the capital of an independent Siamese kingdom.

There can be no doubt that the Company did well by having two Dutchmen in such positions of responsibility, though there were many other compatriots who, though not prominent, nevertheless crewed the English

ships. But regrettably the excellent start that the two made was then dissi-
pated through bad luck and bad judgement in equal parts: Floris, sailing
for London, died there in September 1616, whilst in 1619, asking for re-
employment, Antheuniszoon was refused. Returning to Holland, he set up
in Rotterdam where he was to be prosperously buried in the first week of
February 1640. The loss to the Company of the services of these two was
unquestionably a setback, since their assiduity had helped make a return of
218 per cent for the Seventh Voyage. Working in separate stations, the pair
put tireless effort into establishing contacts between Siam and the Coromandel
coast. These had laid down a base for those who came after. Whilst the
English factory in Japan was to close in 1623, Siam would hum along until
as late as 1685.

What Floris and Antheunis had managed to put together was impressive.
Malaya and Siam were challenging when Europeans struggled to make
anything more than an 'approximate' engagement in such places. Although
Japan was geographically further away, a Western presence in that archipelago for two generations before the Company had arrived had allowed for
some integration within a society that is too often dismissed as always having
been 'closed'. St Francis Xavier, the 'Apostle of Japan', had made an enormous impact during the Azuchi–Momoyama period. Siam, however, was a
different matter. Largely because the language was almost impossible for
Westerners to understand, deals collapsed all too easily. But more fundamental was the realisation that the Company had got there too late. This
Floris ruefully confided to his journal:

Thus being heere with the lawnes [textiles], having no vente att all, which
is greatly to bee wondered, especially for mee who 4 yeares agoe sawe
suche a vente of theym that it seemed the worlde hadde not clothings
enough to provyde this place as was needfull, much lesse to overfill itt,
and that nowe it was so overcloyed that it is hardly possible that in a greate
many yeares they can bee muche requested. Heere it might bee asked
howe and from whence commeth this suddayne change whereas before it
was suche a continuall and proffitable trade, yea, the greateste of all the
Indies. Butt the cause why the same lyethe nowe so under foote is this.
That the Portingalls bring the same quantitye of clothing in Malacca

as heeretofore they have done. Heereuppon followed the Hollanders, who have not onely filled Bantam and Javan butt also the ilands of Molucca, so they have no utterance at Malacca. Besides this there bee some shippes of the Moores which trade for Tanasserin and provyde Siam. Besides this 2 Portingall and a Moores' shipp have founde oute a new haven this laste year called Tarangh [Trang], is a place hard by Keda, and this yeare arryved a Gusarat and another from Nagapatam att Keda, bringing the lawnes overland, and so over filled it that no man ever sawe the lyke.[29]

Whether Floris had been as honest with Smythe as he was to himself, records do not reveal. The 'new haven' of Trang allowed cloths to be brought in just fourteen days, whereas it had taken months to get the same from Tenasserim before the elephant had come into service. Trang had been opened by Indian traders who now gained an unassailable advantage over the Company. But there was much else to blunt the knife. Whereas further west the Company was mastering the Portuguese, in Siam and Cochin China, the Estado continued to reap the benefits of a century-long start. Although 3,835 nautical miles lies between Goa and Macao, as the albatross flies, Macao could not have been sustained without Goa as a stop-off for carracks that had already travelled the 9,710 miles from Lisbon.

Portugal had the infrastructure to support supply lines, whereas the English were hopelessly overstretched and undershipped. In working east of Aden, the Company was sustaining a bridge without supports. Portuguese Macao, which was to repulse a full-scale Dutch assault in 1622, was just too powerful for the Company to enjoy the freedom it needed to make a clear success out of operations up and down the Malay Peninsula. As it was, the great Portuguese settlement of Macao was sufficiently close to Portuguese sub-stations for its traders to summon that help denied the English. In contrast to the propinquity of Macao, the Company's largest base was Bantam. But this was less effective because here the Company was a junior partner to the Dutch. As for the issue of summing help from afar, Surat was under financial siege and London too distant. The English in Malaya, Siam, Cambodia and Vietnam were outgunned, out-supplied and undersold: chests were empty, Bantam would not supply, London could not dispense. Richard Wickham saw it all. So grim was the outlook that perhaps this was why he elected to leave the Company and go private:

> The Honorable Company, as they wright us, make doubt of continewinge there East India trade, beeinge dayly murmored att and scandelised for shipinge awaye soe much mony yearly for India, Bantam etc, and by ther large and hopfull informationes nowe lattly given them of the Japan trade are constantly perswaded that from us all ther factories shall bee stuffed full with silver. For which cause they have sent ther shipping this yeare for Bantam without monyes, the want of which hath bine the cause they have fayled of ther tradinge and are nowe despersed to seecke ther fortunes in other places, which course if the Honourable Company proceed in they only are like to feel the smart therof. I have ever advissed that if they would have silver from this place in any quantitie that they pleassed to send us such staple comodities as are vendible and will att all tymes yeald monyes[30]

If Wickham was sceptical, his doubts were shared by Adam Denton. He told of how 'Pattanie therffore in my openion I hould nott worthie the keapeinge onely upon sale of clothe'.[31] Further complication was how merchants of one voyage furiously competed with those of the next, refusing to share a common pool of goods to complement the garnering of such funds as London had been able to release.

To add to all these difficulties, the quality of employees was lower in the Malay Peninsula than it was in India, whilst with the exception of those two Dutchmen mentioned earlier, factors assigned to this theatre seem to have been less effective than those in Japan – supposing such a thing was possible. Of the traders who manned the South-East Asian stations, undoubtedly the most alarming was John Johnson. He had been master of that same *Globe* that had brought Floris and Antheunis out from London. Floris was astonished at how this 'lewd liver' had been given any responsibility when he was 'so drunk that he could not well stand'. The Dutchman was hardly less contemptuous of Johnson's captain, feeling he should have had Johnson hanged from the yardarm without further ceremony. But with a chronic shortage of personnel, experienced if drunken masters could not be let go.

So Johnson was sent off to Bantam to dry out, only to re-emerge as second in command at Ayutthaya. In contrast to the parlous state of the Company out there, things were good with the Dutch: repair yards craned, workforce cranked, men stretched every sinew to keep a wide variety of vessels up to a high standard of seaworthiness.

There was no comparison between morale on board a Hollander and an Englishman when lingering long off the coast of Singapore. Because the VOC was willing to pour men into the Far East, it did not suffer the same problems of crewing that hobbled the Company when its own operations were overly dependent on Japanese mariners. Just how poorly maintained English ships were is attested by William Eaton, who damns himself as he demolishes the Company. This he does when admitting how he was in the habit of disregarding the exigencies of the monsoon entirely. Trying to get out of Siam too late in the season, Eaton was grounded on mainland Asia for a whole year in 1617.

Missing the wind, though hardly a capital offence, was certainly a crime against the dividend. It ran the risk of retribution when interest rates rose right across the Malay Peninsula. Any Asian moneylender lucky enough to do business with the Company did well: here was an organisation starved of liquidity and in no position to resist a hike. As for these money men, one of them was a woman. The queen of Pattani was an exchange dealer of rare skill. Computed by the English to be sixty if a day, this queen of the Amazons liked nothing more than chasing the buffalo through the bamboo before watching her people dance into the night. When, however, sufficient rack had been drunk by all, what had started as a dance became a reel: 'There were 12 women and childeren to daunce which did effecte it so well that I have not seene better in all the Indies. That being done, all the gentilitie were commanded to daunce, from the greatest to the smalleste, or att least make a shewe or demonstration thereof, which caused no small laughter, which both wee and the Hollanders must do lykewyse, wherewith the Olde Queene was muche rejoiced.'[32]

Bright and early next morning, and none the worse for wear, the 'Old Queen' would be off to her own bank, where the erstwhile revellers of the previous night would be made to dance to a quite other tune. The queen demanded outrageous interest rates, set not according to the value of one currency against another, but with an eye to how serious was the hangover of her supplicants. She lent the Dutch 13,000 rials at 10 per cent per annum, and that was without taking into account the added sweetener of 1 per cent demanded for her treasurer – nor indeed a nice little 'gift' for herself. And so it was with Peter Floris who, after 'mature deliberation', thought that:

> seing that the China wares wente well off from the hand and myselfe being butt meanelye provyded with money, my dettes which were extant to come in very slowly and that the clath att this tyme coulde not stande mee in any steede, I resolved to take upp some money of the Queene to the valewe of 3000 Rs.8, with condition to repaye the same within 3 or 4 months att 6 per cento for the tyme to the Queene and 1 per cento to the treasurer, so that with the gifte and all it amounteth to 7½ per cento.[33]

The queen did well, not only from her land bank but also from the harvest of the sea, levies for anchorage so enormous that they added significantly to overheads for the respective companies. What compounded that aggravation, however, was difficulties experienced in managing multilateral trading at a time when the East India Company at least failed to grasp how factories would survive only where there was a 'privileged' function for each and excellent communication between all, something the Dutch had long understood. With the Hollander, as one port fell upon lean times, others came to shoulder a temporary burden. The Dutch knew that Hirado was never going to subsist on trade alone. For that reason, such sales as there were needed to have value added by the creation of an infrastructure with spare parts and facilities for the repair of carriers coming from all quarters. By contrast, the Company failed to invest men and materiel to create that reciprocity between half a dozen factories so successfully achieved by its rival.

But if the Far Eastern theatre was a disappointment, there was some retrenchment from Siam and its satellites. Here was to be found sappan wood, a capital means with which to promote menstruation and ease the exigencies of confinement. On board the *Globe* was a whole world of delights, some to promote life, some to end it. There were deer skins for the samurai's saddle and ray skins to wrap his handle, in case grip slipped just as an elaborate Japanese code of honour demanded the immediate decapitation of an enemy. Benjamin was supplied to those terrible Buddhist warrior monks known as the Sōhei who, in terrorising Japan for generations, partly through their own actions but also through their surrogates, the Ikkō-ikki, had proved more zealous than the Japanese army itself. Described by the Portuguese as 'a bunch of pederastic hypocrites',[34] when not killing others, or deep in their 'hilarious potations', these demented fellows liked nothing more than to sanctify their temples with the odiferous benjamin. So, too, there was porcelain for that highest of Eastern rituals: the Japanese tea ceremony. Something more carnal, however, was coromandel cloth. There were Siam rubies and Borneo diamonds for kings, and for the kingdom of the kitchen the hold of the *Globe* held: gold, rice, pepper, nutmeg, maize, camphor and 'ningim' or ginseng. For the bedroom there was rhinoceros horn, but for those in serious need of a stiffener elephant tusk. Walking into any Japanese living room, there would be found 'lumra' or black gum which when applied made partitions of paper run with the silkiest of ease. Clarified beeswax and honey-coloured varnish, giving the lacquer its sheen, held the mirror up to the quivering maple beyond. Yet all this was never enough: what was needed was brisk business with China, 'the golden trade of the world'. But only the Jesuits could get in and, as luck would have it, they seemed to be rather more interested in clocks and conversions than in currencies; though that said, whenever coins came their way they proved to be masters of manipulation.

The gathering momentum of the Dutch in the waters east of Bengal took place because the VOC would continue to look east when the EIC was beginning to look west. Soon, indeed, the English became more powerful than the Dutch on the eastern seaboard of the subcontinent. After captains Best and Downton had given the viceroy a good beating, not once but twice, the Company had come to hold the initiative in Gujurat. By contrast, the VOC would eventually dominate the west coast. There the Dutch had marked their arrival by also contesting a long-held Portuguese hegemony. Such heavy investment in the stretch of country between Madras and Orissa as the Dutch were now willing to commit was indicative of how the VOC had foreseen that the local Indian textile industry must be the key to the commercial development of a wider Asia.

If Asians did not really want Western goods, there was such a demand for dyed cotton in Indonesia that Dutch Governor-General Brouwer was moved to describe how Coromandel was the 'left arm of the Moluccas'.[35] Brouwer felt it had to be developed to full capacity if the Spice Islands were to be prevented from 'dying'. It was therefore the VOC rather than the EIC that was the force to be reckoned with all down the eastern seaboard of India, though the VOC could only dominate that vast stretch of coastline at the cost of paying insufficient attention to Gujurat. Before this neglect became apparent, the Coromandel textile industry was central to Dutch success in the Far East. This was because with Coromandel under control, huge possibilities would be afforded the Dutch for the expansion of coastal trading right across Asia. Whereas the English regarded Gujurat as its reservoir of exports to Europe, the Dutch thought Coromandel key to their profits further east. Without Coromandel there would have been no Golden Age; without Gujurat there would have been no British Empire.

10

A THING OF SO MUCH DIFFICULTIE

Elizabeth by the Grace of God Queene of England etc., Most Imperial
and invincible Prince, our honest subject John Newbery the bringer
hereof, who with out favour hath taken in hand the voyage which nowe
hee pursueth to the parts and countreys of your Empire, not trusting
upon any other ground then upon the favour of your Imperial clemency
and humanitie, is mooved to undertake a thing of so much difficultie,
being perswaded that hee having entred into so many perils, your Majestie
will not dislike the same . . .

A letter written by her Majestie to the King of China, in February
1583[1]

John Newbery was a merchant-explorer desirous to break into what London
believed was the fabulous potential of a thousand Chinese markets. Elizabeth I
had been persuaded as to the benefits of the enterprise by either Walsingham
or, most probably, Burghley. Wanli (d. 1620), the longest-reigning emperor of
the Ming dynasty, was never to receive the letter, and so presumably no harm
was done in thus addressing one who was the 'Son of Heaven' as a mere mortal
monarch of a corrupt earth. Regarding Newbery himself, to whom this gilded
missive was entrusted for onward transmission, if not by the fair hand of the
queen herself then likely as not by the tight fist of Lord Burghley, he was
certainly known not only to the English queen but to the more sanguinary
among the brave spirits of Elizabethan commerce.

Newbery was never to meet the 'king of China', but he did do much to
explore the possibilities of opening new Eastern markets beyond that line
described by the crusader castles from Aleppo to Ascalon. Crossing such a
strand in the sand was costly in a whole host of most unwelcome ways: why

then did this late Tudor explorer undertake such hazards? And for that matter, what does a camel train crossing the Tigris in 1580 have to do with Smythe crossing the Adventurers in 1610?

Since the days of Anthony Jenkinson of Bokhara fame the City had become fixed on the need to subsidise the ineffective efforts of the Venice and Turkey companies. This was to be done by the infusion of profit out of the new markets of the Middle East; if only resources could be made to stretch that far. Such dilatory effort as had then followed did nothing to ameliorate the declining fortunes of the Mediterranean companies. So it had been decided that the two should be amalgamated, as we have seen, to form the 'Levant', which thus came upon the scene in the early 1590s.

Whilst such an amalgamation had made for better performance, soon the Levant Company had begun to feel the need to expand out of limitless seas into boundless sands. The question then was how the Levant could reduce pressure and increase profit when it had commitments from Venice to Cairo, from the pillars of Hercules to the gates of Constantinople? Everything pointed to the need to create an independent if dependable company which could complement, as it might subsidise, the efforts of the 'Turks'. Hence why so many Levantines went piling into the inaugural meeting of the East India Company and caused something of a first in British business history: a takeover before a dividend.

Prior to all that, however, City men who had been trading to West Africa were also looking for a means to establish contact beyond the Arab principalities that supplied slaves for the West Indies out of the Sahara. Hence English merchants working out of Guinea looked to East Africa where the 'Mountains of the Moon' and the fabled kingdom of Prester John were surely to be found. Evidently then there were complementary incentives for English adventurers to find their way to the Red Sea and beyond.

Such efforts as the late Elizabethans made to penetrate the Middle East look to have been yet another failure. That said, it is suggested that what happened in the Middle East, but more importantly what didn't happen, was a necessary prelude to the arrival of the East India Company within the oceans of India. Whilst almost nothing tangible came out of the twenty years of desultory English exploration of the Middle East preceding the foundation of the East India Company, such endeavours ensured that the lands between the Mediterranean and the Indian Ocean remained an alluring concept for those who, sensing expansion eastward was needed, could not, alas, achieve the same. If a new and specifically 'Eastern' cartel could only be founded, would not the pickings justify the heroics of Newbery and many others who coming through Tashkent or down the Tigris endeavoured to reach both India and 'Cathay'?

Sporadic attempts to promote English trade through Arabia Felix, as the Middle East was then described, or Arabia Deserta, rather more accurately perhaps, involved traversing a dangerous and largely featureless terrain where a man might as easily drown in sand as the sea; it proved far from 'happy' for the Tudor travelling salesman. Of these, undoubtedly the most dauntless was our intrepid John Newbery, who had had the wind put in his sails by that famous letter from his sovereign.

John appears to have been a relation of the celebrated London publisher Ralph Newbery, a theory deriving from the survival of John's letter to his 'assured good friend' Richard Hakluyt, whose epic *The Principall Navigations* (1589) was to be published by Ralph. The letter was written seven years after John had returned from an odyssey that had taken him down the Euphrates and up the Danube. During these riverine meanderings, John had touched upon Hormuz, Shiraz and Isfahan, before returning to the comforts of Hull via Warsaw. This first of the two odysseys that Newbery was to undertake lasted from March 1579 until August 1582. Newbery's field expedition had been sponsored by Sir Edward Osborne and Richard Staper, who as the two leading English experts on the eastern Mediterranean had long been frustrated by the poor performance of both the English Venice and Turkey companies; returns from which were not as healthy as they should have been. This was because both needed access to new markets in the Middle East. Such then was the thinking of the 'Turks' when Newbery had been tying up in Hull in 1582.

Happily for Staper and Osborne, however, no sooner had Newbery successfully negotiated the Humber than he had begun to think about where he might steer next. Seeing the City still on side, even willing to pay for a new expedition, whilst others were eager to hear about what had happened on his first trip, Newbery was confident he would get the funding he needed to set off again. But he was also savvy enough to know how what was also required was puff and publicity. Among those willing to make the necessary fanfare for a farewell were England's two foremost armchair travellers, John Dee and Richard Hakluyt. According to what Osborne and Staper had told them, it seemed Newbery had visited every historic city between Aleppo and Kabul, and understandably they found this thrilling enough.

In the event, Newbery came to be funded by a merchant, guided by a magician and publicised by a historian. This new expedition would eventually muster five argonauts under Newbery's direction, with orders to make for Baghdad. Among them was Ralph Fitch, whose exploits would be the most astonishing of all. Once at Baghdad, Newbery and Fitch were to take up £400 worth of stock. As they beat a path to the subcontinent it was supposed contacts that they made en route would morph into trading stations. Such then was the hope. But before any of this could be realised, much had to be done in London. Newbery visited the famous Dr Dee on 9 November 1582, though the entry in Dee's diary recording the visit is too brief to give further details.[2] That call finished, it was then time for Newbery to visit Richard Hakluyt, fast becoming cheerleader of English discovery. This meeting produced some writings in Portuguese, in case Newbery was to get into trouble either at Hormuz or Goa where Portuguese strength lay. In what seems to have been a growing postbag, there was also a letter from the English Jesuit Thomas Stevens who, having taken ship at Lisbon in 1579, was settled in Goa administering to his flock. That letter would prove literally a lifesaver, not just for Newbery but for all. Lastly there were illuminated scrolls. Limned in verdigris and orpiment, malachite and gold, with these and other assorted missives it was hoped that new markets all across the East might be opened. With such documents now ready and money raised, it then occurred to someone that it would be no bad thing if a gem-polisher was included among the party. Everyone had heard of the diamond mines of Golconda, and so the assayer William Leach (or Leades) was seconded. Just as each East India Voyage was to have its complement of artists, so here was James Storie. He was a painter who, having confessed a fervent wish 'to see the countries and to seek his fortune', had secured his passage by declaring himself ready to pay his own expenses.

They set off aboard the *Tyger* from Falmouth on 13 February 1583. By the end of April they had disembarked at Tripoli, having somehow evaded the Barbary pirates who cruised the Mediterranean largely unchallenged. At Aleppo they repacked and rethought their strategy. Mindful of the help he had received from Hakluyt, and aware that his patron was the most avid of the collectors among the 'cosmographers', Newberry did not forget Hakluyt's request that he be kept closely informed – less about what was happening but more about what was on offer. So, writing from Aleppo, Newbery braced Hakluyt for a bibliographical disappointment: 'Since my comming to Tripolis I have made very earnest inquirie both there and here for the booke of Cosmographie of Abilfada Ismael, but by no meanes can heare of it. Some say that possibly it may be had in Persia, but notwithstanding I will not faile to make inquirie for it, both in Babylon, and in Balsara [Basra], and if I can finde it in any of these places, I will send it you from thence.'[3]

Sailing down the Euphrates to Falluja thereafter, all made it safely to Baghdad. The journey had been hot, which can hardly have been a surprise to one so well travelled as Newbery. The party visited 'the ruins of the olde tower of Babel . . . sundry times I have gone thither to see it, and found the remnants yet standing above a quarter of a mile in compasse, and almost as high as the stoneworke of Pauls steeple in London, but it sheweth much bigger'.[4] Then, embarking at Basra in August 1583, Newbery, Fitch, Leach and Storie landed at the Portuguese stronghold of Hormuz the following month. At the best of times this might have been unwise, but on this occasion (and unknown to Newbery and his colleagues) the Portuguese garrison had been forewarned of the imminent arrival of an English party. At first things went well; or at least that's what Richard Hakluyt was led to believe when they told him how they had set up a boutique in town.[5] But trouble began soon afterwards. On a previous visit Newbery had had no problems, but now he encountered hostility from the Venetian community provoked by outrages committed by English privateers in the Mediterranean, where Venice felt it had a predominant interest.

'Signor Stropene', who may have been the Venetian consul in Hormuz, had been forewarned about the arrival of Newbery by his brother, who was living in Aleppo. In any event Stropene now denounced the English party to the Portuguese governor. Stropene claimed that these same Englishmen had been in touch with the Portuguese pretender Dom Antonio, possibly lighting on this ruse after overhearing indiscreet talk on the part of Newbery about how his patron Richard Hakluyt had himself met the pretender years before in Paris. This Hakluyt had done when, masquerading as the chaplain to the English embassy, he had in fact been Walsingham's spy. Any talk of Dom Antonio's pretensions was therefore bound to get them all into big trouble. It was nifty work by Stropene. But to slam the door tight shut, he now threw in the suggestion that the four had come to see if 'Ormuz' could be taken by force. All these details come out in a letter sent to John Eldred and William Shals who, still back in Syria, were doing their best to get things moving in Basra. As for the sorry predicament of the boys in Hormuz, this in turn came to be described by Newbery with just that phlegmatic resignation that anyone venturing out of Europe in 1600 needed as a vaccination against despair. Such 'philosophy' could only have been honed because Newbery had already become accustomed to going to bed in a desert wondering whether he would be rising with the sun:

> Right wellbeloved and my assured good friends, . . . the 10 day I with the rest were committed to prison, and about the middle of the next moneth, the Captaine wil send us all in his ship for Goa . . . God knoweth how we shall be delt withall in Goa, and therfore if you can procure our masters to send to the king of Spaine his letters for our releasement, you should doe us great good: for they cannot with justice put us to death. It may be that they will cut our throtes, or keepe us long in prison: Gods will be done.
>
> From out of the prison in Ormuz, this 21 of September, 1583[6]

Dispatched to gaol in Goa just as Newbery had predicted, there they duly arrived on 29 November 1583. Almost at once Newbery was closely questioned by the 'Aveador' about these supposed contacts with Dom Antonio. The conversation then turned to Drake's antics in the faraway Moluccas. When Newbery asked whether he was going to be held responsible for whatever damage Drake may have inflicted on Portuguese pride, he was told not. However, he doubted that was really what they were thinking:

> and there beganne to demaund of me many things, to the which I answered: and amongst the rest, he said, that Master Drake was sent out

of England with many ships, and came to Maluco, and there laded cloves, and finding a gallion there of the kings of Portugall, hee caused two pieces of his greatest ordinance to be shot at the same: and so perceiving that this did greatly grieve them, I asked, if they would be revenged of me for that which Mr Drake had done? To the which he answered, No: although his meaning was to the contrary.[7]

At this point a wholly unexpected thing happened that probably saved their lives. The ecclesiastical authorities swung into action, with the charge being led by Father Thomas Stevens and our old acquaintance Jan Linschoten, both of whom were determined to do what they could to help these English Protestants. As for Archbishop Fonseca, he protested vehemently at their treatment; while shaking his cross in the face of the viceroy, he made it clear that neither Newbery nor his colleagues were to become sacrificial lambs upon the altar of realpolitik. Such good thoughts but better works, Newbery was the first to acknowledge:

> for had it not pleased God to put into the minds of the archbishop and other two Padres or Jesuits of St Paul's colledge to stand our friends, we might have rotted in prison. !e archbishop is a very good man, who hath two yong men to his servantes: the one of them was borne in Hamborough, and is called Bernard Borgers, and the other was borne at Enchuysen, whose name is John Linshcot, who did us great pleasure: for by them the archbishop was many times put in minde of us. And the two good fathers of St Paul, who travelled very much for us, the one of them is called Padre Marke, who was borne in Bruges in Flanders, and the other was borne in Wiltshire in England, and is called Padre !omas Stevens.[8]

Men of the cloth born in Portugal, Flanders, the Empire or England, recruited everywhere and belonging nowhere, they paid scant attention to the conventions of religious observance, still less to the battle lines of international rivalry. Circumnavigating the celestial sphere when Drake was circumnavigating the terrestrial, these 'Soldiers of Christ', as the Jesuits were called, in pursuing conversions were converting prejudice to understanding as they went about their business plucking tolerance out of bigotry. The heroes to emerge from all this are of course Archbishop Fonseca and his traitorous secretary Linschoten.

Father Stevens now began to run around Goa asking old friends to help bail out new friends who couldn't muster the full amount that the bankrupt Portuguese regime was now demanding. Successfully achieved, Stevens was delighted to announce that the four were to be released on one condition: they were not to run off. This, however, proved too much. Once freed, and thinking to hide in the most conspicuous place, Newbery and his fellows hired a shop in the main street. With trading thus started, Fitch could write home how 'if it please God that I come into England, by Gods helpe, I will returne hither againe. It is a brave and pleasant countrey and very fruitfull.'[9] Suddenly things turned sour, though, and a good beginning ground to a shuddering halt. Newbery had made the mistake of asking that their bail money be returned so that the tidy little sum could be invested in the shop. The viceroy Dom Duarte de Menezes (1584–8) was not pleased at all, Newbery declaring how this grandee 'made us a very sharpe answere, and sayd we should be better sifted before it were too long, and that they had further matter against us'.[10] Dom Duarte was in no mood to be accommodating: he had only just arrived and he much resented having to deal with a major diplomatic incident before he had got used to how things were done in Goa. But as far as Newbery was concerned, what Menezes had to say was more than enough. It was time to be off. Alighting on Whit Sunday when everyone would first be in church and then drunk, it was resolved that this would be an excellent moment for flight. By way of preparation, Newbery, Fitch and Leach had set to work by turns, changing cash into gems and sewing other valuables into clothing where they could not be detected. On the morning of the moment, leaving the shop door open so as not to arouse suspicion and setting off for the river, they made a run for it and got clean away.

Not so James Storie. After thirteen days in prison during which he had thoroughly lost his nerve, he had resolved to trade freedom to paint for the restrictions of a life of prayer. He joined the Jesuits. Warmly embraced by the Holy Fathers as the newest of their neophytes, he felt safe enough to begin with, as well he might since any conversion was always cause for much celebration. But if Storie was himself pleased at having exchanged one type of cell for another, satisfaction was not to last for long. Having heard all about Storie, on 12 January 1591 Philip II wrote to Dom Manuel de Sousa Coutinho (1588–91), who had succeeded Duarte de Menezes as viceroy:

> he [the Governor] writes to me of the three Englishmen who went out to those parts in the time of Dom Francisco de Mascarenhas [viceroy 1581–4] two of them were dead, and the other was in Goa practising the profession of a painter, without there being any suspicion of any design in him; nevertheless since it is forbidden that any strangers go to those parts, nor are they allowed there, I do not consider it to my service that he remain. Being an Englishman you should send him home in the first ship to this kingdom that he may go hence to his own country if he desire.[11]

What then happened is not entirely clear. Three ships set out for Lisbon the following season: the *São Bartolomeu* was lost in a storm, the *Santa Cruz* was burned to prevent capture and the *Mãe de Deus*, famously taken, came into Falmouth to make a bevy of London jewellers as rich as any Portuguese viceroy. If Storie was shipped to Portugal in the *São Bartolomeu*, en route for England as King Philip would have allowed, then he went down with the viceroy Coutinho himself, who was returning after having served terms first as governor of Ceylon and then as viceroy of Goa. If, on the other hand, Storie had been lucky enough to have been sent away on the *Mãe*, he would have headed home directly without having to change at Lisbon. This, though, is unlikely, since we do not find the great escape mentioned in the more than 1.76 million words that Hakluyt deploys in the second expanded edition of his *Principal Navigations* (1598).[12] Given how the merman Hakluyt was not only historian but lobbyist, surely he would have found it hard to resist foregrounding such a good story through which he could have suggested how the 'miraculous' escape of honest James was another in the eye of that king of darkness Philip II. No, everything suggests that Storie lies full fathom five, location unknown.

As for Storie's companions, they got safely over the border. Making as much speed as they could heading northwards, they all scrambled into Mughal territory, where Newbery may have presented a letter to Akbar

(d. 1605), the greatest of all the Mughal emperors. If so it is probable that he would have been granted a personal audience with the emperor. What is clear, though, is that Leach took service as a jeweller with the ruler of Fatehpur, who gave him a house and six servants – and that was last we hear of him. Newbery told Fitch to go down the Ganges and explore Portuguese settlements beyond, promising Fitch at his departure 'if it pleased God, to meete me in Bengala within two yeeres with a shippe out of England'.[13] As for Newbery, he was lost in the sand somewhere between Agra and Aleppo while trying to get back home.

Floating down the Jumna with 180 barges carrying salt, opium, asafoetida and lead, Fitch entered Allahabad where, studying Brahmans at the water's edge, he found what he saw so threatening that he dismissed them as 'a kind of craftie people, worse then the Jewes'. With prejudices thus confirmed, Fitch then went up to Bihar to get a look at the Silk Road. Boarding a ship at the mouth of the Ganges, he subsequently struck up the Irrawaddy to make an entry as surprising as it was unwanted into Portuguese Malacca. Denied access to the legendary but locked kingdom of 'Cathay', and so forced westwards, he stayed a full three years at Aleppo, where by popular acclaim he came to be elected consul, before finally returning to London in April 1591. It was not the reception Fitch was hoping for. He had been missing for seven years, and so his family had been legally entitled to declare him dead; this they had done in February 1590, each thinking what she might get out of a fat estate of one who, unmarried, had prospered well in the Leathersellers' Company before he had gone travelling.

Somehow, though, Fitch salvaged both his dignity and estate, recovering sufficiently to enjoy a settled prosperity into old age. Sallying forth from what had once been the Priory of St Helen's but was by now the Leathersellers' Hall, our fearless voyager offered a world of sandy experience to Sir James Lancaster, first of the captains and oldest of the salts upon whom Sir Thomas Smythe was relying to traverse a world getting richer with every voyage. As for any direct input it may be thought that Fitch might have made to the nascent Company, it must be wondered what value he represented. Truth was, Fitch was too old and too tired to do much. That said, he greatly interested the literati of London where, of course, the first to milk him was Hakluyt who, urging him to write before he forgot, marched him off to Lord Burghley.

Though much about the Lord Treasurer's tastes remain a mystery, he clearly enjoyed 'Fitch on the Middle East'. Thus encouraged, Hakluyt inserted the material in his second edition of *Principal Navigations* (1598). What Fitch writes appealed most to proto-anthropologists, though as with so many other travelogues of that time, all is by no means direct experience. In the case of what Hakluyt publishes of Fitch, not a little is refracted through the publications of others, especially the *Viaggio* (1587) of the Venetian merchant Cesar Federici, which Thomas Hickock had translated and published in London in 1588.[14]

What bearing do these adventurers, our 'six merchants', have on the genesis of the East India Company? After the Levant Company was established in 1592, one of the first things the executive of that body set out to do was to claim a monopoly of trade along the caravanserais between Aleppo and the Gulf. Whether anyone paid much attention to such a diktat must be doubted; but then that hardly mattered. What Newbery and Fitch, especially, had achieved by their travels was to get London interested, avaricious and thinking about saffron, indigo and a hundred other powders. What cannot be claimed, however, is that Fitch returned with a messianic prospectus for capturing new markets. Indeed, he is not on the list of those who were the original Adventurers of the East India Company. Though he was not minded to put his wealth into Smythe's hands, he offered a wealth of experience to the EIC by translating Portuguese documents on its behalf. Thus we find him advising the Court of Committees in 1606 as to the best form of words with which to address the new Mughal emperor, Jahāngīr. Now, given the central importance of 'performance' to the Middle East, India and the Far East – in this instance, the extreme formality with which letters from foreign potentates were received especially in regimes outwith Europe – this was a useful contribution in its own right. Although Fitch played no part in the first meetings of the Company, his vicarious role in the fine art of communication was every bit as valuable as any intervention made by others at the Court of Committees.

Sometime the object of Fitch's travels and often the subject of his thoughts, India was only lighted upon by the East India Company after it had failed in its first priority of seizing the Spice Islands. Frustration in the East induced arrival in India by the autumn of 1608. And so with the departure of Ralph Fitch we note the arrival of William Hawkins.

Little is known about the antecedents of this extraordinary man. Captain Hawkins, for that was how he liked to be known, was not the same William Hawkins who as lieutenant-general had so nearly been killed by Sir Edward Fenton on that ill-starred venture to the Moluccas in 1582. Both men did, however, hail from a famous West Country tribe who had made a mountain out of the misery caused by its ruthless prosecution of slavery.

Arriving in India aboard the *Hector* in the late summer of 1608, Hawkins was at once confronted by the governor of Surat who, though addressed as Shah Mukharrab Khan, was known to his friends as 'Hassu', meaning one skilled in surgery. But that had been in a previous life, and now it seemed Hassu thought that stitching a deal was better than sewing a diaphragm. Having made a considerable art out of defrauding Europeans, Mukharrab had done very well from various extortion rackets. Deeply hostile to the English because he already had an 'understanding' with the Portuguese and didn't want that upset, Mukharrab at once began to collude with his friends from Goa. No sooner had Hawkins arrived than the Portuguese resolved to dispatch him forthwith. What they could not know, however, was that their newly identified adversary was much addicted to cloak and dagger: five times in so many weeks were attempts made on his life; five times was he to emerge unscathed:

> The first plot laid against me, was: I was invited by Hogio Nazam to the fraughting of his ship for Mocha, as the custome is, they make at the fraughting of their ships great feasts, for all the principallest of the Towne . . . Out of these Frigats, there came three gallant fellowes to the tent where I was, and some fortie followers Portugals, scattering themselves along the Sea side, ready to giue an assault when the word should be giuen. !ese three Gallants that came to the tents, armed with coats of Buffe downe to the knees, their Rapiers and Pistols by their sides, demaunded for the English Captaine; vpon the hearing of which, I arose presently, and told them that I was the man, and perceiving an alteration in them, I laid hand vpon my weapon. !e Captaine Mogol perceiuing treason towards me, both he and his followers drew their weapons: and if

the Portugals had not been the swifter, both they and their scattered crew (in retiring to their Frigats) had come short home.[15]

Failing upon the shoreline, these would-be assassins now moved to the bazaar. Previously they had cleared it of both goods and sailors, the first sold, the second made prisoner. Assaults various and brutal provoked Hawkins to protest to the Portuguese captain-major. He received the most scatological of replies: 'At the receit of my letter, the proud Rascall braued so much, as the Messenger told me, most vilely abusing his Majestie, tearming him king of Fishermen, and of an Island of no import, and a fart for his Commission scorning to send me any answer.'[16] This was too much for even the rough-tongued Hawkins: 'I told him, that the King of Englands license [to trade at Surat] was as good as the King of Spaines, and as free for his Subjects, as for the king of Spaines, and he that saith the contrary, is a traytor, and a villaine, and so tell your great Captaine, that in abusing the King of England, he is a base villaine, and a traytor to his King, and that I will maintaine it with my sword, if he dare come on shore.'[17]

This was not a war of notes but of nerves. Hawkins found his predicament worsened when, with the *Hector* leaving, he was left with a solitary wool trader named Finch. Retreating into town and barring themselves in a small house, the two spotted a column of cut-throats filing up the narrow alleyway towards their house. They were accompanied by a friar who, staying firmly in the rear, had crucifix at the ready to wave in absolution over whoever had the good fortune to dispatch the heretics. Surviving once more, thereafter Hawkins prepared to conquer the subcontinent, not with broad sword but broad cloth. He left for Agra and, in the face of a better-armed Portuguese force, elected instead to try to defeat them by selling English cloth to Indian merchants.

As threat of imminent death began to recede, fresh problems loomed. Finch had made off with a fardel of indigo that had been promised to Jahāngīr's favourite wife Nūr Jahān, who was a serious trader upon her own account in an age when Muslim women could also be wealthy merchants.[18] Finch was fortunate to survive the imperial fury that followed, though biblical retribution fell soon enough. Having failed to dispose of his bales in Kabul, Finch expired upon the road to Aleppo 'poisoned with the water they drank, in the country of Babylon near Budget [Bagdad] whereinto a multi-tude of grasshoppers fell and poisoned the water whereof drinking they died'.[19] Cut off all too soon, notwithstanding, Finch had had time enough to make himself an authority on the mysteries of indigo, secrets conveyed to colleagues:

> Sarques is distant from Amadavas three coase; the town not big but counted the best and [most?] perfecte soyle in all those partes for the makinge of indicoe, all other places being accompted but counterfeit unto it. The triall of indigo maide here chieflie is by water, and at Amadavas, Jambuzer [Jāmbusar] etc by fire. But at Sarques theie mutch stande upon there former costomes, which by no means theie will break and much boast of the trewenes of their indicoe. Yet found we little difference, but all faithless and circumsisede Moores and glad to have put anie cheating tricks upon us, either in minglienge or otherwise.[20]

Now deprived of support, Hawkins managed to get himself to court none-theless. Once in Agra, though, he was accorded more respect than had been the case in Surat, his step-up helped by the presentation of a little wonder that seemed to defy the laws of nature: 'a small coffer with seven locks, within which were such rare stones that they would lighten the darkest place, no candle being needed'.[21] Rather less welcome to Hawkins's host, however, was the virginals that he also brought along. No sooner had 'Mr Lawes' begun to tinkle the ivories than he was told to desist, and he at once expired from the humiliation of his rejection, or so the documents ask us to believe.[22] Fortunately, there were others with different instruments and better nerves. Of these, Robert Trully so pleased that melancholy emperor with his melo-dies on the cornet that he was invited to conduct the court band.

As for those luminous stones, they promoted the most improbable inti-macy when the grossest of *mésalliances* arose between an erstwhile sailor stained in salt and an emperor dressed in silk. Swimming in his cups and partying until the moon went down, Jahāngīr came up with the suggestion that his new-found friend should marry a girl he had been preparing for just such an occasion – though the subsequent nuptials could hardly have been described as nirvana when the bridegroom was alarmed to see his lady arriving with a camel-train of relatives. Notwithstanding, Hawkins could hardly believe his fortune. Having come to India to find riches, he had found himself a khan of 400 horse instead, and a salary worth £3,200. But then Hawkins was more than a chancer up on his luck. From first arrival he had been much commended for his stout demeanour in the face of the Portuguese, one writing of the admiration all felt: 'Sir, since the receipt of the King's *Firman* sent by your Worship, as also somewhat before, we have lived at our heart's ease.'[23]

Caressed by an emperor and envied by his court, Hawkins now disgraced himself through intemperance. Mukkarab Khan, corrupt governor of Surat and mortal enemy to Englishmen, was as outraged by the growing intimacy between Jahāngīr and Hawkins as he was offended by the former's swinish indulgence of the Englishman. Summoned from his seat of extortion at Surat, Mukkarab proceeded to move against one who, having defied the authorities in Gujurat, was making himself enemies in Uttar Pradesh. When Hawkins was foolish enough to complain about the equity of a compromise over a debt that Mukkarab himself had suggested, this was the indiscretion Mukkarab had been looking for: Hawkins's bad judgement was the beginning of the end for him.

Long in the habit of administering an early morning stiffener, Hawkins appeared at a durbah more than a little squiffy. Banished from the imperial presence and realising his games were up, he was thus obliged to say remorseful farewells to his erstwhile companion of the night. Yet even now all might yet have been well, but for a posse of Englishmen who had debouched from the wreck of the *Ascension*. With the *Union*, the *Ascension* had made up the Fourth Voyage.[24] Once it had arrived in the Bay of Cambaya, with the 'proud, headstrong master' ignoring local advice, the *Ascension* had ended up 'standing, almost full of water, to our great griefe'. For the locals it would have been preferable had the sea done a better job. In the event, however, there had been 'the saving everyman's life in two boats'. By way of thanksgiving, the crew had then proceeded to frolic its way across India, affording such a spectacle of grossness as confirmed in the eyes of the authorities that 'Franks', as Westerners were called, were no more than a rabble of barbarians.[25]

Meanwhile Hawkins, who had been bidden be gone, now suggested to Captain Jourdain, the sometime captain of the *Ascension*, that the two might remove themselves to Goa. In so doing, Hawkins revealed how once in India an Englishman's points of reference too often melted in the heat:

> I told him if he went for Goa his life would not bee longe, because hee had too much disputed against the Pope and their religion, and was apt to doe the like againe there if he were urged thereunto, which would cost him his life, and the sooner because of his goods ... Soe hee was perswaded to goe that waye, and I was perswaded to goe the other waye, although he urdged mee very farre, promising greate wages, but his promises weare of little force, for he was very fickle in his resolucion, as also in his religion, for in his howse he used altogether the custom of the Moores or Mahometans, both in his meate and drinke and other customes, and would seem to bee discontent if all men did not the like.[26]

After Hawkins left the situation drifted until the emergence of Thomas Aldworth, who now determined to establish himself as custodian of English commerce in India. Sometime mayor of Bristol, Aldworth was major-domo of Surat. Before that, however, he had played a central part in generating the expansion of English commerce. In the 1580s Aldworth had done much to set the young Richard Hakluyt on his way when Hakluyt was a student of Christchurch and had received a letter from Sir Francis Walsingham. In this, the Secretary of State had told Hakluyt how he had heard from Aldworth what good things Hakluyt was doing in giving 'much light for the discovery of the Westerne partes yet unknowen'. It had been a busy letter-writing day since no sooner had ink been sanded and sent on its way to Oxford than the quill was off again in scratching congratulations to Aldworth in Bristol: 'Your good inclination to the Westerne discovery I cannot but much commend.'[27] Leaving Bristol and arriving at Surat, Aldworth demonstrated ambition and tenacity. Resolute in the face of aggression, stubborn in argument, careful in management, this most resolute of Company servants might yet have been overwhelmed but for a massive misjudgement on the part of Jerónimo de Azevedo, viceroy of Goa (1612–17).

Nettled by the arrival of the Company and fearful for his fleet, Azevedo conceived the insane idea that he could browbeat Jahāngīr into removing the English by hijacking the *Rahīmī*. This was the largest ship in the entire Indian

Ocean. Capable of transporting 1,500 pilgrims, it belonged to Jahāngīr's redoubtable mother, Mariam-uz-Zamānī.[28] The theft of such a carrier, stowed with money and stuffed with pilgrims, represented the grossest violation of international law. Following this, Jahāngīr ordered the seizure of Daman and the closure of the Jesuit church, the stopping of Portuguese shipping and the freezing of allowances, when all the while Jahāngīr's elephants pawed the dust for battle.

The whole escapade had been a catastrophic error of judgement, the more so because three Mughal princes had recently converted to Christianity: having kissed cadavers in the basilica, they had celebrated their new-found spirituality with all that sottish abandonment recorded in lurid detail by Goa's most famous diarist.[29] Matters might have been still more desperate for Portugal had Jahāngīr possessed even so much as the suggestion of a navy. This was not available from within the resources of the Mughal empire, though; but no matter since the East India Company had one. As a result Jahāngīr came to settle in the rigging of Thomas Best, much to that captain's acute discomfort. As the newest commander in India, Best found himself in serious difficulties with his unwanted guest. Thinking reasonably enough that he had come to run indigo out of India, instead he had arrived in the middle of an international crisis. He was being commanded to prime his powder as Jahāngīr mounted his howdah. What was to be done?

By no reading of the rules could it be construed that Best was permitted to jump into a full-scale war; yet not to do so might threaten all that was to be taken from India. But then what George Orwell would later identify as the single most important weapon in the policing of the British Empire, that is to say the telegraph pole, had not yet been invented and so men could do more or less what they liked. So it was that Best gave Azevedo such a 'banging' as would signal a sea-change in Anglo-Portuguese relations. As for Jahāngīr, he quietly returned his elephants to their barracks without so much as a trumpet to be heard.

Best's ballistic effect was the more remarkable as being accomplished by just two old sea horses: the *Red Dragon* and *Hosiander*. These found themselves pitted against a vanguard of four Portuguese battleships and twenty-five frigates, line astern. Best and his brothers did much more than that, however: they succeeded in giving the Portuguese such a thrashing as was to become the talk of all India. Though the English won handsomely, the sorry truth was that all along the Portuguese must have been hard put even to hit a rowing boat. Lisbon had neglected ballistics when London had been all balls in producing the best gunners in the world.

The Portuguese, realising they were no match for Best's cannon, had attempted to discharge armed soldiery onto English decks. But their pikemen were of little use against the famous English broadside. Such a victory, coming just two years before Downton's own crushing defeat of a Portuguese fleet in these same waters, represented the first of two major disasters for Portugal in so many years. Although the Portuguese commander was beaten off with massive losses, foolishly enough he came back for more and afforded the surgeon of the *Hosiander* some consolation for frustration in finding his saw idle at his side: '[we] steered from one to another, and gave them such banges as maid their verie sides crack; for we neyther of us never shott butt [we] were so neere we could nott misse. We still steered after the *Dragon*, and when she was with one, we weere with another; and the truth is we did so tear them that some of them weere glad to cutt cables and be gone.'[30]

All this was respite for Aldworth, whose self-appointed mission had been to save Surat for the Company. Following victory at sea, Best came into harbour with all pennants flying, gratified to observe how a temporary trade agreement with the Mughal regime was now delivered when previously it had been denied. Accordingly, Best departed east, though not before writing such a triumphalist account of his own performance as to suggest that he was a lot better at sailing than he was at spelling: 'Thus we partted from thes valient champians, that had vowed to do such famous acctts, butt yett [were] content [to] give us over, with greatt shame and infamy redounding unto themselves.'[31] Before leaving, however, Best urged Aldworth also to depart, believing a factory in another place might reduce continual harassment from the Portuguese. But anchorite Aldworth refusing to emerge from his barrel of paprika, reckoned here was a country so large in size and so rich in bounty that for the Portuguese to try to maintain exclusive rights could only court disaster. But was he correct in his thinking?

Was Surat the place to be? Assuredly it was. It was well placed to harvest the fruits of Gujurat, the fattest of all India's provinces until, that is, the place came to be devastated by famine fifteen years later. The city was serviced by a port which the English referred to as 'Swally Hole'. Placed several miles up the Tapti river, Surat could defend itself from punitive raids during any trade war. Once Company sailors had got over their surprise at encountering a hospital for flies run by the Jains, they found themselves gratified by the climate, the drink and the whores. There was a positive hum about the place that they liked, and whilst some were defensive upon finding themselves among the exotics, others took a more positive view of it all. Christopher Farewell admired the way matters were handled amongst 'a mixt people, quiet peaceable very subtill; civill, and universallie governed under one king, but diversly law'd and customed'.[32] But it is Nicholas Downton who offers the most extensive account when writing of how he went:

> a mixt people, quiet, peaceable, very subtille; civille and universallie governed under one king, but diversly law'd and customed' along through many streets (humming like bees in swarmes with multitudes of people in white coates, men and women, close bodied and full of gathering to the mid-leg, with breeches and stocking in one, ruffling like bootes and all of one single callico; this being their generall and most neate or angelicall habite, which sparkles, of their kinde of starching, like silver spangles) untill, almost smothered with clouds of heat and dust, wee came to the English house . . . and all at our honourable masters charge, except our apparell, wherein alone and by our sallaries we differd from common prentises; onely yet (ingenuously) acknowledging a precedencie in our little commonweale for a kinde of representation, to prevent confusion.[33]

Although first the English and then the Dutch set up factories in Surat, the city had always been dominated by dynasties of wealthy Indian merchants, and so it would always remain. Now some of these were richer than Sir Thomas Smythe himself, hard though that is to believe. Of these clans the most famous was the Vora. Known to have made a substantial loan to the English as early as 1630, towards the end of the seventeenth century the Voras would come to control the affairs of the French Compagnie des Indes. Take the Jain Veerji Vora, described as 'the richest merchant in the world': he was to become the indispensable associate of both the English and the Dutch in their Gujarat commerce. Or further afield still there was Mir Jumla of Hyderabad, a politician-merchant whose giant ships from the Coromandel coast were for twenty years the decisive influence at the great entrepôt of Mocha.[34] At Surat, too, there had long been a sizeable community of Jews, Arabs, Armenians, Chinese and Tartars, to whom more recently had come to be added Portuguese, English, Dutch, Danish and French traders. But then dominance of the regional economy by Indians, never Europeans, was by no means peculiar to Surat. Goa itself would have gone bust if 80 per cent of *rendas*, or tax-farming contracts, had not been managed by Hindus during the first seventy years of the seventeenth century.[35] Further south, in Vijayanagara, there were commodity brokers whose deals spanned the entire subcontinent. One such portfolio capitalist gathering was the Malayan family of Telugu merchants, founded by Achyutappa Chetti. Of Achyutappa himself it has been written:

> He had begun serving the Dutch as a translator and broker around 1608. He then became their principal banker. By the 1630s, Achyutappa and his brother Chinnana had become the major procurement agents in Thanjavur and Gingee and both had become shipowners and exporters trading with Sri Lanka, Burma and Malaya. They were major players in developing trade up and down the Coromandel coast and central to the growth of the taxation system.[36]

Tellingly enough, Sesharda, who was a nephew of Achyutappa, later became the powerful chief of the East India Company in Madras. Given the enormous wealth of the indigenous merchant communities of the subcontinent, the East India Company has rightly been described as no more than a flywheel upon an engine until the foundation of Calcutta at the end of the seventeenth century.[37]

Long before all that, thanks to the stalwart effort by Aldworth and good aiming by captains Best and Downton, before the *Lyon*'s sails appeared over the horizon with Roe under them during the early autumn of 1615, prices were low and spirits were high in Surat. At this point the Company's *Hope* signalled farewell to seven sister ships in the harbour. Though much heartened by such traffic, the Company still stood 'between hope and despair . . . whether we should proceed in these countries or no',[38] whilst Hawkins's old adversary Makkarab was reported to be ever more intent on 'discovering the secret rancour of his poisoned stomach, and the hidden malice that he beareth unto our nation'.[39] Despite such impediments, however, seed had been thrown to the winds: William Edwardes had been sent to Ajmer, and others were also busy making their way to Baroach, Dabul and Ahmedabad, this last described as 'the seat of the King of the Guzerats, a great town as spacious as the city and suburbs of London'.[40] Yet as always there were problems, not with being English but with being a trader, one factor remarking that the Mughal's 'greatness cannot descend to affect the title of merchant'.[41] Trust needed to be established with those whose dependability meant the difference between success and failure. Central to all was Edwardes, who had been instructed to pass himself off as a 'leiger' [representative] of his king, 'otherwise it be better that he went not at all and so the voyage to be overthrown' – an arrogation necessary because Paul Canning, Edwardes's unfortunate predecessor, thinking himself honourably taken in the eyes of the world, had been forced to take to his heels after being 'kicked and spurned by the King's porters out of the courte-gates, to the unrecoverable disgrace of our King and nation'.[42] That had happened because Canning had sent in a card announcing that he was a commercial traveller.

While all was abustle in Gujurat, the Gulf was becoming a possible new market. Downton told London how he 'wishes they had some hope of being able to transport their goods by that fair river of Sinde to and from that goodly country near Lahore'.[43] Kerseys were to be bartered where the icy winds of Persia blew the snows of the Zagros mountains over Isfahan. But for the moment India remained the focus, with steady advances in the purchase of calicoes, indigo, cotton and carpets, and lesser businesses of sugar, green ginger and a thousand douceurs. Trade was now spreading throughout Gujurat, up the malachite valleys of Kashmir and onto the stony tablet of Afghanistan, whence lapis lazuli had once been transported to a pharaoh's palace. Aldworth informed Thomas Keridge how 'The Company have sent 15 merchants to remain, all men of civil conversation and good fashion, so there need be no fear of being troubled any more with rascals.'[44]

But if exports expanded, imports were envied. Makkarab Khan had an appetite for English treasures which were meant for the emperor himself. This always remained insatiable, though canny Edwardes somehow managed to slip two portraits past him. The first was of Marlowe's 'scythian shepherd', as the playwright described Tamburlaine. Apparently this was 'one that will content the Mogul above all . . . from whence he derives himself'.[45] The other was of Sir Thomas Smythe. Although the governor somehow lacked the charisma of Tamburlaine, Jahāngīr's artists were required to confess that 'none of them could anything near imitate the same'.[46] But much more was demanded of Edwardes, not least the carrying of metal to where best exchange could be obtained. Since bills of exchange only operated between Europeans, factors had to steer as much as 36,000 rials in one go overland and through defiles so dangerous that Edwards and his colleagues needed a squadron of mounted Pathans to fend off the *thugs* and get them through. Too often these exercises resulted in the sort of ambush that well-nigh overwhelmed Edwardes: on one occasion his party found itself 'sudenlie assaulted by three hundred Rashbootes and more'.[47]

Getting through relatively unscathed, the party now began to think how best to diversify. Quicksilver was promising since a bulk purchase would not 'glut the market'. As for vermilion this was thought 'worth almost as much'. There was a brisk market for English lead, whereas tin was a non-starter; therefore London was told to beware of sending it. A list of dos and don'ts was proceeded by a clear statement that Surat was 'no place for the vent of broadcloth', though whether Persia might not be the 'other place' was worth shout and shot. What should be bought, what stored, what was lacking and how to get £7,000 to Edwardes, 'to be employed against the coming of the next ships', were questions exercising minds busier than ever. There was business too about lost leaders. What might best be shipped from London? What chance for that much-desired drop in the price of indigo? Where was next year's 'winner' to be found? So many questions, so much confusion.

Yet for all the dust of maize and stain of dye, not everyone was taken up with commerce. Some took delight in a place richer, older and more civilised than the country whence they had come:

In this towne are the sepulchers of the Kings of Guyseratt, a verye dellicate churche [i.e. the chief masjīd] and fayer tombes, which are kepte very comelye; whither there is much resorteinge from all parts of the kingdome to vizitt theis toumbes. Allsoe, aboute a myle and a halfe off, there is a verye fayer and pleasante garden, of a myle aboute, which compasseth a very fayre statelye howse, seated dellicately by the river side;

which howse Chon Chon, now the cheifeste nobleman of the Mogull's, builte in memoriall of the greate victorye which hee gott of the last king of Guyseratt. . . . Noe man dwelleth in this howse; only a fewe poore men that are hyred to keepe the orchard clean.[48]

But then there was found more to admire in India than just its buildings. Among the mountains of the Aravalli, rising at Delhi and falling in Rajasthan, was Mount Ararat where Noah's Ark had once come to rest. This mightily pleased those who loved their Old Testament. But for others, preferring the worship of nature to the study of its maker, rarities were in such abundance that many went to fill the menageries or the cabinets of virtuosi back home. In pursuit of just such things, John Oxwick (d. 1615) wrote of how he had just been presented with three antelopes by the governor of Baroach, 'very rare in these parts'. One was for the 'General'. Doubtless this ended legs-up on the table, though the others were spared to enjoy their green thoughts in the green shades of a far-off English park.

Meanwhile, success depended on the grittiness of Aldworth and the energy of Edwardes until, that is, the redoubtable Sir Thomas Roe arrived to represent the Company in the early autumn of 1615. This was the first embassy established anywhere, and Smythe had wanted Roe because he had always taken him to be 'a gentleman of pregnant understanding, well spoken, learned, industrious, of a comely personage, and one of whom there are great hopes that he may work much good for the Company'.[49] Smythe knew of no family that had enjoyed such a close association with the City as had the Roes; in 1569 the Merchant Taylor Sir Thomas Roe had been lord mayor, whilst the member of the Ironmongers' Company, Sir William, had then been elected in 1592 and the stalwart of the senior City company the Mercers', Sir Henry Roe, had served the same office in 1607. Although Sir Thomas Roe the younger was not himself in commerce, he was an Adventurer of some sort and much spirit. That had played well at his interview for the job in India. In 1611 Roe had taken two pinnaces over to South America where, groping through the rain forest, he had reconnoitred the strength of the Spanish. Now if such a man had overcome the Amazon, why could he not be thrust up the Jumna, thought Smythe.

That, however, was the stuff of public debate. There was, though, something that Smythe could play to advantage about Roe's past and about which, indeed, only it would seem Smythe was privy. It was said that in his earlier days Roe had been a notably prodigal son. Wasting a vast inheritance after Oxford, and embarrassed thereby, he badly needed the job. Hobbled with debt, he had just got into marriage and out of Parliament. Financial salvation proffered by the Company might commit this man in servitude to his saviour.

But beyond all this, what could have tipped the balance in a strong field was that out of all the candidates Roe was thought best equipped to prevent the 'plotting' of the Jesuits. For these reasons, then, Smythe was able to persuade the panel to elect him. Nevertheless, the choice needed ratification at the hand of the never-to-be-trusted James I. What if the king was to 'putt vpon them' some courtier who would contemn their authority and deal with their men and goods at his pleasure?[50] Yet royal cooperation was eventually secured, and Roe was able to declare how 'I esteeme it an infinite mercy of God, that when I had fully ended and wasted my patrimony and saw no way but scorne (the reward of folly), before I suffred disgrace, hee vndertooke mee and, beeing as it were new borne, hee restored mee to a new Inheritance and sett me right, for I doubt not to equall my wastes'.[51] Such a 'new birth' took the form of £600 per annum, half reserved in Company stock; expenses for uniforms 100 marks; similar sum to pay debts and £100, lent not given, mind you, wherewith to buy his dinner service. A chaplain was hired for £50 and a surgeon for £24, because in those days what mattered more than temporary affliction was endless damnation. Roe then set about engaging his own retinue on an allowance of £100 a year for wages and £30 for liveries. Here this future Chancellor of the Order of the Garter chose green and red, in which his servants were going to be required to march two by two through what their master fondly assumed would be the admiring bazaar. With tailor visited and plate engraved, Roe was ready to depart. And so began the career of the most successful diplomat of an English early modern world.

11

~~~~

JOSEPH AT THE COURT OF PHARAOH

My Honourable Friends, I was not borne to a life smooth and easy; all
my actions haue beene mingled with crosses and rubbes, that I might
rather say I wrestled then walked toward my Graue.

Sir Thomas Roe to the East India Company, 24 November 1616[1]

On the morning of 2 February 1615, a procession of boats rowed out from
Tilbury towards the fleet of ships lying in the river. The *Lyon*, commanded
by Captain Christopher Newport, was brand new, painted in all the colours
of a Victorian fairground, and indeed seemingly still drying in the sun. It
stood ready to greet Sir Thomas Roe, now about to embark on his own epic
voyage as the first accredited Company ambassador to the court of the great
Moghul. The *Lyon*, *Dragon* and *Peppercorn*, accompanied by their small
supply ship, lost 'sight of England' on 6 March. After a long voyage shorter
than many, on 18 September 1615 the three great ships arrived at Swally
Hole, the port for Surat, Gujurat's shining city of much prosperity and many
peoples. It was the western gateway to an eastern empire.

Now standing off the shores of Asia, Sir Thomas had so recently stood
upon the banks of the Amazon. There, in tracking much of the course of
South America's greatest river, Roe had needed great physical strength but still
more courage. For a man of his temperament that had never been a problem.
But the challenges which India represented to any European certainly would
be. During the four years that Roe was to serve the Company in India he was
to find it much harder to track a path through the labyrinths of a Mughal
court. India was more complex in its tribal customs, and ineffably more superior in its material splendours than that palace perched upon the Thames
where James I had conferred his regal credentials upon Sir Thomas. Predictably

enough, out of the clauses of Roe's instructions had emerged evidence of the darkest ignorance of the ways of India and its mores. There, too, had peeped out the vanities of a famously conceited king whose demand that Roe ensure his master was to be treated as the equal of an emperor of a subcontinent would complicate Roe's attempts to deal with one who recognised no equal and habitually described himself as 'the world beater'. As a result of what became conflicted priorities, well-rounded Roe would come to feel like a bushel of wheat ground between the gritty millstones of a delusional king and a rebellious community of merchants. Phlegmatic and naturally disposed to the understatement (as befits all good diplomats), a powerful sense of frustration is nonetheless detectable towards the end of the embassy and in Roe's rueful reflections upon the difficulties of his station: 'I haue sought to meyntayne vpright your Maiesties greatenes and dignitie, and withall to effect the ends of the Merchant, but these two sometymes cross one another.'[2]

Roe arrived with another, parallel set of instructions from his principal backer and staunch ally Sir Thomas Smythe. First among these demands was that Roe should cleanse the stable that had been abandoned by William Hawkins. After taking bottle and ship and leaving India for Ireland, Hawkins had died during the homeward voyage.[3] Always a law unto himself and ever defiant in the face of his enemies, so too at his last Hawkins appears to have defied Company convention; instead of being tipped over the side, his corpse was lowered into an Irish grave. Perhaps he had so sufficiently pickled himself in Agra that his remains remained inviolate until he got to Waterford.

As for Hawkins's successor, Roe, that September afternoon in Swally Hole Sir Thomas had betrayed no sign of fatigue after his eight-month journey, leaping into the surf to the sound of fife and drum. It was an energetic, loud performance entirely consistent with the high regard in which this man held himself. It did not go down well. The reception party found Roe's performance laughable, and Roe himself came to think the whole thing may have been something of a lapse of judgement. What he could not know was that this was going to be only the first of many an Indian knock to his sense of self-importance: 'At this name of an Ambassador they laughd one vpon another; it beeing become ridiculous, so many hauing assumed that title, and not performed the offices'.[4] Covered in sand but recovering dignity, out of his depth but now on shore, Roe felt obliged to report that 'if it seeme to any that shall heare of my first carriadge that I was either too stiff, too Punctuall, too High, or too Prodigall, let them Consider I was to repayre a ruyned house and to make streight that which was crooked'.[5]

As we have seen, Roe was required to negotiate on behalf of both Company and King. It would be long indeed before Jahāngīr inclined to think about strange pedlars from sea-girt islands, and it might be thought that he never really took James with that seriousness the British monarch craved. Nevertheless, the newly landed Roe was keen to try. Having mustered his men and marched into town, Roe at once dispatched an ultimatum to the Portuguese viceroy declaring that either its recipient should agree to free trade or at least have the decency to come out fighting like a man, adding for good measure that if his correspondent infringed the terms of commerce between England and the Mughal then he should know that 'the same force and spiritt [is] still living in our Nation' [as] 'in the dayes of the blessed and famous Queene Elizabeth'.[6] Not accustomed to being addressed like this, Dom Jerónimo Azevedo, still smarting from his humiliation at the hands of the Company, not once but twice, deigning not to reply, left Roe clicking sparks of fury off spurs of silver. But if Roe's first attempt to cut a figure had failed, it created an impression beyond those shores. In far-away Japan, factors heard about his famously pugnacious letters; the cape merchant Richard Cocks, writing to a friend in Miako, told of how the ambassador 'had pronounced open warrs against the Portingals in the East Indies with fire and sword in the name of the kings maiestie of England'.[7] Unfazed by not hearing from Azevedo, and because he was always opinionated and often self-righteous, Roe went on to tell the archbishop of Canterbury how he was off to conquer the world: 'Neuer were such oportunytyes to dischardge the Portugall from all these Coastes . . . He is declining on all sydes, and a little weyght on his head now layd would sincke him . . . I propound yt to your Grace to make what vse seemes best to your wisedome.'[8]

But that was as far as Roe's war games went. Turning from the 'Portingale' to the 'Mogor', the pressing question now was how to meet the challenge of the Mughal court where others had so signally failed. The sudden appearance in India of Tom Coryate was an unwelcome surprise. Sometime scholar of Winchester and Oxford, after graduation Coryate had taken a job as court jester to Henry, Prince of Wales. That post hadn't lasted long. When leaving behind such precarious distinction as he had ever been able to maintain between reality and fantasy, Coryate left royal service to discover Shakespeare was right: the world is indeed a stage. Embarking on a walking tour of Europe, he subsequently published reminiscences under the title *Coryat's Crudities* (1611). The book was an immediate bestseller and its author was famous.[9]

Roe had got to know Coryate when they had both been members of the Mermaid Club, a group of 'sireniacall gentlemen, that meet on the first Friday of everie moneth, at the Mermaide in Breadstreet'.[10] This was a place Roe had loved and Keats would envy, the Romantic poet composing his 'Lines on the Mermaid Tavern' in tribute to the conviviality of this poet's quarter:

> Souls of Poets dead and gone,
> What Elysium have ye known,
> Happy field or mossy cavern,
> Choicer than the Mermaid Tavern?

Here Roe and Coryate, Ben Jonson and John Donne, Inigo Jones and half a dozen other 'brave spirits' versified. Imbibing vast potations within the convivial atmosphere of London's best literary club, they celebrated England's being part of Europe. But now in this very different station, in the middle of India no less, here was this loon waiting among the reception party at Ajmer when Roe came up to meet the emperor. Such a sudden appearance of one whom Roe had last observed through the tobacco smoke was not an unalloyed pleasure. This was not Bread Street, and Roe had to be on his best behaviour. Although he loved Coryate well enough, he was apprehensive about what were bound to be his japes. Writing to one of the two brothers to whom the First Folio was to be dedicated in 1623, Roe had this to say to the earl of Pembroke:

> Thom Coryat whom the fates haue sent hither to ease mee, and now liues in my house. He came heither afoot, hath past by Constantinople, Jerusalem, Bethlem, Damascus, and breefely thorowgh all the Turkes territory, seene euery Post and Pillar, obserued every Tombe, visited the monuments of Troy, Persia, and this kings dominion, all afoote, with most vnwearied legges, and is now for Samarcand in Tartarya to kisse

Tamberlans Tombe; from thence to Susa, and to Prester Jhon in Ethiopia, wher he will see the Hill Amara, all afoote; and so foote it to Odcombe.[11] His notes are already to great for Portage, some left at Aleppo, some at Hispan [Isfahan] – enough to make any stationer an alderman that shall serue the Printer with Paper. And his exercise here or recreation is making or reapeating orations, principally of my Lady Hartford.[12]

When not delivering speeches to the lovely Lady Hartford, presumably some 3,788 nautical miles away at this point, Coryate was busy diverting his new-found friends. One minute he might be regaling them with stories of how he had provoked a near riot by trying to convert a rabbi in Venice, next telling of problems he had caused in Mecca when he had climbed a minaret to denounce the Prophet. But the attention-seeker was unable to restrain himself. Stopping in Ajmer, stepping before the imperial horse and delivering a speech in Persian, he had so pleased Jahāngīr that the emperor had aimed a bag of rupees at Coryate's pate. The man may have been quite mad but he had Latin, French, Italian, Turkish, Persian and Hindustani, and with such a babbling Tower of Babel to hand Roe found many voices, if not as yet his own.

But then Coryate's life stood for more than just a series of tom-fool japes. The early modern world was one of both ferocious prejudice and marked diversity, surpassing splendour and abject squalor. When Coryate was ambushing the imperial train, the Company was carrying 'Indians', not as crewmen but craftsmen, not as mendicants but merchants. Often consultants, sometimes Brahmans, occasionally both, the advice of such educated men 'was wanted' when a note on file suggested that 'The Indians brought in the *Dragon* . . . be conferred with.'[13] As the *Peppercorn* was preparing, the Court of Committees was agreeing that 'John, the Indian, having by some mishap lost his thumb and not being able to work at his trade of a weaver, to be employed about the ships as he requests.' Crews were as colourful as the ensign, yet of a ship's complement; some pulled the ropes whilst others pooled their discoveries, wandering the world not in pursuit of the nutmeg but of knowledge. Indians were weaving in London long before Frenchmen made Spitalfields their home.

Representing the Company was a task Roe likened to repairing a ruined building. Difficulties abounded when the ambassador spoke not a word of any Eastern language. In the four years of his posting Roe never learned a word of Persian, the official language. Such was Roe's dependence on inter-preters that much of what he committed to paper was itself committed to memory by the spies with which he was hedged about.[14] Part of the chal-lenge Roe faced was understanding how a commercial treaty was to be massaged when such things could only be done between equals. So hard-wired was the idea of Mughal superiority that for the regime to have agreed to sign up to anything permanent with mere merchants was quite unthink-able. Concessions in the form of a *firman*, yes. However, such a thing issued one week could just as easily be rescinded the next.

We are privy to much of Roe's confusion and difficulties because of the happy survival not only of his *Journal* but also of many letters that he sent home. The contradictions of his position are made painfully obvious when on the recto of one letter he might be suspended in admiration about a place he sees as replete with civility, whilst upon the verso, he is contemptuous of a society rank with what he now considers its tyrannical ways. The *Journal* is as richly carved as any Jacobean fireplace: paragraphs where violence is cut in deep relief, passages aflame with description, sentences crackling with indig-nation, much outrageous and yet more outraged. By no means was all this just sound and fury, for it signified much. Parts reflect, as they reflect upon, the beauty of India and the light of its courts. Though sections are lost, the *Journal* not only is the richest of English sources about India, but also, in transcending its time, belongs to ours because it is timeless.

This is hardly surprising given the regard with which Roe's own literary accomplishments had been held at the Mermaid. Ben Jonson, England's greatest playwright after the death of Shakespeare in 1616, had been moved to write two of his hundred-odd *Epigrams* in praise of Roe. If the inspiration and the admonition that Jonson offers his fellow litterateur in these tributes to Roe is intriguing, no less so is the view Roe himself had expressed about the nature of diplomacy in a dialogue with the poet John Donne which Roe had begun just before emerging as a public figure. Under the patronage of Sir Thomas Overbury, the two friends had coined laboured aphorisms about the nature of experience and the expression of truth manifest beneath appear-ances. For Roe, 'circumstances are the Atomies of pollicie, censure the being, Action the life, but successe the Ornament'.[15] Faced with such views, then, any attempt to make Roe the founder of an English school of racism has to be resisted in the face of the complexity, subtlety and ambition of a man who clearly resists easy categorisations. One of the most revealing aspects about Roe, how self-conscious he was about the 'performance' of his embassy, is to be noticed before he ever set foot upon the subcontinent. Writing back to the Company as Keeling's fleet was leaving South Africa to deposit Roe in India, Richard Baker suggests a decidedly theatrical performance on Roe's part. Apparently he set up a pillar on the veldt with an inscription dedicated to his ambitions for India.[16]

As for what was to be discovered in India itself, Roe's imagination was kindled in the face of beauty; ravished by light against a marble basin upon which the gondolier floated and the duck flighted. So, too, with imperial buildings erected by the emperor Akbar. Roe admired the Red Fort of Agra (1565–79), as everyone did; but looking was by no means an unalloyed pleasure: contrasts were painful. Once back home, Roe would come to recollect the tomb of Fatehpur Sikri (1580–1) and compare it with the cenotaph for Anne of Denmark (1618), the first of opalescent marble and filigree screen, the second a pepper-pot of plaster and canvas wobbling upon the floor of Westminster Abbey, fit only for a cloth-horse at the Globe. But if Agra was marble when London was mud, the abandoned and the ruined had a profound effect on the romantic in Roe. During December 1616 he visited Todah, hardly built before abandoned, and by the time that Roe took a walk around the ruins, inhabited only by the cobra and the jackal. Roe passed through under a full moon, coiled statuary splashed with silver to evince the most melancholy of thoughts. Roe described it as

> very strong, had many excellent woorkes of hewed stone about yt excellently cutt, many Tanckes, arched, vawted, and discents made lardge and of great depth . . . full of little Temples and alters of Pagods and Gentliticall Idolatrye, many fountaynes, welles, tanckes, and summer howses of Carued stone, Curiously arched; so that I must confesse a banished englishman might haue beene content to dwell there. But this obseruation is generally that ruine and distruction eates vp all. For since the Proprietye of all is come to the king no man takes care for Particulars, so that in euery Place appeares the vastations and spoyles of war without reparation.[17]

The buildings made the deepest impression, but then Roe was hardly less fascinated by the emperor who was something of a decayed monument himself. Shortly after Roe had started to be favoured with audiences, it became painfully apparent that such was the gulf between the cultures of these two that indirect means was going to have to be found if intercourse was to be maintained. At their first meetings Jahāngīr would stiffen whenever Roe steered talk towards commercial matters. Much to his dismay, Roe then went on to discover that, for Jahāngīr, to the simple issue of boredom was added the serious business of intrigue. Understanding that the throne was an enormous challenge, Roe failed to comprehend the underlying complexities. There were to be found the assorted princes, Khusrú Khurram and Parwiz, whose studied disloyalty served to make Jahāngīr even less effective than he already was. At a loss to make sense of all this, Roe fell back on the disconcerting habit of comparing the intrigues of India with the depravities of Classical Italy, drawing the most improbable of parallels between what he took to be the decadence of the Moghul princes with some of the less salubrious rulers of the Roman Empire's Flavian dynasty:

> The whole Court in a whisper; the Nobility sadd; the Multitude like itselfe, full of tumor and Noyce, without head or foote; only it rages but bendes it selfe vpon noe direct end. The issue is very dangerous; Principally for vs, for among them it matters not who wynns. Though one haue right and much more honor, yet hee is still a moore, and cannot bee a better Prince then his father, who is soe good of disposition that he suffers ill men to gouerne, which is worst then to bee ill; for wee were better beare Iniuryes of Princes then their ministers. So that I may say of this tyme and the constitution of this state as Tacitus did of the Empire of Roome when it was contended for by Otho and Vitellius . . .[18]

But Roe was in Ajmer, not Rome. If he thought he had identified the well-spring of treachery, it was only later that he realised just how Jahāngīr's favourite wife, Nūr Jahān, enjoyed enormous influence behind the scenes. On one occasion Roe spotted her, but the mystery with which he entraps his description suggests his confusion as to how exactly she operated:

At one syde in a wyndow were his two Principall wifes, whose Curiositye made them breake litle holes in a grate of reede that hung before yt to gaze on mee. I saw first their fingers, and after laying their faces close nowe one eye, Now another; sometyme I could discerne the full proportion. !ey were indifferently white, black hayre smoothed vp; but if I had had noother light, ther diamondes and Pearles had sufficed to show them. When I looked vp they retyred, and were so merry that I supposed they laughd at mee.[19]

Never entirely sure just how Nūr Jahān stood within the court of her husband – how could he? – Roe may have been naive in thinking that what was out of sight must be out of notice. Little did he understand how things were disposed; how if Nūr Jahān whispered her enemies were ruined. In these circumstances Roe was at an utter loss as to the best way to conduct himself. Understanding neither Persian nor Turkish, faltering in Spanish and silent in Portuguese, he was obliged to suffer the indignities of 'Iberian whispers' – whatever was said being distorted by Jesuits, who had established a very effective diplomatic presence that allowed them to make a fair stab at interpreting whatever was going on.

As an earnest Protestant, Roe had harboured a profound distrust of Catholics before he had come out to India. But prejudice was dissolved in ways that would have been quite unthinkable at home. Little by little, Roe found himself utterly disarmed by the charm of Francisco Corsi, whom he discovered to be 'a man of severe life, yet of a fair and affable disposition'; just as he also lighted upon the fact that Corsi was as devoted to the Estado as he was to the eucharist. Corsi was not only a regular but a representative of the king of Portugal. A man of suavity and moderation, the very model of pragmatism, this Florentine father suggested that the two could live in amity by avoiding rancorous arguments as to which of them was possessed of the 'true faith'. It is, however, Roe's chaplain, Reverend Edward Terry, who reveals the way in which this most unlikely alliance had come about. What had trumped Rome's instructions to Corsi, which was that he should attempt conversions, was how he and Roe had agreed that the priority for Christians of whatever brand must be to put up a united front in the face of the 'Moor': 'This Jesuit . . . he desired that there might be a fair correspondency betwixt them, but no disputes. And

1. This commemorates Sir Robert Sherley's reception by Pope Paul V in 1609 as envoy from the shah of Persia. From arrival in Persia in 1598 until his death in 1628, Sherley was the shah's special adviser on Europe. The East India Company dealt with Sherley after it began trading in Persia from 1616.

2. The tomb of Sir Thomas Smythe, England's most powerful businessman and first governor of the Company. Smythe oversaw the birth of the EIC, presided over capital growth, and championed it against both James I and Parliament when hostile to its monopoly on Eastern trade.

3. Portrait of Sir Thomas Roe, first East India Company ambassador to India (1615–19). Roe stabilised English trade by refusing to be ignored at the Mughal court. On returning, he was asked to preside over the Company in the Far East, but refused.

4. Roe addressing the Emperor Jahāngīr at a durbar. Painted shortly after the Amritsar Massacre (1919), and given canonical status in the House of Lords, this monument to imperialism was the expression of a belief about English superiority which was once widely held.

5. European and Asian traders haggle in the foreground whilst ships of Spain, the Dutch Republic and England ride at anchor. Their rivalry was central to the emergence of the Company in the broader context of European expansion into Asia.

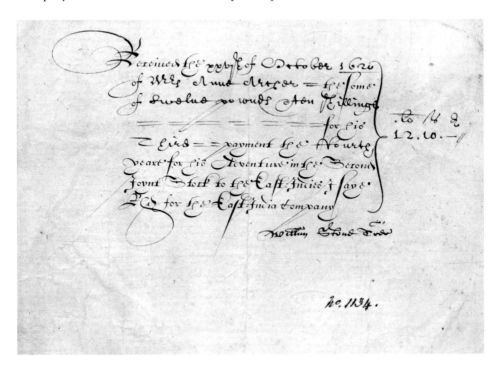

6. A handwritten receipt for Mrs Anne Archer, an 'Adventurer' in the Third Joint Stock. It suggests the role of women in the founding narrative, while the comparatively small amount (£12 10*s*) indicates the wide social base underpinning investment in the Company.

7. Itakura Katsushige presided over a trial after the head of the East India Company factory in Japan denounced two Spanish missionaries masquerading as merchants. Fray Luis Flores and Fray Pedro de Zuñiga were burned to death as a result.

8. In the bottom left foreground, James I gazes out at the spectator, seemingly ignored by Jahāngīr in favour of a Sufi sheikh. An accurate likeness, it is based upon an unidentified portrait of the king which records reveal Roe presented in the hope of obtaining a *firman*, or pass, to permit the Company to trade in India.

9. Naqd 'Ali Beg was sent by Shah Abbas I to London in 1624 to shadow Sir Robert Sherley, the shah's adviser on Europe. Sherley had been sent to promote the export of silk, but was suspected of trying to sell its monopoly to whoever would bribe him most.

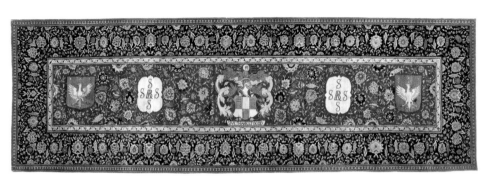

10. The Bell Carpet was presented to the Girdlers' Company by Robert Bell in 1634. Prominent in the East India Company, Bell was Warden of the Girdlers. Possibly made in Lahore, this magnificent carpet stands as a symbol of the intimate commercial and cultural ties between the City of London and the Company.

11. Jan Pieterszoon Coen presides over the main square of Hoorn, one of six founding 'chambers' of the Dutch East India Company (est. 1602). Coen was governor general of the Dutch East Indies, and hated the English. His merciless rule has sparked contemporary debate about the removal of the statue.

12. These Dutch ships are notable for the elaborate carving of bow and stern. Such decoration was also the most striking feature of the *Peppercorn*, whose adventures in sailing to Japan and back feature prominently in the book.

13. Governor general of the Dutch East Indies (1616–19), Laurens Reael tried unsuccessfully to negotiate a settlement after the East India Company occupied Pulau Run in 1615. One of the Moluccas, Pulau Run was the earth's most valuable real estate, stuffed with boundless stocks of mace and nutmeg.

14. Fort Victoria on Amboyna, another fabulously well-endowed Spice Island. This was the theatre for the Massacre of Amboyna (1623) which marked the end of Anglo-Dutch rivalry in the Spice Islands. Resentment of the Dutch was ever-present in the councils of the Company.

15. Dockyards at Deptford where the East India Company had facilities complementing its vast 13-acre site at Blackwall, which only disappeared in the 1980s. The building on the far right, of early seventeenth-century date, might be an allusion to Company offices built at Blackwall during the governorship of Smythe.

16. Sets of tapestries woven at Mortlake were sent both to Persia and India between 1625–35. Depicting an episode in the story of Vulcan and Venus, this would have been fabulously expensive to manufacture. Company directors thought such luxuries had a special appeal in Eastern markets.

further, his desire was that those wide differences 'twixt the Church of *Rome* and us might not be made there to appear; that Christ might not be seen by those differences to be divided among men professing Christianity.'[20] Just such a view as this had always been the default of the Company at a time when a desire to evangelise was almost non-existent.

Through Corsi's efforts, Roe came to discover that he shared a mutual passion for music and painting with Jahāngīr. What began as incomprehension and a failure to connect, 'grounded in geo-cultural distance and deepened by contrasting political objectives', gave way to an 'arrival at mutual understanding . . . the outgrowth of proximity fuelled by basic human curiosity, and achieved by means of fortuitous cultural convergences.' As William Pinch acutely observes, 'The tension in their relationship was not simply a function of one party being European and the other Indian. It was a productive tension which animated and animates still, all social relations.'[21] Indeed, later, as Levant Company ambassador to the Sublime Porte in Constantinople (1621–9), Roe would turn to a comparison between what he experienced in India and what he was experiencing in Turkey. At his first posting he had 'treated with an affable and courteous prince . . . I alway saw a free and noble jollity, accompanied with infinite riches and greatness; briefly, the Mogoll is in greatness of revenue, in bravery of court, in multitude of attendance, in state abroad, in riches, in elephants, in his sports, and, which is most honorable, in his conversation, a man that lives humanely with men, very much to be preferred [to how business was conducted in Constantinople]'.[22] Evidently, then, Roe was able to see the comparative strengths and weaknesses of cultures which if he found alien he always confessed were absorbing. And, little by little, Roe's attributes succeeded in transforming him in the eyes of his Indian hosts from an absurdity for standing upon dignity and a bore for talking about calico, to one whose company came to be enjoyed by the one to whom he had presented his credentials. This was unquestionably of value, weighing against the abiding irrelevance of the EIC to a civilisation older and more sophisticated than the one from where the Company issued.

The imperial atelier was the more attractive because it was the only place where Roe enjoyed an advantage over ambassadors who mattered vastly more to the regime than he.[23] Indeed, Roe's problem went way beyond linguistic ineptitude, and in justice to him, it was one which would have afflicted the best of Western observers: all and any 'Frank' was competing with representatives of regimes more powerful and princes of more interest to the Mughals than these men from Europe, a place where no one had ever been and none wanted to go. Truth was, because of the essential irrelevance of Western regimes to the foreign policy of Mughal India, neither Roe nor for that matter even the Jesuits, so much the suaver negotiators, could ever have been said to have been within the frame. Beyond that, Roe's wholesale ignorance of the symbolism of signs and signals inclined him, if never those wily old Jesuits, to dismiss as little more than mummeries upon marble such 'performance' as habitually greased the wheels of the Mughal court. Roe had been scandalised to see the Persian ambassador Reza Beg perform the *sujūd* and *taslim*, things that Roe understood were reserved for the worship of the Prophet alone

> At euening I went to the Durbar to visitt the king, wher I mett the Persian Embassador with the first muster of his Presentes. Hee appeared rather a Iester or a Iuggler then a Person of any grauety, running vp and downe, and acting all his woordes like a mimicke Player. Now indeed the Atashckannoe [*tosha-khána*] was become a right stage. Hee deliuered the Presentes with his owne handes, which the king [with] smiles and Cherfull Countenance and many woordes of Contentment receiued. His toong was a great aduantage to deliuer his owne busines, which hee did with so much flattery and obsequiousnes that it Pleased as much as his guift: euer calling his Maiestie King and Commander of the world, forgetting his own master had a share in yt; and on euery little occasion of good acceptation hee made his Tezelims. When all was deliuered for that day hee prostrated himselfe on the ground, and knocked with his head as if hee would enter in.[24]

Jahāngīr had given Roe presents but what had Roe given him? This was a time when diplomacy hung less on the conviction of a discourse than on the carat of a diamond. In contrast to that Persian ambassador who provoked envy and contempt in equal measure in Roe, for his part he could offer only third-rate *bijoux*. Among a selection of paintings, more notable for incongruity than artifice, was the mysterious 'Lady Rich'.[25] Whatever the purpose of this and other pictures, present-giving was of great importance, and yet this, too, was something in which Roe found himself constantly eclipsed. What shipped from London could rival Beg's largesse, when Roe found himself obliged to stand aside as porters took ten days to unpack a camel-train of treasure dispatched from Isfahan?

> Hee brought for Presentes 3 tymes 9 horses of Persia and Arabia, this beeing a Ceremonius Number among them, 9 mules very fayre and Lardg, 7 Camells laden with veluett, two Sutes of Europe Arras (which I suppose was Venetian hanginges of veluett with gould, and not Arras), two Chestes of Persian hanginges, on Cabinett rich, 40 Muskettes, 5 Clockes, one Camell laden with Persian Cloth of gould, 8 Carpettes of silke, 2 Rubyes ballast, 21 Cammelles of wyne of the Grape, 14 Camelles of distilld sweet waters, 7 of rose waters, 7 daggers sett with stones, 5 swoordes sett with stones, 7 Venetian looking glasses, but these soe faire, so rich that I was ashamed of the relation.[26]

Apparently, only the partridge in the pear tree was missing. Although Roe was discomfited within the courts of luxury, he pursued the nicest questions as to where feet fell in relation to the imperial person; that is to say, the unseemly business of standing upon various dignitaries and their dignities, before 'Himselfe in a Coate of Cloth of siluer, embrodered with great Pearle and shining in Diamondes like a firmament'.[27] During such longueurs, Roe was forever conquering new territory by the strategic application of a spur, forcing those who were less well armed than himself to beat a lateral retreat. By such means did he become unrivalled in the resolution of millimetric issues of where a man might best place himself under that glittering star.

But despite his best efforts, Roe could never have achieved a commercial treaty with all that would have implied in terms of equality between parties. How could the representative of a nation wholly irrelevant to the concerns of the Mughal empire possibly expect to be regarded as equal to a man who went about calling himself 'the world-beater'? In short there could be no treaty where there could be no equality. Hardly less important was how for the most part the Mughals despised trade. Although both Nūr Jahān and Jahāngīr's father-in-law Āshaf Khān were up to their arms in indigo, Jahāngīr utterly disdained such sordid concerns.

Dislike for trade and the idea of getting wet was no idiosyncratic prejudice on the part of Jahāngīr but something hardwired into his genes: Babur,
the founder of the dynasty, had never seen the sea, whilst Akbar got his first
peek at the Indian Ocean when thirty. As for Jahāngīr, the sequinned slipper
would never be stained by the salty brine. But if imperialism disdained the
waters, absence was an opportunity for others; Company acquisition of the
ferry trade to Mecca was a welcome subsidy when new powers either threatened those who surfed the waters unarmed or else contested hegemony with
the navies of Europe. The Mappilas of Malabar and Western Ceylon was an
armed and aggressive group that gave much trouble to the Portuguese. As for
the Yaruba of Oman, this was a force that had to be kept at bay when its
soldiers mounted raiding parties along the Gulf of Hormuz and over the sea
to Zanzibar.[28] Far to the east and on Malay's Peninsula, Aceh's startling
expansion during a period of triumphant Muslim resurgence frustrated what
might otherwise have been domination by Portugal east of Bengal.[29]

Roe had to fall back on patience, distraction and luxury when pressing
his suit upon an emperor too often drunk, drugged or plain indolent. With
both men passionate about the arts, hours spent listening to English viols,
nights comparing the relative merits of artists, intervals passed imbibing
copious draughts, all this and more allowed Roe to insinuate himself into a
position of trust. But then it was not just to do with indulgence. Roe's determination never to be cowed induced in his nocturnal host the gradual inclination to pass from contempt for one who had bored him with talk of cloth
to admiration for a gentleman who could discourse about the arts.

And so it was that one evening the two got down to playing 'Real or
Fake?'. Now this was a parlour game that both men much enjoyed. It went
as follows. Two 'identical' miniatures might be laid upon a table: one English
and the other its Indian copy. The trick was to discover which was which.
Getting it right, Jahāngīr pinched himself with delight, declaring that 'I am
so fond of pictures and have such discrimination in judging them that I can
tell the name of the artist whether living or dead.'[30] But there were a number
of health hazards associated with all this. Tiring of such diversions, Jahāngīr
would fall 'to drincking of our Allegant, giuinge tasts [toasts] to diuers, and
then sent for a full bottle, and drincking one Cup sent it to mee; that it
beegan to sower soe fast it would spolyd before hee could drincke all, and

that I had none. So hee turned to sleepe: the Candles were poppd out and I groppd my way out of doores.'[31]

The next day there was an immediate cure for the Roe hangover. Without notice the diplomatic corps were obliged to follow the imperial train on a 'progress' with 'Honest Thom' as the queen of Bohemia would call him, sweating upon a pachyderm in toiling up such mountains as might have given even Hannibal pause for thought. But Roe did not give up. In every sense he had qualified the hard way to become an officer in the royal regiment of hangers-on:

> Wee Passed through woodes and over Mountayns, torne with bushes, tyred with the incommodityes of an impassible way, wher many Camells perished. Many departed for Agra, and all Complayned. I lost my Tents and Cartes but by midnight wee mett. The king rested two dayes, for that the *leskar* could not in lesse tyme recouer their order, many of the king's woemen, and thowsandes of Coaches, Carts and Camells lyeing in the woody Mountaynes without meate and water; himselfe gott bye on a small Eliphant which beast will Clime vp rockes and passe such streightes as noe horse nor beast that I know can follow him.[32]

Roe never quite knew what he might encounter next. During strenuous efforts to catch up with the emperor, he was assaulted by a camel train carrying severed heads. A long time before, these had belonged to some three hundred rebels, but now they were on their way to Jahāngīr as a thoughtful tribute sent by the governor of Kandahār. They proved both impediment to progress and challenge to stomach.[33] But it was not all so ghoulish. Although the roads could be choked with heads and hangers-on alike, out of dust and blood could come geometry and control in the span of a single afternoon. For the thousands who were required to service such a chaotic enterprise as the Mughal progress, accommodation was provided by the *leskar*. This was an encampment the size of London; erected in just half a day, it had a plan Roe found mighty pleasing:

> Returning I viewed the *Leskar* which is one of the woonders of my little experience that I had seene yt finished and sett up in 4 howers (except

some of great men that haue double prouision) the Circuitt beeing little
lesse than 20 English mile, the length some wayes 3 *Course*, compre-
hending the skirtes; and [in?] the middle, wherin the streets are orderly,
and tents Joynd, are all sorts of shopes and distinguished so by rule that
euery man knowes readely were to seeke his wants, euery man of qualetye
and euery trade beeing limited how farr from the kinges tentes he shall
Pitch, what ground hee shall vse, and on what syde, without alteration;
which as it lyes togither may equall almost any towne in Europe for
greatnes.[34]

A *leskar* took hours to put up, Jahāngīr much less time to reinvent himself.
At the centre of a vast building site one moment, he might be closeted with
a 'prophet' the next. To begin with Roe discounted these fakirs, like the one
with whom Jahāngīr was now in deep conclave, dismissing him as 'a poore
silly ould man, all ashd, ragged and patched'. But then as Roe watched the
emperor not in his castle but certainly with a poor man at his feet, prejudice
dissolved and humility quickened: 'I mention with envye and sorrow, that
wee having the true vyne, should bring forth such Crabbes, and a bastard
stock [of] grapes: that either our Christian Princes had this deuotion or that
this Zeale were guided by a true light of the Gospell.'[35]

Roe had burgeoning respect for mystics but he condemned astrologers,
on one occasion if only because he badly needed a rest after a long day's
riding. He was greatly irritated when they reached the ruins of Mandur, and
'no man was suffered to goe in before hee was set, by the aduice of his
Astrologers'.[36] Stuff and nonsense, thought Roe. Eventually permission was
granted, only for Roe to be galled upon finding that someone else had bagged
the mosque that he thought he had booked. Promptly kicking him out, Roe
was less than pleased to discover that his quarters came with a lion and wolf
thrown in. Soon enough the lion appeared, and sallying forth armed with
only a broadsword wherewith to do battle, he was just in time to see his
adversary vault the fence with Roe's poodle in its mouth. Mourning his dog,
Roe was able to take it out on the wolf.

Eventually the imperial train returned to Agra, where Roe began to feel
that he was gaining ever more respect for the Company. Then, much to his
dismay, it was reported from Surat that the VOC ship *Nassau* had docked,

come to explore the possibilities of opening more Dutch factories. Roe was not pleased, suggesting to the Court of Committees that the newcomers would 'use us worse than any brave enemy would or any other but unthankful drunkards that we have relieved from cheese and cabbage, or rather from a chain with bread and water. You must speedily look to this maggot; else we talk of the Portugal, but these will eat a worm in your sides.'[37] Such fears proved exaggerated; if only because the Dutch did not have the resources to run all after they had thrown almost everything they had had at the Spice Islands. Yet despite profound misgivings, Roe worked well with his opposite number, Pieter Van Ravesteyn. Discovering Roe to be 'a very peace-loving man', Ravesteyn declared how he 'is very sorry for the differences between us and the English and would gladly see an agreement arrived at'.[38] Although global relations would crash with the Massacre of Amboyna, at this point it looked as if an accommodation might still be reached, and with Amsterdam warmly thanking Roe for all that he was doing.

Before the VOC had been founded in 1602, two men of the Middelburg Company (soon to be incorporated into that larger concern) had arrived in India from Aceh, a full six years before the EIC began its settlement at Surat. Had the Dutch consolidated their affairs at that moment, then the English would surely have fared as badly in India as they were currently doing in the Malay archipelago. But in April 1603 the Middelburg factors had been put to death by the Portuguese. When Admiral Malatief detailed two ships to call at the Gulf of Cambay, in order to reopen prospects, the Portuguese had so harassed their head man that he shot himself. A further hiatus had then ensued until the moment when the *Nassau* arrived at Surat, and Roe overreacted.

The berthing of the *Nassau* was the signal for Ravesteyn to travel up from Masulipatam to look for the possessions of those who had been previously murdered and seek a *firman* from Jahāngīr. There would be no *firman* and no bodies. However, missing stock was relocated, only to be abandoned because infrastructure to store it was lacking. On returning to Masulipatam, Ravesteyn lost no time in telling Coen out in Bantam what a chance they were missing by neglecting Gujurat. To this Coen responded by sending Pieter van den Broecke, with instructions to expand operations. Admiral Broecke arrived in August 1616. Failing also to get the much-sought-after

245

firman, and with his ships *Middelburg* and *Duyve* sinking off Daman, he returned to Bantam in July 1617. Thus was Ravesteyn abandoned to make the best of things. Such a failure of nerve by what had hitherto been nerveless Dutchmen served to let slip a fine chance. For long, Dutch braggadocio had been a most formidable weapon, as for the most part it would remain. Not in India, though. Nevertheless, it transpired that the 'red-haired barbarians', as the Dutch were called, were actually suffering just the same lack of confidence that so debilitated the English. Despite flights of steps and squads of palms to make the bravest of parade grounds out of a Dutch settlement, Coen's letters offer a sobering corrective to any assumptions that a Dutch victory in the East was a foregone conclusion. Coen's correspondence is as replete with stories of empty chests as that of any English factor. Letters full of woeful tales of ruined harvest, lack of supplies and missed opportunities all added up to what one Dutch observer confessed was 'water . . . at the factors' lips but they could not drink it'.[39]

Recalled by the Court of Committees in April 1619, Roe returned with William Baffin. During their long months at sea, these two worked on what came to be known as the 'Roe Map'. Once published, it became the standard reference work for the geography of the subcontinent. Whereas Mercator demonstrated just how little had been known as to the relative positions of Indian cities and geographical features, the 'Roe Map' allows the Indus to take its proper shape, correctly identified with the river entering the ocean near Laribandar. The whole of western and the greater part of central India is portrayed with reasonable accuracy. What these two achieved was only to be superseded in 1715 with the appearance of François Catrou's *Histoire générale de l'empire du Mogul*.

With the map finished and the Thames entered, a grand delegation was waiting for Roe at Tilbury, everything in streamers and all ready to pull the consul up Poplar High Road in a triumph that lacked only an elephant and tiger to make it as Roman as anyone could have wished. At first all went well. Roe amused himself in deploying his Indian spoils between London and his house in Gloucestershire, including a vast Lahore carpet spangled with his arms and a crest with the family motto, 'Tramite recta'.[40] It represented what had been both the problem and the solution in India. In never deviating from his path, Roe had been unable to adapt to a culture that he found deeply repellent and wondrously attractive by turns. And yet at the same time his achievement in firming up the Company was because of this very intransigence.

'Having duly weighed his [Roe's] carriage and behaviour from the beginning till this present,' the Company recorded, 'they esteemed him a very worthy gent, that hath husbanded things exceedingly well, and very moderate in his expenses, and one that by his modesty, honesty and integrity hath given good satisfaction.'[41] The Court of Committees then gave Roe the rarest gift at their disposal: its members elected him to a seat on their own body. Following this, Smythe informed him that the Company's wish was that he would go as governor-general to the Far East. Here the intention was that he would take on that most formidable of Dutch opponents, none other than Jan Pieterszoon Coen himself. Roe refused.

It is not clear whether he might have accepted if all had been equal. But soon enough, alas, it turned out that they were becoming very far from that. As the weeks passed, the Company woefully mishandled Roe's return. What had been mooted as a gratuity of £2,000 was then reduced to £1,500. Now the thing that galled Roe about this was how the reduction had been accompanied with the wholly implausible claim that it was too little, compared with his deserts, but their smale retournes pleaded partly their excuse.[42] No sooner had this been said than the Company treasurer had declared to the assembled Court of Committees, with Roe listening to all this, that the profit of Surat was reckoned at £200,000, or 120 per cent of the capital employed, though by another calculation it was £210,860. Roe might have overlooked all this had the reduction not been followed by the cancellation of a £200 pension.[43] Mortified by those whom he had served so strenuously, he marched off to the Levant to take sail for Constantinople instead.

Unquestionably there is something of a riddle about the Company's treatment of Roe. Here was praise offered with the right hand but with the sinister, crabbed meanness and confusion of message. What, however, cannot be in doubt is the steady regard with which Sir Thomas Smythe held Roe. Both men had always believed in caution, had set their face against overreach and were content with a steady intelligent accretion of wealth. It may be that Smythe lamented treatment about which he could now do little, but the result was that the East India Company lost the services of arguably their most talented recruit. Despite his disastrous debut during his early days in India, Roe would graduate *cum laude* as the most experienced and skilful English diplomat of early modern Europe – but only after leaving the subcontinent. Roe achieved much there, even when outplayed by those who could understand the culture because they could either speak the language or subscribed to the same religious faith as the regime. And though Smythe himself lamented how, shortly after Roe's return, 'our affairs in India lye a bleeding', the corpse was not yet dead; such vitality as the Company managed to retain in India had been due to the curious mix of courage, magnanimity, obstinacy, officiousness and self-importance which comprised that obese little man who was Sir Thomas Roe.

Aside from 'Clive of India' (d. 1774) and Warren Hastings (d. 1818), no one in the history of the EIC has generated as much controversy as Roe. There has long been a determination to see him as the founder of a school of prejudice and prime mover behind the creation of the later British Empire. But such an argument can only be sustained at the cost of eliding context in pursuit of reductionism. Roe's testamentary record is too allusive to allow a monolithic construction, and, as we have argued, the East India Company had absolutely no interest in 'empire building'. Roe was forced to respond in ways chosen for him when the resonate command of a king rang like tinnitus in the ear. His instruction to impress the greatness of a monarch upon the Mughal required the selling of a line cast over the waters by James I whose notorious vanity blinded him to the essential irrelevance of his kingdoms in either the wars of Europe or the magnificence of India. To a king convinced that he was 'a Terror to all other Nations', not to mention 'not only absolutely obeyed but universally beloved and admired of all our People',[44] Roe wrote things he did not believe whilst his 'emperor' read things he wanted to credit.

With the expansion of empire came the inflation of reputation. Those who thought most highly of Roe and his performance in India were the same who much later persuaded Parliament to remember him in painting. But what was commissioned is now both deeply offensive and blushingly embarrassing. Ironically enough, this is by the Jewish painter Sir William Rothenstein (d. 1945), and it comes with the sententious title *Sir Thomas Roe, envoy from King James I of England to the Mogul Emperor, succeeds by his courtesy and firmness at the Court of Ajmir in laying the foundation of British influence in India* (1925). With chest puffed out and calf thrust forward, Roe takes such a posture as Julius Caesar might have adopted when addressing the senate in Shakespeare's play of that name. Roe stands with legs akimbo before an emperor, luminous in cambric and shining like the firmament, surrounded by courtiers bound in their ropes of pearl. Attendant upon a master perched upon a marble shelf in the *dandasana* pose, all listen with deference to a lesson on international relations delivered by a well-muscled representative of what is, clearly implied here, a superior race.[45]

Such a view was propounded by the distinguished 'imperial' historian Sir William Foster, for whom Roe represented the finest example of 'the upstanding Englishman', a species that had become endangered with the onset of the Stuarts. According to Foster, Roe had been the first to shake off the coils of Oriental despotism to lay down the lineaments of England's manifest destiny in India, that discreet geopolitical expression of a broader 'white man's burden'. In contrast to such an uncomplicated view is an altogether more nuanced interpretation offered by the doyen of post-colonial historians of India, Sanjay Subrahmanyam, and other revisionist scholars.[46] For him, and from the first, the Company was a presence that, when not wholly irrelevant to the concerns of a great power, was disabled with prejudice.

If Roe cannot be credited with transforming the Company, by showing that he was not to be trifled with he earned gradual grudging respect. That was important when even in his day success in Anglo-Indian relations depended upon finding congruities, as E.M. Forster would later claim. But if Forster, that most subversive student of Indian affairs, was to have profound doubts about the British in India, he might have felt less troubled about so troubling a history had he but known how Roe too had set his own face against any form of subjugation. Like Forster, Roe deplored colonisation. This had nothing to do with the lack of respect colonisation implies, but all to do with the lack of profits that would ensue from making such an improvident investment as, in Roe's view, colonisation necessarily incurred. Roe saw things in black and white and would have had no understanding whatever of Forster's views as to the morality of taking what belonged to others. Nevertheless, in surveying the scene in 1615, Roe was certain that the building of forts and the taking of towns must be rejected because of the ruinous costs involved. To the extent that Roe's views were respected in London and settlement was indeed eschewed, in warming the seed of English trade he allowed it to germinate thereby. Nurturing such modest beginnings, therefore, Roe has a critical place in the establishment of the English in India, though hardly in that grotesque sense in which his 'achievements' had come to be depicted in the corridor of the English Parliament during the dying days of Empire.[47]

Roe often suffered the agonies of frustration, around which he spun his protective garments: 'Roe's achievement owed more to his adaptations at the scene of Moghol power than to his constancy to the role drafted in London' is the verdict of one who goes on to add: 'The mission achieved fundamental strategic aims. It won the respect of the Emperor; contested Portuguese interest at court and eventually secured provisional rights for the East India Company.'[48] In seeing Roe massaging a bruised *amour propre*, Subrahmanyam suggests epigrammatically enough that he 'turned diplomatic failure into rhetorical success'.[49] But whatever Roe truly thought about Mughal civilisation, his predicament surely provokes sympathy. It had been an impossible job, and it is to be doubted that anyone could have done it another way.

Surely the best measure of Roe's legacy, with its suggestion of something solid if never spectacular, belongs to Roe's chaplain Edward Terry. This godly man's verdict, exuding whiff of complacency and swell of satisfaction, suggests how the English could be said to have arrived with Roe; but they would conquer only with Clive – and then only after generations of Englishmen had crumbled into the dust of India.

> Yet we Englishmen did not at all suffer by that inconstancy of his [Jahāngīr], but there found a free trade, a peaceable residence, and a very good esteem with that King and people; and much the better (as I conceive) by reason of the prudence of my Lord Ambassador, who was there (in some sense) like Joseph in the Court of Pharaoh, for whose sake all his nation there seemed to fare the better.[50]

12

＞∼

THIS HOPEFULLEST TRADE

Persia is like a big caravanserai which has only two doors, one towards the side of Turkey by which silver from the West enters [in the form of] piastres which come from the New World to Spain, from there to France . . . [and] leaving France through Marseilles, they enter into Turkey, from where they arrive here [Iran], where one recasts them into abbasis . . . Some carry their piastres until the Indies . . . The other door of exit is Bandar Abbas . . . for going to the Indies, to Surat, where all silver of the world unloads, and from there as fallen into an abyss it does not re-emerge . . .[1]

The unstoppable flow of silver from the Americas eastwards made for chronic tension between Turkey and Persia. Despite its colossal size and military resources, which represented a real and present threat to the Holy Roman Empire, Turkey was in serious financial trouble by 1617. Just at the moment, therefore, when the Company was preparing to make its first foray into Persia, the 'Ottoman Porte' declared war on the 'Sublime Sophy', Ahmed I (d. 1617) claiming that Abbās I (d. 1629) had reneged on delivering the amount of silk Persia had agreed to supply Turkey.[2] Whilst the Ottomans had a surplus of metal in the form of specie with Europe, this had always been outweighed by a deficit with both Persia and India. As for the subcontinent, many Westerners thought Surat was made of silver. Between 1588 and 1602 some 124 tons had arrived in India, whilst a third of all silver coming into Europe between 1600 and 1750 ultimately reached the subcontinent. And all this when inflation in India was never more than 0.3 per cent. Here the contrast with Persia was grievous. The Persian *shaki* weighed 9.22 grams during the reign of Shah Esmāʿīl (d. 1524), but only 2.30 grams when

Shah Abbās the Great came to power (1588), such had been the depreciation of the currency in sixty years.

As for the Company, very soon after it had made landfall in India its factors understood how the 'wealth stream' flowed inexorably eastwards. As early as August 1609 a paper was submitted to London from the factory at Surat, recommending the sorts of gifts the 'king', as the shah of Persia was here being described, might like. Due diligence would need to be exercised, since the emperor 'wants not worldly wealth or riches possessing an inestimable treasury, and is, it is thought, herein far exceeding the great Turk'.[3] What this suggests is that the East India Company had long had its eye on Persia. Although the Company arrived in Persia when Abbās was also having huge difficulties with his own economy, in the face of serious revenue-raising problems, he had in fact set about reforms some time before and these were now having a transformative effect:

> The chief reason why the country at present is without money, is because of the wars between the Turk and the King [the shah of Persia]; no merchant or caravan can pass to or fro in safety. The Banians, in return for their linens, carry most of the silver and gold out of this country, which being prohibited, if taken they suffer death, and this happened to several when the English were at Kasbin, one of Connok's[4] dear friends being the principal person who suffered. This King is a tyrant and will not suffer any of his subjects to be rich; he caused one of the richest merchants in Ispahan to be beaten to death with cudgels, took away his estate, and then had him hanged up in the Midan, to the annoyance of any coming near, and no man knows the cause . . . The King is a merchant, and has the refusal of all goods that come to town, forcing his subjects to take them at his price.[5]

The 'King' was indeed a merchant whose earlier military campaigns against internal enemies had been so successful that he was able to prompt commerce thereafter. Posterity considers him, Abbās I, the most effective of all the shahs. With a spirit of entrepreneurship unparalleled among rulers of the world in his day, Abbās summoned Chinese porcelain workers to establish his own manufactories, while he promoted a dozen regional schools for the production of rugs. Renegotiating commercial treaties to do with silk, or re-orientating the paths for export of what was Persia's most valuable asset, Abbās went on to create breaks for outsiders and roads for insiders, building caravanserais and banking canals, all in the spirit of transforming what had once been a war machine into an empire of commerce. Disciplined, pertinacious, cautious now impetuous then, this imperial psychopath combined subtlety with boldness in the promotion of internal prosperity and external reputation. Relocating whole peoples with a ruthlessness that Stalin would have applauded, Abbās moved Arminians from their ancestral lands at Old to New Julfa, where at the end of a spear he induced these refugees to build him the world's first business park.

Looking at all this from over the ocean, soon enough the factors of Surat believed it was time for them to enter the world's most exciting market. Despite such optimism, Roe considered it a folly to suggest such an incursion into Persia. For him the Red Sea would always be the market of choice. Syria or Persia: which then was it to be? For those who could listen to this argument with equanimity, what was clear enough was that something urgently needed to be identified so that what were meagre sales in India to date could be supplemented by the reciprocity of markets either side of the Indian Ocean.

But why did Roe favour the Red Sea when he had certainly read an admonitory text which had been written by Sir Henry Middleton shortly after the horrors he had endured at the hand of the Turk in the Yemen. That broken general had superscribed a letter of advice to all English ships to shun the Red Sea'.[6] Circulated after the forced march to San'aa during the troubled Sixth Voyage, Middleton had argued that a man must hazard his life in sailing into the Red Sea. Despite the risks Middleton had spelled out in his state paper, Roe was convinced that another voyage would prove worth it after all. In all this, however, he came to be confounded by the president of Surat and the king of disaffection Thomas Keridge.

In the eyes of Roe, Keridge was guilty of disloyalty, even though the degree of independence that the Company allowed the president of Surat was never very precisely defined. Nevertheless, the fact that no one had thought what the demarcation lines should be meant that there would be friction between the embassy and the presidency as surely as the sparks fly up. Keridge had convened a meeting at which he had pressed the case for the Gulf against Roe's advocacy of the Red Sea. Keridge having suborned subordinates to attend a subversive gathering aboard the *Charles*, subsequent discussion had by no means gone all his way: some had real misgivings about going behind Roe's back, whilst others demurred when Keridge proposed sending to Jask 'divers commodities not vendible in these parts'. Eventually, though, Keridge was able to exert sufficient pressure on colleagues to get them to dismiss a letter from Roe in which the ambassador had been 'earnestly persuading them to desist' from sending a Company ship up the Persian Gulf. This in a sense signalled that Keridge had won the day; though the start to Persian operations which then ensued could hardly have been described as impressive. When Roe got the details of what Keridge had dispatched he was concerned that the goods would 'disgrace their great promises and hopes'. If the grand vizier of Persia was to think that this was the best England could muster, 'hee [the shah] will reiect vs quite and cast off all thought of vs, and eyther the more constantly resolue to goe thorough with the Spaniard or to make Peace with the Turke; One of them he must doe'.[7] But there were anxieties closer to home for Roe. To put it at its simplest, Keridge was threatening the very foundations of his authority; as he himself ruefully informed a correspondent, 'Your factors loue to runne without mee, I will looke out to mend their faults, and like patient Job, pray and sacrifice for them, as he did for his sonnes whiles they banquetted'.[8]

Soon enough, however, the power struggle came to the notice of London when Roe appealed for the resolution of a most unfortunate state of affairs. After much deliberation, Smythe came down for Roe, in turn provoking Roe to write to Keridge with characteristic magnanimity how 'you shall all fynde me a tame lyon, you shall see I will use [my authority] with all modestie (or rather neuer lett you see but in case of Necessitie) hoping you will suffer mee to aduise, and either follow it, or show mee a good reason wherin I err, which for me is very easie'.[9] What such a document eloquently demonstrates is that Roe was always careful to maintain that separation so vital to the successful prosecution of diplomacy: he was ever clear as to the crucial distinction between matters of opinion and representation. Accordingly, he now got behind the boys in the boats by writing to the shah's jeweller, the

Englishman William Robbins: 'wee ayme nott at gnatts and small flyes, but at a Commerce Honorable and Equall to two so mighty Nations'.[10]

But as if the Company had not had enough difficulties with a 'house divided' in India, there had long been another hazard, in the form of the infamous 'Sir' Robert Sherley. Having appointed himself ambassador to the shah, indeed having awarded himself that spurious English knighthood, Sherley had spent the last ten years stymieing English efforts to get into Persia. What the Court of Committees knew of Sherley, but still more what it suspected, had done much to complicate relations and delay a long-planned entry of the Company into Persia at a time when, to all appearances, such a thing had looked so promising a venture. Proving as devoid of loyalty as he was devoted to his own chances, Sherley might be suggesting to the shah one moment that it should be the English who ought to be given 'most favoured nation' status and the next lobbying on behalf of the Spanish instead. In all this inconsistency there was, however, one consistency. Everything depended on who at any moment was offering Sherley the largest bribe.

But trouble with Persia was not confined to Isfahan only: it broke out 1,200 miles away in Aleppo where the Levant Company had its main factory. How Persia might affect things on the Mediterranean littoral was an urgent question when relations between the two English companies had long been held in suspended if animated tension. Such had been the consternation over what might be termed the respective spheres of interest of the two companies that the 'Turks' (as merchants of the Levant Company came to be known in London) had commissioned a policy statement that positively smokes with resentment at what the East India men were contemplating: 'all spices, silks, indigo, and goods of the Indies, which used to be brought through Persia into Turkey, and from thence to this realm, are now brought direct from the Indies'.[11] Was the Levant expected to stand aside, whilst their own partnerships that had been so long in the spinning were now to be snapped at the behest of their younger sibling the East India Company? If that happened, then there would certainly be sanctions imposed by the Ottoman regime on the Levant Company itself. Assuredly, too, such a shift in the dynamic of Middle Eastern trade relations as must follow a broad enlargement of East India Company commerce would diminish business right across the Ottoman

Empire. As for any treaty between the EIC and the shah, who could say what effect this would have on the profits of the Levant Company? And what if a caravan of 100,000 camels, making its way from Kandahar to Constantinople, were to find the Ottoman authorities closed against it?

But if there was growing tension between these two London cartels, impasse with Isfahan was quite suddenly relieved by the unexpected news that Sherley had left for Madrid to screw better terms for silk out of Philip III than he reckoned would ever be forthcoming from James I. This was the spur to assemble a Persian team. It was mustered under Edward Connok (d. 1617) as cape merchant and Thomas Barker (d. 1619) as number two. This done, Roe was still far from convinced that things were going to work out. But then there was little he could do when his original instructions had made it clear that he would be required to give the factors the latitude they needed to make the calls as to where and when new markets should be established.

Thrust onto the sidelines, Roe was forced to address William Robbins, his own contact in Isfahan, in a second letter. He assured his correspondent that his 'honest and good affection to his country will not go unrecompensed by the East India Company', before suggesting that profit could not accrue by landing goods at Jask, only to have them then transported up to Isfahan, which would surely incur further charges. Roe thought that it would be essential to secure a better port 'free for them alone or all indifferently'. There were going to have to be privileges and a settled agreement as to prices. No less important was surety from the 'King' that he would allow silk to be brought to a specified outlet for its onward transmission round the Cape to England. This way, it would be possible to circumvent Aleppo, since in recent months it had been invested by a nest of hostile Turks. As for the Spanish and Portuguese, Robbins would do as well to 'open the King's eyes that hee bee not blynded with the smoky ayer of Spanish greatnes'. Finally Roe advised his correspondent to behave like a 'faythful englishman'.[12]

What was projected in Isfahan came to be promoted in London. The courtly geographer Lord Carew confessed to Roe how with India 'All novelties of the country will be welcome, especially books and coins, but not to trouble himself about loadstones', before he got on to how a project for opening Persia had been greeted with much enthusiasm. It had been decided in London that a trial should be made of Persian textile because 'there is suche a madnes in England to be clothed in silk as thatt we cannott endure our home-made clothe'.[13] That Persia rather than Turkey was now the location of choice for silk was confirmed when Roe received a letter from James I. In this, he learned how what he was doing by way of 'an entrance of a treaty' had given the king 'very good contentment, being resolued to retain in a gratious memory the dilligences and dexterity you haue vsed in your negociations there'. The letter went on to authorise a treaty of commerce 'without further circumstance' that 'shalbe by vs foorthwith ratified'.[14] But how to carry out these royal urgings when Connok, who was described as 'a valiant and discreet man as sufficient for a merchant as any can be and an excellent penman', turned out to be neither brave nor tactful? Far from this, he was positively delusional.[15] Attracted to this job so that he could make statecraft not silk his business, the measure of Connok's determination to abandon the caravanserai for the council was the very first letter he sent to Smythe. It is replete with things in which he had no business meddling.

The letter begins with a reference to the departure of Sherley for Spain 'to contract for all the Persian silks'. If this was successful, Connok went on, that would allow England's traditional enemy to monopolise 'the only richest yet known in the world'. As Smythe cast old eyes over new paragraphs, he read about the dangers faced if the shah was to allow 'the Spaniard to have footing on his shore'. But then for Smythe alarm gave way to anger upon finding himself upbraided by this pipsqueak Connok. In Connok's opinion the English were 'the ablest nation for shipping', and therefore he couldn't understand why he had been denied access to the 'yearly required sums of money'. If Smythe would only fund factories properly, annual import of Persian silk might amount to £1 million. Not content with criticising the boss, Connok proceeded to discourse about how he and not Sherley should be made the chief adviser to the shah upon European affairs, on whom, indeed, Connok threatened to call 'with reasons unanswerable possess this prince what society, honor, benefit he may attain in freeing his gulfs of its present slavery, by taking Ormuz into his possession, an act worthy himself, easily performed, and whereby he may be Lord of his own'.[16] Here was a mere merchant making wholly unauthorised proposals that, if acted upon, threatened to drag the whole Middle East into crisis. But if Connok was prepared to contemplate hostilities, Roe wanted to avoid conflict; making a prediction that in the event would prove hopelessly wrong: 'that wee will take Ormus and beate the Portugall out of those seas; these are vanityes'.[17]

As the missives flowed in, so Connok swelled up, by subscribing letters with a touch of the quixotic and a peck of melodrama wholly consistent with his feeling that he was right in the middle of things: 'From the Persian Court and army near the confines of the Turk, 25 days journey from Ispahan.' If there was a flourish, there was a frenzy about how the king of Spain by 'large lies' had attempted Connok's own 'dismission'. The Spanish ambassador, Connok went on, had denounced him as an impostor who was carrying forged credentials. An enormous diplomatic row now ensued that required the intervention of the shah himself – a Solomon, not of the Temple but the camp, who prided himself on his capacity for smoking out a fraud. Had he not placed a baker in his oven and mounted a butcher on his spit when he had caught both doctoring weights? But in this case he deemed no such terminal measures appropriate. The surest method to establish the veracity of anyone's papers was to give them a jolly good sniff, and so 'In presence of the whole court the King took his Majesty's letter, put it to his mouth, then on his head, examined the manner of the sealing of it, and then opened it, satisfied that it was a true letter, and demanded what his Majesty chiefly required'. Turning to the Spaniard, the shah warned that tonsured friar with admonitory and chilling looks: 'Let him split in ten thousand pieces that tells me lies!' Thereafter the issue was wrapped up to Connok's satisfaction at any rate, when the shah proceeded to declare that 'the English were a people free from lying or deceit, but that the Portugals had any time these 20 years told him not one true word'.

But no sooner had the scandalous claims of the Spaniard been dismissed than Connok began to raise his own canard. He accused the senior Spanish diplomat in Persia, Don García de Silva, of plotting against him.[18] Shortly afterwards, seeing de Silva and his retinue riding towards him and convinced that he was about to be attacked, he decided it would unwise to try the issue, and so set 'spurs to his horse and with as much speed as their horses could carry them, directed their course towards an adjacent village to the great dis-reputation of our King and nation, he being in the opinion of these people, an Ambassador'.[19] Subsequently asked why he had behaved in a way that was hardly consistent with his status as cape merchant of the Company, Connok protested that he had done this because the don had 'intended to have seized and murdered him'.

That was unlikely when Don García de Silva was one of the founding fathers of Celtic studies and something of a fan of all things British. During a course of assiduous reading, de Silva had been intrigued to learn how in battles between the English and the Picts both sides had included a high proportion of women in their armies. As for now, the affronted Spaniard was rather more interested in early Persian burial practices than in burying Connok. Dismayed and bemused, he was 'much grieved that they being Christians should raise such false scandal on each other to the disgrace of the Christian profession, and that he should be ready to do any service in his power for the subjects of the King of Great Britain with whom the King of Spain had concluded a perpetual peace, league, and amity'.[20] Notwithstanding his neuroses, the least of Connok's difficulties was the king of Spain. Far more serious was his own dysfunctional relationship with Thomas Barker, who had been number two at Surat. Problems had begun because Barker had been passed over for the top job, which had of course gone to Connok instead, and when it was obvious to anyone who knew what they were talking about that Barker should have had it in the first place. This disappointment had then been followed by general disillusionment at a prospect none relished: '[These] merchants sent [to Persia] to reside in the country who were unable any longer to endure the insolence, outrages and indiscreet government of the Factory at Surat, and had resolved rather than live another year so hellish a life, to have gone home.'[21] But relations between these English merchants deteriorated by the week. The hatred Connok cultivated for Barker and the jealousy Barker nurtured for Connok made for the most extreme rancour, a sense of just how office politics was going being suggested by a rebuke that Connok fired at Barker: 'and to speak particularly to you, Mr Barker, (now the chief director and manager thence of these neglects), remember yourself, you know by our commission you ought to be by me directed, and since it so ought to be, so shall be, be you assured'.[22] This was hardly the tone needed to pacify one who not only had the experience that Connok lacked, but was also endowed with a gift for languages such as he could never have claimed; Barker was fluent in Turkish, Arabic, Persian,

Italian and Spanish. More generally, however, in a small community where everyone knew everyone else's business, Connok's rebarbative tone merely made others say, not only to themselves but also to their colleagues, 'Me next?'

Matters had not been helped by the choice of Jask as base camp, against Roe's advice. Described as a 'very poor fisher town', it had somehow contrived to find itself a mile from the sea. The place had a castle but no ordnance, walls of clay but 'doors so weak that a man might break them down with his foot'.[23] It was difficult to see how something little better than a barn was going to be defended against determined Portuguese assault. But then Connok 'would rather hazard ships, goods and men than be disappointed of his employment'.[24] Problems of location were eased when five of the six top men expired and the last, having been rendered insane by too much sex, had set off through the desert somehow hoping to get to London. The first to go was Connok himself. As his end approached, he protested how Edward Monox had poisoned him. But then, with a last exhalation, he made a still more shocking revelation: he had gone over to Rome. For those waiting to steal his money, certain damnation now came to be added to the sins of what had clearly been a wicked life.

But if Persia was dysfunctional, it was successful. It had a fecund combination of strong domestic demand and attractive exports. However disastrous the start-up, whatever the quality of personnel, it would have needed particularly foolish men to have driven the Company into the wastes of Baluchestan. Besides the variety of its products and the appetites of its people, the Safavid Empire was presided over by one deeply interested in bringing Europe to Persia. Abbās I may have 'cut off heads every hour', as Connok had written in warm approval, but he had never cut off the Company.[25] From the first, he had encouraged settlement at that shiny new trading estate of amber and mosaic that he had made the Armenians build. There, too, the Company had been accorded every encouragement. Indeed, Abbās went out of his way to accommodate its needs. William Bell had managed an exchange deal that, having served to devalue the currency, caused Abbās to strike off the head of his mint master rather than risk embarrassing the English. If that could hardly be said to have made for a revaluation, it certainly cleared the air with the Company:

The Sophy 'now in quiet', and hath no wars, but sometime of his own people he cutteth off head, hands, and feet of some, and of others he openeth their bellies to see if they have any evil disease in their hearts. This some doth term tyranny, but without this the crown would not stand long upon his own head, whose life we have just cause to pray for, as if he should die before his subjects had experience of the honest intents of the English they would much fear woeful times.[26]

Given such a sanguinary state of affairs, factors could never relax, ever watchful as this masterful tyrant manipulated foreign relations. A dozen nations vied with one another for the next commercial advantage. A posse summoned to his presence found that he had 'made his secret entrance into this city by private and unknown passages'. Wrong-footed, all now awaited 'the King, that he might the better divulge and demonstrate the magnificent state of his court, deferred it until he had prepared a princely and sumptuous banquet, whereto he invited all foreign ambassadors resident in his Court viz. the Spanish, Indian, Turkish, Russian, Tartarian and Uzebeck'. As Company representatives approached the throne, each observed the courtly rituals of obeisance, whilst for his part, the Sophy condescended to accept a letter from James I, 'glorying no doubt to have it published in an assembly of so many repugnant and discrepant nations, that it hath pleased so potent and yet so remote and diffident a prince to direct his royal letters to him'. With that ritual over, now was judged the time to gain an advantage over the Portuguese by telling tales, not out of but in court. Abbās was having none of it, though. When asked for support by the English he refused them. He was never going to extend protection to either nation since their 'disunion' was his rejoicing, 'for that if our forces were united the whole world would be insufficient for us'.[27] But then what followed seemed a gross act of bad faith. Abbās claimed he had kept a compact agreed with the Company that was to stop export of silks through Aleppo and send it out of the Gulf instead. This was palpably untrue, and so it was clear the regime was playing divide and rule: Turk against Frank.

But what of Abbās's capital, to which had been added that state-of-the-art industrial park down by the river? It was the world's most elegant city, a carpet of flowers where at 'intervals palaces emerged from gardens named after thrones, nightingales, dervishes, mulberries and paradise itself. Its shaded walks made it an extended pergola. The verdict of foreigners was unanimous: no contemporary city in the world could rival Isfahan; and these were men familiar with the greatest cities of Europe.'[28] For many a sober Protestant, the *maidan*, or public square, of Isfahan was to be preferred to the piazza of St Peter's. The pleasure domes of Isfahan stood for well-mannered reticence and noble geometry amidst a city of cool abstraction and considered under-statement. Here were to be enjoyed walkways lambent in gold and dyed in azurite, embroidered with tendril and floored in marble. Dome, cone, column and spire, all relieved by shady plane tree, plashing fountain, pergola of tama-risk and cedar of Lebanon; the *mise en scène* conspiring to instil a pleasing sense of cerebral abstraction and calculated tranquillity. When John Fryer (d. 1733) visited Isfahan, unchanged from the days of its creator Abbās I, he found the Royal Bazaar 'the surpizingest piece of Greatness in Honour of Commerce the whole world can boast of, our *Burses* being but Snaps of Buildings to these famous *Buzzars*'.[29]

But New Julfa was very different. Lying the other side of the city, here were to be had Tabriz carpets bartered for Novgorod hides, saffron from the Zagros weighed against silver from Potosí, and all exchanged against such a tumult of tongues as made New Julfa Old Babel. But whilst the Company secured its own footing in a place where profit justified investment, there was never to be the same dividend here as might have been extracted from the Spice Islands. Nevertheless, there was a product to hand that sold in Persia as nowhere else. Cloth would remain the staple of English exports to the Safavid Empire. To begin with, however, things went slowly: 'the reason is not the heat of this climate for it is as cold both for extremity and permanency as France, England, and other parts of Christendom which have more northerly latitude'.[30] Barker thought that there should be no problem in disposing of 400 to 500 bales of cloth annually, in return for a commitment by the Company to take 8,000 bales of silk of 180 pounds avoirdupois per bale. This would represent 1,000 tons stowage for a homeward-bound fleet. Silk exports to Europe could amount to about £1 million per annum, 'but half of it has not yearly been exported, being spent and wrought in Persia in making sundry sorts of stuffs'. Somehow silk exports to Europe never achieved the momentum that the English expected and the Persians promised.[31] But there can be no doubt that Persia was proving a fine investment and Keridge's boldness in advocating entry was proving to be a good call. Such optimism was entirely justified. Smythe had recently presided over a Court of Committees that had been summoned to look at the rise in Company customs returns. During the 'Customer's' time, that is to say during the lifetime of Smythe's own father, total revenue for all of England's imports coming into the Port of London had amounted to £12,000 per annum. In 1615, however, it was being reported by Smythe that in 1613 customs taxes levied from just the last two returning East India ships had been a staggering £14,000. As for the previous year of 1614, the Company had been obliged to disgorge £13,000.[32]

Besides silk, out of Persia came rhubarb, musk, carpets, velvets, satins, damask, tafettas, gold and silver cloths, bezoar stones, opium and fruits; from England, cloth, tin, brass, 'morse teeth' (elephant tusks), Muscovy hides, vermilion, quicksilver, lead, coney skins, cochineal, coral beads, iron, copper and sword blades. As for India, she received from Persia steel, ginger, sugar, all kinds of preserves, saffron, gumlac, indigo, copper, iron, camphor, sugar candy, opium, tamarinds, paper, cords and cotton wool. Further afield, from Indonesia, the Spice Islands, Cambodia, Burma, China and Japan arrived in their due seasons pepper, spices, china dishes and 'all sorts of china ware', tin, sandal and logwood, camphor and ginger. No wonder it was said of Persia that 'this trade, the hopefullest without exception that ever England enjoyed'.[33] Such optimism was entirely justified.

When Isfahan expanded, Aleppo contracted, and relations with the Levant Company soured accordingly. Since the foundation of the Levant, Aleppo had been the nodal point for silk coming out of Persia. Not any longer, however. Now there was talk of it all going to Europe round the Cape. Such a redirection had been mooted ever since Abbās had resolved to use the Company as leverage against the Ottomans when he had found himself unable to subdue his adversary by arms alone. Now Abbās was threatening to extend a trade war by diverting silk from Syria to reduce Ottoman tax revenues: '[It is] probable that the King [of Persia] may treat with other Princes for diverting the trade of his silk other ways than through the Turk's dominions because he would impoverish his enemy by exhausting such an annual treasure yet as to a peace being concluded with the great Turk, there is no appearance of it at present, neither is the king so effeminate or such a lover of peace, that he will make peace on dishonorable terms.'[34] This was further bad news for the Levant when the viability of its operations out of Aleppo had already been threatened. One thing was certain, though. If Abbās really did impose sanctions, the sultan could hardly be expected to make a distinction between those who worked for the East India and for the Levant.

By now, that is to say in 1617, it was simply too dangerous for Levantines to look out for East Indians: if scouts were caught they were killed. There had once been a time when Libby Chapman, an experienced and well-respected consul in Aleppo, had been able to transmit as many commercial secrets as he could find informants to bribe, but not any longer. Now it was a question of sending 'two of the Arabian nation who are accustomed to, and they only do know the passage through the desert'.[35] Chapman's position gave some protection, but not for William Nelson. Dispatched from Isfahan when bound for Aleppo, Nelson was met by 'a Frenchman fifty days since within three days' journey of Aleppo', the writer Edward Pettus then adding that 'if he accomplish his journey he escapes fair, considering the great wait laid for Englishmen and their letters; if any, of what nation soever, be taken carrying letters for England, nothing more sure than death'.[36] As for Turkish merchants in Aleppo, they were all 'hurly-burly' about this 'new intended trade of the English'.[37] Business confidence was at a low ebb, and people were so on edge that the Levant was obliged to make urgent representations to London. There the respective governors spent three days in close discussion of the crisis.

Sir Thomas Smythe and Sir Thomas Lowe were well matched. Lowe had found himself in Aleppo by coming at it from Venice, where for years he had been making his money importing goods out of Frankfurt. Smythe, by contrast, had chosen quite another route: sailing down the Volga to Astrakhan, from there he had crossed the Caspian and so approached the Middle East via Azerbaijan. But now they were both in London and locked behind heavy doors, so no one would hear what they were saying. But it was no good. Soon enough their palpable differences were widely known as their painful deliberations came to be closely observed:

In December last, (as in the Gazette of thatt moneth you may see,) I related vnto you how yll our men are vsed att Constantinople, and as farre as I canne judge there yll usage is liklier to continew then receve amends; yf we shall settle a trade in Persia, how farre forth the Grand Signor may be irritated to the confiscation of all the Englishe marchants goodes (throughout his dominions) is to be feared, whereby the kingdome shall receive great damage, and a profitable trade destroyed.[38]

Chapman had warned Lowe that Abbās had told the Turkish ambassador how he was minded to 'embrace' the trade of the East India Company. Knowing this, Lowe made clear to Smythe that he must stop using his factors 'for the conveyance of their letters, because of the dangers that may befall'.[39] But then matters went way beyond safety. As Carew indicated in his letter quoted above, there was a growing tension which though regrettable, was entirely predictable. To begin with the Levant had been solicitous parent but now the East India Company was the obstreperous teenager rebelling against the authority of those who if older were no longer thought the wiser. Carew's fears were shared by many since it was commonly taken that if Aleppo fell the Levant would fall. But the doubters were plumb wrong, for Aleppo survived. Raw-silk imports, which had stood at approximately £12,000 at the accession of Elizabeth in 1559, had grown tenfold by 1620. The truest measure of how these mighty men stitched things up is best suggested, though, by events in the late 1620s. By then, some 90 per cent of all raw silk imported into Europe was carried by the two companies working in concert. Just before the Civil War an astonishing 220,000 pounds of raw silk was arriving at English ports. All this suggested that the difficulties between the two companies had always been more apparent than real. Exports carried by the EIC made little impact on either the size or the profitability of the Levant. By 1628–9 the East India Company carried 41 per cent of silk exports, compared with 56 per cent accounted for by the Levant. By 1634 the dominance of the Levant was absolute: of Europe's annual purchase of 191,000 pounds of silk, the Levant held a staggering 71 per cent and the Company a mere 17 per cent. In the end the supposed 'threat' of the East India impugned neither the commercial integrity nor the profitability of the Levant.[40] That said, much later in the century relations between the two became rather more strained than in the days of Messrs Smythe and Lowe. The nexus between what would emerge as England's most profitable international companies of the pre-industrial world has been summarised thus:

> Although the Levant and East India Companies were tightly connected for much of the first half of the seventeenth century, the two bodies emerged as commercial and political rivals in the latter part of the century . . . The growing trade of the East India Company also turned it into a direct competitor of the Levant Company, as shipments of silk from Bengal provided a cheap alternative to the Persian silks that Levant merchants brought to England from Ottoman ports.[41]

Nevertheless, in a short time and during a period of acute crisis, relations were tense and problems grew with every post. Messrs Chapman and Saville declared how business had become so fraught that they could no longer freight, 'excusing themselves for conveying in future, letters for Persia, the one being a principal man of the Turkey Company, the other agent for many merchants, because if anything should be discovered, their goods would be in danger'.[42] Having had one narrow escape, the two much regretted that 'some other course to be thought upon,[43] . . . Apparently this was because of the danger to the messenger, who is liable to lose his life and goods as well as he who sent him'.[44] How to circumvent these new difficulties was the question. The answer was to hire Georgians and Armenians who in disguise had much more chance of being taken for locals, and who could adopt a 'character' or cypher whenever letters contained hazardous material.[45]

But then another solution was found. This was George Strachan of the Mearns whose many talents included ingenuity in deciphering. His recruitment would greatly help, if only because he was a phenomenal linguist. But there was more to Strachan than a tongue for languages; he also had a nose for danger. He was brave; as was acknowledged by a colleague who wrote: 'the bearer, Strachan, has had a violent burning fever and fifteen fits already, which have much weakened him, and he much fears if he stay here it will cost him his life, for he has been very grievously handled'.[46] Such an aside suggests that Strachan had endured an experience similar to the one that had come William Nelson's way when he had been picked up running letters out of Isfahan through Syria. Once they had captured him, Nelson's tormentors had threatened to burn him alive, but he had been rescued by Strachan, who used his fluent Arabic to spirit him away.[47]

The two years that Strachan was to spend at Isfahan was more than enough regarding his service with the Company. He could abide neither the coarseness of his colleagues nor the sermons of Robert Jefferies, from whose bullying he begged to be relieved 'that he may have justice, and his innocent and honest life restored to him free from the malicious craftiness of this wicked man, or else license to go out of this house and the Company's service'.[48] What had decided Strachan to leave the Company was because Jefferies had lighted upon two shady 'Portingales' who, for a little something, had been all too willing to blacken Strachan's name. Pietro Chevart and Estefano de Sant Jaque testified that they had overheard Portuguese friars swear that Strachan had poisoned Roe's correspondent, the jeweller William Robbins. Having dispatched Robbins, according to these same informers, Strachan had then finished off Thomas Barker. But this was not the end of it. The two also swore that Strachan was ready to 'poison all the English in Ispahan'.[49]

Jefferies liked nothing more than denouncing the sins of his colleagues. This was because he had been chosen by the Lord to recover all these lost sheep of Persia. Jeffries warmed with much enthusiasm to the process of making a misery of lives that in all honesty were sufficiently miserable already. One such 'saving' involved marshalling purse-lipped colleagues into making declarations 'against dice playing and other misdemeanours'. Those caught were to give their winnings to the poor and themselves be 'dismissed from the Company's table'.[50] That established, Jefferies made for an easy target: the Reverend Matthew Cardrowe. Though a minister, and thus taken to be a 'painful man', Cardrowe had proved hardly that. As the years passed, he had begun to think that the ways of Persia were strewn with mimosa and not the thorn. Always good-natured, often venal, Cardrowe could be called upon less for a good sermon than a good bottle. As the first to pull the cork he was the last to condemn fellow sinners. This most amiable of men was ever ready to bestow indulgence upon the depravities of the fallen. When a brace of sailors got so drunk that 'wine bereaved them of their footmanship', he had earned the enmity of Jefferies for 'interfering' just as the Pharisee was poised to administer condign punishment.

But it transpired that with Cardrowe, charity was less Christian than calculated. Kindness was an insurance policy against the moment when it would be discovered that the priestly finger had not always been in the prayer book. By January 1624 there were charges about missing rials and rows about 'the weight and measure of several commodities'. After Cardrowe's dishonesty came to be exposed following his death, the blame for what had happened was squarely laid at the door of the English compound in Isfahan. Yet that was not really fair since it subsequently emerged that within the Court of Committees 'there was once great suspicion of the Minister Mr Cardro now with God'. That was all very well, thought Edward Monox, now cape merchant in Persia and making a damn good job of it too. His feeling was that if London had long suspected Cardrowe of having been up to no good, at least they should have said so. Thus in the light of Isfahan's discovery about the suspicions London had harboured but hidden, Monox was moved to write to the Court of Committees on behalf of his brethren to point out how 'it grieves them exceedingly to find their worships so bitter with them'.[51]

As for Jefferies, however, where he lived was less the empire of Persia than the realms of Satan. Jask, Shiraz and Isfahan, all were consumed in blasphemy and sunk in fornication, swimming in sodomy and drowned in drunkenness. The Court of Committees was astonished when Smythe read out how Jefferies had endeavoured:

> a reformation of weak, diseased and unmerchantly carriage and his discovering the unreasonable, unconscionable corruption of Edward Monox in certain parcels of iniquity, there hath been (with the dispensation of the devil) a triple treachery begotten against him by their critical agent Ed. Monox, their carnal minister Cardro, and Strachan, their infernal physician; the world, the flesh and the devil, whose conspiracy hath caused these lines to take their being.[52]

Eventually, however, the kingdom of righteousness fell when in denouncing gaming, Jeffries made the mistake of turning on Monox, himself a great man for the cards. As Jefferies fulminated so Monox became furious. The timing was not propitious: Persia was doing well, and the last thing now required was to allow Jefferies to continue to do his rounds upsetting everyone. In July 1620 futures to the value of £12,000 had been solicited from cloth, kerseys and other goods 'lately sold to his [the shah's] treasurer Lalabegg'.[53] That was equivalent to the entire customs charges which the English Crown extracted from the Port of London for one whole year. And so Monox waited until his chance came. This happened at Jask, when the master of *London's Hope* recorded how 'Edward Monox did, on the 22 Dec. last, publicly pronounce aboard the *London* in Jask Road, that Jefferies should not leave the ship, for that he did commit him there prisoner for the King.' At first Jefferies tried to counter, declaring That 'he could have had forty witnesses more, but excused them, for Monox spake it first in the great cabin and afterwards upon the half-deck, working Jefferies' disesteem among strangers to publish his disgrace so much as possibly he could'. But with persecutors unconvinced and Jefferies now determined to play the martyr, the prisoner endorsed the warrant: 'God pardon him; his practices have been foolish and infernal, from whom the Lord will deliver.'[54] Monox was not bothered. He had far more important things to worry about than any pardon from the Lord. After all, he was about to seize the Straits of Hormuz!

What became a famous victory, conducted by Persian army and Company fleet, had been slow to muster. As early as October 1619 Barker had been telling the Court of Committees how 'sometimes he [Abbās] would secretly whisper unto us that he had a resolution to take Ormuz from the King of Spain and deliver it unto the English nation'.[55] When, however, Abbās subsequently found the English to be evasive, he evolved an altogether more sinister stratagem. He told Monox that unless he cooperated, first goods and then people would be sold to the highest bidder. Although the prospect of war was contrary to the whole ethos of the Company, Monox could not but agree with a colleague out in Indonesia who wrote: 'If the Company may have possession of Ormuz, and will send means to maintain it, they have gotten the key of all India, which will be a bridle to our faithless neighbours the Dutch, and keep all the Moors in awe of us.'[56]

Neither Persian army nor English navy could prevail without the other. But once they were united, Monox was confident of the outcome, writing to Keridge:

As we increase so doth Ormuz decrease; for the very report of the arrival of five English ships in Jask did strike such terror and amazement into these hen-hearted inhabitants, that even their own houses and churches escaped not the fury of their mattocks and pickaxes, fearing lest the English in landing should possess themselves of the said churches and houses, and therein lay siege and battery into their invincible fort. [As for the future, greater commerce with India would add] more vigour to this our infant trade.[57]

And indeed, come the spring of 1622, it fell after a siege of six weeks.

The subjugation of Hormuz caused a sensation in Europe, not least because of desperate accounts of smoking ruins and appalling butchery. At Madrid, the English ambassador the earl of Bristol was summoned 'to treat with the lords of the Junta',[58] whilst his counterparts in London, the Marquis Yinjiosa and Don Carlos Coloma, were instructed to demand redress for what was considered outrage against Iberia and larceny against the Estado. To start with, Spain was gratified at the speed with which its protest was taken up in London, with not just the one but both Secretaries of State furiously scribbling between Greenwich and Hampton Court; depending on where James I was residing at any given moment and so where each of the two had to hover with paper and quill.

In truth, however, Lords Conway and Baltimore were only going through the motions since London had not the least intention of satisfying the aggrieved party. Why should they? Holland was the power to be reckoned with now, and Spanish pride, or whatever its Portuguese variety might be, could go hang. Conway at Greenwich, wrote to Baltimore how he had been closeted with the king, who 'recommends to his judicious handling the intimations to the merchants of the serious and grievous complaints of the Ambassadors of Spain, and otherwise of the great wrongs and spoils made by them to their infinite enriching, at Armuse'. No sooner written than he rowed back, with Conway adding: 'These complaints are new and pressed hard, the issue of which must be attended to, and can do no hurt if men be well warned.'[59] Here Conway was making the Company privy to confidential exchanges, so Smythe could dodge the bullet. No longer governor himself, he was standing in for Sir William Halliday who, always ill, was often absent.

Next morning and writing from St Martin's Lane, back came Baltimore with how he had already 'intimated to the merchants of the East India Company the King's commands touching Ormuz, but will send tomorrow for the Governor himself and let him know the King's pleasure'.[60] Whether Smythe bothered to turn up is doubtful, though Abbott, Bell and Secretary Bacon certainly did. At the Court of 4 July, less than a week since the issue had become live, Smythe reported how he had talked to Baltimore in the Star Chamber. There he had learned how the Spanish had 'pressed the King touching the business'.[61] As for his part, Conway had asked Smythe to send 'in writing such satisfaction as they can at present give, taking knowledge of what he had said unto them'.[62] But Smythe prevaricated: 'The Court took consideration of this business, which being weighty (all circumstances considered), they conceived there could not be too much caution used in the very entrance, and therefore thought fit to forbear writing, but entreated Mr Deputy and Mr Bell to repair to Mr. Sec [Conway] at Windsor, and the Company's secretary to attend them.'[63]

With the threat of reparations receding, caution was still needed. This was emphasised by the Court of Committees when it began to rehearse arguments that might put a better gloss on things. It was noted on 6 August how 'The Court thought fit that a report to be delivered to his Majesty be drawn up by some well chosen civilians but that it be verbal and not in writing, unless the King command it.'[64] After that everyone began to relax. Deputy-Governor Abbot related how Conway 'did not conceive that it [the petition from the Spanish delegation] was much pressed at the instant, that the King would be in London on Wednesday, when, if there were cause, Secretary Conway would send for them'.[65] The minute then wanders off to consider offers for mace, nutmegs and indigo 'at certain prices'. But if relations with Portugal's minder Spain had been severely strained, there was still more repair work to be done in a quite other sphere. This was to recover from the damage inflicted on the East India Company after a largely fruitless decade trying to make a success of a Japanese station.

13

SEVEN MERCHANTS OF JAPAN

It was April 1622, and the worthies of the City, led in procession by that sometime treasurer of the Virginia Company Sir Thomas Smythe, filed into a church made famous by everyone's model merchant, who was of course fabulous Dick Whittington. This was Bow Bells, no less. And here they all were to celebrate England's first investment in America, to hear what the Reverend Patrick Copland had to tell them about the comforts of the next life as these were refracted through the vicissitudes of this. Doubtless many thought that the whole thing was merely going to be a chance to sleep through a sermon, but such cynics were in for a big surprise. Climbing into the pulpit, Copland let fire with such hell and brimstone so that all sat up agape:

"Will you yet see the great danger of Sea men, I will leade you along to weigh it by an experience and tryal of mine own in a *Typhoon*, or cruel tempest, that I met with off of the islands of Macqau, adioyning to the Continent of *Chyna* . . . In this *Typhoon*, or storme, our goodly *Vnicorne*, (a ship of 800: Tunne), was cast away upon the Continent of *Chyna*; but all the people (blessed be God) saved . . . In this Tempest wee lost also our *Pinnance*, with 24 or 30 men in her, which we had sent before us to *Firando* . . . to giue notice of our comming, of whom we never heard newes; wee cut off our long Boate, and let her goe; we sunk our Shallop, with two men in her, who were swallowed vp by the waues. Such was this Storme, as if *Ionah* had been flying unto *Tharshish*. The ayre was beclouded, the heavens were obscured, and made an Egyptian night of fiue or six dayes perpetual horror. The experience of our Sea-men was amased, the skil of our Mariners was confounded, our *Royal James* most violently and dangerously leaked, and those which pumped to keepe others from

272

drowning were halfe drowned themselves with continuall pumping. But God that heard *Ionah* crying out of the belly of Hell, and who heere is sayd *to turne a storme into a calme*; hee pitied the distresses of his servants; hee hushed the Tempest, and brought us safely to *Firando*, our wished Haven."[1]

None of this can have made easy listening for Smythe: some ten years before this sermon was delivered, he had been so taken with an address from the emperor of Japan that he had pushed through the Court of Committees the big idea of opening a factory in what Copland calls 'Firando' and we call Hirado. Among Smythe's critics had been those who had thought that to open a stall in Japan would be to stretch resources too thinly, whilst others had considered Japan would distract from the ultimate prize of 'Cathay'. Nevertheless, Smythe had pressed on with his own thinking that Japan could be the tradesman's entrance to China. But in getting his way Smythe lost it, since once it had been penetrated, Japan had proved impenetrable. When the single factory that had been started in 1613 came to be closed in 1623, money had been lost and hostility gained. Occasional landfall was made by the Company thereafter, though even that ceased when the Company's *Return* was refused permission to trade in 1673.

Failure in Japan was both commercial and cultural. The Japanese had very little interest in buying English goods when with each passing month the shogunate was developing deep hostility to the West because of the Jesuits, who had been gaining alarming numbers of proselytes for well-nigh two generations. The 'Apostle of Japan', St Francis Xavier, had landed at Kagoshima in 1549. After eighteen months spent converting thousands, he had provoked internal debate among Japanese warlords about whether the country should stay the closed society that instinct dictated or instead throw open its ports indiscriminately.

The Company made its first physical contact with Japan when Edward Saris arrived aboard the *Clove* on 12 June 1613, carrying Richard Cocks as cape merchant and five others: Tempest Peacock, Richard Wickham, William Eaton, Walter Cawarden and Edmund Sayers. Matters got off to the best possible start, with visitors swarming all over the *Clove*, and for those with a professional interest there was a chance to note the differences between a Western galleon and an Eastern junk. Saris, who was to become that famous authority on Japanese pornography, was much taken when the women fell upon their knees in front of what they took to be a vision of Mary. But this was no Virgin in the manger; it was Venus lying naked in a verdant landscape which if the iconography is anything to go by, the painter would have rendered as delicious as any Garden of Eden. The *geishas* blushed and Saris laughed:

> There came contynuallye such a worlde of people aboard, boath men and women, as we weare not able to goe upone the decks, and all about the shipp was covered with boates full of people, admiring much our head and starne. And giving leave to divers of the better sort of women to com into my cabbin, where the picture of Venus hung, verye lasiviously sett out and in a great frame, they fell downe and worshiped it for our ladye, with showes of great devotyon, whereby we perceaved them to be of the Portingale made papestes.[2]

Junketings stopped soon enough when it became clear that 'Firando' was the wrong place for a base: it turned out to be little more than a 'poor fisher town'. Waiting on the quayside were the representatives of the *daimyō*[3] of Hirado and the *bugyō*[4] of Nagasaki, the first incorrigibly greedy and the second inveterately hostile. The *bugyō* was forever expecting sweeteners, requiring not only a little something for himself but also for his entourage. Cocks was driven mad by demands that could never be satisfied:

> And in Nangasaque [Nagasaki] there is noe king nor nobleman, but only the Emperour's bongew (or governar) of the place, soe that we need not to geve presentes to more then one at any shipp's entring. But at Firando there is the king hymselfe, w'th two of his brothers, and 3 or 4 of his uncles besides many other noblemen of his kindred, all w'ch look for presentes or else it is no living amongst them; and that w'ch is more, they are all wais borowing and buying but sildom or neaver make paym't except it be the king hymselfe. So that it maketh me altogether a-weary to live amongst them.[5]

In Japan presentation mattered every bit as much as presents, but our seven merchants were wholly ignorant of the fine art of social intercourse as it was

274

practised in one of the most formal cultures in the world. Matsuura Takanobu (d. 1614), *daimyō* of Hirado, was a man of high refinement who found himself quite at a loss as to what to say to Cocks, the son of a Staffordshire yeoman. Dauntless in battle, Shigenobu lived in fear lest one of Cocks's smelly 'watter spaniels' upset the china. Shigenobu had served abroad where, when not wielding the *wakizashi*, he liked to observe the rituals of the tea ceremony, as it could be measured through the austere merits of Korean pottery. Once home from campaigning, Shigenobu had done his best to encourage the Japanese ceramic industry. This he had contrived by offering Korean prisoners the simplest of choices: decapitation or relocation.

As for Saris, he was back in Bantam by December 1613. Made 'general' for the voyage to Japan because of long familiarity with Indonesia, Saris's appointment had been confirmed because of the assumption that as he knew Bantam he must know Bungo. But the very first thing he did once he got to Hirado was to make the disastrous mistake of spurning the advice of William Adams, who as tutor in mathematics and naval architecture to the emperor was the only Westerner wholly accepted by that suspicious regime. Achieving *hatamoto* status and acquiring an estate at Edo, Adams might have run things for the Company too, had Saris allowed it.[6] Adams had suggested Nagasaki was the better base for Company operations, as being one of the best deep-water harbours in all of Japan. But no: Saris pronounced it must be Hirado. He would not take the advice that Adams was offering partly because he was out of his depth, and also because he felt mightily insecure in the company of one who had spent ten years ingratiating himself with the shogunate. That said, Saris's reluctance was in some sense understandable; if only because Adams seemed all things to all nations at a time when the newly arrived English contingent was decidedly defensive. It was noticed with some concern that whereas Adams had worked for the precursor of the VOC, he had never served the EIC. What also damned him in the eyes of Saris, who had by then endured years of being humiliated by the Dutch, was not only that Adams fraternised with the 'enemy', but that he was in the habit of asking Spanish, Portuguese and Japanese over for *sake* whenever he was in town. What was more, Adams always stayed with his Japanese friends. If only Adams had been heeded but his habits ignored, what was a ship of fools might have become a junk of profit.

How was anyone to know what Japanese women would buy next year when there was huge difficulty in anticipating requirements for this? There was real difficulty responding to a clientele whose tastes were as nuanced as 'whites' on a Farrow and Ball chart. But there was a difference. Nowadays industry dictates the market, but then the 'Japanner' was a law unto herself. There was no 'industry' in a place where English goods could only be sold piecemeal; no way in which the Company could create a fashion that none could resist. Japan was a hideously difficult market to understand, with its complexities compounded by a trans-Asian trading network that reached west to Arabia and east to Mexico. Given the sophistication of the Japanese market, much of what Saris recommended proved of little interest. After textiles were: 'Pictures, paynted, some lacivious, others of stories of warrs by sea and land, the larger the better'.[7] Following these came: 'vermilion; Payntinge for women's faces; Syvett; China sowinge-gould; Sugar candie; amber; waxe; Huny; Nuttmedges; Campher; Sanders and Collombacke wood; Elliphantes' teeth; Rhenosseroes' hornes, Hartes' hornes and Roach allome'. In due course however, Richard Wickham dismissed all that Saris had recommended 'as so much galley-pot rubbish: A cargazon of Gen'll Saris his invention, having, as appeareth by the Ho' Compa' l'res, given such admirable hopes of this places that yf we were lerned alchimists we could not so soone turne mettles into silver as the Hon'ble Compa' (being deluded) are bouldly confident that we can turne these idle commodytys into mony with a woord speaking'.[8]

Of things saleable there was too little, but of the unsaleable too much. If cape merchant Cocks knew nothing about Japan, he knew about wool; but even so, the stuff was devilishly difficult to shift. There was a niche market for under-saddles and the wrapping of weapons such as the *katani* and *jinboari*, but that was about it. By contrast, Indian piece goods did better, as between December 1613 and January 1617 they yielded a gross profit of 38 per cent. This compares with the best lines: sappan wood from Siam at between 200 and 230 per cent, and Chinese silk even better at 300 per cent, though the Company could never get enough of that to make it a market-changer. It was Coromandel textiles that kept this factory alive. There was also a very small movement in European prints that gave 400 per cent, though it was a nice question as to how many wrestlers wanted to see Hercules squeezing the life out of Antaeus.

Taking the overall figures to January 1617, cloths and remnants were valued at £2,509, but sales returned only a measly £1,566.[9] As to the effect this had on morale, one of the factors sighed as he confided: 'the people soe mutable that that w'ch is a good comoditie this yeare will prove a drugge another yeare'.[10] Clients preferring 'sad' colours, the same recommended stocking up with cinnamons and straw-coloured cloth, sober blues and violets, but not the primary and the powerful. As for blacks, whites and greens, sales were much slower, whilst it seems anything red or pink induced a positive seizure in all clients. Fastidiousness became something of a cult. White spots on blue or black were all right, but white on red not on your life: these were best reserved for winding the dead. While the wrong spots induced a rash, goods were attractive only when expensive: 'the nature and condition of these Japaners . . . is to buy those comodytys that are most rare and at the time when they are most dearest . . . So likwise doe they enquire after all sortes of new stuf fantastically paynted or striped, such as are not usually brought heather.'[11] And yet fussiness was never exclusive to Japan. Take the great mystery of the sugar cube that would come to exercise the Company in a later generation. After leaving Japan, the Company imported West Indian cube sugar into Persia. It then occurred to someone that the business might become a whole lot easier if the stuff came in loose. This was not so: one disgruntled emir protested that his coffee was not sweet enough without that reassuring geometry he had always known. The market collapsed accordingly.

As for what was happening in Japan in 1613, middlemen deflated profits by insisting on a fixed price, refusing to decrease it even when gains grew to upwards of 200 per cent. Although there were things for which there was demand, these were not English: they were Indian textiles. Hirado depended on 'coastal trading' more than was the case with any other station where the Company had dropped anchor. *Peppercorn* would leave London and make first deposit at Surat. Leaving, Coromandel cotton was acquired, and so venturing on to Siam a first tranche of textiles was traded against perfumed wood, benjamin and animal skins. The rest went on to Hirado for distribution across Japan and beyond.

The burning issue was entry into China. If only this could be effected, then Japan could become viable overnight. Accordingly, Cocks invested in Li Tan (d. 1625), the leading Chinese merchant at Nagasaki. Domiciled in one country, dominant everywhere, Li's contacts were legion, power extensive and funds inexhaustible. Moving between the cultures of Europe and Asia, Li had European clients across all Asia. Here was a man who was a lot more than just a facilitator. Though acting for Asian supplier and European buyer, he was also something of a broker in both politics and war. Without the local knowledge of Li, and his nephew Zheng Zhilong, European companies could never have been successful. Extracting concessions from this regime, facilitating the policies of that tyrant, Li was politician and purveyor to anyone prepared to pay enough. 'Rey Chino' to the Portuguese, 'Captain China' to the Dutch, 'Andrea Dittis' to the English, Li was the croupier at the casino.

He is first encountered in Manila, where he was having difficulty with the authorities, claiming he had stolen 40,000 rials from them. Condemned to the galleys but slipping his tether, he made his way to Kyushu, where he had established himself as the leading man between Japan and China. No waters in the seventeenth century were more threatening to the regular conduct of business than those between China and Japan. The poison was pollution from that dangerous waterborne parasite, the Japanese pirate. Infesting Formosa (Taiwan) and the Pescadores, these descendants of the *Wakko* or 'dwarf-pirates', blood-encrusted cut-throats to a man, would sally forth to feast upon the fat of such junks that had been improvident enough to have plied unarmed the hazardous way between Amoy and Kyushu. But then, if the missionary Fra Martínez is to be believed, Li was not above a little of the strong-arm stuff himself: he controlled, if he did not always command, a fleet of eighty junks.[12]

Although the English had nothing to fear from pirates, they had everything to gain from Li, or so they fondly thought. Li was going to get them into China because he had been identified at the highest level as the instrument of a new pro-China policy that had just been promoted by Tokugawa Ieyasu, who

was quick to recognise that there were great profits in the China trade. Instead of leaving that trade to Portuguese-Dutch rivalry he decided that

Japanese merchants should recruit Chinese to help them. A new system of trade permits was introduced to cut down on the European dominance of this trade. And it was during this period that Li Dan [sic] and Zheng Zhilong built up their maritime forces and the island of Taiwan [Formosa] was opened up as a useful trading base by the Chinese and then the Dutch and Spanish.[13]

Besides having the ear of Ieyasu, Li possessed a powerful combination of charm and ruthlessness: as with one he disarmed, whilst with the other he stripped the East India Company of such assets as it had assembled for the Chinese market. Leading Cocks up the garden path, far into the bamboo indeed, Li assured his good friend 'Kapitan Ruicharu Kaksu sama' that it could only be but a matter of weeks before a cloud of sails came drifting into Hirado, though, for reasons that Li could not explain nor Cocks dared to ask, those famous junks somehow failed to materialise. However, it should be added in defence of the Japanese operation that this sort of thing was going on all over the Far East. The Chinese screwed Europeans wherever they could induce Westerners to do so foolish a thing as enter into a contract. For example, George Cokayne stationed at Jakarta reported to one George Ball (who was himself busy reporting Cocks to London) how 'Trade is now "hugger mugger among the Chinese caterpillars", for they handle all, make price with the Landaks as they please, and bring the stones to us at the price they please. The Landak people prevented from trading with the Company's people, for it is to the advantage of the Chinese that the English be kept from trading with the Landaks themselves.'[14]

Endowed with wealth but bereft of principle, Li bankrupted the Japanese operation. As Li grew rich and Cocks grew torpid, disgrace rattled along behind. That same George Ball who was the correspondent of George Cockayne, himself boss to Cocks and 'president' of all, looking on from Bantam, was now beginning to ask awkward questions: where was the money and where was the profit? As for Cocks, he was quite unable to identify a single stable commodity that sold quickly whilst yielding a high return. Silk might have been just the thing; indeed, profits could have been high had the English broken into the silk run between Macao and Nagasaki. But the heavily armed battleships that were needed to force such an issue were unavailable. And so it was that the contingent of English merchants in Japan came to be reduced to pedlars choked with trifles. Struggling with their packs, they also laboured under far heavier misapprehensions. Upon arrival they were wholly not to say lamentably ignorant of the fact that Japan had a far older culture than could be found in all Europe. After all, when marauding animal-skinned tribesmen of the Borders had been staining their bottoms with woad, the artists of Japan had been painting their walls with blossom.

A degree of ignorance about Japan could have been avoided if only anyone back in London had thought to look up the Spanish ambassador, favourite among the diplomatic corps then hovering about the sacred person of James I. Diego Sarmiento de Acuña, 1st conde de Gondomar, was amassing one of the great libraries of Spain and would have been only too happy to lend books written by the Jesuits which told of Japan and China alike.[15]

What made matters worse was how the collective experience which the Company had accrued en route to the Far East now came to be applied to Japan – where it was wholly inapplicable. It will be recalled that voyages stopped at the Cape where stones could be inscribed, letters retrieved and health restored. At the Cape it was always easy to stock up with anything needed to allow the voyage to proceed in relative health when it was merely a case of a rattle for a ram or a pin for a penguin.[16] It was therefore naively assumed that much the same would prevail the further east the ships sailed. It came as a tremendous shock therefore to discover just how difficult trading really was when the Japanese disdained to be fobbed off with the baubles and trinkets which the Indigenous of South Africa had received with such uncomplicated pleasure. However, the challenge which the East India Company faced in Japan went far beyond a mutual failure at cultural reciprocity. There was no incentive for the Japanese to buy anything from the English when they had long-distance connections with the Malay Peninsula in one direction, the Philippines and Mexico in the other.

But if there was no 'need' for the Japanese, there was no 'way' for the English. It was never going to be possible for the East India Company to break into the Chinese market. Thus, what had seemed a positively celestial chance when back in 1613 Smythe had spun his terrestrial globe to alight on Japan, now turned out a delusion. There could never be a grand joined-up stratagem which might have made out of the endeavours of the East India Company not a globe but a polyhedron: not just trade between England and Japan but a multifaceted business including not merely China but Cochin China (Vietnam), Korea and lands beyond.

Given such grievous disappointments, then, how exactly did the fortunes of the Company unravel as the seven contrived their plans to roll their bolts in the markets of Nagasaki and their ray skins under the awnings of Edo? In December 1614 Richard Wickham, of the Bristol store, sailed out of Hirado as chief merchant on a junk named the *Sea Adventure*. It was an escapade no one relished since it seemed to many waiting apprehensively on the quayside that the *Adventure* liked to spend more time *under* than *on* the water. The voyage failed and, forced to over-winter at Okinawa island, the party was back empty-handed two years after the Company had first arrived in Japan. Time spent on higher seas than anyone felt comfortable with meant that setting forth for business was an extraordinarily hazardous undertaking in itself, and one which was not helped by having to pilot a way through 6,852 islands. Happily, however, and on this occasion at least, William Adams had been the man delegated to do just that: best helmsman in Europe, he had been the first to bring in the Dutch.

Adams was pilot and Wickham cape merchant when together they competed in a triathlon of wind, storm and mutiny: 'Tewesdaye, wee did nothing but walk mallincolly and meues sollitari.' Perhaps if crew could only be persuaded to remain 'solitary', all might yet be well. But so far from that, as lassitude bore down, so the men grow fretful. As commanders Wickham and Adams faced imminent disaster, with backs to the taft-rail, they were forced to draw their swords: 'all our offessers, mariners and passengers risse up in armes to a ffought on w'th another, but by my great p'sswasion and Mr Wikham and Sr Edward Saris . . . did so p'sswad on both sides as ther wasse no bludshed of no p'tty, thankes bee to Allmyghty God for ever amen.' Gratitude was premature and troubles far from over, however: '[I] could not mak an end but hoped the nixt day to mak pece.' The end falling on Easter night, this merely served to provoke the most laconic of entries in the ship's journal: 'he that had been the cass of the great muttini being still fooull of desperate partes, this night Shobe Donno killed hime. This day fayr wether, the wind northerlly.'[17] As for Shobe Donno, he seems to have settled the weather on board quite as well. Once he had managed to cut the throat of the chief miscreant the throng was quieted. Murder, larceny, sexual and physical assaults, drunkenness and insubordination, these and more required pragmatism, clemency and resolution when crews might be calm one day and mad for blood the next. This was the world of the *Ancient Mariner*.[18]

The inexact science of navigation could mean being a cable's length from the razor of a reef before anyone knew it. Wickham's companion Edward Sayers, another of the group sent out to Japan, attempting Siam – which it was hoped might prove a market to subsidise the poor returns from Japan – found the *Sea Adventure* had the nasty habit of simply drifting helplessly onto rocks: 'Thene wee fell with an illand, having allmoste stumbelled upon it. Butt we halled of our sheetts close and with God's geiftt wee goot clere of it, with great danger of castinge away the jounke and oursellfes . . . There bee 3 of theme in all, butt nether pillett nor anye other knewe whatt ilandes theay ware, but geseinge theme to bee soum ilandes of the Leuckes.'[19] Conditions aboard the *Sea Adventure* veered from numbed indifference to stark terror in less time than it took to unfurl a sail, a state of tension confounded by confusion when no one could remember the days of the month. For his part, Sayers seems to have thought that there are only thirty days in December, but that this state of affairs was then made up with thirty-one for September! For him, if for no one else, 27 July 1619 turned out to have been both a Monday *and* a Tuesday. What, however, we must take on trust was that on 19 July the *Adventure* was breezing past an island that Sayers describes as looking like a cardinal's cap. As land slipped by, Sayers slipped into a trance, mesmerised by the devotions of his Chinese captain: 'This day the capten of the jounke binge a Chenye, mayed a sakerifise with a hene and porke and wine and a littell jounke withall and all theis with vittells and wine and ofered it to the pagod ashore, atope of a mountane, and seitt itt under sall in the see with many seremones.'[20] But the gods were in a bad mood that day, since three weeks later and the hapless crew were still in a sea of trouble:

Nowe wee havinge many mene secke, and thay wind binge soo steife aganste us, thay ware agreed agane to goe for Macaue, thoe I intreatted theme to staye untell tomorowe to see if the wind would favere us. Thene wee came to one mell a daye and one gucke of watter for a mane a day to drese veittelles and to drienke to. Thene theay desyered my monkey to bee throne overebourd, which I gave hime to theme to doo whatt thay would with hime. Soo thaye caste hime over-bourd. This the wind continueinge stell verye stronge thatt wee bracke the other rope of our mane roudere, soo wee had boutt one to truste unto to save oure lyves, wee steringe away all this night eeste and by soath and eeste south eeste.[21]

Happily, their predicament was unexpectedly eased when one 'morninge wee toacke 2 greatt sharkes which refreshed all the compeny very wille'.[22]

In Japan, as everywhere in the Far East, the Dutch deeply resented the English, whom they thought of as trading without paying for the overheads involved, not only in policing seas but also in coughing up for joint operations based at Hirado. All of that, however, was sitting precariously on top of a whole raft of historic tension. For example, one day Richard Cocks bumped into his opposite number, the director of the Dutch factory:

Yes, said he [Harmanson], but what recompence shall be made for the lives of our dead men? Unto w'ch I [Cocks] replied that yf the Hollandrs would reccon aright they rested much indebted to the English nation in that part, for that for one Hollander that had lost his lyfe in conquest of the Molucos (as they termed it) their had 20 Englishmen lost their lyves in driveing the Spaniardes out of the Loe Cuntries and making the Hollanders a free state. Unto w[hi]ch he know not well to answer, but laughed it out.[23]

If relations between Cocks and Harmanson were at best tricky, Cocks's relationship with Adam Westerwood were murderous, or so Westerwood was hoping they would become. Things had not got off to a good start because Cocks went around mocking Westerwood's 'noble parentage' as the son of a 'close-stool maker'. In a letter to the Clothmakers Company about what Westerwood and his gang were up to, Cocks wrote of how:

We are much molested . . . w'th the unruly Hollanders, whoe have procleamed open warrs against our English nation both by sea and land . . . geving 3 assalts against us in one day, they being 100 of them to I Englishman. Yet God preserved us from them, the Japoneses, our neighb'rs, taking our partes. So that then their Generall or cheefe comander, called Adam Westarwood, sett my life at sale, promesing fifty rialles of 8 to anyone would kill me, and 30 of the like for the life of each other English m'rchant, w'th many other stratagems they used against us too long to be repeated.[24]

Quite suddenly, though, everything changed. With the creation of that Anglo-Dutch Fleet of Defence (1621–2), which was discussed in Chapter 9, Cocks at last found himself able to sleep through another day.

As if managing the Dutch was not difficult enough, Cocks was required to control subordinates and discourage depravities. Japanese brothel keepers were especially aggressive towards him since Company employees were their most reliable customers. On one occasion, Cocks was unwise enough to march into a whorehouse where he was not looking to be serviced but to save. Finding himself bounced out, he went on to record how: 'Bastian which keepeth the whore house gave it out, that if I came any more into his house to seeke for our people, he would kill me.' Outraged, at once Cocks complained to the 'king'. He in turn sent word to the master of those particular ceremonies that:

> it should be lawfull for me, or any other that accompanied me to go into any Iapans house to seek for our men, without any molestation, and that they themselves should aide and assist me: and if the doore were not opened at my comming, I might lawfully breake them downe: and a souldiour was sent to Bastian to signifie unto him, he should take heed he did not molest or disturbe me in my proceedings; for if he did, he should be the first that should pay for it.[25]

Having endured such a school of hard knocks, thereafter Cocks was wise enough to let things hang, and so no more is heard of these nocturnal prowlings. But so disruptive was the European presence in brothel, bar and bagnio that the 'Bongo' (*Bugyō*) forbade Europeans to visit any 'house' after dark, which 'angred our people in such sort, that some of them gave it out, they would drinke in the fields, if they might not bee suffered to doe it in the Towne; for drinke they would'.[26]

Cocks's own arrangements seemed to be going well, however. He prided himself on not needing a brothel: in contrast to others, he could always go home to what he fondly thought would be the undivided attentions of his obliging mistress Matinga. Soon enough, though, he was sorely disabused after it was discovered that she was running three other lovers besides Cocks himself. Kicking her out, Cocks transferred his lusts to what today would be regarded as under-age girls, parents either selling them in the market or, more profitably still, direct to their European clients. Shame-faced but triumphant, Cocks confided in Wickham:

> I bought a wench yisterday, cost me 3 taies, for w'ch she must serve 5 yeares and then repay back the three taies, or som frendes for her, or else remeane p'petuall captive. She is but 12 yeares ould, over small yet for trade, but yow would littell thynke that I have another forthcominge that is more lapedable[27] yet it is true, and I think a gentelwoman of your accoyntance. Yow must be no blab of your tonge, yet I make no dowbte but Sturton [Nealson] and yow eather are, or else will be, p'vided shortly.[28]

All seven needed lots of sex, some choosing bigamy, others brothels and the rest under-age girls. As for 'the naturalized Japanner' William Adams, he ran one family in Stepney and another in Edo. He had become a bigamist when Ieyasu, the first shogun of the Togukawa dynasty, and with whom Adams was on the best of terms, had told him that he was just too valuable to the regime to be allowed to leave. Unable to return to his wife Mary and daughter Deliverance, Adams was meticulous about sending money home, even after he had made his new arrangements.

Among the very few to be unsullied by all this was Richard Watts, purser of the *Bull*. He deplored the depravity that he observed, and notified Smythe: 'Pray you p'don my boldnesse in writtinge of the truthe, for dutie that I owe your Worships makethe me soe bolde. Itt would make any honest harte to lamentthe times that wee live in this sinefull Sodome of Jappon.' He went on: 'for w'th reverence I write itt to your Worships, and to our great shame, that this house of yours is more like a puteree [brothel] then a m'chantes' factory, everie man for the p'te afected to his owne pleasure or his private p'fitte rather respectinge their owne private then your Worships' bussines, as per accompts will to your Worships one day appeare of the great expence and littell gayne.'[29] But what was Smythe to do about it when any rocket he might launch in response to Watt's revelations would take at least a year to land, and then fail to explode?

Death was never far from Cocks's mind, and it was fluency in Spanish that came to his rescue when, quite suddenly, he chanced upon two friars buried under rice in the bottom of a junk. In spotting them Cocks saw his chance. Here was a grand opportunity to claim the reward that the shogun had just announced for anyone lucky enough to catch a missionary by his cassock. If you handed one of these over, in turn you were handed the entire cargo of the ship in which the wretched man had been apprehended.

Brought before a tribunal, Fray Luis Flores and Fray Pedro de Zuñiga swore upon all the deities of Japan that they were merchants, not men of God. Listening carefully to the claims of both parties, the judges ordained that he who lied died. Coming up with proof only hours to go before sentence was to be pronounced, Cocks clinched his case. Later he was pleased to hear how 'The two fryers w'ch were in the friggatt . . . were rosted to death att Nangasaque [Nagasaki]i, and 12 other marriners of the friggatt beheaded before their faces before they were executed'.[30] Regarding the unhappy sea captain, he adopted the much approved custom that was expected of any self-respecting 'Japonner' in trouble. This was to 'cut your belly' before someone thought to do it for you. As for Cocks, he had got the money and he had survived, if only just. Not long afterwards he came to discover what a risk he had taken – how close he himself had been to death. The 'Chief Justice of Japan' Itakura Katsuhige,[31] taking a walk and running into Cocks, ran through what had been going through his own mind at the trial:

had [we] not absolutely proved the Portingalls to be padres, that th' Emperour ment to have put Capt' Leonard Camps [Dutch commander] and me to death and to have sezed on all we had in the cuntrey, and yf any resistance had byn made, to have burned all our shiping and put us all to the sword. God send us well out of Japon, for I dowbt it wilbe every day worse then other.[32]

But if terror lingered long in the memory of Cocks, soon enough it fades for us, his tribulations giving way to tales summoned up from within the priceless pages of Cocks's diary. Although it is all too easy to see how prone to hyperbole and plain untruth was this most intemperate of men, the diary remains the most important and most vivid of all Western accounts of the Tukogawa shogunate (1603–1868) in its earliest years. Out of diary and letters alike steps one who is memorable for his incompetence but admirable in courage. Impulsive and disorganised, warm one moment splenetic the next, Cocks rides in triumph through disgrace. Unrivalled in the colours with which he stains his page, his writings from Japan are of such gross and indulgent amplitude that they must surely contribute at least one of those 8 miles now making up the business of the EIC on the shelves of the British Library. Like a disappointed teacher dismissing the scholarship boy who has failed him, the president of the Indies, in writing from Bantam, describes Cocks's extravaganzas as 'copious but not compendious, large, but stuffed with idle and needless matter, ill beseeming one of Cocks' place, years, and experience'.[33] How right President Ball was, but how wrong would we be not to notice this priceless monument of a living history.

Wherever they went, our seven merchants faced colossal difficulties. Tempest Peacock is next; now there's a name not even Ben Jonson could have invented for one so obviously stiff with pride and swollen with avarice! In the short time Peacock had left to live after first arriving at Hirado in 1613, he proved as contemptuous of the 'native' as gin-sodden Ellis in Orwell's *Burmese Days*. Peacock travelled to Cochin China less than a year after arriving in Japan. Invited to dinner by one who was gracious enough to send his own son with the invitation, Peacock, who was then well on with his nightly potations, confronting what he took to be the grovelling delegate of a despised race, tore up the invitation and, dancing upon it, dismissed the snivelling boy with orders to wait outside. That was his death sentence. When shortly afterwards he was nosing up the Perfume River to Hué, hired assassins hiding in the reeds emerged to ram his skiff. Different accounts followed: was Peacock harpooned; was his skull cracked? In stuffing rials into his breeches and so sinking like silver, had this wretched man not received condign punishment for incorrigible greed? Nobody knew. But if Peacock provoked his own end, Walter Cawarden must solicit more sympathy. He was left behind to 'look after the house', but the killers went after him too. Fleeing in haste, but managing to duck the billhooks, Cawarden made the coast, only to be drowned when his junk sank returning to Hirado. The death of two out of the seven merchants within months of arriving was the most grievous of blows.

Four years later Smythe was still trying to find out what had happened to Peacock, to whom he seems to have been close. Edmund Sayers sent statements from the crime scene: a 'Jappaner and a mandarin, now secretary to the great King' told him that 'the greatest occasion of their making away' was because of the money and goods they were carrying. Peacock had been enticed up river with the promise of a fine parcel of silk, whereupon they had 'stembelled his boote and oversette him into the revere, and afterwards kielled him with thare lances in the watere, thay presentlye reportinge to the Kinge that thaye ware cast awaye by mere meschance'.[34] Confirming that Cawarden had indeed been 'cast away in a great storm', he added some spicy detail that would otherwise have gone unnoticed: 'this Japaner, whoum mayed Mr Pecoke awaye, binge ferfull that wee woold secke joustes of the Kinge againste him, . . . [with] 30 Japanes . . . pout into Chena not fare from Macawe, where the Chenas have coote all thayere throtes. . .'[35] That was something at least. Finally it was reported how 'this mandarene seckaratare to the Kinge, binge ferfoull of lousinge his heed, [obtained] prevelegese verey large'.[36] And so it would seem that Messrs Peacock and Cawarden may not have died in vain after all.

Our fourth samurai is Richard Wickham, a survivor and a success, much of the latter finding its way into his own pocket. Living like a despot, Wickham was never so unfeeling as to ignore the absence of a family with whom he had had no contact for nigh on ten years. He had started with the Company in December 1607. Bound for Persia upon the Fourth Voyage, he had been taken prisoner and shipped to Goa, whence he had been transported to Lisbon aboard the *Nossa Senhora da Piedade*. A fine linguist, Wickham quickly made friends with the Persian ambassador who was bound for Spain on that same ship. No sooner had the *Piedade* arrived in Lisbon, however, than having been encouraged to 'escape' by his new-found friend, Wickham made a run for the docks and for Deptford; mightily relieved to have escaped the Inquisition. No sooner home than sent to Japan, Wickham was given responsibility for Edo (Tokyo), only to be promoted cape merchant on the *Sea Adventure*, that terrible thing so full of holes.

Spending more time at Ōsaka and Kyōto than in Edo itself, Wickham is to be spotted puffed up like a robin in the snow, roosting under the pines during what the dendrochronologists have told us has been until now the coldest winter in the history of the world. Notwithstanding that, Wickham hunkered down with Suetonius in the original and turned the pages of Sir Walter Ralegh's *History of the World*, bestseller then but infinitely tedious now. Wickham found the indispensable aid to Ralegh was his copy of Ortelius's celebrated *Theatrum Orbis Terrarum*, the greatest geography book of the sixteenth century. This *Theatrum* was not just sitting on his desk as a complement to global history: he needed it close by if he was to please those cartographers back home who were clamouring for his thoughts on what Japan looked like, being expected to contribute his own researches as to the nature of a Globe with a capital 'G'. Stocked with a good travelling library, Wickham's study was also stuffed with bottles of rack for the cold and pouches of Virginia to disperse the fumes of melancholy that too often settled upon this unhappy man. After longueurs of self-reliance, moods of despair and pulses of danger, Wickham took passage aboard the *Advise* for a new life in Bantam. Here at last he openly became that private trader he had always been. Ever the snappy dresser, he was decidedly snappy himself. More often frozen by gloom than with the snow, Wickham could never forget the black dog of depression. Writing to his 'Most dear and loving mother' and proffering her 'My most humble duty remembered with the friendly remembrance of all my sisters and loving frendes in generall', he moves on to lament how forgotten he felt since:

> not once in 7 yeares' time [had his family thought] to remember me with
> a fewe lines, and unto whom I have not bin so sparing of inke and paper
> . . . Good mother, comend me unto my 2 sisters Anne and Mary in
> Ludlow yf they be living, and tell them my earnest request unto them is
> only to remember me in theyre dayly prayers, and whether I live or die,
> God willing, I will not be unmindfull of them, neyther of the rest of my
> sisters, unto whom I pray comend me, with my brother Lewes and my

sister, with all the rest in generall; and thus, by the mercy of God hoping
to see you once more before I die, to your exceeding comfort, I remayne
allways,

Your obedient sonne till death,

R. Wickham Bantam, 10 June 1617[37]

But such hopes were dashed when Wickham came to be dished the very next
year. By the summer of 1618 he had succumbed to the 'bloody flux', or
dysentery. As the actuaries arrived to do the post-mortem inventory, matters
were found to have been most irregular. When the counting was over,
London was forced to conclude that much of the spoils that Wickham had
accumulated had been what is best described as 'midnight merchandise'.
How could anyone have acquired quite so many kimonos without being
up to no good was what the Court of Committees was forced to conclude.
The whole thing was acutely difficult since Wickham had been close to Sir
Thomas Smythe no less. And so it came about that the governor found
himself in the embarrassing position of having to sue the executors of an old
friend. But by now the old man was well used to dealing with every sort of
difficulty, and such was the sum it was reckoned that Wickham had run off
with it had to be done. Furthermore, the £1,400 the Company alleged was
theirs represented a test case about the whole principle of 'private trade'. For
years factors had been leaching wealth, and now the Court of Committees
felt it was the time for it to stop.

Resolution or not, neither Smythe nor his Court of Committees had
reckoned with old Mother Wickham who, as the principal beneficiary of her
son's will, was going to be damned rather than let a groat get out of her
grasp.[38] Mrs Wickham's claims were just one of three suits that made for
'very heavy businesses' in the early weeks of 1622. One of the others involved
a no less determined woman, 'Dame Dale', as her husband Sir Thomas used
to call her, in hot pursuit of the money he had sunk in the Indies and which
she was claiming the Company had trousered.

When a hearing on the Wickham case finally came to be conducted by
Sir Julius Caesar in February 1622, it emerged that Elizabeth Wickham had
been pursuing her claim against the Company for two and a half years.
Clearly the Company had always felt that her son Richard had been up to no

good. Indeed they claimed that when he had first gone out to Japan he had been no more than 'a silly young man' on a wage of £20 a year, and could only have acquired such a large estate by the time of his death either by private trading or through plain stealing. His mother's case was that he had gone to Japan with a sizeable estate of his own.[39] The Court of Committees' verdict had been that since Richard 'had gained it by employing the Company's stock, and it amounted to [£]1400, it was resolved not to give way to this private trade and to defend the detaining thereof, wherewith no ways satisfied she refused to submit herself, and so departed'.[40]

The Company stood by its allegations, but as a concession, was prepared to pay whatever wages had been due to Wickham to his mother, and, if it could be proved, the value of the stock that Mrs Wickham had alleged her son had originally taken out to Japan back in 1613.[41] This did no good. The Company tried to shut her up on 13 March through £300 'for quietness sake',[42] perhaps with Sir Julius's advice ringing in their ears so as to avoid the bad publicity which must follow too hot a pursuit of the plaintiff. Sir Julius, it seems 'showed much love and respect to the Company, and in his advice to them said that they were not generally well thought of, and though he utterly misliked private trade, yet he wished them to connive at small matters lest they be unfurnished of worthy men to serve them'.[43]

That offer as a final settlement having been refused, the Company's solicitor began to look about him as to how to undermine Mrs Wickham's case. All too aware that her principal witness was that formidable George Ball – erstwhile president of the Indies no less, but who was himself then being prosecuted for gross malfeasance during his presidency – the solicitor advised that a delaying tactic might just work, suggesting to Committees 'to use means to put off her cause until Ball's cause in Star Chamber may first be heard, presuming it will fall out so foul against Ball as will much weaken his testimony'.[44] That ruse failed. On 24 November 1624 the Company's solicitors were instructed that a 'Warrant be prepared for payment of the money forthwith into Chancery', and with that, Mrs Wickham's case rested. However, there had been losers too. Wickham had given £250 to the Mayor and Corporation of Bristol, his hometown, but legal fees had to be paid out of his estate before anything could be released. It may well be thought that some beneficiaries were happy enough: had the whole hearing not cost so much, the boys of Bristol Grammar School would have had to plough through £100-worth of books. With subsequent court expenses this was reduced to £68, the balance used 'to give satisfaction to such that were employed about the recovery of the same'.[45]

Although the Company had lost, Smythe was clear that the Court of Committees should move firmly against private trading. Mrs Wickham had taken advantage of the Company's lenity in allowing mariners to fill up one chest with Eastern goods. These they were then permitted to sell on their own behalf once back in London, something Mrs Wickham had pointed out to justify her son's private trade. That having been the case, it now be 'ordered that private trade in mariners shall be wholly forborne, but with power to the Court to tolerate it where they see cause'.[46] Despite Smythe's best efforts, though, private trading could never be stopped. Had the Company been able to do so, the most famous impeachment in English history would never have arisen. This was to be the trial of Warren Hastings in 1787.[47]

So much, then, for the most conflicted of our group. Next up is William Eaton: recipient of the finest collection of nautical instruments east of Plymouth. These had come to him after the famous pilot William Adams had expired in the house of his friend Yasimon Dono. Before then, however, and in Ōsaka and Sakai, Eaton had been shocked to discover 'nowe there is noe more Christians of Jappaners in these partes'.[48] But if a Christian risked toasting, Eaton faced freezing: 'Most loving and kind friend,' he wrote to Cocks. 'Tomorrow morning I doe purpose, if I have not my fitt of the agew, to goe, God willing, for Sackeye [Sakai] to see if I can put of my lead, the w'ch I hope to doe . . . I wishe I had shuch another furde cape [fur cap] as my mate gave you, for that I am nowe so extreme could one my head, besides all the parte of my boddy is in shuch a case that all the clothes I can put one will not kepe me warme.'[49] But cold was better than rats: these Eaton came to know intimately when, in May 1616, he shared his cell with quite a lot of them. He had found himself banged up when, after going to buy timber in Ōmura, he had killed one 'Japoner' and severely wounded another after the three had fallen out about who owned a piece of second-hand rope.

Carted off to Akuno-ura jail, there Eaton put in a plea of manslaughter. Although the *daimyō* allowed this, what was going to happen next depended on the survival of the 'Japoner' he had sorely wounded. In the end he pulled through, a salvation Eaton lost no time in conveying to the drunkard William Nealson: 'The man I hurte is indeferent well and, thankes be to God, theare is noe danger of his life . . . w'ch I am wonderfull glad of, for sence the tyme that the deed was donne, I have scarse eaten a bitt of meate for verey greave, w'ch hath brought mee soe loe that at present I am not well.'[50] Given a sentence of three weeks for murder was, Eaton thought, quite enough, since he was 'kept prisoner . . . in a vile and extreme manner'. He was clearly shaken, but it is no less clear that this was not for long. Once the sand had dried on the account of his troubles, Eaton's accounts become full of ships and manifests: the *Thomas* had arrived from the Moluccas; the *Advice* was rumoured to be coming for Japan; Captain Elkington had gone home in the *New Year's Gift*; Edward Dodsworth was in the *Merchant's Hope*.

As for Edmund Sayers, he was charged with penetrating Korea. Remotest station in the whole repertoire of the Company, no Englishman had ever visited this, the strangest of lands. But what could be made of the Koreans? Unknowable, stranger than the 'Japonner' even, these outlandish men could be identified because 'every one having a head attire of a redish culler w'th a littell mark of silver, lyke a fether, in it'.[51] But then what Sayers said Cocks embellished, thrilled to discover how the Koreans didn't have horses and carts; preferring to whizz about in sleighs with sails instead.[52] Surviving Korea, Sayers endured numerous voyages in the *Sea Adventure*. Thus it was something of an irony that it would be a nasty little experience in the backstreets of Hirado that nearly did for him. Strolling with friends, he was assaulted by thugs who, knocking him to the ground, 'wounded [him] very sore'. Had his group not managed to stagger into a house and bolt the door, that would have been that. The *bugyō* banished the assailants whilst Sayers was dispatched to Nagasaki, there to remain on 'pain of death'. Eventually leaving with the remnant of the English factory, Sayers left a daughter born to his Japanese mistress Maria. Father and daughter would never meet again. As for Sayers himself, he met his fate far from home. Starting a new life as a merchant in Surat, he died in 1626, having successfully dodged his debtors. Of these, easily the crossest was a Captain Goodal, who wanted to know what had happened to 'the diamonds pawned to him by Edward Sayers'.[53]

The last of the Japanese contingent was unsinkable William Eaton. Like Sayers, Eaton stopped off in India, there to reinvent himself as the model team-worker. If President Keridge had heard what Eaton had done, he cared not to listen. After all, he said to himself, who didn't have a past, if few could hope for a future? And so it was that the new Eaton, well shorn and well turned out, eventually appeared in the boardroom in London to tell the Court of Committees all about the Japanese fiasco: 'Captain Clevenger, Commander of the *Jonas*, and Eaton a factor from Japan, who went out with Captain Saris 15 years since in the *Hector*, presented themselves, but the Court having not leisure to confer with them they were referred to another time.'[54] Doubtless with Eaton there had been a considerable amount of rewriting of history, but he was determined not to welsh on Cocks, who had been a good friend to him:

> Examination of Eaton in London on 2nd December 1626 concerning his services in the Indies and what he knew of the carriage and condition of Cocks, how he died, what number of servants were in the Company's house, what entertainment they had and by what means so great an estate of the Company's was spent by Cocks, and such like, and making but cold and uncertain answers, was dismissed for the present, but desired that he would recollect his memory and name a short journal of his service and employment.[55]

But if such answers were 'cold and uncertain', that was sufficient. No more was said. Six months later Eaton's name was cleared, suggesting that the Company was prepared to forget misdemeanours in one who had made a decent stab at the Siam market. Doubtless it was upon proceeds from Siam that Eaton put his son through Trinity College, Cambridge. As for himself, he became a consultant. When a subcommittee was charged with assessing the chances of reopening Japan as late as 1668, it heard how 'Mr Eaton who was Second at Japan is living, and dwelleth at Highgate, [and] may be able to give full satisfaction as to the trade there and of the civility of the people'.[56]

So much for seven lives, but what of the end of the whole show? The president of the Indies had not just suspected but long known that Cocks was up to no good, repeatedly writing about how he found Cocks 'most extreme hott in passeon and most miserabell could in reason, but as your choller moves mee nott, soe your careles regard of my love wronges me not . . . your own perversenes layes in the way, blynding your understanding that you know nether knowe how to macke choyce of a frind nor to use men as men are'.[57] Cocks cared nothing for this when there was 3,000 miles between himself and the noxious George Ball. Shrugging his shoulders, he merely moaned how this man 'never gave me roast meate but he did beate me w'th the spitt'.[58] But Ball was right: Cocks was grossly incompetent at a time when Japan was turning its face against the West. Difficulties mounted, aggression rose, resolution fell. The Jesuits had been expelled, whilst as for the Company, it not only found itself restricted to Hirado and Nagasaki, but also debarred from trading to Portuguese Macao and the inland countries. All this meant further demands from Bantam that things be closed down:

> For whereas in our last letters sent Mr Cox we absolutelie charged him, with Sayres and Eaton, to cleere all remaines and to come away from thence, leaving a matter of 5000 taies in the factory with John Osterwick, the said Cox and the rest scarce so much as take notice of our order and requirie, neither in answer can shew any lawfull excuse for their stay there. Their accompts also, which wee have for 2 yeares so earnestlie required from them, are not sent, and it is to be doubted they can gave none. And if all be true which wee heare reported of them, it is a misery to know that men of such antique years should be so miserablie given over to voluptuousness, regarding not what they consume therein[59]

Eventually these 'most wanted men' were taken off by the *Bull*: Cocks, Sayers and Eaton were sent to London, while others were left to pursue the hopeless business of recovering 'desperate debts', of which by far the largest was a small matter of 6,636 *taels* still owed by Li Tan. Put aboard the *Anne Royal*, but dying on 27 March 1624, Cocks was at once unceremoniously tipped over the side somewhere in the middle of the Indian Ocean. Such then was the end for him, and his demise was also terminal for the Company as far as Japan was concerned.

Not so with the Dutch: they agreed to live on an artificial island called Dejima. This had been so devised as to prevent the Japanese from being contaminated by the 'red-haired barbarians', as they called the Dutch. And here the VOC would remain for the next two hundred years: confined to a space measuring 400 by 250 feet. Despite what would appear to have been limited prospects, they were happy enough when a diet of noodles and prostitutes was pushed through a wicket gate. Such allurements would not have been to the taste of the Company, however. As Hirado closed, so it came to be discovered that the Dutch were tougher. This was why the 'Hollander' won the East Indies and the English relinquished them.

14

GOODNIGHT AMSTERDAM

Although the East India Company's expulsion from Japan was humiliating, it is to be doubted whether anyone really envied the VOC for its miserable mat of seaweed, from whence for the next two centuries the Dutch would fish for scraps like those tame cormorants Richard Cocks had loved to watch on Hirado Bay. But an allotment in the harbour of Nagasaki was about the sum total of any concession the Court of Committees was prepared to make the Heeren XVII. Truth was, the Englishman hated the Hollander, and the feeling was mutual. Such a steady state of animosity would persist from the foundation of the Vereenigde Oostindische Compagnie in 1602 until the 'Glorious Revolution' of 1688. That is not to say that there weren't many instances of private accord and cultural sympathy. Sir William Temple, notable essayist and competent diplomat, showered the most extravagant of encomia upon this new people, and there would always be fertile exchanges on the level of spiritual belief and material culture. Yet the strained relations between England and Holland at a governmental and company level deeply affected the supposed progress of the East India Company.

One who could never find a friend among the Dutchmen was Sir George Downing, an American immigrant to England who glided into the circle of English government. From thence he proceeded to conduct such a campaign of vituperative hostility against the 'Boor' as must have won the grudging admiration of that monster Jan Pieterszoon Coen, who if anything, despised the English still more than Downing the Dutch. It was an animosity provoked, sustained and inflamed by Downing's uneasy awareness, which soon enough would morph into a burning resentment, that the Dutch were much better at everything than his own compatriots.

The Restoration of 1660 gave the East India Company the break it badly needed. Finally, every appetite that a Puritan dispensation had suppressed, the Caroline age now encouraged. As 'Moho' came to Soho,[1] so that little black bean from Mocha – upon which the East India Company looked with the most jealous eye – created the wherewithal for the coffee house to replace the tavern and brought about a sea-change in sociability.[2]

One of those who haunted these new-found establishments and was often to be seen coming out of Pasqua Rosee's Head off Cornhill, the earliest of the coffeehouses as dating from 1652, was the extraordinary Sir George Downing. Downing was the most unprincipled figure of the Restoration.[3] Given the standards that prevailed in that louche age, that is quite a claim. The famous diarist Samuel Pepys, who had the misfortune to work under Sir George at the Navy Board, considered him 'a perfidious rogue' and 'most ungrateful villaine',[4] whilst the historian Gilbert Burnet dismissed his subject as 'a crafty fawning man . . . Ready to turn to every side that was uppermost and to betray those who . . . thought they might depend on him'.[5] A graduate of Harvard, Downing was dismissed as 'an obscure New England fanatick' whose manners 'were as rude as those of an Iroquois in whose neighbourhood he was bred'.[6] For all that, he was the first Englishman to understand that Dutch economic miracle, the VOC. His reward would be the naming of a modest London street in his memory.

If Jan Huyghen van Linschoten had been guilty of gross deceit in stealing for the Dutch from the Portuguese, Downing must in turn stand condemned for the most grievous lapse of manners with, as it happens, the Dutch. It is Pepys himself who tells the tale. After attending chapel at Whitehall in December 1668, the diarist took a turn in the park, only to run into Sir George who was briefly back from Holland. As they strolled among the parterres, Downing suggested that he was getting the measure of the 'enemy': 'He told me that he had so good spies, that he hath had the keys taken out of De Witts[7] pocket when he was a-bed, and his closet opened and papers brought to him and left in his hands for an [hour], and carried back and laid in the place again and the keys put in his pocket again.'[8]

Perhaps partly as a result of reading the private correspondence of Johan De Witt (d. 1672), Grand Pensionary of Holland no less, 'Downing's lasting contribution to England's economic destiny was that he brought to bear his observation of Dutch economic practice on English theory and policy'.[9] As for what Downing himself thought, he was in no doubt that a little commercial espionage must always trump the norms of diplomatic convention. Writing to Lord Arlington in February 1664, Downing had remarked that 'if England were once brought to a Navigation as cheape as this Country, good night Amsterdam'. Although night was yet a long way off, it would not be long before twilight descended upon Amsterdam and dawn rose in London. Thanks to loathsome Sir George's wholesale reforms to the Treasury and his recasting of the English taxation system, Calcutta could afford to be founded in 1684 and the Bank of England was formed in 1696. With these things the East India Company would be on its way.

For all Downing's nightly perambulations, the origins of Dutch financial hegemony were to be found less in the transactions of the bourse than in the transformation of an environment. Geography and that most important of all Dutch conquests, the mastery of an impossible terrain, had set the terms for future greatness generations before Downing came to deploy bad manners and intrepid larceny. From a huge enterprise of reclamation, the inception of which can be dated centuries before the arrival of the 'Golden Age', there arose within the Low Countries a culture of notable public enterprise. The subjugation of wetlands stretching to desolate limitless horizons had from the first required cooperation between those urban settlements that had been able to thrust their roots beneath the reeds. The most fruitful expression of this mutuality was the steady emergence of a sophisticated tax system that in allowing for the raising of capital had induced firmness upon the land and fraternity between the peoples. A vast communal effort had been required to reclaim the islands from the sea. By the middle of the sixteenth century, the inhabitants of the northernmost seven provinces had bonded so effectively that with no little pride they were able to declare themselves the 'United Provinces'.

Managing vast reclamation, a cooperative enterprise unequalled in the history of Europe, such a triumph of hydraulics won universal if grudging admiration from the enemies of Holland. But if the rewards were there for all to see and many to profit from, the miracle of turning water into money bequeathed a legacy that would prove of inestimable value. Separate towns came together in what would develop into the prosecution of commercial warfare upon the Far East. And so there arose an unquenchable spirit of public commitment, which, having developed into something more cooperative than anywhere else on the face of the earth, provoked in turn 'the remarkable "inter-urban" initiative of digging and exploiting "*trekvaarten*" (canals) between cities'.[10]

Dutch towns, famous for their civic guards, medical schools and diversity of industry, made for a nice balance between provincial identity and national purpose. Each centre was big enough for local pride but small enough for coherence, distant enough from others to be independent yet close enough for an identity of values. The short journeys required to travel to local assembly or States-General meant that the high proportion of Dutchmen who had been university educated were exceptionally well informed as to the business of a new country in which they not only had a stake but a make. The connections between Dutch cities was conducive to high levels of public revenue. The size of the country, the proportion of agricultural land to urban space, easy communication between the border with the Holy Roman Empire to the east and maritime provinces abutting the North Sea to the west: all promoted common purpose.

As for the reclamation, no less than 60 per cent was accomplished between 1590 and 1650. Yet for centuries a system of public finances had evolved that would be the essential precondition for the successful launch of the VOC in 1602. As regards the issue of public finance, where the English fell out the Dutch fell in. Even in the thirteenth century, the debts of the counts of Holland were guaranteed by the multitude of prosperous little cities that would one day defy the Spanish Crown. In England, by contrast, a long and conflicted relationship between the king and his peoples may be traced to a famous quarrel at Runnymede. In 1215, the disaffected had sought to oppose the philosophy of the Angevins that was based upon their belief in the probity of *vis et voluntas*: the force inherent in kingship, legitimate because the will of its holder is above the law. Though Magna Carta has always been celebrated as the *fons et origo* of individual liberty, constant breach of its provisions had served only to point to how the English Crown was centuries away from creating a system of raising funds that met with the agreement of its subjects. By contrast, the United Provinces fell upon a method to fund the obligations of the state and the ambitions of its proconsuls that gathered to itself universal conformity and patriotic accord. The failure of the English Crown to find an equivalent means with which to prosecute the obligations of the executive ensured that lack of funding and issues of taxation caused the outbreak of Civil War in 1642 and the downfall of the monarchy. Let us now amplify these contrasts that caused the VOC to triumph and the EIC to trip.

What has been described as the 'fiscal fecundity'[11] of the United Provinces needs to be considered if the success of the Dutch and the failure of the English is to be understood. When people are to be taxed, they have to agree, not on the precise terms and exact amounts, but upon the principle that instincts for greed and pursuit of ease be tempered by a willingness to contribute to the *res publica*. This was exactly what the Dutch had subscribed to during the latter part of the sixteenth century. Why then did they behave with more fiscal responsibility than any corresponding nation in Europe? Why were they to be rewarded by the appearance in Amsterdam of a system of public finance, town hall accountability, banking and debt servicing that turned out to be a hundred years ahead of anything the English could conceive?

By the time the VOC was launched, following the amalgamation of half a dozen 'town companies' that had hitherto competed, there already existed such a system of raising revenue. There was far greater capitalisation for the VOC than for the EIC. What has been described as the Dutch 'tax revolution', beginning in around 1574, announced itself with the universal introduction of what came to be known as the General Means. Raised on commodities that everyone consumed, by such equity came to be avoided the divisive nature of taxes in France. There, privileged classes either declined to pay or passed their obligations on to those least able to bear them. The Dutch General Means was a phenomenal success. The list of things deemed of broad consumption and therefore taxable was grain and its milling, herring, salt, horned beasts and cloth. In 1575 the General Means brought in 300,000 *gulden* but by 1608 a handsome 4 million. Although the United Provinces would remain the most heavily taxed country in Europe until the French Revolution, such was the buoyancy of the economy that people complied willingly enough. It might justly be said that if Holland had a uniquely efficient tax system, it was also alone in having investors queuing up to yield what was requested. So secure were its interest payments, so safe its capital, that Holland's most ardent English admirer, Sir William Temple, would remark how 'when they [the state authorities] put off any part of the principal, those it belongs to receive it with tears, not knowing how to dispose it to interest with such safety and ease'.[12]

Immediately after the foundation of the EIC in 1600, the City of London was doing well enough, though public finances remained in disarray after the best attempt at a solution to the bankruptcy of the executive had been rejected. Salisbury's last act was his proposed Great Contract. Mooted in 1611, it was mauled in 1613. Had the Contract been adopted, monopolies would have been surrendered in return for an annual subsidy provided by Parliament. But such a rational scheme had been eschewed by a body that saw something sinister behind the Crown's wish to be free of parliamentary leverage. In lieu of that contract, therefore, the Crown's methods of raising cash came to be seen as by turns vexatious, illegal and piratical. In the period 1560–1640, between 73 and 76 per cent of revenue was the result of non-parliamentary taxes, something in the order of 25 per cent being raised from direct taxes via parliamentary grants. This was as dangerous as it would be disastrous. Unable to meet debt or obligation, fettered in the process of funding new policies yet fearful of reform, the Crown was forever devising inventive but illegal methods of revenue-raising. Non-parliamentary income, accounting for 75 per cent of total revenue, was a cause of concern at a time when Charles I was resisting accountability.[13]

Take, for example, the matter of forced loans. These, necessarily erratic, were adopted by the Crown to pressurise its subjects into lending. The system compared unfavourably with the sober, reliable and respectable conduct of the States-General. By the 1630s, in the absence of Parliament, the Crown would become overly dependent on forced loans and customs revenues. Unhappily, however, the Exchequer almost never paid interest, let alone sustained any ambition to redeem capital sums extracted from provident scrivener or wealthy widow. In contrast, the States-General had evolved a reliable, popular and uncontentious system of loans and public debt. In the Low Countries interest was always promised and always paid. Furthermore, 'Debt Paper' was issued on forced loans, which did not mention the name of the creditor. These could thus be easily transferred, sold or 'used as collateral for cash loans between private persons'.[14] What made the system a force for good in Holland was the privatisation of the means to satisfy the government's creditors. Those who gathered the taxes collected the loans. In Holland the taxman was empowered to prioritise interest payments with the discharge of interest obligations. These were extracted from tax revenues before whatever sums remaining were sent into government. The loan-farmers created a cooperative enterprise unequalled in early modern Europe.[15] In the absence of grants from Parliament, in England customs revenue became ever more important, and also ever more burdensome on the overseas companies.[16] By contrast, the Dutch looked to excise. This meant that whereas the profits of the EIC were taken at the Customs House, what the VOC bore home was secured from the predation of government officials. The chaos of royal finances in England had a most deleterious effect when profits began to stall with the onset of economic depression in 1618.

The English capital was a house divided. London consisted of the City of Westminster and the 'City': places which meant far more than titles of topography graven by the burin's mark upon a bird's-eye view. During the reigns of the early Stuarts there arose an insurmountable barrier between Westminster and the City. This was not made of brick – such a thing would have to wait until the Civil War to appear – but of abandoned promissory notes. Issued out of the City for the benefit of the Crown's ailing finances, for forty years these bonds would be constantly reneged upon at Westminster and Whitehall with the result that between the foundation of the East India Company and the outbreak of the Civil War, a great weight of resentment settled upon the shoulders of those men of business who made up the Court of Committees. If the East India Company was a capital mess, then by contrast in Holland the 'Compagnie' was a national union. Here the six chambers making up the federated structure of the VOC were bound with hoops of steel and a philosophy which proclaimed *un pour tous, tous pour un.*

But with the Dutch it was not all drains and taxes; other developments gave enormous opportunity for wealth creation. Dutch coastal waters, once cold, had now become warm. Vast fields of cod and herring, previously located around Iceland and the Lofoten islands, elected in 1600 to take up station off the coast of Holland, allowing the home economy an expansion that was industrial in scale. With such marked profits came a rise in per capita income followed by a hike in investment for the nascent VOC.

But as the fish moved so too did the Dutch, though in the case of the burghers it was to the Baltic. From the fifteenth century onwards profit generated in the north was the precondition of dominance in the south. Known in Holland as the 'mother trade', the Baltic was all about basics. As pitch and pine, grain and fur shuffled around the Mediterranean, what had poked its way through the Danish straits provoked one observer into declaring how the great Baltic Sea was 'the soul of our commerce as a whole, upon which all other trades and processing industries depend'.[17] Record of tolls exacted for passage through the Danish Sound at the end of the fifteenth century reveal how early and firmly the Dutch had seized the neck of that particular bottle. From penetration came power as the 'Hollander' became the broker between Denmark and Sweden. Beyond that, however, Low Country merchants even managed to supplant the cereal-growers of Picardy as main suppliers to the markets of Scandinavia. Although French cereals were unequalled in quality and yield, such were the costs of shipping from Seine to Sound that the Dutch were not only able to undercut traditional suppliers, but also to begin to deliver those same cereals themselves. All of this demanded new types of boats. Thus it was that out of the shipyards of Middelburg and Enkhuizen arose a critical spirit of innovation vital to the VOC:

> The carveel made possible the completion in one sailing season of a triangular circuit (*deurgande vaart*) from Holland to the bay of Biscay (to load salt and wine) to the Baltic (to load grain and timber), and back to Holland. For the more northerly Hanse merchants, the shipping season usually began too late to complete such a voyage, requiring them to winter in southern Europe . . . The Portuguese were hampered by the fact that their spice-laden fleets arrived in Lisbon too late to be shipped all the way to the Baltic in the same season.[18]

But luck was also on the side of the Dutch. A commercial crisis arising in southern Europe at the end of the sixteenth century allowed its fleet to build upon achievements and know-how that Dutch mariners had accumulated in more northerly waters since the late Middle Ages. When once the Spanish had supplied Italy with her cereals, now the increasingly meagre yields of

Valencia and Navarre meant that for a second time and in a second location the Dutch were ready to take advantage of changes in the European economy. The difficulties of the Spanish economy and the demand for bread in Spain's Italian dependencies conspired to ensure that the prices of wheat, rye and barley rose to unprecedented heights.

And yet there is a great mystery about all this. How did Holland manage to become a world power during the very years when its peoples came to endure the longest civil war in history? In truth the fratricide was less destructive, less burdensome and less pernicious than some who invented Dutch history allowed. Of these, the American John Lothrop Motley (d. 1877) remains the master chronicler of the nascent republic with his justly celebrated *The Rise of the Dutch Republic* (1855). Subtle in massaging sources when he was not neglecting them, Motley, full-time diplomat and part-time historian, spun the most elevating of narratives out of an agenda that had been settled in mind before our creative historian settled to his researches. The intention was to provide an affecting allegory, universal in its application, about the triumph of democracy over obscurantism. The *Rise* is an epic about a heroic people striving to defend their birthright and obtain freedom. Published in three volumes by a passionate Abolitionist, nothing is allowed to impede the argument that the emergence of the Republic was an affecting story of a new people seeking a life free from the constraints of bigotry. According to Motley's narrative, the great struggle had been the breaking of chains. Significantly enough for a liberal American, however, all this had happened at the very moment when the Pilgrim Fathers had elected to settle in America by sailing in the *Mayflower*.

In contrast, recent historians have consulted the sources with an assiduity Motley neglected to apply to his own researches; but then his problem was that he could not read Dutch. Among many a corrective to the master narrative has been the suggestion that the Eighty Years' War was less long and much less bloody than Motley was prepared to allow. Whilst there can be no doubt of the outrages graphically recorded first by Brueghel and last by Rubens, nor that this theatre of conflict was indeed the '*place d'armes et escole guerrière à toute l'Europe*',[19] a more important truth has emerged since Motley's day. This is that by the end of the sixteenth century the parties to the conflict were bent upon making peace, not war: the archdukes Albert and Isabella for Spain; Jan van Oldenbarnevelt, the Grand Pensionary, and his protégé Hugo Grotius for the Republic. There was so little fighting after 1600 that the VOC emerged in 1602 not from a forest of pikes but a field of commerce. As with all wars of independence, there were significant areas where life had continued as normal. Given the strength of the Dutch fleet, the United Provinces could never be assaulted in her own waters, whilst the six chambers of the VOC were notable for continuity of voyage and momentum of business. In short, the most destructive phase of fighting was long over by the time that the VOC sent out its first flotillas.

The most gifted of all the regents of the Spanish Netherlands, Archduchess Isabella was earnest in pressing her nephew Philip III to be more open to the power of compromise than had ever come naturally to any king of Spain. Thus was Oldenbarnevelt offered independence and freedom of worship, without being required to reciprocate a single concession over the vital question of a Dutch withdrawal from the East Indies. What upset the Spaniards, however, was less the principle than the practice of gaining assent; largesse that offered everything for nothing was impossible to sell to the knightly caste of Castile. They were adamant to the last breastplate in resisting generosity towards the rebels. Contrary to our orthodoxy about Spain's orthodoxy, what mattered more to Philip III than purity of faith was the profit of commerce. Both sides had long recognised that he who held the Indies held the future. But if the regent Isabella would make Philip III apprehensive as to what the next dispatch might contain, Oldenbarnevelt was persuaded to make something of a gesture. Not wishing to provoke Spain any further, Oldenbarnevelt threatened to liquidate the Dutch West India Company, the Geoctrooieerde Westindische Compagnie, though opponents forced him to abandon so radical a move before matters could go further.[20]

If there was not much fighting between the end of the Twelve Years' Truce in 1621 and the Peace of Westphalia in 1648, there was a more lively movement of goods within the United Provinces than could have been generated even in peacetime, if only because the place had long filled with inflated and fixed garrisons, each of which required generous supplies. But then these citadels, and such desultory sieges as they attracted, were located far away from those provinces of Holland which marched with the North Sea and which were never threatened by war. All of this made it eminently possible for the VOC to flourish within that wartime economy. Indeed, such a state of hostilities as formally prevailed until 1648 was as productive of growth as it was provocative of communitarianism. Men came together, contracting for defence and expanding for commerce, in ways they would not have done but for civil war.

If the archduchess could not be the handmaid of peace, she aspired to be the mother of plenty. It was Isabella's willingness, as it was Philip III's support, that allowed for the promulgation of the Twelve Years' Truce. Lasting from 1609 to 1621, such a cessation of hostilities gave further encouragement to Dutch trade as when that blessed interlude which was provided came to be of permanent value to the VOC. As hostilities resumed in 1621, a moment when no one wanted to leave their barracks, over 800 Dutch ships were coming in and out of Iberian and southern Italian ports 'whilst of all the ships entering the Baltic in the years 1609–1620, 70% were Dutch'.[21] Just before this felicitous moment the Dutch had created Europe's most sophisticated banking system, deposit accounts with the Exchange Bank of Amsterdam growing faster in the years 1609–20 than in the whole span of its existence, 471 depositors registering in those twelve years of peace.[22]

But then the truce had its enemies within, for whom war had been the best of friends. The revival of the cereal industry in the Southern Netherlands, which had been contingent upon the cessation of hostilities, heralding as it did enhanced exports to the Peninsula and Italy, meant financial pressure on the markets of the United Provinces. Concurrently, a hike in prices within Holland itself, as a result of increased competition for cereals from southern Europe, proved to be greater than in any other decade of the century. The northern Netherlands had been the only place in all of Europe where wages had either kept pace with or outstripped prices. No longer. Prices now overtook wages.

There was also the 'West India interest' within Holland; something that did not exist in England. Oldenbarnevelt had tried to expunge this not because it had vehemently opposed his overtures for peace but because he felt that he had identified an interest group that was worth throwing as a sop to the Spaniards, if only to preserve the East Indies from reintegration with Iberia. The Dutch West Indies Company, whose most vociferous apologists were Reynier Pauw and Willem Usselincx, created significant difficulties at a time when the exigencies of international diplomacy denied them such latitude in the Atlantic as their rivals had so long enjoyed in the Pacific. The Geoctrooieerde Westindische Compagnie, closely modelled upon the VOC, with a Heren XIX and its own regional chambers, had been created in 1602. Because of the political situation in the years before the temporary peace of 1609, though, it would only come to be chartered in 1621 with the end of the Twelve Years' Truce. The Dutch West Indians, already slave masters but wanting to master the sugar trade too, were hardly less angry about what the truce was doing for the home economy than they were frustrated at having their ambitions stalled for reasons of state:

> Usselincx argued that the war had buttressed nascent Dutch industries; effectively creating trade barriers with the imposition of the *licenten*; system whereby the Flemings had had to pay licenses to be allowed to import the wools from Germany and England with which its weavers had to be supplied. With peace the *licentens* would be removed and so Dutch industry would be exposed to the full force of competition from the east and the south.[23]

Evidently, then, tensions within the United Provinces existed, though those between the provinces never threatened the union per se. Difficulties, and they could be acute, were either between commercial companies or between religious confessions. Such political differences as existed within the United Provinces were never conducted with that rancour that arose over the failure of Salisbury's Great Contract. But then by comparison with England this united cause of Holland was sustained by a trio whose several but federal distinctions proved to be decisive in the great struggle with the East India Company.

Prince Maurits of Nassau (d. 1625), Stadtholder of the Republic, was a fine military commander. Presiding over fifty-one battles, though, as he would have been the first to say, always a man for the siege rather than the set-piece, Maurits was as effective in filling out borders as in facing down enemies. But if the Republic owed much to Maurits, Maurits owed more to Johan van Oldenbarnevelt. The most *politique* of all Dutch statesmen, for thirty-two years Oldenbarnevelt had been the hoop around the barrel; keeping the staves of provincialism bound within the cause of nationalism.

But then Oldenbarnevelt is hardly less celebrated for being the first to notice the genius of Hugo Grotius (d. 1645). As a fifteen-year-old, Grotius had been taken to Paris by the Grand Pensionary himself. Meeting Henri IV at the Louvre in 1598, a boy whose voice had only recently broken blushed to hear the fiercely anti-intellectual Henry of Navarre declare to a suppliant entourage how the youth now quivering before them was 'the miracle of Holland'. When some three years later the Dutch authorities resolved that new nations have to invent a past, but declined to appoint a greybeard as their 'historiographer', they gave the palm instead to the beardless Grotius. Only seventeen, Grotius repaid their faith by giving the world that powerful web of sophistry that is his *Mare Liberum*. Prompted to write by the exigencies of the VOC, Grotius argues that men's relationship with the land is different from that with the sea: 'The air belongs to this class of things [common property] for two reasons. First, it is not susceptible of occupation; and second its common use is destined for all men. For the same reasons the sea is common to all, because it is so limitless that it cannot become a possession of any one, and because it is adapted for the use of all, whether we consider it from the point of view of navigation or of fisheries.'[24]

In writing thus, Grotius was challenging the claim of the English fishing lobby that was desperate to protect its home waters against the incursions of other nations. As for the Dutch themselves, the implications of what Grotius had to argue also allowed the VOC to establish to its own satisfaction, if hardly to anyone else's, a legal basis for greed. Predictably enough, the EIC would attempt to refute Grotius's claims with the appearance of John Selden's *Mare Clausum*. Although distributed for many years in manuscript only, this was read by all who went fishing in troubled waters. Selden argued the exact opposite to Grotius, declaring the right of nations to close their coastal waters. This he did in order to exclude the Dutch herring fleets that appeared in English waters like a murmuration of starlings. Whilst there could be no congruence between the arguments of the two greatest jurists in Europe, they were mutually respectful, with Grotius laying the foundation of maritime law as Selden created the concept of territorial waters.

In contrast to the identity between the VOC and the public institutions of Holland, the EIC looked in vain for support from above. Where Holland had Maurits, England had James I. Afraid of his own shadow, James made absolutely sure he never went near any sort of siege, rattling a tin sabre that never came out of its scabbard. As for Lord Salisbury, he failed to offer the same close interest in the promotion of trade that his father Lord Burghley, the Oldenbarnevelt of England, had so famously championed. But where the two countries also diverged was with the dominance of a plutocracy in Holland in contrast to the transitory and baneful presence of 'favourites' in England. Corruption associated with the earl of Somerset, first and most disastrous of these royal favourites, did irreparable damage to the Stuart dynasty. But Buckingham was worse: more able than Somerset, possessed of towering ambition, during the 1620s he was to bring every sort of difficulty into the path of the East India Company.

And yet there were complementarities between the EIC and the VOC. The respective constitutions were strikingly similar, though more surprising perhaps was the large presence of the other's nationals amongst the respective Adventurers, crews, pilots and factors. For historic reasons, there had been a bigger presence of the Dutch in London than the English in Amsterdam. With the institution of the Spanish Council of Blood in 1568, many Flemings had made a home for themselves in East Anglia, London and the South-East. The Dutch church in Austin Friars was a major centre of European worship, whilst Sir Noël de Caron (d. 1624), Dutch ambassador to England for no fewer than forty-one years, was the cultural event of South Lambeth.

Fleming by birth, born before Henry VIII had thought to dump Katherine of Aragon, de Caron had come to London to offer a Dutch crown to Elizabeth I, though having too many, she had demurred. He had settled and became an honorary Englishman, knighted by James I in 1607. He died so old and so rich that in casting about as to what to do with it all he would leave the lot to Prince Charles, but not before founding 'almshouses at Vauxhall, in what is now Fentiman Road, about a half a mile from his own house. Over the gate was a Latin inscription informing the visitor that it was founded in the thirty-second year of Sir Noel's embassy, "as an insignificant monument of what he owed to the glory of God, in gratitude to the nation, and in munificence to the poor".'[25]

De Caron developed a deep respect for his neighbours, though that was not difficult since he only had one: John Tradescant the Elder (d. 1638), famous gardener and a person of startling originality and deep intelligence, who shared the heron-haunted marsh that was then Lambeth. In a moment of rare largesse, Elizabeth I, England's most parsimonious monarch, had presented de Caron with this plot, enough ground wherewith to make something of *'firmitas, utilitas et venustas'* (fitness, commodity and delight), as Sir Henry Wotton, England's ambassador to Holland, suggested must be the chief support of any good building.[26] So upon a royal patch de Caron had built a house that, though never an embassy, was always a hotel with well-appointed guest rooms and a splendid picture gallery.[27]

Here the old anglophone developed his famous garden. Knowing James I to have a special devoted to eating cherries, de Caron was mindful to provide satiety to this, one of only a hundred pleasures with which this most profligate of kings indulged himself. And so it came to pass that under de Caron's boughs they would discuss the fruits of a joint grafting, considering what was ripe and what was sour across a field of Europe where they had so often worked in concert. Doubtless it was on just such an occasion that de Caron suggested how the two East Indian companies should amalgamate so as to create the world's biggest global enterprise: 'Sir Noell hath also made a Motion to join their East India trade with ours; but we fear that in case of joyning, if it be upon equal Terms, the Art and Industry of their People will wear ours out.'[28] De Caron also proposed the two countries set about North America by combining their respective experience to sort out the mess that was Jamestown. This also failed because of the same insecurity that scotched any real idea of a joint East India Company.

But if, one way or another, de Caron's overtures were rejected, there had always been Englishmen willing to work for the VOC, as there were Dutch serving the EIC. Of these the most notable, not to say notorious, must be William Adams, whose adventures amidst the seas of Japan had caught the fancy of Sir Francis Bacon (see Chapter 4). Then there was famous Henry Hudson who paddled along the river that still bears his name. In 1609 Hudson had joined the Dutch when the Compagnie commissioned him to find that ever-allusive north-east route to China. Leaving Amsterdam in April 1609, he had sailed up to Norway, but failing to push through pushed on to America. Whilst snooping about Chesapeake Bay, Delaware and Albany, Hudson established Dutch claims to the island of New Amsterdam, which became Manhattan. This was the future base for the Dutch colony of New Netherland (est. 1625). Eventually this would come to be traded for legal ownership of Pulau Run by the VOC, that atoll where Nathaniel Courthope had plunged to his heroic death amidst the azurite waters.[29] As for things going the other way, the presence in Siam of the Dutchmen Flors and Atheunsioon, sent out there by the Court of Committees to jointly run such a show as could be mustered, makes it abundantly clear that people trafficking between the two companies happened all the time.[30]

England and the Republic were more closely entwined than either with any other European power. If it had not been for learning the art of war as a mercenary in the Low Countries, Lord Fairfax could never have become the leading Parliamentary general of the English Civil War, whilst the stimulus that Burghley had given to English commerce had depended as much upon Dutch input as English initiative.

But it was not just with the profession of arms or the pursuit of riches that the United Provinces became so central to English concerns. The confession of faith was central to the conversation. Generous provision in Holland for nonconformity, forthcoming since Tyndale had fled to the Low Countries to escape oppression in the 1530s, had been of immeasurable importance to the cultural life of England. More recently, however, there had been something of a civil war within the new Dutch Republic, albeit one involving the throwing of prayer books rather than the brandishing of pikes. In 1618 the English ambassador to the United Provinces, Sir Dudley Carleton, found himself cast as Solomon at the Synod of Dort. This general assembly of ecclesiastics was convened to decide which of two strands of Calvinism would best suit the needs of Holland.

The presence of a strong English delegation led by the ambassador and his cousin George Carleton, bishop of Carlisle, materially helped to shift the delegates against the moderate party at the Synod. The moderates were the Remonstrant party, supporting the views of the theologian Jacobus Arminius who, before dying in 1609, had espoused a kinder form of Calvinism that he had hoped might be adopted as the official religion of the United Provinces. The Remonstrant party was opposed to the uncompromising confession of faith whose principal spokesman was Franciscus Gomarus of the University of Leiden. These more hardline theologians were called the Counter-Remonstrants.

The Remonstrants were supported by Oldenbarnevelt and Grotius whilst the Counter-Remonstrants could look to help from the Stadtholder Prince Maurits. Had the English not swung behind the more uncharitable of these alternatives, Oldenbarnevelt himself would not have swung: he was hanged on the Binnenhof at The Hague on 13 May 1619 for the crime of advocating tolerance and supporting difference. As for Grotius, he was luckier: it was life imprisonment for him. Immured in a castle but entombed in books, Europe's most learned man not only made a virtue out of scholarship but an escape from gaol. Ordering yet more tomes, he emptied the trunk in which they arrived, got in, closed the lid, and off he went to Paris. There he would spend the rest of his life regretting that he was not in Holland.

If the disputatious Synod of Dort was immediately remote to the concerns of the English, that all changed. Soon enough debates over 'Arminianism', as support for Jacobus Arminius's views was called in England, became the chief concern of the country's Puritans and Charles's critics. Provoked by the thrust for conformity promoted by the archbishop of Canterbury, William Laud (beheaded 1644), Arminianism became an ecclesiastical badge of loyalty to the absolutist regime by the 1630s. During the years of so-called Personal Rule, when for eleven years Charles I ruled without Parliament, the hierarchy of the Church promoted Arminianism with disastrous consequences. This contributed profoundly to the breakdown of order and the breakout of chaos in 1642. Whilst some historians think religion was the cause of the English Civil War, others feel the threat of bankruptcy was still more important, but what cannot be disputed is how Arminius's disease had been imported from Holland.

England and Holland impinged upon one another in so many ways. Yet there was a critical difference: the Dutch believed in themselves and the English did not. This is suggested by how little of a memorial nature has come down from the earliest days of the EIC. In contrast the Dutch never stopped congratulating themselves on their astounding achievements. Take Rembrandt's *The Shipbuilder and his Wife* (1633), a portrait of Jan Rijksen and his wife Griet Jans. Rijksen was a shareholder in the VOC and from 1620 its principal shipbuilder. Here he is then, drafting the profile elevation of a cross section through a ship's hull as, with dividers in hand, he turns to his wife who has interrupted him with a letter.[31] By contrast, such memorabilia as survives from the first years of the EIC could be tipped into one archaeologist's barrow. It consists of a fragment of a coat of arms displaying three ships: a chip off an old block which has in recent times been identified as the keystone over the main entrance to Blackwall Dock. Something of a relic to be revered by the disciples of business history, assuredly this is no work of art, only surfacing when the dock was finally closed in 1987. Belonging to the Museum of London, the repository of the capital's archaeology is, understandably enough, disinclined to allot precious gallery space to so mournful a talisman of the most splendid commercial enterprise in the history of the City.[32]

Dutch culture was for export. The portrait of Shakespeare forming the frontispiece to the First Folio was etched by a Dutchman, just as his bust in Holy Trinity, Stratford, was chiselled by Gheerart Janssen (active in England 1612–23, his father having been chased out of Holland by the duke of Alva). If we have all heard of the 'bard', few can afford to dispense with an introduction to Edward Grimeston (d. 1640). He was the first notable English historian who treated Europe as an aggregate of separate national histories; beginning his literary work with *A True History of the Memorable Siege of Ostend* (1604).[33] In 1609 Grimeston's *A Generall Historie of the Netherlands* appeared, richly illustrated with copperplate portraits by yet another Dutch artist, Karel van Sichem. The first ever historical series of English portraits, Henry Holland's *Baziliωlogia* (1618) was made up of engravings mainly by Dutch and Flemish artists, whilst Holland's second compendium, his more famous *Herωologia Anglica* (1620), described as being a 'Protestant Pantheon', was published in two volumes in Holland.

It is in the field of portraiture, though, that Dutch bravura and English equivocation are best sensed. Always complacent, often pretentious, sometimes plainly ridiculous, portraits of the first Dutch governor-generals of Batavia are to be found by the battalion in the Rijksmuseum, though we must look in vain for an English equivalent at the National Maritime Museum.

Take the portrait of Laurens Reael (d. 1637), which is indeed in the Rijksmuseum, an artwork redolent of the huge difference between an English and a Dutch way of doing things. Reael was that man, it will be recalled, whose vain attempt to propitiate Nathaniel Courthope was chronicled in

Chapter 9.[34] Returning to Europe after serving as governor-general of Batavia (1616–19), Reael had this likeness taken in Holland in 1620. At first glance, his appearance suggests a rich, well-blended trifle of pretension, permanence and promise. Wearing black silk, the sleeves so rolled in black and gold as to make wasps out of arms, and a Gunpowder Plot hat, circumference described by gold chain, Reael stands before sheets of carnation draped here and dropped there, creating an air of plenitude that tempers the sable of authority with the triumph of opulence. Such an exuberance of heavy silk would have been entirely natural for a mansion on the IJssel, but hardly we may suppose in Batavia, where humidity was such that had the poor man actually stuck his head into that coal scuttle of a helmet we see upon a side table he must have called for a ventilator. But empires are absurd, and clanking around a parade-ground in steel whilst blinded by sweat was no more egregious a folly than when the EIC would come to require its staff to wear tweed in Calcutta. Here, however, heroics all in red and black make for a lack of conviction that cannot solely be attributed to the brush of its jejune creator, Cornelis van Der Voort (d. 1624). The eye begins to perceive how swagger can neither banish doubt any more than sash can bind the truth. And paper reveals what canvas conceals: documents which make up Reael's apologia speak to the sitter's profound doubts as to either the efficacy or indeed the ethics of what he was doing as a colonial administrator, surrounded as he was by those for whom killing the 'native' was of no more consequence than killing the deer. So if indeed this species of 'conviction painting' actually lets the regime down by insinuating Reael's grave doubts about the 'culture' of the VOC, then this attractive exemplum of the Dutch governing class might surely be said to have possessed more in common with the irenic Roe than the irascible Coen.

Striking indeed is the congruence of the two proconsuls. Although both Reael and Roe were strenuous in defence of the nation, each was an intellectual *au fond*. Messing about at Oxford, Roe made a deeply serious contribution to the cultural life of London thereafter. As for Reael, although he was to make a surprise move into the VOC, before then he had obtained a doctorate and so was no less at home in the high culture of Holland than Roe had been in frequenting the Mermaid Club. Reael was the epitome of the rounded humanist. Both Reael and Roe were men of peace, though never afraid of war.

That said, Roe was more fortunate than Reael in pursuit of clemency. With the Company owning a fixed determination to avoid either conquest or colonisa- tion, Roe was never required to face a choice between career and conscience; though he and his wife together put up a mighty resistance to Barbary corsairs when off Malta on 8 August 1628 the brigands tried to board Roe's ship returning from his embassy in Constantinople.[35] Not so with Reael. Deeply troubled by the dogs of war that the Heren XVII were unleashing upon the Indonesian archipelago, Reael resigned as governor-general on 31 October 1617 – though it would be 21 March 1619 before his successor Coen could begin to destroy everything Reael had tried to create.

As a jurist by training, Reael would be driven out of the VOC by equivo- cation in the face of the treatment that he was expected to meet out to those who were considered to be a threat to Dutch mastery of the Spice Islands. Like Admiral Steven van der Haghen with whom Reael worked, he felt commerce should be pursued by all means peaceful. But then, as the brother-in-law of Jacobus Arminius, whose espousal of an irenic Calvinism had so provoked the Synod of Dort, Reael also felt deeply ambivalent about coming home, knowing that as the moderates had fled, so the light of Holland had been cowled. Nevertheless, as an ardent patriot, Reael resumed a high-profile career, serving as vice-admiral of Holland and West Friesland before commanding the Dutch contingent in a joint Anglo-Dutch force that fought a nine-month engage- ment with the Spanish along the length of the Barbary coast. In 1637 Reael was being considered as admiral for the Confederate Fleet when he died of the plague, something he had caught from his two boys who had predeceased him.

But if Reael was a naval man, he was a man of parts in that epic drama of nation-building that came to be refracted through the steely rise of the VOC. Just as Roe would read poetry sheltering from the heat in his howdah, so when Reael could not be found in his cabin he was to be discovered in his cabinet.[36] There he much enjoyed the company of the Republic's best writers. Like Roe, Reael was a connoisseur of poetry, recipient no less of a 'Lof de Zeevart' ('Ode to Seafaring') by the celebrated Joost van den Vondel. In much the same vein, Roe had been dedicatee of two epigrams by Ben Jonson – one, it may be suspected, composed with India in mind[37] – the affinity between the poet and the diplomat the fruit of scepticism and the dictate of revulsion in the face of rank corruption which had come in with the Stuarts.[38] Reael and Roe were each guardian of the national honour: the former was delegated to represent the United Provinces at the coronation of Charles I, while the latter was appointed to maintain the dignity of the Kingdom of England in his capacity as Chancellor of the Order of the Garter.

Such then is the compelling parallel between this remarkable pair. Yet more noteworthy, though, is the bonding between seventeenth-century England and Holland. The congruities and contrasts, the victories and vicissitudes that made for this particular means of exchange suggest how Anglo-Dutch relations even managed to defy the laws of chemistry in being both holistic and atomistic at one and the same time.

15

DEADLOCK

Pieter Both (d. 1615) was the first governor-general of the Dutch East Indies and the first to explicitly promote a stratagem of violence towards the Indigenous of East Asia. Both's appointment may have come as a surprise since he did not hail from a marine family. He had been born at Amersfoort, which even when Holland was such a watery world had been safe enough from the sea. Both had started as a member of the Brabant Company before its absorption within the larger portfolio of the VOC. Having taken four ships out to the East Indies in 1599, he was deemed ready to preside over the East Indies, which he did between 1610 and 1614. Having conquered Timor and driven the Spaniards out of Tidore, he looked to have all the makings of becoming as ruthless as Coen in the extermination of indigenous peoples. But if Both had been approved for a second spell, that was never to materialise, because returning home he was drowned at Flic-en-Flac when two out of the four ships in his flotilla went down off Mauritius. They never found him, of course, but his family found consolation in having the second-highest elevation in Mauritius named Pieter Both Mountain.

If the Dutch mourned one whom the more fervent nationalists regarded as a great man, the English must have rejoiced in the disappearance of a great menace. When Both had been sent to Bantam in 1609 he had been armed not only with cannons but also with directives. Of these the most startling had ordered him to make 'the spice-islands fast to the United Company, so that nothing of them can fall into the hands of any other nation in the world'.[1] Faced with such a degree of intransigence, what was the Company to do following Both's arrival in the Far East in 1610? The obvious answer was discussion and negotiation. Gradually animosities between the EIC and the VOC had been gathering momentum, and so towards the end of Both's time as governor-general there began a decade of negotiation as to how an accommodation with the Hollander might be accomplished. For the most part these talks, now in London now in The Hague, were overseen from the London end by Smythe; when, that is, he was not actively sapping the morale of the English delegation by muttering things under his breath about the perfidy and dishonesty of the other side.

The trouble was how Governor Smythe had been harbouring a deep dislike of the Hollander since at least 1604. As ambassador to Moscow he had discovered the Dutch trying to infringe the monopoly that the Muscovy Company had hitherto enjoyed on trade between Europe and Russia. But as far as Smythe was concerned, there were problems with these same people and far closer to home. Smythe was principal promoter of the English fishing industry and, much to his fury, the Dutch were endlessly interfering with his boats in the North Sea. Hobbled with cynicism and bridled with doubt, Smythe would consistently fail to offer convincing leadership during the three conferences over ten years that would be convened to settle the differences between the EIC and the VOC.

Smythe was not alone, however; indeed, few in England were inclined to think well of the Dutch. The fixed hostility of Englishmen to the Hollander was well said by Sir Thomas Overbury who, before he had succumbed to the dark arts of poisoning, had had just enough time to express the commonly held view. This was that with the Dutchman you must expect nothing but trouble:

> There belong to that State twenty-thousand Vessels of all Sorts, so that, if the Spaniards were entirely beaten out of those Parts, the Kings of France and England would take as much Pains to suppress, as ever they did to raise them; for, being our Enemies, they are able to give us the Law at Sea, and eat us out of all Trade, much more than the French, having at this Time three Ships to our one, though none so good as our best.[2]

From the first, Smythe did his best to sabotage initial overtures when he acquainted 'the state with their [Dutch] wrongs and crave redress'. This he did by drawing up a petition to the Privy Council. It was full of how the Dutch were monopolising trade by 'maintaining now for law by strong hand that which lately they esteemed unreasonable, for the Portugal to challenge a more special property in any of those parts, than themselves or any other nation whatsoever'.[3] Despite Smythe's damaging intervention, however, the head of this first delegation was nonetheless able to persuade the Court of Committees to be allowed to proceed. This was to be on the basis that the Dutch were not only capable of good faith but also interested in viable solutions:

> so we might peaceably proceed to trade jointly together without troubling of either states (to right conceived injuries) or giving such an advantage to others (who would willingly take the opportunity of fishing in the troubled streams of our divisions and dissensions). So that (upon conference) they are willing to join commissioners, with such as you shall substitute here, to salve and put a remedy to all griefs past, and consider of some indifferent course to be continued betwixt us hereafter, for the good and benefit of either part.[4]

But despite best efforts and better thoughts, Amsterdam now took so long to respond to English overtures that Smythe could take pleasure in venting his prejudices. Writing to Sir Ralph Winwood, who was English ambassador at The Hague, he now declared: 'I can expect no other but that they intend to proceed by delays, as they have been accustomed to do and to give reasonable answers, but perform nothing in substance.'[5] Actually Smythe was wrong, or so Winwood thought. In reporting how the VOC wanted amalgamation with the EIC, Winwood told Smythe how he had been persuaded that there could be a 'good correspondence': 'here [it] is taken to be the surest course both to live together in good amity and to be master over the Portugall in those islands'.[6] But despite that view from The Hague, all the while in London, Smythe held himself in a state of permanent scepticism. Nevertheless, serious talking began in London during April 1613, the first plenary session of the commissioners being held at Smythe's own house which was where many important meetings were held in those days. The Dutch delegation consisted of Reynier Pauw, Jacob Boreel and Dirck Meerman, representing the three towns of Amsterdam, Middelburg and Delft. These were men whose experience at making a fortune and running the most important cities in Holland made their selection not only natural but also challenging in the highest degree. Five years later and Rainier Pauw would be central to the defeat of the Remonstrants at the Synod of Dort, where his influence would play a major role in sending Oldenbarnevelt up the scaffold (Chapter 14). Grotius was of the London party too, infiltrated at the last moment by Oldenbarnevelt himself, who had sent him along as the best legal mind the Dutch possessed.

By contrast, the English delegation was much less impressive. Sir Daniel Dun (d. 1617) was an Oxford academic and certainly no sailor; he was a judge in the Court of Admiralty. Even less well qualified was Sir Christopher Perkins (d. 1622). Somehow he had contrived to be forgiven for having been a Jesuit in the age of the Gunpowder Plot. Putting such earlier spiritual indiscretions aside, Perkins had subsequently begun to earn fat fees as a Master of Requests in the prerogative courts. These courts worked in equity, not civil law, and that, unfortunately, was the legal language that the Dutch best understood. Finally on the English side was Sir Clement Edmondes (d. 1622), who did at least have first-hand acquaintance with the Low Countries. Son of a Shropshire yeoman, Edmondes had entered All Souls as a chorister. After graduation he had moved on to become adviser to Sir Francis Vere, the commander of English mercenaries in the Netherlands. To these were added four Adventurers from the Company.[7]

The Dutch commissioners were received in audience by James I, to whom Grotius now opened proceedings, tracing the history of the Dutch and the Portuguese in the East at inordinate length. This he did on the basis that long usage creates present law. Although Grotius's agenda was to make the United Provinces impregnable, he at last drew breath in conceding how it was now 'time for the nations to agree together like Abraham and Lot'.[8]

These talks lasted from early April until the end of May 1613, during which time Grotius was able to persuade James I that the quarrel was not just a fight between merchants but a matter of state. As Grotius continued to front the Dutch argument, he was able to persuade James that how the Dutch behaved in the Indies had as much to do with international relations as it did with profit. This reinforced James's instinct to favour the Dutch over his own subjects. In so skilfully unpicking the knots that tied James to the Company, Grotius deployed the argument that the strong arm wielded by the Dutch had more to do with defying the exclusive claims of the Portuguese than it did with excluding the English from a Dutch sphere of dominance. Dutch forts and Dutch battles were entirely legitimate, Grotius suggested, because without them the Iberians would not allow so much as one English ship beyond the Malay Peninsula. What was more, the Dutch had every right to recoup the vast outlay in building forts and maintaining fleets, not by imposing a universal ban on trade but by excluding rivals from those limited number of places where the Dutch had sunk money and were looking for salvage. But the difficulty for the English was that these same redoubts had been planted on just those islands that provided the largest return in profit of any spot on the face of the earth. Throwing up their hands, the Dutch protested that they had never been bent upon exclusion. All his compatriots wanted, Grotius assured his English interlocutors, was to be allowed to recoup the vast expense his countrymen had been put to in forcing access to the spices.

But after six weeks of Latin it became apparent that no accord was going to emerge, so the Dutch summarised both what they could offer and what they hoped for by way of understanding and cooperation from the English. In his final summing up, Grotius plainly stated that the Dutch were looking for war with Spain: 'In its nature Indian commerce is far different from European. European commerce does not need our support, but Indian cannot (since the Spaniards oppose it) be obtained except by fighting.'[9] He then added what all knew to be untrue; that the Indian trade was scarcely profitable. With this Grotius was pleading that the Dutch be allowed to deploy a 'fortress India' *mentalité* since, according to him, what was needed was strength to prosecute the fight against the Spaniard. It was only because of the threat of Spain, Grotius added, that the indigenous were kept under subjugation, much of the effort having to be directed at the end of a pike so that the precious plantations might be preserved. By way of an intermediate offer to the English party, however, Grotius then suggested there should be mutual aid and freedom of trade between Holland and England, neither nation should encourage the allies of the other and no arms should be supplied to each other's enemies.

None of this went down well – that is, if marginalia to be found in a manuscript of these first proceedings is a true record of English reaction. Entitled 'Briefe of the Proceedings', this is a copy of Grotius's summing up

322

in which he sought to justify the position of the VOC. The critique drips with asperity, as it also suggests the supposed justification for Dutch aggression was regarded as thoroughly specious by the English. Grotius's argument is found to be wholly unpersuasive. As to his nonsense that the Dutch treated the indigenous as equals, such a preposterous claim solicited the following response: 'Their inviolable contracts, if there be any, were forced from them by violence and therefore no injustice if they break them.' Opposite the words 'we think it very honest to defend oppressed people' is the interjection 'against their will'. As for the claim that 'reasonable conditions in the sale of merchandises may be obtained of us', the same writes: 'The contrary whereof we find by experience, that our cloves being sold [to others] they raise the price of theirs to an unreasonable rate (although both wet and rotten) and therefore do no doubt of any reasonable conditions from them.'[10]

No one was persuaded, none able to jump such a chasm of mistrust. But that was not the worst of it. As the talks collapsed, relations corroded. When the king was granting the Dutch delegation a farewell audience on 21 May 1613, there occurred a robust exchange of views. Standing aside, James listened as Smythe accused his adversaries of pig-headedness and also censured them for omission from their instructions of any power to enter into a formal watertight agreement. Whilst Smythe was first to lament how matters had not progressed, he could not refrain from pointing out that the Dutch had studiously ignored his proposals that the conference be resumed: 'By all which it appeareth that their purpose and intent is to exclude His Majesty's subjects from the trade of spices in the East Indies and to engross the same wholly to themselves.'[11] Now untrammelled access to Eastern spices was 'of great importance to the state, as well in respect of free and open trade and employment of shipping and mariners, as of the inconvenience which will fall upon us if the Hollanders should give the law unto us for such commodities as come from those parts, and by primitive right do belong as well unto us as unto them or to any other nation of Europe.'[12]

Speaking in Latin, James manoeuvred Grotius into a corner, only to find himself in a still tighter one. Assuring the Dutch jurist that he would give orders for his subjects to maintain friendly relations with the Dutch and now beckoning Smythe over, he told Smythe the gist of what had been said. Having listened carefully, Smythe replied that the order would be good; but only if the English were permitted to trade freely in all places without exception. The Dutch had told the king that they would not interfere with the English in those places where they had neither forest, factories nor allies. Furthermore, they would avoid other locations where they did not already have a presence. But Smythe was having none of that, suspecting such 'generosity' to be more apparent than real.

In Smythe's jaundiced view it would only be when the Dutch had finished strangling the well-spiced goose that the English would be permitted to pick up such feathers as might still be left blowing about. Burdened with settled prejudices as he was, Smythe then went on to say that the terms the Dutch were offering were contrary to the rights of the EIC. The Company ought to be allowed to trade as freely in Dutch stations as the English did in Holland and Zeeland, though Smythe conceded that in doing so the Company would have to be willing to pay duties (*gabellen*).[13] None of this convinced James, who told Smythe that the Dutch could not continue the expenditure that would be needed to keep the Spanish at bay, if by sharing trading places their income was reduced. Nothing could have made clearer to Smythe a sad fact: his king had more sympathy with the VOC than with the EIC. Thus broke up the first of three conferences. Whether matters might have been different had James not been so partisan must be doubted, though, if only because there was an ocean of resentment between the two peoples. If little had been accomplished between such traders in hostility as were the EIC and the VOC, the king had succeeded in reinforcing a growing sense of mistrust within the counsels of the Company towards himself.

James failed to support the EIC because Grotius had worked upon his vanity. Prior to arriving, Grotius had corresponded with the celebrated Isaac Casaubon (d. 1614), a brilliant intellect who, having enjoyed distinguished academic posts in Geneva, Montpellier and Paris, had been courted by all the parties to the religious disputes of Europe; each hoping to recruit this prodigy to their own persuasion. Since 1611, however, Casaubon had been in England, where he had suffered from spiritual claustrophobia as a result of the attentions of a king who could never stop congratulating himself on having stolen such a prize as Casaubon represented from Marie de' Medicis. She had been courting the divine with all the energy that James himself was giving to the cause. As for the king, he often sent for his pet theologian. This he did to stroke him with compliments as the two discussed the strands, the stridencies and the strains of European Protestantism.

Before the first round of talks had begun, Casaubon had shown the king a letter from Grotius in which the Dutch jurist had suggested to the Swiss divine how there should be a world council of Churches under the presidency of James no less. Regarding himself as a reincarnation of King Solomon, James took pride not only in his theology but also in his wisdom. Nothing could have been more calculated to provoke the sin of self-love than the flattering invitation that Grotius was now proffering him. The letter from Grotius to Casaubon, the unctuous flattery of Grotius to James, both suggested to the king that he alone was qualified to reconcile those of this world who were unable to agree about the precise nature of the next.[14] As far as the Company was concerned, however, all this talk regarding a straight way to salvation could have been more profitably directed towards discovering with the Dutch delegation how to navigate safely the Straits of Sunda. Nevertheless, in so artfully flattering James with thoughts about how he might take Europe not by force but argument, together with assurances of a peculiarly Dutch regard for his gracious person, Grotius made of James a very puffball of conceit. Thus had Grotius contrived to have the man who should have been the stoutest supporter of an English East India Company cast instead the fondest of eyes upon those Dutch arguments that Grotius was concurrently marshalling in defence of the VOC. By likening James I to the most revered of the patriarchs, Grotius distracted as he disarmed. It was an extraordinary achievement: having won the admiration of a king of France, now he had succeeded in gaining the gratitude of a king of England. The reward for Grotius was how henceforth James would be persuaded that the Dutch must be allowed to remain armed. Always better accoutred than the English, the Dutch alone could assume the mantle of war, if only to dismantle the pretensions of Spain and dash the hopes of England.

Grotius now did a little spiritual calling. This did not go well at Lambeth to be sure, however enthusiastically he may have been greeted within the halls of the rich. The incumbent of the palace was of course George Abbot, whose creative passion had always been cosmography. But although both men could have been said to have world views in their separate ways, Grotius received the coolest of receptions from the prelate. This was hardly surprising since George's brother Maurice was shortly to become deputy-governor of the East India Company. Accordingly, the archbishop could hardly have been expected to take a charitable view of its rival the VOC, which was about to take over the East Indies.

But then there was much else that must have been calculated to make this decidedly awkward. Abbot was the most intractable of Calvinists, one for whom, therefore, Grotius's moderate view of predestination was a species of anathema. But their temperaments grated too. Abbot considered this objectionable young man who had had the sauce to call upon him to be impertinent, prolix and conceited. True enough. But there was more to Abbot's antipathy towards Grotius than merely dislike of a bumptious youth. There was hurt pride. The king had become increasingly disenchanted with his archbishop, whose brand of Calvinism he found offensive. Although Abbot was *ex-officio* senior privy councillor, he had been increasingly sidelined, obliged to shuffle amidst the patristics of Lambeth library rather than attend the king in his councils. This mattered to him in all sorts of ways, but hardly more so than when England's commercial expansion seemed to be at hazard. Here was one who had he been robed in kersey not cambric would have presided beneath the beams of the Drapers' Hall and not among the cloisters of Lambeth: Abbot's father had been an illiterate cloth worker from Guildford. As for his son George, when he was not thinking about God he thought about Goa. 'My Lord of Canterbury' cared passionately about his brother Maurice's East India Company. As for Grotius's presence in London as chief spokesman for the VOC, Abbot had an uneasy sense that the Dutch jurist was running rings around the English delegates. And so it was that after Grotius had called, Abbot relieved himself of such a degree of asperity as may be thought inconsistent with the principles of his office. Abbot informed Winwood: 'at his [Grotius's] first coming to the King, by reason of his good Latine *Tongue*, he was so *tedious* and full of *tittle-tattle* that the King's judgement was of him, *that he was some pedant full of words and of no great judgement*'.[15] In so saying there was a degree of irony, doubtless lost upon one who was more notable for an absence of humour than the presence of spiritual wisdom. This was a time when men said of King James I that he was either a pedant on a royal scale or, much the same thing, 'the wisest fool in Christendom', as Henri IV of France had described him back in 1604.

Although it would not be long before the more accommodating members of the Court of Committees moved for new talks after the Dutch went home in the high summer of 1613, with Smythe there was little or no movement. From the breakdown of talks in 1613 to the breakout of war in 1620, he was balancing his commitments to the East India Company whilst attempting to discharge obligations to the Muscovy. Under the first came the demand from the English that they be allowed to help themselves to the riches of the East. As for the Muscovy, it symbolised the aspiration of British fishermen that the Dutch be thrust out of the waters of the north, banned from the Arctic to protect the Company and its whales from the harpoons of others. Forced to argue that in one ocean the English must be given free trade, whilst in another they should be allowed to exclude those whose favour in the south the English were simultaneously expecting to be granted, was a contradiction not even serpentine Smythe was able to resolve. Hobbled with cynicism, bridled with doubts, unable to beat wings caught in the sticky web of conflicted interest, confusing private ambition with public duty, Smythe failed to offer convincing leadership when no fewer than three conferences were convened to settle the differences between the EIC and the VOC.

Such a dilemma demanded that at one and the same time Smythe should clamour for a *mare liberum* in the south as he called for a *mare clausum* in the north. This created paralysis in command and confusion in the ranks. Was it to be freedom to buy cloves in southern zephyrs *and* the power to prevent the catch of cod under northern lights? If the Dutch listened to English arguments against exclusion in the Moluccas, they were quick to point out how the EIC could not play the same card in the seas of the north. Because there were no princes residing in the Lofoten islands, its waters must be free for all. By contrast, every archipelago had its sultan, with whom, as the Dutch declared sanctimoniously, it would always be necessary to come to a treaty; though as the English had always inferred, their rivals had some mighty odd ideas as to what constituted a 'treaty'.

As for those ice fields and their whales about the Lofoten islands, all that Smythe could do was to fall back on claims of 'prior discovery'. He argued that rights came with a first discovery by the English of the whaling grounds to which the Dutch countered by suggesting that because there was no policing them and therefore there were no overheads they had no wish to keep the English away, as was certainly the case in the Spice Islands where the overheads were massive. What the Dutch wished to have off the Grand Banks was freedom to fish unmolested, side by side with whoever else might care to join them. Here, as the Dutch had long pointed out, the French had been the first, yet they had never striven to exclude anyone. And so there for the time being matters rested.

On 13 January 1615 Smythe addressed the Court of Committees. He began by saying that the king was displeased with both parties for not agreeing to an amalgamation. Although Smythe had gone to some length to explain to the king why this would not do, he now felt it necessary to elaborate on what he had told him:

> He conceived it dangerous to cross his Majesty's interests and yet impossible for the Company to join with the Hollanders. They maintained their merchandise 'with their state', and having concluded a joint stock for ten years, had paid no dividends but some small matter, whereas the London Company remained at the pleasure of the king and would be discouraged without present profit. The court considered how, if the king imposed upon them a joint stock, it might be prevented; deciding in the end not to wait until His Majesty's instructions might be seen.[16]

With a second round of Anglo-Dutch talks beginning in 1615, still less came to be achieved than had been accomplished in 1613. London opened aggressively with Deputy-Governor Maurice Abbot pushing out his first pawn. Abbot stood by the final English proposal from two years previously: that there must be an agreement for mutual relations in the Indies. But as the Dutch commissioners now pointed out, the States-General had never given them authority to deliver on that. The English then announced that they had no intention of withdrawing their claim to freedom of commerce in the Indies; a demand that the Dutch thought gratuitously brusque. All the while Smythe knew full well that the idea of a war with Spain was being actively discussed in secret conversations between James I and the Dutch delegation: talks from which he was being deliberately excluded. Despite the obvious import of so drastic an initiative, the prospect of war had never been a substantive point on any agenda; rather, it had been something raised in two notes that the Dutch commissioners of 1613 had communicated directly to the king whilst concealing them from Smythe. Clearly there were parallel talks going on, one about England's commerce and the other about its foreign relations. Smythe's position was now impossible. As chief spokesman of the City he found himself talking to a king who clearly thought international relations more important than nutmegs. Just how duplicitous James was is suggested by the gratification that the Dutch felt at his positive response to one of their predictions. This was that if the EIC got its way the Spaniards would be masters of all the Indies, a threat they put over with a degree of condescension by implying that Smythe had failed to grasp the complexities of the great game: '*Ce que nous esperons avoir este bien compris par la tres singuliere sagesse et prevoyance de sa Majeste, et partant, Messieurs, nous attendrons de vous quelque overture*' ('Which we hope to have been well understood by virtue of the very singular wisdom and foresight of His Majesty; and therefore, Sirs, we await your proposals').[17]

With this second round of talks in The Hague, the English tried to hold a line, Abbot claiming that the Dutch had avoided conceding freedom of commerce by raising *arguments de discours* or canards. This could be demonstrated by looking at four 'indubitably true and consequently indisputable maxims' that Abbot had extracted from a paper published in the United Provinces in favour of freedom of commerce.[18] Abbot then went on to refer to the convention that the English had made with Ivan the Terrible. With this, Smythe argued, the Muscovy Company could have behaved as the Dutch were now doing in the Indies. Then the Muscovy would have been quite justified in excluding the Dutch from trading not only at Archangel, but also right down to the Persian border where the English alone had traded between 1553 and 1587. But in its earliest days the Muscovy Company had had no wish to exclude competition, so why should the Dutch do so now?

This was a new argument for freedom of commerce. Something dressed up afresh, though, was the claim that Drake had go to the Moluccas first and therefore English rights to the Spice Islands predated those of the Dutch. To give a little zest to this argument, the English commissioners cited the Spaniard Bartolomé Leonardo y Argensola's *Conquista de las Islas Malucas* (1609). In this book mention is made of Drake's supposed treaty with the sultan of Ternate. Now to quote such a source was not a smart move, since as

329

the Dutch gleefully pointed out, the Spanish historian had simply copied a view that the English had themselves aired prior to Argensola's own publication. As for the Dutch argument, which was that were it not for their military presence in the Far East the Spanish would prevent anyone from trading, '*nous faisons peu d'estime de ce que l'Espaignol peut attenter la contre nous . . . nous eusmes trafficq en ces endroicts devant que vous en sceusiez seulement le chemin et le maintenons encores par la force en des lieux eminents la ou voz Armes ne furent ne furent oncquez*' ('we have little fear of what the Spaniards may try to do against us there . . . we traded in these places before you even knew they existed; and our trade continues to this day, protected by our own armed forces, in important trading stations where your army has never even been').[19]

Once again, matters ended with no further progress. Leaving The Hague on 30 April 1615, the English delegation was back by 13 May. At this point it discovered that the king had gone horse-racing at Newmarket. Before the Company could send up its own findings, Tobias de Coene had slipped over from Holland to brief de Caron and then the two, received by James I, had told him of an important shift in the Dutch position vis-à-vis Spain, a change that may have been something of a concession to the East India Company's refusal to back proactively a Dutch war with Spain. The Dutch continued to want cooperation against Spain; though they were now ready to agree that England could join them for defensive operations only, should these be necessary. For his part the king assured de Caron that he would send for Smythe and pressurise him into agreeing to a union between the EIC and the VOC, something James had wanted from the first. Meanwhile, the commissioners for the EIC, knowing nothing of this and pressing ahead with their own report, produced a document that represented an essential prelude to any union: common capital of £12,000–15,000; control of prices; reduction of expenses, presents and taxes to local princes; the opening of the China trade; and the restraint of Chinese, Malay and Javanese traders in the Moluccas. If this last point could be maintained, then '*Estants unis et associez ensemble nous pourrons aisement empescher le trafficq a toutes nations de l'Europe*' ('United and working together, we will easily be able to prevent all other nations of Europe from trading in the area').[20]

The king was deeply interested by all this, and so instructed the respective ambassadors to initiate matters along the lines proposed. However, documentation that the EIC produced under great pressure in no way represented the different strands of opinion causing discord within the Court of Committees. Indeed, a minority paper now appeared. Entitled 'Reasons showing the Inconveniences and Impossibilities of a Joint Stock to be held with the Hollander', it pointed out how the English were merchants and the Dutch warriors: the VOC were given state subsidies, the EIC not. Abbot went on to point out how an amalgamation would never work. In the first place, to exclude the rest of the world from the Moluccas, as the Dutch wanted, simply would not work. Secondly, in the technical sphere, differences between Dutch and English weights and measures would make accounting very difficult. For the EIC, the best way to exclude the Iberians was not to exclude but to excel – to sell more cheaply, not only in 'coastal' but also in European trade.

More substantive was a third and final push for peace that began in 1618. For the English, it attracted men with much higher profiles than before, perhaps a sign that the Company was at last in real earnest. Representing the government were Sir Julius Caesar, Master of the Rolls, Sir Henry Marten, Judge of the High Court of Admiralty, and Sir Edward Coke. To these were added Smythe and Abbot, together with Sir Clement Edmondes. Meanwhile, with talks looming, Sir Dudley Carleton, now the British ambassador at The Hague, suggested the odds of getting things done and the means to do it:

> A ship, richly laden, newly arrived in Zealand from the East Indies, the eighth this year, all valued at ten millions of florins. No small question whether their good success and prosperity will help or hinder the business of the conjunction of the Companies. The deputies have given them full power to treat and conclude, whereas Grotius and those who went to England some fews years since had only commission to talk and dispute. Those who know them, and have interest in the advancement of the business, say they must be roundly dealt with, and rather by way of intimidation than persuasion or inducement.[21]

At once it became apparent that the Dutch had dropped their insistence on union. Instead there should be trade open to both, input of capital at the discretion of each company, prices to be rigged and a 'Fleet of Defence' that would also need rigging.[22] There was much here pleasing to the English party; after all, matters had come a long way in five years. But then that was part of the whole problem: things had gone on too long and the English were unable to trust their rivals. Furthermore, the EIC now insisted on its right to construct its own fortresses; if only to ensure that the Dutch did not take advantage of a greater military preparedness. Predictably enough, this caused new arguments for old problems. Thus for the third and last time, the companies abandoned any full-blown attempt at reconciliation.

But even supposing matters had gone better, what might have been agreed in Europe would have been disowned in Asia. If in the West it was possible to talk, albeit at interminable length, as some of the more irascible of the English delegates sometimes felt, the huge pressures imposed upon the servants of the respective companies out East meant that talking there could all too easily be cast aside by the more decisive expedient of coming to arms. By now Dale and Coen had fired upon each other, hoping that matters so long in contention could at last be resolved in the gunroom and not the boardroom. Coen, recognising the English and not the Spanish as the 'enemy', set about bullying the Heren XVII with his characteristic and toxic mix of low obeisance with hectoring arrogance. As his masters' voice, he stated his belief that the Heren had opened the sluice when, had they but locked those gates, that hateful enterprise which was the EIC must have been frustrated:

> Praised be to God, who directs all things to good, the means never failed thereto. Yet it seems that if your worships had had this faith, we should not have been so hastily bridled with so hard a bit, nor would so many of your rightful conquests been surrendered ... Why was it forgotten so soon that you had lately sent out sixteen such excellent ships? Was this haste to prevent bloodshed? We recognise that it is no business of the servant what his master does ... but (under correction) your lordships have gone too fast.[23]

After the final breakdown of talks in 1619 and the break-up of the Fleet of Defence in 1622, matters drifted on until early 1623. There then arose what stands for all time as the most serious crisis in the history of Anglo-Dutch relations: the notorious Massacre of Amboyna. The events of February 1623 have been described, somewhat portentously it may be thought, as 'a turning point of the British Empire':[24] a 'turning point' because over the centuries 'historians had come to argue, a massacre had transpired that explained the ultimate configuration of the British Empire'.[25] By this is meant that as a result of the massacre the East India Company turned its face away from the Far East and towards India.[26]

This, the boldest of claims about an atrocity that resulted in fewer deaths than an American school shooting, may stand for a beginning. Yet it was also closure, though hardly in the sense of a resolution of trauma as understood in today's terms. Overreaction in England to the news of the so-called massacre of ten English factors in Amboyna, as it began to filter out in the spring of 1624, stood not only for the atrophy of ambition in the East but looked for a perilous few days at least as if it might be the outing of pent-up fury against the Dutch community in London. For so many years the English had perceived themselves as having suffered the basest humiliation in the face of arrogance and barbarism, and so this fury provoked by that 'massacre' threatened to get quite out of hand.

Amboyna, a small but fabulously lucrative spice island, had been captured from the Portuguese by Steven van der Hagen in 1605, with not a shot fired. Very soon it was realised that this tiny carbuncle was the richest stone in the jeweller's window. As time passed, Amboyna became another name for cloves, which were to be found in more abundance and in better quality than anywhere else upon the face of God's earth. But then what had been a happy discovery came to be shadowed by anxiety as triumph among the soldiers turned to paranoia for the planters. This was not all: the island mattered emotionally too. It had been the headquarters of the VOC until Coen had come along and stuck his flag into what had traditionally been known as Jakarta, but which with nationalism foregrounded, Coen had renamed Batavia in 1619. With such an appellation Coen had been hoping to revive among his neo-Batavians that spirit which had invested the heroes of old Batavia, whose tales had come down to a latter-day Dutchman from his reading of Caesar's *Comentarii de Bello Gallico* and Tacitus' *Germania*.

Burdened with the enormous value of Amboyna, the Dutch authorities had become more defensive with each passing year. Over the winter of 1622 much had seemed to be happening to arouse the suspicions of Amboyna's governor, Herman van Speult. The sultan of Ternate was being thoroughly tiresome in threatening to switch his nominal allegiance to the VOC, to an accommodation with the Spanish, encouraged to do so by the English. To add to Speult's sense of unease was his conviction that an international conspiracy was afoot. Come February 1623, and looking for trouble, Speult found it easily enough. He was able to persuade himself that a *ronin*, or mercenary samurai, was taking measurements of Fort Victoria to discover whether it might be possible to seize the redoubt. Like the ghost of Hamlet's father, 'a *Japoner* Souldier of the *Dutch* in their Castle of *Amboyna*, walking in the night upon the wall, came to the Sentinel (being a *Hollander*,) and there, amongst other talk, asked him some questions touching the strength of the Castle, and the people that were therein'.[27] The fuse to the barrel had been loose talk, which had caused Speult to think that this had been the general signal for assault. Moving immediately, Speult seized those Englishmen who were on the island and sent for others stationed nearby.

On the face of things it is surely hard to believe that ten English men of business, some doubtless debilitated by the tropics,[28] not a single muster-master among them, could possibly have contemplated forcing the gates of a Dutch fort.[29] But such an assumption is without reckoning with the presence on the island of a contingent of samurai for whom killing was an exercise of honour. Just possibly these fearsome swordsmen may have been persuaded by the English to move against Speult and his guardsmen. There is justification therefore in keeping an open mind as to whether the English were harbouring treacherous designs after all, an answer to which could not be resolved then and certainly cannot now. All that can be said with any certainty, however, is that there were quite enough Japanese soldiers to take the fort, as indeed there was sufficient motivation for Speult to destroy the English.[30]

As it was, prior to all this Speult had been having difficulty with the cape merchant George Muschamp, who had a long and deep hatred of the Dutch and as headman on Amboyna was certainly in a position to affect the thinking of his subordinates. In the perennial contest for a share in the spoils between the EIC and the VOC, Muschamp had lost his leg and with that, perhaps, he had also been parted from some of his professional dignity.[31] Muschamp had been present when the *Hound* and *Sampson* had been taken and the late lamented president of the Indies John Jourdain had been assassinated, almost certainly on the say-so of Coen who regarded his opposite number as 'a very clever fellow [who] left no means untried which would in any way serve his designs'.[32] As for Muschamp, fighting with desperate resolve aboard the *Sampson*, he had endured the agony of having that right leg of his 'dismembered'. Eighteen months later and here he was, reported as stumping and stomping around Amboyna, muttering every sort of imprecation against those scoundrels up at the fort.[33] As for Speult, he felt no less humiliated than Muschamp because he had been forced to carry out the execution of a compatriot at the behest of Muschamp himself. The English cape merchant had demanded that a Dutch corporal be executed for contravening the terms of the treaty that was supposed to regulate the conduct of the two nations.[34] Speult had had no option but to comply with Muschamp's merciless demand.

This Speult had done by personally shooting David Jost. Exactly a year before this deeply distressing episode, Muschamp had written a letter to Bantam on 12 June 1621, 'according to the order given him . . . [enclosing] the true platform of the castle, with the length, breadth, and number of munition'.[35] Why had he done this? Perhaps because he had actually been laying plans, literally as well as metaphorically, for the assault that Speult would convince himself was in the offing come February 1623.

But whatever may or may not have been intended, as far as Speult was concerned, this lot had had it coming to them, and come it did. Gabriel Towerson and his nine colleagues were rounded up and put to the bucket and the candle – waterboarded first and burning candles applied thereafter. Still alive, most were executed. By 9 March 1623 Towerson's mangled head had become a silhouette against the setting sun, where it became as blue and yellow as the VOC colours. Together the two represented a tableau of triumph and an ensign of revenge that would resonate down the years, as with the passage of time what had been an incident became a massacre.

The whole process of the supposed unmasking but certain torture of these ten English martyrs was over in less than a month, though the outrage would be remembered for more than a century. Although Speult had done irreparable damage by his act of insular barbarity, relations might not have become quite so bad had he only thought to have done his job properly.

He should have murdered the lot, but instead he found four not guilty. In thus freeing them, Speult had condemned himself: when these wretches got back home, the cripples threatened to call down such a firestorm upon the defenceless heads of the London Dutch as public safety demanded that the Trained Bands come out as the prospect of war came in.

In rattling the drum the Company deliberately overreacted. Its own factors had been guilty of the most unspeakable depravities when the Company had been part of the Fleet of Defence.[36] Thus it was that the reception of Amboyna in England had less to do with fingernails than frustration. Fundamentally, English reaction over the supposed massacre was in essence a projection of accumulated disappointment at Dutch success. The 'massacre', to allow Amboyna its common misnomer, coincided with a painful period of self-awareness. The Dutch had snatched the diadem: the VOC not the East India Company had come to dominate what were not only the world's most profitable crops, but also those that were impregnable because they grew only on tiny islands the Company could never hope to take. Reaction had less to do with the murder of the factors than the death of the future. Gliding about Paul's Walk, where scandal flew out as pigeons flew in, news-mongers found themselves handling the hottest news since Guy Fawkes had been unmasked. John Chamberlain was the most prominent of these broadcasters, writing to Dudley Carleton of how the East India Company:

> informed the counsaile the last weeke of divers yll presages, among the rest of a sermon newly printed by one Wilkenson, which I know not what relation yt can have to this late accident, (for I have not read yt) but the epistle or preface made by a minister is bitter enough; then of a play or representation of all the busines of Amboyna redy to be acted: and of a large picture made for our East Indian companie describing the whole action in manner and forme wherupon the counsaile gave order the picture shold be supprest, the play forbidden, and the booke called in: and withall for a strong watch of 800 men extraordinarie against Shrove Tewsday to see the citie be kept quiet.[37]

The picture referred to was by Richard Greenbury, painter of choice whenever the Company wished to have a record of such exotics as might come stalking up Leadenhall Street carrying their *rupiyas*.[38] What one notices, another elaborates: 'The East India Company have ordered Greenbury, a painter, to paint a detailed picture of all the tortures inflicted on the English at Amboyna, and would have had it all acted out in a play; but the Council was appealed to by the Dutch Ministers, and stopped it; for fear of disturbance this Shrovetide.'[39] But that was far from the full story.

The Court of Committees had been so outraged when they heard about the atrocity that Greenbury had been instructed to produce the most powerful condemnation he could devise. But when it became known more widely what Greenbury was intending, there was considerable unease around the Privy Council table. On 18 February 1625 Greenbury was called in by the Company and 'ordered not too much to hasten the finishing of it', just as he was also requested to 'put out the petition therein inserted, being that delivered by the Netherlanders to Queen Elizabeth to succour them in their distress'.[40] At this point there arose the sort of full-scale crisis that so often enveloped the Company when international relations came to the fore. As it had been with the Spanish over Hormuz, so now with the Dutch at Amboyna: the Court of Committees found itself in Westminster hearing the government's instruction to retract too damaging an account of the incident. The king feared rightly enough that the Dutch community in London 'may be greatly endangered by the fury of the people'.[41]

So far the inventory of outrage had included: a book; a 'pamphlet' that was in fact the printed text of the sermon by Wilkinson to which Chamberlain was referring; a play (the text of which has not come down to us); and this very large Greenbury picture 'wherein was lively, largely and artificially, set forth those several bloody tortures and executions inflicted upon our people at Amboyna'.[42] When asked about these four items at the Privy Council, the Court of Committees could hardly deny that it had directly commissioned the painting when there it was, hanging on its premises: 'but for the fourth, they confessed ingeniously [it] to be their act; not with intent to stir up the people to tumult, but thereby to keep in their own house, a perpetual memory of that most bloody and treacherous villany'.[43] Emboldened despite the pressure it was under, the Court of Committees now rallied behind all that they had either encouraged, endorsed or commissioned. As for the anonymous *A True Relation of the Late Cruel and Barbarous Tortures and*

Execution Done upon the English at Amboyna, which had been published in London the year before (1624), 'they see nothing in that book worthy of reprehension'.[44]

In crises such as this, however, resolution can change to retreat within the hour, and indeed only three days after that grilling in Westminster, Abbot told the Adventurers how Greenbury's picture had so offended the Council that it had been agreed it should be locked in the room where it was being displayed until further notice. Ever since the evil May Day riots of 1517, holidays had made the authorities extremely nervous, and on this occasion it was feared that when the apprentices came out the gallows might go up, leading to the very massacre James I was fearing.[45] A further week, and with rumours flying between London and Amsterdam, Abbot felt compelled to write to Carleton asking him to assure the Dutch how the Company 'for their parts have denied to show their picture to divers knights and people of worth because it should not provoke them as it hath many who heretofore have taken view thereof'.[46] But with no sign of interest abating, and just ten days after the furore had begun, Buckingham sent word to Abbot that he must come to York House with Greenbury himself and a full turn-out of the Committees.[47] Buckingham had heard that the Heren XVII had made representations to Carleton as to how offensive they found those four last things that previously the Privy Council had picked out as threatening international relations.

Everyone was now under colossal strain, so much so that Abbot fell out with Greenbury. When Greenbury put in a bill of £100, the Court of Committees tried to make him responsible for the whole disaster. Thereafter, Robert Bell and Thomas Mun decided what the Company was willing to pay.[48] It turned out not much when Greenbury was deemed 'worthy to be blamed for permitting such a multitude to have the sight of it in his house, for by the view thereof not only that picture was taken away, but divers other conceipts upon the same subject were quashed; that it was a question whether they should pay for it, but if he will make a reasonable demand they will think upon him'.[49] This was rank hypocrisy when Greenbury had been urged to do his worst. Understandably aggrieved, Greenbury asked 'What about ninety?' To which answer was returned that someone had 'proffered' to reproduce the painting in brass for £30; a process Greenbury was now misinformed would require an awful lot more work than he had put into a painting that once commissioned was now disowned. A furious row ensued when Greenbury, upon being informed that his demand for £90 'was a great deal too much', was offered £40 instead. Hardly surprisingly, 'he, not therewith contented, departed'.[50] But then he needed the money and so, when by a show of hands he was offered the same a week later, he accepted.

Some of those who had seen the painting before it was burned on the orders of Buckingham had taken perverse pleasure in examining the various ways in which Towerson and Co. had met their terrible ends. But for others it had provoked mournful thoughts of a broader less transient nature. For such as eschewed sensationalism, the painting had been not so much history as allegory, when Greenbury's painting had stood as an epitome of just those attributes that the Dutch had mastered but the English could not muster; differences that many predicted would result in the VOC winning not just the day but the century. It could have been said that the whole sorry business of Greenbury's *Amboyna* demonstrated how the Company needed to be better armed against the enemy at home than the rival abroad. As the next thirty years would demonstrate, the EIC was to experience ever more acute difficulties with the Crown. How Sir Maurice Abbot at home had been browbeaten by Buckingham over one painting was an ominous portent of the way in which the Company would continue to be frustrated abroad.[51]

As for the outrage of Amboyna itself, sheriffs had been right to offer the besieged Dutchmen of London all the protection they could summon. Seven years later men were still looking for revenge, though hardly for either redress or reparation. In 1631 Thomas, Lord Fairfax, then busy learning the art of killing for Protestantism, found himself staying in Frankfurt: listening to two captains in their cups, he heard of the horrors that they had just committed deep in a gothic forest:

> One Mr Fairfax writes from Frankford to Sir Thomas Gore of Yorkshire his kinsman, that eighteen Hollanders (whereof three had their hands in torturing our people to death at Amboina in the East Indies) lying one night in the same town as they were going toward Strasbourg, being at supper in the midst of their cups and jollities, those three discoursed to the rest how bravely they had triumphed over the English at Ambonia,

and what justice they had done upon them etc. This discourse of theirs came suddenly to the ears of two English captains of horse serving under the Emperor being then in town. Who the next morning with a troop of horse met those Hollanders in a wood and bid them prepare themselves; for they must die. The Hollanders said they hoped otherwise for all the money they had was at their command. We seek not your money (said they) you may throw it upon a dunghill, if you please; tis your lives we must have in revenge of the blood of a kinsman of ours and other English which you tortured to death at Amboina, and if we had time we would inflict all those tortures of fire, water etc upon you; but being scanted thereof you shall die an easier death. You three shall be hanged first for being actors and the residue after you for being applauders and justifiers of the tragedy. After they had hang'd up sixteen they made the two surviving to cast the dice which of them should escape to carry the news into Holland. Whom, they bid to tell his Master, the States, what justice two English captains had done upon those heinous malefactors which they had suffered so many years to go unpunished.[52]

Subsequent violence seems to have been confined to the page, not the rope. The afterlife of Amboyna takes the lamentable story of Anglo-Dutch relations deep into the pages of *Gulliver's Travels* (1726), such was the folk memory of that famous outrage. In Book Three, the eponymous hero leaves Japan on the *Amboyna* where, once aboard, he fears his throat will be cut. That does not happen, but if you had asked your average Hanoverian what he thought about Gulliver trusting himself to a Dutchman of all people, he would have replied by saying that Gulliver had only himself to blame. As for life before Swift, relations between the Company and the Crown continued to deteriorate, whilst the disruption of the English Civil War represented crisis of a quite new magnitude. When England joined Holland in becoming a republic, only then would the Company begin to think it might yet find the twin supports of salvation and solvency.

Although some financial compensation was forthcoming from the Dutch over Amboyna, it was Cromwell who would give the succour that had been looked for in vain from Charles I. Cromwell's decision not to give up but to ante up was conditioned by decidedly mixed motives. Primarily, though, he wished to destroy the Dutch so England could become the pre-eminent maritime power. Therefore a strong East India Company made a lot of sense in the calculus of advantage. But however mixed Cromwell's motives may have been, the 'Protector' protected what had long been taken to be a national asset: recasting clauses, regranting charter, relaunching business. It is then upon the high road to republicanism we travel as we consider how perilously close the Company came to immolation, not only at the hands of Levellers but also as a result of the absolutist policies of Charles I.

16

DELIVERANCE

When Sir Thomas Smythe relinquished office in July 1621 there were many who thought he should have gone long before. Nevertheless, despite a plummet in his popularity in his last years, such was his vast experience that he would be retained as consultant until he died from the plague in the autumn of 1625. (Somehow it was appropriate that he went within six months of his old sparring partner James I, against whom for so many years he had wrestled to save the Company from royal predatory designs.) The choice of Sir William Halliday as Smythe's successor, and who duly took office in July 1621, had been something of a surprise. Sir Maurice Abbot had been the obvious choice. Deputy since 1615, Abbot had played a prominent part in the third round of negotiations with the VOC, though it could hardly have been said he had deported himself with the restraint that might fairly have been expected from one who was representing what had become a national institution. On the contrary, Abbot, by then an influential figure in the City, had not helped those who looked for peace with the Dutch by letting it be known that he thought them never to be trusted. This was not wise. Because of such intemperance, what had hitherto seemed an unstoppable rise within the East India Company had been stalled.

It cannot have been easy for Halliday with Smythe still active, still less when Halliday himself became so ill that the king was 'exceeding sorry to hear of the great indisposition of Sir Wm. Holladay . . . a very worthy and well deserving magistrate and minister'.[1] Clearly in pain and consequently underperforming, Halliday began by making a poor fist of reassuring Adventurers who were nervous about encroachment upon the recently captured Hormuz. There the Dutch had dashed in to join other 'Foreigners, soldiers and merchants, [to] threw off all restraint in the indulgence of their

342

passions . . . [and where] Avarice was made a science'.[2] Halliday's failure to think strategically was confounded by his inability to act decisively. A proposition that the Company should buy the entire stock of Persian silk recently come into London was no sooner made than withdrawn because 'one bale [had] disparaged the whole parcel'. Silk turned into calico and frustration into shouting as 'there rested £47,555 worth to be divided'.[3] This was enough to have made the whole City one of those canvas *leskars* that Jahāngīr pitched and Roe admired. Some thought that the stock of calico should be sold to domestic syndicates, others favoured re-export to Europe, whilst the boldest considered making tents in the desert, to which the calico could be shipped with the cooperation of the Levant Company.

But once again Halliday dithered until the point when 'Sir Randall Cranfield had given out very uncivil speeches of the Governor, Deputy and committees, which reached higher than to them, as particular men, and trenched deep into the government'. That was not the end of it, however. Damning the crew, Cranfield shot the captain through having 'offered personall disgraceful words' aimed at Halliday himself.[4] Although those who ran the Company also ran the gauntlet of abuse, this was different. It was reported that the dying Halliday was 'much grieved at a message sent him from Sir Randall Cranfield which was to have his money, or otherwise he would come by it how he could'.[5] The whole thing was the more upsetting because Randall was not only on the Court of Committees but also brother of Lionel, the powerful Lord Treasurer and earl of Middlesex. Mercifully for Halliday himself, he died before he could be harried any further.

The two men who now put themselves forward for the governorship were Sir Maurice Abbot and Sir William Cockayne. Surprisingly, it seems the latter's unhappy 'Project' of 1614, by which he aimed to satiate his own greed and increase the royal coffers, but which had surely brought forward a looming recession by turning England's most important industry upside down (see the Introduction), did not affect the appropriateness of his candidacy in the eyes of a large swathe of Adventurers.

Given the fierce competition to succeed Halliday, some of the bolder spirits among the generality had suggested something that they called the 'ballot box' should be adopted as the best means to express a general will. This was thought by the Court of Committees to be a very bad idea indeed.

Had it not fought for years to keep the hoi polloi under firm control, so why throw that up now? Thus the idea of using a box came to be 'dismissed as an innovation and alteration in the government of the company', condemned as serving nothing but the 'endangering and subversion thereof'.[6] Reaching for the strongest term of abuse that the scandalised executive could think up to dismiss such a dangerous novelty, the box was condemned as being an 'Italian device'.[7]

Once the Court of Committees saw that the General Court had come to its senses, then the election proceeded by 'erection of hands'. Thus it was that in July 1624 Abbot would be duly confirmed in what one commentator had once described in the days of old Smythe as the 'warme seat'.[8] So arose for Abbot the ticklish business of what on earth to say about the hardly lamented if recently deceased Halliday. How was the awkward transition to be massaged when some were expecting eulogy but others felt only exasperation at what they had taken to be his ineffectiveness? In the end Abbot wrapped things up faster than Halliday had been wrapped himself; a valediction damning the man not with faint but no praise at all: 'it might be expected he should say something in commendation of their late Governor, who is with God, but he should not sully his virtues through want of due expression, and therefore he would be silent'.[9] Quite so.

At the time of Halliday's death a major confrontation arose between the Company and the king's favourite, the duke of Buckingham, over what had happened when Hormuz had been taken; events which must be noticed if what Abbot came to be confronted with in the 1624 Parliament is to be properly understood. Here we have to go back almost a year to May 1623 when news arrived in London of the fall of Hormuz in 1622; that moment when the Spanish ambassador had made those vigorous protests described in Chapter 12. As we shall see, the consequences of a seemingly impetuous action on the part of the Company – without which, however, it could have been thrown out of Persia altogether for failing to do the shah's bidding – now became a major issue in the hugely conflicted Parliament of 1624.

When news of Hormuz broke in London in 1623, the king and his favourite had seen their chance. It was easy enough for Buckingham to claim that the Company had acted *ultra vires* in agreeing to attack Hormuz in a joint amphibious operation which had combined an East India Company fleet and a Persian army. As the months passed, Buckingham, gathering his forces and well armoured within his regalia as lord high admiral, had no compunction in attacking the East India Company by taking it through the High Court of Admiralty. This he elected to do for the way in which it had acted without reference to himself as the titular head of the English navy. Here lawyers argued that by virtue of Buckingham's office, his permission should have been asked before the Company had attacked. Since it had not thought to do so, a stonking financial penalty had now become payable. To reinforce that demand, fetters were promptly slapped upon the annual fleet, which as bad luck would have it was just ready to leave for the Indies during the spring of 1624. But then with a famous peremptoriness for which Buckingham was notorious, the Lord High Admiral at once forbade it to move at all.

It was by far the most serious confrontation between the Crown and Company to date. Despite this being nothing more than bribery dressed up as due process, the Court of Committees had no choice but to address so serious a crisis in its affairs. There had been unanimous agreement that the duke should get £2,000 'as well for favor shown in the business of the Dutch as to sweeten him for their future occasions, and particularly for that of Ormuz'.[10] When that was refused, the Court brought in a certain Dr Steward, presumably a specialist in maritime law, who proceeded to give it as his opinion 'that the tenth part of custom belongs to the Lord Admiral if he give any commission, but said there was no written law for it'.[11] A sizeable rump of Adventurers, now thinking it most unwise to provoke the ire of so dangerous a man as Buckingham, were all for stumping up. Nevertheless, the Court had elected to hold out, hoping it would be possible to 'give reasons that of right no tenths are due to his Lordship'.[12]

Someone had then come up with the bright idea that they should all be guided by what went on in Holland. There, whenever prizes were taken or captures made they normally handed over 5 per cent to the States and the same to the Prince of Orange. But that suggestion had been thrown out, and when the king had been petitioned to lift the warrant he had made it clear that this would not happen until there was £10,000 on the table for him and the same for his favourite. Hearing thereafter how the Company had still not come up with a straight answer, the king spluttered at Smythe, 'Did I deliver you from the complaint of the Spaniard, and do you return me nothing?'[13] Referring to what the Company had got up to in the Persian Gulf, the king also accused Smythe of doing no more than nurturing a crow's nest of pirates. So angry had the king indeed become that he proceeded to raise his demands from £10,000 to £15,000. Calming down at last, maudlin and lachrymose by turn, he then protested how he was no tyrant but would allow his subjects 'the benefit of law, and would have it so tried'.[14] This was little comfort to the ex-governor, however. Smythe had spent his life trying to keep the Company out of the courts but now he had come to feel that there was nothing for it but capitulation. And so he had scurried off with his purse between his legs. But the penalty might have been a lot worse: at least he had extracted a promise that his ships would be released for their annual departure.

Thus it had come about that the embattled Abbot had found himself fending off Buckingham's creatures in Parliament. So began such a fracas as Smythe had never had to endure. Furious gales buffeted the Company in the House as a hundred voices shouted: 'stay the Money that they send out of this land'. Here the members were raising that old canard that in exporting metal the Company was fatally weakening the sinews of the nation. This was followed up by the claim that what was represented was no less than £80,000.[15]

What ensued was a triumph for the enemies of the Company in the face of a disastrous defence mounted by those who had been inserted to defend privileges long enjoyed yet never justified. First came Robert Bateman (d. 1644), the Company's treasurer, solicitor, Master of the Skinners' Company but certainly no master of debate. Bateman sat as one of four MPs for London, and, having more ships than electors, might have been expected to sail to the rescue. Not a bit of it, because he hauled down his colours at the first cannonade. Harried by cries of 'Search the books! Search the books!', Bateman was only able to bleat about how 'he could not precisely satisfy them of the just sum', though he was fairly sure Leadenhall Street had agreed £30,000 in rials were to be sent out; provided, that was, 'His Grace' would only untie those ropes!'[16] As for another London MP, Martin Bond (d. 1643), he was reckoned less reliable than Bateman because he had backed the earl of Warwick who had defenestrated Smythe during a colossal row over the running of the Virginia Company back in 1619. But whatever Bond's true colours, the anger of the rabble could no longer be abated when it was found that 'Mr Bond . . . did but whisper a few words to the gentleman next to him and was cried to speak out else to the bar'.[17] That meant standing at the bar of the Commons to be accused of contempt of the House.

What had maddened Abbot and the braver spirits was the thought that Buckingham could yet have been forestalled if only Thomas Keridge had done what he had said he would. Keridge, abrasive sparring partner of Roe, had not only recently returned from India but had also been put on the Court of Committees when he had been delegated to get this famously frozen fleet away. Once 'extremely trusted', overnight Keridge had come to be thought 'haughty and given to avarice', though his problems were those positively medieval vices of sloth and acedia; instead of leaving the City for Blackwall with his urgent commission to throw the ropes into the Thames and get things moving by all means, Keridge had simply sat on his bottom in Botolph Lane doing absolutely nothing at all.[18] As for what Keridge's old enemy Sir Thomas Roe, who was also on the Court of Committees, thought about all this, he passed his time in Constantinople watching with some bemusement economies being undertaken at the seraglio where one official after another came to be strangled on a quotidian basis.

Back in London and up in Parliament, hearing the motion to stay the ships, Abbot, 'growing hot', now 'stood up, and made known . . . he was ready to give answer to the house what they require'.[19] With Thomas Mun as prompter on the bench beside him, Abbot pointed out how the Company did 'carry out not so much as they bring in, and not half of what they are allowed to carry'. Let no man think that the Company was getting away with anything illicit! It may have been intending to take out £40,000, but when returns were not 'interrupted', as Abbot put it euphemistically, these could be '£400,000 per annum in good real commodities, as calicoes, indigo, silk and such like, whereof calicoes alone save the kingdom the expense of at least £200,000 yearly; in cambric, lawns and other linen cloth'.[20]

Asking the House to congratulate him upon both his patriotism and his personal wealth, with some complacency Abbot informed his fellow members how after accumulating 60 pounds of gold upon his personal account, profit stemming from re-export of 'Indian commodities', he had deposited that same amount in the Royal Mint as nest egg for the nation. But then came a revelation that, if less provocative, was the more startling. He declared that out of imports valued at £400,000 'about £100,000 serves this kingdom, and the rest being exported, works itself home again, either in money, or commodities that would cost money'. The EIC had become a net exporter, not merely within Asia but to Europe and beyond. Finally the governor roundly declared 'that the Company will be ready to make this appear to the House whensoever it shall be their pleasure to call them'.[21] In the face of Bateman's collapse and Bond's censure, the governor had succeeded in hauling his company off the shoals of public opprobrium.

Having rallied things in the face of heavy parliamentary censure, Abbot's high stock was renewed when news of Amboyna arrived in London during May 1624. Adventurers had always been inclined to vote for anyone who in the modern age might have headed their flyers with 'Hate the Dutch!' in blood-red capitals. Not only could Abbot have claimed that rousing one-liner, but with news of Amboyna now breaking like hail across London, he also had no compunction in declaring how of 'their [the Dutch] treating . . . [he] found nothing but tricks to delude' and that 'all the treaties with the Dutch are but so many treacheries'.[22] So it was that Abbot came to be assured of the governorship of the EIC not for one but for fourteen years. During what was to be a tenure almost as long as Smythe had either enjoyed or endured, Abbot was to face just a single confidence vote before finally clambering out of the chair and into mayoralty. Installed at the Guildhall in 1638, from thence Abbot was to go in search of an easier life, though hardly a richer one, since for long he had been the uncrowned king of Golconda as London's principal dealer in Indian diamonds.

After the 1624 Parliament, it looked as if Abbot might find favour with the new king. First to be knighted under the new regime, 'Sir Maurice', as he had now become, at once offered his sovereign a cut diamond at the bargain price of £8,000.[23] This was a simply colossal amount of money, enough indeed to equip one grand boat to Japan and back, though if it could be identified today the 'Abbot diamond' might have outsized, outshone indeed, even the Koh-i-Noor. But amity between Charles I and Sir Maurice was not to last. What was a multifaceted relationship rarely sparkled, but was cut this way and that during what were to be long years of association which paralleled if they could not mirror that long contested relationship between

James I and Sir Thomas Smythe. Neither Sir Maurice nor his brother Archbishop George could forget what they had suffered at the hands of the regime: humiliation for Morris at the hands of Buckingham, abasement for George as isolated from James I. Disaffected Maurice and despised George, governor and archbishop alike, now fell upon the remedy of impeaching the great duke himself, though these two were merely prominent among an army of Buckingham's enemies.

The opening morning of the drama was 8 May 1626, its theatre St Stephen's Hall, Westminster. Here Buckingham stood accused of 'high crimes and misdemeanours'. As for the Company, some felt that the stakes were as high for them as for the favourite when upon the outcome of this impeachment might depend not only reputation but also survival. Matters began with Sir Dudley Digges, former ambassador to Russia and member of the Court of Committees, who spoke to Article V of the charges. The longest clause Buckingham faced, it concerned the way the favourite had treated the Company. Digges was then followed by Sir John Glanville, who as MP for Plymouth had a close interest in the proceedings since Company fleets often stopped in his constituency. Glanville argued that those who regarded the Company as being merely a sectional interest were mistaken; Parliament's grievances were the Company's grouses when, for the first time in the history of the Company, these two aggrieved powers came together against what they perceived to be ready and present danger. In threatening the Adventurers, Buckingham threatened all. If Buckingham's fiat went unchallenged, how stood the surety of the nation in the face of what Glanville argued were the whimsical, arbitrary and unaccountable actions of this pernicious man? Members feared that Buckingham was going to try to ordain whether an investor might be allowed to commit capital to a Company voyage or not – a potential exercise in prohibition, or so Glanville was arguing in the Chamber. With the Member for Plymouth, as for the whole tribe of Buckingham's enemies, the favourite's actions were but a first step towards interfering with much broader liberties than those involved in the business of an Adventurer deciding where exactly they might put their money:

> And though his Lordship may perhaps call his Act therein, a lawful
> Composition, I must crave pardon of your Lordships to say thus, That if

his supposed Right had been good, this might peradventure have been a fair Composition: The same pretence being unsound, and falling away, it was a mere naked Bribe, and an unjust Extortion; for if way should be given to take Money by colour of Releases of pretended rights, men great in power, and in evil, would never want means to extort upon the meaner sort at their pleasures, with impunity.[24]

After Glanville had sat down, the great Selden weighed in by referring to the term 'territorial waters' which he had invented and Buckingham had neglected. As Lord High Admiral, Buckingham should have done much more to protect those living in West Country constituencies who were the victims of privateer and pirate alike. As for the Dutch, Selden added that Buckingham was responsible for how they were going to be wholly unpunished for the outrage of Amboyna. This was prescient. Although there was a promise to arrest the homeward-bound Dutch East Indies fleet and escort it into Portsmouth harbour, soon enough James I would steer away from such a course: no sanctions were imposed, and nothing happened to make the VOC pay for what they had done to those poor English martyrs.

Impeachment failed. Yet if the Company lost, the cost was much higher for the Crown. Out of this trial opened a road to the Petition of Right (1628), Civil War (1642–7) and that glint on frozen steel when, upon a raw morning in January 1649, the king's head would fall from the block. As for the impeachment itself, it was now taken over by a 'Committee of the Whole House'.

Despite the failure of the main business, this move persuaded the more naive Adventurers into believing that a realignment of tectonic plates had somehow taken place. Some of them, despite the failure of the principal cause, were still determined to think well of the proceedings. And so it was that such optimists came to believe that as a result of this parliamentary challenge to the unconstitutional power of the royal favourite things had been repositioned. Whereas in the past it had been Crown and Parliament versus the Company, it now looked as if it was Parliament and Company against Crown. No lasting change took place in fact. Yet the Company had played for the highest stakes, and the prominence that it had gained from taking Buckingham head on served to shift perceptions about the place of

350

the Company in English life. Before this impeachment, the Company had never been entirely secure. But from now on it was part of the nation.

If either the cause of liberty or the promotion of dividend had brought odd fellows together, fusion was brief, benefits being forgotten in the face of renewed attacks upon the Company that had more to do with sin of greed and sourness of temperament than what anyone could discover about principle. These began when three members of the Lords moved against it: Lord Saye, the earl of Warwick and Lord Brooke. William Twisleton-Wykeham-Fiennes, 1st viscount Saye and Sele, a man of the left, described by Lord Clarendon as he 'who had the deepest hand in all the evils that befel this unhappy kingdom . . . of a proud, morose and sullen nature', had long had it in for what he regarded as an outfit making unconscionable amounts of money with little compunction and less doubt.[25] As for the dashing Warwick, he had no such worries: for him it was all about ensuring that he could sink the ships of others in order to get his own into the harbour instead.[26] Inveterate scourge of the Company, Warwick had encouraged his sister to marry Smythe's son whilst himself helping Sir Edwin Sandys eject Smythe from the Virginia Company. Of 'My Lord Brooke', however, he was merely sour at the good fortunes of others, one of many who had failed in that impossible business of being Chancellor of the Exchequer to a Stuart king.

All the while Charles I was encouraging Warwick to undermine the Company's 'ownership' of the Indian Ocean, despite himself knowing full well that the proprietary rights of the EIC had always been upheld with each renewal of its charter. Never mind scrolls: the Stuarts would always be better at inventing than respecting the law. The first indication that Charles was no friend to the Company came in June 1628 when Warwick was encouraged to claim a staggering £28,000. This Warwick demanded as 'compensation' for the seizure of two of his ships by the Company in Swally Roads; but since it had been proved that the EIC had acted only in accordance with the terms of its charter, the plaintiff got away with a mere £4,000.[27] With the failure of this government-sponsored raid, the Crown moved further from the Company towards the interlopers, of whom Warwick would always be the most dashing and the most plausible.

Warwick was mustering allies when things were not going well in the City. At this point the Company's Adventurers threatened something worse than mutiny. Many began to let it be known that they were giving up and selling up. Thus there began a thirty-year programme of systematic disruption whereby 'the sporadic resistance of the small investors and gentry [grew] into a systematic movement of opposition to the old-merchant leadership'.[28] Abbot was having a rocky time: rubbed by the king and chaffed by Parliament, he was abused by the Adventurer as he was envied by all for that colossal wealth of his. But then Abbot would always prove the most robust of governors. When about this time the Crown itself came to attack his private wealth, he had no compunction whatever into moving into the street to do battle.

The highpoint of Abbot's defiance came in the autumn of 1628, following a demand by the king for an additional levy of 2s 2d on currants imported by a syndicate including Abbot. What the Crown demanded the City denied. With an impasse settling in, Sir Nicholas Leate, governor of the Levant, Sir Morris Abbot, governor of the East India, and Sir William Garraway, fixer of just about everything else, together with two others, took it upon themselves to break into the Customs House. There, five rich men set about seizing sacks impounded by the Crown because they had flatly refused to pay the levies demanded of them. With the five now arrested, the earl of Portland appeared at the Court of Exchequer, rising to declare how the felonious 'had unmannerly and ungratefully disturbed his Majesty's gracious intentions; ungratefully . . . because that company viz. trading for Turkey, received continual favours from his Majesty, having their petitions daily granted at the council board'.[29] Of the five, Richard Chambers, lowest in profile was highest in anger. Believing this 'imposition' had made donkeys of them all, Chambers now began to bray about how 'Merchants in no part of the world are so screwed and wrung as in England. In Turkey they have more encouragement!!'[30]

If such intemperance was startling to some, to the cynical it all seemed so much expedience concealed within a sack of principle. To those who stood by these oligarchs, such a break-in had been no heist but a defence of the inalienable rights of property. Where five merchants defied the Crown, five thousand applauded intrepid men whose defiance had been fed less by greed than by a wish to uphold what they saw as a vital principle: their fixed belief that nothing should be yielded unless sanctioned by Parliament – a constitutional point that the five hoped might be conceded when they took out 'suits of replevin' against the Crown.[31] With this device came to be announced to a watching world how it is possible for very rich men indeed to eschew compensation in favour of making good law instead.

Whatever the motives of Abbot and his associates, people now began to say that the balance of the 'commonweale' had been disturbed by their actions. Yet in some ways nothing had changed. Court and City still needed each other if they were to promote their separate endeavours. Having conceded the Petition of Right, what was now to be Charles I's lonely quest for solvency, his rule without Parliament, made it still more urgent he try to make the overseas companies disgorge a moiety of their wealth. But if the king thought the money was for the taking, according to the City it was only for the talking. And so it was that the two parties fell into a fifty-year dialogue, lasting until Crown finances came to be put upon a rational basis at the Glorious Revolution. Half a century before then, however, the Crown was looking to profit and the EIC to privilege, the first needing money, the second monopolies.

The Company strained to meet demands for forced loans, whilst the king tried to break the stranglehold the EIC was maintaining upon India. Factories were awash with rumour of what might happen next whilst home base was hardly more secure. Blackwall had never justified itself financially and redundancies now had to be made: salary cuts of between 20 and 50 per cent were pushed through and traditional 'New Year's gifts' were suspended, except one for the king's master chef. After all, what would happen if he refused to sprinkle the twenty-six different dishes served up at the royal table with Company cinnamon or clove? Dockers were paid off, and it was decided to stop building ships but instead acquire them on leasehold as one way to further economies.

If it made little sense to build ships, it made less to hold Blackwall. Although it contained the largest workforce in London, the yards had always run at a loss. In 1630–1 a 'little new dock' had been built to the east of the original dry dock: the 'great' or 'double dock'. When that 'little dock' had to be widened and new gates fitted three years later, the Company's shipwright had submitted an estimate of £150. However, the project had run more than four times over budget. Springs under the foundations had begun to seep through tarpaulins that had been laid as a base for pulverised clay: this was meant to be watertight but wasn't. The whole thing was a hydraulic nightmare. From its creation in 1618 Blackwall had always been an infernal nuisance. In 1628 Adventurers had argued that 'ships by the great [fixed price] should be built in other men's docks as the Turkey [Levant] Company do'.[32] By the mid-1630s it was generally agreed how 'Blackwall doth daily exhaust their treasure in a very great proportion'. Thus it was that in 1652 Blackwall would come to be knocked down to Sir Henry Johnson (d. 1683) for £4,350 when it had actually been valued at £6,000 only two years before. The relatively disappointing sum which came to be realised . . . may have been because the Company had failed to interest the Royal Navy which had use for neither yard nor plant. Johnson himself would certainly have known about this failed negotiation and thus been in position, to some extent at least, to dictate terms notably favourable to himself.[33] Johnson therefore did very well in getting such an attractive price, for with this he acquired ten acres, three docks, two launching slips, a causeway, two cranes, a residence in red brick, storehouses and workshops in abundance. Whilst the Company was to remain one of Johnson's most important customers, he was able to produce ships far more economically than the EIC had ever done. This would be something he was to achieve with his system of 'ships' husbands' as managers for multiple projects.[34] In retrospect it must have been obvious just how badly the EIC had run its principal capital resource.

If the Company could do indigo it was hopeless with real estate. Although Smythe had been a notably intelligent manager of industrial relations, after his departure theft, strikes and over-long lunch hours (when men would wander up to Poplar High Street to booze all afternoon) meant that by Abbot's day not so much as a peck of pepper was to be found in all Blackwall. Storage had been scattered between warehouses in Leadenhall Street and cellars in the City instead.

As for head office, that had been Smythe House to begin with. But as from 1621 affairs had become marginally less disorganised when Lord Northampton's mansion in Bishopsgate, known as Crosby Hall (built 1466 as Crosby Place), became available to rent.[35] Thereafter, and still in the environs of Leadenhall Street, everyone shifted to rent down the road, first to the house of the East India Company governor Sir Christopher Clitherow, and then from 1648 to an adjoining property which was named Craven House after a former lord mayor, Sir William Craven, though the house had been built by a still earlier holder of that office, Sir Robert Lee.[36] The Company's new perch was still not giving the impression of housing a multinational though. In 1661 alterations were made across the clapboard front, where there now suddenly appeared a vast painting of a ship getting to India faster than the *Peppercorn* had ever managed. Upon the pediment above stood a factor with legs akimbo and stick in hand, body language suggesting a harassed teacher rapidly losing control of his class. Below were two giggling dolphins cavorting this way and that, while under them was the royal arms, and further below still, those of the Company. Had anyone been able to stand back, something impossible when the City was as tight as a box hedge, Craven House looked uncommonly like the stern of a ship: at least that was appropriate even if the office space within was not.

In 1710 a contract was signed to buy the property, but by now such was its perilous condition that it was decided to pull it down. Plans were drawn up by the merchant and amateur architect Theodore Jacobsen. By 1729 the Company had at last exchanged gingerbread Elizabethan for the pompous and the Portland. Between 1796 and 1800 Henry Holland and Richard Jupp gave the Leadenhall Street frontage its definitive vice-regal fifteen-bay front. Finally filled to its fullest dimensions, Holland's creation was to function as a truly international headquarters, but then only until 1858 when upon the closure of the East India Company, the proconsular magnificence of pediment and column came to be rendered dust in demolition.[37]

As for Abbot, he was less concerned about his accommodation than an accommodation with the king. But this was never going to be easy when Charles I had decided to destroy the Company by backing what he misguidedly decided might become its rival: the so-called Courten Association of Sir William Courten (d. 1636). Emerging from humble origins in Pudding Lane, greasy William had made his money between London, Amsterdam and Antwerp. Sent as an apprentice to Holland, by means of the most artful of alliances he had thereafter found his way to frauds ingenious and scams bounteous. Working among the bleaching fields of Haarlem, he had married the deaf and dumb daughter of his master and the Dutch merchant Peter Cromling. Was this a love match, an act of charity or a provident investment, who could say? But whatever the truth none could deny that out of such a union came the most handsome of rewards, a dowry that was worth £60,000 at a conservative estimate. Sticking those *stuivers* into the mire and extracting handsome returns thereby, Courten moved on to run a nice little business dedicated to the illegal export of gold from London. Heavily fined, £20,000 was Courten's loss but his gain much more.

Once a bounder but now by the 1620s something of an adventurer, with a very small 'a', Courten, together with his business partner Captain John Powell, tried unsuccessfully to lay claim to Barbados. But here the two found themselves frustrated because:

> In July 1627 the king issued a grant to James Hay, first earl of Carlisle, of the Caribbee Islands, which included Barbados. Courten tried to protect his interests by relying on a powerful supporter at court, Philip Herbert, first earl of Montgomery and fourth earl of Pembroke, who was awarded a patent for the island in February 1628. Within a month Carlisle had acquired a second patent which made it clear that Barbados was included in his original grant. Although the legal confusion caused violent turmoil in Barbados, by the end of 1628 Carlisle had asserted his authority over the island; it remained in his hands, and those of his successors, until 1646. Later efforts by Courten's descendants to receive compensation for his losses were fruitless.[38]

The debacle here was typical of Courten everywhere. This was a man forever taking a ship further than leaky timbers would allow. Finding himself frustrated in the West and turning to the East Indies instead, Courten was hoping that in contesting the monopoly of the Company there, he might destroy profit and pretension everywhere. As for what Charles I was thinking, with the Courten Association now arising in the waters of the Indian Ocean, the king began to hope that should his creature indeed succeed in ridding him of that turbulent Company, then for its part the Crown might yet reduce the EIC to such a state of privation as would require it to comply with his arbitrary demands. By such means would the Exchequer find that solvency of financial salvation which it had for so long been denied.

But if the support the king was offering for a major exercise in private enterprise to contest a larger privilege might have appeared magnanimous to the observer, the whole thing was something of an induced birth. The monarch had been slipped £10,000 with which the wily suborner Sir William now hoped to buy royal support for his various projects. As for the king, he believed that in taking trade from a source out of which he had never been able to extract sufficient funds, the Association would deliver where the Company had demurred. Charles I fell in with these interlopers because he had fallen out with the Company, thinking that a new presence in the East Indies would have the double advantage of doing what it was told and providing him with much-needed funds.

Although the Courten Association only hit the water in 1636, the year of Sir William's death, having been taken over by his son, the presence of the Association in waters contingent to the East India Company seemed at first to represent a quite new order of threat. At the start of that year, the Association fielded the *Dragon, Planter, Sun, Katharine, Anne* and *Discovery* to do commercial battle with the Company. In number this hostile assemblage represented exactly twice the complement that the EIC normally assigned to its annual fleet. Just how serious a threat the Association appeared to be has been nicely put:

> the activities of the Courten Association indicate that it was much more than a simple, if unexpectedly well-organized, group of interlopers. The Courten Association was essentially the mirror image of the East India Company: it was granted many of the same rights and privileges, but its charter was to a small group of aristocrats and merchants with direct and close ties to Charles and the royal court. In fact, the Association was a sign of a carefully orchestrated breakdown of the alliance between crown and the Company that had characterized the latter's activities in the early 1600s. It represented Charles's attempt essentially to dismantle the Company and remake the East Indies trade via a body constructed to work not with the crown, like the Company, but for the crown.[39]

But what made matters much more perilous for the Company was how Courten had found ready acceptance among disaffected Adventurers, from whom for years Abbot had been successfully concealing the real state of the Company's finances.[40] In May 1635 a row had broken out over a demand that the plain Adventurer be allowed to see where his money stood. Dissatisfied with prevarication, a committee of investigation was set up, consisting of Adventurers from the General Court but with no one on it 'pricked' from the Court of Committees. The fixers at the top of the Company regarded this as an outrageous move, and so provoked Abbot that at once he ordered books be cooked, and for fellow members of the Court of Committees to be enjoined to absolute silence about what by now was, in truth, the dire state of Company finances. Further to that, however, it was also proposed that the minutes be doctored, 'impertinent passages and discourses omitted', and a general attack be taken to this enemy within the gates:

> There are and ever have been, a malignant popular and malicious party among that Company, who only reign at their general or quarterly courts and these have ever been clamorous against the government and committees; and these either being the poorer sort and not able to bear the loss, or the envious and greater part, have in their general courts the power and concluding voice; and seeing that they could never obtain their ends, by complaint to become directors and managers, because the State countenanced the best men, it is they that now seek their revenge, to break the Company and so to have their wills by a general ruin.[41]

While Abbot was trying to beat down his critics, Charles was crying up his rivals. The king confirmed a commission under the great seal to Captain Weddell to trade at 'Goa, Malabar and China'. But worse was to follow. In June the Courten Association was permitted to 'sell in His Majesty's dominions any good imported from the East, without let or hindrance of the East India Company or others'.[42] In all this, however, there was one important concession: this was that no interloper be allowed to trade where the Company had factories. That alone may well have prevented the Company from actually going bust at this perilous moment in its affairs.

And yet things were never quite as bad as it served Abbot's turn to pretend. The Courten Association did not possess sufficient capital, boats or firepower to represent a fatal threat when the EIC owned powerful warships and lateral support. It had a wide network of contacts and entrepôts that Courten could neither rival nor use. For instance, cargo could be sent by Cairo *and* the Cape. In short, the Association was not able to break the back of the Company; indeed, for all its supposed threat, it was singularly ineffective in denting the profitability of the EIC. Nevertheless, its attempt to rival Abbot's show served to foreground the deep resentment felt by those who saw themselves as excluded from the privileged world of Crosby House. Courten had served to expose a near-fatal combination of complacency and lack of management that was alive and well where privileges were unjustified by performance and the Adventurer delayed in his dividend. The uncovering of inertia and conservatism, the exposure of complacency and myopia now announced the arrival upon the scene of a quite new species. This was the so-called new merchant, who was determined to make a *mare liberum* out of what had always been a *mare clausum*:

> The Company's monopoly had been used not merely to cut out potential competitors within its own sphere of operations, which was bad enough; it had also been used to systematically stymy those who wished to promote other, undeveloped aspects and regions of the Eastern trade. In particular, the East India Company leadership had refused to plant colonies in the East and tried to prevent others, notably the new merchants, from doing so; it had confined its trade to India, whereas the new merchants and others had long been intent on once again penetrating the East Indies, and particularly on establishing trade with the island of Pulo Run; it had ignored the Guinean trade, which the new merchants had used for its gold and ivory to complement the East Indian commerce; and it had refused to establish well-fortified settlements in India itself.[43]

What then of these supposed colonies that the Company denied and others demanded? What was the Company's position in the face of widespread demand that it adopt at least some of the practices long prosecuted by the VOC? At this juncture the Company was notably defensive, despite growing pressure to try in India what was being attempted in America. As for the Crown, it had diametrically opposed views to those of the Company, believing in colonial settlements because Charles I longed to make a tropical entrance into the theatre of empire. Whatever fantasies Charles may have entertained, however, St Helena only would be acquired by the Company at this juncture. This was because that island was the rendezvous for recovery after rounding the Cape, just as the other island Madagascar had always been the anchorage before mustering the strength needed to go on for India.

Abbot left office in 1638; leaving his successor, Sir Christopher Clitherow, in a disastrous bind. Company business collapsed alongside 'the King's Great Business': Charles I's ambition to build the most powerful fleet in the world upon the proceeds of his hated Ship Money tax. That world-beating fleet never materialised, whilst the failed exercise of raising the money to pay for it all raised hell instead. Significant interest groups were permanently disaffected, and the expedients upon which Charles now fell landed most heavily on the East India Company. Staring ruin in the face, Charles now turned upon the City to demand colossal 'Forced Loans', upon which, it was known, neither interest nor capital would ever be paid. As if the Court of Committees had not mishandled things badly enough, it now resolved to hand over to the king the entire pepper import for 1640, 607,552 pounds, for which the Crown paid 2s 1d per pound, giving itself a liability to the Company of £63,283 11s 1d.[44] Only £13,000 would ever be recovered, and then solely because the Company would hold back the equivalent in customs levies. Such improvidence, such debt, so serious an embarrassment served to ensure that the more radical of the Adventurers were better able to infiltrate the boardroom.

By 1640 it had become much easier for critics of the Company to dismantle the wall of secrecy that the Court of Committees had maintained for so long. What the radicals wanted was to trade on their own initiative; what they suggested was that the Company should provide support not command, offering storage, insurance and social care for employees who would be free to run voyages as they saw fit. In effect this would have meant becoming more like the Levant Company. But whilst Smythe would not have recognised the East India as it stood on the outbreak of war, the serious burdens under which the Company still worked between the Civil War and the Protectorate served to frustrate these new men who, thinking that they had manoeuvred themselves into the direction of the Company's affairs, could do little to reconstitute how its procedures operated.[45] After actual fighting broke out and confusion broke in following the rising of the king's standard at Nottingham in 1642, so chaotic became the state of finances that not even Newton could have done the maths. There were many syndicates and much confusion. As the radicals took over, they found syndicates running side by side: Fourth Joint Stock started in 1642, with a nominal capital of about £105,000 upon which no dividend had been declared, while the Second General Voyage was established in 1641 and the United Joint Stock in 1649. Although these tiles overlapped, water came pouring in nonetheless.

As for that court of conspiracies, the Court of Committees, it was in the most desperate trouble. Ordinary adventurers had obliged it to stand as collateral for loans that the Company had made to the royalist government at the outset of the troubles. But despite the enormous personal fortunes that each of the twenty-four members continued to enjoy, they were never going to be able to pay back the loans for which they alone stood surety. Much to their chagrin, the twenty-four suddenly discovered that the king had marched off to the Tower to seize their private supplies of gold, which each had fondly supposed was well guarded behind the portcullis.[46] As collateral, and between them, they owed the Company £276,146. That was never going to be found.

Of these radicals, none was more exceptional than Maurice Thomson: intimate of Cromwell and enemy of the Company. Adventurer since the 1630s, Thomson had exerted colossal pressure by developing his Assada Company. From the first, Thomson had conceived this as something of a rival to the EIC. It had been created out of the tattered remnants of the Courten Association, which had collapsed when Charles had thrown over his old friends in extortion.[47] Through the 1640s the Assada had tacked menacingly astern the East India Company. Armed with demonic energy, elevated with a vision of globalism revolving about an axis of self-interest, Thomson represented present threat not only to the old ways but also to the old sea-lanes of the EIC. Although the Company had no interest whatever in making money out of slavery, unlike Thomson who was a major slaver, it could have been said he represented all the EIC might have been had it only bestirred itself sooner.[48] Intrepid risk-taker and adventurer across four continents, Thomson made gold by shipping slaves to America, whilst at the same time standing as the tireless defender of liberties, providing those he represented were white. Thomson never fought a battle but he certainly laid siege to the Company. Standing on its head that famous aphorism of Coen's that war without trade and trade without war could not be accomplished, Thomson's own *obiter dictum* might have been this: trade needs colonisation as colonisation needs commerce. Bold, dictatorial and passionate, in 1644 he dispatched his own *Sun, Hester* and *James* 'to erect a new commonwealth in Madagascar'.[49]

Elected governor of the East India Company in 1645, Thomson hoped India would become the global player she had never been, and he promoted fruitful exchanges between the subcontinent, Africa and the Americas. Such lateral networks were something the Company had never contemplated before. Although Thomson's tenure as governor of the EIC lasted only two years, his friendship with Cromwell survived longer. Indeed it may have been Thomson himself who made the Protector look upon the EIC with more sympathy than he might otherwise have afforded it. Without one such as Maurice Thomson, whose revolutionary credentials not even Cromwell himself could doubt, the Protector might have sided with those who wished to dismantle the whole control system of oceanic trade. Instead, Thomson had worked to save the Company, and so in 1657 a new charter was issued. The document has not survived and so its details escape us, though its effects do not. If trade is as much about confidence as cash, with perception as profit, Cromwell's reissue certainly did the business. Years of lobbying now ended and a silver age began. Rials sailed in and ships sailed out, as Cromwell's new charter created such an impact as had not been experienced since Cumberland had banged the gavel back in 1600. Immediately following that fillip to confidence given by the new charter, £739,782 10s came to be subscribed to a new issue.[50] This was the most enormous amount of money, representing more than the three existing syndicates put together.

Meanwhile, how was the Company doing elsewhere? Persia was making steady progress, whilst returns out of Bantam permitted the retention of a factory there. The most hopeful zone of all, however, was the subcontinent, where one man had held things together. This was William Methwold, who now lies under Kensington Church Street having once lain under the stars of Sumatra.[51] Nothing if not a gentleman, William 'knew Latin, became fluent in Dutch and French, and later could converse in Persian'.[52] As a twenty-five-year-old, he had set off for India aboard the *Unicorn*, and during six months at sea had the uncomfortable experience of sharing a table messing with Edward Conok, whom we last encountered accusing the Spanish ambassador to Persia of trying to poison him. Duly arriving at his drop-off in Surat, Methwold had been dispatched to Tiku, where he had swept up the pepper as dysentery swept off the crew. If survival in Sarawak was cause for self-congratulation, success in India was greeted with the loudest huzzahs. Fusing husbandry with acumen, Methwold went on to so transform things in the kingdom of Golconda that his achievement might have merited a statue of 'Methwold of Musalipatnam' alongside that of 'Clive of India', which is to be found at the bottom of the Foreign Office steps close to Horse Guards Parade.

Musalipatnam was known to Ptolemy as 'Maisolos', from which the word 'muslin' derives, but it was Methwold who was the first to recognise fabric strong enough to sustain the full weight of the rials that the Company would eventually invest in that spinning city. Between May 1618 and October 1622, Methwold made the Company rich before doing openly what others did discreetly. He became so prodigious a private trader as demanded his uncountable, unaccountable wealth become the subject of an official enquiry.[53] Not only was Methwold required to answer charges of embezzlement, but he was also told to explain how he had managed to lose a sack of diamonds. Shrewd in business, skilled in diplomacy, Methwold accepted the freedom of the EIC when in June 1628 he was invited to head up Persia. Others would have found the salary of £500 irresistible; not him, however.

Appointed president of Surat instead, there Methwold came to be charged with recovering trade after the apocalyptical famines of 1629–32 had succeeded in killing seven million people in Gujurat and the Deccan alone. Although the famine was over by the time that Methwold arrived, all about him was valley of bones and bowl of dust. As part of his recovery programme of 1635, he engineered an accord with the Portuguese that allowed entrée to Portuguese ports, protection under its fortresses and access to its stores. The Methwold Treaty was decisive. At the Restoration the Company was able to move from the equivalent of a confined cellar in Surat to splendid reception rooms in Madras. Although the ceding of those Portuguese concessions would be part of the marriage treaty between Charles II and Catherine of Braganza (1661), the Crown might never have looked to Portugal but for how Methwold had massaged his contacts. At the General Court of the East India Company held in Merchant Taylors' Hall on 12 March 1640, in turning to Methwold, Clitherow asked him to speak to the state of India:

> The latter, after excusing himself, he not having come prepared to address the Court, says that he has been employed twenty-five years by the Company, the last seven as President at Surat, where on arriving he found everything in a miserable condition and strangely altered from when he was first in India, the people dead, the towns depopulated and all things incredibly dear; but now all is different, since the famine and pestilence ceased, the people have come down from remote parts of the country and settled again in the towns, spinners, weavers, merchants and artificers; so that manufactures are as plentiful and cheap as formerly. The peace concluded with the Portuguese is of great consequence and advantage to the Company because now the Portuguese ports are open and free, and the charge of shipping is consequently greatly reduced. Then also there is the enlargement of trade with Synda, which place yields indigo, calicoes and many other commodities, and it is of additional value because the Portuguese will not allow the Dutch to trade there. In these respects and many others Mr Methwold alleges that the trade of India etc was never in a more hopeful condition.[54]

Methwold's felicitous handling of Portugal before the Civil War was so assured that he would come to be offered the ambassadorship at Madrid in 1649. He refused. Nevertheless, by the time that he left this life and his farm on the Cromwell Road in 1653 he had found his way through pestilence in Malaya, famine in India and war in England to an assured place in Anglo-Lusitanian relations. In 1634 he had secured peace with *ultramarino* Portugal, whilst when he was acting as deputy-governor of the Company in 1639, Madras had been purchased from the South Indian *nayak* Damarla Venkatappa. Beyond that, Bombay was to be leased by the Company from the Crown in 1668. Charles II's marriage to a princess from the house of Braganza, which had provided a viceroy of Goa, had given the Company unparalleled opportunity to re-found and re-find itself. As the sand dried upon the ink of that marriage contract between England and Portugal, vast possibilities had opened to Englishmen who at the beginning of our story had fought the Portuguese carracks for a place on the ocean. Various possessions that now came England's way with Catherine of Braganza's dowry meant that England succeeded in securing the naval base of Tangier, the seven islands of Bombay, trading privileges in Brazil, and beyond that, if anything could be 'beyond' the Portuguese Empire, religious freedom for British residents in Portugal's territories.

All this represented vast promise, more likely of accomplishment because the robust policies that Cromwell had initiated Charles II now promoted. These were the great and sanguinary naval wars against the Dutch that, begun by the genius of Admiral Blake under the Protectorate, were continued with the notable courage of the duke of York under the Crown. Such hellish encounters now meant that whereas fighting between England and Holland had once been confined to the oceans of the East, henceforth the same were to be conducted upon the waters of the West. At last the Dutch were taken on with the full might of the state thrown into the hazard; not with ships shuffling in a mangrove creek but smoking on the Southern Bight and the Broad Fourteens, those submarine kingdoms that describe the waters of the North Sea lapping upon the Low Countries.

What was attempted by force was reinforced by statute. This was the celebrated Navigation Act of 1651,[55] the purpose of which was to ensure that:

> By its provisions no goods of Asiatic, African or American origin could be introduced into any part of the British dominions, except in vessels owned by Englishmen or English colonists, and manned by crews of which a majority were English nationality; while goods of European origin could only be imported either in English ships or in the ships of the countries actually producing the articles. Moreover, salt-fish could only be imported or exported in English vessels – a proviso specially prejudicial to the interests of the Dutch fishermen.[56]

It was because Charles II amplified policies the regicides had promoted that a puissant Company began to gather its strength. In 1674 the Court of Committees ordained that Bombay ought to be 'settled in the way of a colony', whilst ten years later that same city came to be decreed as the 'principal seat of our trade as well as of our power'.[57] But if there was one moment that represented a decisive break from the nostrums of old Sir Thomas Smythe, this became apparent only in 1687. This was the year when the Court of Committees acknowledged that everything had now changed. Once a factor had needed only a long grasp of commerce and a short residence in India, or as one observer put it, 'little other science was necessary when we wee [were] in the State of mere trading Merchants. But the case is altered from that since his Majestie has been pleased by his Royall Charters & during his Royall Will & Pleasure to forme us into the condition of a sovereigne State in India.'[58]

Sovereign? What was that? The only 'sovereign' Smythe would have recognised must have been that lambent disk of gold that Henry VII had ordered his Mint to strike for the first time in 1489. Though Smythe might have been incredulous at how much the EIC had changed since his day, he would have been gratified by the transformation of its balance sheet. At the end of the reign of Charles II, the East India Company was the undisputed master of European commerce in India. Success had been due to the assumption of a more rounded awareness of India than Smythe's monstrous regiment of men could have been expected to have possessed. *Homo mercatorius*, as that species had evolved, now succeeded in mustering indigenous acquaintance, mastering the exigencies of land law and mulling over the idiosyncrasies of local custom. Whereas the first English factories had cultivated little more than fibrous growths which for their very frailty might have been identified as forget-me-nots, by 1687 scattered trading stations had come to resemble that indigenous Indian rhizome which is the *Iris milesii*. Fleshy and dense, part lying on the surface part growing fingers to feel and fiddle deep into the rich compost of ethnic trading, by the late 1680s such bulbous excrescences had begun to thrust out lateral roots from whence new emergent plants made connected yet independent growth.

Thus it was that by the Glorious Revolution, 'The Worshipful Company of Merchants of London Trading into the East Indies' had become the aorta of national commerce. Fifty years later and we find Joseph Addison, England's first journalist, loving nothing better than to see the 'ministers of commerce' bring their world to his metropolis, a delight that this most urbane man of letters expressed with all the elegance that such a master of the topical essay could muster:

There is no place in the town which I so much love to frequent as the Royal Exchange. It gives me a secret satisfaction, and in some measure gratifies my vanity, as I am an Englishman, to see so rich an assembly of countrymen and foreigners consulting together upon the private business of mankind, and making this metropolis a kind of emporium for the whole earth. I must confess I look upon high-change to be a great council, in which all considerable nations have their representatives. Factors in the trading world are what ambassadors are in the politick world; they negotiate affairs, conclude treaties, and maintain a good correspondence between those wealthy societies of men that are divided from one another by seas and oceans, or live on the different extremities of a continent. I have often been pleased to hear disputes adjusted between an inhabitant of Japan and an alderman of London, or to see a subject of the Great Mogul entering into a league with one of the Czar of Muscovy. I am infinitely delighted in mixing with these several ministers of commerce, as they are distinguished by their different walks and different languages; sometimes I am jostled among a body of Armenians: sometimes I am lost in a crowd of Jews; and sometimes make one in a group of Dutchmen. I am a Dane, Swede or Frenchman at different times; or rather fancy myself like the old philosopher, who upon being asked what countryman he was, replied, that he was a citizen of the world.[59]

CONCLUSION

The East India Company survived because of the enormous profit margins that accrued from the return of just a single voyage. This meant that the Company could absorb the chaos, disorganisation and embezzlement that characterised the earliest years that have been covered in this account. Whilst profits were astounding until the depression of 1618–21, despite the knock-back those years entailed, England was a rich country, even if the Company was never a well-run organisation. England was a prosperous society with standards of living rising, cities growing and communal identities ever more sharply focused with every crisis that arose between Crown and Commons.

The great historian Lord Clarendon, who was both the central witness of the reign of Charles I and the shrewdest observer of the 'unhappy troubles' that followed it, thought the years of Charles I's 'Personal Rule' felicitous indeed,[1] a time when Europe's greatest painter Sir Peter Paul Rubens had been busy with his allegories of 'Peace' and 'Plenty' on the ceiling of the Banqueting House in Whitehall Palace. Here on these canvas roundels, Rubens had alluded to exactly those symbols that had allowed the East India Company to make its profits. The huge resources of English wealth, of which so much came to be poured into 'adventures', gave the Company both the latitude and capacity it needed to survive. That acknowledged, however, had it not been for a steady rise in per capita income, something that had been accruing for two generations or more, a series of egregious errors of management and periodic difficulties in raising capital must have resulted in a wholesale failure in that most daring of ventures: the East India Company.

The first twenty years proved the most profitable, after which the dark interval between the depression of the late 1610s and the issue of a new charter in the 1650s threatened all. Following the marriage of England and

Portugal in 1661, India, and with that the survival of the East India Company, was at last assured, even though for years before then the Company had been a national and a public affair.

The Company was fortunate in the nature and capacities of its first two governors: different temperaments for different times.[2] Sir Thomas Smythe had accrued vast experience in running City businesses, whilst relationships his family had cultivated for three generations meant that he was able to raise the money in Leadenhall Street as no one else could have done. In so narrow a compass as was the City of London in 1600, the contacts that Smythe inherited as he cultivated were of the broadest. The place Smythe occupied, first as deputy and then as governor of the Muscovy Company, turned out to be an ideal complement to the EIC. His presence within the highest counsels of the Levant Company was invaluable too, for early notice of price differentials in markets contingent to the EIC.

Whether Smythe presided over the first 'global business' remains a matter for debate, but it was 'Governor' Smythe to whom the government turned when it wanted to know about Russia; as it was to Smythe too that James I looked for the creation of a British America. Smythe's role as treasurer of Virginia, his most fraught appointment, was for all that the best of investments. Although Jamestown and its discontents disgorged violent men such as Sir Thomas Dale, one who if he did not directly sink a fleet certainly sunk its prospects, English America created such EIC stalwarts as Martin Pring and Christopher Newport. Schooled in crossing the Atlantic, in crossing the indigenous of Virginia such men emerged as commanders in the fields of East Asia.[3] Smythe's investment in America paid the richest dividends when those who had worked the Atlantic sailed the Pacific. That said, what exactly the relationship was between experience in America and endeavour in Asia is a study waiting to be written.

Smythe knew how survival was going to depend upon the East India Company keeping sweet with the Levant. Had it not been for adroit handling of such tensions as arose when these two had adjacent stalls in the same bazaar, the older company might have viewed the upstart as threat, not ally. Above all, however, it was Smythe's determination to preside over a business run by businessmen and not the landed classes that allowed his merchants to make their money, as it left those aristocrats to raise their flag. This was the critical distinction between England's graft and England's glory. It was something that saved the Company from dilution of purpose and confusion of priorities. Throughout the 'years of endurance' covered in this book, Smythe was ever for commerce and never for colony.[4]

Smythe's de facto successor, Abbot, was a very different animal. It must be doubted whether Smythe could have faced down the colossal threat that the Crown represented to the Company by the 1620s. Many a time Smythe had been forced to repel borderers when Parliament had first begun to demand control; before it had gone on to call for closure of what to many seemed little more than a parasite upon the body politic. But then with the supreme crisis of 1624, in rising to his feet, Abbot rose to such a level of oratory as Smythe could never have matched. So persuasive was Abbot's eloquence in those freighted and fretted days of a tumultuous Parliament that it can fairly be suggested that he alone saved the Company.

Although Smythe was always one for consensus when oratory was beyond his capacity, notwithstanding he was often bridled by disloyalty in ways that Abbot was never to experience. In part this was Smythe's own fault. When he had agreed to serve as governor from 1607, he had made it clear that he would act only in a part-time capacity; multifarious business interests allowed no other choice. That in turn had encouraged his detractors to get at him when matters got tough, as of course happened increasingly with the passing of the years.

Although Abbot was always controversial, Adventurers questioned neither his competence nor his commitment; they merely hated how he went about things. By contrast, there was a lingering suspicion about Smythe when in the view of many an Adventurer he had too many interests to give the Company the focus it demanded. But where both came together was how each became enormously courageous, not only in defying the Crown but also in keeping the great unwanted out of the Company. The metal of these two men was of the strongest. Here was Smythe, summoned to Whitehall Palace, where he would be confronted by a vision nicely described by Thomas Carlyle in his *Historical Sketches*:

This King James, with his large hysterical heart, with his large goggle-eyes, glaring timorously-inquisitive on all persons and objects, as if he would either look through them, and, so to speak, start forth into them, and spend his very soul and eyesight in the frustrate attempt to look through them, – remains to me always a noticeable, not unlovable, man. For every why he has his wherefore ready; prompt as touchwood blazes up, with prismatic radiance, that 'stonishing lynx-faculty.[5]

In the most fraught of audiences, Smythe would inform James how the Company would not collude in his latest scam, at the same time as, hardly 500 yards away, Abbot was facing down those in Parliament who howled for closure.

Maurice was replaced by Maurice, though things were very different when Abbot gave way to Thompson. Such a prodigy of ambition as Thompson proved allowed the most audacious to gather to themselves all those countless frustrations that others had experienced when locked out, fed up and put down; it allowed the successors to the 'dispossessed' at last to break through those barriers that Smythe had so laboriously constructed, precisely to keep them all out. Notably abrasive and fearless in challenge, Thompson endeavoured to change the nature of the Company root and branch. This happened in the 1640s when his tribe of 'new merchants' tried to stand the Company on its end. Though in many respects that revolution failed, Thompson led to Cromwell who, leading the nation in a national struggle, made the predictable decision that if England was to be the first maritime power, it had to support the first in profitability within the City. Hence the 1657 renewal of the charter that changed everything.

In this account much has been accounted for, though more remains to be explored. The place of women requires foregrounding in any future study.[6] Women were important investors, and an unknown number took their fights to the enemy: many occasions of injustice provoked wives, mothers and widows to go to law. We think of Mrs Wickham coming up from Bristol to the London law courts where she conducted an aggressive campaign for redress over a period of three years – and won. But the part women played was not merely litigious. There were many female investors among the Adventurers, and some among the rentiers too; women to whom the Company was beholden in many an important respect. For example, the Court Minutes of 15 February 1625 begin with a record of how the countess of Warwick 'had willingly condescended to pleasure the Company with the loan of her house for the entertainment of the Persian ambassador gratis betwixt this and Lady Day next, but if for any longer time she would expect rent'. It was then ordered that an inventory be taken of 'such goods and household stuff as the Countess lends to the Company upon this occasion'.[7] Unlike with the VOC, where women regularly travelled out to Dutch colonies in the Far East, English women were not allowed to live in Asia, but it would appear that they were free enough to lord it in the City.

The Company may have made London a far more racially mixed community. If all the business was importing those famous spices, what became a lot hotter than any paprika was the controversy that arose out of the import of new ethnicities. If some think 'global' a wholly anachronistic word to describe businesses in the early modern world, it is fair to describe *Peppercorn* as a multinational. Such was the decimation caused by death and disease on board our favourite ship that there was always a high proportion of aliens making up the crew of any voyage from which *Peppercorn* returned. Much to the regret of the poor law authorities who were charged with the unenviable task of making sure London did not go up in smoke because of social unrest, many of these 'Japoners', 'Negars' or 'Moors' coming to Blackwall aboard the *Peppercorn* returned neither to Bantam nor Bungo.

This was not a 'problem' that had been solely caused by the Company, though its activities certainly exacerbated such tensions as may have arisen from too many people of different cultures living in the cramped and sordid tenements of east London. Rather, much immigration had been as a result of political unrest and war in the Mediterranean and North Africa. Displacement caused by twenty years of intermittent fighting between England and Spain had caused so many illegal immigrants to risk their all in getting to England that by the turn of the seventeenth century the government had come to feel it imperative to reduce the numbers by whatever means available. Among the Cecil papers is what is described as a 'Minute'. Dated 1601, the same year in which Smythe sent off his first voyage, the paper shows an irritated Elizabeth I reaching out to a well-tried people-trafficker who might sink the problem without trace:

> Whereas the Queen's Majesty is discontented at the great number of
> negars and blackamoors which are crept into this realm since the troubles

between her Highness and the King of Spain, and are fostered here to the annoyance of her own people, which want the relic consumed by these people, who are mostly infidels without understanding of Christ and his Gospel, in order to discharge them out of this country, her Majesty hath appointed Caspar Van Zeuden, merchant of Lubeck, for their transportation and a man who at his own charge has brought from Spain several Englishmen who otherwise would have there perished: this is to require you to assist him to collect such negroes and blackamoors for this purpose; and if any refuse to deliver such blackamoors to him, you are to persuade them to comply and if they will not to certify their names to us.[8]

In a recently published study of how commerce worked between the accession of James I and the outbreak of Civil War, it has been suggested that overlap between the various trading bodies of the City was critical.[9] Doubtless so, but without a synoptic account of how precisely the East India and the Levant operated in their adjacent zones, something we currently lack, it is impossible to know just how the East India Company competed for investment if not markets. Writing about what that same author describes as the rising status of the merchant class, a markedly more complacent view is offered than mine as to the relationship between the City of London and the City of Westminster. Although Smythe and Abbot were often closeted with the king, such voyages from one end of London to the other were usually pilgrimages of grief rather than causes for congratulation. Truth is, there was always a huge cultural divide between court and commerce no man could reconcile. This was that period in the history of England's financial institutions when statesmen looked in vain for the means wherewith to put Crown finances on regulated, proportionate, predictable and clear foundations.

Take the baneful career of Lionel Cranfield, from whose family Smythe was to buy his estate at Sutton Sutton-at-Hone. Baltic merchant and main mast of the Eastland Company, Cranfield became first Chancellor of the Exchequer then Lord Treasurer. That said, he was never the courtier because every fibre in his merchant's body was set against the profligacy that characterised the royal household. Duly ennobled as an improbable first earl of Middlesex, Cranfield himself came to be undone by enemies in Parliament who, finding themselves unable to countenance his attempts at retrenchment, impeached him. Cranfield's 'crime' had been his determination to make the executive live within its means; something that no company in the City could afford to ignore if it was to survive. But whilst it may be doubted whether relations between the City and the Court were as positive and productive as have been suggested, there were a number of families who, within just two generations, moved with silken ease from the counting house to the country house.

What, too, of the social origins of that most interesting group to emerge from the Adventurers: the factors? What sort of men were they? Had their souls been lost to Mammon? Were they simple misfits or simply incorrigible romantics? Maybe all three rolled into one? Could they have been like little John Milton who, brought up in Bread Street, could never read enough about Richard Cocks and his drunken friends? For Milton, the Far East was Paradise and Pandemonium rolled into one. So taken was England's first poet with all things east of Aden that he was crazy enough to think of editing Hakluyt and Purchas, writers whose combined output comes in at about two million words.

One of the contrasts between the VOC and the EIC is the rich deposit of material culture belonging to the former and its relative absence from the latter. We recall that portrait of Laurens Real for which no equivalent exists within the galleries of Britain. Why not is a question worth trying to answer. So too, we have all those bird's-eye views of Dutch forts fronded in palms and framed less as works of art than badges of history. They don't exist in England because English forts did not exist in the East Indies. Wander and wonder at the Rijksmuseum's collection of *Delfts blauw* (after 1620), ceramic jars upon which might be observed an elephant dancing a gig or 'Confucius' sitting easy with his nice medley of narcotics at the end of a hookah. Such things are entirely absent from the cultural inventory of the early East India Company. But what is absent within the British Museum is present within the churches and graveyards of the realm. Second only in ubiquity to the memorials to the fallen of the two great wars are the tributes to those who served in the Company. What is suspended from an aisle or secluded under an oak suggests a rich deposit of word and image. From St Mary's Carisbrooke to the East Kirk of Cromarty, from 1625 to 1825, from the internment of Governor Smythe to the apotheosis of Officer Thomson, is to be found the abundant archaeology of this once great enterprise.[10]

That conceded, Governor Smythe was a voracious collector of the exotic. Whilst no inventories have survived to tell us what he owned, in our imaginations we have many a 'night piece' to summon up. Lingering in the mind's eye, if not on the walls of the National Gallery, are pictures of auctions suggesting what delights must have regaled these merchants when lots came up for sale. Men crouched in the lantern light as a ten-bay Japanese lacquer screen fell to a candle under the shadowed vault, these were fabulous treasures that having come into the Pool of London came up for grabs in the precincts of the Royal Exchange. Sometimes such things would be *nature-morte*, though often enough the lots were very much alive in tooth and claw: parrots and marmosets, lyre birds and lions, all to be distributed between the aviaries of the Strand and the cages of the Tower. What part, then, did the East India Company play in making for that marked contrast between the interior of Shakespeare's lodgings in Silver Street and Pepys's house in Seething Lane during the sixty years that separated the respective lives of these famous authors? Their dwellings were only a mile apart, but were the appearances a great deal further than that? What effect did the activities of the Company have on social intercourse in the seventeenth century? Such aspects of material culture, and how the Company affected taste in early modern England, assuredly needs further excavation.

These then are just a few of so many questions which, like pepper bursting from a sack in the hold of the *Peppercorn*, spill out of every file in the East India Company library. Meanwhile, it is to be hoped that some light has been thrown on what was the improbable triumph of the Adventurers. These were men, and women too, whose energies created what by 1657 had set itself on the road to becoming the most successful and also the most challenging business organisation the world has ever witnessed. But it is crucial to note that if there was much 'anarchy' in the rise of the EIC, assuredly there had been nothing 'relentless' about its genesis.[11] The East India Company was from its earliest days a parlous, improbable institution which survived a hazardous birth, but only just. As Orpheus counselled Eurydice, historians do well to look resolutely forwards, not backwards.

TIMELINE

Date	Events in England	Events in Europe	Events in Africa, Asia and the Americas	England in Africa, Asia and the Americas	Europe in Africa, Asia and the Americas
1405–33			Explorer and diplomat Zheng He extends China's maritime and commercial influence over the Indian Ocean		
1488					Bartolomeu Dias sails round the Cape of Good Hope
1492					Columbus lands in the West Indies, believing it an outlier of Asia
1493		Papal bull issued by Alexander VI divides maritime world between Spain and Portugal			
1494		Treaty of Tordesillas confirms Iberian 'rights' to the oceans			
1509–15					Afonso de Albuquerque creates Portuguese colonies from Arabia to China
1511–12					Portugal takes Malacca and establishes ties with the Moluccas or 'Spice Islands'

1520			First Portuguese embassy arrives in China, to be expelled two years later
1526	Babur becomes first Mogul emperor		
1533	Henry VIII's *Act of Supremacy* declares 'This realm of England is an empire'		
1536	Dissolution of the monasteries followed by massive transfer in land ownership, leading to profound economic and social change		
1544	Henry VIII establishes the Navy Board, signalling the rise of an English marine		Spanish discovery of silver mines in Potosí, Peru
1553–4		Richard Chancellor discovers an all-sea route to Russia; Ivan IV grants English merchants 'free marte with all free liberties throughout my whole dominions'	

Date	Events in England	Events in Europe	Events in Africa, Asia and the Americas	England in Africa, Asia and the Americas	Europe in Africa, Asia and the Americas
1554	Marriage of Queen Mary and Philip II, entangling England with Spain				
1555	Founding of the Muscovy Company (6 February)			Richard Chancellor attempts to find a way to 'Cathaia' from Moscow	
1556			Accession of the Mughal emperor Akbar		
1557				Antony Jenkinson leads trade delegation to Moscow	Portuguese settle at Macao
1558	Elizabeth I succeeds Mary; Sir Thomas Smythe probably born	First Russian trade delegation reaches London			
1562			African slave trade initiated by Sir John Hawkins	Jenkinson travels to Persia and has an audience with the Shah at Kazvin	
1565	Tobacco introduced into England, a narcotic which would later be the staple export of the English colony of Virginia (Charter: 1606)		Fall of the Vijayanagar empire in central India		First Spanish settlement on the Philippines which would become the city of Cebu

1566	Dutch begin 'Revolt of the Netherlands' against Spain				
1567		Muscovy Company given monopoly over White Sea trade			
1569			Introduction of the Mercator Projection, assisting mariners to steer a course over long distances		
1570				Publication of the world atlas *Theatrum Orbis Terrarum* by Abraham Ortelius; with some material supplied by English cartographers, Jenkinson among them	
1571		Royal Exchange opened by Elizabeth I as rival to Antwerp's Bourse			Defeat of the Ottoman navy at Lepanto	The Spanish create capital in Philippines at Manila
1573		Sir John Hawkins made Treasurer of the Navy Board, pruning corruption and improving hygiene aboard English vessels			Akbar conquers Gujurat	

Date	Events in England	Events in Europe	Events in Africa, Asia and the Americas	England in Africa, Asia and the Americas	Europe in Africa, Asia and the Americas
1576			Akbar conquers Bengal	Sir Martin Frobisher sails in quest of a north-west passage to China	
1577				Sir Francis Drake sets out in the *Pelican* (*Golden Hind*) to circumnavigate the globe	
1579	Christopher Saxton publishes the first English national atlas		Akbar invites the Jesuits to his court	John Newbery's first journey into the Middle East	Portuguese set up trading station in Bengal
1580		Philip II seizes the throne of Portugal		William Harborne sent to Constantinople as ambassador, creating the conditions for the founding of the Levant Company; Muscovy Company unsuccessfully seeks a north-east passage	
1581			Akbar conquers Afghanistan	Sir Francis Drake returns from his circumnavigation	
1582	Richard Hakluyt publishes *Divers Voyages touching the Discovery of America*			Sir Edward Fenton's disastrous voyage to the East Indies	First Jesuit mission to China; the Jesuits already claim 150,000 converts in Japan

1583			John Newbery and Ralph Fitch depart for Newbery's third journey to the East	
1585	Treaty of Nonsuch grants Elizabeth I sovereignty over the United Provinces, which she rejects	Alessandro of Parma sacks Antwerp and so destroys its commercial pre-eminence in Europe		
1586	William Camden publishes *Britannia*		Abbās the Great becomes shah of Persia and breaks the power of internal enemies	Ralph Fitch reaches Pegu (Bago, Myanmar)
1587	Christopher Marlowe's *Tamburlaine* romanticises the 'East'		Akbar annexes Kashmir; Hideyoshi issues an edict banning missionaries but allowing traders to remain: Japanese gesture politics	
1588	Spanish Armada hugely boosts the confidence and reputation of the English marine; Publication of Anthony Ashley's translation of Waghenaer's *Spieghel der Zeevaerdt* as *The Mariners Mirrour*			

Date	Events in England	Events in Europe	Events in Africa, Asia and the Americas	England in Africa, Asia and the Americas	Europe in Africa, Asia and the Americas
1589	Richard Hakluyt publishes first edition of *Principall Navigations*				
1591				Sir James Lancaster becomes the first Englishman to make a commercial survey of the East Indies (returns 1594); Fitch returns to London after travels spanning more than eight years and as far as Malacca	
1592	Foundation of the Levant Company, following amalgamation of Turkey and Venice Companies; Edward Wright and Emery Molyneux construct first English globes; Portuguese carrack *Mãe de Deus* is towed into Falmouth with its fabulous hoard	Jan Linschoten publishes his *Itinerario*, a triumphant exercise in commercial espionage			

1595					Cornelis de Houtman takes the first Dutch fleet to the East Indies
1596			Peace treaty between Japan and China after Japan fails in its invasion of South Korea		
1598	Hakluyt publishes second enhanced edition of *Principall Navigations*	Death of Philip II of Spain	Hideyori comes to power in Japan		
1599–1600	Foundation of the EIC; Publication of Edward Wright's *Certaine Errors in Navigation*				
1600	Russian trade delegation arrives at Gravesend; First Charter of the EIC (31 December)			Elizabeth I asks Akbar for English trading privileges in India	English pilot William Adams brings the Dutch to Japan for the first time
1601	Sir Thomas Smythe, first governor of the EIC and sheriff of London, is sent to the Tower on 2 March 1601 for supposed complicity in the Essex rebellion; EIC's First Voyage				

Date	Events in England	Events in Europe	Events in Africa, Asia and the Americas	England in Africa, Asia and and the Americas	Europe in Africa, Asia and the Americas
1602		Foundation of the VOC		EIC is established at Bantam (Banten)	
1603	James I succeeds Elizabeth		Ieyasu, first shōgun of the Tokugawa dynasty	Sir Thomas Smythe, as ambassador to Russia, gains a new grant for the Muscovy Company	
1604	Treaty of London ends twenty-year war with Spain	Henri IV founds the Compagnie des Indes Orientales			
1606	Charter of the Virginia Company: Sir Thomas Smythe elected first Treasurer	Publication of the *Mercator-Hondius Atlas*: it runs to fifty editions in multiple languages during the seventeeth century			
1608				EIC's Third Voyage arrives in India and the EIC opens for business there; William Hawkins represents the Company at the Moghul court	

1609	Renewal of the East India Charter	Publication of Hugo Grotius's *Mare Liberum*; Twelve Years' Truce between Spain and the United Provinces begins		VOC establishes a base at Hirado in Japan and at Pulicat on the Coromandel coast
1610	EIC's Sixth Voyage		Portuguese fall out of favour in Japan; henceforth the Dutch and Spanish are permitted to trade with 'red seal passes'	
1611	Salisbury's 'Great Contract' fails; subsequently Crown attempts to milk EIC for money; First performance of Shakespeare's *The Tempest*, inspired by shipwreck story of Sir Thomas Gates of the Virginia Company	Robert Middleton sent to Amsterdam to seek accord between the EIC and the VOC	EIC establishes a factory at Masulipatam on the Coromandel coast	
1612			Captain Best defeats a large Portuguese naval force off the coast of Gujurat	

Date	Events in England	Events in Europe	Events in Africa, Asia and the Americas	England in Africa, Asia and the Americas	Europe in Africa, Asia and the Americas
1613	Adoption of medium-term 'joint-stock' financing for EIC; First round of talks to settle differences between EIC and VOC held in London (15 April)			Arrival of the *Clove* in Hirado; EIC opens for business in Japan; EIC establishes a factory at Surat	
1614	Disastrous Cockayne project initiates trade war with the Dutch and depresses the English cloth trade for decades		Tokugawa shogunate issues a decree ordering the exclusion of Christian missionaries, with serious repercussions for Western companies' prospects within Japan		Jan Pieterszoon Coen arrives at Bantam
1615		Second round of talks to settle EIC–VOC differences held in The Hague		EIC dispatches the *Dragon, Peppercorn* and (carrying Roe and his retinue) *Lyon* to India; Roe begins his four-year embassy to the 'Great Mogul'; Downton defeats a large Portuguese naval squadron off the coast of Gujurat	

Year					
1616			Persecution of Christians in Japan begins in earnest, following resumption of sole power by shōgun Hidetada; Restriction of European ships to Nagasaki and Hirado only		Dutch establish their factory at Surat
1618	Major economic depression in England; EIC opens Blackwall Dock	Thirty Years' War begins		Sir Dudley Digges negotiates a loan to the Russian government with funds by the Muscovy and EIC	
1619	Joiners strike at EIC docks in Blackwall; The *Royal Anne* sinks and with it, the reputation of Smythe; Third round of talks to resolve EIC–VOC dispute held in London				VOC and EIC establish factories at Pegu (Bago, Myanmar); Jan Pieterszoon Coen founds Batavia (Jakarta) for the VOC
1621	Sir William Halliday elected governor of the EIC; Publication of *The Lawes or Standing Orders of the East India Company*, the EIC rule book; Smythe's ally Lord Chancellor Bacon successfully impeached by Parliament			Roe begins seven-year embassy to the 'Grand Sophy' at Constantinople	

Date	Events in England	Events in Europe	Events in Africa, Asia and the Americas	England in Africa, Asia and the Americas	Europe in Africa, Asia and the Americas
1622				Persian army and EIC fleet take Hormuz from the Portuguese	
1623		Failure of the 'Spanish Match'		Massacre of Amboyna (Feb–Mar); English factory at Hirado closes; First commercial treaty with Russia negotiated by Sir John Merrick	
1624	Sir Morris Abbot elected governor of the EIC; Death of Sir Noël de Caron, hugely influential Dutch ambassador to England; Smythe's long-term business ally and friend, Lord Treasurer Middlesex, successfully impeached for corruption by Parliament			James I makes Virginia a Crown colony, taking it out of the hands of private enterprise	VOC establishes factory on Formosa (Taiwan) in the hope of breaking into China
1625	Charles I succeeds James; Death of Sir Thomas Smythe (4 September)				

1626	The representatives of the EIC in Parliament take the lead in the attempted but unsuccessful impeachment of Buckingham			
1627	Posthumous publication of Sir Francis Bacon's *New Atlantis*, in part inspired by pilot William Adams;			
1628	Petition of EIC grievances submitted to the Commons			Spanish treasure fleet captured by the Dutch at Matanzas Bay, Florida
1633		Beginning of *sakoku*, the Japanese exclusion policy	William Methwold arrives in Surat as 'President', transforming EIC prospects in Gujurat after the Great Famine	
1634	Charles I imposes Ship Money to pay for the Navy			

Date	Events in England	Events in Europe	Events in Africa, Asia and the Americas	England in Africa, Asia and the Americas	Europe in Africa, Asia and the Americas
1635	Creation of the Courten Association to try to break the monopoly of EIC				Dutch oust the Portuguese from Formosa
1636					Dutch established in Ceylon
1637				EIC sets up a factory at Canton	
1638	Sir Christopher Clitherow elected governor of EIC Maurice Thomson founds the Assada Company out of the shell of the Courten Association				
1639				Madras purchased by EIC from the South Indian *nayak* Damarla Venkatappa; EIC establishes a factory at Fort St George, Madras	Portuguese forbidden to enter Japan
1640		Portugal gains independence from Spain		EIC found a factory on the Hooghly River in Bengal	

Year			
1641	Marriage of William, son of Frederick Henry of Orange, to Mary, daughter of Charles I: so begins a congruence of the ruling families of England and Holland		Malacca captured from the Portuguese by Van Diemen; members of a Portuguese mission to Japan beheaded for ignoring the exclusion laws
1642	English Civil War begins (22 August)		Dutch in Japan confined to Dejima, an artificial island in Nagasaki Bay
1644			
1647	Maurice Thomson becomes a director of EIC then its governor		
1648		Peace of Westphalia closes the Thirty Years' War; formal recognition of the United Provinces	
1649	William Methwold negotiates merger between EIC and Assada Company		
1650			EIC annexes St Helena

Date	Events in England	Events in Europe	Events in Africa, Asia and the Americas	England in Africa, Asia and the Americas	Europe in Africa, Asia and the Americas
1651	First Navigation Act, aimed at protectionism for English shipping				
1652	First Anglo-Dutch War				Dutch found Cape Town
1653	England and Portugal move into accord with a commercial treaty				
1657	Cromwell renews the EIC charter; massive capital subscription follows; EIC introduces permanent joint-stock funding				
1662	Marriage of Charles II and Catherine of Braganza; Tangier and Bombay ceded to British Crown as a result; Royal Society obtains royal charter			The Company of Royal Adventurers Trading into Africa set up by Charles II under a royal charter	

Year		
1664	Colbert establishes French East and West Indies companies as rivals to England	
1668		Bombay and its seven islands leased by EIC from the Crown; EIC builds Fort William on site later known as Calcutta
1674		EIC Court of Committees ordains 'Bombay be settled in the way of a colony'
1685		Outbreak of war between EIC and Emperor Aurangzeb
1687		EIC transfers its headquarters from Surat to Bombay
1688	William of Orange becomes king of England	
1689		Foundation of English factory at Calcutta

NOTES

PREFACE

1. Anna Winterbottom, *Hybrid Knowledge in the Early East India Company World*, Basingstoke, 2015, p. 60.
2. For the survival of material culture associated with the Dutch East Indies at this time, see: Julie Berger Hochstrasse, *Still Life and Trade in the Dutch Golden Age*, New Haven and London, 2007, *passim*.

INTRODUCTION

1. It would be more accurate to say that there were 101 interested parties since there is sometimes more than one person against a number: for instance, '81. Augustine Skinner, Robert Brooke and Thomas Westwray'. W. Noël Sainsbury, ed., *Calendar of State Papers Colonial* (hereafter Sainsbury, *Papers*): *East Indies, China and Japan, 1513–1616*, London, 1862, no. 256, 22 September 1599, p. 101: 'The Names of such person as have written with their own hand, to venture in the pretended voyage to the East Indies (the which it may please the Lord to prosper), and the sums that they will adventure, the xxii September 1599, viz.'
2. Astrid Friis, *Alderman Cockayne's Project and the Cloth Trade*, Copenhagen, 1927, *passim*.
3. For Hicks as lender to the Crown, see Robert Ashton, *The Crown and the Money Market*, Oxford, 1960, *passim*.
4. T.D. Whitaker, *The History and Antiquities of the Deanery of Craven, in the County of York*, ed. A.W. Morant, Leeds and London, 1878, vol. 2, p. 354.
5. Sainsbury, *Papers, 1513–1616*, no. 268, 'Court Minutes of the East India Company', 1 October 1600.
6. Ibid., no. 286, 3–28 February 1601, under 17 February.
7. Sir William Wilson Hunter, *History of India: From the First European Settlements to the Founding of the East India Company*, New York, 2011 (reprint), vol. 7, p. 4.

1. THE SMOKY AYER OF SPANISH GREATNES

1. For the tentative then tyrannical engagement of the Portuguese with the ancient peoples of the Atlantic, see David Abulafia, *The Discovery of Mankind: Atlantic Encounters in the Age of Columbus*, New Haven and London, 2008, *passim*.
2. Daniela Bleichmar, Paula De Vos, Kristin Huffine and Kevin Sheehan, eds, *Science in the Spanish and Portuguese Empires, 1500–1800*, Stanford, 2009, p. 90.
3. 'New Christians' were Jews who had converted to Christianity, usually to avoid persecution.
4. A.R. Disney, *A History of Portugal and the Portuguese Empire*, vol. 2: *The Portuguese Empire*, Cambridge, 2009, p. 158.

5. Bernardo Gomes de Brito, ed., *História trágico-marítima, em que se escrevem cronologicamente os naufrágios que tiveram as naus de Portugal, depois que se poz em exercício a Navegação da Índia*, 2 vols, Lisbon, 1735–6.

6. No historian, as opposed to economist, would have such an influence on the thinking of the East India Company as Hakluyt until the early nineteenth century when Mill and Macaulay published books as sententious as they were influential. From the very first, Hakluyt hovered in the office as the ghost behind the desk. See Sainsbury, *Papers, 1513–1616*, no. 286, 16 February 1601: 'Warrants, including 10l (£), to Mr Hakluyt, for his travels, taken in instructions, and advices touching the preparing of the voyage, and for his former advices in setting the voyage in hand the last year'; also '30s for three maps by him provided and delivered to the Company'.

7. Donald F. Latch, *Asia in the Making of Europe: A Century of Wonder*, vol. 2, book 1: *The Visual Arts*, Chicago, 1970, p. 13.

8. M.N. Pearson, *The New Cambridge History of India*, vol. 1: *The Portuguese in India*, Cambridge, 1987, p. 78.

9. Anna Jackson and Amin Jaffer, eds, *Encounters: The Meeting of Asia and Europe, 1500–1800*, London, 2004, cat. no. 18.15: 'Six-panel screen depicting the arrival of a Portuguese ship', ink, colour and gold leaf on paper, Japan, *c.* 1603–10.

10. Latch, *The Visual Arts*, pp. 64–5.

11. Pearson, *The Portuguese in India*, pp. 43–4.

12. Ibid., p. 44.

13. K.N. Chaudhuri, *Trade and Civilisation in the Indian Ocean: An Economic History from the Rise of Islam to 1750*, Cambridge, 1985, p. 69.

14. David Veevers, 'Gender', in William A. Pettigrew and David Veevers, eds, *The Corporation as a Protagonist in Global History, c. 1550–1750*, Leiden and Boston, 2019, ch. 19, p. 195.

15. Pearson, *The Portuguese in India*, p. 118.

16. Georg Schurhammer, *Francis Xavier: His Life, His Times*, Rome, 1973–82, vol. 2, p. 540.

17. António da Silva Rego, intro., *As Gavetas da Torre do Tombo*, Lisbon, 1960–70, vol. 3, p. 213.

18. For Jerónimo Xavier's biography see Jorge Flores, ed., *The Mughal Padshah: A Jesuit Treatise on Emperor Jahangir's Court and Household*, Leiden and Boston, 2016, pp. 14–15 and 43–44.

19. 'A Jesuit priest with a book, folio from the Selim Album', attrib. to the artist Kesu Das. Chester Beatty Library, Dublin, inv. no. 44.5. This is from an album of thirty miniatures which had been assembled into a small album for Prince Salim, as Jahangir was called, when he resided at his own court in Allahabad.

20. Flores, ed., *The Mughal Padshah*, p. v and Fig. 3.

21. Nathan Wachtel, 'The Marrano Mercantilist Theory of Duarte Solis Gomes', *Jewish Quarterly Review*, vol. 101, no. 2 (Spring 2011), pp. 164–88.

22. Pieter Emmer and Femme Gaastra, eds, *An Expanding World: The European Impact on World History 1450–1800*, vol. 13: *The Organization of Introceanic Trade in European Expansion 1450–1800*, Aldershot, 1996, pp. 59–60.

23. Sir William Foster, ed., *The Embassy of Sir Thomas Roe to the Court of the Great Mogul, 1615–1619, as Narrated in his Journal and Correspondence*, 2 vols, Hakluyt Society, 2nd ser., part 1, 1899 (hereafter Foster, *Roe Journal*), vol. 1, p. xxxiv.

24. Niels Steensgaard, 'The Dutch East India Company as an Institutional Innovation', in Emmer and Gaastra, eds, *An Expanding World*, pp. 133–55: p. 152.

25. Sanjay Subrahmanyam, *The Portuguese Empire in Asia, 1500–1700: A Political and Economic History*, London and New York, 1993, p. 108.

26. Ibid., p. 7.

27. For the first appearance of this immensely influential view see Max Weber, *Die protestantische Ethik und der Geist des Kapitalismus*, Tübingen, 1904–5, *passim*.

28. Niels Steensgaard, *Carracks, Caravans and Companies: The Structural Crisis in the European-Asian Trade in the Early 17th Century*, Copenhagen, 1973, p. 93.

29. See Duncan T. Bentley, 'Niels Steensgaard and the Europe–Asia Trade of the Early Seventeenth Century', *The Journal of Modern History*, vol. 47, no. 3 (Sep. 1975), pp. 512–18: p. 512. For a still greater upbeat and more forthright view of Portuguese achievements see 'Sanjay' Subrahmanyam, *The Portuguese Empire in Asia*, p. 142, in which the writer confidently posits the argument that 'the hypothesis of "decline" can be contested with the greatest of ease'.

30. Stephen Alford, *London's Triumph: Merchant Adventurers and the Tudor City*, London, 2018, p. xiii.

31. Ibid., p. 9.

32. Ibid., pp. 138–9.

33. See Byron's *Don Juan*, and Richard Ford's contemptuous dismissal of Spain's roads in his *Handbook for Travellers to Spain*, London, 1845, *passim*. Ford's *Handbook* established in the British mind, as no other publication in English has ever done, the topos of the amiable, idle and incompetent Spaniard, the afterlife of which extended to the witless Spanish waiter Manuel in John Cleese's *Fawlty Towers* (BBC, 1st series 1975, 2nd series 1979).

34. John Guy, *Gresham's Law: The Life and World of Queen Elizabeth I's Banker*, London, 2019, pp. 140–2.

35. 'Contemporaries claimed that as many as 18,000 people were slaughtered in Antwerp, though the death toll may have been in the hundreds.' Ritchie Robertson, *The Enlightenment: The Pursuit of Happiness, 1680–1790*, London, 2020, p. 86.

36. 'By the mid-seventeenth century Portuguese Brazil was far more important to the home land than the tottering Estado da Índia.' C.R. Boxer, *Portuguese India in the Mid-Seventeenth Century*, Delhi, 1980, p. 4.

37. Sir William Foster, *England's Quest of Eastern Trade*, London, 1933, pp. 136–7.

2. NORTH SEA NATIONS

1. Guy, *Gresham's Law*, p. 123, describes the wheel-lock as 'one of the landmark technological innovations of the sixteenth century'. Its portability alone provoked fear of easy assassination during the French Wars of Religion. Perhaps it is this pistol and not that proficiency in languages that so many of the earliest factors of the East India Company possessed in abundance which accounts for the survival of the early modern English travelling salesmen, intrepid enough to traverse the steppes of Central Asia, of which there were so many instances during the sixteenth century.

2. Lance Jenott, ed., 'Anthony Jenkinson's Explorations on the Land Route to China, 1558–1560', https://depts.washington.edu/silkroad/texts/jenkinson/bukhara.html.

3. Ibid.

4. Natasha Glaisyer, *The Culture of Commerce in England 1660–1720*, Woodbridge, 2006, *passim*.

5. Although a north-west passage was only to be achieved in 1908 by Roald Amundsen, Baffin's ghost might have been consoled to learn that the accuracy of Baffin's tidal and astronomical observations taken from the *Discovery* would be verified when Sir William Parry was to sail through the same waters in 1821.

6. Foster, *England's Quest*, pp. 8–9.

7. Sophie Lemercier-Goddard, 'George Best's Arctic Mirrors: A True Discourse of the Late Voyages of Discoverie . . . of Martin Frobisher (1578)', in Frédéric Regard, ed., *The Quest for the Northwest Passage*, London, 2013, p. 57.

8. Foster, *England's Quest*, p. 34.

9. It is impossible to be precise about the damage that the English marine inflicted on Iberia. During the war (1585–1604) it cannot be doubted massive disruption was caused to Spanish trade in home waters. However, it would appear that just seven really big fish were either captured or destroyed in the period 1585–97: *Santa Maria de San Vicente* (1585), *Espírito Santo* (1590), *Santa Cruz* (Azores, 1592), *Nossa Senhora Mãe de Deus*

(Azores, 1592), *Cinco Chagas de Cristo* (Azores, 1594), *São Pedro* (coast of Brazil, 1594), *São Francisco* (Azores, 1597). For a general account of English attacks on Iberian shipping, see Duncan T. Bentley, 'Navigation Between Portugal and Asia in the Sixteenth and Seventeenth Centuries', in Om Prakash, ed., *European Commercial Expansion in Early Modern Asia*, Aldershot, 1997, pp. 1–25.

10. In eighty-two years of warfare, the *Carriera* lost twenty-three ships to enemy action: 3.8 per cent of 595 voyages attempted.
11. The Museu de Marinha in Lisbon has a reconstruction of what the *Mãe* might have looked like. https://en.wikipedia.org/wiki/Madre_de_Deus.
12. Sanjay Subrahmanyam, *Empires Between Islam and Christianity, 1500–1800*, Albany, 2019, p. 225.
13. Robert J. Antony, 'Turbulent Waters: Sea Raiding in Early Modern South East Asia', *The Mariner's Mirror*, vol. 99, no. 1 (2013), pp. 23–39: p. 26.
14. Ibid., p. 189.
15. Ibid., p. 191.
16. Ruth A. McIntyre, 'William Sanderson, Elizabethan Financier of Discovery', *William and Mary Quarterly*, vol. 13 (1956), pp. 184–201: p. 193.
17. Ibid., p. 197.
18. Matthew Dimmock, *Elizabethan Globalism: England, China and the Rainbow Portrait*, New Haven and London, 2019, p. 131.
19. Foster, *England's Quest*, pp. 137–8.
20. Tony Campbell, 'Martin Llewellyn's Atlas of the East' (*c.* 1598), www.maphistory.info//llewellyn.html.
21. See www.rmg.co.uk/discover/behind-the-scenes/blog/all-about-portolans: 'Portolan charts are a type of navigational sea chart, concerned with coastlines and ports, rather than features inland. They functioned primarily by judging the direction and distance between ports. A key feature of almost all portolans, therefore, is the compass rose.'
22. Campbell, 'Martin Llewellyn's Atlas of the East'.
23. Ibid.
24. Ibid.
25. Despite the dominance of the printed word in early modern Europe, much of utilitarian value and more of cultural worth was spread about through the circulation of manuscripts: the logs of Captain Nicholas Downton and the poems of Dr John Donne, the newsletters of Mr John Chamberlain and the sermons of Archbishop George Abbot, among such miscellanea.
26. Sarah Tyacke, 'Gabriel Tatton's Maritime Atlas of the East Indies, 1620–21: Portsmouth Royal Naval Museum, Admiralty Library Manuscript, MSS 352', *Imago Mundi*, vol. 60, no. 1 (2008), pp. 39–62.
27. Ibid., p. 44.
28. Owen Feltham, *Batavia, or, The Hollander displayed in brief characters & observations of the people & country, the government of their state & private families, their virtues and vices: also, A perfect description of the people & country of Scotland*, London and Amsterdam, 1675, pp. 1, 7.
29. Joep Leerssen, *National Thought in Europe: A Cultural History*, Amsterdam, 2020, p. 103.
30. 'Rutters' were sailing manuals, some printed, others manuscript, which advised routes and hazards ocean-going merchantmen might be expected either to follow or avoid. In addition, however, they could provide rudimentary information about what a visitor might find when tying up in a particular port.
31. For the best account of Linschoten, the genesis of his work and the influence of his publications, see Nuno Vila-Santa, 'Jan Huygen van Linschoten and the *Reys-gheschrift*: updating Iberian Science for the Dutch expansion', *Historical Research*, vol. 94, no. 216 (Nov. 2021), pp. 736–57.
32. Ibid., p. 738: 'Linschoten's acquisition of Iberian Science during his years in Goa and the Azores (between 1583 and 1591) should not be seen as a spy mission.'

33. https://www.uu.nl/en/special-collections/collections/early-printed-books/geographical-descriptions/itinerario-by-jan-huygen-van-linschoten.
34. Sainsbury, *Papers, 1513–1616*, no. 266, 'Foulke Greville to Secretary Sir Robert Cecil', 10 March 1600.
35. Vila-Santa, 'Jan Huygen van Linschoten', p. 737.
36. Ibid., p. 753.
37. Sir Ernest Mason Satow, ed., *The Voyage of Captain John Saris to Japan, 1613*, Hakluyt Society, 2nd ser., part 1, 1900, p. 188.
38. For a summary of Linschoten's life in Goa and the influence of his *Itinerario* see Harold J. Cook, *Matters of Exchange: Commerce, Medicine and Science in the Dutch Golden Age*, New Haven and London, 2007, pp. 121–8.
39. Foster, *England's Quest*, p. 143.
40. Standards of hygiene in England were still more gross than in Holland. When in 1665 Charles II returned to London, having fled to Oxford during the plague, it was remarked how courtiers went, 'leaving at their departures their excrements in every corner, in chimneys, studies, coal houses, cellars'. Andrew Wear, 'The History of Personal Hygiene', in W.F. Bynum and Roy Porter, eds, *Companion Encyclopedia of the History of Medicine*, London, 1993, vol. 1, pp. 1283–1308: p. 1301.
41. A 'privateer' was a private individual or syndicate permitted to attack an enemy in wartime, 'licensed' to do so by 'letters of marque' or a royal commission. By contrast, an 'interloper' had no such official backing but worked independently of any official sanction, in the hope of breaking in upon lucrative trade routes.
42. Robert Ashton, *The City and the Court, 1603–1643*, Cambridge, 1979, p. 75.
43. Rupali Mishra, *A Business of State: Commerce, Politics, and the Birth of the East India Company*, Cambridge, MA, 2018, p. 73.
44. The Company arms was granted by the historian William Camden in his capacity as Clarenceux King of Arms on 4 February 1600.

3. MERCHANTS OF LIGHT

1. J.R. McCulloch, *Early English Tracts on Commerce*, Cambridge, 1954, pp. 11–12.
2. Francis Bacon, *The Advancement of Learning and New Atlantis*, intro. Thomas Case, Oxford, 1974, where at p. 296 Bacon has the father of 'Saloman's house' speak to the narrator 'in the Spanish tongue': 'For the several employments and offices of our fellows, we have twelve that sail into foreign countries under the names of other nations (for our own we, conceal), who bring us the books and abstracts, and patterns of experience of all other parts. These we call Merchants of Light.' This passage had been preceded (p. 288) with the same 'father' having declared how 'The end of our foundation is the knowledge of causes, and secret motions of things; and the enlarging of the bounds of human empire, to the effecting of all things possible.'
3. Sonia P. Anderson, 'Roberts, Lewes', in *Oxford Dictionary of National Biography* (hereafter *ODNB*).
4. Edmond Smith, *Merchants: The Community That Shaped England's Trade and Empire*, New Haven and London, 2021, p. 210.
5. Dimmock, *Elizabethan Globalism*.
6. Ibid., p. 203.
7. Joan Thirsk, *Economic Policy and Projects: The Development of a Consumer Society in Early Modern England*, Oxford, 1978, pp. 52–3.
8. Ibid., p. 58.
9. Ibid., p. 8.
10. It is an unfortunate aspect of Tudor history that too many people were called 'Sir Thomas Smythe'. This one is not to be confused with our very own 'Smythe', Sir Thomas Smythe, first governor of the East India Company, nor for that matter with 'Sir Thomas Smythe', the father of the governor, who thankfully was known less often as 'Sir Thomas Smythe'

than as 'Customer Smythe', a none-too-respectable allusion to how the 'Customer' had cornered an extremely profitable little business squeezing the customs revenues in his capacity as their 'Farmer'.

11. Elizabeth Lamond and William Cunningham, eds, *A Discourse of the Common Weal of this Realm of England*, Cambridge, 1893, pp. 64–5.

12. John Stow, *The Survey of London*, London, 1912, p. 161.

13. The *Golden Hind* had disintegrated by about 1650. However, John Davies of Camberwell, in charge of naval stores at Deptford, had a chair made from its timbers. Improbably enough, this somehow ended up in the Bodleian Library, Oxford.

14. This was the resting place of Hājjī Mahmūd Shāhsavār, who visited London and, liking what he saw, became a permanent resident, dying there in August 1626. W. Toldervy, *Select Epitaphs*, London, 1755, pp. 104–5.

15. Ibid., 1633 edition, p. 780.

16. Ian W. Archer, *The Pursuit of Stability: Social Relations in Elizabethan London*, Cambridge, 1991, p. 81.

17. Smith, *Merchants*, p. 64.

18. Archer, *The Pursuit of Stability*, pp. 1–2.

19. Ibid., p. 216.

20. Ibid., p. 242.

21. Ibid., p. 217.

22. Ibid., p. 204.

23. Ibid., Table 5.8, p. 181.

24. Edward Terry, *A Voyage to East-India With a Description of the large Territories under the subjection of the Great Mogol*, London, 1655, p. 2.

25. Thirsk, *Economic Policy and Projects*, p. 119, n. 31.

26. There were very few urban dynasties in London. See Archer, *The Pursuit of Stability*, p. 51, where the author writes that 'most of the City's rulers were first generation inhabitants recruited from relatively modest provincial backgrounds . . . a high level of social mobility into the elite helped sustain popular confidence in the idea of metropolitan opportunity which was so potent in the popular literature of the period'.

27. Theodore K. Rabb, *Enterprise and Empire: Merchant and Gentry Investment in the Expansion of England, 1575–1630*, Cambridge, MA, 1967, p. 6.

28. Thirsk, *Economic Policy and Projects*, p. 118.

29. Ibid., pp. 174–5.

30. 'Elizabeth I 1533–1603', in Susan Ratcliffe, ed., *Oxford Essential Quotations*, online edition 2016, www.oxfordreference.com/view/10.1093/acref/9780191826719.001.0001/q-oro-ed4-00004114.

31. There is a certain irony here. It was Russian, not English, painters who were taken with the romance of commerce when what the English had sold the Russians would celebrate. See for example Alexander Litovchenko's *Ivan the Terrible Showing His Treasures to the English Ambassador Sir Jerome Horsey* (1875). This was bought by the czar for his collections in St Petersburg.

32. These phrases are taken from the most notorious contribution to *Hymns Ancient and Modern*, the songbook of the Anglican establishment. This battle-hymn of British evangelism with its title 'From Greenland's Icy Mountains' was composed by Reginald Heber (d. 1826) who as bishop of Calcutta (1823–6) was the most high-profile missionary in all India. Mercifully the hymn only has four relatively short verses, since after inventorying the topographies of the British Empire the good bishop concludes his first verse with the exhortation: 'They call us to deliver. / Their land from error's chain.'

33. For the mercantilist debate in Jacobean England see Mark Blaug, ed., *The Early Mercantilists: Thomas Mun (1571–1641), Edward Misselden (1608–1634) and Gerard de Malynes (1568–1623)*, Cheltenham, 1991, *passim*.

34. It may be as well at this juncture to indicate the relative values of the main currencies imported into India against the Indian mahmudi: rial of eight (Seville) = 4s 6d (sterling)

= 4 (Indian) mahmudi 23.5 pices (1m = 1s); rial of eight (Mexican) = 4s 6d = 4 mahmudi 21 pices; lion dollar of Holland = 4s = 4 mahmudi 21½ pices; Zealand dollar = 2s 8d. = 3¼ mahmudis; Venetian dollar = 4s 6d = 5 mahmudis; Hungarian dollar = £3 13s 0d = 31¼ mahmudis; English 20s = 21¾ mahmudis. K.N. Chaudhuri, *The English East India Company: The Study of an Early Joint-Stock Company, 1600–1640*, London, 1965, p. 116, Table IV: 'Some Exchange rates Between European, English and Indian Currencies'.

35. For an accessible summary of these ideological differences see 'The Discourse of Trade: Print, Politics and the Company in England', in Miles Ogborn, *Indian Ink: Script and Print in the Making of the English East India Company*, Chicago, 2007, pp. 104–57.

36. Thomas Mun, *A Discourse of Trade, from England unto the East Indies*, London 1621, p. 26.

37. 'The "Grand Sophy" [the Shah of Persia] was an ardent Shia whereas the "Great Turk" [the Sultan of Turkey] was a fanatical adherent of the Sunni form of worship'; C.R. Boxer, *The Portuguese Seaborne Empire, 1415–1825*, London, 1969, p. 41.

38. William A. Pettigrew and Mahesh Gopalan, eds, *The East India Company, 1600–1857: Essays on Anglo-Indian Connection*, London, 2017.

39. Ibid., p. 39.

40. Emily Erikson, *Between Monopoly and Free Trade: The English East India Company, 1600–1757*, Princeton and Oxford, 2014, p. 45.

41. Sainsbury, *Papers: East Indies, China and Japan, 1617–1621*, London, 1870, no. 1152, Court Minutes, 12 November 1621.

42. Ibid., no. 1154, Court Minutes, 14–16 November 1621.

43. Sir William Foster, *A Supplementary Calendar of Documents in the India Office Relating to India or to the Home Affairs of the East India Company 1600–1640*, London, 1928, no. 464.

44. On 6 February 1621, 'Parliament took into consideration the scarcity of coin in England'. In response, probably in June of that same year, Mun lodged with the Company, 'Reasons to prove that the trade from England unto the East Indies doth not consume but rather increase the treasure of this kingdom'. Sainsbury, *Papers, 1617–1621*, no. 1023.

4. ENLARGING THE BOUNDS OF HUMAN EMPIRE

1. Quoted by Margaret Pelling and Charles Webster, 'Medical Practitioners', in Charles Webster, ed., *Health, Medicine and Mortality in the Sixteenth Century*, Cambridge, 1979, pp. 185–6.

2. I.G. Murray, 'Clowes, William', in *ODNB*.

3. Ibid.

4. Pelling and Webster, 'Medical Practitioners', in Webster, ed., *Health, Medicine and Mortality*, p. 165.

5. Paré's knowledge was distilled into four books translated as Ambroise Paré, *The workes of that famous chirurgion Ambrose Parey translated out of Latine and compared with the French. by Th: Johnson*, London, 1634.

6. W.H. Brock, 'The Biochemical Tradition', in Bynum and Porter, eds, *Companion Encyclopedia of the History of Medicine*, vol. 1, pp. 153–8: pp. 155–6.

7. C. Webster, 'Alchemical and Paracelsian medicine', in Webster, ed., *Health, Medicine and Mortality*, pp. 301–34: p. 327.

8. Cromwell had constructed for himself a fifty-eight-room mansion running along the river and over the remains of the great Augustinian priory which after its dissolution in 1538 was known as 'Austin Friars'.

9. Frederick C. Beiser, *The Sovereignty of Reason*, Princeton, 1996, p. 46.

10. Brodie Waddell, *God, Duty and Community in English Economic Life, 1660–1720*, Woodbridge, 2012, p. 141.

11. W.S. Holdsworth, 'English Corporate Law in the 16th and 17th Centuries', *Yale Law Journal*, vol. 31, no. 4 (Feb. 1922), pp. 382–407.

12. For the place of Coke in public law or common law, see Stephen Sedley, *Lions Under the Throne: Essays on the History of English Public Law*, Cambridge, 2015.
13. M.R.L.L. Kelly, 'Common Law Constitutionalism and the Oath of Governance: An Hieroglyphic of the Laws', *Mississippi College Law Review*, vol. 28, issue 1, article 7 (2009), pp. 122–79: p. 137.
14. For how Coke and Bacon represented the polarities of the law in early Stuart England, see Damian X. Powell, 'Why Was Sir Francis Bacon Impeached? Lawyers and the Chancery Revisited', *History*, vol. 81, no. 264 (Oct. 1996), pp. 511–26.
15. Henry S. Turner, *The Corporate Commonwealth: Pluralism and Political Fictions in England, 1516–1651*, Chicago and London, 2016, p. 17.
16. Virginia Woolf, 'The Elizabethan Lumber Room', in *The Common Reader*, 1st ser., New York, 1948, p. 65.
17. 'Shakespeare is the first to bring a wide range of sea terms into drama and poetry. He is at ease in an idiom unknown to most and his scope and precision can be adequately illustrated only in an analytical glossary'; A.F. Falconer, *Shakespeare and the Sea*, London, 1964, p. 149.
18. 'William Tyndale *c.*1494–1536', in Susan Ratcliffe, ed., *Oxford Essential Quotations*, online edition 2016, https://www.oxfordreference.com/view/10.1093/acref/9780191826719.001.0001/q-oro-ed4-00011088.
19. Robert Tombs, *The English and Their History*, London, 2014, p. 196.
20. Third Institute, *Proeme, 1642–4: Institutes of the Lawes of England, 1628–42* , cited by Allen D. Boyer, 'Sir Edward Coke', in *ODNB*.
21. Bacon, *The Advancement of Learning and New Atlantis*, p. xiv.
22. Ibid., p. x.
23. Thomas Babington Macaulay, *Critical and Historical Essays: Contributed to the Edinburgh Review*, London, 1852, p. 403.
24. 'Of Seditions and Troubles', in Francis Bacon, *Essays*, intr. Oliphant Smeaton, London, 1906, p. 46.

5. RAISING THE MONEY

1. Karen Hearn, ed., *Dynasties: Painting in Jacobean and Tudor England 1530–1630*, London, 1995, cat. nos. 58–60.
2. Robert Devereux, earl of Essex, *The arraignment, tryal and condemnation of Robert Earl of Essex and Henry Earl of Southampton, at Westminster the 19th of February, 1600 . . .*, London, 1679, p. 16.
3. Ibid., p. 24.
4. https://www.british-history.ac.uk/cal-cecil-papers/vol11/pp100-119 under: 2 March 1600/01. It is not clear when precisely Smythe came to be released from the Tower. He was still there on 23 December 1603, though bizarrely enough he was knighted within its precincts on 13 May 1604. Presumably that was the moment for release since he had been appointed Receiver for the Duchy of Cornwall in April 1604. For details see Basil Morgan, 'Smythe, Sir Thomas', in *ODNB*.
5. *Calendar of Cecil Manuscripts*, vol. 11, ed. Roberts, p. 530, Sir Thomas Smythe to Sir Robert Cecil, 'endorsed. Mr Smith, The Tower of London', 23 December 1601.
6. *Calendar of Cecil Manuscripts*, vol. 23: *Addenda, 1562–1605*, ed. G. Dyfnallt Owen, London, 1973, p. 87, 'Before February 17, 1600–1'.
7. Sir Edward Michelborne was a famous interloper, first a creature of Essex and later a client of Lord Treasurer Buckhurst, who pressurised without success the EIC into making Michelborne 'general' of the First Voyage in preference to Sir James Lancaster. Spurned by the Company for his financial embarrassments, Michelborne turned to the Crown, from which in June 1604 he obtained a licence 'to discover the countries of Cathay, China, Japan, Corea, and Cambaya, and to trade there' in defiance of the 1st Charter of

the East India Company. Mary Anne Everett Green, ed., *Calendar of State Papers Domestic: James I, 1603–1610*, London, 1857, p. 121.

8. For Mikulin in London see N.E. Evans, 'The Meeting of the Russian and Scottish Ambassadors in London in 1601', *Slavonic and East European Review*, vol. 55, no. 4 (Oct. 1977), pp. 517–28.

9. 'Portrait of G.I. Mikulin', State Historical Museum of Russia, see http://nav.shm.ru/en/exhibits/1731/.

10. I am grateful to the licensor, Marion E. Colthorpe, for permission to quote this and following citations from the Folger Library's *Folgerpedia* webpage, 'The Elizabethan Court Day by Day', https://folgerpedia.folger.edu/The_Elizabethan_Court_Day_by_Day, extract dated 14 October 1600.

11. Smythe's official instructions for the embassy, National Archives, Kew, PRO SP/91/196.

12. Unless otherwise stated, all accounts of the embassy are taken from *Sir Thomas Smithes voiage and entertainment in Rushia . . .*, London, 1605 (unpaginated).

13. Ibid.

14. For an excellent modern account of Smythe's embassy see Sotheby's, *English Silver Treasures from the Kremlin: A Loan Exhibition*, London, 1991, *passim*.

15. *Calendar of Cecil Manuscripts*, vol. 17: *1605*, ed. M.S. Giuseppi, London, 1938, p. 69, Sir Thomas Smythe 'In the Musco' to Lord Cecil in London, 25 February 1605.

16. Ibid.

17. For this prodigious object, presented by Smythe to Boris Godunov on 11 October 1604 and still to be seen in the Moscow Kremlin Armoury Museum, see *English Silver Treasures*, Fig. 5.

18. Smythe to the earl of Salisbury, 24 September 1605, ibid., p. 433.

19. For comparison of the Amsterdam and London money markets in about 1600, see Carl Wennerlind, *Casualties of Credit: The English Financial Revolution, 1620–1720*, Cambridge, MA, 2011, *passim*.

20. Sainsbury, *Papers, 1513–1616*, no. 902, Court Minutes, 16 February 1615.

21. Ibid., p. lxxvi.

22. Ibid., no. 912.

23. Robert Kayll, *The trades increase*, London, 1615, p. 53.

24. Sir Dudley Digges, *The defence of trade in a letter to Sir Thomas Smith Knight, governor of the East-India Company etc, From one of that societie . . .*, London, 1615, pp. 52–3. For the best summary see Ogborn, *Indian Ink*, pp. 107–20.

25. John Wood, *The trve honor of navigation and navigators: or, Holy meditations for Sea-men . . .* (London, 1618), in Catherine Pickett, *Bibliography of the East India Company: Books, Pamphlets and Other Materials Printed Between 1600 and 1785*, London, 2011, p. 14.

26. Sainsbury, *Papers, 1617–1621*, no. 238, Court Minutes, 9 January 1618.

27. Sainsbury, *Papers, 1513–1616*, no. 700, Court Minutes, 10 March 1614.

28. Aylesbury (1597), Dunwich (1604), Sandwich (1614) and Saltash (1621).

29. See Peter Lefevre, 'Smythe, Sir Thomas (c. 1558–1625)', in Andrew Thrush and John P. Ferris, eds, *The History of Parliament: The House of Commons 1604–1629*, Cambridge, 2010.

30. N.E. McClure, ed., *The Letters of John Chamberlain*, Philadelphia, 1939, vol. 1, no. 185, p. 488, John Chamberlain in London to Sir Dudley Carleton at The Hague, 25 November 1613.

31. John Cramsie, *Kingship and Crown Finance under James VI and I, 1603–1625*, Woodbridge, 2002, *passim*.

32. Ibid., p. 152.

33. Mary Anne Everett Green, ed., *Calendar of State Papers Domestic: James I, 1619–23*, London, 1858, vol. 123, Sir Thomas Smythe, Sir Thomas Lowe and Sir William Cockayne to the Privy Council, no. 13, 5 October 1621.

34. William Pettigrew and Edmond Smith, 'Corporate Management, Labor Relations, and Community Building at the East India Company's Blackwall Dockyard, 1600–57', *Journal of Social History*, vol. 53, no. 1 (2019), pp. 133–56.

35. For the positive nature of industrial relations within the East India Company, see ibid.
36. East India Company, *The Lawes or Standing Orders of the East India Company*, London, 1621, reprint Farnborough, 1968, p. xcvi.
37. Ibid., p. cix.
38. Ibid., p. ccviii.
39. Ibid., p. cclii.
40. Ibid., p. cclv.
41. Ibid., p. cclxxxvi.
42. McClure, ed., *Letters of John Chamberlain*, vol. 2, no. 292, p. 154, John Chamberlain in London to Sir Dudley Carleton at The Hague, 1 April 1618.
43. Ibid.
44. For a comprehensive account of the Scottish East India Company and its travails both in Edinburgh and London see Joseph Wagner, 'The Scottish East India Company of 1617: Patronage, Commercial Rivalry, and the Union of the Crowns', *Journal of British Studies*, vol. 59 (July 2020), pp. 582–607.
45. Ibid., p. 599.
46. McClure, ed., *Letters of John Chamberlain*, vol. 2, no. 284, pp. 134–5, John Chamberlain in London to Sir Dudley Carleton at The Hague, 31 January 1618.
47. Sainsbury, *Papers, 1617–1621*, no. 657, John Chamberlain in London to Sir Dudley Carleton at The Hague, 24 April 1619.
48. Ibid., no. 677, 31 May 1619.
49. McClure, ed., *Letters of John Chamberlain*, vol. 2, no. 329, p. 244, John Chamberlain in London to Sir Dudley Carleton at The Hague, 5 June 1619.
50. Sainsbury, *Papers, 1617–1621*, no. 705, 15 July 1619.
51. Ibid., no. 826, 20 March 1620.
52. Kent County Record Office, Cranfield Papers, U1115/C15, Thomas, Lord Egerton, to Richard Brown, 7 July [1620].
53. McClure, ed., *Letters of John Chamberlain*, vol. 2, no. 386, p. 388, John Chamberlain in London to Sir Dudley Carleton at the Hague, London, 14 July 1621.
54. Ibid., vol. 2, no. 394, p. 405, John Chamberlain to Sir Dudley Carleton, London, 10 November, 1621.
55. J.F. Wadmore, 'Sir Thomas Smythe, Knt. (A.D. 1558–1625)', *Archaeologica Cantiana*, vol. 20 (1893), pp. 82–103: p. 101.
56. For Donne's famous sermon delivered at the obsequies of Cockayne see Peter McCullough, 'Preaching and Context: John Donne's Sermon at the Funerals of Sir William Cockayne', in Hugh Aldington, Peter McCullough and Emma Rhatigan, eds, *The Oxford Handbook of the Early Modern Sermon*, Oxford, 2011, pp. 1–57.
57. Edmund Waller, 'Of English Verse', lines 14–16.
58. Rodney Shewan, ed., *The Life of Samuel Johnson By James Boswell*, London, 1968, 2 vols, vol. 1, p. 566.
59. Samuel Purchas, *Hakluytus Posthumus or Purchas his Pilgrimes*, London, 1625–6, p. 487.

6. RUNNING THE OFFICE

1. Robert Brenner, *Merchants and Revolution: Commercial Change, Political Conflict, and London's Overseas Traders, 1550–1653*, Cambridge, 1993, pp. 21–2.
2. Sainsbury, *Papers, 1513–1616*, p. lii.
3. Given that the Muscovy Company was Smythe's first and last love (he left it most in his will) we should expect many letters within its archive. However, Sir Percival Griffiths, *The History of English Chartered Companies*, London and Tonbridge, 1974, p. 19, wrote of how the Great Fire of 1660 'destroyed the Minute Books of the Russia Company and [another of] 1838 destroyed many of the rest'.
4. Most of the collection was housed at his residence in Deptford which went up in smoke in 1619.

5. Smith, *Merchants*, p. 114: 'Merchants' grand halls were ideal for holding larger gatherings, including corporate activities. Many meetings of the Spanish Company were "held at the dwelling house of Mr Thomas Wilford", while the Levant Company's directors met at Sir Thomas Lowe's house during his period as governor'.

6. Guy, *Gresham's Law*, p. 39.

7. Sainsbury, *Papers, 1513–1616*, pp. 314–15, Court Minutes, August 2–19, August 9.

8. Samuel Pepys was present in the Navy Office on 6 November 1660 when the *Indian* and the *Halfe moone* were knocked down for £1300 and £850 'by the candle': 'This was the usual method of auction-sale. A section of wax an inch in length was lit for each lot, and the successful bidder was the one who shouted immediately before the candle went out'. Robert Latham and William Matthews, eds, *The Diary of Samuel Pepys*, London, 1970–1983, vol. 1, p. 284 and note 2.

9. Sainsbury, *Papers, 1513–1616*, no. 443, 23–30 May 1609.

10. Ibid., no. 1009, 28 July 1615.

11. John Strype, ed., *Survey of London*, London, 1720, vol. 1, book 2, p. 88.

12. Sainsbury, *Papers, 1617–1621*, no. 192, Court Minutes, 11 November 1617.

13. Sainsbury, *Papers, 1513–1616*, no. 431, Court Minutes, 15 March 1609.

14. Ibid., no. 702, Court Minutes, 22 March 1614.

15. Ibid., no. 691, Court Minutes, 9 February 1614.

16. For the argument that we owe more to the intellectual achievements of the seventeenth century than to those of the Renaissance see A.C. Grayling, *The Age of Genius: The Seventeenth Century and the Birth of the Modern Mind*, London, 2016, *passim*.

17. For a biography of Wickham see Anthony Farrington, *The English Factory in Japan 1613–1623*, London, 1991, vol. 2, p. 1576.

18. Ibid., vol. 1, no. 289, 'An inventory of the goods of Mr Ric' Wickham, m'rchant, deceased in Bantam the 12th November 1618', pp. 729–36.

19. To get a sense of what Wickham's lacquerware might have looked like, see Julia Hunt, 'Asia in Europe: Lacquer for the West', in Jackson and Jaffer, *Encounters*, pp. 234–49.

20. For Aubrey's account of Whitson's escapades, from cellar to Guildhall, see John Aubrey, *Brief Lives with an Apparatus for the Lives of our English Mathematical Writers*, ed. Kate Bennett, Oxford, 2015, vol. 1, pp. 711–14.

21. His three daughters having pre-deceased him, Whitson provided in his will a sufficiency to accommodate '40 poor women and children' in what presumably must have been not just a school but something of a 'hospital': part dispensary, part alms house. Whitson went on to add that all were to be 'apparelled in red'. Today pupils wear a red blazer with a badge displaying a sunflower (for Spain perhaps?) and above the prow of a ship is a sail; an allusion to Whitson as Bristol's most successful merchant until the arrival upon the scene of the notorious Edward Colston.

22. For Whitson's testamentary dispositions see Bristol Archives, 33041/BMC/6, and Patrick McGrath, *John Whitson and the Merchant Community of Bristol*, Bristol, 1970, *passim*.

23. There is a delightful memorial to Martin Pring. It is an auricular tablet, all in glutinous alabaster and crisp armorial, hanging like a sail off the wall of St Stephen's Bristol. It looks like a wedding cake which has been left out in the rain. Mermaid and merman, seemingly made out of melting marzipan, bend as they begin to slither into the lap of congregation below. The reader may wish to be spared the inscription; though if not, it can be found at www.speel.me.uk/sculptplaces/bristolststephen.htm.

24. There is indeed an engraving of the English factory in Surat, something often taken to represent what it looked like in the days that concern us. However, this image must date from towards the end of the seventeenth century at the earliest and is therefore unreliable for our purposes.

25. Mark Morton, *Cupboard of Love: A Dictionary of Culinary Curiosities*, 2nd edn, Toronto, 2004, p. 47.

26. John Davies, trans., *The Voyages and Travells of the Ambassadors from the Duke of Holstein to the Grand Duke of Muscovy and the King of Persia in Seven Books . . .*, *The First Book*, London, 1642, pp. 17–18.

27. Edward Wright, *Certaine errors in nauigation, arising either of the ordinarie erroneous making or vsing of the sea chart, compasse, crosse staff, and tables of declination of the Sunne, and fixed stars detected and corrected. By E. W.* London, 1599.

28. For ways in which Wright improved and 'translated' the work of Mercator and others, see 'The Wright Approach', in Mark Monmonier, *Rhumb Lines and Map Wars: A Social History of the Mercator Projection*, Chicago, 2004, ch. 5, pp. 63–79.

29. Turner, *The Corporate Commonwealth*, p. 109.

30. Charles Bricker et al., *Landmarks of Mapmaking*, Oxford, 1976, p. 31.

31. Sainsbury, *Papers, 1513–1616*, no. 702, Court Minutes, 14 March 1614.

32. Thomas Smith, *Catalogus Librorum Manuscriptorum Bibliothecae Cottonianae*, Oxford, 1696, p. 126; British Library, Cotton Mss. Titus B VIII, fols. 242–69.

33. F.C. Danvers, *Letters Received by the East India Company from its Servants in the East*, vol. 1: *1602–1613*, London, 1896, letter no. 48, p. 96, Lawrence Femell to 'Sir Henry Middleton in Moha, 14 May 1611'.

34. Farrington, *The English Factory in Japan*, vol. 1, p. 241.

35. Sainsbury, *Papers, 1513–1616*, no. 871, Minutes, 10 January 1615.

36. Helen Wallis, 'Purchas's Maps', in L.E. Pennington, ed., *The Purchas Handbook: Studies of the Life, Times and Writings of Samuel Purchas 1577–1626*, London, Hakluyt Society, 2nd ser., part 2, 1997, vol. 1, ch. 3, p. 154: Saris' map which was 'four foot one way and almost five foot the other' was 'by Captain Saris . . . gotten at Bantam of a Chinese, in taking a distress for debts owing to English merchants, whose being him careful to convey away a box, was the more careful to apprehend it, and therein found this Map'. It is now in the Biblioteka Czartoryskich Cracow. It was perhaps the earliest map of China from Chinese sources to be published in Europe.

37. J.K. Laughton and G.G. Harris, 'Keeling, William', in *ODNB*.

38. Strachan, *Sir Thomas Roe*, p. 60.

39. Ibid., pp. 60–1.

40. Foster, *Roe Journal*, vol. 1, p. 18.

41. Strachan, *Sir Thomas Roe*, p. 62.

42. Sainsbury, *Papers, 1513–1616*, no. 912, Court Minutes, 22 February 1615.

43. See https://en.wikipedia.org/wiki/William_Keeling. Smythe wanted Keeling for great things, but Keeling only wanted his wife. Sent out to the Far East no fewer than three times, and with the presidency of the Indies his for the taking, Keeling took early retirement and the keepership of Carisbrooke Castle. After his early death aged forty-two, Anne erected surely the most beguiling of all early memorials to Company servants: a pedimented wooden board like those tabernacles to be found in old churches with the Ten Commandments all tricked out in gold, but instead of 'Our Lord' with Anne's lord all painted in leaf! Ploughing the seas, the vessel trails a string of deplorable couplets that have something of a generic resemblance to those ditties dedicated to old Smythe down in Sutton-at-Hone; suggesting perhaps, that as well as retaining Richard Hakluyt as Company historian and Samuel Purchas as archivist, Smythe may have appointed the equivalent of an obituary writer – or Company bard? Moving, charming, funny and ridiculous all at once, what is left of Keeling leaves no doubt that he and his ilk were men of substance in communities willing enough to celebrate the far-off far-past achievements of those lucky enough to sink into the bosom of the earth and not the ocean's waves:

> Fortie and Two years in this Vessel fraile
> On the Rough Seas of Life did Keling Saile
> A Merchant Fortunate A Captains Bould
> A Courtier Gratious yet (Alas) not Old.
> Such Wealth Experience Honour and High Praise

Few Winne in Twice Soe Manie Yeares or Daies
But what the World Admird he deemed but Drosse
For Christ, Without Christ all his Gaines but losse
For him and his dear Love With merrie Cheere
To the Holy Land his last course he did Steere
Faith served for Sailes the Sacred Word for Card [marine charts]
Hope was his Anchor Glorie his Reward
And this with Gales of Grace by happie Venter,
Through sreights of Death heaven's harbor he did ENTER

44. Sainsbury, *Papers, 1513–1616*, no. 476, John Chamberlain in London to Dudley Carleton, 30 December 1609.
45. Sir William Foster, ed., *The Voyage of Nicholas Downton to the East Indies, 1614–15, as Recorded in Contemporary Narratives and Letters*, Hakluyt Society, 2nd ser., part 1, 1939 (1938), p. 50.
46. Mary Anne Everett Green, ed., *Calendar of State Papers Domestic: James I, 1611–18*, London, 1858, vol. 98, no. 28, 19 July 1618: 'Petition of Bridget Gray to the Council, that her grandson, John Throckmorton, prisoner in Newgate for felony, may be discharged, it being his first offence, and Sir Thos. Smythe being ready to convey him beyond seas. With order thereon, that on certificate by the Lord Mayor and Recorder, that John Throckmorton was not convicted for murder, burglary, highway robbery, rape, or witchcraft, a warrant be made for his banishment. Also certificate of the Mayor and Recorder that his crime was aiding in stealing a hat worth 6s., for which his accomplice, Robt. Whisson, an old thief, was hanged.'
47. Sainsbury, *Papers, 1513–1616*, no. 1003, Court Minutes, 11 July 1615.
48. Ibid., no. 616, 26 July 1612.

7. A VOYAGE EXCEEDINGLY TROUBLESOME

1. Chaudhuri, *The English East India Company*, p. 107.
2. 'He who unto the sea commits his bodies [is] either poore, or desp'rat or a noddie'; Randle Corgrave, *A Dictionary of the French and English Tongues* (London, 1611), quoted by Vincent V. Patarino, Jr., 'The Religious Shipboard Culture of Sixteenth- and Seventeenth-Century English Sailors', in Cheryl A. Fury, ed., *The Social History of English Seamen, 1485–1649*, Woodbridge, 2012. ch. 6, p. 142.
3. Samuel Johnson, 16 March 1759, quoted in James Boswell, *Life of Samuel Johnson*, 1791, p. 207.
4. Andrew B. Appleby, 'Diet in Sixteenth-Century England: Sources, problems, possibilities', in Webster, ed., *Health, Medicine and Mortality*, pp. 97–117: p. 98.
5. Orwell joined the Indian Imperial Police in 1922 and resigned in 1928.
6. In 1626, en route to his great house at St Albans, Sir Francis stopped at Lord Arundel's villa at Highgate. Venturing into the garden to stuff a chicken with snow, his lordship caught a cold, retired to bed and promptly died. See Freeman Dyson and Timothy Beecroft, 'Francis Bacon and the Frozen Chicken', *New York Review of Books*, 31 May 2007.
7. 'Hardly less of a hazard, if however it was not a terminal experience, has to be what happened to the *Senhora de Nazaré*. She put into Luanda in Angola in 1651 "*cuidando estar já na India, due tal piloto levavá*" ("thinking to be in India such was the pilot it had")'; Boxer, *Portuguese India*, p. 25.
8. Sainsbury, *Papers: East Indies and Persia, 1630–1634*, London, 1892, no. 432, Court Minutes, 26 April 1633.
9. Sainsbury, *Papers, 1617–1621*, no. 608, Court Minutes, 26 February 1619.
10. Ibid., no. 789, Court Minutes, 20 December 1619. 'An unspecified number of mariners died as a result of this scandal'.

11. Sainsbury, *Papers, 1513–1616*, no. 448, Court Minutes, 5 July 1609, p. 188.

12. Ibid., no. 472, Court Minutes, 11 December 1609.

13. Sainsbury, *Papers, 1617–1621*, no. 883, p. 384, Thomas Brockedon, Augustine Spalding and George Muschamp in Jakarta to the Company in London, 20 July 1620.

14. The breakdown of provisions and costings is taken from Sir George Birdwood and Sir William Foster, eds, *The Register of Letters etc of the Governour and Company of Merchants of London Trading into the East Indies, 1600–1619*, London, 1893, pp. 95–106.

15. All the figures in this paragraph are taken from ibid., pp. 95–106, 'A Computation of the charge for setting forth to Sea vpon a third voyadge to Bantam and the Moloccos vpon a new accompte and for discouy of furder trade and other places wch the Dragon Hector and a Pinnace as ffoloweth'.

16. For example, 'stammel' from the French word *estamel*, cheap woollen material dyed red, as in 'Red-hood, the first that doth appear / In Stammel. Scarlet is too dear': Ben Jonson, *Love's Welcome*.

17. Danvers, *Letters Received by the East India Company*, vol. 1, p. 242.

18. Sainsbury, *Papers, 1513–1616*, no. 682, p. 271, Court Minutes, 20 January 1614.

19. Sainsbury, *Papers, 1617–1621*, no. 774, Court Minutes, 22 November 1619.

20. Nicholas Downton, 'Journal of the voyage of the *Peppercorn* from Bantam to Waterford', in Danvers, *Letters Received by the East India Company*, vol. 1, pp. 241–51: pp. 244, 246.

21. Robert Parthesius, *Dutch Ships in Tropical Waters: The Development of the Dutch East India Company (VOC) Shipping Network in Asia, 1595–1660*, Amsterdam, 2010, p. 62. The great English collector Lord Arundel got very cross when, unloading a case of ancient Greek statues, he not only discovered that some clown had packed jars of olive oil against his cases, but when he tried to remove the oil, it was 'never to be gotten out'.

22. Downton, 'Journal of the voyage of the *Peppercorn*', in Danvers, *Letters Received by the East India Company*, vol. 1, *passim*.

23. Boies Penrose, 'Some Jacobean Links between America and the Orient', *The Virginia Magazine of History and Bibliography*, vol. 49, no. 1 (January 1941), pp. 51–61: p. 58.

24. Donald McDonald, *Surgeons Twoe and A Barber: Being Some Account of the Life and Work of The Indian Medical Service (1600–1947)*, London, 1950, pp. 23–5.

25. Bernard S. Cohn, *Colonialism and Its Forms of Knowledge*, Princeton, 1996, p. 19.

26. Ogborn, *Indian Ink, passim*.

27. Miles Ogborn, 'Writing Travels: Power, Knowledge and Ritual on the English East India Company's Early Voyages', *Transactions of the Institute of British Geographers*, vol. 27, no. 2 (2002), pp. 155–71: p. 168.

28. Sainsbury, *Papers, 1513–1616*, no. 479, Court Minutes, 15 January 1610.

29. Hazel Forsyth, *The Cheapside Hoar: London's Lost Jewels*, London, 2013, p. 215.

30. Sainsbury, *Papers, 1513–1616*, no. 439, Court Minutes, 13 April 1609.

31. Ibid., no. 479, Court Minutes, 13 January 1610.

32. Ibid., no. 700, Court Minutes, 19 March 1614.

33. Ibid., no. 762, Court Minutes, 19 August 1614.

34. Ibid., no. 359, Court Minutes, 16 January 1607.

35. Birdwood and Foster, eds, *The Register of Letters*, pp. 328–47, Clause 3: p. 328. 'A Commision sette downe by VS the Governor Deputy and Comittees for the Marchants of London tradeinge to the East Indies for better direccon of or loueinge freind Sr Henry Middleton. . . . in this our intended VIth voyadge [to] the East Indies which we humblie beseech Almightie God to blesse with a happie conclucion.'

36. Sainsbury, *Papers, 1513–1616*, no. 867, Court Minutes, 4 January 1615.

37. Birdwood and Foster, eds, *The Register of Letters*, pp. 328–48, Clause 1, p. 329.

38. Ibid., Clause 3, p. 329.

39. Ibid., Clause 4, pp. 329–30.

40. Ibid., Clause 8, p. 331.

41. John Chamberlain 'To my assured Goode friend Master Dudley Carleton gave these at Eton', London 23 January 1609, McClure, ed., *Letters of John Chamberlain,* vol. 1, pp. 282–3.
42. Chaudhuri, *Trade and Civilisation in the Indian Ocean,* p. 25.
43. Geoffrey Parker, *Global Crisis: War, Climate Change and Catastrophe in the Seventeenth Century,* New Haven and London, 2013, p. 68.
44. 'Popingay', so-called after the common green and red parrot that Italians once called the *pappagallo* or 'talking cock'. The weavers of Gloucester especially were famous for the production of this much sought-after cloth together with 'Murrey's graine' (mulberry coloured), 'violet graine', grass greens, 'flame coullors' and Venice reds.
45. For the relationship of world currencies it is as well to consult Chaudhuri, *The English East India Company,* Table 6.

8. OCEANS OF WEALTH

1. Minutes from which the account of preparations has been taken are missing 18 January 1610 to 4 January 1614.
2. See *South African Railway Magazine,* 1907, www.theheritageportal.co.za/article/workmen-discover-hidden-steps-and-centuries-old-post-office-stones-1906, and 'An Inscribed Rock at Sierra Leone', *Geographical Journal,* vol. 64, no. 2 (Aug. 1924), pp. 139–41.
3. Clements R. Markham, ed., *The Voyages of Sir James Lancaster, Kt., to the East Indies, with Abstracts of Journals of Voyages to the East Indies, during the Seventeenth Century, preserved in the India Office. And the Voyage of Captain John Knight (1606), to seek the North-West Passage,* Hakluyt Society, 1st ser., part 2, 1877, p. 159.
4. Ibid., p. 155.
5. Robert Kerr, *A General History and Collection of Voyages and Travels,* Edinburgh, 1824, vol. 8, p. 410.
6. Ibid., p. 411.
7. Ibid., p. 417.
8. Ibid., p. 371.
9. Ibid., p. 418.
10. Ibid., p. 380.
11. Danvers, *Letters Received by the East India Company,* vol. 1, letter no. 25, pp. 56–7, Pemberton to Middleton.
12. Ibid., letter no. 27, p. 60, Pemberton to Middleton.
13. Ibid., letter no. 31, p. xx, p. 64, Pemberton to Middleton.
14. Ibid., letter no. 30, p. 63, Downton to Middleton.
15. In 1626 Buckingham presented Henrietta Maria with Lord Minimus, a dwarf who sprang out of a pie at a banquet.
16. Kerr, *Voyages and Travels,* vol. 8, p. 387.
17. Danvers, *Letters Received,* vol. 1, letter no. 45, p. 91, Femmell to Middleton, 14 May 1611.
18. Ibid., letter no. 68, p. 123, 23 May 1611, Middleton to Femmell.
19. Michael Jinkins, 'Perkins, William', in *ODNB.*
20. Farrington, *The English Factory in Japan,* vol. 2, no. 402, Extracts from the East India Company's commission to John Saris for the Eighth Voyage, 4 April 1611, Clause 41, p. 983.
21. Kerr, *Voyages and Travels,* vol. 8, p. 394.
22. Ibid., p. 432–3.
23. Sanjay Subrahmanyam, *Europe's India: Words, Peoples, Empires, 1500–1600,* Cambridge, MA, 2017, p. 111.
24. Kerr, *Voyages and Travels,* vol. 8, p. 434.
25. Ibid., p. 435. The Ormondes were the most powerful family in Ireland during the reign of James I.
26. Ibid.

27. The weaknesses which her captains would all notice in *Peppercorn* would now come to be exacerbated as a result of this refit, with Captain Keeling informing the Company: 'The *Peppercorn* more fit for peace than for these voyages; she cannot carry her ordnance but in very smooth water; being deeply laden she is a slug, but jocund; she saileth well. They lost many days by the sluggishness of the *Peppercorn* at the first.' Danvers, *Letters Received*, vol. 2, letter no. 16, p. 190, Captain Edward Keeling at Saldania Bay, to the East India Company in London, 19 June 1615.

28. Sainsbury, *Papers, 1617–1621*, no. 127, Thomas Mitford 'From aboard the *Peppercorn*' to the East India Company in London, 8 August 1617.

29. Ibid., no. 643, Captain Martin Pring 'Aboard the *James Royal* near the isle of Becie in the straits of Sunda' to the East India Company, 23 March 1619, p. 266.

30. Ibid.

31. Ibid., no. 775, Augustine Spalding 'Aboard the *Unicorn* Masulipatam Road' to the East India Company in London, 23 November and 9 December 1619.

32. For what Spalding got up to and what he got away with see Birdwood and Foster, eds, *The Register of Letters*, pp. 95–6, note 1.

33. Sainsbury, *Papers, 1617–1621*, no. 842, Captain Robert Adams 'Aboard the *Bull* in Jakarta Road' to the East India Company in London, 2 May 1620.

34. Ibid., no. 845, John Rowe 'Aboard the *Globe*, Jacatra Road' to Sir Thomas Smythe in London, 2 May 1619.

35. Ibid., no. 671, 'Minutes of a Court held aboard the Moon', 21 May 1619.

36. Sainsbury, *Papers: East Indies, China and Japan, 1622–1624*, London, 1878, no. 70, 'Minutes of Consultations by the Council of the Fleet of Defence off the Manillas', 3 April to 2 August 1622.

37. Farrington, *The English Factory in Japan*, vol. 2, no. 353, Richard Cocks to Sir Thomas Smythe and the East India Company in London, 4 October 1621, p. 858.

38. Ibid., vol. 2, no. 422, Consultations of the Fleet of Defence at Hirado and on board ship, 10 September 1621–11 March 1622.

39. Ibid., vol. 1, p. 12.

40. Ibid., vol. 2, no. 381, p. 925, Richard Fursland, Thomas Brockedon and Augustine Spalding at Batavia to the East India Company in London, 9 February 1623.

41. Ibid., vol. 2, no. 350, Robert Adams at Hirado to Sir Thomas Smythe and the East India Company in London, 27 September 1621, p. 846.

42. Ibid., vol. 2, no. 351, Richard Cocks at Hirado to Sir Thomas Smythe and the East India Company in London, 30 September 1621, p. 849.

43. Ibid., vol. 2, no. 363, p. 882, Joseph Cockram at Hirado to Richard Fursland at Batavia, 6 September 1622.

44. R.S. Magurn, trans. and ed., *The Letters of Peter Paul Rubens*, Cambridge, MA, 1955, letter no. 77, Brussels, 15(?) February 1626.

45. Farrington, *The English Factory in Japan*, vol. 2, no. 366, p. 895, Richard Cocks at Hirado to Sir Thomas Smythe and the East India Company in London, 7 September and 14 November 1622.

46. Sainsbury, *Papers, 1622–1624*, no. 261, Edward Lenmyes 'From Aboard the *Elizabeth*, Jacatra' to the East India Company at London, 8 February 1623.

9. THE FLYING DUTCHMEN

1. Jonathan Israel, *The Dutch Republic: Its Rise, Greatness, and Fall, 1477–1806*, Oxford, 1995, pp. 219–20.

2. Mishra, *A Business of State*, p. 26.

3. Sainsbury, *Papers, 1513–1616*, no. 253, 'News Letter', 8 August 1597.

4. Parthesius, *Dutch Ships in Tropical Waters*, p. 34.

5. Ibid., p. 67.

6. McClure, ed., *The Letters of John Chamberlain*, vol. 2, no. 467, pp. 601–2, John Chamberlain in London to Sir Dudley Carleton at The Hague, 26 February 1625.

7. Parthesius, *Dutch Ships in Tropical Waters*, p. 67.

8. Philip F. Alexander, *The Earliest Voyages Round the World, 1519–1617*, Cambridge, 1916, p. 116.

9. See www.americanforeignrelations.com/E-N/Freedom-of-the-Seas-Origins-of-the-concept-of-freedom-of-the-seas.html.

10. For the best modern account of Fenton, see James McDermott, 'Fenton, Edward', in *ODNB*.

11. For the narrative of Fenton's expedition see E.G.R. Taylor, ed., *The Troublesome Voyage of Captain Edward Fenton, 1582–1583, Narratives and Documents*, Hakluyt Society, 2nd ser., part 2, Cambridge, 1959 (1957), *passim*.

12. Anon., 'An Inscribed Rock at Sierra Leone', *Geographical Journal*, vol. 64, no. 2 (Aug. 1924), pp. 139–41. This rock is noticed in *Wanderings in West Africa* (1863) by the famous African explorer and East India Company soldier, Sir Richard Burton KCMG, authority on the art of Eastern love-making – as had become known to him from applying in the field, tips found out of those scandalous texts the *Karma Sutra* and *The Perfumed Garden*.

13. Sainsbury, *Papers, 1516–1616*, no. 231, '1583', p. 92.

14. Foster, *England's Quest*, pp. 127–8.

15. Kerr, *Voyages and Travels*, Edinburgh, 1824, vol. 8, http://www.columbia.edu/itc/mealac/pritchett/00generallinks/kerr/vol07chap09sect07.html.

16. Foster, *England's Quest*, p. 256.

17. Ibid.

18. William Foster, ed., *The Journal of John Jourdain, 1608–1617, describing his Experiences in Arabia, India, and the Malay Archipelago*, Hakluyt Society, 2nd ser., part 1, 1905, p. liv.

19. Vincent C. Loth, 'Armed Incidents and Unpaid Bills: Anglo-Dutch Rivalry in the Banda Islands in the Seventeenth Century', *Modern Asian Studies*, vol. 29, no. 4 (Oct. 1995), pp. 705–40: p. 710.

20. Foster, *England's Quest*, p. 257.

21. Ibid.

22. Om Prakash, *The Dutch Factories in India, 1617–1623*, Delhi, 1984, p. 13.

23. Foster, *England's Quest*, p. 266.

24. Ibid., p. 267.

25. Ibid.

26. Ibid., p. 268.

27. Ibid., p. 269.

28. For the work these Dutchmen did for the EIC see: W.H. Moreland, ed., *Peter Floris his Voyage to the East Indies in the Globe, 1611–1615*, Hakluyt Society, 2nd ser., part 1, 1934, *passim*.

29. Anthony Farrington and Dhiravat Na Pombejra, *The English Factory in Siam 1612–1685*, London, 2007, vol. 1, no. 8, 'Peter Floris' Journal of the *Globe* at Patina and Ayutthaya in the East India Company's Seventh Voyage, 22 June 1612–22 October 1613', p. 84, 6 September 1612.

30. Ibid., vol. 1, no. 67, p. 219, Richard Wickham at Hirado to Benjamin Farie at Ayutthaya, 15 January 1617.

31. Ibid., vol. 1, no. 27, p. 144, Adam Denton at Pattani to Sir Thomas Smythe and the East India Company in London, 5 October 1614.

32. Ibid., vol. 1, no. 8, 'Peter Floris' Journal', p. 97, 1 January 1613.

33. Ibid., pp. 105–6, 5 June 1613.

34. For a nice study of these manic Buddhist men of war see 'The Jesuits in Japan', in Hugh Trevor-Roper, *Historical Essays*, London, 1957, ch. 18, pp. 119–24.

35. J.R. Bruijn, F.S. Gaastra and I. Schöffer, eds, *Dutch-Asiatic Shipping in the 17th and 18th Centuries*, The Hague, 1987, vol. 1, p. 128.

10. A THING OF SO MUCH DIFFICULTIE

1. Richard Hakluyt, *The Principal Navigation, Voiages, Traffiques and Discoueries of the English Nation*, 2nd edition, London, 1598, vol. 2, p. 245.
2. J.O. Halliwell, ed., 'The Private Diary of Dr John Dee', *The Camden Society*, 19 (1842), p. 18.
3. Richard Hakluyt, *Voyages*, intr. John Masefield, London, 1907, 'John Newbery to Richard Hakluyt, Alepo, the 28 of May 1583', vol. 3, p. 271.
4. Ibid., 'The Voyage of M. John Eldred to Trypolis in Syria by sea, and from thence by land and river to Babylon and Balsara. 1583', vol. 3, pp. 324–5.
5. Dimmock, *Elizabethan Globalism*, p. 147.
6. Hakluyt, *Voyages*, intr. Masefield, 'The Voyage of M. John Eldred', vol. 3, p. 275.
7. Ibid., [Ralph Fitch], 'His third letter to Maister Leonard Poore, written from Goa', p. 277.
8. Ibid., pp. 277–8.
9. Ibid., 'A letter written from Goa by M. Ralph Fitch to Master Leonard Poor abovesaid', p. 281.
10. Ibid., 'The voyage of M. Ralph Fitch Marchant of London by the way of Tripolis in Syria, to Ormuz, and so to Goa in the East India . . .', p. 287.
11. William F. Sinclair and Donald Ferguson, 'The Travels of Pedro Tixiera', Hakluyt Society, 2nd ser., part 1, no. 9, London, 1902, p. xxx.
12. '"World enough, and time": Richard Hakluyt and the Renaissance Discovery of the World', https://hakluytsociety.wordpress.com/2017/06/19/world-enough-and-time-richard-hakluyt-and-the-renaissance-discovery-of-the-world/.
13. Hakluyt, *Voyages*, intr. Masefield, 'The Voyage of M. Ralph Fitch, marchant of London by the way of Tripolis in Syria, to Ormus, and so to Goa in the East India . . . 1583', vol. 3, p. 290.
14. Trevor Dickie, 'Fitch, Ralph', in *ODNB*.
15. Clements R. Markham, 'The Hawkins Voyages during the Reigns of Henry VIII, Queen Elizabeth, and James I', Hakluyt Society, 1878 (1877), pp. 395–6.
16. Ibid., p. 393.
17. Ibid.
18. For this incident see Ellison B. Findlay, 'The Capture of Maryam-uz-Zamani's Ship: Mughal Women and European Traders', *Journal of the American Oriental Society*, vol. 108, no. 2 (1988), pp. 227–38: p. 233.
19. Sainsbury, *Papers, 1513–1616*, no. 650, Thomas Keridge at Agra to Thomas Aldworth and Council at Surat, 7 September 1613.
20. Foster, ed., *The Voyage of Nicholas Downton*, pp. 111–12.
21. Sainsbury, *Papers, 1513–1616*, no. 449, William Finch at Surat to Captain William Hawkins, Surat, 12 July 1609.
22. Ibid., no. 650, Thomas Keridge at Agra to Thomas Aldworth and Council at Surat, 7 September 1613. 'Lawes' may perhaps have been a relative of the celebrated Henry Lawes who was to write the music for Milton's *Comus*.
23. Ibid., no. 449, William Finch at Surat to Captain William Hawkins, Surat, 12 July 1609.
24. After the *Union* was wrecked on the coast of Brittany when returning from the East, the Sixth Voyage became a total write-off.
25. Sainsbury, *Papers, 1513–1616*, no. 459, Unknown to the East India Company, 15 September 1609.
26. Foster, ed., *The Journal of John Jourdain*, pp. 161–62.
27. For the relationship between Aldworth, Hakluyt and Walsingham, see Hakluyt, *Voyages*, intr. Masefield, pp. 78–9.
28. For the significance of this crisis in Mughal–Portuguese relations see Findlay, 'The Capture of Maryam-uz-Zamani's Ship', *passim*.
29. See G. Havers, trans., *The travels of Sig. Pietro della Valle, a noble Roman, into East-India and Arabia Deserta. In which, the several countries, together with the customs, manners,*

traffique, and rites both religious and civil, of those Oriental princes and nations, are faithfully described: in familiar letters to his friend Signior Mario Schipano. Whereunto is added a relation of Sir Thomas Roe's voyage into the East-Indies, London, 1665.

30. Foster, *England's Quest*, p. 237.
31. Ibid., pp. 237–8.
32. Christopher Farewell, *An East India Collation or a Discourse of Travels*, London, 1633, reprinted in Foster, ed., *The Voyage of Nicholas Downton*, p. 143.
33. Ibid., p. 134.
34. For the impact of Mīr Jumla on the fortunes of the EIC see: Sir William Foster, *The English Factories in India, 1618–1669*, Oxford, 13 vols, 1906–27, vol. 11, 1661–64, *passim*.
35. Pearson, *The Portuguese in India*, p. 113.
36. Burton Stein, *Vijatanagara*, vol. 1, part 2, *The New Cambridge History of India*, Cambridge, 1989, p. 139.
37. Subrahmanyam, *The Portuguese Empire in Asia*, p. 105.
38. Sainsbury, *Papers, 1513–1616*, no. 846, Thomas Mitford to Sir Thomas Smythe, Governor, and Committees of the East India Company, 24 December 1614.
39. Ibid., no. 847, John Crouther, Ahmedabad, 26 December 1614, to the Governor and Committees of the East India Company.
40. Ibid., no. 846, Thomas Mitford to Sir Thomas Smythe, Governor, and Committees of the East India Company, 24 December 1614.
41. Ibid., no. 856, Edward Dodsworth, Ahmedabad, to the East India Company, 30 December 1616.
42. Richmond Barbour, *Before Orientalism: London's Theatre of the East 1576–1626*, Cambridge, 2003, p. 148.
43. Sainsbury, *Papers, 1513–1616*, no. 796, Captain Nicholas Downton, 'Aboard the *New Year's Gift*, Swally Road', to the East India Company, 20 November 1614.
44. Ibid., no. 778, Thomas Aldworth at Surat to Thomas Keridge at Agra, 22 October 1614.
45. Ibid.
46. Ibid., no. 848, William Edwardes at Ahmedabad to Sir Thomas Smythe, Governor of the East India Company, 26 December 1614.
47. Foster, ed., *The Voyage of Nicholas Downton*, pp. 116–17.
48. Ibid., p. 112, note i.
49. Sainsbury, *Papers, 1513–1616*, no. 765, Court Minutes, 7 September 1614, p. 318.
50. Foster, ed., *Roe Journal*, vol. 1, p. iv.
51. Ibid., vol. 1, p. vi.

11. JOSEPH AT THE COURT OF PHARAOH

1. Foster, ed., *Roe Journal*, vol. 2, p. 343.
2. Ibid., pp. 496–7, Sir Thomas Roe, 'The Camp of Ghehangeer Sha, greate Mogoll', to James I, 15 February 1617–[18].
3. Sainsbury, *Papers, 1513–1616*, no. 810, Nicholas Downton to Sir Robert Sherley in Persia, Nov.? 1614.
4. Foster, ed., *Roe Journal*, vol. 1, p. 45.
5. Ibid., p. 46.
6. Ibid., pp. 76–7.
7. Ibid., p. 78.
8. Ibid., p. 124, Sir Thomas Roe to 'The Lord Bishop of Canterbury', 'Adsmere' [Ajmer], 29 January 1615–[16].
9. Thomas Coryate, *Coryat's Crudities Hastily gobled up in five months travells . . . Newly digested in the hungry aire of ODCOMBE in the County of Somerset and now dispersed to the nourishment of the travelling Members of the Kingdome*, London, 1607.

10. Michael Strachan, 'Roe, Thomas', in *ODNB*.
11. Coryat's father was vicar of Odcombe, a village in Somerset where Coryat had retreated to write *Crudities*. It was upon the whitewashed arcades of St Peter and St Paul that Tom had hung his odiferous walking shoes – or did he regard them as his spurs ? – after returning from Europe. Here these had been something of a send-up of those who, more self-important if hardly as self-publicising as Tom himself, might instead have suspended their own armorials.
12. Foster, ed., *Roe Journal*, vol. 1, n. 3.
13. Sainsbury, *Papers, 1513–1616*, no. 474, Court Minutes, 19 December 1609.
14. Among the forbidden books held in the library of St Paul's College, Goa was '*um comentario pequeno que trata do Imperio del Rei Mogol e sua magnificênca, autor Thomas Reus fidalgo ingles*'; Flores, ed., *The Mughal Padshah*, p. 8, n. 12. As for the Dutch, they too took the closest interest in Roe's correspondence and his *Journal*, though it would not be until 1656 that Jacob Benjamin of Amsterdam published the *Journael van de Reysen*, with Roe's name appearing on its handsome frontispiece. Even the Italians, who can hardly have been said to have had a stake in India, were familiar with Roe's *sententiae*. We find excerpts from Roe in Valerio Zane's *Il Genio Vagante* (Parma, 1792).
15. Roe had been part of the circle that orbited around the precocious and brilliant Sir Thomas Overbury, whose murder in 1615, which touched upon James I, would be the greatest royal scandal of the seventeenth century. In Overbury's *Newe and Choise characters of severall authors together with that exquisite and unmacht poeme written by Syr Thomas Ouerberie with the former characters and conceited newes, all in one volume Printed by Thomas Creede in Pauls Churchyard, 1615*, we find 'Country Newes' by 'Sr T. R.', immediately followed by 'Newes from the very Country' by 'I. D': authors identified as Roe and Donne respectively. See Evelyn M. Simpson, 'John Donne and Sir Thomas Overbury's CHARACTERS', *Modern Language Review*, vol. 18, no. 4 (Oct. 1923), pp. 410–15, and Alastair Bellany, *The Politics of Court Scandal in Early Modern England: News, Culture and the Overbury Affair, 1603–1660*, Cambridge, 2002, *passim*.
16. Sainsbury, *Papers, 1513–1616*, no. 991, letter from Richard Baker to the East India Company, '20 June [1615] Saldanha'.
17. Foster, ed., *Roe Journal*, vol. 2, p. 361.
18. Ibid., p. 294.
19. Ibid., p. 321.
20. G. Havers, *A Relation of Sir Thomas Roe's Voyage into the East Indies*, London, 1665, pp. 477–8.
21. William R. Pinch, 'Same Difference in India and Europe', *History and Theory*, vol. 38, no. 3 (Oct. 1999), pp. 389–407: p. 407.
22. Samuel Richardson, ed., *The Negotiations of Sir Thomas Roe to the Ottoman Porte*, London, 1740, Sir Thomas Roe in Constantinople, to George, Lord Carew in London, 3 May 1622, pp. 37–8.
23. Roe receives not so much as a mention in Jahāngīr's voluminous memoirs.
24. Foster, ed., *Roe Journal*, vol. 2, p. 300. The *tosha-khána* was properly the repository in which articles received as presents, or intended to be given as presents, were stored; but here as in a subsequent entry, Roe uses the term to mean the royal place of audience. Foster, idem., p. 300, note 1. The *al-sujūd* is the ritual of touching the forehead on the ground as a sign of humility before Allah. The *taslim* is the concluding ritual of prayer.
25. John Keay, *The Honourable Company: A History of the English East India Company*, London, 1993, p. 19.
26. Clara Cary Edwards, 'Relations of Shah Abbās the Great, of Persia, with the Mughal Emperors Akbar and Jahangir', *Journal of the American Oriental Society*, vol. 35 (1915), pp. 247–68. Foster, ed., *Roe Journal*, vol. 2, pp. 296–7.
27. Ibid., p. 320, 1 November 1616.
28. Erikson, *Between Monopoly and Free Trade*, p. 11.
29. Subrahmanyam, *The Portuguese Empire in Asia*, p. 108.
30. Foster, ed., *Roe Journal*, vol. 1, p. 213, n. 1.

31. Ibid., pp. 214–15.
32. Ibid., vol. 2, p. 368.
33. Ibid., p. 360.
34. Ibid., p. 363.
35. Ibid., p. 367.
36. Ibid., p. 391.
37. Strachan, *Sir Thomas Roe*, p. 112.
38. Prakash, *The Dutch Factories in India*, p. 91.
39. Ibid., p. 151.
40. Something very similar can still be seen in the Hall of the Girdlers' Company. On 12 August 1634 it was reported at Committees how 'Mr Bell having given order . . . for the making of a Lahore carpett, containing seven yards longe and three and a half yards broad . . . with his own and [the] Girdlers Armes thereon': John Irwin, *The Girdlers' Carpet*, Hove, 2019, p. 3.
41. Sainsbury, *Papers, 1617–1621*, no. 765, Court Minutes, 12 November 1619.
42. Foster, ed., *Roe Journal*, vol. 2, p. 528.
43. See 'ROE (ROWE), Sir Thomas (1581–1644)', in *The History of Parliament: the House of Commons 1604–1629*, ed. Andrew Thrush and John P. Ferris, 2010 [unpaginated], www.historyofparliamentonline.org/volume/1604-1629/member/roe-sir-thomas-1581-1644.
44. Sainsbury, *Papers, 1513–1616*, no. 852, 'Instructions for Sir Thos. Roe, knight, authorised by us, under our great seal of England, to repair as our ambassador to the Great Magoar [or emperor of the Oriental Indies]', 29 December 1614.
45. http://www.parliament.uk/worksofart/artwork/william-rothenstein/sir-thomas-roe-at-the-court-of-ajmir-1614/2598.
46. 'The Company and the Mughals Between Sir Thomas Roe and Sir William Norris', in Sanjay Subrahmanyam, *Mughals and Franks: Explorations in Connected History*, Oxford, 2005, pp. 143–72.
47. Historians depend much, as we all do, on the journal that Roe kept in India. It has attracted a notoriety hardly surpassed in the corpus of English writing on India. But those who choose to see Roe's papers as first of a whole library of hostile texts from an Englishman about India are missing the point. The *Journal* is in no sense a confessional, fixed or private enterprise; indeed, from the first Roe knew it would be read by the twenty-four members of the Court of Committees once he got home. Roe's *Journal* is no Pepys, with all his dirty groping secrets. Rather, it is the work of a diplomat who weaves patterns to please the multitude of clamorous, ignorant and prejudiced patrons at home in the hope of gaining the preferment that this most ambitious of men craved. Accordingly, it makes little sense to extract one passage here, one sentence there, to convict this man of being the *fons et origo* of a nascent English 'superiority' in the face of Indian civilisation. The irony of the embattled positions taken up about Roe is that the very *Journal* upon which such judgements are founded can be read both as an incunable of imperialism and something that anticipates that famous mantra of E.M. Forster: 'only connect'. In the end, from the entangled hedgerow of Roe's *Journal*, with all its compactions and convolutions, you pluck what you will; so various, so dense is that gross vegetation that Roe cultivated to vent frustration, air prejudice, admire 'the other', but above all, perhaps, to sanctify and satisfy himself in the eyes of one man in Philpot Lane and another in Whitehall Palace.

There is no doubt that Roe's reputation has suffered a vertiginous drop in the twentieth century. Yet we should avoid looking at the man through the wrong end of the telescope: 'To project [Roe's] findings backward,' argues Richard Barber (*Before Orientalism*, p. 3), 'to read precolonial ethnography as if its rhetoric bespoke European dominance of the world, or its defensive tropes necessarily foretold aggressive expansion is anachronistic.' And, quite simply, the intransigence, intolerance, superciliousness and insecurity that stain the pages of his *Journal*, while notable, are predictable given the intolerable pressures under which Roe had laboured. It is all too easy to engage, not to say indulge, a process of applying the norms, or better the aspirations, of supposed twenty-first-century tolerance to condemn what was said 400 years ago.

48. Barbour, *Before Orientalism*, p. 146.
49. Subrahmanyam, *Mughals and Franks*, pp. 158–62.
50. Foster, ed., *Roe Journal*, vol. 1, pp. xliv–xlv.

12. THIS HOPEFULLEST TRADE

1. Najaf Haider, 'Precious Metal Flows and Currency Circulation in the Moghul Empire', *Journal of the Economic and Social History of the Orient*, vol. 39, no. 3 (1996), pp. 298–364: p. 307.
2. Stephen F. Dale, *The Muslim Empires of the Ottomans, Safavids and Mughals*, Cambridge, 2010, p. 115.
3. Sainsbury, *Papers, 1513–1616*, no. 455, 30 August 1609, Surat.
4. Edward Connok was to be the first cape merchant appointed in Persia; not on the grounds that he knew anything about merchandise but because he had shown conspicuous bravery in boarding a Portuguese carrack when the English flotilla carrying him to Surat had engaged the enemy.
5. Sainsbury, *Papers, 1617–1621*, no. 446, Edward Pettus at 'Ispahan', 27 September 1618, to the East India Company at London.
6. Sainsbury, *Papers, 1513–1616*, no. 570, Middleton's 'A Letter of Advice to all English ships to shun the Red Sea', May 1611, Mocha.
7. Foster, ed., *Roe Journal*, vol. 2, p. 353.
8. Ibid., p. 354, Sir Thomas Roe, 'From the way midnight', 27 November 1616, to Sir Thomas Smythe at London.
9. Ibid., p. 426, note 2, Sir Thomas Roe, 'Mandoa, 8 November 1617, 'To the Factors at Surat'.
10. Ibid., p. 374, Sir Thomas Roe to William Robbins at 'Ispahan', 17 January 1616 [1617].
11. Sainsbury, *Papers, 1513–1616*, no. 342, Nov. 1604, 'Observations on the two special causes mentioned in the petition of the Turkey Merchants, of the decay of their trade into the Levant'.
12. Foster, ed., *Roe Journal*, vol. 2, p. 374, Sir Thomas Roe to William Robbins at 'Ispahan', 17 January 1616 [1617].
13. John Maclean, ed., *Letters from George Lord Carew to Sir Thomas Roe Ambassador to the Court of the Great Mogul 1615–1617*, Camden Society, vol. LXXVI, 1859, Carew to Roe, 'Savoy, this 18 January 1616', pp. 78–9.
14. Foster, ed., *Roe Journal*, vol. 2, p. 556, James I to Sir Thomas Roe, Giuen vnder our signet at our Pallace of Westminster, the 4th of February 1616[–17].
15. Chaudhuri, *The English East India Company*, p. 80.
16. Sainsbury, *Papers, 1617–1621*, no. 56, Edward Connok, 'Ispahan' to the East India Company at London, 2 April 1617.
17. Foster, ed., *Roe Journal*, vol. 2, p. 406, Sir Thomas Roe, 'Mandow' to William Robbins, 21 August 1617.
18. Da Silva became a student of Zoroastrianism after travelling to Shiraz, Qom and Isfahan. Though he would expire at Mozambique, en route for Spain, his mission had a fruitful afterlife, with the publication of his posthumous *Totius legationis suae et Indicarum rerum Persidisque commentarii*. This was the first book to make the West aware of Persepolis when the manuscript came to be translated into French by the Dutch diplomat Abraham de Wicquefort in 1667.
19. Sainsbury, *Papers, 1617–1621*, no. 339, April 1618, Thomas Barker to Sir Thomas Roe.

20. Ibid.
21. Ibid., no. 54, William Lesk, 'On board the *Globe*', to the East India Company at London, March 1617.
22. Ibid., no. 68, Edward Connok to Thomas Barker, Pley, Pettus, at 'Ispahan', and William Bell at Shiraz, 8 May 1617.
23. Ibid., no. 37, Thomas Doughty at Surat to the East India Company at London, 26 February 1617.
24. Ibid.
25. Ibid., no. 59, Edward Connok, at 'Ispahan' to George Pley, 10 April 1617.
26. Ibid., no. 811, Edward Monox, Robert Jefferies and Thomas Barker Junior, at 'Ispahan' to Thomas Keridge and the factors at Surat, 3 March 1620.
27. Ibid., no. 753, Thomas Barker, Edward Monox, William Bell, and Thomas Barker, jun., at 'Ispahan' to the East India Company at London, 16 October 1619.
28. Robert Hillenbrand, 'Safavid Architecture', in P. Jackson and L. Lockhart, *The Timurid and Safavid Periods*, vol. 6, *The Cambridge History of Iran*, Cambridge, 1986, p. 777.
29. Roger Savory, *Iran under the Safavids*, Cambridge, 1980, p. 166.
30. Sainsbury, *Papers, 1617–1621*, no. 339, April 1618, Thos. Barker to Sir Thomas Roe.
31. Ibid.
32. Sainsbury, *Papers, 1513–1616*, no. 1021, Court Minutes, 12 September 1615.
33. Ibid., no. 340, Thos. Barker and Wm. Bell, at 'Ispahan', 28 April 1618, to Thomas Keridge at Surat.
34. Sainsbury, *Papers, 1617–1621*, no. 339, p. 158, Thomas Barker to Sir Thomas Roe, April 1618.
35. Ibid., no. 91, Edward Connok, George Pley, and William Tracy, at 'Ispahan' to the East India Company at London, 2 June 1617.
36. Ibid., no. 446, Edward Pettus at 'Ispahan' to the East India Company at London, 27 September 1618.
37. Ibid.
38. Maclean, *Letters from Carew*, 'Savoy, this 18 January 1616', pp. 78–9.
39. Sainsbury, *Papers, 1617–1621*, no. 489, Court Minutes, 17–20 November 1618, p. 212.
40. Brenner, *Merchants and Revolution*, Cambridge, 1993, Table 1.3.
41. William A. Pettigrew and Tristan Stein, 'The Public Rivalry between Regulated and Joint Stock Corporations and the Development of Seventeenth-Century Corporate Constitutions', *Historical Research*, vol. 90, no. 248 (May 2017), pp. 341–62: p. 351.
42. Sainsbury, *Papers, 1617–1621*, no. 526, Court Minutes, 1 January 1619.
43. Ibid.
44. Ibid., no. 535, Court Minutes, 8 January 1619.
45. Ibid., no. 600, Court Minutes, 23 February 1619.
46. Ibid., no. 848, William Bell at Shiraz, 8 May 1620, to Edward Monox at 'Ispahan'.
47. Ibid., no. 828, George Strachan at 'Ispahan', 25 March 1620, to the East India Company at London.
48. Ibid., no. 893, George Strachan, August 1620, to Edward Monox and the factors in Persia.
49. Ibid., no. 894, Declaration by Pietro Chevart and Estefano de Sant Jaque at 'Ispahan', 8 September 1620.
50. Ibid., no. 871, Consultation held at 'Ispahan', present: Robert Jefferies, William Bell, John Purefey and John Benthall, against dice playing and other misdemeanours, 3 July 1620.
51. Sainsbury, *Papers, 1622–1624*, no. 330, William Bell and others at 'Ispahan' to the East India Company at London, 15 October 1623 and 9 January 1624, p. 163.
52. Sainsbury, *Papers, 1617–1621*, no. 992, Robert Jefferies at Surat, 14 March 1621 to the East India Company at London.
53. Ibid., no. 880, Consultation held at Ispahan, 18 July 1620, present: Robert Jefferies, William Bell, Thomas Barker, John Purefey and John Benthall.

54. Ibid., no. 972, Certificate signed by William Baffin, master of the *London*, John Woolhouse, and Bartholomew Symonds, surgeon, 10 February 1621.
55. Ibid., no. 753, p. 304, Thomas Barker and others at 'Ispahan', 16 October 1619, to the East India Company at London.
56. Sainsbury, *Papers, 1622–1624*, no. 143, p. 64, Richard Fursland, Thomas Brockendon and Augustine Spalding at Batavia, 27 August 1622, to the East India Company at London.
57. Sainsbury, *Papers, 1617–1621*, no. 811, Edward Monnox, Robert Jefferies and Thomas Barker at 'Ispahan', 3 March 1620, to Thomas Keridge and the factors at Surat.
58. Sainsbury, *Papers, 1622–1624*, no. 248, John Digby, earl of Bristol at Madrid, 28 January 1623, to George Calvert, viscount Baltimore at London.
59. Ibid., no. 297, Viscount Conway at Greenwich, 30 June 1623, to Viscount Baltimore.
60. Ibid., no. 298, Baltimore, St Martin's Lane, 1 July 1623, to Conway.
61. Ibid., no. 301, p. 121, Court Minutes, 4–23 July 1623.
62. Ibid.
63. Ibid.
64. Ibid., no. 311, p. 135, Court Minutes, 30 July–6 August 1623.
65. Ibid., no. 301, p. 123, Court Minutes, 4–23 July 1623.

13. SEVEN MERCHANTS OF JAPAN

1. Patrick Copland, *Virginia's God be thanked, or a sermon of thanksgiving for the happie successe of the affayres of Virginia this laste yeare. Preached by Patrick Copland at Bow Church in Cheapside, before the Honorable Virginia Company, on Thursday, the 18 of April, 1622*, printed for I.D. for William Sheppard and John Bellamie, London, 1622, pp. 5–7.
2. Farrington, *The English Factory*, vol. 2, p. 991, Extracts from John Saris' journal of the Eighth Voyage, 9 June–5 December 1613.
3. *Daimyōs* were powerful feudal lords who were endowed with extensive hereditary lands. From the tenth century until the fall of the Tokugawa dynasty in 1868, they carved up Japan between themselves.
4. By contrast, a *bugyō* tended to be less sanguinary; a samurai, certainly, he would often hold an official governmental office such as the magistracy of a town like Hirado.
5. Farrington, *The English Factory*, vol. 1, no. 319, p. 793, Richard Cocks at Nagasaki, 10 March 1620, to Sir Thomas Smythe and the East India Company at London.
6. Richard Lloyd Parry wrote of how out in Japan, it is thought that the grave of William Adams has been found: 'Final Resting Place of Sailor who Inspired TV's Shogun', *The Times*, 3 April 2019.
7. Farrington, *The English Factory*, no. 70, vol. 1, p. 209, John Saris on board the *Clove* at Plymouth to the East India Company in London, 17 October 1614.
8. Ibid., no. 235, vol. 1, p. 585, Richard Wickham at Hirado, 'January 1617', to John Jourdain at Bantam.
9. Ibid., no. 427, pp. 1260–8, extracts from Richard Cocks's account book of the Eighth Voyage, 28 June–3 December 1613. Just as the astronomical dividends which Adventurers received look impressive on paper, but need to be divided by the number of years between investment and return, so too caution is required in the interpretation of these figures: the gross sum has to be divided by at least four to represent the number of years during which the EIC had been trying to dispose of its stock.
10. Ibid., no. 133, p. 341, Richard Coppendale at Hirado to the East India Company's agent in Siam, 5 December 1615.
11. Ibid., no. 43, pp. 161–3, Richard Wickham at Edo to Richard Cocks at Hirado, 25 May 1614.
12. José Eugenio Borao, *The Spanish Experience in Taiwan, 1626–1642: The Baroque Ending of a Renaissance Endeavour*, Hong Kong, 2009, p. 138.

13. Wang Gungwu, 'Merchants Without Empire: The Hokkien Sojourning Communities', Chapter 3, pp. 420–1, in James D. Tracy, ed., *The Rise of the Merchant Empires: Long Distance Trade in the Early Modern World*, Cambridge, 1990.

14. Sainsbury, *Papers, 1617–1621*, no. 101, George Cokayne at Succadana to President Ball at Bantam, 15 June 1617.

15. For Gondomar as a bibliophile, see María Luisa López-Vidriero and Pablo Andrés Escapa, *Correspondencia del Conde de Gondomar*, Madrid, 4 vols, 1999–2003, *passim*.

16. Penguins much intrigued Roe as he clambered about Robben Island en route for India. They made good steaks but better lamps. Their oil burned in the glass that towered above the taft rail – so big it could hold a man like a fly in amber. The 'great lantern' remained alight through the long watches of the stormiest of nights. If it was extinguished then so too was hope of ever finding that ship which had held it – as those watching the fate of the *Penelope* on that English voyage back in 1591 under George Raymond had ruefully noted in their ship's log.

17. Farrington, *The English Factory*, vol. 2, no. 409, pp. 1057–59, William Adams's journal of his voyage to the Ryukyu islands in the *Sea Adventure*, November 1614–November 1616.

18. Coleridge read Wickham's accounts of life in Japan before writing *The Rime of the Ancient Mariner* (1798), https://www.bl.uk/collection-items/purchas-his-pilgrimage-or-relations-of-the-world-and-the-religions.

19. Farrington, *The English Factory*, vol. 2, no. 410, Edmund Sayers's journal of his voyage from Hirado to Siam in the *Sea Adventure* and of his return in a chartered junk, with accounts of presents and goods in Siam, 7 December 1615–22 November 1616, p. 1097.

20. Ibid., p. 1087.

21. Ibid., p. 1094.

22. Ibid., p. 1099.

23. Ibid., vol. 1, no. 149, p. 383, Richard Cocks at Hirado to the East India Company in London, 25 February 1616.

24. Ibid., no. 317, pp. 775–6, Richard Cocks at Nagasaki to the Governor and Company of Clothworkers of London, 10 March 1620.

25. Ibid., vol. 2, no. 435, p. 1517, Cock's Diary, 7 August–6 November 1613, 17 September 1613.

26. Ibid., p. 1517.

27. 'Lapedable': obsolete term for sexual intercourse.

28. Farrington, *The English Factory*, vol. 1, no. 30, Richard Cocks at Hirado to Richard Wickham at 'Edo, Shizuoka or elsewhere', 9 March 1614, p. 140.

29. Ibid., vol. 2, no. 348, p. 843, Richard Watts at Hirado to Sir Thomas Smythe and the East India Company in London, 22 September 1621.

30. Ibid., no. 364, p. 887, Richard Cocks at Hirado to Richard Fursland at Batavia, 7 September 1622.

31. For a portrait of Itakura Katsuhige see https://en.wikipedia.org/wiki/Itakura_Katsushige#External_links.

32. Farrington, *The English Factory*, vol. 2, no. 366, p. 898, Richard Cocks at Hirado to Sir Thomas Smythe in London, 7 September and 14 November 1622.

33. Sainsbury, *Papers, 1617–1621*, no. 106, George Ball, President at Bantam, to Richard Cocks at 'Firando', 3 July 1617.

34. Farrington, *The English Factory*, vol. 1, no. 270, p. 698, Edmund Sayers at Hirado to Sir Thomas Smythe in London, 16 February 1618.

35. Ibid.

36. Ibid., p. 699.

37. Ibid., vol. 1, no. 245, pp. 613–14, Richard Wickham at Bantam to his mother in England, 10 June 1617.

38. Sainsbury, *Papers, 1622–1624*, *passim*. 'Elizabeth Wickham' is wrongly described as the wife of Richard Wickham. 'Elizabeth' was Wickham's mother; he never married. 'William', described as a son, was Richard's brother.

39. Ibid., no. 29, Court Minutes, 13 February 1622.
40. Ibid., no. 13, Court Minutes, 23 January 1622.
41. Ibid., no. 29, Court Minutes, 13 February 1622.
42. Ibid., no. 50, Court Minutes, 13 March 1622.
43. Ibid., no. 30, Court Minutes, 15 February 1622.
44. Ibid., no. 454, Court Minutes, 26 May 1624.
45. National Register of Archives, Public Record Office: R.A. C2/Jas.I/W1/52: Elizabeth Wickham (*administratix*) v Sir William Halliday and others. Wickham had clearly died a very rich man. Sainsbury, *Papers, 1622–1624*, no. 231, '1622. Petitions to the East India Company of Persons who solicit Employment, Increase of Wages, Payment of Wages due to their Relatives in the Company's Service', under '5 June 1622' is the following entry: 'Mayor and Commonalty of Bristol: A legacy of 250l from Richd. Wickham'. This would appear to be a separate sum from what had been assigned to Bristol Grammar School to buy books.
46. Sainsbury, *Papers, 1622–1624*, no. 409, Court Minutes, 9 February 1624.
47. All London was at the impeachment of Hastings for corruption. The legal sensation of the reign, this great public drama was notable for two things. Edmund Burke emerged as the finest public orator in what was the golden age of parliamentary debate, whilst for his part, Hastings remained steady in the face of those elegant periods of his adversary. Such indeed was the defendant's sang-froid during proceedings which were to last seven years that many came to support him. Eventually, he would be acquitted.
48. Farrington, *The English Factory*, vol. 1, no. 28, p. 136, William Eaton at Ōsaka to Richard Wickham at Edo, 1 March 1614.
49. Ibid., no. 71, p. 215 William Eaton at Ōsaka to Richard Cocks at Hirado, 27 October 1614.
50. Ibid., no. 165, p. 415, William Eaton in prison at Akuno-ura to William Nealson, 22 May 1616.
51. Ibid., no. 267, pp. 670–1, Richard Cocks at Hirado to Sir Thomas Smythe and the East India Company in London, 15 February 1618.
52. As described by Milton in *Paradise Lost* III.431–6:

> Here walk'd the Fiend at large in spacious field.
> As when a vulture on Imaus bred,
> Whose snowy ridge the roving Tartar bounds,
> Dislodging from a region scarce of prey
> To gorge the flesh of lambs or yeanling kids,
> On hills where flocks are fed, flies toward the springs,
> Of Ganges or Hydaspes, Indian streams;
> But in his way lights on the barren plains
> Of Sericana, where Chineses drive
> With sails and wind their canny wagons light:
> So on this windy sea of land, the Fiend
> walked Up and down alone, bent on his prey.

It has been suggested that Milton's sources for this passage were to be found in Juan Gonzales de Mendoza's *Historia de las cosas mas notables, ritos y costumbres del gran reyno dela China* (*The History of the Great and Mighty Kingdom of China and the Situation Thereof*: tr. R. Parke, 1588). This book, by the Augustinian monk and bishop of Popayán, 'aroused European interest' in this pollution-free mode of transport. Grotius himself rode in one of the copies constructed by the Dutch scientist Steven, whilst Jacques de Gheyn III made a celebrated engraving which he entitled *The sailing-car of Prince Maurice of Orange*. John Milton, *Paradise Lost*, ed. Alastair Fowler, London, 1998, p. 193.
53. Sainsbury, *Papers, 1625–1629*, no. 375, pp. 265–66, Court Minutes, 22 November 1626.
54. Ibid., p. 266, Court Minutes, 24 November 1626.
55. Ibid., no. 379, p. 276, Court Minutes, 2 December 1626.

56. Farrington, *The English Factory*, vol. 2, p. 1555.
57. Farrington, *The English Factory*, vol. 1, no. 247, George Ball at Bantam to Richard Cocks at Hirado, 9 June 1617.
58. Ibid., vol. 1, no. 319, Richard Cocks at 'Nangasaque in Japon' to Sir Thomas Smythe and the East India Company in London, 10 March 1620.
59. Farrington, *The English Factory*, vol. 2, no. 381, p. 925, Richard Fursland, Thomas Brockedon and Augustine Spalding at Batavia to the East India Company in London, 9 February 1623.

14. GOODNIGHT AMSTERDAM

1. 'Moho' was the Company's name for Mocha, from whence the EIC imported its first coffee. Commonly supposed to have been a 'Restoration' drink, the fact that Lawrence Femmell was mighty taken with it back in 1614 suggests that it had long been enjoyed by the more discriminating of English palates – before, that is to say, the first coffee house in London was founded.
2. Brian Cowan, *The Social Life of Coffee: The Emergence of the British Coffeehouse*, New Haven and London, 2005, p. 93.
3. For Downing and Anglo-Dutch rivalry, see Jonathan Scott, ' "Good Night Amsterdam": Sir George Downing and Anglo-Dutch State Building', *English Historical Review*, vol. 118, no. 476 (Apr. 2003), pp. 334–56.
4. 'A Perfidious Rogue', *Spectator*, 15 August 1925.
5. Scott, ' "Good Night Amsterdam" ', pp. 335–6.
6. Ibid., p. 335.
7. Johan De Witt was for twenty years (*c.* 1650–70) Grand Pensionary and leading Republican politician in Holland in the post-Stadtholder era. Together with his brother Cornelis, Johan was first murdered and then partially eaten by an Orangist mob who, tiring of the De Witts' dominance over the affairs of the Republic, had resolved to dispense with their services.
8. Latham and Matthews, eds, *The Diary of Samuel Pepys*, vol. 9: *1668–69*, p. 402.
9. Scott, ' "Good Night Amsterdam" ', p. 337, quoting Charles Wilson, *Profit and Power: A Study of England and the Dutch Wars*, The Hague, Boston and London, 1978, p. 95.
10. Wantje Fritschy, *Public Finance of the Dutch Republic in Comparative Perspective: The Viability of an Early Modern Federal State (1570s–1795)*, Leiden and Boston, 2017, p. 19.
11. See Marjolein't Hart, 'The United Provinces, 1579–1806', in Richard Bonney, ed., *The Rise of the Fiscal State in Europe c. 1200–1815*, Oxford, 1999, pp. 309–27.
12. Ibid., p. 289, n. 114.
13. Ibid., p. 273.
14. Ibid., p. 289.
15. Ibid., p. 309.
16. Ibid., p. 275.
17. Jan de Vries and Ad van der Woude, *The First Modern Economy, Success, Failure and Perseverance of the Dutch Economy, 1500–1815*, Cambridge, 1997, p. 374.
18. Ibid., pp. 352–3.
19. Jonathan Israel, *The Dutch Republic and the Hispanic World 1606–1661*, Oxford, 1982, p. 3.
20. Ibid., p. 6.
21. Ibid., p. 45.
22. Ibid., p. 47.
23. Ibid., p. 36.
24. Hugo Grotius, *The freedom of the seas: or, The right which belongs to the Dutch to take part in the East Indian trade / a dissertation by Hugo Grotius; translated with a revision of the*

Latin text of 1633 [Grotius's *Mare Liberum*], ed. James Brown Scott and trans. Ralph Magoffin, New York, 1916, p. 28.

25. Roberta Anderson, 'Caron, Sir Noel de', in *ODNB*. For an illustration of these alms-houses pulled down in 1852, see a watercolour by Thomas Hosner Shepherd: British Museum Collections inv. no. 1880,1113.5496.

26. This is what Wotton recommends from his reading of Vitruvius, whom Wotton was to popularise for an English readership in his *Elements of Architecture collected . . . from the Best Authors and Examples*, London, 1624.

27. Though nothing is known as to what hung in Sir Noël's picture gallery, his largesse to artists is attested by the existence of an etching of the Laocoön by Jacques de Gheyn III. This has a four-line inscription in which this brilliant Dutch printmaker thanks Sir Noël for having him to stay. The print was made in 1619 and published by Henrick Hondius in 1631: British Museum Collections inv. no. 1917,1208.499.

28. Edmund Sawyer, *Memorials of Affairs of State in the Reigns of Queen Elizabeth and James I*, London, 1725, vol. 3, p. 239, John Moore to Sir Ralph Winwood, London, 15 December 1610.

29. The English had continued to claim Pulau Run, the site of Calthorpe's last stand, for most of the seventeenth century; although the Dutch had been de facto master of the island since they had shot Calthorpe dead in 1622.

30. The exploits of William Adams in Japan became the inspiration in America for *Shogun* (1980), an irresistible concoction of drama and bath-house love which not only proved the most successful programme in the history of the NBC but has been credited with that important cultural event: the rise of the sushi house in Middle America.

31. Royal Collection: https://www.rct.uk/collection/405533/the-shipbuilder-and-his-wife-jan-rijcksen-15602-1637-and-his-wife-griet-jans.

32. Museum of London ID: DK87-136.

33. G.N. Clark and W.J.M. Van Eysinga, *The Colonial Conferences between England and the Netherlands in 1613 and 1615*, Leiden, 1951, p. 8.

34. Rijksmuseum, Amsterdam inv. no: SK-A-3741.

35. Roe was rightly proud of his wife's stoutness (Richardson, ed., *Negotiations*, pp. 825–6):

> she sat upon the deck among the guns and was often forced to tack as the enemy came upon our quarters. This glory she hath, that she showed no fear nor passion; but seeing it was her portion, but resolved that she would bear it. Some great shot fell about her, which moved her not; only while I was with her, to see her, I got a bruise with piece of wood over the back which felled me; and this amazed her; but when I rose and had no harm, but pain, she said the chance of the day was past; the bullet came dangerously right with me, but was diverted.

The two recuperated sightseeing in Florence, where Roe ordered *pieta dura* tables from the *botteghe* of the Pitti Palace, inlaid with semi-precious stones and displaying the Roe coat of arms. See David Howarth, 'Samuel Boothouse and Artistic Enterprise in Seventeenth-Century Florence', *Italian Studies*, vol. 32 (1977), pp. 83–96.

36. A 'cabinet' was to the seventeenth century what a study is today, though with this difference: Reael's would have been groaning with stuffed animals, dusted with dried plants and adorned by artefacts plucked from the indigenous cultures of the East. Just as both the VOC and the EIC created a taste for the Oriental in the seventeenth century, with such delights as porce-lain from China and rugs from Persia, *objets* that both Pepys and Evelyn record in their respective diaries, so in the next century would emerge the Chinoiserie aesthetic.

37. These are 'Epigrammes' XCVIII and XCIX in: *The Workes of Benjamin Jonson, London Printed by Richard Bishop and are to be sold by Andrew Crooke, in St Paules, Church-Yard*, London, 1640, 2 vols, vol. 1.

38. Roe was to be MP for Tamworth. He resigned in despair after the Addled Parliament of 1614 and, shaking English dust off his heels, headed to the dust of India, there to reinvent himself.

15. DEADLOCK

1. Clark and Van Eysinga, *The Colonial Conferences*, p. 34.
2. Ibid., p. 35.
3. Ibid., p. 43.
4. Ibid., p. 44.
5. Ibid., p. 50.
6. W.S.M. Knight, 'Grotius in England: His Opposition There to the Principles of Mare Liberum', in *Transactions of the Grotius Society*, vol. 5, 1919, pp. 1–38.
7. Clark and Eysinga, *The Colonial Conferences*, p. 49.
8. Ibid., pp. 61–2.
9. Ibid., p. 76.
10. Ibid., p. 73.
11. Ibid., p. 67.
12. Ibid., p. 76.
13. Ibid., p. 78.
14. Ibid., p. 79.
15. Knight, 'Grotius in England'.
16. Clark, *The Colonial Conferences*, p. 96.
17. Ibid., p. 102.
18. Ibid., p. 103.
19. Ibid., p. 104.
20. Ibid., p. 121.
21. Sainsbury, *Papers, 1617–1621*, no. 485, Carleton at The Hague to Sir Robert Naunton at London, 14 November 1618.
22. Clark, *The Colonial Conferences*, p. 13.
23. Ibid., p. 135.
24. Alison Games, *Inventing the English Massacre: Amboyna in History and Memory*, Oxford, 2020, p. 2.
25. Ibid., p. 181.
26. Ibid., Chapter 6, 'Legacies: Reinvention and the Linchpin of Empire', *passim*.
27. Anon., *A True Relation of the Late Cruel and Barbarous Tortures and Execution Done upon the English at Amboyna*, London, 1624, p. 4, https://ota.bodleian.ox.ac.uk/repository/xmlui/bitstream/handle/20.500.12024/A95286/A95286.html?sequence=5&isAllowed=y.
28. Sainsbury, *Papers, 1617–1621*, no. 346, George Cokayne and John Hayward at Jakarta to President Ball Bantam, 6 May 1618, reporting how the humidity had eaten three tons of iron nails. What then can the climate have done to a man's stomach before the appearance of morphine, quinine and penicillin?
29. Games does not exclude the possibility that there was indeed a conspiracy involving the English and the Japanese against the Dutch.
30. Games, *Massacre*, pp. 53–5.
31. Ibid., pp. 33–4. Over a six-day period in February–March 1621, Speult had forced all the *orang-kayaks* (local leaders) of the islands in his orbit to pay homage to the Stadthouder Prince Maurice. But then he had also forced Muschamp to witness these rituals of obeisance.
32. William Foster, 'Coen's Narrative of the Visit of the *Darling* to Amboyna and Ceram', in Foster, ed., *The Journal of John Jourdain*, p. 336.
33. For Muschamp, his pain and his anger, see Games, *Massacre*, pp. 13, 33–4, 40–2, 46, 49–50.
34. Ibid., pp. 40–1.
35. Sainsbury, *Papers, 1617–1621*, no. 1021, George Muschamp at Amboyna to the President and Council of Jakarta, 12 June 1621; and Games, *Massacre*, p. 33.
36. Games, *Massacre*, p. 58, points out how the principal martyr, Gabriel Towerson, had taken part in the torture of someone who had allegedly stolen some EIC papers.

37. McClure, ed., *Letters of John Chamberlain*, vol. 2, no. 467, Chamberlain in London to Carleton at The Hague, 26 February 1625.

38. One such was Naqd 'Ali Beg whose portrait by Greenbury hangs at St Pancras: inv. No. British Library F23. For this see 'Stitched up with Silk: Naqd 'Ali Beg's journey to London in 1626', London, British Library blog post, 11 June 2013, https://blogs.bl.uk/asian-and-african/2013/06/stitched-up-with-silk-naqd-%CA%BBali-begs-journey-to-london-in-1626.html. Mildred Archer, *The India Office Collection of Paintings and Sculpture*, London, 1986, pp. 28–9; and unpublished notes by William Foster, dated 7 November 1903, in the India Office Records (IOR/L/R/6/248).

39. Mary Anne Everett Green, ed., *Calendar of State Papers Domestic: James I, 1623–25*, London, 1859, vol. 184, Calendar, no. 64, p. 481, Thomas Locke in London to Sir Dudley Carleton at The Hague, 21 February 1625.

40. Sainsbury, *Papers, 1625–1629*, no. 59, Court Minutes, 18 February 1625.

41. Ibid., no. 61, Sir Maurice Abbot and ten members of the Court of Committees in London to Sir Dudley Carleton at The Hague, 19 February 1625.

42. Ibid.

43. Ibid.

44. Ibid.

45. Ibid., no. 65, Court Minutes, 21–23 February 1625.

46. Ibid., no. 70, Sir Maurice Abbot and five members of the Court of Committees in London, 26 February 1625, to Sir Dudley Carleton at The Hague.

47. Ibid., no. 73, Court Minutes, 28 February 1625.

48. It is Robert Bell's fabulous carpet that still survives at the Girdlers' Company. See Plate 10.

49. Sainsbury, *Papers, 1625–1629*, no. 105, Court Minutes, 8 April 1625.

50. Ibid., no. 127, Court Minutes, 6 May 1625.

51. In this narrative of how 'Amboyna' unfolded in England, as from spring 1624, the present author offers a quite different view to that of Edmond Smith. In his *Merchants*, pp. 210–11, Smith argues that 'In the months following news of the massacre, the East India Company took careful control of the collection, interpretation and distribution of news of the event.' For this writer, the Company was wholly out of control.

52. John Pory to Sir Thomas Puckering, 21 April 1631, British Library, Harleian Ms. 7000, ff. 326–8. Games suggests that the executioners did their best to replicate how the English factors had died upon Amboyna, given that waterboarding was not an option in the middle of a German forest.

16. DELIVERANCE

1. Sainsbury, *Papers, 1622–1624*, no. 319, Secretary of State, Lord Conway, to Attorney General Coventry, 21 August 1623.

2. Henry James Coleridge, *The Life and Letters of St. Francis Xavier 1506–1556*, 2 vols, London, 1935, vol. 2, p. 106.

3. Sainsbury, *Papers, 1622–1624*, no. 333, Court Minutes, 22 October 1623.

4. Ibid.

5. Ibid., no. 388, Court Minutes, 12 January 1624.

6. Smith, *Merchants*, pp. 57–8.

7. The box in question now belongs to the Saddlers' Company. See ibid., Plate 12.

8. McClure, ed., *The Letters of John Chamberlain*, vol. 2, no. 386, p. 388, John Chamberlain in London to Sir Dudley Carleton at The Hague, 14 July 1621.

9. Sainsbury, *Papers, 1622–1624*, no. 433, 'Minutes of a General Court of the East India Company for the election of a Governor', 23 March 1624.

10. Ibid., no. 303, Court Minutes, 23 June–23 July 1623, p. 125.

11. Ibid., no. 413, Court Minutes, 18–23 February 1624, p. 247.

12. Ibid., p. 248.
13. Mishra, *A Business of State*, p. 204.
14. Sainsbury, *Papers, 1622–1624*, no. 303, Court Minutes, 23 June–23 July 1623.
15. Ibid., no. 425, Court Minutes, 8 March 1624.
16. Ibid.
17. Ibid.
18. Ibid., no. 435, Court Minutes, 26 March 1624.
19. Ibid., no. 425, 8 March 1624.
20. Ibid.
21. Ibid.
22. Ibid., no. 708, p. 469, Court Minutes, 10 December 1624; Andrew Thrush, 'Abbot, Sir Maurice', in *ODNB*.
23. Thrush, 'Abbot', *ODNB*.
24. John Rushworth, 'Historical Collections: The impeachment of Buckingham (1626)', in *Historical Collections of Private Passages of State*, vol. 1: *1618–29*, London, 1721, pp. 302–58.
25. Earl of Clarendon, *The History of the Rebellion and Civil Wars in England Begun in the Year 1641*, ed. W. Dunn Macray, vol. 2, Oxford, 1969 edn, section VI.209.
26. There can be no portrait by Van Dyck painted with more brio than that of Warwick, now in the Metropolitan Museum in New York. Accession no: 49.7.26
27. Sainsbury, *Papers, 1625–1629*, no. 672, Court Minutes, 27 June 1628.
28. Brenner, *Merchants and Revolution*, p. 274.
29. Ibid., p. 233.
30. Ibid., pp. 231–4.
31. A 'Suit of Replevin' is action to recover personal property that was wrongfully taken or detained.
32. 'Blackwall Yard: Development, to c.1819', in *Survey of London*, vols 43 and 44: *Poplar, Blackwall and Isle of Dogs*, ed. Hermione Hobhouse, London, 1994, pp. 553–65, fn. 50, *British History Online*, http://www.british-history.ac.uk/survey-london/vols43-4/pp553-565.
33. For details of the negotiations see ibid., pp. 553–65.
34. Ibid.
35. Its Great Hall still exists: it was translated from the City to Cheyne Walk, Chelsea, in 1910. For a wonderful sense of what the interior of Crosby Hall looked like, at a time when its hammer-beam roof would not have disgraced Hampton Court, see *Interior of Crosby Hall, Bishopsgate*, watercolour by John Sell Cotman, 1831. Victoria and Albert Collections, acc. no. P.19-1927.
36. For the appearance of Craven House after its makeover, see https://en.wikipedia.org/wiki/East_India_House#/media/File:Old_East_India_House.jpg.
37. For the final manifestation of the East India Company, when at last it had come to look like the giant corporation which by then it was, see *East India House* by Thomas Malton the Younger, Paul Mellon Collection, Yale Center for British Art, Yale University, New Haven, CT, acc. no. B 2001.2.1001.
38. John C. Appleby, 'Courten, Sir William', in *ODNB*.
39. Mishra, *A Business of State*, p. 273.
40. Sainsbury, *Minutes*, vol. 1: *1635–1639*, 'Quarterly General Court, 12 June 1635', pp. 64–5.
41. Ibid., p. 270: 'Informations and Observations that the East India Company are resolved to divide and leave the Trade'.
42. Ibid., pp. 274–6: 'Reasons to move the King to confirm under the Great Seal Captain Weddell's Commission'.
43. Ibid., p. 611.
44. Ibid., vol. 2: *1640–1643*, p. xii.

45. Following the execution of Charles I in January 1649, there had been an interval of parliamentary government until Parliament was dismissed by Cromwell and he assumed power. The 'Protectorate' followed the chaotic experiment of Parliaments without a king. The 'Protectorate', or 'Interregnum' to royalists, was when the British Isles and its dependencies was ruled as a republic by the 'Lord Protector', Oliver Cromwell. The protectorate lasted from 1653 to 1659.
46. Sainsbury, *Minutes*, vol. 2: *1640–1643*, p. ix.
47. Ibid., vol. 1: *1635–1639*, p. xxviii.
48. Slavery within the EIC during this period was not yet an industry. The number of slaves traded within the Indian Ocean for the period 1600–99 has been estimated at 50,324–65,024 within the Dutch trading community, but only 1,811–1,819 among the English. If the sceptic may raise their eyebrow at such exact numeration, extracted before the invention of the census, and when many a Robinson Crusoe was living embowered in prelapsarian bliss, sequestered alike from either control or observation. Notwithstanding we must surely accept the principle of difference between what was a Dutch and an English state of affairs. For the fruits of painful tabulation, see Richard B. Allen, *European Slave Trading in the Indian Ocean, 1500–1850*, Athens, OH, 2014, p. 19, Table 2.
49. For the most recent assessment of Thomson's energy, reach and range of business interests see David Brown, *Empire and Enterprise: Money, Power and the Adventurers for Irish Land during the British Civil Wars*, Manchester, 2020, *passim*.
50. Sainsbury, *Minutes*, vol. 6: *1655–1659*, p. xx.
51. Methwold is buried in St Mary Abbot's, at the bottom of Kensington Church Street. Where exactly within the church he lies is not, however, known.
52. Michael Strachan, 'William Methwold', in *ODNB*.
53. Methwold's will is PRO PROB-11-231-31.
54. Sainsbury, *Minutes*, vol. 2: *1640–1643*, pp. 26–7.
55. J.E. Farnell, 'The Navigation Act of 1651, the First Dutch War, and the London Merchant Community', *Economic History Review*, vol. 16, no. 3 (1964), pp. 439–54.
56. Sainsbury, *Minutes*, vol. 5: *1650–1654*, p. xiii.
57. Ibid., vol. 10: *1674–1676*, pp. 107–8; Court of Committees to Surat, 28 October 1685, IOR E/3/91 fols 5–6. Quoted by Philip J. Stern, ' "A Politie of Civill & Military Power": Political Thought and the Late Seventeenth-Century Foundations of the East India Company-State', *Journal of British Studies*, 47, no. 2 (Apr. 2008), pp. 253–83.
58. No. 146, Court of Committees to FSG, 28 September 1687, IOR E/3/91, fol. 209. Quoted in Stern, ' "A Politie" '.
59. Joseph Addison in *The Spectator* (19 May 1711).

CONCLUSION

1. See Clarendon, *The History of the Rebellion*, *passim*.
2. I am ignoring Sir William Halliday, whose illness and death precluded his making much of an impact.
3. For a rather more positive assessment of Sir Thomas Dale, see Smith, *Merchants*.
4. See ibid., pp. 207–29. Smith argues that there was more collaboration between merchant and colonist than is suggested above, though his argument centres on the 1640s and beyond.
5. 'James I of England, James VI of Scotland', http://www.explore-parliament.net/nssMovies/04/0454/0454_.htm.
6. A start has been made, though only for the second half of the seventeenth century, by Aske Laursen Brock and Misha Ewen, 'Women's Public Lives: Navigating the East India Company, Parliament and Courts in Early Modern England', *Gender and History*, vol. 33, no. 1 (2020), pp. 52–83.

7. Sainsbury, *Papers, 1625–1629*, no. 260, Court Minutes, 17 February 1626.

8. *Calendar of Cecil Manuscripts*, vol. 11, 1906, p. 569.

9. Smith, *Merchants, passim*.

10. In a corner of the kirkyard at Cromarty East Church is a notice commemorating John Thomson. He was a nineteen-year-old officer of the East India Company whose actions aboard the *Kent*, carrying 600 souls bound for India, were extraordinary. On 1 March 1825 the *Kent* caught fire in a force 10 gale. At the sighting of another ship Thomson commanded a cutter which endured nine hours in mountainous seas crossing between the ships and carrying people to safety. His actions, so the memorial states, helped to save 547 lives. I would like to thank Keith and Philippa Atkey for bringing this commemoration to my notice.

11. See the title and subtitle of the most recent study of the EIC: William Dalrymple, *The Anarchy: The Relentless Rise of the East India Company*, London, 2019.

BIBLIOGRAPHY

MANUSCRIPT SOURCES
BRISTOL CITY ARCHIVES

33041/BMC/6: Bristol Municipal Charities Record: Alderman John Whitson's Charities

BRITISH LIBRARY

Cotton Mss. Titus B VIII
Harleian Ms. 7000: John Pory to Sir Thomas Puckering, 21 April 1631
IOR/L/R/6/248: Sir William Foster, unpublished notes, 7 November 1903

KENT COUNTY RECORD OFFICE, MAIDSTONE

U1115/c15: Cranfield Papers

NATIONAL ARCHIVES, KEW

SP/91/196: 'Instructions for Sir Thomas Smythe knight authorised by his Matys. Under the great seal of England to repair as Embassadour to ye Emperour of Moscovie'

PREROGATIVE COURT OF CANTERBURY

PROB-11-147-84: Will of Sir Thomas Smythe
PROB-11-138-271: Will of William Nealson
PROB-11-147-536: Will of William Eaton
PROB-11-145-315: Will of George Ball
PROB-11-151-750: Will of Richard Cocks
PROB-11-139-459: Will of Richard Wickham
PROB-11-126-143: Will of Tempest Peacock
PROB-11-137-60: Will of Sir Thomas Dale
PROB-11-231-31: Will of William Methwold

PRIMARY SOURCES AND EARLY PRINTED BOOKS (PRE-1800)

Birdwood, Sir George, and Sir William Foster, eds, *The Register of Letters etc of the Governour and Company of Merchants of London Trading into the East Indies, 1600–1619*, London, 1893
Calendar of the Salisbury (Cecil) Manuscripts, Historical Manuscripts Commission, 24 vols, London, 1883–1976 [*Calendar of Cecil Manuscripts*]

Danvers, F.C., *Letters Received by the East India Company from its Servants in the East*, 6 vols, London, 1896–1902

Farrington, Anthony, *The English Factory in Japan 1613–1623*, 2 vols, London, 1991

Farrington, Anthony, and Dhiravat Na Pombejra, *The English Factory in Siam 1612–1685*, 2 vols, London, 2007

Foster, Sir William, *A Supplementary Calendar of Documents in the India Office Relating to India or to the Home Affairs of the East India Company*, London, 1928

Sainsbury, E.B., *A Calendar of the Court Minutes of the East India Company 1635–1679*, 11 vols, Oxford, 1907–38

Sainsbury, W. Noël, ed., *Calendar of State Papers Colonial* [Sainsbury, *Papers*]:
— *America and West Indies, 1574–1660*, London, 1860
— *East Indies, China and Japan, 1513–1616*, London, 1862
— *East Indies, China and Japan, 1617–1621*, London, 1870
— *East Indies, China and Japan, 1622–1624*, London, 1878
— *East Indies, China and Persia, 1625–1629*, London, 1884
— *East Indies and Persia, 1630–1634*, London, 1892

Alexander, William, *An Account of the Diseases, Natural History, and Medicines of the East Indies, Translated from the Latin of James Bontius Physician to the Dutch Settlement at Batavia; To which are added Annotations by a Physician*, London, 1769

Anon., *Addison's Essays from The Spectator*, London, 2007 (1882), no. 24, 'Benefits of Commerce', pp. 78–81

Anon., *East Indian Trade Selected Works, 17th Century*, Farnborough, 1969

Anon., *An Impartial Vindication of the English East India Company*, London, 1688

Anon., *The Petition and Remonstrance of the Governor and Company of Merchants of London Trading to the East Indies, Exhibited to the Honorable the House of Commons assembled in Parliament Anno 1628*, London, 1628

Anon., *Sir Thomas Smithes voiage and entertainment in Rushia . . .*, London, 1605

Anon., *A True Relation of the Late Cruel and Barbarous Tortures and Execution Done upon the English at Amboyna*, London, 1624

Asher, G.M., *Henry Hudson the Navigator: The Original Documents in which his Career is Recorded*, Hakluyt Society, 1st ser., no. 27, London, 1860

Barker, A., *A True and Certaine Report of the Beginnings, Proceedings Overthrowes and Now Present Estate of Captaine Ward and Danseker, Pirates*, London, 1609

Bontius, Jacobus, *De Medicina Indorum*, Leiden, 1642

Boswell, James, *Life of Samuel Johnson*, 1791, p. 207.

Boxer, C.R., ed., *The Tragic History of the Sea 1589–1622: Narratives of the Shipwrecks of the Portuguese East Indiamen São Thomé (1589), Santo Alberto (1593), São João Baptista (1622) and the Journeys of the Survivors in South East Africa*, Hakluyt Society, 2nd ser., part 2, vol. 112, Cambridge, 1959

Brito, Bernardo Gomes de, ed., *História trágico-marítima, em que se escrevem cronologicamente os naufrágios que tiveram as naus de Portugal, depois que se poz em exercício a Navegação da Índia*, 2 vols, Lisbon, 1735–6

Burnell, Arthur Coke, *The Voyage of John Huyghen van Linschoten to the East Indies. From the Old English Translation of 1598. The First Book, containing his Description of the East*, Halkuyt Society, 1st ser., part 2, vol. 70, London, 1885 (1884)

— *The Voyage of John Huyghen van Linschoten*, Hakluyt Society, 1st ser., part 2, vol. 71, 1885 (1884)

Bynum, W.F., and Roy Porter, eds, *Companion Encyclopedia of the History of Medicine*, 2 vols, London, 1993

Cardim, Antonio Francisco, *Batalhas da Companhia de Jesus na sua gloriosa Provincia do Japão*, [1650] Reprint Lisbon,1894

Clarendon, earl of, Edward Hyde, *The History of the Rebellion and Civil Wars in England Begun in the Year 1641*, ed. W. Dunn Macray, 6 vols, Oxford, 1969

Clowes, William, *A Profitable and Necessarie Booke of Obseruations, for all those that are burned with the Flame of Gun powder, Etc, and also for curing of wounds made by Musket and Caliuershot, and other weapons of war commonly vsed at this day both by sea and land, as heerafter shall be declared*, London, 1596

Coleridge, Samuel Taylor, *The Ryme of the Ancient Mariner*, London, 1798

Collinson, Richard, ed., *The Three Voyages of Martin Frobisher, in search of a Passage to Cathaia and India by the North-West, A.D. 1576–8*, Hakluyt Society, 1st ser., part 1, vol. 38, London, 1867

Copland, Patrick, *Virginia's God be thanked, or a sermon of thanksgiving for the happie successe of the affayres of Virginia this laste yeare. Preached by Patrick Copland at Bow Church in Cheapside, before the Honorable Virginia Company, on Thursday, the 18 of April, 1622.* printed for I.D. for William Sheppard and John Bellamie, London, 1622

Corney, Bolton, ed., *The Voyage of Sir Henry Middleton to Bantam and the Maluco islands; being the Second Voyage set forth by the Governor and Company of Merchants of London trading into the East-Indies. From the Edition of 1606*, Hakluyt Society, 1st ser., part 1, no. 19, London, 1855 (1856)

Coryate, Thomas, *Coryat's Crudities Hastily gobled up in five months travells . . . Newly digested in the hungry aire of ODCOMBE in the County of Somerset and now dispersed to the nourishment of the travelling Members of the Kingdome*, London, 1607

Davies, John, trans., *The Voyages and Travells of the Ambassadors from the Duke of Holstein to the Grand Duke of Muscovy and the King of Persia in Seven Books . . .*, London, 1642

Devereux, Robert, earl of Essex, *The arraignment, tryal and condemnation of Robert Earl of Essex and Henry Earl of Southampton, at Westminster the 19th of February, 1600 . . .*, London, 1679

Digges, Sir Dudley, *The defence of trade in a letter to Sir Thomas Smith Knight, governor of the East-India Company etc, From one of that societie . . .*, London, 1615

Dryden, John, *Amboyna: A Tragedy*, London, 1673

Duffus Hardy, Sir Thomas, *Syllabus of the Documents relating to England and other kingdoms confined in the Collection known as 'Rymers Foedera'*, 2 vols, London, 1869

East India Company, *The Lawes or Standing Orders of the East India Company*, London, 1621, repr. Farnborough, 1968

Feltham, Owen, *Batavia, or, The Hollander displayed in brief characters & observations of the people & country, the government of their state & private families, their virtues and vices: also, A perfect description of the people & country of Scotland*, London and Amsterdam, 1675

Foster, Sir William, ed., *The Embassy of Sir Thomas Roe to the Court of the Great Mogul, 1615–1619, as Narrated in his Journal and Correspondence*, 2 vols, Hakluyt Society, 2nd ser., part 1, 1899 [Foster, *Roe Journal*]

— ed., *The Journal of John Jourdain, 1608–1617, describing his Experiences in Arabia, India, and the Malay Archipelago*, Hakluyt Society, 2nd ser., part 1, 1905

— ed., *The Voyage of Nicholas Downton to the East Indies, 1614–15, as Recorded in Contemporary Narratives and Letters*, Hakluyt Society, 2nd ser., part 1, 1939 (1938)

— ed., *The Voyage of Sir Henry Middleton to the Moluccas, 1604–1606*, Hakluyt Society, 2nd ser., part 1, vol. 88, London, 1943

— ed., *The Voyage of Thomas Best to the East Indies, 1612–14*, Hakluyt Society, 2nd ser., part 1, vol. 75, London, 1934

— ed., *The Voyages of Sir James Lancaster to Brazil and the East Indies, 1591–1603*, Hakluyt Society, 2nd ser., part 1, vol. 85, London, 1940

Green, Mary Anne Everett, ed., *Calendar of State Papers Domestic: James I, 1603–10*, London, 1857

— ed., *Calendar of State Papers Domestic: Elizabeth, 1595–97*, London, 1869

— ed., *Calendar of State Papers Domestic: Elizabeth, 1598–1600*, London, 1869

— ed., *Calendar of State Papers Domestic: Elizabeth, 1601–1603*, London, 1870

— ed., *Calendar of State Papers Domestic: James I, 1611–18*, London, 1858

— ed., *Calendar of State Papers Domestic: James I, 1619–23*, London, 1858

— ed., *Calendar of State Papers Domestic: James I, 1623–25*, London, 1859

Grey, Edward, *The Travels of Pietro della Valle in India. From the old English Translation of 1664, by G. Havers*, Hakluyt Society, 1st ser., part 2, vol. 84, I, London, 1892 (1891)

— *The Travels of Pietro della Valle in India*, Hakluyt Society, 1st ser., part 2, vol. 85, II, London, 1892 (1891)

Grotius, Hugo, *The freedom of the seas: or, The right which belongs to the Dutch to take part in the East Indian trade / a dissertation by Hugo Grotius; translated with a revision of the Latin text of 1633* [Grotius's *Mare Liberum*], ed. James Brown Scott and trans. Ralph Magoffin, New York, 1916

Hakluyt, Richard, *The Principal Navigations, Voiages, Traffiques and Discoueries of the English Nation, . . .*, 3 vols, 2nd edn, London, 1598–1600

— *Voyages*, intr. John Masefield, 8 vols, London, 1907

Havers, G., *A Relation of Sir Thomas Roe's Voyage into the East Indies*, London, 1665

— trans., *The travels of Sig. Pietro della Valle, a noble Roman, into East-India and Arabia Deserta.: In which, the several countries, together with the customs, manners, traffique, and rites both religious and civil, of those Oriental princes and nations, are faithfully described: in familiar letters to his friend Signior Mario Schipano. Whereunto is added a relation of Sir Thomas Roe's voyage into the East-Indies*, London, 1665

Herbert, Thomas, *A Relation of Some Yeares Travaile Begunne Anno 1626*, London, 1634

Johnson, Robert, *Nova Britannia*, London, 1609

Johnson, Thomas, trans., *The workes of that famous chirurgeon Ambrose Parey translated out of the Latine and compared with the French. by Thomas Johnson*, London, 1634

Kayll, Robert, *The trades increase*, London, 1615

Kent, Countess of, *A Choice Manual of Rare and Select Secrets in Physick and Chyrurgery . . . as also Most Exquisite Ways of Preserving, Conserving, Candying etc*, London, 2nd edn, 1654

Kerr, Robert, *A General History and Collection of Voyages and Travels*, 18 vols, Edinburgh, 1824

Knolles, R., *The General Historie of the Turkes*, London, 1631 edn

Lamond, Elizabeth, and William Cunningham, eds, [Sir Thomas Smith], *A Discourse of the Common Weal of this Realm of England*, Cambridge, 1893

Latham, Robert, and William Matthews, eds, *The Diary of Samuel Pepys*, 11 vols, London, 1970–83

Lee, Maurice, *Dudley Carleton to John Chamberlain, 1603–1624: Jacobean Letters*, New Brunswick, 1972

López-Vidriero, María Luisa, and Pablo Andrés Escapa, eds, *Correspondencia del Conde de Gondomar*, Madrid, 4 vols, 1999–2003

Maclean, John, ed., *Letters from George Lord Carew to Sir Thomas Roe Ambassador to the Court of the Great Mogul 1615–1617*, Camden Society, vol. LXXVI, London, 1860

McClure, N.E., ed., *The Letters of John Chamberlain*, 2 vols, Philadelphia, 1939

McCulloch, J.R., *Early English Tracts on Commerce*, Cambridge, 1954

Malynes, Gerard de, *Consuedo, vel, Lex Mercatoria: or, The Law Merchant: Divided into three parts, according to the Essential Parts of Traffick Necessary for All Statesmen, Judges, Magistrates, Temporal and Civil Lawyers, Mint-Men, Merchants, Mariners and Others Negotiating in all Places of the World*, London, 1622

Markham, A.H., ed., *The Voyages and Works of John Davis the Navigator*, Hakluyt Society, 1st ser., part 2, 1880 (1878)

Markham, Clements R., ed., *The Hawkins Voyages during the Reigns of Henry VIII, Queen Elizabeth, and James I*, Hakluyt Society, 1878 (1877)

— ed., *The Voyages of Sir James Lancaster, Kt., to the East Indies, with Abstracts of Journals of Voyages to the East Indies, during the Seventeenth Century, preserved in the India Office. And the Voyage of Captain John Knight (1606), to seek the North-West Passage*, Hakluyt Society, 1st ser., part 2, 1877

— ed., *The Voyages of William Baffin, 1612–1622. Edited, with Notes and an Introduction by Clements R. Markham*, Hakluyt Society, 1st ser., part 2, vol. 63, London, 1881 (1880)

Martin, Priscilla, intr., *William Tyndale's New Testament*, Ware, 2002

Milton, John, *Paradise Lost*, ed. Alastair Fowler, London, 1998

Misselden, Edward, *The Circle of Commerce*, 1623

Moreland, W.H., ed., *Peter Floris his Voyage to the East Indies in the Globe, 1611–1615*, Hakluyt Society, 2nd ser., part 1, 1934

— ed., *William Methwold, Relations of Golconda in the Early Seventeenth Century*, Hakulyt Society, 2nd ser., part 1, vol. 66, London, 1931

Moreland, W.H., and P. Geyl, trans., *Jahangir's India: The Remonstratie of Francicso Pelsaert*, Cambridge, 1925

Morgan, Edward Delmar, ed., *Early Voyages and Travels to Russia and Persia by Anthony Jenkinson and other Englishmen. With some Account of the First Intercourse of the English with Russia and Central Asia by Way of the Caspian Sea*, ed. Edward Delmar Morgan, Hakluyt Society, 1st ser., part 2, vol. 72, I, London, 1886 (1885)

— *Early Voyages and Travels to Russia and Persia*, Hakluyt Society, 1st ser., part 2, vol. 73, II, London, 1886

Mun, Thomas, *A Discourse of Trade, from England unto the East Indies*, London, 1621

— *Englands' Treasure by Foreign Trade, or the Balance of Our Foreign Trade is the Rule of our Treasure*, London, 1664

— *The Petition and Remonstrance of the Governor and Company of Merchants of London Trading to the East Indies*, London, 1628

Overbury, Sir Thomas, *New and Choice Characters of Several Authors Written by Sir Thomas Overburie*, London, 1615

Page, Samuel, *Divine Sea Service*, London, 1616

Pearsall Smith, Logan, *The Life and Letters of Sir Henry Wotton*, 2 vols, Oxford, 1907

Phillip, William, ed., and William Rogers, trans., *John Huighen van Linschoten. His discourse of voyages into ye Easte and West Indies Deuided into four bookes*, London, 1598

Purchas, Samuel, *Hakluytus Posthumus or Purchas his Pilgrimes*, London, 1625–6

— *Hakluytus Posthumus or Purchas His Pilgrimes*, ed. Cyril Wild, 20 vols, Glasgow, 1907

Rego, António da Silva, intr., *As Gavetas da Torre do Tombo*, 7 vols, Lisbon, 1960–70

Richardson, Samuel, ed., *The Negotiations of Sir Thomas Roe to the Ottoman Porte*, London, 1740

Roberts, Lewes, *The Merchants Mappe of Commerce*, London, 1638

— *The Treasure of Traffike or a Discourse of Forraigne Trade*, London, 1641

Roe, Sir Thomas, *Journael van de reysen ghedaen door . . . Sr T. Roe . . . afgevaerdicht naer Oostindien aen den Grooten Mogol . . . Uyt het Engels vertaalt, ende met copere figuren verciert*, Amsterdam, 1656

— *Sir Thomas Roe his speech in Parliament wherein he sheweth the cause of the decay of coyne and trade in this land, especially of merchants trade, and also propoundeth a way to the House, how they may be increased. Printed in the year 1641*

Rundall, Thomas ed., *Memorials of the Empire of Japon in the XVI and XVII Centuries*, Hakluyt Society, 1st ser., part 1, no. 8, London, 1850

— *Narratives of Voyages towards the North-West, in Search of a Passage to Cathay and India. 1496 to 1631*, Hakluyt Society, 1st ser., part 1, vol. 5, London, 1849

Rushworth, John, *Historical Collections of Private Passages of State*, 8 vols, London, 1721

Sandys, Sir Edwin, *Europae Speculum*, London, 1632

Satow, Sir Ernest Mason, ed., *The Voyage of Captain John Saris to Japan, 1613*, Hakluyt Society, 2nd ser., part 1, 1900

Sawyer, Edmund, *Memorials of Affairs of State in the Reigns of Queen Elizabeth and James I*, 3 vols, London, 1725

Sinclair, William F., and Donald Ferguson, 'The Travels of Pedro Tixiera', Hakluyt Society, 2nd ser., part 1, no. 9, London, 1902

431

Skinner, John, *A true and large discourse of the voyage of the whole fleete of ships set forth the 20. of April 1601. by the Gouernors and Assistants of the East Indian Merchants in London, to the East Indies*, London, 1603

— *A true relation of the vniust, cruell, and barbarous proceedings against the English at Amboyna in the East-Indies, by the Neatherlandish gouernour and councel there.: Also the copie of a pamphlet, set forth first in Dutch and then in English, by some Neatherlander; falsly entituled, A true declaration of the newes that came out of the East-Indies, with the pinace called the Hare, which arriued at Texel in Iune, 1624. Together with an answer to the same pamphlet. / By the English East-India companie. Published by authoritie*, London, 1624

Smith, John, *A sea grammar: with the plaine exposition of Smiths Accidence for young sea-men, enlarged: diuided into fifteene chapters: what they are you may partly conceiue by the contents*, London, 1627

Smith, Thomas, *Catalogus Librorum Manuscriptorum Bibliothecae Cottonianae*, Oxford, 1696

Smith, Sir Thomas attrib., ed. Mary Dewar, *Discourse of the Commonwealth of this Realm of England*, Charlottesville, 1969

Stevens, Henry, *The Dawn of British Trade To the East Indies as recorded in the court minutes of the East India Company 1599–1603, Concerning an account of the formation of the Company The first Adventure and Waymouth's Voyage in search of the North-West Passage*, London, 1886

Strachey, William, *A true reportory of the wracke, and redemption of Sir Thomas Gates Knight; vpon, and from the Ilands of the Bermudas: his comming to Virginia, and the estate of that Colonie then, and after, vnder the gouernment of the Lord La Warre, Iuly 15. 1610*, in Samuel Purchas, *Purchas his Pilgrimes*, London, 1625 (circulated in London as a manuscript from 1610)

Stow, John *A Survey of London, Contayning the Originall, Increase,Moderne Estate and description of that Citie written in the yeare 1598 by John Stow Citizen of London.Also an Apology (or defence) against the opinion of some men, concerning that Citie the greatnesse thereof with an appendix, containing in Latine, Libellum situ e nobilitate London: Written by W. Fitzstephen in the raigne of Henry the second*, London, 1598

— *The Survey of London*, London, 1912, with an intro. by Henry B. Wheatley

Strachan, Michael, and Boies Penrose, eds, *The East India Company Journals of Captain William Keeling and Master Thomas Bonner, 1615–1617*, Minnesota, 1971

Strype, John, ed., *Survey of London*, 2 vols, London, 1720

Taylor, E.G.R., ed., *The Troublesome Voyage of Captain Edward Fenton, 1582–1583, Narratives and Documents*, Hakluyt Society, 2nd ser., part 2, Cambridge, 1959 (1957)

Temple, Sir Richard Carnac, *The Travels of Peter Mundy, in Europe and Asia, 1608–1667*, Hakluyt Society, 2nd ser., part 1, vol. 17, I, London, 1907 (1905)

— *The Travels of Peter Mundy II: Travels in Asia, 1628–1634*, Hakluyt Society, 2nd ser., part 1, vol. 35, II, London, 1914

Terry, Edward, *A Voyage to East-India With a Description of the large Territories under the subjection of the Great Mogol*, London, 1655

Thackston, Wheeler M., ed. and trans., *The Jahangirnama: Memoirs of Jahangir, Emperor of India*, New York, 1999

Thompson, Sir Edward Maunde, *Diary of Richard Cocks Cape-Merchant in the English Factory in Japan 1615–1622 with Correspondence*, Hakluyt Society, 2nd ser., part 2, vol. 66, II, London, 1883

— *Diary of Richard Cocks*, Hakluyt Society, 2nd ser., part 2, vol. 67, London, 1883 (1882)

Tiele, P.A., *The Voyage of John Huyghen van Linschoten*, Hakluyt Society, 2nd ser., part 2, vol. 70, II, London, 1885 (1884)

Toldervy, W., *Select Epitaphs*, London, 1755

Vasconcellos, Padre Simão de, *Chronica da Companhia de Jesv do estado do Brasil: e do qve obrarão sevs filhos nesta parte do Novo mvndo. Tomo primeiro: da entrada da Companhia de Jesv nas partes do Brasil. Edos fvndamentos qve nellas lançârão, & continuàrão seus religiosos em quanto alli trabalhou o padre Manoel da Nobrega, fundador, & primeiro Prouincial desta*

Prouincia, com sua vida, & morte digna de memoria: e Algũas Noticias Antecedentes curiosas, & necessarias das cousas daquelle estado, pello, Lisbon, 1663

Vega, Lope de, *Fuenteovejuna*, 1619

Wheeler, John, *A Treatise of Commerce: wherein is shewed the commodities arising by a well ordered and ruled trade, such as that of the Society of Merchants Adventurers is proved to be*, London, 1601

Wood, John, *The true honor of navigation and navigators: or, holy meditations for sea-men Written vpon our sauiour Christ his voyage by sea, Matth. 8. 23. &c. Whereunto are added certaine formes of prayers for sea trauellers, suited to the former meditations, vpon the seuerall occasions that fall at sea. By Iohn Wood, Doctor in Diuinitie*, London, 1618

Woodall, John, *The surgeons mate or Military & domestique surgery Discouering faithfully & plainly ye method and order of ye surgeons chest, ye uses of the instruments, the vertues and operations of ye medicines, with ye exact cures of wounds made by gunshott, and otherwise as namely: wounds, apos fumes, ulcers, fistula's, fractures, dislocations, with ye most easie & safest wayes of amputation or dismembring. The cures of the scuruey, of ye fluxes of ye belly, of ye collicke and iliaca passio, of tenasmus and exitus ani, and of the calenture, with A treatise of ye cure of ye plague. Published for the service of his Ma. tie and of the com:wealth. By John Woodall Mr. in chyrurgerie*, 3 vols, London, 1639

Wotton, Sir Henry, *Elements of Architecture collected by H.W. kt, from the Best Authors and Examples*, London, 1624

Wright, Edward, *Certaine errors in nauigation, arising either of the ordinarie erroneous making or vsing of the sea chart,compasse, crosse staff, and tables of declination of the Sunne, and fixed stars detected and corrected. By E.W.*, London, 1599

MODERN SOURCES

Abulafia, David, *The Discovery of Mankind: Atlantic Encounters in the Age of Columbus*, New Haven and London, 2008

Alexander, Philip F., *The Earliest Voyages Round the World, 1519–1617*, Cambridge, 1916

Alford, Stephen, *London's Triumph: Merchant Adventurers and the Tudor City*, London, 2018

Allen, Richard, *European Slave Trading in the Indian Ocean, 1500–1850*, Athens, OH, 2014

Anderson, Christina M., ed., *Early Modern Merchants as Collectors*, London, 2019

Andrews, Kenneth R., 'Christopher Newport of Limehouse, Mariner', *William and Mary Quarterly*, vol. 11 (1954), pp. 28–41

— *Elizabethan Privateering: English Privateering during the Spanish War, 1585–1603*, London, 1964

— 'The Elizabethan Seaman', *Mariner's Mirror*, vol. 68 (1982), pp. 245–62

— *Ships, Money and Politics: Seafaring and Naval Enterprise in the Reign of Charles I*, Cambridge, 1991

— *Trade, Plunder and Settlement: Maritime Enterprise and the Genesis of the British Empire, 1480–1630*, Cambridge, 1984

Anon., 'An Inscribed Rock at Sierra Leone', *Geographical Journal*, vol. 64, no. 2 (Aug. 1924), pp. 139–41

Antony, Robert J., 'Turbulent Waters: Sea Raiding in Early Modern South East Asia', *Mariner's Mirror*, vol. 99, no. 1 (2013), pp. 23–39

Aparicio, Ángel Alloza, de Bunes Ibarra, Miguel Ángel, and Martinez, José Martinez, eds, *Peso de todo el Mundo* (Madrid, 1622) and *Discurso sobre el aumento de esta monarquía* (Madrid, 1625) by Sir Anthony Sherley, Madrid, 2010

Appleby, Joyce Oldham, *Economic Thought and Ideology in Seventeenth-Century England*, Princeton, 1978

Arasaratnam, S., *Merchants, Companies and Commerce on the Coromandel Coast*, Delhi, 1986

Archer, Ian W., 'The Arts and Acts of Moralisation in Early Modern London', in J.F. Merritt, ed., *Imagining Early Modern London: Perceptions and Portrayals of the City from Stow to Strype, 1598–1720*, Cambridge, 2001, pp. 89–113

— *The Pursuit of Stability: Social Relations in Elizabethan London*, Cambridge, 1991

Archer, Mildred, *The India Office Collection of Paintings and Sculpture*, London, 1986

Armitage, David, *The Ideological Origins of the British Empire*, Cambridge, 2000

Ashton, Robert, *The City and the Court, 1603–1643*, Cambridge, 1979

— *The Crown and the Money Market*, Oxford, 1960

— 'The Parliamentary Agitation for Free Trade in the Opening Years of the Reign of James I', *Past and Present*, vol. 38, no. 1 (1967), pp. 40–55

Aslanian, Sebouh David, *From the Indian Ocean to the Mediterranean: The Global Trade Networks of Armenian Merchants from New Julfa*, Berkeley, 2014

Aubrey, John, *Brief Lives with an Apparatus for the Lives of our English Mathematical Writers*, ed. Kate Bennett, 2 vols, Oxford, 2015

Aylmer, G.E., *The State's Servants: The Civil Service of the English Republic*, London, 1973

Bacon, Francis, *The Advancement of Learning and New Atlantis*, intr. Thomas Case, Oxford, 1974

— *Essays*, intr. Oliphant Smeaton, London, 1906

Barber, W.J., *British Economic Thought and India 1600–1858*, Oxford, 1975

Barbour, Richmond, *Before Orientalism*: *London's Theatre of the East 1576–1626*, Cambridge, 2003

Barbour, Violet, *Capitalism in Amsterdam in the 17th Century*, Michigan, 1963

Bard, Nelson P., 'The Earl of Warwick's Voyage of 1627', in N.A.M. Rodger, ed., *The Naval Miscellany*, vol. V, London, 1984, pp. 15–94

Bath, Bernard Hendrik Slicher, 'The Economic Situation in the Dutch Republic during the Seventeenth Century', in Maurice Aymard, ed., *Dutch Capitalism and World Capitalism*, Cambridge, 1982

Beach, Milo Cleveland, 'The Mughal Painter Abu'l Hasan and some English Sources for his Style', *Journal of the Walters Art Gallery*, no. 38 (1980), pp. 6–33

Beiser, Frederick C., *The Sovereignty of Reason*, Princeton, 1996

Bellany, Alastair, *The Politics of Court Scandal in Early Modern England: News, Culture and the Overbury Affair, 1603–1660*, Cambridge, 2002

Bentley, Duncan T., 'Niels Steensgaard and the Europe–Asia Trade of the Early Seventeenth Century', *The Journal of Modern History*, vol. 47, no. 3 (Sept. 1975), pp. 512–18

Berkeley, Michael, *They Came to Japan: An Anthology of European Reports on Japan, 1543–1640*, Berkeley, 1965

Blaug, Mark, ed., *The Early Mercantilists: Thomas Mun (1571–1641), Edward Misselden (1608–1634) and Gerard de Malynes (1568–1623)*, Cheltenham, 1991

Bleichmar, Daniela, Paula De Vos, Kristin Huffine and Kevin Sheehan, eds, *Science in the Spanish and Portuguese Empires, 1500–1800*, Stanford, 2009

Borao, José Eugenio, *The Spanish Experience in Taiwan, 1626–1642: The Baroque Ending of a Renaissance Endeavour*, Hong Kong, 2009

Borschberg, Peter, *Hugo Grotius, the Portuguese and Free Trade in the East Indies*, Singapore, 2011

Bouza, Fernando, Pedro Cardim and Antonio Feros, *The Iberian World, 1450–1820*, London and New York, 2020

Bowen, H.V., Margarette Lincoln and Nigel Rigby, *The Worlds of the East India Company*, Woodbridge, 2002

Boxer, C.R., *Dutch Merchants and Mariners in Asia, 1602–1795*, London, 1988

— *The Dutch Seaborne Empire, 1600–1800*, London, 1973

— *The Great Ship from Amacon*, Lisbon, 1959

— *Jan Compagnie in Japan, 1600–1817*, Oxford, 1968

— *Portuguese India in the Mid-Seventeenth Century*, Delhi, 1980

— *The Portuguese Seaborne Empire, 1415–1825*, London, 1969

Brenner, Robert, *Merchants and Revolution: Commercial Change, Political Conflict, and London's Overseas Traders, 1550–1653*, Cambridge, 1993

— 'The Social Basis of English Commercial Expansion, 1550–1630', *Journal of Economic History*, vol. 32 (1972), pp. 361–84

BIBLIOGRAPHY

Brentjes, Sonja, *Travellers from Europe in the Ottoman and Safavid Empires, 16th–17th Centuries*, Farnham, 2010

Brett-James, Norman G., *The Growth of Stuart London*, London, 1935

Bricker, Charles, et al., *Landmarks of Mapmaking*, Oxford, 1976

Brock, Aske Laursen, and Misha Ewen, 'Women's Public Lives: Navigating the East India Company, Parliament and Courts in Early Modern England', *Gender and History*, vol. 33, no. 1 (2020), pp. 52–83

Brook, Timothy, *Mr Selden's Map of China*, London, 2013

— *Vermeer's Hat: The Seventeenth Century and the Dawn of the Global World*, London, 2008

Broomhall, Susan, and Jacqueline Van Gent, *Dynastic Colonialism: Gender, Materiality and the Early Modern House of Orange-Nassau*, Abingdon, 2016

Brotton, Jerry, *This Orient Isle: Elizabethan England and the Islamic World*, London, 2016

Brown, David, *Empire and Enterprise: Money, Power and the Adventurers for Irish Land during the British Civil Wars*, Manchester, 2020

Bruijn, J.R., F.S. Gaastra and I. Schöffer, eds, *Dutch-Asiatic Shipping in the 17th and 18th Centuries*, 3 vols, The Hague, 1979–87

Bull, Hedley, Benedict Kingsbury and Adam Roberts, *Hugo Grotius and International Relations*, Oxford, 1992

Canny, Nicholas, ed., *The Origins of Empire: British Overseas Enterprise to the Close of the Seventeenth Century*, vol. 1: *The Oxford History of the British Empire*, Oxford, 1998

Chancey, Karen, 'The Amboyna Massacre in English Politics, 1624–1632', *Albion*, vol. 30, no. 4 (1998), pp. 583–98

Chaudhuri, K.N., 'The East India Company and the Export of Treasure in the Early Seventeenth Century', *Economic History Review*, new ser., vol. 16, no. 1 (1963), pp. 23–8

— 'The East India Company and the Organization of Its Shipping in the Early Seventeenth Century', *Mariner's Mirror*, vol. 49, no. 1 (1963), pp. 27–41

— *The English East India Company: The Study of an Early Joint-Stock Company, 1600–1640*, London, 1965

— *Trade and Civilisation in the Indian Ocean: An Economic History from the Rise of Islam to 1750*, Cambridge, 1985

— *The Trading World of Asia and the English East India Company, 1660–1760*, Cambridge, 1978

Chaudury, Sushil, and Michel Morineau, eds, *Merchants, Companies, and Trade: Europe and Asia in the Early Modern Era*, Cambridge, 1999

Chester, Joseph Lemuel, ed., 'The reiester booke of Saynte De'nis, Backchurch parishe (city of London) for maryages, christenyges, and buryalles, begynnynge in the yeare of Our Lord God 1538: The Register Book of St Dionis Backchurch 1538–1754', *The Harleian Society*, vol. 3, 1878

Chitty, Herbert, 'Thomas Stevens "Primus in Indis" ', *Wiltshire Archaeology and Natural History Society*, vol. 22 (1902), pp. 22–3

Clark, G.N., 'Grotius's East India Mission to England', *Transactions of the Grotius Society*, vol. 20, *Problems of Peace and War: Papers Read before the Society in the Year 1934*, Cambridge, 1934, pp. 45–84

Clark, G.N. and W.J.M. Van Eysinga, *The Colonial Conferences between England and the Netherlands in 1613 and 1615*, Leiden, 1951

Clark, Peter, *The Cambridge Urban History of Britain*, vol. 2, *1540–1840*, Cambridge, 2000

Clulow, Adam, *The Company and the Shogun: The Dutch Encounter with Tokugawa Japan*, New York, 2014

Cohn, Bernard S., *Colonialism and Its Forms of Knowledge*, Princeton, 1996

Coleridge, Henry James, *The Life and Letters of St. Francis Xavier 1506–1556*, 2 vols, London, 1935

Cook, Harold J., *Matters of Exchange: Commerce, Medicine and Science in the Dutch Golden Age*, New Haven and London, 2007

Corbett, Margery and Ronald Lightbown, *The Comely Frontispiece: The Emblematic Title Page in England, 1550–1660*, London, 1979

Cowan, Brian, *The Social Life of Coffee: The Emergence of the British Coffee House*, New Haven and London, 2005

Cramsie, John, 'Commercial Projects and the Fiscal Policy of James VI and I', *Historical Journal*, vol. 43 (2000), pp. 345–64

— *Kingship and Crown Finance under James VI and I, 1603–1625*, Woodbridge, 2002

Craven, W.F., *Dissolution of the Virginia Company: The Failure of a Colonial Experiment*, New York, 1932

Croft, Pauline, 'English Mariners Trading to Spain and Portugal, 1558–1625', *Mariner's Mirror*, vol. 69 (1983), pp. 251–66

— 'Englishmen and the Spanish Inquisition, 1558–1625', *English Historical Review*, vol. 87, no. 343 (Apr. 1972), pp. 249–68

Cust, Richard, 'Charles I, the Privy Council and the Forced Loan', *Journal of British Studies*, vol. 24, no. 2 (1985), pp. 208–35

Dale, Stephen F., *The Muslim Empires of the Ottomans, Safavids and Mughals*, Cambridge, 2010

Dalrymple, William, *The Anarchy: The Relentless Rise of the East India Company*, London, 2019

Dari-Mattiacci, Giuseppe, Oscar Gelderblom, Joost Jonker and Enrico C. Perotti, 'The Emergence of the Corporate Form', *Journal of Law, Economics, and Organization*, vol. 33, no. 2 (May 2017), pp. 193–236

Das, Anil Kumar, 'Sir Thomas Roe and the Prospects of English Trade in Bengal', *Proceedings of the Indian History Congress*, vol. 28 (1966), pp. 228–35

Das, Nandini, *Sir Thomas Roe: Eyewitness to a Changing World*, Hakluyt Society Annual Lecture, 2017, London, 2018

Davies, Margaret Gay, *The Enforcement of English Apprenticeship: A Study in Applied Mercantilism 1563–1642*, Cambridge, MA, 1956

Davis, J.S., *Essays in the Earlier History of American Corporations*, Cambridge, MA, 1917

Dillon, Janette, *Theatre, Court and City 1595–1610: Drama and Social Space in London*, Cambridge, 2000

Dimmock, Matthew, *Elizabethan Globalism: England, China and the Rainbow Portrait*, New Haven and London, 2019

Disney, A.R., *A History of Portugal and the Portuguese Empire*, 2 vols, Cambridge, 2009

Donaldson, Ian, *Ben Jonson: A Life*, Oxford, 2011

Donno, Elizabeth Story, ed., *Marvell: The Complete Poems*, Harmondsworth, 1986

Dyson, Freeman, and Timothy Beecroft, 'Francis Bacon and the Frozen Chicken', *New York Review of Books*, 31 May 2007

Earle, Peter, *The Pirate Wars*, London, 2003

Edwards, Clara Cary, 'Relations of Shah Abbās the Great, of Persia, with the Mughal Emperors Akbar and Jahangir', *Journal of the American Oriental Society*, vol. 35, (1915), pp. 247–68

Edwards, Philip, and Colin Gibson, *The Plays and Poems of Philip Massinger*, Oxford, 1976

Emmer, Pieter, and Femme Gaastra, eds, *An Expanding World: The European Impact on World History 1450–1800*, vol. 13: *The Organization of Introceanic Trade in European Expansion 1450–1800*, Aldershot, 1996

Epstein, M., *The Early History of the Levant Company*, London, 1908

Eraly, Abraham, *The Mughal Throne*, London, 2003

Erikson, Emily, *Between Monopoly and Free Trade: The English East India Company, 1600–1757*, Princeton and Oxford, 2014

Evans, N.E., 'The Meeting of the Russian and Scottish Ambassadors in London in 1601', *Slavonic and East European Review*, vol. 55, no. 4 (Oct. 1977), pp. 517–28

Falconer, A.F., *Shakespeare and the Sea*, London, 1964

Farnell, J.E., 'The Navigation Act of 1651, the First Dutch War, and the London Merchant Community', *Economic History Review*, vol. 16, no. 3 (1964)

Farrington, Anthony, *A Biographical Index of East India Company Maritime Officers: 1600–1834*, London, 1999
— *Trading Places: The East India Company and Asia 1600–1834*, London, 2002
Ferrier, R.W., 'The Armenians and the East India Company in Persia in the Seventeenth and Early Eighteenth Centuries', *Economic History Review*, vol. 26, no. 1 (1973), pp. 38–62
— 'An English View of Persian Trade in 1618', *Journal of the Economic and Social History of the Orient*, vol. 19, no. 1 (1976), pp. 182–214
Findlay, Ellison B., 'The Capture of Maryam-uz-Zamani's Ship: Mughal Women and European Traders', *Journal of the American Oriental Society*, vol. 108, no. 2 (1988), pp. 227–38
Finkelstein, Andrea, *Harmony and Balance: An Intellectual History of Seventeenth-Century Economic Thought*, Ann Arbor, 2000
Fisher, F.J., *London and the English Economy, 1500–1700*, London, 1990
Flores, Jorge, 'Distant Wonders: The Strange and the Marvelous between Mughal Indian and Habsburg Iberia in the Early Seventeenth Century', *Comparative Studies in Society and History*, vol. 49, no. 3 (July 2007), pp. 553–81
— ed., *The Mughal Padshah: A Jesuit Treatise on Emperor Jahangir's Court and Household*, Leiden and Boston, 2016
Flores, Jorge, and Nuno Vassallo e Silva, *Goa e o Grão-Mogol*, Lisbon, 2004; trans. as *Goa and the Great Mughal*, Milan, 2011
Forsyth, Hazel, *The Cheapside Hoard: London's Lost Jewels*, London, 2013
Foster, Sir William, *Early Travels in India, 1583–1619*, London, 1921
— *The East India House: Its History and Associations*, London, 1924
— *England's Quest of Eastern Trade*, London, 1933
— *The English Factories in India, 1618–1669*, Oxford, 13 vols, 1906–27
— *John Company*, London, 1926
— *A Supplementary Calendar of Documents in the India Office Relating to India or the Home Affairs of the East India Company, 1600–1640*, London, 1928
Freedman, Paul, ed., *Food: The History of Taste*, Berkeley, 2007
Friis, Astrid, *Alderman Cockayne's Project and the Cloth Trade*, Copenhagen, 1927
Fury, Cheryl A., ed., *The Social History of English Seamen, 1485–1649*, Woodbridge, 2012
Games, Alison, *Inventing the English Massacre: Amboyna in History and Memory*, Oxford, 2020
— *The Web of Empire: English Cosmopolitans in an Age of Expansion, 1560–1660,* Oxford, 2008
Gelderblom, Oscar, 'From Antwerp to Amsterdam: The Contribution of Merchants from the Southern Netherlands to the Rise of the Amsterdam Market', *Review* (Fernand Braudel Center), vol. 26 (2003), pp. 247–83
— 'The Organization of Long-Distance Trade in England and the Dutch Republic, 1550–1650', in O. Gelderblom, ed., *The Political Economy of the Dutch Republic*, Aldershot, 2009, pp. 223–54
Gelderblom, Oscar, Abe de Jong and Joost Jonker, 'An Admiralty for Asia. Isaac le Maire and Conflicting Conceptions about the Corporate Governance of the VOC', in J.G.S. Koppell, ed., *The Origins of Shareholder Advocacy*, New York, 2011, pp. 29–60
— 'The Formative Years of the Modern Corporation: The Dutch East India Company VOC, 1602–1623', *Journal of Economic History*, vol. 73, no. 4 (2013), pp. 1050–76
Gelderblom, Oscar, and Joost Jonker, 'Completing a Financial Revolution: The Finance of the Dutch East India Trade and the Rise of the Amsterdam Capital Market, 1595–1612', *Journal of Economic History*, vol. 64, no. 3 (Sept. 2004), pp. 641–72
Glaisyer, Natasha, *The Culture of Commerce in England, 1660–1720*, Woodbridge, 2006
Glete, Jan, *War and the State in Early Modern Europe: Spain, the Dutch Republic and Sweden as Fiscal-Military States, 1500–1600*, London, 2002
Grafe, Regina, *Distant Tyranny: Markets, Power and Backwardness in Spain, 1650–1800*, Princeton, 2012
Grassby, R., 'The Personal Wealth of the Business Community in Seventeenth-Century England', *English Historical Review*, vol. 23, no. 2 (Aug. 1970), pp. 220–34

— 'Social Mobility and Business Enterprise in Seventeenth-Century England', in Christopher Hill, D.H. Pennington and Keith Thomas, eds, *Puritans and Revolutionaries*, Oxford, 1978, pp. 355–81

Grayling, A.C., *The Age of Genius: The Seventeenth Century and the Birth of the Modern Mind*, London, 2016

Griffiths, Sir Percival, *The History of English Chartered Companies*, London and Tonbridge, 1974

Gross, G.W., *The Diary of Baron Waldstein: A Traveller in Elizabethan England*, London, 1981

Gupta, Ashin Das, 'Indian Merchants and the Western Indian Ocean: The Early Seventeenth Century', *Modern Asian Studies*, vol. 19, no. 3 (1985), pp. 481–99

Guy, John, *Gresham's Law: The Life and World of Queen Elizabeth I's Banker*, London, 2019

Guy, John, and Deborah Swallow, *Arts of India 1550–1990*, London, 1999

Habsburg, Francesca von, ed., *The St Petersburg Muraqqa': Album of Indian and Persian Miniatures from the 16th through the 18th Century and Specimens of Persian calligraphy by 'Imad al-Hasani*, Milan, 1996

Haider, Najaf, 'Precious Metal Flows and Currency Circulation in the Mughal Empire', *Journal of the Economic and Social History of the Orient*, vol. 39, no. 3 (1996), pp. 293–364

Hakluyt's Collection of the Early Voyages, Travels and Discoveries of the English Nation, 3 vols, London, 1810

Halliwell, J.O., ed., 'The Private Diary of Dr John Dee', *The Camden Society*, 19 (1842)

Harkness, Deborah E., *The Jewel House: Elizabethan London and the Scientific Revolution*, New Haven and London, 2007

Harris, G.G., *The Trinity House at Deptford 1514–1660*, London, 1965

Hart, Marjolein't, 'The United Provinces, 1579–1806', in Richard Bonney, ed., *The Rise of the Fiscal State in Europe c. 1200–1815*, Oxford, 1999

Hearn, Karen, ed., *Dynasties: Painting in Jacobean and Tudor England 1530–1630*, London, 1995

Heath, J.B., *Some Account of the Worshipful Company of Grocers of the City of London*, London, 1829

Hebb, D.D., *Piracy and the English Government, 1616–1642*, Aldershot, 1994

Helgerson, Richard, *Forms of Nationhood: The Elizabethan Writing of England*, Chicago, 1992

Henderson, Paula, 'Sir Francis Bacon's Essay "Of Gardens" in Context', *Garden History*, vol. 36, no. 1 (Spring 2008), pp. 59–84

Hinton, R.W.K., 'The Mercantile System in the Time of Thomas Mun', *Economic History Review*, new ser., vol. 7, no. 3 (1955), pp. 277–90

Hobhouse, Hermione, ed., *Survey of London*, vols 43 and 44, Poplar, Blackwall and Isle of Dogs, London, 1994

Hochstrasser, Julie Berger, *Still Life and Trade in the Dutch Golden Age*, New Haven and London, 2007

Holdsworth, W.S., 'English Corporate Law in the 16th and 17th Centuries', *Yale Law Journal*, vol. 31, no. 4 (Feb. 1922), pp. 382–407

Houghton, W.E., 'The History of Trades: Its Relation to Seventeenth-Century Thought', in P.P. Wiener and A. Noland, eds, *Roots of Scientific Thought: A Cultural Perspective*, New York, 1957, pp. 354–81

Howarth, David, 'Samuel Boothouse and Artistic Enterprise in Seventeenth Florence', *Italian Studies*, vol. 32 (1977), pp. 83–96

Hudson, Douglas, *Half Moon: Henry Hudson and the Voyage That Redrew the Map of the New World*, New York, 2009

Hudson, W.H., *Macaulay's Essay on Lord Clive*, London, 1910

Irwin, John, *The Girdlers' Carpet*, Hove, 2019

Israel, Jonathan, *Dutch Primacy in World Trade, 1585–1740*, Oxford, 1989

— *The Dutch Republic: Its Rise, Greatness, and Fall, 1477–1806*, Oxford, 1995

— *The Dutch Republic and the Hispanic World, 1606–1661*, Oxford, 1982

Ittersum, Martina Julia van, *Profit and Principle: Hugo Grotius, Natural Rights Theories and the Rise of Dutch Power in the East Indies*, Leiden, 2006

Jack, S.M., *Trade and Industry in Tudor and Stuart England*, London, 1977

Jackson, Anna, and Amin Jaffer, eds, *Encounters: The Meeting of Asia and Europe, 1500–1800*, London, 2004

Jackson, P., and L. Lockhart, *The Timurid and Safavid Periods*, vol. 6, *The Cambridge History of Iran*, Cambridge, 1986

Jones, J.R., *The Anglo-Dutch Wars of the Seventeenth Century*, London, 1996

Katouzian, Homa, *The Persians: Ancient, Mediaeval and Modern Iran*, New Haven and London, 2009

Keay, John, *The Honourable Company: A History of the English East India Company*, London, 1991

Kelly, M.R.L.L., 'Common Law Constitutionalism and the Oath of Governance: An Hieroglyphic of the Laws', *Mississippi College Law Review*, vol. 28, issue 1, article 7 (2009), pp. 122–79

Kelsey, Harry, *The First Circumnavigators: Unsung Heroes of the Age of Discovery*, New Haven and London, 2016

Kingsford, C.L., 'The Taking of the Madre de Dios, 1592', *Naval Miscellany*, vol. 2, Edinburgh and London, 1912, pp. 85–122

Knight, W.S.M., 'Grotius in England: His Opposition There to the Principles of the Mare Liberum', *Transactions of the Grotius Society*, vol. 5 (1919), pp. 1–38

Koeman, C., *Flemish and Dutch Contributions to the Art of Navigation in the XVI Century*, Lisbon, 1988

Landwehr, John, ed., *VOC: A Bibliography of Publications Relating to the Dutch East India Company, 1602–1680*, Utrecht, 1991

Lane, Kris, *Colour of Paradise: The Emerald in the Age of Gunpowder Empires*, New Haven and London, 2010

Lang, R.G., 'Social Origins and Social Aspirations of Jacobean London Merchants', *Economic History Review*, second ser., vol. 27, no. 1 (1974), pp. 28–47

Larkin, James F., and Paul L, Hughes, *Stuart Royal Proclamations*, vol. 1: *Royal Proclamations of King James I 1603–1625*, Oxford, 1973

Latch, Donald F., *Asia in the Making of Europe: A Century of Wonder*, vol. 2, book 1: *The Visual Arts*, Chicago, 1970

Lawson, Philip, *The East India Company: A History*, Abingdon, 2013

Leerssen, Joep, *National Thought in Europe: A Cultural History*, Amsterdam, 2020

Leng, Thomas L., '"His neighbours land mark": William Sykes and the Campaign for "Free Trade" in Civil War England', *Historical Research*, vol. 86, no. 232 (May 2013), pp. 230–52

Logue, John, 'The Revenge of John Selden: The Draft Convention on the Law of the Sea in the Light of Hugo Grotius' Mare Liberum', *Grotiana*, vol. 3 (1982), pp. 27–56

Lombard, Denys, and Jean Aubin, eds, *Asian Merchants and Business Men in the Indian Ocean and the China Sea*, Oxford, 2000

Loth, Vincent C., 'Armed Incidents and Unpaid Bills: Anglo-Dutch Rivalry in the Banda Islands in the Seventeenth Century', *Modern Asian Studies*, vol. 29, no. 4 (Oct. 1995), pp. 705–40

Macaulay, Thomas Babington, *Critical and Historical Essays: Contributed to the Edinburgh Review*, London, 1852

McCullough, Peter, 'Preaching and Context: John Donne's Sermon at the Funerals of Sir William Cockayne', in Hugh Aldington, Peter McCullough and Emma Rhatigan, eds, *The Oxford Handbook of the Early Modern Sermon*, Oxford, 2011, pp. 1–57

McDonald, Donald, *Surgeons Twoe and A Barber: Being Some Account of the Life and Work of The Indian Medical Service (1600–1947)*, London, 1950

McGrath, Patrick, *John Whitson and the Merchant Community of Bristol*, Bristol, 1970

MacGregor, Arthur, *Company Curiosities: Nature, Culture and the East India Company, 1610–1874*, London, 2018
— ed., *Naturalists in the Field*, Leiden, 2018
MacGregor, Neil, *A History of the World in a Thousand Objects*, London, 2010
McIntyre, Ruth A., 'William Sanderson, Elizabethan Financier of Discovery', *William and Mary Quarterly*, vol. 13 (1956), pp. 184–201
MacKay, Ruth, *'Lazy, Improvident People': Myth and Reality in the Writing of Spanish History*, Ithaca, 2006
MacLean, Gerald, *The Rise of Oriental Travel: English Visitors to the Ottoman Empire, 1580–1720*, Basingstoke, 2004
Magurn, R.S., trans. and ed., *The Letters of Peter Paul Rubens*, Cambridge, MA, 1955
Malament, Barbara, 'The "Economic Liberalism" of Sir Edward Coke', *Yale Law Journal*, vol. 76, no. 7 (June 1967), pp. 1321–58
Mather, James, *Pashas: Traders and Travellers in the Islamic World*, New Haven and London, 2009
Matthee, Rudolph, *The Politics of Trade in Safavid Isfahan: Silk for Silver 1600–1730*, Cambridge, 1999
Melo, Joao Vicente, *Jesuit and English Experiences at the Mughal Court, c.1580-1615*, Cham, 2022
Melville, Charles, ed., *Safavid Persia: The History and Politics of an Islamic Society*, London, 1996
Merritt, J.F., ed., *Imagining Early Modern London: Perceptions and Portrayals of the City from Stow to Strype, 1598–1720*, Cambridge, 2001
— 'Puritans, Laudians, and the Phenomenon of Church-Building in Jacobean London', *Historical Journal*, vol. 41 (1998), pp. 935–60
Milton, Giles, *Samurai William*, London, 2003
Mishra, Rupali, *A Business of State: Commerce, Politics, and the Birth of the East India Company*, Cambridge, MA, 2018
Monmonier, Mark, *Rhumb Lines and Map Wars: A Social History of the Mercator Projection*, Chicago, 2004
Morton, Mark, *Cupboard of Love: A Dictionary of Culinary Curiosities*, 2nd edn, Toronto, 2004
Motley, John Lothrop, *The Rise of the Dutch Republic: A History*, 3 vols, Oxford, 1906
Muchmore, Lynn, 'A Note on Thomas Mun's "England's Treasure by Foreign Trade"', *Economic History Review*, vol. 23, no. 3 (Dec. 1970), pp. 498–503
Muldrew, Craig, *The Economy of Obligation*, Basingstoke, 1998
Murdoch, James and Yamagata, Isoo, *A History of Japan during the Century of Early Foreign Intercourse (1542–1651)*, vol. 2, Kobe, 1925
Newman, Andrew J., *Safavid Iran: Rebirth of a Persian Empire*, London, 2006
Nicholl, Charles, *The Reckoning: The Murder of Christopher Marlowe*, London, 1992
Nicoll, Fergus, *Shah Jahan*, London, 2009
North, Michael, ed., *Artistic and Cultural Exchanges between Europe and Asia, 1400–1900*, Farnham, 2010
O'Connell, John, *The Book of Spice: From Anise to Zedoary*, London, 2015
Ogborn, Miles, *Indian Ink: Script and Print in the Making of the English East India Company*, Chicago, 2007
— 'Writing Travels: Power, Knowledge and Ritual on the English East India Company's Early Voyages', *Transactions of the Institute of British Geographers*, vol. 27, no. 2 (2002), pp. 155–71
Parker, Geoffrey, *Global Crisis: War, Climate Change and Catastrophe in the Seventeenth Century*, New Haven and London, 2013
Parker, John, *Books to Build an Empire: A Bibliographic History of English Overseas Interests to 1620*, Amsterdam, 1965
Parry, Glyn, *The Arch-Conjuror of England: John Dee*, New Haven and London, 2011

BIBLIOGRAPHY

Parry, Richard Lloyd, 'Final Resting Place of Sailor Who Inspired TV's Shogun', *The Times*, 3 April 2019

Parthesius, Robert, *Dutch Ships in Tropical Waters: The Development of the Dutch East India Company (VOC) Shipping Network in Asia, 1595–1660*, Amsterdam, 2010

Pearson, M.N., *Coastal Western India*, New Delhi, 1981

— *The Indian Ocean*, London, 2003

— *The Portuguese in India*, vol. 1: *The New Cambridge History of India*, Cambridge, 1987

Pennell, S., 'Consumption and Consumerism in Early Modern England', *Historical Journal*, vol. 42 (1999), pp. 549–64

Pennington, L.E., ed., *The Purchas Handbook: Studies of the Life, Times and Writings of Samuel Purchas 1577–1626*, 2 vols, London, Hakluyt Society, 2nd ser., part 2, 1997

Penrose, Boies, *The Sherliean Odyssey*, Taunton, 1938

— 'Some Jacobean Links between America and the Orient', *Virginia Magazine of History and Bibliography*, vol. 49, no. 1 (Jan. 1941), pp. 51–61

Pettigrew, William, and Mahesh Gopalan, eds, *The East India Company, 1600–1857: Essays on Anglo-Indian Connection*, London, 2017

Pettigrew, William, and Edmond Smith, 'Corporate Management, Labor Relations, and Community Building at the East India Company's Blackwall Dockyard, 1600–57', *Journal of Social History*, vol. 53, no. 1 (2019), pp. 133–56

Pettigrew, William A., and Tristan Stein, 'The Public Rivalry between Regulated and Joint Stock Corporations and the Development of Seventeenth-Century Corporate Constitutions', *Historical Research*, vol. 90, no. 248 (May 2017), pp. 341–62

Pettigrew, William A., and David Veevers, eds, *The Corporation as a Protagonist in Global History, c. 1550–1750*, Leiden and Boston, 2019

Pickett, Catherine, *Bibliography of the East India Company: Books, Pamphlets and other Materials Printed Between 1600 and 1785*, London, 2011

Pieres, P.E., *The Dutch Power in Ceylon 1602–1670*, Colombo, 1929

Pinch, William R., 'Same Difference in India and Europe', *History and Theory*, vol. 38, no. 3 (Oct. 1999), pp. 389–407

Pinto, M.H., Mendes, *Biombos Namban*, Lisbon, 1988

Powell, Damian X., 'Why Was Sir Francis Bacon Impeached? Lawyers and the Chancery Revisited', *History*, vol. 81, no. 264 (Oct. 1996), pp. 511–26

Powell, William S., *John Pory 1572–1636: The Life and Letters of a Man of Many Parts*, Chapel Hill, 1977

Prakash, Om, *The Dutch Factories in India, 1617–1623*, Delhi, 1984

—, ed., *European Commercial Expansion in Early Modern Asia*, Aldershot, 1997

Price, Jacob M., Review of Theodore Rabb, *Enterprise and Empire,* Cambridge, MA (1967), *Economic History Review*, new ser., vol. 22, no. 1 (April 1969), pp. 130–1

Pye, Michael, *The Edge of the World: How the North Sea Made Us Who We Are*, London, 2014

Quinn, D.B., 'Sir Thomas Smith (1513–1577) and the Beginnings of English Colonial Theory', *Proceedings of the American Philosophical Society*, vol. 89 (1945), pp. 543–60

Quinton, Anthony, *Francis Bacon*, Oxford, 1980

Rabb, Theodore K., *Enterprise and Empire: Merchant and Gentry Investment in the Expansion of England, 1575–1630*, Cambridge, MA, 1967

— *Jacobean Gentleman, Sir Edwin Sandys 1561–1629*, Princeton, 1998

Ramsay, G.D., 'Clothworkers, Merchant Adventures, and Richard Hakluyt', *English Historical Review*, second ser., vol. 92 (1977), pp. 504–21

Ranke, Leopold, trans. Walter K. Kelly, *The Ottoman and the Spanish Empires in the Sixteenth and Seventeenth Centuries*, Philadelphia, 1845

Ray, Nihar-Ranjan, *Dutch Activities in the East*, Calcutta, 1954

Regard, Frédéric, ed., *The Quest for the Northwest Passage*, London, 2013

Richards, R.D., *The Early History of Banking in England*, London, 1929

Roberts, R.S., 'The Personnel and Practice of Medicine in Tudor and Stuart England Part I', *Medical History*, vol. 6 (1962), pp. 363–82

— 'The Personnel and Practice of Medicine in Tudor and Stuart England Part II', *Medical History*, vol. 8 (1964), pp. 217–34

Robertson, Ritchie, *The Enlightenment: The Pursuit of Happiness, 1680–1790*, London, 2020

Robins, Nick, *The Corporation That Changed the World: How the East India Company Shaped the Modern International*, London, 2012

Rodger, N.A.M., 'Queen Elizabeth and the Myth of Sea-Power in English History', *Transactions of the Royal Historical Society*, vol. 14 (2004), pp. 153–74

Ruigh, Robert E., *The Parliament of 1624: Politics and Foreign Policy*, Cambridge, MA, 1971

Sadler, A.L., *The Maker of Modern Japan: The Life of Tokugawa Ieyasu*, London, 1937

Savory, Roger, *The History of Shah Abbās the Great*, 2 vols, Persian Heritage Series, vol. 28, Boulder, 1978

— *Iran under the Safavids*, Cambridge, 1980

Scammell, G.V., 'European Seamanship in the Great Age of Discovery', *Mariner's Mirror*, vol. 68 (1982), pp. 357–76

— *The First Imperial Age*, London, 1989

— 'Manning the English Merchant Service in the Sixteenth Century', *Mariner's Mirror*, vol. 56 (1970), pp. 131–54

Schrader, Stephanie, ed., *Looking East: Rubens's Encounter with Asia*, Los Angeles, 2013

Schurhammer, Georg, *Francis Xavier: His Life, His Times*, 4 vols, Rome, 1973–82

Scott, Jonathan, *England's Troubles: Seventeenth-Century English Political Instability in European Context*, Cambridge, 2000

— '"Good Night Amsterdam": Sir George Downing and Anglo-Dutch State Building', *English Historical Review*, vol. 118, no. 476 (Apr. 2003), pp. 334–56

Scott, W.R., *Constitution and Finance of English, Scottish and Irish Joint-Stock Companies*, 3 vols, Cambridge, 1910–12

Screech, Timon, '"Pictures (the Most Part Bawdy)": The Anglo-Japanese Painting Trade in the Early 1600s', *Art Bulletin*, vol. 87, no. 1 (2005), pp. 50–72

Sedley, Stephen, *Lions Under the Throne: Essays on the History of English Public Law*, Cambridge, 2015

Sen, S.P., 'The Role of Indian Textiles in Southeast Asian Trade in the Seventeenth Century', *Journal of Southeast Asian History*, vol. 3, no. 2 (1962), pp. 92–110

Senning, Calvin F., 'Piracy, Politics, and Plunder under James I: The Voyage of the "Pearl" and Its Aftermath, 1611–1615', *Huntington Library Quarterly*, vol. 46, no. 3 (Summer 1983), pp. 187–222

Simpson, Evelyn M., 'John Donne and Sir Thomas Overbury's CHARACTERS', *Modern Language Review*, vol. 18, no. 4 (Oct. 1923), pp. 410–15

Singh, Jyostna, *Colonial Narratives/Cultural Dialogues: 'Discoveries' of India in the Language of Colonialism*, London, 1978

Slack, Paul, 'Material Progress and the Challenge of Affluence in Seventeenth-Century England', *Economic History Review*, vol. 62, no. 3 (2009), pp. 576–603

Smith, Edmond, *Merchants: The Community That Shaped England's Trade and Empire*, New Haven and London, 2021

Smith, Pamela H., and Paula Findlen, *Merchants and Marvels: Commerce, Science and Art in Early Modern Europe*, New York and London, 2001

Solomon, Julie, Robin Solomon and Catherine Gimelli Martin, *Francis Bacon and the Refiguring of Early Modern Thought: Essays to Commemorate the Advancement of Learning (1605–2005)*, Aldershot, 2005

Sotherby's, *English Silver Treasures from the Kremlin: A Loan Exhibition*, London, 1991

Steensgaard, Niels, *Carracks, Caravans and Companies: The Structural Crisis in the European-Asian Trade in the Early 17th Century*, Scandinavian Institute of Asian Studies Monograph Series, no. 17, Copenhagen, 1973; reissued as *The Asian Trade Revolution of the Seventeenth Century: The East India Companies and the Decline of the Caravan Route*, Chicago, 1975

Stein, Burton, *Vijayanagara*, vol. 1, part 2: *The New Cambridge History of India*, Cambridge, 1989

Stern, Philip J., *Corporate Sovereignty and the Early Modern Foundation of the British Empire in India*, Oxford, 2011

— '"A Politie of Civill & Military Power": Political Thought and the Late Seventeenth-Century Foundations of the East India Company-State', *Journal of British Studies*, vol. 47, no. 2 (Apr. 2008), pp. 253–83

Stern, Philip J., and Carl Winnerlind, *Mercantilism Reimagined: Political Economy in Early Modern Britain and Its Empire*, Oxford, 2014

Stocker, J.J., "Pedigree of Smythe of Ostenhanger', *Archaeologica Cantiana*, vol. 20 (1893), pp. 76–81

Strachan, Michael, *Sir Thomas Roe: A Life*, Wilton, 1989

Stradling, R.A., *Europe and the Decline of Spain*, London, 1981

Stronge, Susan, *Painting for the Mughal Emperor: The Art of the Book, 1560–1660*, London, 2002

Subrahmanyam, Sanjay, *Courtly Encounters: Translating Courtliness and Violence in Early Modern Eurasia*, Cambridge, MA, 2012

— *Empires Between Islam and Christianity, 1500–1800*, Albany, 2019

— *Europe's India: Words, Peoples, Empires, 1500–1600*, Cambridge, MA, 2017

— *Mughals and Franks: Explorations in Connected History*, Oxford, 2005

— 'Persians, Pilgrims and Portuguese: The Travails of Masulipatnam Shipping in the Western Indian Ocean, 1590–1665', *Modern Asian Studies*, vol. 22, no. 3 (1988), pp. 503–30

— *The Portuguese Empire in Asia, 1500–1700: A Political and Economic History*, London and New York, 1993

Supple, Barry E., *Commercial Crisis and Change in England, 1600–1642*, Cambridge, 1959

— 'Thomas Mun and the Commercial Crisis, 1623', *Bulletin of the Institute of Historical Research*, vol. 27 (May 1954), pp. 91–4

Takamizawa, T., and O. Okamoto, *Namban Byobu*, Tokyo, 1970

Taylor, E.G.R., *Late Tudor and Early Stuart Geography, 1583–1650*, London, 1934

Tawney, R.H., *Business and Politics under James I: Lionel Cranfield as Merchant and Minister*, Cambridge, 1958

Teltscher, Kate, *India Inscribed: European and British Writing on India, 1600–1800*, Oxford, 1995

Thirsk, Joan, *Economic Policy and Projects: The Development of a Consumer Society in Early Modern England*, Oxford, 1978

Thirsk, J., and J.P. Cooper, eds, *Seventeenth-Century Economic Documents*, Oxford, 1972

Thompson, D.W., 'Japan and The New Atlantis', *Studies in Philology*, vol. 30, no. 1 (Jan. 1933), pp. 59–68

Thrush, Andrew, and John P. Ferris, eds, *The History of Parliament: The House of Commons 1604–1629*, Cambridge, 2010

Tielhof, Milja van, *The Baltic Grain Trade in Amsterdam from the late 16th Century to the Early 19th Century*, Leiden, 2002

Tombs, Robert, *The English and Their History*, London, 2014

Toomer, G.J., *John Selden: A Life in Scholarship*, 2 vols, Oxford, 2009

Tracy, James D., ed., *The Rise of the Merchant Empires: Long Distance Trade in the Early Modern World*, Cambridge, 1990

Trautman, Thomas R., *Aryans and British India*, New Delhi, 2005

Trevor-Roper, Hugh, *Archbishop Laud, 1573–1645*, London, 1940

— *Historical Essays*, London, 1957

— 'Hugo Grotius and England', in *From Counter-Reformation to Glorious Revolution*, London, 1992, pp. 47–83

Trivellato, Francesca, *The Familiarity of Strangers*, New Haven and London, 2009

Turley, Jeffrey S., and George Bryan Souza, *The Commentaries of Dom García de Silva Y Figueroa on his Embassy to Shah 'Abbās I of Persia on Behalf of Philip III, King of Spain*. Leiden and Boston, 2017

Turner, Henry S., *The Corporate Commonwealth: Pluralism and Political Fictions in England, 1516–1651*, Chicago and London, 2016

Tyacke, Sarah, 'Gabriel Tatton's Maritime Atlas of the East Indies, 1620–21: Portsmouth Royal Naval Museum, Admiralty Library Manuscript, MSS 352', *Imago Mundi*, vol. 60, no. 1 (2008), pp. 39–62

Varadarajan, Lotika, 'The Brothers Boras and Virji Vora', *Journal of the Economic and Social History of the Orient*, vol. 19, no. 2 (May 1976), pp. 224–7

Vaughan, Virginia Mason, and Alden T. Vaughan, eds, *The Tempest*, The Arden Shakespeare, London, 2014

Vila-Santa, Nuno, 'Jan Huygen van Linschoten and the Reys-gheschrift: Updating Iberian Science for the Dutch Expansion', *Historical Research*, vol. 94, no. 216 (Nov. 2021), pp. 736–57

Vinal Smith, George, *The Dutch in Seventeenth-Century Thailand*, Detroit, 1977

Vries, Jan de, and Ad van der Woude, *The First Modern Economy, Success, Failure and Perseverance of the Dutch Economy, 1500–1815*, Cambridge, 1997

Wachtel, Nathan, 'The Marrano Mercantilist Theory of Duarte Solis Gomes', *Jewish Quarterly Review*, vol. 101, no. 2 (Spring 2011), pp. 164–88

Waddell, Brodie, *God, Duty and Community in English Economic Life, 1660–1720*, Woodbridge, 2012

Wadmore, J.F., 'Sir Thomas Smythe, Knt. (A.D. 1558–1625)', *Archaeologica Cantiana*, vol. 20 (1893), pp. 82–103

— 'Thomas Smythe of Westenhanger, commonly called, Customer Smythe', *Archaeologica Cantiana*, vol. 17 (1887), pp. 193–208

Wagner, Joseph, 'The Scottish East India Company of 1617: Patronage, Commercial Rivalry, and the Union of the Crowns', *Journal of British Studies*, vol. 59 (July 2020), pp. 582–607

Wallis, Helen M., 'The First English Globe: A Recent Discovery', *Geographical Journal*, vol. 117, no. 3 (Sept. 1951), pp. 275–90

Walton, Steven, 'State Building through Building for the State: Foreign and Domestic Expertise in Tudor Fortification', in Eric H. Ash, ed., *Expertise: Practical Knowledge and the Early Modern State*, Georgetown, 2010, pp. 66–84

Wantje, Fritschy, *Public Finance of the Dutch Republic in Comparative Perspective: The Viability of an Early Modern Federal State (1570s–1795)*, Leiden and Boston, 2017

Warner, Oliver, *English Maritime Writing: Hakluyt to Cook*, London, 1958

Waters, David W., *The Art of Navigation in England in Elizabethan and Early Stuart Times*, London, 1958

— *The Iberian Bases of the English Art of Navigation in the Sixteenth Century*, Lisbon, 1970

Watson, Bruce, 'Fortifications and the "Idea" of Force in Early East India Company Relations with India', *Past and Present*, vol. 88, no. 1 (1980), pp. 70–87

Weber, Max, *Die protestantische Ethik und der Geist des Kapitalismus*, Tübingen, 1904–5

Webster, Charles, ed., *Health, Medicine and Mortality in the Sixteenth Century*, Cambridge, 1979

Weis, René, *Shakespeare Revealed*, London, 2007

Weissbourd, Emily, ' "Those in Their Possession": Race, Slavery, and Queen Elizabeth's "Edicts of Expulsion" ', *Huntington Library Quarterly*, vol. 78, no. 1 (Spring 2015), pp. 1–19

Wennerlind, Carl, *Casualties of Credit: The English Financial Revolution, 1620–1720*, Cambridge, MA, 2011

Whitaker, T.D., *The History and Antiquities of the Deanery of Craven, in the County of York*, ed. A.W. Morant, 2 vols, Leeds and London, 1878

Wilde, Marc De, '*Fides publica* in Ancient Rome and its Reception by Grotius and Locke', *Legal History Review*, vol. 79 (2011), pp. 455–87

BIBLIOGRAPHY

Willes, Margaret, *The Making of the English Gardener: Plants, Books and Inspiration, 1560–1600*, New Haven and London, 2011

Wilson Hunter, Sir William, *History of India: From the First European Settlements to the Founding of the East India Company*, 9 vols, reprint, New York, 2011

Wilson, Mona, Johnson, *Poetry and Prose*, London, 1969

Winterbottom, Anna, *Hybrid Knowledge in the Early East India Company World*, Basingstoke, 2015

Wood, A.C., *A History of the Levant Company*, Oxford, 1935

Woolf, Virginia, 'The Elizabethan Lumber Room', in *The Common Reader*, 1st ser., New York, 1948, pp. 61–8

Wright, L.B., *English Explorers' Debt to the Iberians*, Coimbra, 1980

ONLINE SOURCES

https://www.alexander-ene.co.uk/the-history-of-double-entry-bookkeeping-system.htm

https://www.americanforeignrelations.com/E-N/Freedom-of-the-Seas-Origins-of-the-concept-of-freedom-of-the-seas.html

https://archive.org/

http://baroqueart.museumwnf.org/database_item.php?id=object;BAR;pt;Mus11_A;48;en

https://www.bl.uk/collection-items/purchas-his-pilgrimage-or-relations-of-the-world-and-the-religions

https://www.bl.uk/collection-items/stracheys-a-true-reportory-of-the-wreck-in-bermuda

https://www.bl.uk/collection-items/thomas-mores-history-of-king-richard-iii

https://ota.bodleian.ox.ac.uk/repository/xmlui/bitstream/handle/20.500.12024/A95286/A95286.html?sequence=5&isAllowed=y

https://www.british-history.ac.uk/survey-london/vols43-4/pp553-565

http://www.columbia.edu/itc/mealac/pritchett/00generallinks/kerr/vol07chap09sect07.html

https://contentdm.lib.byu.edu/digital/search/collection/JohnDonne/mode/all

http://thedutchgoldenage.nl/people/governours%20of%20the%20voc%20and%20wic.html

http://www.explore-parliament.net/nssMovies/04/0454/0454_.htm

https://folgerpedia.folger.edu/The_Elizabethan_Court_Day_by_Day

https://www.hathitrust.org

https://www.theheritageportal.co.za/article/workmen-discover-hidden-steps-and-centuries-old-post-office-stones-1906

https://www.historyofparliamentonline.org

https://collections.libraries.indiana.edu/lilly/exhibitions/exhibits/show/portuguese-speaking-diaspora/india

https://www.maphistory.info//llewellyn.html

https://blog.nationalarchives.gov.uk

http://nav.shm.ru/en/exhibits/1731/

https://www.oxfordreference.com/view/10.1093/acref/9780191826719.001.0001/q-oro-ed4-00004114

http://www.parliament.uk/worksofart/artwork/william-rothenstein/sir-thomas-roe-at-the-court-of-ajmir-1614/2598

https://proquest.libguides.com/eebopqp [Early English Books Online (EEBO)]

'Stitched up with Silk: Naqd 'Ali Beg's journey to London in 1626', London, British Library blog post, 11 June 2013, https://blogs.bl.uk/asian-and-african/2013/06/stitched-up-with-silk-naqd-%CA%BBali-begs-journey-to-london-in-1626.html.

https://www.uu.nl/en/special-collections/collections/early-printed-books/geographical-descriptions/itinerario-by-jan-huygen-van-linschoten

'"World enough, and time": Richard Hakluyt and the Renaissance Discovery of the World', https://hakluytsociety.wordpress.com/2017/06/19/world-enough-and-time-richard-hakluyt-and-the-renaissance-discovery-of-the-world/

BIBLIOGRAPHY

https://www.proquest.com/eebo/docview/2240906336/23828342/CABC7917E9BA45FAPQ/2?accountid=25070

https://www.rct.uk/collection/405533/the-shipbuilder-and-his-wife-jan-rijcksen-15602-1637-and-his-wife-griet-jans

https://www.rmg.co.uk/discover/behind-the-scenes/blog/all-about-portolans

https://depts.washington.edu/silkroad/texts/jenkinson/bukhara.html

INDEX